NetBeans IDE Programmer Certified Expert Exam Guide

(Exam 310-045)

NetBeans IDE Programmer Certified Expert Exam Guide

(Exam 310-045)

Robert Liguori
Ryan Cuprak

New York   Chicago   San Francisco   Lisbon   London   Madrid
Mexico City   Milan   New Delhi   San Juan   Seoul   Singapore   Sydney   Toronto

The McGraw·Hill Companies

Cataloging-in-Publication Data is on file with the Library of Congress

McGraw-Hill books are available at special quantity discounts to use as premiums and sales promotions, or for use in corporate training programs. To contact a representative, please e-mail us at bulksales@mcgraw-hill.com.

NetBeans IDE Programmer Certified Expert Exam Guide (Exam 310-045)

1234567890 DOC DOC 109876543210

ISBN: Book p/n 978-0-07-173877-4 and CD p/n 978-0-07-173878-1
of set 978-0-07-173880-4
MHID: Book p/n 0-07-173877-0 and CD p/n 0-07-173878-9
of set 0-07-173880-0

Sponsoring Editor Tim Green	**Copy Editor** Jan Jue	**Illustration** Lyssa Wald
Editorial Supervisor Jody McKenzie	**Proofreader** Andrea Fox	**Art Director, Cover** Jeff Weeks
Project Editor Emilia Thiuri	**Indexer** Karin Arrigoni	**Cover Designer** Peter Grame
Acquisitions Coordinator Meghan Riley	**Production Supervisor** James Kussow	
Technical Editor Brian Leonard	**Composition** Apollo Publishing Service	

To Patti and Ashleigh
—Robert J. Liguori

To Elsa
—Ryan Cuprak

Robert Liguori is a computer scientist and has been developing, maintaining, and testing air traffic management systems since 1996. He is currently providing web services assistance for air traffic management systems in support of the Federal Aviation Administration. Liguori is a software engineer with STG Technologies, Inc.

Liguori has a bachelor's degree in computer science and information technology from Richard Stockton College of New Jersey. He is a Sun Certified NetBeans IDE Specialist, Sun Certified Java Associate, and Sun Certified Java Programmer. He is currently pursuing various other certifications.

In 2008 Liguori worked closely with Edward Finegan to produce the book: *SCJA Sun Certified Java Associate Study Guide* (CX-310-019) (McGraw-Hill, 2009). The book targets preparation for the SCJA exam.

In 2007 Liguori spent his free time with his wife, Patricia Liguori, coauthoring a handy Java reference guide: *Java Pocket Guide* (O'Reilly Media Inc., 2008). The book captures Java's fundamentals in a companion-size book.

Liguori enjoys spending time with his family, as well as surf fishing for rockfish (striped bass), kingfish, bluefish, and flounder along the East Coast of the United States. He can be contacted at robert@gliesian.com.

Ryan Cuprak is an e-formulation analyst at Enginuity PLM and president of the Connecticut Java Users Group that he has run since 2003. At Enginuity PLM he is focused on developing data integrations to convert clients' data and also user interface development. Prior to joining Enginuity he worked for a startup distributed-computing company, TurboWorx, and Eastman Kodak's Molecular Imaging Systems group, now part of Carestream Health. At TurboWorx he was a Java developer and also a technical sales engineer supporting both presales and professional services. Cuprak earned a BS in computer science and biology from Loyola University Chicago. He is a Sun Certified NetBeans IDE Specialist. He can be contacted at rcuprak@acm.org.

About the Technical Editor

Brian Leonard is a principal software engineer at Oracle, where he currently focuses on Oracle Solaris technologies. Prior to joining the Solaris team, Leonard spent four years evangelizing the NetBeans IDE. During that time the NetBeans community grew from thousands to hundreds of thousands of users, and Brian falls to sleep at night assuming he played some small part in fueling that growth.

Leonard began his career working as a systems engineer with EDS at Enron, but claims no responsibility for Enron's ultimate demise. Always wanting to experience California, he moved from Houston to Silicon Valley in 1991, just in time to ride the dot-com wave. In 1997 Leonard joined the startup NetDynamics, which was pushing a new concept called an application server. In 1998 NetDynamics was acquired by Sun, and soon after, J2EE (now Java EE) was born. Leonard then spent the rest of his career working in the application server space before his boss suggested he consider joining the then left-for-dead NetBeans team. The rest, of course, is history. Leonard can be contacted at william.leonard@oracle.com.

About LearnKey

LearnKey provides self-paced learning content and multimedia delivery solutions to enhance personal skills and business productivity. LearnKey claims the largest library of rich streaming-media training content that engages learners in dynamic media-rich instruction complete with video clips, audio, full motion graphics, and animated illustrations. LearnKey can be found on the Web at www.LearnKey.com.

CONTENTS AT A GLANCE

Part I
NetBeans IDE Fundamentals

1   General Configurations   3

2   Builds and Controls   77

3   Java SE Desktop Applications   171

Part II
NetBeans IDE Development Support

4   Java EE Web Applications   259

5   Database Connectivity   309

6   Source Editor   339

7   Refactoring Support   387

Part III
NetBeans IDE Application Tools

8   HTTP Server-Side Monitor   437

9   Local and Remote Debuggers   471

10 Testing and Profiling   511

Part IV
Appendixes

A   NetBeans Versions   609

B   NetBeans Installations   617

C   NetBeans Keymap   629

D   NetBeans Code Templates   639

E   About the CD   649

Glossary   653

Index   671

CONTENTS

Preface . . . . *xix*
Acknowledgments . . . . *xxv*
Introduction . . . . *xxvii*

Part I
NetBeans IDE Fundamentals

1   General Configurations **3**

Configuring IDE Functionality 5
    Options Window 5
    Plugin Manager 34
    Exercise 1-1: Installing the Sun SPOT NetBeans Plugin . . . 42
Working with Configuration Files and Directories 43
    Exercise 1-2: Changing the Default Java Heap Size 46
Debugging with External Libraries 46
    Classpath Types 48
    Library Manager 49
    Project Libraries 51
    Library Sharing 54
    Exercise 1-3: Configure a Global Library and Import 56
Developing with the JDK 57
    Exercise 1-4: Configuring a Second JDK 60
    ✓   Two-Minute Drill 64
    Q&A   Self Test 66
    Self Test Answers 70

2   Builds and Controls **77**

Understanding Free-Form Projects 78
    Creating a Project 79
    Editing Project Properties 87
    Integrating JUnit 91
    Profiling 91
    Debugging 93
    Exercise 2-1: Creating a Free-Form Project 94

Using Version Control Systems 95
    Visual Feedback 99
    File Diff Utility 100
    CVS 102
    Subversion 116
    Exercise 2-2: Checking Out a Subversion Project 132
    Mercurial 133
    Exercise 2-3: Creating a Mercurial Project and Cloning . . . 141
    Local History 141
    Exercise 2-4: Experimenting with Local History 145
Working with Build Files and Processes 145
    Project Structure 147
    Running Targets 149
    Customizing Ant Scripts 150
    Exercise 2-5: Creating a Free-Form Project 153
Configuring the JDK into the Project 154
    Exercise 2-6: Back in Time to an Older JDK 157
    ✓ Two-Minute Drill 159
    Q&A Self Test 161
    Self Test Answers 165

3 Java SE Desktop Applications **171**
Creating Desktop Applications from Existing Sources 172
    Step 1: Choose Project 174
    Step 2: Name And Location 174
    Step 3: Existing Sources 176
    Step 4: Includes & Excludes 176
    Exercise 3-1: Creating a Java Program
    with Existing Sources 178
Managing Classpaths for Compilation and Debugging 180
    Understanding Classpath Types 181
    Editing Java SE Project Classpaths 182
    Understanding Project Classpath Differences 188
    Configuring Classpath Variables 189
    Exercise 3-2: Managing the Classpath 190
Creating Forms with the GUI Builder 191
    Touring the Editor 192
    Creating Forms and Adding Components 205
    Working with Layouts 205

Exercise 3-3: Free Design Layout 212

Exercise 3-4: Free Design Layout Using GridBag Layout . 213

Navigating Generated Code 213

Generating Event Listeners 218

Understanding Beans Binding 222

Exercise 3-5: Beans Binding and JavaBeans 225

Exercise 3-6: Beans Binding and Swing Components . . . 229

Understanding Internationalization Support 229

Packaging and Distributing Java Desktop Projects 230

Creating an Executable JAR 231

Deploying via Java Web Start 234

Exercise 3-7: Using Java Web Start 239

Exercise 3-8: Creating an Executable JAR 240

✓ Two-Minute Drill 242

Q&A Self Test 246

Self Test Answers 250

Part II
NetBeans IDE Development Support

4 Java EE Web Applications **259**

Creating Web Applications from Existing Sources 260

Step 1: Choose Project 261

Step 2: Name And Location 262

Step 3: Server And Settings 262

Step 4: Existing Sources And Libraries 263

Exercise 4-1: Creating a Web Program
with Existing Sources 264

Adding and Using NetBeans-Available Web Frameworks 265

Adding Web Frameworks 266

Understanding Web Frameworks 268

Exercise 4-2: Making Use of JavaServer Faces Libraries . . . 272

Understanding the Visual Web JSF Framework 272

Visual Web Frameworks 273

Exercise 4-3: Working with a Visual Web JSF Sample
Application 278

Deployment Descriptor Visual Editors 279

Working with Server Instances 281

Registration 282

Exercise 4-4: Integrating an Application Server
with a NetBeans Server Plugin 284
IDE/Server Integration 284
Building and Deploying Web Applications 286
Common Development Tasks 286
Configuring Build Settings 288
Deployment Processes 293
✓ Two-Minute Drill 298
Q&A Self Test 301
Self Test Answers 304

5 Database Connectivity **309**
Working with Databases in the IDE 310
Database Explorer 312
Exercise 5-1: Registering a JDBC Driver 315
Database Support Components 319
Exercise 5-2: Interfacing with the Sakila Database Through the
Database Explorer 323
✓ Two-Minute Drill 329
Q&A Self Test 330
Self Test Answers 333

6 Source Editor **339**
Modifying Behavior of the Source Editor 341
Editor Panel Configurations 341
Fonts & Colors Panel Configurations 350
Keymap Panel Configurations 354
Exercise 6-1: Changing Behavior of the Source Editor .. 356
Understanding Error Highlighting and Correction 357
Projects Window Diagnostic Icons 357
Source Editor Left Margin Annotation Diagnostic Glyphs ... 358
Source Editor Diagnostic Highlighting 358
Exercise 6-2: Highlighting Errors in Source Code
and Related Files 360
Error Stripe Diagnostic Marks 360
Output Window Diagnostic Messages 361
Using Editor Hints 362
Class Importing Hints 363
Missing Methods, Fields, and Variable Hints 364

Inherited Methods Implementation Hints 366

Exercise 6-3: Inserting a Cast from an Editor Hint 366

Exercise 6-4: Producing Annotation Glyph Icons
in the Left Margin 367

Generating Code 368

Code Completion 368

Code Templates 370

Exercise 6-5: Creating a HelloWorld Project
in 30 Seconds 371

Live Code Templates 372

Exercise 6-6: Writing Descriptions for Code Templates . . . 375

✓ Two-Minute Drill 377

Q&A Self Test 379

Self Test Answers 382

7 Refactoring Support **387**

NetBeans Refactoring Architecture 389

Exercise 7-1: Understanding the NetBeans Refactoring
Process 391

Refactoring Source Code 391

Best Practices Refactorings 394

Simplification Refactorings 402

Generalization and Realization Refactorings 404

Organizational Refactorings 412

Refactoring Management 419

Exercise 7-2: Becoming Familiar with the Refactoring
Catalog 421

✓ Two-Minute Drill 422

Q&A Self Test 424

Self Test Answers 428

Part III
NetBeans IDE Application Tools

8 HTTP Server-Side Monitor **437**

Using the HTTP Server-Side Monitor 438

The HyperText Transfer Protocol Standard 439

HTTP Server-Side Monitor Setup 443

Exercise 8-1: Monitoring HTTP Requests
Against GlassFish 446
HTTP Server-Side Monitor Usage 447
✓ Two-Minute Drill 461
Q&A Self Test 462
Self Test Answers 465

9 Local and Remote Debuggers **471**

Debugging Local Applications 472
Session Establishment 473
Breakpoint Settings 475
Exercise 9-1: Applying Conditions to Breakpoints 484
Code Stepping 485
Debugging Support Windows 487
Debugging Remote Applications 494
Differences Between Local and Remote Debugging 494
Web Application Debugging 497
Exercise 9-2: Debugging Various Files in a Web
Application 500
✓ Two-Minute Drill 501
Q&A Self Test 503
Self Test Answers 506

10 Testing and Profiling **511**

Testing Applications with JUnit 512
Understanding JUnit Basics and Versions 513
Creating JUnit Tests and Suites 517
Managing Testing Classpath 524
Running JUnit Tests 524
Exercise 10-1: Running Unit Tests 527
Exercise 10-2: Creating Unit Test 528
Configuring Continuous Integration Support 528
Exercise 10-3: Unit Testing with Hudson 532
Using the NetBeans Profiler 533
Optimizing Java Applications 535
Launching the Profiler 537
Attaching a Profiler to a Local Application 541
Exercise 10-4: Attaching the Profiler 547
Monitoring a Desktop Application 547

Exercise 10-5: Deadlocking Thread 557
Understanding CPU Performance 559
Using Profiling Points 569
Understanding Memory Usage 577
Exercise 10-6: Memory Profiling 586
Using the HeapWalker 587
Exercise 10-7: Memory Profiling 593
✓ Two-Minute Drill 596
Q&A Self Test 599
Self Test Answers 602

Part IV
Appendixes

A NetBeans Versions **609**

NetBeans IDE Versions 610
Supported Technologies 611
New Features 612

B NetBeans Installations **617**

NetBeans IDE Installations 618
Microsoft Windows 620
OpenSolaris 623
Mac OS X 624
Linux 627
OS Independent Zip 627

C NetBeans Keymap **629**

NetBeans IDE 6.1 Keymap 630
File Shortcuts 630
Code Folding Shortcuts 631
Navigation Shortcuts 631
Source Shortcuts 632
Refactoring Shortcuts 632
Run Shortcuts 633
Debugging Shortcuts 633
Debugging Window Shortcuts 634
Profiling Shortcuts 634

Window Shortcuts 634
Traditional Editor Functions Shortcuts 635
Miscellaneous 637
Help Shortcuts 637
Function Key Shortcuts 637
Shortcut Reference Documentation 638

D   NetBeans Code Templates **639**
NetBeans IDE 6.1 Code Templates 640
Java Code Templates 641

E   About the CD **649**
About the CD 650
System Requirements 650
Installing and Running MasterExam 650
MasterExam 650
Electronic Book 651
Bonus Appendixes 651
NetBeans IDE Installation Bundles 651
Help 651
Removing Installation(s) 652
Technical Support 652
LearnKey Technical Support 652

Glossary **653**

Index **671**

This book is designed to help you acquire the appropriate knowledge to become a NetBeans Programmer Certified Expert for the NetBeans IDE. This preparation will familiarize you with the necessary knowledge related to the many features of the NetBeans IDE that are represented on the exam. The scope of this book is to help you pass the exam. As such, objective-specific areas are detailed throughout this book. Peripheral information, which is not needed to pass the exam, may be presented in a limited fashion. Since this book covers a lot of information about the NetBeans IDE, you may also wish to use it as a general reference guide away from the certification process.

How hard is the exam? Considering that there are just 28 straightforward objectives, and you only need to get 36 of 61 questions right, you may guess that it's a walk in the park. It's not. You must have extensive experience with the IDE in all the basic areas such as desktop development, web development, database integration, versioning, configurations, testing, debugging, monitoring, profiling, and general usage of the IDE. Many people may feel that they have this experience, or that their experience with other IDEs would help them out. This is generally not the case. As an example, when asked to cite the specific means of accessing a needed dialog box for an IDE feature, you either know what menus to traverse (from usage) or you don't.

In regard to the general expertise needed with the NetBeans IDE to pursue the certification, we recommend the pursuit for the following types of candidates:

- Java SE developers familiar with the NetBeans IDE and the Swing API
- Java EE developers familiar with the NetBeans IDE and various enterprise frameworks
- NetBeans module/plugins developers
- Software programmers familiar with monitoring, profiling, and debugging tools with the NetBeans IDE
- Software testers familiar with the NetBeans IDE and the JUnit test tool
- Software architects familiar with the NetBeans IDE
- Configuration management experts familiar with the NetBeans IDE including version controls systems and IDE configuration
- High school, college, and university students wishing to get certified after taking a class on the NetBeans IDE. Note: Students may wish to discuss with their professors the adoption of this book as part of their IDE-supported curriculum.

Achieving the NetBeans IDE certification will clearly distinguish you as an expert with the IDE.

Sun Certification Program

Oracle now offers Sun certifications in a variety of technical areas supporting many of their own tools and technologies (Table 1).

In This Book

This book has been designed to present you with the NetBeans IDE information needed to complement your skill sets and expertise to get you certified. The objective-related information has been organized in a cohesive manner across the four parts of the book. This book was written with the help of various NetBeans sample projects, some open-source projects, and a few homegrown ones. Various desktop applications are used in Part I, and a primary web application (Rockfish Reports) is used in Part II. Various NetBeans sample projects are used in Part III. Part IV is reserved for peripheral information such as appendixes and the glossary.

In regard to content specifics, Part I covers NetBeans IDE desktop-related fundamentals including configurations, builds and controls, and general development against a primary desktop application. Part II covers NetBeans IDE development areas and general fundamentals including database connectivity, the source editor, refactoring, and web development. Part III covers application tools used with the IDE including the HTTP Server-Side Monitor, local and remote

TABLE I   Sun Certification Program

Certification Tool/Technology	Certification Overview
NetBeans IDE	Single certification targeting the NetBeans Integrated Development Environment
Java Programming Language	Eight certifications targeting Java in regard to entry level, professional, specialized, and enterprise expertise
Solaris Operating System	Four certifications targeting Solaris OS in regard to entry level, system, network, and security administration expertise
MySQL	Four certifications targeting MySQL RDMBS in regard to entry level, database developer, DBA, and Cluster DBA expertise
OpenOffice.org	Three certifications targeting OpenOffice.org Writer, Calc, and Impress expertise
Sun Cluster	Single certification targeting Sun Cluster Administration
Java CAPS	Single certification targeting Java CAPS
Sun Identity Manager	Single certification targeting Sun Identity Manager

debuggers, the JUnit test tool, and the application profiler. Finally, Part IV wraps things up with a useful glossary and a variety of appendixes containing information on versions, the installation process, keymaps, code templates, database integration, sample projects, and NetBeans-related resources.

On the CD

For more information on the CD-ROM, please see "About the CD-ROM" at the back of the book.

Exam Readiness Checklist

At the end of the Introduction you will find an Exam Readiness Checklist. This table has been constructed to allow you to cross-reference the official exam objectives with the objectives as they are presented and covered in this book. The checklist also lets you gauge your level of expertise on each objective at the outset of your studies. This should allow you to check your progress and to make sure you spend the time you need on more difficult or unfamiliar sections. References have been provided for the objective exactly as the vendor presents it, the section of the study guide that covers that objective, and a chapter and page reference.

In Every Chapter

We've created a set of chapter components that call your attention to important items, reinforce important points, and provide helpful exam-taking hints. Take a look at what you'll find in every chapter:

- Every chapter begins with **Certification Objectives**—what you need to know to pass the section on the exam dealing with the chapter topic. The Objective headings identify the objectives within the chapter, so you'll always know an objective when you see it!

- **Exam Watch** notes call attention to information about, and potential pitfalls in, the exam. These helpful hints are written by authors who have taken the exams and received their certification (who better to tell you what to worry about?). They know what you're about to go through!

exam
watch

Note that unlike the Options window, the Plugin Manager window only has a Close button. This means that plugin updates, installs, deactivations, and uninstalls happen immediately, as soon as you click the button. Also note that some plugins may require that you restart NetBeans for the changes to take effect.

■ **Step-by-Step Exercises** are interspersed throughout the chapters. These are typically designed as hands-on exercises that allow you to get a feel for the real-world experience you need to pass the exams. They help you master skills that are likely to be an area of focus on the exam. Don't just read through the exercises—they are hands-on practice that you should be comfortable completing. Learning by doing is an effective way to increase your competency with a product.

■ **On the Job** notes describe the issues that come up most often in real-world settings. They provide a valuable perspective on certification- and product-related topics. They point out common mistakes and address questions that have arisen from on-the-job discussions and experience.

■ **Inside the Exam** sidebars highlight some of the most common and confusing problems that students encounter when taking a live exam. Designed to anticipate what the exam will emphasize, getting inside the exam will help ensure you know what you need to know to pass the exam. You can get a leg up on how to respond to those difficult-to-understand questions by focusing extra attention on these sidebars.

■ **Scenario & Solution** sections lay out potential problems and solutions in a quick-to-read format.

SCENARIO & SOLUTION

You wish to perform refactoring operations on a class. What commands are available?	Rename, Move, Copy, Safely Delete, and Use Supertype Where Possible
You wish to perform refactoring operations on a field. What commands are available?	Rename, Safely Delete, Pull Up, Push Down, Extract Superclass, and Encapsulate Fields
You wish to perform refactoring operations in regard to unnesting inner classes. What commands are available?	Move Inner To Outer Level and Convert Anonymous To Inner

■ The **Certification Summary** is a succinct review of the chapter and a restatement of salient points regarding the exam.

■ The **Two-Minute Drill** at the end of every chapter is a checklist of the main points of the chapter. It can be used for last-minute review.

■ The **Self Test** offers questions similar to those found on the certification exams. The answers to these questions, as well as explanations of the answers, can be found at the end of each chapter. By taking the Self Test after completing each chapter, you'll reinforce what you've learned from that chapter while becoming familiar with the structure of the exam questions.

Some Pointers

Once you've finished reading this book, set aside some time to do a thorough review. You might want to return to the book several times and make use of all the methods it offers for reviewing the material:

- *Reread all the Two-Minute Drills*, or have someone quiz you. You also can use the drills as a way to do a quick cram before the exam. You might want to make some flash cards out of 3×5-inch index cards that have the Two-Minute Drill material on them.

- *Reread all the Exam Watch notes and Inside the Exam elements.* Remember that these notes are written by authors who have taken the exam and passed. They know what you should expect—and what you should be on the lookout for.

- *Review all the S&S sections* for quick problem solving.

- *Retake the Self Tests.* Taking the tests right after you've read the chapter is a good idea, because the questions help reinforce what you've just learned. However, it's an even better idea to go back later and do all the questions in the book in one sitting. Pretend that you're taking the live exam. When you go through the questions the first time, you should mark your answers on a separate piece of paper. That way, you can run through the questions as many times as you need to until you feel comfortable with the material.

- *Complete the Exercises.* Did you do the exercises when you read through each chapter? If not, do them! These exercises are designed to cover exam topics, and there's no better way to get to know this material than by practicing. Be sure you understand why you are performing each step in each exercise. If there is something you are not clear on, reread that section in the chapter.

ACKNOWLEDGMENTS

The NetBeans exam covers information from basic IDE configuration to building web applications. For this project, the divide-and-conquer authoring approach was taken by splitting up the chapters based on individual experience, expertise, and preference. Ryan led the chapters related to the core IDE including all of Part I (IDE configurations, builds and controls, and Java SE desktop applications) as well as the chapter on JUnit and the Profiler in Part III. Robert focused on four areas that he had a heightened interest in: web applications, database connectivity, the source editor, and refactoring. He also led up the HTTP Server-Side Monitor and debugging chapters in Part III of the book.

NetBeans IDE Project Team Acknowledgments

We would like to express our gratitude to all of the people who have played technical roles in the development of this book including:

The McGraw-Hill and Support Team: Timothy Green, Meghan Riley, Jody McKenzie, Jim Kussow, Brian Leonard, Melinda Lytle, Emilia Thiuri, Jan Jue, Lyssa Wald, Andrea Fox, and Apollo Publishing.

Informal Reviewers: Sally Baldwin, Paul Caron, and Willis Morse.

Personal Acknowledgments

I would like to acknowledge my parents , Joseph Liguori and Joan Marie Liguori, my father-in-law Leo Shearn, and my mother-in-law Florence Shearn, for their continuous guidance and support. I would also like to thank all of my friends and family with special regards to those who have been there for me in recent times: Michael Liguori, Joseph Liguori, Dennis and Elizabeth Wilson, Chris and Lisa Loeb, Robert Derosa, Martin Suech, Jack Wombough, and Paul Caron. Special thanks and appreciation go to Patti and Ashleigh for supporting me while writing this book. Finally, I would like to thank my coauthor, Ryan Cuprak, for digging in deep with the content of his chapters to make this book an invaluable NetBeans IDE certification resource.

—Robert Liguori

Writing this book would not have been possible without the support of family and friends. I would especially like to thank the love of my life, Elsa, who has supported and encouraged me throughout the long, arduous process and the many long nights I was hunched over the computer. I would also like to thank Brian Leonard for encouraging me years ago to try out NetBeans. In addition, special thanks go to Willis Morse and Sally Baldwin for their invaluable corrections and suggestions. Finally, I would like to thank my coauthor, Robert, for recruiting me to this project and guiding me through the process.

—Ryan Cuprak

INTRODUCTION

This NetBeans IDE study guide has been designed to assist you in preparation of passing the NetBeans IDE Programmer Certified Expert exam. The information in this book is presented through textual content, coding examples, exercises, and more. Code examples have been validated on Windows Vista, Windows 7, and Macintosh OS X operating systems. In this book, information is covered in detail for all exam objectives. The main areas covered are as listed:

- General NetBeans IDE Configurations
- Builds and Controls
- Desktop Application Development
- Web Application Development
- Database Integration
- Source Editor Functionality
- General Refactoring
- HTTP Server-Side Monitoring
- Local and Remote Debugging
- JUnit Testing
- Application Profiling

The targeted NetBeans IDE version for the exam is 6.1. However, a good portion of the book was written against version 6.8 to take advantage of bug fixes, enhancements, and new features. NetBeans IDE 6.1 was used if the changes to the subsequent versions were significant enough to affect your study preparation and/or exam score. Table 2 details which NetBeans versions were used for each chapter and appendix.

TABLE 2

NetBeans
Versions Used
for Each Chapter
and Appendix

Chapter/Appendix	NetBeans Version
Chapter 1—General Configurations	NetBeans 6.8
Chapter 2—Builds and Controls	NetBeans 6.8
Chapter 3—Java SE Desktop Applications	NetBeans 6.8
Chapter 4—Java EE Web Applications	NetBeans 6.1, 6.9
Chapter 5—Database Connectivity	NetBeans 6.8
Chapter 6—Source Editor	NetBeans 6.8
Chapter 7—Refactoring	NetBeans 6.1
Chapter 8—HTTP Server-Side Monitor	NetBeans 6.8
Chapter 9—Local and Remote Debugging	NetBeans 6.8
Chapter 10—Testing and Profiling	NetBeans 6.8
Appendix A—NetBeans Versions	Recent versions
Appendix B—NetBeans Installations	NetBeans 6.8
Appendix C—NetBeans Keymap	NetBeans 6.1
Appendix D—NetBeans Code Templates	NetBeans 6.1
On the CD—NetBeans Database Integration	NetBeans 6.8
On the CD—NetBeans Sample Projects	NetBeans 6.8
On the CD—NetBeans Resources	All versions

Specifics about the NetBeans IDE Certification Exam

Oracle and Sun certification specifics about the NetBeans IDE exam objectives are detailed on their website at http://education.oracle.com/. Specifics about the exam process are supplied by Prometric when you enroll. However, we detail in the following sections the important information you will need to know to take the exam.

Dynamics of the NetBeans IDE Exam

The NetBeans IDE exam is geared toward software programmers and developers with extensive experience developing Java-based desktop and web applications with the NetBeans IDE. There are no prerequisites for this exam. You must get 36 of 61 questions correct, having a passing percentage of at least 59 percent. The designated time limit is 75 minutes. The exam is strictly multiple-choice questions and answers.

The current U.S. price to take the exam is $300.00 but is subject to change. If you are employed by a technical organization, check to see if your company has an educational assistance policy. For education-related areas that do not return a "grade" such as an exam, employers may require that the candidate pass the exam with a certain percentage. Candidates receive their percentage immediately following the exam and are sent a detailed summary of how they did on the exam with an overall percentage, as well as percentages per objective. This information breakdown can be beneficial when considering retaking the exam or when considering restudying weak areas. Oracle and Sun certification allow you to publish their credentials through the certification manager website at http://certmanager.net/sun/. Publishing credentials involves your selecting certification information to publish and forwarding that information via a form to e-mail recipients whom you wish to share the information with. The received e-mail will provide a link and password to view the published credentials from a secured server for a period of two weeks. It is important to note that the published credentials, also known as the Credential Verification Report, only provide a certified result, not the actual percentage of how a candidate has scored, as shown in Figure 1.

FIGURE 1   Published credentials example

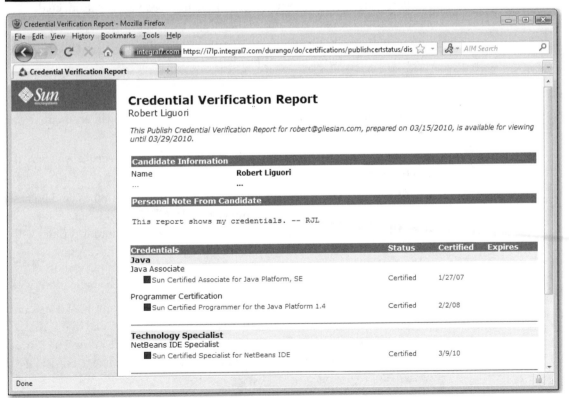

Scheduling the NetBeans IDE Exam

You will need to sign up for and schedule the test through the Prometric website (www.prometric.com or www.2test.com). The exams are given by Prometric at Authorized Prometric Testing Centers.

Preparing for the NetBeans IDE Exam

Getting a good night's rest before the exam and eating a healthy breakfast will contribute to good test marks. Don't cram for the exam the night before. If you find you need to cram, you should reschedule the exam since you should be more prepared for it.

You will need to bring a few things with you for the exam *and* leave a few things behind. Let's take a look at some dos and don'ts.

Dos

- *Do* bring two forms of identification. Valid identification includes a valid passport, current driver's license, government-issued identification, credit cards, and check-cashing cards. At least one item must include your photograph. Make sure not to "shorthand" your signature when you sign in since it must match your identification.

- *Do* show up early, from 15 to 30 minutes before your exam's scheduled start time. You may find that the center needs to set up several people for exams. Getting in early may get you set up early, or at the least it will ensure that you don't start late.

- *Do* print directions to the test facility. Or let your GPS navigator lead you, if you have one.

- *Do* use the restroom ahead of time. The exam is only 75 minutes, and breaks are frowned upon and may be disallowed. You can't pause the time you've been allocated if you need to take a break. However, a countdown timer will be on the screen if you need to know how much time you have left.

Don'ts

- *Don't* bring large items. Large storage may not be available for book bags and jackets. So the more items you can leave in your car, dorm, and so on, the less you'll have to worry about once you get to the testing facility. The testing facilities typically do have small securable lockers for your usage, but you'll have to ask to use one.

- *Don't* bring writing supplies. The test center will likely provide laminated paper with a dry erase marker. You will not be able to keep these.

- *Don't* bring your laptop, cell phone, or other similar device.
- *Don't* bring drinks or snacks since they are not allowed.

Taking the NetBeans IDE Exam

When you begin the exam, you will likely be presented with an optional computer-based survey. This survey will ask you about your technical background and other related information. A common misconception is that the answering of these questions may be related to which exam questions you will be presented with. Taking the survey is not related to the exam questions you will receive. The survey can take 20 to 30 minutes to complete. The information gathered is important for those developing and refining future exams, so answer the questions honestly.

After you have completed the exam, your results may or may not appear on the screen. In some cases, you may need to wait for the testing personnel to retrieve your results from the printer. You will need to sign your results once completed. The point here is that *you should not leave* once you have completed the exam, stay and get your results.

Within a few weeks after your exam, if you pass, you will receive a certificate, a pin, and a congratulation letter. If you should unfortunately fail the exam, you will receive only the knowledge you gained from the studying and experience. That's okay, though, just sign up for the test again, study your weak areas, and give it another go.

We would like to know how you did on the exam. You can send us an e-mail at examresults@gliesian.com.

Rescheduling the NetBeans IDE Exam

Rescheduling is easy. Just go to the Prometric site and follow the rescheduling prompts; it's an online process. It is not uncommon for work, school, personal events, and other priorities to delay your readiness for the exam. You may reschedule the exam as often as you like. Just try to do the rescheduling of your exam at least two days prior to the existing scheduled exam date.

Oracle's Certification Program in NetBeans IDE Technology

This section maps the exam's objectives to specific coverage in the study guide.

Exam Readiness Checklist

Official Objective	Study Guide Coverage	Ch #	Pg #	Beginner	Intermediate	Expert
NetBeans IDE Fundamentals						
1.1 Demonstrate the ability to configure the functionality available in the IDE including using, enabling, and disabling functionality and using the Plugin Manager.	Configuring IDE Functionality	1	5			
1.2 Explain the purpose of the user directory and the netbeans.conf file and how these can be used to configure the IDE.	Working with Configuration Files and Directories	1	43			
1.4 Describe how to integrate external libraries in the IDE and use them in coding and debugging your projects.	Debugging with External Libraries	1	46			
1.6 Describe how to integrate and use different versions of the JDK in the IDE for coding, debugging, and viewing Javadoc documentation.	Developing with the JDK	1	57			
2.1 Describe the characteristics and uses of a free-form project.	Understanding Free-Form Projects	2	78			
2.2 Demonstrate the ability to work with version control systems and the IDE (what VCSs are available, which ones you need an external client for, how to pull sources out of a repository, view changes, and check them back in).	Using Version Control Systems	2	95			
2.3 Describe the ways in which you can change the build process for a standard project, such as configuring project properties and modifying the project's Ant build script.	Working with Build Files and Processes	2	145			
2.4 Configure your project to compile against and run on a specific version of the JDK.	Configuring the JDK into the Project	2	154			
3.1 Demonstrate the ability to create NetBeans projects from the source code of an existing Java SE program.	Creating Desktop Applications from Existing Sources	3	172			
3.2 Describe how to manage the classpath of a Java SE project, including maintaining a separate classpath for compiling and debugging.	Managing Classpaths for Compilation and Debugging	3	180			

Exam Readiness Checklist
(continued)

Official Objective	Study Guide Coverage	Ch #	Pg #	Beginner	Intermediate	Expert
3.3 Demonstrate the knowledge of the NetBeans GUI Builder and the ability to layout and hook up basic forms using it.	Creating Forms with the GUI Builder	3	191			
3.4 Demonstrate the ability to package and distribute a built Java Desktop project for use by another user.	Packaging and Distributing Java Desktop Projects	3	230			
NetBeans IDE Development Support						
4.1 Describe how to create a NetBeans project from the source code of an existing Web application.	Creating Web Applications from Existing Sources	4	260			
4.3 Demonstrate knowledge of which web frameworks are available in NetBeans IDE and how they are added to and used in a web application.	Adding and Using NetBeans-Available Web Frameworks	4	265			
4.2 Distinguish between a visual web application and a web application.	Understanding the Visual Web JSF Framework	4	272			
1.3 Demonstrate the ability to work with servers in the IDE, such as registering new server instances and stopping and starting servers.	Working with Server Instances	4	281			
4.5 Demonstrate a knowledge of basic tasks related to building and deploying web applications to a server, such as changing the target server and undeploying an application.	Building and Deploying Web Applications	4	286			
1.5 Demonstrate knowledge of working with databases in the IDE, including registering new database connections and tables running SQL scripts.	Working with Databases in the IDE	5	310			
5.2 Describe how to use the Options window to change the default appearance and behavior of the Source Editor.	Modifying Behavior of the Source Editor	6	341			
5.3 Describe the ways the IDE highlights errors in source code and the tools the IDE offers for correcting those errors.	Understanding Error Highlighting and Correction	6	357			
5.4 Demonstrate the ability to use editor hints, such as implementing all the methods for an implemented interface.	Using Editor Hints	6	362			

Exam Readiness Checklist
(continued)

Official Objective	Study Guide Coverage	Ch #	Pg #	Beginner	Intermediate	Expert
5.5 Demonstrate the ability to use live code templates such as automatic generation of constructors, try/catch loops, and getters and setters.	Generating Code	6	368			
5.1 Describe the purpose and uses of refactoring and demonstrate the ability to perform basic refactoring on Java source code.	Refactoring Source Code	7	391			
NetBeans IDE Application Tools						
4.4 Describe how to monitor HTTP requests when running a web application.	Using the HTTP Server-Side Monitor	8	438			
6.2 Describe how to debug a local (desktop) application, including setting breakpoints and stepping through code.	Debugging Local Applications	9	472			
6.3 Describe the difference between local and remote debugging and describe how to debug a remote (web) application.	Debugging Remote Applications	9	494			
6.1 Demonstrate the ability to work with JUnit tests in the IDE, such as creating JUnit tests and interpreting JUnit test output.	Testing Applications with JUnit	10	512			
6.4 Describe the purpose of profiling applications and how to profile a local desktop application in the IDE.	Using the NetBeans Profiler	10	533			

Part I

NetBeans IDE Fundamentals

CHAPTERS

1   General Configurations

2   Builds and Controls

3   Java SE Desktop Applications

1

General Configurations

- Configuring IDE Functionality
- Working with Configuration Files and Directories
- Debugging with External Libraries

- Developing with the JDK
- ✓ Two-Minute Drill
- Q&A Self Test

Congratulations on deciding to learn and master the NetBeans Integrated Development Environment (IDE), an incredibly powerful development tool. NetBeans not only helps you get your job done faster, but also improves your understanding of code and your software architecture skills.

Tool proficiency is just as important as development language competency. Too often developers muddle along with only a rudimentary grasp of their tools, digging deeper only when confronted with an intractable problem in production. Undoubtedly many developers' first exposure to the NetBeans profiling tool is after a production server has repeatedly run out of memory, and the initial solution of increasing the Java heap size has backfired.

This book contains detailed explanations of the features in NetBeans and comprehensive practice test questions. The accompanying CD contains additional practice exam questions. The discussions in this book are tied back to real job situations that have confronted the authors. By the end of this book you will not only be a master of NetBeans but also a master troubleshooter able to leverage this powerful tool.

NetBeans has come a long way since 2004, when Sun released version 4.0 to mark a gigantic leap forward for the world-class Java IDE. In fact, NetBeans has become an application platform. NetBeans provides excellent support for developing solutions using Grails, C, C++, JavaScript, Groovy, Python, and PHP among others. The breadth of the features in NetBeans is daunting. Since version 6.0, the features in the core IDE have mushroomed. The test, however, focuses on the core of the IDE and on developing Java-based applications.

This chapter focuses on the core tasks of configuring the IDE, to familiarize you with the Options window and all of its settings. You will also learn about the IDE directories, including their layout and purpose. In addition, you will master defining external libraries and configuring Java Development Kits (JDKs) for development. These skills will serve as your foundation for exploring NetBeans further.

CERTIFICATION OBJECTIVE

Configuring IDE Functionality

Exam Objective 1.1   Demonstrate the ability to configure the functionality available in the IDE including using, enabling, and disabling functionality and using the Plugin Manager.

The NetBeans certification exam typically devotes several questions to IDE configuration and the Plugin Manager. Success on these questions is contingent on having an excellent working knowledge of the Options window and also of the Plugin Manager. The exam asks very specific questions about these features and the content of the screens. This objective is split into two sections:

- Options Window
- Plugin Manager

Options Window

The NetBeans Options window, shown in Figure 1-1, configures most aspects of the IDE. This window configures global IDE settings and is not project specific. To open the Options window, choose Tools | Options. On Macintosh OS X (Mac OS X), choose NetBeans | Preferences. The Preferences dialog box has a row of icons going across the top for the different logical configuration groups. Configuration changes are saved back to the `.netbeans/6.X` directory found under a user's home directory. If different versions of NetBeans have been installed, a different directory with the version number appears under the `.netbeans` directory. Deleting the configuration directory before launching NetBeans resets the IDE to its default settings.

| **FIGURE I-I** | NetBeans Options window |

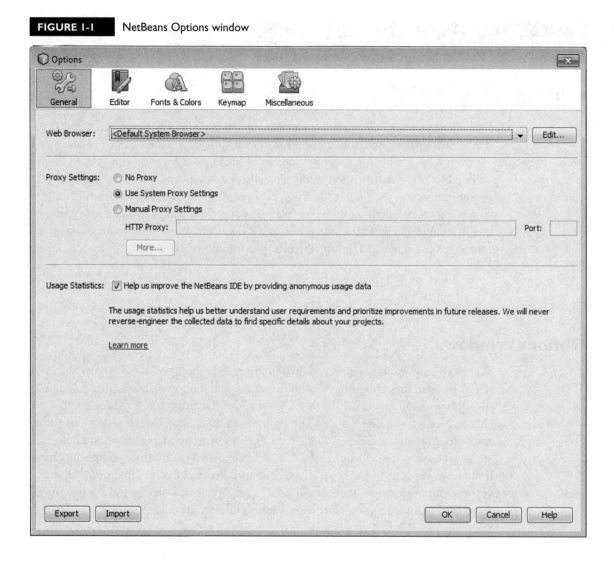

Table 1-1 lists the different configuration groups whose icons appear across the top of the Options window, a brief description of each group, and the chapter where it is covered. This chapter focuses on configuration settings not covered in other sections of this book, specifically the General and Miscellaneous groups. Syntax highlighting and key bindings are covered in Chapter 6 along with the source editor.

When you click a group icon at the top of the Options window, its content panel appears. Often the content panel contains tabs with a multitude of settings. Changes are applied only after you click the OK button.

| TABLE 1-1 | Options Window Configuration Groups | |

Group	Description	Chapter
General	Configures the default web browser and proxy settings for corporate networks.	1
Editor	Practically every aspect of the editor can be configured. This includes templates, coding formatting, code completion, etc.	6
Fonts & Colors	Fonts and colors to be used for syntax, highlighting, and code differences.	6
Keymap	This panel controls the shortcut keys. If you are more familiar with another editor, you can use that editor's key bindings to simplify your transition.	6, Appendix C
Miscellaneous	This is a catchall collection of configuration settings for various plugins and IDE extensions.	1

Two important buttons are at the bottom of the Options window: Export and Import. The Export button opens the dialog box in Figure 1-2 to save selected configuration settings out to a ZIP file, which you can reimport into the IDE using the Import button. This makes it possible to easily share IDE configurations among members of a development team and it works across platforms.

For instance, many companies have strict coding conventions that dictate tab sizes, brace placement, file templates, and so on. The import/export functionality provides a simple mechanism to propagate these conventions among the group without laborious documentation and setup instructions. NetBeans keeps track of changes that differ from the default settings. NetBeans exports settings only if changes have been made. Thus, settings that have not changed appear disabled in the Export dialog box.

General

The General configuration group appearing in Figure 1-1 is one of the simplest panels in the Options window. From this group, three things can be configured:

- Web Browser
- Proxy Settings
- Usage Statistics

The default web browser for the NetBeans IDE can be selected from the Web Browser drop-down list. You can use the selected web browser for previewing the

FIGURE 1-2

NetBeans options
export dialog box

output from web applications, as well for viewing IDE documentation and links. On the Windows platform, two options are available by default: <Default System Browser> and Internet Explorer. If Firefox is installed, it also appears on the list.

Click the Edit button to configure additional web browsers. The Default System Browser selection uses the default browser as configured for your operating environment (for Windows this is configured in the Control Panel). Selecting Internet Explorer sets the browser as Internet Explorer (IE), regardless of the default browser.

The Proxy Settings primarily pertain to corporate environments where network traffic is routed through a firewall. You have three options:

- **No Proxy** Choose this option for direct connection to the Internet with no outgoing traffic filtering.
- **Use System Proxy Settings** Under most circumstances this option suffices.
- **Manual Proxy Settings** Use this option to configure proxy username/ passwords, SOCKS proxy, and hosts to exclude from a proxy. The Advanced Proxy Options dialog box is depicted in Figure 1-3.

Proxy settings are company specific. The proxy settings affect solely the IDE; external tools including Maven may need to be configured separately. Proxy server

FIGURE 1-3

NetBeans proxy
server settings

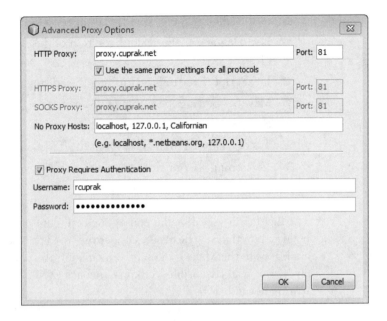

settings are not propagated to child processes. So if you are writing an application
that accesses external resources, you have to write your own code to handle
configuration of the proxy server.

The third group on the General panel is Usage Statistics. It is highly unlikely that
this will be covered on the exam. Enabling this feature by selecting the checkbox
sends feature usage information to the NetBeans developers.

Miscellaneous

The Miscellaneous group is a collection of other features and plugins that can be
configured in the IDE. This configuration group continues to grow with each release
of NetBeans. NetBeans 6.8 contains the following tabs:

- **Ant** Apache Ant configuration settings including Ant version as well as
classpath.
- **Appearance** Look-and-feel settings for the IDE.
- **Diff** File comparison settings such as ignoring whitespace/line endings.
- **Files** Settings for file extensions and Multipurpose Internet Mail Extensions
(MIME) type handling.
- **GUI Builder** Settings related to the user interface (UI) of the GUI Builder.

- **Issue Tracking**   Settings for connecting to Bugzilla.
- **Java Debugger**   Basic configuration of the debugger including exception filters.
- **JavaScript**   Settings controlling the editing and testing of JavaScript.
- **Maven**   Settings pertaining to Maven.
- **Profiler**   Settings related to the Profiler.
- **Tasks**   Patterns that show up in the Tasks panel.
- **Versioning**   Configuration of the different version-control systems.

Ant

The first tab in the Miscellaneous group configures Ant. Ant is a common Java build system that NetBeans uses under the hood to compile, run, and test code. It is analogous to the Make tool commonly used in the C/C++ world. However, it uses an easy-to-read Extensible Markup Language (XML) file format. You extend Ant by writing new subclasses.

To give you a flavor of Ant, an example Ant file follows. In this listing we create a clean directory in which we build, compile, and package the classes into a JAR file. We can see two of the basic building blocks of an Ant file—a target and a task. A *target* contains a list of tasks such as compiling classes, manipulating the file system, and launching external programs. Specifying dependencies upon previous targets controls the order of target execution. You can invoke a target from the command line by passing the target name as a parameter to the Ant executable, or invoke the entire set of tasks by invoking the Ant executable without any parameters. The website http://ant.apache.org provides an excellent source of documentation on Ant, as well as references to related books.

```
<project name="SequenceTools" default="package" basedir=".">
  <target name="clean">
    <delete quiet="true" dir="classes"/>
    <mkdir dir="classes"/>
  </target>
  <target name="compile" depends="clean">
    <javac srcdir="src" destdir="classes">
      <classpath path="lib">
        <fileset dir="lib">
          <include name="**/*.jar"/>
        </fileset>
      </classpath>
    </javac>
```

```
    </target>
    <target name="package" depends="compile">
      <jar destfile="SequenceTools.jar" basedir="classes"/>
    </target>
  </project>
```

As mentioned previously, NetBeans uses Ant under the hood as its build system. If you are creating a new NetBeans project from one of its templates, NetBeans automatically generates the Ant build file for you. If you already have a mature project with its own Ant build files and directory structure, you can use the Free Form Project wizard to integrate your existing project's build file into NetBeans. Chapter 2 contains a detailed discussion of NetBeans Ant files. The Ant panel provides an interface for configuring:

- File system location of the Ant executable and resources
- Interaction between NetBeans and Ant's external process
- Extensions to Ant's class path
- Additional Ant environment properties

Figure 1-4 shows the contents of this panel. The Ant Home setting allows you to pick the version of Ant to be used by NetBeans. Projects sometimes have requirements for specific versions of Ant on which their build process has been validated. Take care in selecting significantly older or newer versions of Ant, as compatibility issues with NetBeans may arise. NetBeans does not have the ability to configure the version of Ant used on a project-by-project basis. Information about the version of Ant being used appears below the Ant Home field.

The next set of checkboxes under Ant Home controls several important features of the Ant integration. The first option, Save All Modified Files Before Running Ant, saves all unsaved documents prior to running an Ant task. Since Ant is used to build, run, and test code, clearing this checkbox means that you have to explicitly save your changes in order for them to take effect when compiling, running, testing, and so on. The Reuse Output Tabs From Finished Processes option reduces clutter by recycling the Output tab. If the checkbox is cleared, a new tab is created each time an Ant target is invoked. The third option, Always Show Output, causes NetBeans to switch to the Output tab when an Ant task is invoked.

The Verbosity Level controls the output from the build process. You can choose Quiet, Normal, Verbose, or Debug. The quiet mode displays only output generated by your application. The verbose and debug modes output copious amounts of information including classpaths, working directories, VM parameters, and so on. The latter two are indispensable when troubleshooting problems with custom Ant tasks.

FIGURE 1-4 NetBeans Options window: Ant

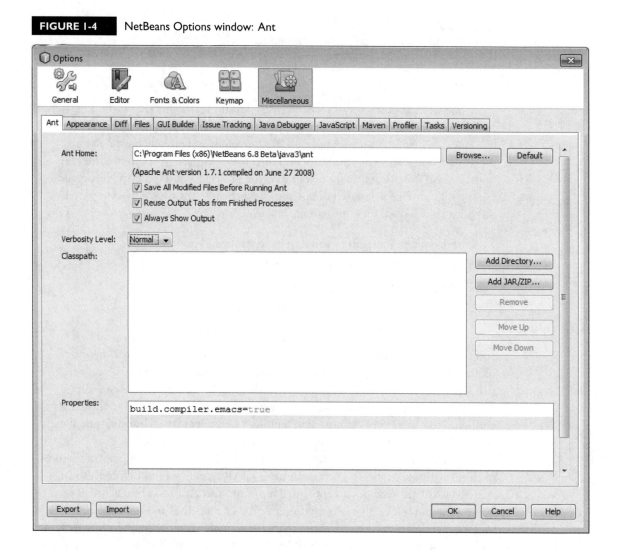

The Classpath list box provides a mechanism for adding additional Ant tasks to Ant. Many of the optional Ant tasks have external library requirements that must be added to the classpath. Adding libraries to Ant in this Options window makes the Ant task available to all projects in NetBeans. For instance, the svn Ant tasks from SvnAnt (http://subclipse.tigris.org/svnant.html) require five external libraries. If these libraries are missing, Ant will report the error: "Problem: failed to create task or type svn."

The Properties text area is used to enter system properties that configure Ant's core classes or that can be consumed by Ant build files. Examples of built-in parameters that you can change can be found in Ant's online documentation (http://ant.apache.org/manual/running.html). For instance, the URLs for SvnAnt could be defined in this field.

Appearance

The Appearance tab, shown in Figure 1-5, controls several user interface–related settings. Depending upon features available on your Java Development Kit (JDK) and operating system (OS) platform, any of the first three checkboxes may be disabled. The first three checkboxes are

- Drag Window Image
- Transparent Drag Window Image
- Transparent Floating Windows

These checkboxes control the overall NetBeans appearance. When the Drag Window Image option is on, NetBeans displays an image of a panel (such as Tasks, Properties, or Projects) during a drag. With this option off, you see only a red outline. If you are working on an older computer or your project is taxing the computer resources, disabling this feature can improve the NetBeans responsiveness. The Transparent Drag Window Image option makes an undocked window transparent as you drag it. The Transparent Floating Windows option, added in NetBeans 6.1, does the same for floating windows (undocked windows). Making windows transparent during dragging helps when undocked and floating windows overlap each other. These last two features cannot be enabled on Mac OS X, Linux, or OpenSolaris, and although they appear checked, they are not supported on these platforms.

The Close Activates Most Recent Document option switches focus to the previously viewed document when you close the frontmost document. If this is not enabled, closing a document causes the document to the right to become selected. The last two options, Snapping Floating Windows and Snap To Screen Edges, constrain the position of floating windows as you drag them.

Diff

The Diff panel in Figure 1-6 configures the file difference engine used to compare files. Performing file comparisons (see Chapter 2) is heavily leveraged by version control integration. By default, NetBeans uses its built-in diff engine. NetBeans

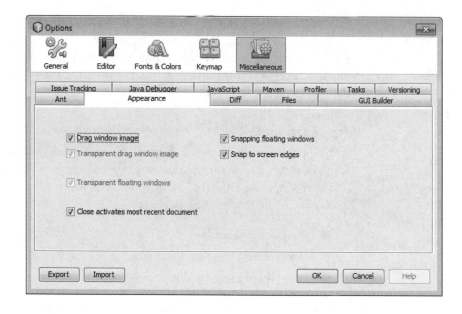

can also use the command-line diff utility available on POSIX (Portable Operating System Interface for Unix)-based systems such as Red Hat Linux, Solaris, and Mac OS X. The Unix diff tool is much more powerful than the NetBeans engine in terms of features and is possibly faster when working with large files. The diff engine generates output that NetBeans then uses to render in the file comparison window.

The internal diff engine supports three configuration parameters:

■ **Ignore Leading And Trailing White Space** Ignores whitespace (tabs/space) at the beginning and end of a line. For example, if you converted a file that uses tabs for indenting to spaces, checking this would show only real code changes.

■ **Ignore Changes In Inner Whitespace** Ignores changes to whitespace within a line. For instance, some developers like to include spaces within parentheses, as in (_int_a_), where an underscore represents a space.

■ **Ignore Changes In Case** Ignores capitalization modifications.

The file system location of the external diff engine (Unix diff command) can be selected by clicking the Browse button. On Unix systems the diff command is normally on the path, so browsing for it is unnecessary. On a Windows system with Unix environment installed such as Cygwin (http://www.cygwin.com/), you must select the executable. Parameters to diff follow the path to the executable. The {0}

FIGURE 1-6

NetBeans
Options window:
Diff

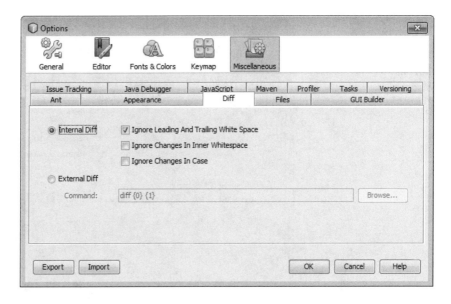

and {1} parameters must be present because they are placeholders representing the
files being compared.

Files

The Files tab in Figure 1-7 is used to configure file associations and file exclusions.
In this tab file extensions such as `.java`/`.xhtml` are mapped to MIME types.
MIME types, define the type of the file, and NetBeans uses the MIME types to
determine which editor should be used to open a file. For example, the `.xhtml`
file extension is mapped to the MIME type *HTML files (text/html)*, which opens
the NetBeans HTML editor. Switching the MIME type to *plain/text* would cause
XHTML files to be opened in NetBeans' text editor.

This tab can also be used to configure new file extensions and to associate them
with a MIME type and hence an editor. For example, if your application used the
extension `.config` for application-specific XML configuration files, you would add
the file extension by clicking the New button and then selecting the MIME type
XML File text/xml. Files with the `.config` extension would then open in NetBeans'
XML editor. If you inadvertently change the MIME type on a file extension, clicking
the Default button reverts your change.

This tab also can be used to configure files or directories that NetBeans ignores.
Files ignored by NetBeans do not appear in the Files or Projects windows. These files
won't be indexed or searched. For example, a global find/replace would break the

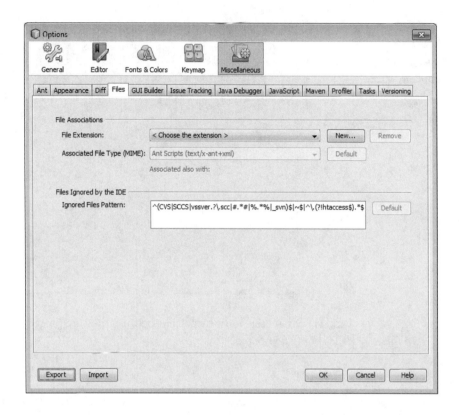

version-control system integration files found in `.svn/CVS` directories. By default, NetBeans also ignores the Unix hidden directories that start with a period. The ignored-files pattern takes a POSIX regular expression.

GUI Builder

NetBeans includes the powerful GUI Builder for designing and constructing Swing user interfaces. It supports most of the built-in Java layouts, such as GridBag and FlowLayout among others, and also adds an intuitive free-form layout. NetBeans goes a step further and also integrates Beans Binding (JSR 295) to shuttle values back and forth between the GUI controls (`JTextFields`, `JRadioButtons`) and the domain model. Under the hood, the NetBeans GUI Builder generates the copious amount of Java code necessary to construct a user interface that supports internationalization and can adapt to changing platform appearances. The GUI Builder is covered in Chapter 3; this section discusses configuration of this feature shown in Figure 1-8. For a more in-depth understanding of the GUI Builder refer to Chapter 3. The following features of the GUI Builder can be configured:

- Location of component declaration
- Access modifiers
- Listener generation style
- Internationalization (i18n)
- Layout generation
- Setting of a component's name
- Qualified name usage

on the
Job

JSR 295 Beans Binding (https://beansbinding.dev.java.net/) is a framework for binding user interface components directly to the data model. This saves significant amounts of time because large amounts of UI code are usually devoted to setting and retrieving values on Swing components. NetBeans integrates extensively with Beans Binding.

FIGURE 1-8

NetBeans
Options window:
GUI Builder

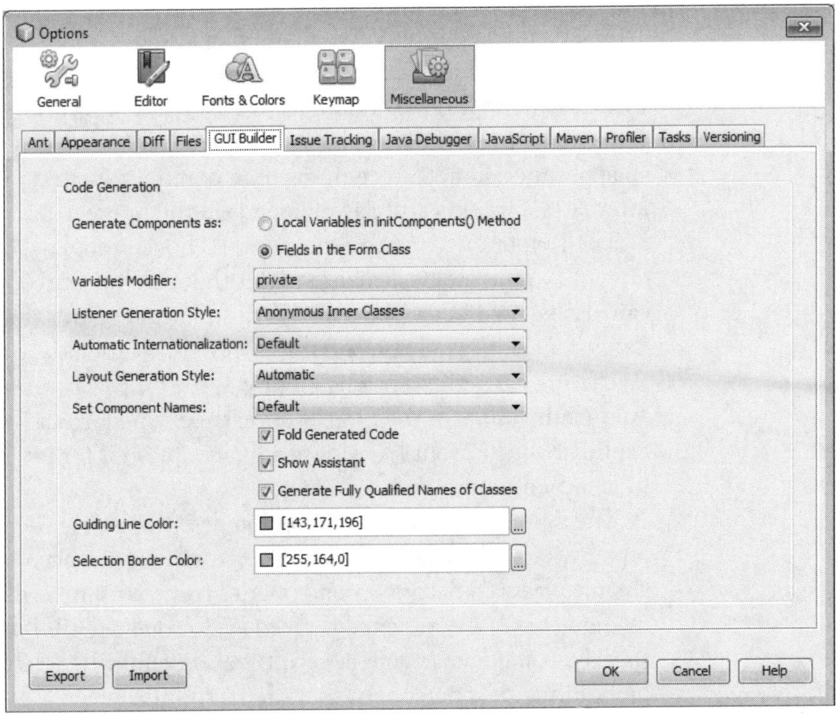

![Options window screenshot]

The Generate Components As radio button group controls whether a class variable (field) is created for each component dropped onto a screen. For example, if a `JTextField` is dropped onto a screen, then a member variable for that `JTextField` is created in the class if "Fields in the Form Class" is selected. If "Local Variables in initComponents() Method" is chosen, the component is instantiated and accessible only within the `initComponents()` method of the form. In this case other methods in the form class cannot access the components. Lack of a class variable isn't a limitation if `SwingBindings` is being utilized to its fullest potential.

If a component is generated as a field in the form class, the Variables Modifier option comes into play. This drop-down list controls whether the field is declared as default, private, protected, or public. The Listener Generation Style option determines how the listener logic is implemented. A number of different listeners can be registered for each Swing component, such as `ActionListener`, `FocusListener`, `MouseListener`, and so on. These listeners are on the Events tab in the Properties window. Three different options are available. The complexity of the form determines which of the three options should be selected. The options are documented in Table 1-2 with sample code. In all cases, a method on the form's class is created to handle the listener.

The Automatic Internationalization option controls whether text is automatically added to a resource bundle. For example, if a `JLabel` is dropped on a screen with automatic internationalization enabled, text typed into the GUI Builder is automatically inserted into the resource bundle. It is much easier to internationalize an application from the beginning than to retrofit it afterwards. Enabling automatic internationalization will pay dividends in the future.

The Layout Generation Style controls how GroupLayout code is generated. GroupLayout is a new layout manager that was integrated into Java 6. However, it can also be used in pre–Java 6 with the addition of an external library (Swing Layout Extensions library). There are three options: Automatic, Standard Java 6 Code, and Swing Layout Extensions Library. If the project is configured for Java 5, using Automatic results in the project using the Swing Layout Extensions library. The explicit Swing Layout Extensions Library option is for projects that are also deployed to Java 5 environments.

The Set Component Names option determines whether to set the name property of a Swing component. The `java.awt.Component` class possesses a name property. Setting a component's name is useful if the component tree is manipulated or interrogated from code. Automated GUI testing tools often require that the component name be set. It is also useful when debugging Swing GUIs and pinpointing the component that fired a specific event.

| TABLE 1-2 | Listener Generation Style |

Anonymous Inner Classes

```
public class Example1 extends javax.swing.JPanel {
  private void initComponents() {
    ...
    jCheckBox1.addActionListener(new java.awt.event.ActionListener() {
      public void actionPerformed(java.awt.event.ActionEvent evt)
        jCheckBox1ActionPerformed(evt);
      }
    });
  }
  private void jCheckBox1ActionPerformed(java.awt.event.ActionEvent evt) {
    // TODO add your handling code here:
  }
}
```

One Inner Class

```
public class Example2 extends javax.swing.JPanel {
  private void initComponents() {
    ...
    FormListener formListener = new FormListener()
    jCheckBox1.addActionListener(formListener);
  }
  private class FormListener implements java.awt.event.ActionListener {
    FormListener() {}
    public void actionPerformed(java.awt.event.ActionEvent evt)
      if (evt.getSource() == jCheckBox1) {
        Example2.this.jCheckBox1ActionPerformed(evt);
      }
    }
  }
  private void jCheckBox1ActionPerformed(java.awt.event.ActionEvent evt) {
    // TODO add your handling code here:
  }
}
```

Main Class

```
public class Example3 extends javax.swing.JPanel implements ActionListener {
  private void initComponents() {
    ...
    jCheckBox1.addActionListener(this);
  }
  public void actionPerformed(java.awt.event.ActionEvent evt) {
    if (evt.getSource() == jCheckBox1) {
      Example3.this.jCheckBox1ActionPerformed(evt);
    }
  }
  private void jCheckBox1ActionPerformed(java.awt.event.ActionEvent evt) {
    // TODO add your handling code here:
  }
}
```

The GUI Builder tab also includes three checkboxes:

- **Fold Generated Code**   Code generated in design mode is automatically folded when switching to the source mode. Thus, the only code that is expanded is code that you can edit.
- **Show Assistant**   Enables the GUI assistant. The assistant appears in a bar above the GUI designer but below the toolbar.
- **Generate Fully Qualified Names Of Classes**   Components are declared/instantiated without imports. If this option is checked, then you see `javax.swing.JTextField` instead of `JTextField` in the generated source.

The last two settings, Guiding Line Color and Selection Border Color, control the colors in the GUI editor. The first option controls the color of the guiding lines to help you align components with other components. The second option determines the color of a control's border when it is selected.

Issue Tracking

NetBeans integrates with the Bugzilla issue tracking system. Using this integration you can see information such as which issues have been assigned to you. Issue-tracking systems are added and removed by right-clicking the Issue Trackers item in the Services window. The Issue Tracking tab in the Options window, depicted in Figure 1-9, configures the frequency with which NetBeans connects and refreshes the list of open items. At this time, NetBeans only supports Bugzilla—undoubtedly more issue-tracking systems will be added in the future.

Java Debugger

The Java Debugger tab in Figure 1-10 configures the basic behavior of the debugger in NetBeans. Tweaking these settings can simplify the troubleshooting of those intractable problems that often crop up at the last minute. The NetBeans debugger is covered in depth in Chapter 9. This Java Debugger tab divides the configuration of the debugger into three categories:

- **General**   Miscellaneous settings
- **Step Filters**   Control when the debugger should step into code
- **Variable Formatters**   Format the display of variables to make them more readable

FIGURE 1-9

NetBeans
Options window:
Issue Tracking

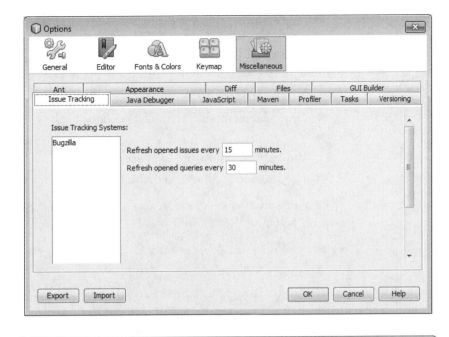

FIGURE 1-10

NetBeans
Options window:
Java Debugger

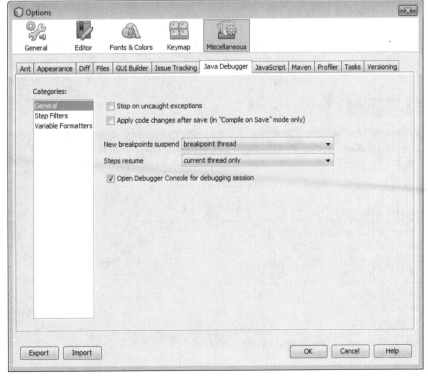

The first category, General, configures several key behaviors of the debugger. These are outlined in Table 1-3.

The second Java Debugger category, Step Filters, shown in Figure 1-11, controls what methods you do *not* want NetBeans stepping into. You can block stepping into with the following method types:

- Synthetic methods   Methods generated by the compiler
- Static initializers   A block of code that executes when a class is loaded. It can be used to initialize static variables.
- Constructors   A method that is executed when a class is created.

Disabling method stepping can also be done by class name. By default, NetBeans does not step into the following classes:

- `java.lang.ClassLoader`
- `java.lang.StringBuffer`
- `java.lang.StringBuilder`
- `java.lang.AbstractStringBuilder`
- `sun.*`
- `sunw.*`

Additional classes can be added to this list. Choosing the "Step through the filters to reach unfiltered code" option steps into the next class available that isn't in the filtered list.

TABLE 1-3   Debugger General Category

Debugger Behavior	Description
Stop on uncaught exceptions	Dynamically creates a breakpoint when an uncaught exception is thrown.
Apply code changes after save (in Compile On Save mode only)	Changes to code are automatically reloaded into an application without restarting the application.
New breakpoints suspend: ■ All threads ■ Breakpoint thread ■ No thread (logging)	Defines the behavior of new breakpoints. Editing the properties on a specific breakpoint can change this behavior.
Steps resume: ■ All threads ■ Current thread only	Stepping over a line can resume either the current thread or all of the threads.
Open Debugger Console for debugging session	If this is checked, the debug console is displayed when using the debugger.

FIGURE 1-11

NetBeans
Options window:
Java Debugger
Step Filters

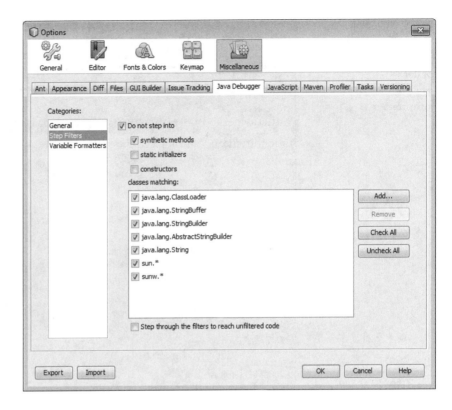

The last category on the Java Debugger tab, shown in Figure 1-12, is the Variable Formatters. This is useful when viewing complex data types in the debugger. For example, in the debugger when you browse a `Map` type, you expect to see keys and their values, not the internal data structures of a `HashMap`. NetBeans ships with the following variable formatters:

- Default `Collection` Formatter
- Default `Map` Formatter
- Default `Map.Entry` Formatter

Clicking either the Add or Copy button can create new formatters. This displays a dialog box where a code snippet is entered to format a specific data type specified using a fully qualified class name.

NetBeans
Options
window: Variable
Formatters

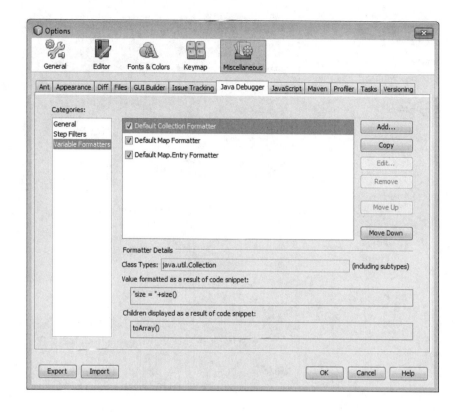

JavaScript

NetBeans provides an excellent editor and debugger for JavaScript. At the heart
of any Ajax-enabled website is JavaScript, which has traditionally been hard to
debug. The configuration tab in Figure 1-13 lists the various browsers supported by
NetBeans and whether they are enabled. Also, the minimum JavaScript version
supported per browser can be chosen. The default JavaScript version, regardless of
browser, can also be configured.

Maven

Maven is a project management tool that not only compiles code but also handles
packaging and dependency management. More information on Maven can be found
on Maven's official website: http://maven.apache.org. Maven integration wasn't
available in NetBeans 6.1, so it won't be on the current exam. However, Maven is
growing quickly in popularity, and with each release of NetBeans it is more tightly
integrated. At some point in the future it will likely be added to the exam. Current

FIGURE 1-13

NetBeans
Options window:
JavaScript

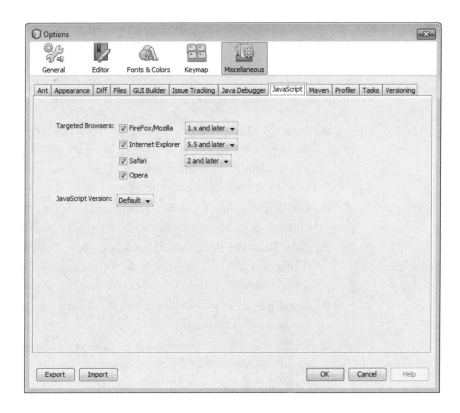

releases of NetBeans can now use the Maven POM (Project Object Model) file as a substitute for the NetBeans project files. Since many open source projects such as Apache Tomcat use Maven for their build system, it is now easy to dive into these projects and expend minimal effort setting up a development environment.

Maven excels at managing dependencies. Add the open source object/relational mapping tool Hibernate (www.hibernate.org), and Maven downloads the myriad of dependencies. It tracks the dependencies of the dependencies and can warn of conflicts. Using Maven, the version of each dependency is known, and the dependency graph can be traced and understood. Maven helps bring sanity to the task of tracking and managing an application's dependencies. Maven also provides a common project structure.

Maven standardizes many of the operations and functions that integrated development environments try to address and control. The major IDEs including NetBeans, Oracle JDeveloper, Eclipse, and IntelliJ IDEA all provide their own interfaces for managing dependencies, building projects, and packaging the output. Maven standardizes these operations and introduces the concept of repositories where dependencies can be published and queried. Using Maven to define projects greatly simplifies the task of sharing projects with other IDEs.

NetBeans integration with Maven has been improving with each release. NetBeans comes with Maven 3.0 built in. The Maven configuration tab in Figure 1-14 configures the integration. On this panel the following items can be configured:

- **External Maven Home** Just as NetBeans can be configured to use a different version of Ant, it also can be configured to use a different version of Maven. NetBeans searches the PATH environment variable on startup and uses the system-specific version if available.

- **Global Execution Options** Clicking the Add button provides a list of valid options. Additional options can be entered directly into the list.

- **Skip Tests For Any Build Executions Not Directly Related To Testing** Checking this causes NetBeans to pass the parameter `-Dmaven.test.skip=true` when running the `mvn` command.

- **Local Repository** NetBeans uses the default local repository as configured by the Maven installation.

- **On Project Open** Contains three drop-down boxes that configure the default behavior when NetBeans opens a Maven project. NetBeans can attempt to download project binaries, a Javadoc of dependencies, and sources of dependencies when a project is opened. Depending on the size of the project and network connection, these three settings can have a significant performance impact.

- **Index Update Frequency** Controls the interval with which NetBeans polls the Maven repositories for updates.

- **Include Snapshots In Local Index** Specifies whether the index of the repository includes snapshot artifacts.

The Edit Global Custom Goal Definitions button opens a dialog box, shown in Figure 1-15, where custom Maven goals can be defined. These can then be executed from the Custom menu when right-clicking the project in the Project window. In Figure 1-15, we create a quick-test menu option under the Custom menu in the Project window. Clicking this menu item executes three Maven goals. Profiles and properties can also be passed in as a part of the custom action. These are advanced Maven configuration options.

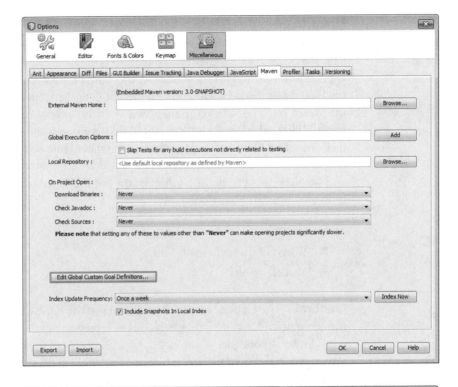

FIGURE 1-14

NetBeans
Options window:
Maven

FIGURE 1-15

NetBeans
Options window:
Maven goal
definitions

Profiler

NetBeans includes an excellent code profiler that is covered in Chapter 10. The NetBeans code profiler can be used to profile the current project or remote applications running on another machine. The Profiler is an invaluable tool for tracking down memory leaks and inefficient code. Since the Profiler is tightly integrated into the IDE, profiling is easy to do on a daily basis. NetBeans provides HeapWalker, which searches memory dumps for potential memory leaks. A common misconception is that garbage collection obviates the need to manage memory and references.

The NetBeans Profiler is configured on the Profiler tab as shown in Figure 1-16. It is divided into three sections:

- General
- When Profiling Session Starts
- Miscellaneous

General   The General section configures both the JDK to be used when profiling and the communication port. The specified JDK is used to run the application being profiled if it is local. To configure additional JDKs, click the Manage Platforms button. The port setting specifies the Transmission Control Protocol (TCP) port the target JVM should listen on.

When Profiling Session Starts   The section When Profiling Session Starts configures when the telemetry overview and threads view windows are opened. They can be opened Always, For Monitoring Only, or Never. The last setting configures when the Live Results window is opened, which can be for central processing unit (CPU) and/or memory profiling.

Miscellaneous   This section controls four separate pieces of profiler functionality. The first field, When Taking Snapshot, configures the behavior when a snapshot is generated. Its three options are self-explanatory:

- Open New Snapshot
- Save New Snapshot
- Open And Save New Snapshot

The next setting, On `OutOfMemoryError`, controls what the Profiler does when a `java.lang.OutOfMemoryError` is thrown. The Profiler has four On OutOfMemoryError options:

- Do Nothing
- Save Heap Dump To Profiled Project
- Save Heap Dump To Temporary Directory
- Save Heap Dump To <File Chosen By Browser>

If the Enable Rule-Based Heap Analysis checkbox is checked, NetBeans analyzes a heap snapshot by using HeapWalker to locate memory leaks. The Reset button reverts the Do Not Show Again checkboxes in dialog boxes.

FIGURE 1-16

NetBeans
Options window:
Profiler

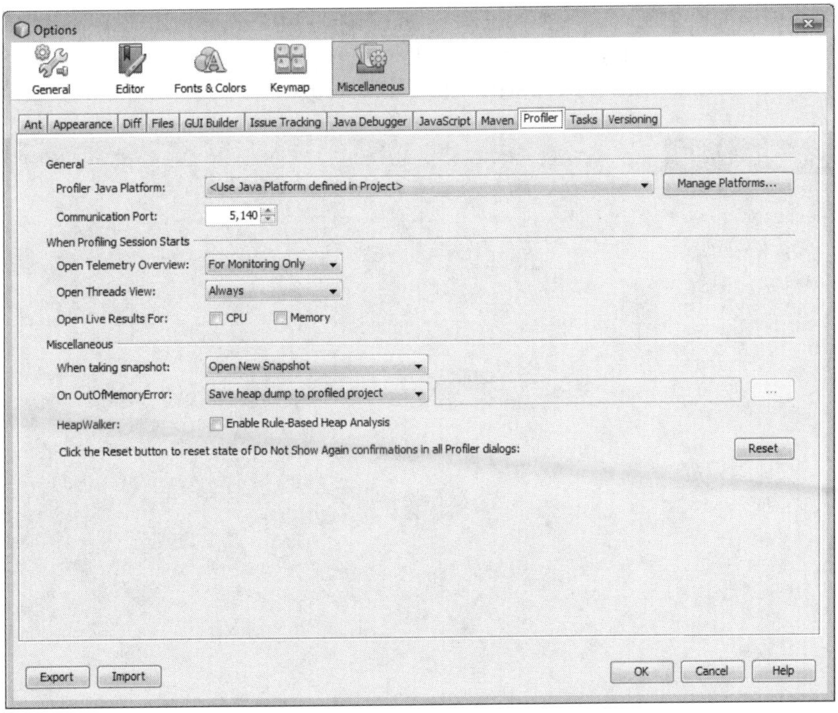

Tasks

The Tasks tab in Figure 1-17 configures the patterns that NetBeans uses to search code and comments for ToDo notes. These ToDo notes are displayed in the Tasks tab along with the file and location. Double-clicking a ToDo in the Tasks tab causes NetBeans to open the source code file and to place the cursor on the ToDo. Tasks are a handy way to keep daily track of work in progress—for instance, to record at the end of the day where you left off or to record some bit of functionality that must wait for a less hurried day. If Show ToDos From Comments Only is selected, only patterns in comments are pulled into the Tasks tab. Thus, the following would not be flagged:

```
System.out.println("TODO replace with logger!")
```

Versioning

NetBeans ships with integrated support for three version-control systems including Concurrent Versions System (CVS), Mercurial, and Subversion. NetBeans also includes a local version control system, Local History, which tracks code changes for a limited period. The Versioning tab, depicted in Figure 1-18, configures the integration with these different systems.

FIGURE 1-17

NetBeans
Options window:
Tasks

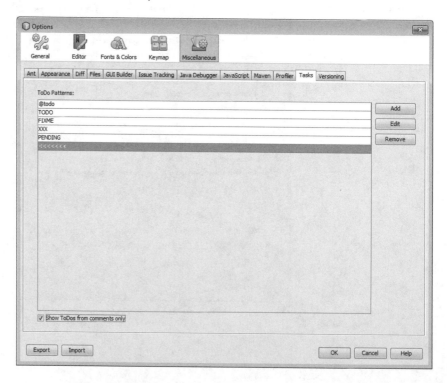

CVS is an open source revision-control system that has been around for a long time. It is the first version-control system that appears in the list. Settings that can be configured include:

- **Status Label Format** Defines the status label shown beside the file in the CVS window
- **Apply "Exclude From Commit" On New Files Automatically** Excludes new files from automatically being committed to the server
- **Wrap Commit Messages To** Wraps commit messages to the specified length
- **Automatically Prune Directories After Checkout** Deletes empty directories after an update or checkout operation

The Local History feature comes in handy when you accidently delete code or want to revert changes you made recently that weren't committed to one of the other version-control systems. Local History has one configuration parameter, and that is the number of days the history is cached. The configuration of this feature is shown in Figure 1-19.

FIGURE 1-18

NetBeans
Options
window: CVS

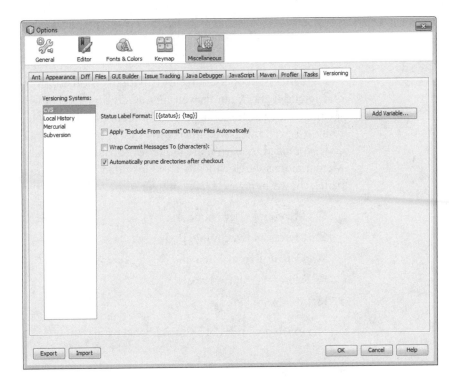

FIGURE 1-19

NetBeans
Options window:
Local History

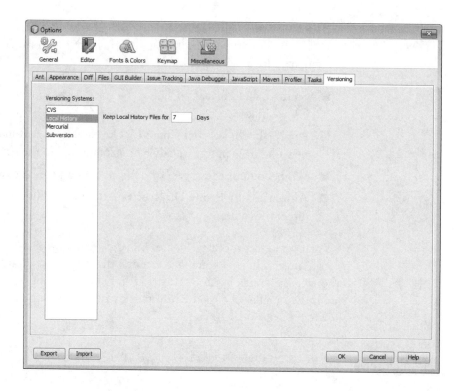

Mercurial is an open source distributed version control. For more information on Mercurial check out its website for additional documentation: http://mercurial. selenic.com. It is the source control system used by the NetBeans project, and as a result it is well integrated into NetBeans. If you intend to examine the NetBeans code, you need to learn more about Mercurial. Before using Mercurial in NetBeans, Mercurial must be downloaded and installed on your computer. The Mercurial panel, shown in Figure 1-20, configures the following settings:

- Mercurial User Name
- Mercurial Executable Path
- Default Export Filename
- Mercurial Status Labels
- Mercurial Extensions

The exam does not delve into these settings.

FIGURE 1-20

NetBeans
Options window:
Mercurial

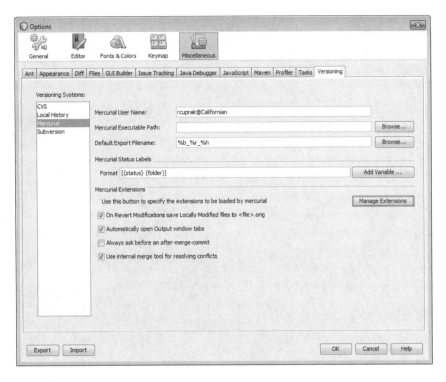

Subversion is another key open source version-control system that NetBeans supports. It was written as a replacement for CVS. More information on Subversion can be found at http://subversion.tigris.org. As with Mercurial integration, NetBeans requires that the native Subversion binaries be installed on the computer. The panel for configuring NetBeans' Subversion support is shown in Figure 1-21 and has the following settings:

- **Path To The SVN Executable File**   Path to the svn.exe file. NetBeans automatically detects the path to Subversion in some environments.
- **Subversion Status Labels | Format**   Informational label to be displayed next to files in the Subversion window.
- **Automatically Open Output Window Tabs**   Causes the Subversion window to be automatically displayed when an SVN operation is performed.

Additionally, the "Define {folder}" button can be used to define the naming pattern for branches and tags. The Manage Connection Settings button is used to manage the list of repositories NetBeans has previously connected.

FIGURE 1-21

NetBeans
Options window:
Subversion

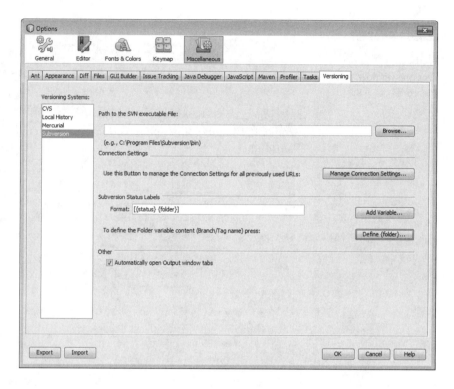

Plugin Manager

The NetBeans IDE can easily be extended and upgraded with the Plugin Manager.
Although NetBeans started out as a Java IDE, it has followed the same trajectory
as Eclipse and has evolved into a general-purpose tool and application platform.
Early in the development, the NetBeans development team had the foresight to
modularize the IDE while also delivering a tightly integrated solution. The NetBeans
IDE is really just a prepackaged collection of plugins. Starting in NetBeans 6.8,
when the IDE first loads, it now prompts for feature activation.

Thus, a C++ developer can elect to activate only C++ plugins. Demonstrating
the power of this plugin architecture, entire applications have been written using
the NetBeans Platform. These applications are completely unrelated to software
development. The Plugin Manager administers the plugins and provides a clean
and intuitive interface.

The Plugin Manager in Figure 1-22 is opened from Tools | Plugins. The
window may take some time to load because the Plugin Manager connects to one
or more remote update centers to check for new plugins as well as for updates to
existing ones. Plugins, or "modules" in the older terminology, can be pulled either
from remote update centers or from the local file system. Plugins that have been

downloaded usually have the file extension .nbm for "NetBeans modules." NBM files are JAR/ZIP archives. The plugins are usually signed with a certificate, and NetBeans warns if the certificate is invalid or cannot be verified. The Plugin Manager has five tabs:

- **Updates**   Lists updates for plugins presently installed
- **Available Plugins**   Lists plugins from the registered update centers that can be installed
- **Downloaded**   Lists plugins that have been manually downloaded
- **Installed**   Shows current list of installed plugins
- **Settings**   Manages the list of update centers and basic update settings

Updates

The Updates tab appearing in Figure 1-22 lists the available updates for plugins already installed. Clicking the Reload Catalog button forces a check of the update centers. The list box on the left displays the list of available updates. Clicking an update populates the panel on the right with a description of the update. First check the update and then click the Update button to apply updates.

FIGURE 1-22   NetBeans Plugin Manager: Updates

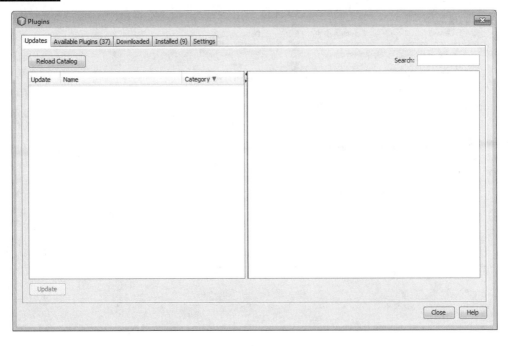

Available Plugins

The Available Plugins tab in Figure 1-23 lists all of the uninstalled plugins from the configured update centers. The left pane displays the plugin Name, Category, and Source. Sources are configured on the Settings tab; each source has its own icon. Clicking an update displays more information in the right pane including the version, date of release, source name, description, and home page for additional information. Plugins are installed by choosing the checkbox next to the plugin and clicking the Install button. A wizard displays the license and prompts the user to confirm that they have read it. This is done for each selected plugin. Once a plugin is installed, it disappears from this list. To force an update of the plugin catalog, click Reload Catalog.

FIGURE 1-23   NetBeans Plugin Manager: Available Plugins

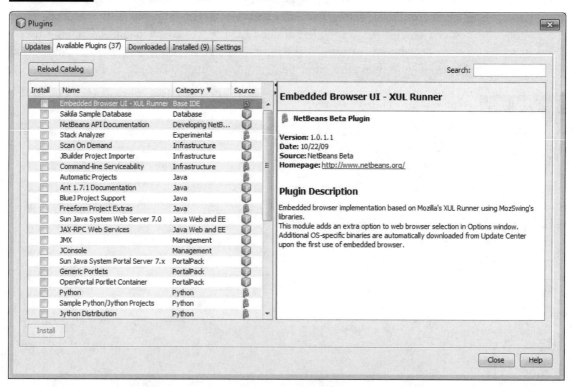

Downloaded

The Downloaded tab in Figure 1-24 contains the plugins that were manually downloaded. Clicking the Add Plugins button displays a file browser for selecting a downloaded plugin in the file system. Adding a plugin to this list does not actually install it; this just makes the plugin available for installation. The Install button installs the plugin and activates it. To summarize, the sequence for using a manually downloaded plugin is twofold:

1. Download and add the plugin on the Downloaded tab.
2. Click the Install button to install the plugin and activate it.

The two-step process allows you to review the metadata in the description panel prior to installing and activating the plugin.

FIGURE 1-24   NetBeans Plugin Manager: Downloaded

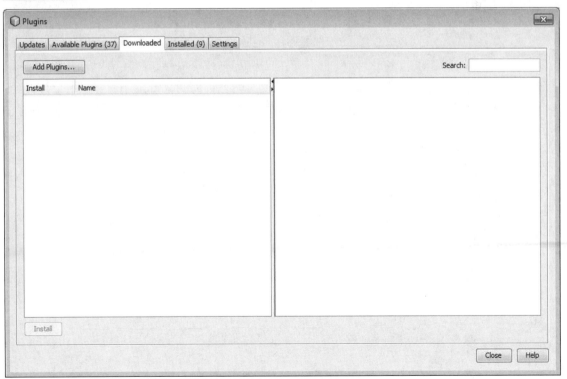

Installed

The Installed tab in Figure 1-25 lists all of the plugins that have been either installed from an update center or downloaded manually and added via the Downloaded tab. The Installed tab:

- Lists all plugins currently installed
- Lists the current status of the plugins installed
- Can activate or deactivate a plugin
- Can deactivate or uninstall a plugin

To activate, deactivate, or uninstall a plugin, the plugin must first be selected in the list by selecting its checkbox. The Search box filters the list of installed plugins. Note: the search functionality is available on all of the tabs except Settings.

FIGURE 1-25   NetBeans Plugin Manager: Installed

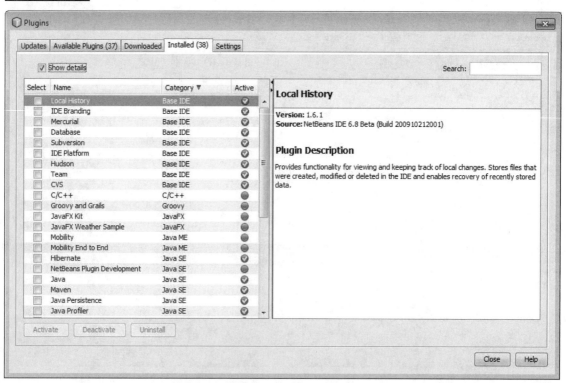

The Show Details checkbox toggles between macro features and the plugins that compose those features. Highlighting a plugin row displays information about the plugin in the right-hand pane. The pane provides key information on a plugin including:

- Plugin version
- Source of the plugin

There is a subtle difference between deactivating and uninstalling a plugin. *Deactivating* a plugin simply turns the plugin off, so NetBeans loads only plugin metadata to display in the Plugin Manager. When a plugin is *uninstalled*, it is completely removed from NetBeans and deleted from the file system. Once a plugin is removed, the only way to use it again is to download and install it—either manually or through an update center.

The Plugin Manager displays the status of plugins with several different icons listed in Table 1-4. Deactivating some plugins requires restarting NetBeans. The Plugin Manager gives you the option of restarting immediately or deferring. If restarting is deferred, the plugins cannot be reactivated until NetBeans is restarted.

Settings

The Settings tab in Figure 1-26 configures several key features of the Plugin Manager including:

- Update centers
- Auto-update check interval
- Proxy servers
- Shared plugin directory

	Icon	Description
TABLE 1-4 Installed Plugin Icon Descriptions	✓	The plugin/feature is installed and activated.
	●	The plugin is installed but deactivated.
	⟳	The plugin is deactivated, but the IDE must be restarted to take effect.

FIGURE 1-26   NetBeans Plugin Manager: Settings

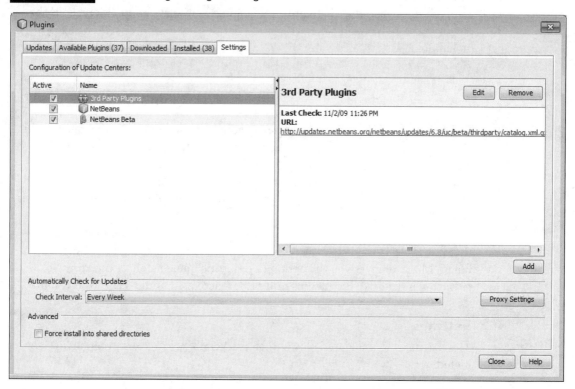

The left panel lists the update centers. Each update center can be deactivated by clearing the Active checkbox. Deactivating an update center stops NetBeans from polling the update center for updates or downloading the list of available plugins. The three buttons Edit, Remove, and Add manage the update center list.

The Check Interval drop-down list specifies the gap between checks for updates. NetBeans can poll for updates on Startup, Every Day, Every Week, Every Two Weeks, Every Month, or Never. Next to this drop-down list, a button configures the proxy settings. This brings up the General configuration tab (Tools | Options | General).

on the **job**

The NetBeans Plugin Portal (http://plugins.netbeans.org) is an excellent source of information on plugins. It contains invaluable reviews from other users and some documentation. If you develop your own plugin, you can easily promote it here.

By default, plugins are installed into the NetBeans user directory under a user's home directory. Plugins downloaded and installed in this directory are not available to other users on the computer. Plugins can be shared between users by selecting Force Install Into Shared Directories. Shared plugins are installed under the NetBeans installation directory in `extras/module`. To install plugins in the shared directory, you must be running NetBeans under an account with administrative permissions.

e x a m

ⓦ a t c h   *Note that unlike the Options window, the Plugin Manager window only has a Close button. This means that plugin updates, installs, deactivations,* *and uninstalls happen immediately, as soon as you click the button. Also note that some plugins may require that you restart NetBeans for the changes to take effect.*

The following Scenario & Solution will help solidify your understanding of the NetBeans Plugin Manager.

SCENARIO & SOLUTION

You want to see what updates are available for NetBeans.	Click the Update tab.
You want to browse available plugins.	Click the Available Plugins tab.
You have chosen a feature to install by selecting the checkbox next to it. You want to install the feature.	Click the Activate button on the Installed tab.
You want plugins to be installed in a shared directory for all users.	On the Settings tab, select "Force install into shared directories."

EXERCISE I-I

Installing the Sun SPOT NetBeans Plugin

The Sun Labs group at Sun Microsystems developed an innovative embedded platform, Sun SPOT (http://www.sunspotworld.com/), which has the Java Virtual Machine (JVM) running directly on hardware. SunSpots can be wired up to motors, sensors, lights, and so on, and can communicate with each other wirelessly. Many exciting home robotics projects have been built with them. To facilitate development, Sun has provided a NetBeans plugin. The NetBeans plugin comes with a user interface for monitoring the SunSpots as well as project templates and additional tools. In this exercise, you install this plugin. This exercise does not require a SunSpot kit.

1. Open the Plugin Manager and add an update center for the SunSpot plugin:

   Name: Sun Spot World

   URL: http://www.sunspotworld.com/NB6/updates.xml

2. Switch to the Available Plugins tab.

3. Search for "SunSpot" and checkmark the following plugins:

   a. SpotRenameRefactoring

   b. Sun SPOTs Info

   c. SunSpotHostApplicationTemplate

   d. SunSpotApplicationTemplate

   e. SPOTModulesUpdateCenter

4. Click Install and accept the licenses. Note the SunSpot plugins are not signed.

5. Select File | New Project | Java | Sun SPOT Application to create a new SunSpot application.

Working with Configuration Files and Directories

Exam Objective 1.2   Explain the purpose of the user directory and the netbeans.conf file and how these can be used to configure the IDE.

The NetBeans user directory and `netbeans.conf` file are integral to the functioning of NetBeans and very important to understand. A NetBeans user directory is created for every user that runs NetBeans. NetBeans stores configuration settings, plugins, and so on in this directory. The NetBeans user directory is located under a user's home directory and is named `.netbeans`. The `netbeans.conf` file is a configuration file that is consulted prior to launching the IDE. It is used to determine the JDK, the default location of a user's NetBeans directory, to set system properties including heap space, and so on. There can be two `netbeans.conf` files, one under the installation directory in `etc` or another in a NetBeans user's directory to customize the settings for a particular user.

e x a m

ⓦ a t c h   *The exam may ask specific questions about how to cleanly uninstall NetBeans, uninstall a specific NetBeans version, or how to wipe clean changes made to an installation. It is important to remember that simply reinstalling the same version of NetBeans may not fix or revert a configuration change that has been saved to the NetBeans user directory. A NetBeans uninstaller cannot fix this problem. NetBeans may be installed on a network share, and thus the user directories are spread out over a network and on multiple machines.*

The NetBeans user directory is named `.netbeans` and is created under a user's home directory the first time NetBeans is run. The location of a user's home directory varies by operating system. On Windows 7 the NetBeans user directory appears under `C:Users\<username>\.netbeans`. On Windows XP it probably is `C:\Documents and Settings\<username>\.netbeans`. On Mac OS X it is `/Users/<username>/.netbeans`. Many different permutations are possible depending upon the prerogatives of the IT department and the computing environment. Under the `.netbeans` directory, a separate directory for each version of NetBeans is created. Thus, multiple versions of NetBeans can be run simultaneously on the same computer.

The NetBeans-specific directories beneath the NetBeans user directory store user-specific configuration settings, installed plugins, cache files, and log output. For instance, the startup log can be found under `.netbeans/<version>/var/log/messages`. Plugins, formerly known as modules, are downloaded to `.netbeans/<version>/modules`. Cache files, which include the local history, are stored under `.netbeans/<version>/var/cache`. The exam tests at a high level; it is not necessary to be an expert on every configuration and cache file in this directory.

While multiple instances of NetBeans can be run on the same computer, it can be dangerous to share projects between these versions. A newer version of NetBeans upgrades an older project, possibly causing problems when launching the older version of NetBeans.

The `netbeans.conf` file plays an integral role in NetBeans startup. As mentioned earlier, there can be two `netbeans.conf` files. The global `netbeans.conf` is found in the installation directory under `etc`. On a Windows 7 installation the `netbeans.conf` file is found in `\Program Files (x86)\NetBeans 6.8\etc\netbeans.conf`. On Mac OS X the file is slightly harder to find: `/Applications/NetBeans/NetBeans 6.8.app/Contents/Resources/NetBeans/etc/netbeans.conf`. A user-specific `netbeans.conf` file gets stored under `<user home directory>/.netbeans/<netbeans version>/etc/netbeans.conf`. The settings in the user-specific `netbeans.conf` file override the global file.

The `netbeans.conf` file controls the JDK used to launch NetBeans. Separate JDK/JREs (Java Runtime Environments) can be used for projects regardless of this setting. Command-line parameters to NetBeans and the JVM are also specified in this file. For instance, in large projects it is often necessary to set the Java heap size. Following is an example NetBeans 6.8 global configuration file:

```
# ${HOME} will be replaced by JVM user.home system property
netbeans_default_userdir="${HOME}/.netbeans/6.8beta"
# Options used by NetBeans launcher by default, can be
# overridden by explicit command line switches:
netbeans_default_options="-J-Dorg.glassfish.v3ee6.installRoot=\\
"C:\Program Files (x86)\glassfish-v3-b68\" -J-client -J-Xverify:\
none -J-Xss2m -J-Xms32m -J XX:PermSize=32m -J-XX:\
MaxPermSize=200m -J-Dnetbeans.logger.console=true -J-ea \
-J-Dapple.laf.useScreenMenuBar=true \
-J-Dsun.java2d.noddraw=true"
# Note that a default -Xmx is selected for you automatically.
# You can find this value in var/log/messages.log file
# in your userdir.
# The automatically selected value can be overridden by
# specifying -J-Xmx here
# or on the command line.
# If you specify the heap size (-Xmx) explicitly, you may
# also want to enable
# Concurrent Mark & Sweep garbage collector. In such case add
# the following options to the netbeans_default_options:
# -J-XX:+UseConcMarkSweepGC -J-XX:+CMSClassUnloadingEnabled
-J-XX:+CMSPermGenSweepingEnabled
# (see http://wiki.netbeans.org/wiki/view/FaqGCPauses)explore
# Default location of JDK, can be overridden by using
# --jdkhome <dir>:
netbeans_jdkhome="C:\Program Files (x86)\Java\jdk1.6.0_14"
# Additional module clusters, using ${path.separator}
# (';' on Windows or ':' on
Unix):
#netbeans_extraclusters="/absolute/path/to/cluster1:/absolute/\
path/to/cluster2"
# If you have some problems with detect of proxy settings, you
# may want to enable detect the proxy settings provided by
# JDK5 or higher.
# In such case add -J-Djava.net.useSystemProxies=true to the
netbeans_default_options.
```

EXERCISE 1-2

Changing the Default Java Heap Size

Large NetBeans projects have the potential to cause out of memory errors (`java.lang.OutOfMemoryErrors`). NetBeans indexes project files in order to provide code completion and precompile syntax checking. These features come at a hefty price. Once the memory telemetry monitor in NetBeans 6.8 shows a razor-thin margin and forcing garbage collection isn't improving performance, it is time to increase the Java heap space. The memory telemetry monitor can be displayed by choosing View | Toolbars | Memory.

1. Navigate to the `netbeans.conf` file in your installation directory.
2. Add `-J-Xmx400m` to the `netbeans_default_options` property.
3. Restart NetBeans.
4. Verify that the parameter was passed to the JVM; search `<user home>/.netbeans/<NetBeans version>var/log/messages.log` for `-Xmx400`.

CERTIFICATION OBJECTIVE

Debugging with External Libraries

Exam Objective 1.4   Describe how to integrate external libraries in the IDE and use them in coding and debugging your project.

NetBeans provides powerful support for external library management. The IDE tracks classpath dependencies and constructs the appropriate classpaths for compilation, testing, and execution. This is important since as the Java ecosystem has vastly expanded, so has the number of dependencies for the typical Java application. Managing large sets of dependencies is not a trivial task and is one of the key reasons for using an advanced IDE such as NetBeans. Each dependency in turn has its own list of dependencies. It isn't uncommon for a Java application to include dozens of JAR files and possibly platform-specific native libraries. These dependencies must be efficiently tracked, shared, and debugged. The IDE leverages its knowledge of a project's libraries to provide support for robust code completion, error detection, code refactoring, and supportive pop-ups that display the documentation for a given method, parameter, or class. Thus, a developer should rarely click compile to discover that a dependency is missing, a class wasn't imported, or a parameter of an invalid type was passed to a method.

Before diving into the material for this objective, it is important to first define what is meant by an external library dependency in NetBeans. An *external library dependency* is either a single JAR file, collection of JAR files, or nested directory of classes and shared libraries. Shared libraries are native code libraries accessed via JNI. A project may also depend upon other projects; this topic is discussed further in project configuration. Common examples of external libraries include log4j, Hibernate, JavaServer Faces (JSF), and SwingX. If you are accessing the parallel or serial port, you might use the RXTX library (http://users.frii.com/jarvi/rxtx/) that includes native shared libraries for Windows, Linux, and Mac OS X. Once the RXTX JAR files and shared libraries are added as a library dependency to a project, code in the project may use RXTX classes to talk to serial and parallel ports. When an external library is added to a project, NetBeans indexes the library and all of its class files to provide auto-completion and error checking to make your life easier while editing.

When adding libraries to a NetBeans project, consider the following:

- Will the libraries be shared across multiple projects?
- Will each project get its own copy of the libraries?
- Should a library be divided into interfaces and implementation?

These issues are important to consider. Sharing libraries across multiple projects helps to ensure project consistency. It reduces the chances that one project will end up with a slightly older or newer version of a library such as log4j or Hibernate. Configuring each project so that it gets a copy of a library simplifies development when multiple developers are involved and where project dependencies change over time. Storing external libraries with projects eases integration with continuous integration tools such as Hudson and CruiseControl. Splitting libraries into interface and implementation libraries forces the use of interfaces during development. For example, if you are using JPA, you obviously want to keep JPA implementation separate and available only at runtime so that you don't inadvertently import Hibernate or TopLink classes directly.

The following topics will be covered for this objective:

- Classpath types
- Library Manager
- Project libraries
- Library documentation and source
- Library sharing

Classpath Types

Most projects have at least two distinct classpaths (Table 1-5)—a compile/runtime classpath and a test classpath. The *test* classpath usually includes a unit testing framework such as JUnit, TestNG, or jMock, the test code itself, and possibly mock objects and test-specific configuration files. The *compile/runtime* classpath is used to compile and run the application. The test dependencies are kept separate so that they are not distributed with the application. The distinction between classpaths is a developer best practice/convention. This distinction is not enforced by the Java language or runtime.

In NetBeans, upwards of four classpaths for a Java project (Table 1-5) can be configured. These are not four independent classpaths. The compile classpath is the root classpath. The remaining three classpaths add further dependencies to the compile classpath. The compile classpath is used not only for compiling the project but also for auto-completion in the editor. Only classes added to the compile classpath are available in the editor unless you are working with test sources. The compile test classpath is used for compiling test source code files. External test libraries are added to the compile test classpath. External libraries added to the compile test classpath can only be utilized from test source code files.

The run and run test classpaths contain external dependencies that are only available at runtime. For instance, if you were using JPA (Java Persistence API), you would place the JPA interfaces in the compile classpath and the implementation

TABLE 1-5	Classpath	Description
	Compile	Used for compiling as well as importing and auto-completion
Classpath Types	Compile test	Used for compile test sources
	Run	Used for running a project
	Run test	Used for running unit tests

classes (Hibernate/TopLink) into the run classpath. This would ensure that you do not accidently import the Hibernate classes directly, thus circumventing the standard JPA interfaces. Whenever possible it is always best to code to interfaces.

Library Manager

There are two user interfaces in NetBeans for configuring external libraries. Project-specific library configuration is done via the Project Properties dialog box. By right-clicking the Libraries or Test Libraries nodes in a project, you can access this dialog box. Defining libraries for use across multiple projects or any of the open projects is the province of the Library Manager, depicted in Figure 1-27. The Library Manager can be opened by choosing Tools | Libraries.

FIGURE 1-27   Library Manager

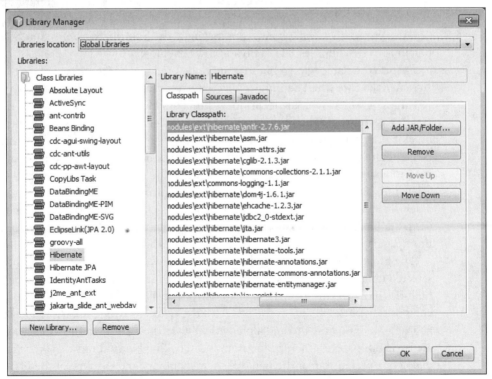

The user interface for the Library Manager can be split into three parts, as shown in the Library Manager window:

- **Libraries Location** This drop-down list selects a library set to be displayed/ edited.
- **Libraries** This box lists the libraries in the current project or global repository. In NetBeans 6.8, libraries are grouped into either Class Libraries or Server Libraries.
- **Classpath tab** This panel displays the contents of the library selected in the Libraries list.

The Libraries Location list contains the library locations for each project appearing in the Projects tab and includes Global Libraries. The Library Classpath box displays the full path for each library, leaving you to make the leap from path to project. Only projects that have a libraries folder defined appear in this box. The next section on project properties explains this further. The Libraries Location list always has at least one entry, Global Libraries. *Global libraries* are libraries that can be shared and used between multiple projects. Global libraries also encompass libraries provided by IDE plugins. For instance, the Sun Microsystems Sun SPOT plugin adds two libraries, SPOTlib and SPOTlibHost.

Despite the name, global libraries are not stored in a central location on the file system. Take care when defining a new library, because the IDE does not copy the JAR files or folders to a safe location within a directory controlled by the IDE. It is very easy to delete the library files out from under the IDE. Projects that depend on global libraries that have been corrupted fail to either build or run. For instance, if the library were a JPA persistence implementation added to the run classpath, the project would compile but fail to run due to the missing JPA implementation. Global libraries are not managed in a version-control system nor can they be shared. They are local to the machine on which they are set up, unless a network share is used. Global libraries back many of the project templates in NetBeans such as the Enterprise application, EJB module, Grails application, and so on.

The Libraries list on the left of the window shows all of the libraries for the selected library location. The libraries are grouped into Class Libraries and Server Libraries in NetBeans 6.8. Clicking a library, such Beans Binding, displays the composition of the library in the panel on the right. Only one library can be selected at a time. Libraries are ordered alphabetically. At the bottom of the Library Manager are two buttons, New Library and Remove. Clicking New Library displays a modal dialog box prompting for the name of the new library and the type of the library:

Class or Server. The new library is immediately created and selected. The Remove button deletes a library. At this time the Remove button does not confirm the request to delete a library—it immediately deletes the selected library. The only way to roll back changes in the Library Manager dialog box is to select Cancel.

The main panel, at right, displays the contents of the library including the library classpath, library sources, and library Javadoc. JAR files and directories of class and share libraries are added to the library classpath. The full path to the library is displayed in the Library Classpath list box. The order of the libraries added is important, because the Java interpreter and compiler observe this order when resolving dependencies. Buttons on the right allow dependencies to be reordered.

Adding source and Javadoc JARs to a library is optional. However, the extra time spent configuring source and documentation definitely pays dividends during development. Most open source libraries, such as log4j, are distributed with their documentation and source. Adding source documentation allows you to drill into the code in NetBeans. Once source code has been attached to a library, you can delve into classes and methods by CTRL-clicking or placing the cursor on the item of interest and selecting Navigate | Go To Source. If the library was compiled with the debug flag, then you can also see the values of the instance variables.

Project Libraries

To access project libraries, as shown in Figure 1-28, right-click the top-level node of a project in the Project window and select Properties. In the Project Properties dialog box in the Categories box, select the Libraries category. Using this dialog box, libraries can be pulled in from several different sources including global libraries and other projects, and new libraries can also be defined. The Java platform and library storage directory can be selected in this dialog box and will be discussed later in this chapter. This dialog box has tabs for the four different classpaths: Compile, Run, Compile Tests, and Run Tests. Each of these tabs has seven buttons along the right side of the dialog box:

- **Add Project**   Adds another NetBeans project as a dependency
- **Add Library**   Adds a global library as a project dependency
- **Add JAR/Folder**   Adds an individual JAR or folder of class files to a project
- **Edit**   Edits an existing classpath entry
- **Remove**   Removes a classpath entry
- **Move Up**   Moves a classpath entry up in the ordering
- **Move Down**   Moves a classpath entry down in the ordering

FIGURE 1-28   NetBeans project libraries

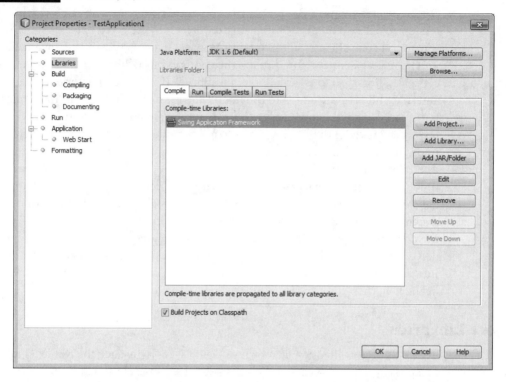

Using the Add Project button, other NetBeans projects can be added as a dependency. Only the output of another project (its JAR files) is added to the classpath. The checkbox at the bottom of the screen, Build Project On Classpath, causes project dependencies to be built when the current project is compiled. Dividing a project into multiple pieces is a good approach to modularizing code. This allows pieces of the system to be built independently and fosters good overall design. Alternatively, NetBeans projects can be created for external libraries if the sources are available.

The Add Library button opens two different dialog boxes, shown in Figure 1-29 and Figure 1-30, depending upon whether a project-specific libraries folder has been configured. A project-specific libraries folder is discussed in the next section; dependencies are copied into and are stored with the project. If a project-specific library directory is not configured, then the Add Library dialog box shown in Figure 1-29 prompts for a global library. It has a button to create a new global library that displays a dialog box similar to the one in Figure 1-27. The new global

e x a m

ⓦ a t c h   *The exam focuses a*
significant amount of attention on the
free-form project type. Free-form projects
will be covered in Chapter 2. In a free-
form project all of the hooks into the
NetBeans project must be defined. This
gives NetBeans the freedom to edit existing

projects with their own structure and build
system without imposing any structural
requirements. If a free-form project is to be
used as a project dependency, its output
must be configured first in its Project
Properties dialog box. If you don't do this,
nothing will be added to the classpath.

library can be managed afterward via the Library Manager. When a project-specific
library directory is configured, the dialog box in Figure 1-30 is displayed. From this
dialog box, libraries that have already been imported to the project may be added.
Generally the libraries in this list match the libraries already added to the project,
with the exception of libraries that have been removed. The Import button in this
dialog box copies a global library into this project. The Add JAR/Folder button
opens a standard file chooser to select either a folder or a JAR file to be added to the
classpath. If a libraries folder is configured, the selected JAR files will be copied to
the folder. Selecting a folder to be added to the classpath is useful for directories of
class files or directories containing shared libraries (DLLs).

FIGURE 1-29

NetBeans Add
Library: global
libraries

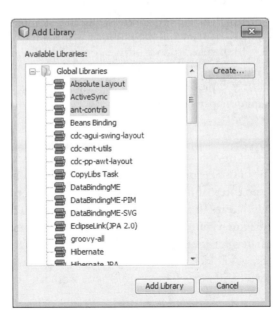

FIGURE 1-30

NetBeans Add
Library: project
libraries

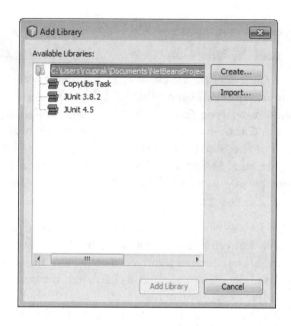

The Edit button edits an existing library. Using this button you can attach sources and Javadoc as well as add/remove JAR dependencies. If the libraries aren't being stored with the project, the changes are made to the global libraries. The Remove button removes the library.

The Move Up and Move Down buttons reorder the library dependencies. Dependency ordering is important because it influences what class is picked up by the ClassLoader when multiple copies of the class are on the classpath. Generally it isn't a good idea to have multiple copies of a class on the classpath or to have multiple copies of a library. Depending on classpath, ordering for behavior creates a maintenance nightmare.

Library Sharing

One of the key technical aspects that has been glossed over thus far is the location of the external libraries in relation to the project. By default, when adding JARs and libraries to a project, the files are left in their current location. This can cause problems when sharing projects. The paths to the libraries and JAR files are specific to a developer's machine. In Figure 1-28, the Project Properties library contains a Libraries Folder setting. By clicking the Browse button, you can select a directory in which libraries for the project are stored. The reference to this directory can be either relative to the project or absolute. The directory doesn't have to be under the root of the project. In fact, the libraries directory could be on a network share. If the libraries directory is on a network share, then an absolute path can be used, allowing the project to be stored anywhere on the computer, providing that all developers use a common mount point for the shared library. If the libraries directory is under the root of the project—in a lib directory, for instance—then a relative path should be used.

Once a libraries folder has been selected, all external libraries for a project are stored in this directory. Any existing library dependencies are copied into it. There is no undoing this operation. Once a libraries folder is selected and the changes are committed by clicking the OK button, you cannot go back.

NetBeans creates an `nblibraries.properties` file in the libraries directory. The contents of this file are shown in Figure 1-31. This file configures the project libraries. Each library is stored in its own directory.

FIGURE 1-31	NetBeans nblibraries.properties

```
libs.swing-app-framework.classpath=\
    ${base}/swing-app-framework/appframework-1.0.3.jar:\
    ${base}/swing-app-framework/swing-worker-1.1.jar
libs.swing-app-framework.javadoc=\
    ${base}/swing-app-framework/appframework-1.0.3-doc.zip
libs.Log4j.classpath=\
    ${base}/Log4j/log4j-1.2.15.jar
libs.Log4j.javadoc=\
    ${base}/Log4j/apidocs/
libs.Log4j.src=\
    ${base}/Log4j/java/
libs.OpenMap.classpath=\
    ${base}/OpenMap/milStd2525_png.jar:\
    ${base}/OpenMap/omcorba.jar:\
    ${base}/OpenMap/omj3d.jar:\
    ${base}/OpenMap/omsvg.jar:\
    ${base}/OpenMap/openmap.jar
libs.junit.classpath=\
    ${base}/junit/junit-3.8.2.jar
libs.junit.javadoc=\
    ${base}/junit/junit-3.8.2-api.zip
libs.junit_4.classpath=\
    ${base}/junit_4/junit-4.1.jar
```

EXERCISE 1-3

Configure a Global Library and Import

Apache Commons IO is an open source library that provides numerous input/output utility classes and methods. Useful utilities in this package include routines for copying directories, deleting directories, writing a Java String to a file, and so on. In this exercise, you create a new global library for Apache Commons IO using the Library Manager and add it to a project. You also configure the source and Javadoc for this library to facilitate development and debugging.

1. Download the Apache IO binary from the Apache Jakarta website:

   http://commons.apache.org/downloads/download_io.cgi

2. In NetBeans select Tools | Library.

3. Select New Library.

4. Name the new library **ApacheIO** and set its type as Class Libraries.

5. Add content to the new library:

   a. On the Classpath tab, click Add JAR/Folder and add the `commons-io-<version>.jar` file.

   b. On the Sources tab, click Add JAR/Folder and add the `commons-io-<version>-sources.jar` file.

   c. On the Javadoc tab, click Add JAR/Folder and add the `commons-io-<version>-javadoc.jar` file.

6. Right-click the project in the Projects window and select Properties. In the Categories panel, select Libraries.

7. Browse for a libraries folder. Create a new folder under your project and name it **lib**. Set the path to be relative. Libraries will now be stored locally with the project and can be checked into version control and shared among developers. If you zip up the project and send it to someone else, it now has all of the required dependencies.

8. On the Compile tab, select Add Library. This displays the Add Library dialog box shown in Figure 1-30. Click Import and from the list of Global Libraries, select the ApacheIO library you created previously and click Import. With ApacheIO selected in the Add Library dialog box, click Add Library to add it to the project.

9. Click OK to confirm the changes to the Project Properties.

10. Create a new class `ApacheIOTest` with the following content:

```
import java.io.File;
import org.apache.commons.io.FileUtils;
public class ApacheIOTest {
  public static void main(String args[]) {
    FileUtils.sizeOfDirectory(new File("/"));
  }
}
```

11. To view the Javadoc for `FileUtils`, click `FileUtils` and press CTRL-SHIFT-SPACEBAR. The Javadoc for this class should appear in a little window.

12. To view the source of the `sizeOfDirectory` method, CTRL-click `sizeOfDirectory`. A new tab opens in the editor with the source of the method.

13. To debug this new library, set a breakpoint on `FileUtils`
`.sizeOfDirectory(...)` and choose Debug | Debug File.

14. The debugger will stop on the line; click "step-into," which brings you once again to the source of the `FileUtils.sizeOfDirectory(...)` method.

Using the steps outlined in this exercise you can now debug just about any open source project. This skill is extremely valuable when troubleshooting or trying to understand how an external library works.

CERTIFICATION OBJECTIVE

Developing with the JDK

Exam Objective 1.6   Describe how to integrate and use different versions of the JDK in the IDE for coding, debugging, and viewing Javadoc documentation.

A developer using NetBeans is not tied to using the version of JDK used to run NetBeans. This is an important distinction to understand. Upgrading to a new version of NetBeans does not require nor necessitate a transition to a newer JDK/JRE. Java was first released in 1995, and major enhancements have been made to the language, runtime, and supporting class library every couple of years. With each release, bugs are fixed, hopefully fewer new bugs are introduced, and new features are added. The reasons for using a different version of Java are many and diverse. Moving a large application to a newer version of Java requires extensive testing. Older code sometimes had to work around bugs in Java, or it inadvertently or intentionally exploited bugs. Often other tools such as application containers or external libraries dictate the version of Java used. Alternatively, NetBeans may be used with newer versions of Java to experiment with upcoming features and changes, or to evaluate the impact that a migration might have on a project. Note that the NetBeans editor might not be able to leverage the newer JDK features, however.

In addition to working with older or newer versions of Java, you can use alternative JDK implementations including:

- **OpenJDK** (http://openjdk.java.net/)   A complete, open source implementation of the JDK.
- **JRockit** (http://www.oracle.com/technology/products/jrockit/index.html)   A high-performance JDK used in a server environment
- **IBM® WebSphere® Real Time** (http://www-01.ibm.com/software/webservers/realtime/)   A real-time JDK

Sun Microsystems licenses Java to other companies that in turn implement the language specification. Apple Computer licenses the language specification and implements Java for the Macintosh platform. Several of the implementations mentioned earlier target high-availability or read-time environments.

In addition to registering Java Standard Edition JDKs, you can also register Java Micro Edition JDKs. If you are developing for the embedded world for devices such as cell phones, set-top boxes, printers, and other embedded devices, you would use a Java ME SDK. These are configured into NetBeans the same way as Java SE SDKs.

Integrating new Java versions is a straightforward process. In NetBeans parlance, the different Java versions are referred to as *Java platforms*. To add/remove Java platforms, select Tools | Java Platforms. This displays the Java Platform Manager shown in Figure 1-32. Using this window, you can register Java SE and Java ME platforms with the Add Platform and Remove buttons. The Platforms list along the left shows the registered JDKs. Clicking a JDK displays information about the JDK in the panel on the right. The panel has three tabs: Classes, Sources, and Javadoc. The contents of the Classes tab cannot be changed; however, sources and Javadoc can be attached on the subsequent tabs. Older JDKs, such as 1.3, require a separate download for the Javadoc.

FIGURE 1-32

NetBeans Java
Platform Manager

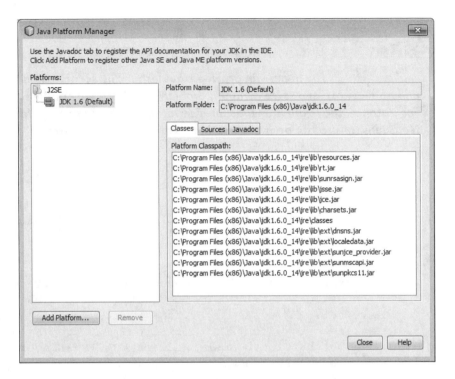

After the Java platforms have been configured, configure the Java platform for a project by opening the project's properties (File | Project Properties) and selecting the Libraries category as depicted in Figure 1-28. The list of available Java platforms appears in the Java Platform drop-down list. The Manage Platforms button at right provides another shortcut to accessing the Java Platform Manager.

on the
Job

The source and binary format do not necessarily have to be in sync with the Java platform configured for a project. For instance, you can use JDK 1.6 to generate binaries that are compatible with JDK 1.3. This setting is configured on the bottom of the Sources category in Project Properties. Take care: this doesn't prevent you from using new JDK classes not present in the older JDK.

After the JDK has been changed for a project, debugging and viewing Javadoc comments is no different from any other external library. CTRL-clicking a built-in class such as `String` will take you to its source. Javadoc will appear for methods when using auto-completion or when using the key shortcut CTRL-SHIFT-SPACEBAR. The local variables are not available when stepping into the JDK since the JDK was not compiled with the source flag.

exam

ⓦatch   *The exam will provide troubleshooting scenarios and expect you to be able to diagnose and solve common problems arising from configuration and deployment. For instance, the exam may present a situation where an application compiled in NetBeans fails to run on a test machine with the following error:*

```
Exception in thread "main"
java.lang.UnsupportedClassVersionError: racing/Main
(Unsupported major.minor version 49.0)
  at java.lang.ClassLoader.defineClass0(Native Method)
  at java.lang.ClassLoader.defineClass(ClassLoader.java:488)
  at java.security.SecureClassLoader.defineClass
(SecureClassLoader.java:10
6)
  at java.net.URLClassLoader.defineClass(URLClassLoader.java:243)
  at java.net.URLClassLoader.access$100(URLClassLoader.java:51)
  at java.net.URLClassLoader$1.run(URLClassLoader.java:190)
  at java.security.AccessController.doPrivileged(Native Method)
  at java.net.URLClassLoader.findClass(URLClassLoader.java:183)
  at java.lang.ClassLoader.loadClass(ClassLoader.java:294)
  at sun.misc.Launcher$AppClassLoader.loadClass(Launcher.java:288)
  at java.lang.ClassLoader.loadClass(ClassLoader.java:250)
  at java.lang.ClassLoader.loadClassInternal(ClassLoader.java:310)
```

In this particular case, the application was compiled with Java 6 in NetBeans and deployed on a machine with an older version of the JRE (1.3). The project can either be switched back to using the 1.3 JDK, or the source/binary format can be set to 1.3.

EXERCISE 1-4

Configuring a Second JDK

In this exercise, you are going to configure the Java 5 (JDK 1.5) with NetBeans. Many applications still use Java 5. The steps used in this exercise work with other JSDK releases as well. This exercise will work on Linux and Windows;

Mac OS X provides preinstalled copies of the JDK under `/System/Library/`
`Frameworks/JavaVM.framework/Versions`.

1. Download the Java 5.0 JDK from http://java.sun.com. Java 5 can be found
   on the Previous Releases page. The exact download link continues to change
   and now requires registration.

2. Run the JDK 5 installer.

3. Launch NetBeans.

4. Select Tools | Java Platforms to display the Java Platform Manager window
   and click Add Platform.

5. Browse and select the JDK 1.5 directory as shown next:

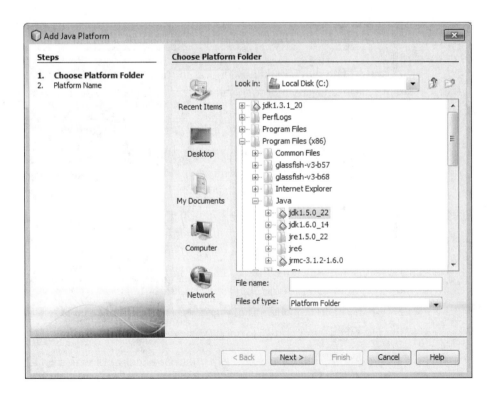

6. Name the platform and click Finish to complete adding the JDK:

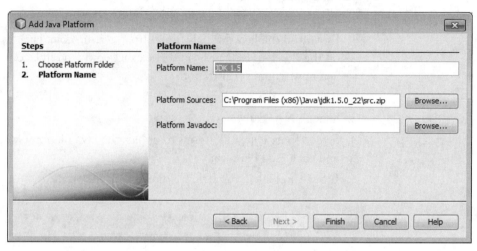

7. The JDK should now appear in the Platforms list of the Java Platform Manager window, as shown next. It is ready to be used in a project.

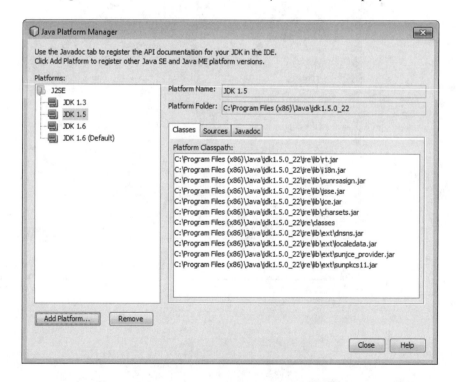

8. Change the JDK of the main project by selecting File | Project Properties and clicking the Libraries category.
9. Select JDK 1.5 from the Java Platforms box.
10. Click OK—the project is now using Java 5.

CERTIFICATION SUMMARY

This chapter focused on NetBeans configuration ranging from IDE user settings to configuration files, external libraries, and Java Development Kits (JDKs). Starting out with configuration provides a firm base on which to delve further into the IDE.

✓ TWO-MINUTE DRILL

Configuring IDE Functionality

❑ NetBeans is configured from the Options window by selecting Tools | Options.

❑ Changes are applied by clicking the OK button in the Options window.

❑ Configuration settings can be exported and imported.

❑ The top-level configuration panels are General, Editor, Fonts & Colors, Keymap, and Miscellaneous.

❑ The Miscellaneous configuration group configures the following features: Ant, Appearance, Diff, Files, GUI Builder, Issue Tracker, Java Debugger, JavaScript, Maven, Profiler, Tasks, and Versioning.

❑ Ant features that can be configured include Ant home, classpath, and verbosity.

❑ Appearance tab controls the docking behavior of NetBeans windows such as Projects, Files, Services, and so on.

❑ Diff tab configures the file diff support including ignoring trailing whitespace, inner whitespace, and changes in case. An external diff engine can also be configured.

❑ Files tab associates file extensions with MIME types. This determines which file editor will be used for a specific file extension.

❑ GUI Builder tab configures GUI Builder code generation.

❑ Issue Tracking tab configures refresh rates for Bugzilla.

❑ Java Debugger tab configures thread suspension, step filters, and default variable formatters.

❑ JavaScript tab configures targeted browsers for testing JavaScript code.

❑ Maven tab configures Maven home, local repository, custom goal definitions, and index update frequency.

❑ Java Profiler tab configures profiler platform, communication port, actions to perform when starting a profiling session, and what to do on an OutOfMemoryError.

❑ Tasks tab configures text patterns to be tracked in the Task window.

❑ Version tab configures the version-control system as well as the local history settings.

❑ The Plugin Manager extends NetBeans.

❑ Plugins can be loaded either from an update site or from the local disk.

❑ Plugin changes are applied immediately.

❑ Clicking Install or Update immediately installs and activates a plugin.

Working with Configuration Files and Directories

❑ Each NetBeans user has a NetBeans user directory, `.netbeans`, in their home directory.

❑ The NetBeans user directory stores user preferences, cache, logs, and local file history.

❑ The `netbeans.conf` file, found under the installation directory, configures the JVM to be used by NetBeans, heap settings, JVM parameters, and the default location and name of the NetBeans user directory.

❑ `netbeans.conf` can be overridden for a user by placing a `netbeans.conf` file in a user's NetBeans user directory.

Debugging with External Libraries

❑ External libraries can be added to the Library Manager to be shared among projects or directly to a project.

❑ Global libraries are managed from Tools | Libraries.

❑ Project-specific library configuration is managed from File | Project Properties | Libraries.

❑ External libraries can be configured with sources and Javadoc to facilitate debugging.

❑ JAR files can be ordered to control the order in which the classloader locates classes.

❑ Libraries can be added to four classpaths: Compile, Run, Compile Tests, and Run Tests.

❑ Configuring a libraries folder for a project triggers the IDE to store all external libraries for a project under a common directory structure.

Developing with the JDK

❑ Multiple Java SE and Java ME JDKs can be registered with NetBeans.

❑ Each project can be configured to use a specific SDK.

❑ Sources and Javadoc can be attached to the SDK to facilitate debugging and development.

❑ Java Platforms are managed from Tools | Java Platforms.

SELF TEST

The following questions will help you measure your understanding of the material presented in this chapter. Read all the choices carefully because there might be more than one correct answer. Choose all correct answers for each question.

Configuring IDE Functionality

1. A project imported as a free-form project requires a specific version of Ant in order to build. Where would this be configured?

   A. Select File | Project Properties | Build | Compiling, and change the path to the required version of Ant.

   B. Configure the PATH and ANT_HOME environment variables.

   C. Edit the build.properties in the NetBeans user directory.

   D. Select Tools | Options | Miscellaneous | Ant, and change the default Ant directory.

2. An application uses the .config file extension for its XML configuration files. By default, NetBeans opens this file in its text editor. How can the developer configure NetBeans to always open the file using the XML editor?

   A. NetBeans will auto-detect the file type and use the appropriate file editor.

   B. Right-click the file and set the file MIME type.

   C. Configure a MIME type for the file in Tools | Options | Miscellaneous | Files.

   D. Add the .xml extension to the end of the file.

3. A developer doesn't want to step into the static initializer of classes while debugging. How can the developer disable this feature?

   A. This feature cannot be disabled.

   B. Set breakpoints in the constructors and run to the breakpoints instead of stepping into the constructor.

   C. Enable the step filter for static initializers by selecting the checkbox in File | Project Properties | Debug.

   D. Enable the step filter for static initializers by selecting the checkbox in Tools | Options | Miscellaneous | Debugger.

4. After installing a plugin in NetBeans, when does it become available?

   A. Once the plugin has been activated on the Installed tab of the Plugin Manager.

   B. Only after Apply has been clicked in Plugin Manager dialog box.

C. Only after the IDE has been restarted.

D. Unless the plugin specifically requests a restart of NetBeans, it is available as soon as it is installed.

5. On a remote system the default profiling port is already occupied by another process. Where can the TCP port be configured?

A. Set the `jpda.port` property in the `netbeans.conf` file.

B. Change the JPDA port setting in File | Project Properties | Profiler.

C. Use the shared memory connector instead to connect to the remote process. Configure the remote process to use the shared memory connector.

D. Change the port in Tools | Options | Miscellaneous | Profiler.

Working with Configuration Files and Directories

6. A developer is working on a large project with thousands of files. NetBeans has been running into heap problems trying to index the project. How can the developer increase the available heap size for NetBeans?

A. Right-click the Java executable in Explorer and increase the size property.

B. Right-click the NetBeans icon in Explorer and increase the heap size property.

C. Change the default heap size in Tools | Options | General and restart NetBeans.

D. Edit the `netbeans.conf` file and add `-J-Xmx400m` to `netbeans_default_options`.

7. After playing around with the settings in the Options window, a developer wants to revert NetBeans back to its original factory default settings. How can this be accomplished?

A. Delete the NetBeans user directory.

B. Open up regedit on Windows, search for nodes with NetBeans as the text, and delete.

C. Click the Revert button in Tools | Options to revert NetBeans to its initial state.

D. Uninstall NetBeans and then reinstall it.

8. A developer installs a new JDK and wants to run NetBeans using this JDK. How does this developer go about running NetBeans with a different JDK?

A. NetBeans ships with its own JDK, and this cannot be changed without breaking the IDE.

B. Change the `netbeans_jdkhome` property in the `netbeans.conf` file to point to the correct JDK.

C. Change the `JAVA_HOME` and `PATH` environment variables to point to the new JDK.

D. Uninstall the current JDK and install the JDK to be used with NetBeans.

Debugging with External Libraries

9. A developer checks a new project into version control. Another developer checks out the project, but is unable to compile or run the project due to missing dependencies. The paths in the project are specific to the original developer's machine. What should the original developer do to remedy the situation?

   A. Define shared libraries in the Library Manager for these dependencies, and then commit the project to version control.

   B. Define global libraries in the Library Manager for these dependencies, and then commit the project file to version control.

   C. Use absolute paths when adding library dependencies.

   D. Configure a libraries folder in File | Project Properties | Libraries and recommit the project.

10. The Java Persistence API (JPA) provides an abstract interface for object-relational mapping tools such as Hibernate and TopLink. If a user codes to only the JPA interfaces, then they can easily switch between JPA providers without having to recompile their code, and the code remains vendor agnostic. In which classpath should the JPA vendor libraries be added so that the code the developers write doesn't accidentally import vendor-specific classes?

    A. Compile

    B. Run

    C. Compile Tests

    D. Run Tests

11. While troubleshooting a bug in some code, a developer needs to step into an open source library to figure out what it is doing. How can the developer debug the external library?

    A. NetBeans will automatically decompile the external library, allowing the developer to step into it.

    B. The external library needs to be compiled with debug flags.

    C. The developer needs to add the sources from the open source project to his project and then recompile.

    D. The developer should attach the source directory for the open source project to the JAR file in File | Project Properties | Library Or Tools | Libraries depending on the project and library configuration of the project.

Developing with the JDK

12. An old project requires JDK 1.3 to compile and run. NetBeans 6.8 is being used and was installed with JDK 1.6. How can the old project be compiled and run?

   A. Download and install JDK 1.3. Update the `PATH` and `JAVA_HOME` environment variables to point to 1.3.

   B. Download and use NetBeans 3.1 and open the project.

   C. NetBeans cannot be used with a JDK other than 1.6.

   D. Download and install JDK 1.3. In NetBeans, select Tools | Java Platforms and register the 1.3 JDK. In Project Properties for the project, select the 1.3 JDK.

13. Which of the following SDKs cannot be registered as a Java Platform?

   A. JRE 6

   B. JDK 1.3

   C. Java ME 3.0

   D. JRockit JDK 3.0

SELF TEST ANSWERS

Configuring IDE Functionality

1. A project imported as a free-form project requires a specific version of Ant in order to build. Where would this be configured?

   A. Select File | Project Properties | Build | Compiling, and change the path to the required version of Ant.

   B. Configure the `PATH` and `ANT_HOME` environment variables.

   C. Edit the `build.properties` in the NetBeans user directory.

   D. Select Tools | Options | Miscellaneous | Ant, and change the default Ant directory.

   ☑ **D. The path to Ant is configured in the Options window.**

   ☒ **A, B,** and **C** are incorrect. **A** is incorrect because Ant isn't configured on a project-by-project basis. **B** is incorrect because NetBeans does not consult environment variables in order to locate Ant. **C** is incorrect because `build.properties` doesn't configure Ant's location.

2. An application uses the `.config` file extension for its XML configuration files. By default, NetBeans opens this file in its text editor. How can the developer configure NetBeans to always open the file using the XML editor?

   A. NetBeans will auto-detect the file type and use the appropriate file editor.

   B. Right-click the file and set the file MIME type.

   C. Configure a MIME type for the file in Tools | Options | Miscellaneous | Files.

   D. Add the `.xml` extension to the end of the file.

   ☑ **C. File associations are configured in Tools | Options | Miscellaneous | Files.**

   ☒ **A, B,** and **D** are incorrect. **A** is incorrect because NetBeans does not attempt to guess at the content type of a file. **B** is incorrect because there is no option to set the MIME type by right-clicking. **D** is incorrect because changing the file extension is not necessary.

3. A developer doesn't want to step into the static initializer of classes while debugging. How can the developer disable this feature?

   A. This feature cannot be disabled.

   B. Set breakpoints in the constructors and run to the breakpoints instead of stepping into the constructor.

C. Enable the step filter for static initializers by selecting the checkbox in File | Project Properties | Debug.

D. Enable the step filter for static initializers by selecting the checkbox in Tools | Options | Miscellaneous | Debugger.

☑ **D.** Stepping into static initializers can be disabled in Tools | Options | Miscellaneous | Debugger.

☒ **A, B,** and **C** are incorrect. **A** is incorrect because stepping into static initializers can be disabled. **B** is onerous and places an unneeded burden on the developer. **C** is incorrect because debugger settings are not configured on a per-project basis.

4. After installing a plugin in NetBeans, when does it become available?

   A. Once the plugin has been activated on the Installed tab of the Plugin Manager.

   B. Only after Apply has been clicked in Plugin Manager dialog box.

   C. Only after the IDE has been restarted.

   D. Unless the plugin specifically requests a restart of NetBeans, it is available as soon as it is installed.

   ☑ **D.** Unless the plugin specifically requests a restart of NetBeans, it is active as soon as it is installed.

   ☒ **A, B,** and **C** are incorrect. **A** is incorrect because a plugin does not need to be activated after it is installed. **B** is incorrect because the Plugin Manager does not have an Apply button. **C** is incorrect because NetBeans does not need to be restarted unless the plugin specifically requests the operation.

5. On a remote system the default profiling port is already occupied by another process. Where can the TCP port be configured?

   A. Set the `jpda.port` property in the `netbeans.conf` file.

   B. Change the JPDA port setting in File | Project Properties | Profiler.

   C. Use the shared memory connector instead to connect to the remote process. Configure the remote process to use the shared memory connector.

   D. Change the port in Tools | Options | Miscellaneous | Profiler.

   ☑ **D.** The default port for the Profiler is configured in the Options window.

   ☒ **A, B,** and **C** are incorrect. **A** is incorrect because `netbeans.conf` configures the startup parameters of NetBeans, not the Profiler. **B** is incorrect because profiler settings are not configured in Project Properties. **C** is incorrect because the Profiler uses TCP ports for communication.

Working with Configuration Files and Directories

6. A developer is working on a large project with thousands of files. NetBeans has been running into heap problems trying to index the project. How can the developer increase the available heap size for NetBeans?

   A. Right-click the Java executable in Explorer and increase the size property.

   B. Right-click the NetBeans icon in Explorer and increase the heap size property.

   C. Change the default heap size in Tools | Options | General and restart NetBeans.

   D. Edit the `netbeans.conf` file and add `-J-Xmx400m` to `netbeans_default_options`.

   ☑ **D.** The loader prior to instantiating NetBeans consults the NetBeans config file.

   ☒ **A, B,** and **C** are incorrect. **A** is incorrect because the Java heap size is not changed by right-clicking `java.exe` and editing a property. **B** is incorrect because you cannot edit the heap properties of NetBeans in Windows Explorer or in the Finder on Mac OS X. **C** is incorrect because the heap settings cannot be configured within NetBeans.

7. After playing around with the settings in the Options window, a developer wants to revert NetBeans back to its original factory default settings. How can this be accomplished?

   A. Delete the NetBeans user directory.

   B. Open up regedit on Windows, search for nodes with NetBeans as the text, and delete.

   C. Click the Revert button in Tools | Options to revert NetBeans to its initial state.

   D. Uninstall NetBeans and then reinstall it.

   ☑ **A.** Deleting the NetBeans user directory will delete all user preferences.

   ☒ **B, C,** and **D** are incorrect. **B** is incorrect because settings for NetBeans are not stored in the registry. **C** is incorrect because there is no Revert button. **D** is incorrect because reinstalling will not clear the NetBeans user directory.

8. A developer installs a new JDK and wants to run NetBeans using this JDK. How does this developer go about running NetBeans with a different JDK?

   A. NetBeans ships with its own JDK, and this cannot be changed without breaking the IDE.

   B. Change the `netbeans_jdkhome` property in the `netbeans.conf` file to point to the correct JDK.

   C. Change the `JAVA_HOME` and `PATH` environment variables to point to the new JDK.

   D. Uninstall the current JDK and install the JDK to be used with NetBeans.

☑ **B**. Setting the `netbeans_jdkhome` property in the `netbeans.conf` file does change the JDK.

☒ **A, C**, and **D** are incorrect. **A** is incorrect because NetBeans can be run on different versions of Java including Java 5 and 6. **C** is incorrect because NetBeans uses the value stored in the `netbeans_jdkhome` property that is specified in the `netbeans.conf` file. **D** is incorrect as this will not change the paths specified in the `netbeans.conf` file.

Debugging with External Libraries

9. A developer checks a new project into version control. Another developer checks out the project, but is unable to compile or run the project due to missing dependencies. The paths in the project are specific to the original developer's machine. What should the original developer do to remedy the situation?

    A. Define shared libraries in the Library Manager for these dependencies, and then commit the project to version control.

    B. Define global libraries in the Library Manager for these dependencies, and then commit the project file to version control.

    C. Use absolute paths when adding library dependencies.

    D. Configure a libraries folder in File | Project Properties | Libraries and recommit the project.

    ☑ **D**. Creating a libraries directory under the project and committing it to version control will enable other developers to easily check out the project.

    ☒ **A, B**, and **C** are incorrect. **A** is incorrect because there is no shared library feature. **B** is incorrect because global libraries are local to a developer's machine. **C** isn't a solution because absolute paths won't help the developers if they don't have the libraries.

10. The Java Persistence API (JPA) provides an abstract interface for object-relational mapping tools such as Hibernate and TopLink. If a user codes to only the JPA interfaces, then they can easily switch between JPA providers without having to recompile their code, and the code remains vendor agnostic. In which classpath should the JPA vendor libraries be added so that the code the developers write doesn't accidentally import vendor-specific classes?

    A. Compile

    B. Run

    C. Compile Tests

    D. Run Tests

    ☑ **B**. The libraries should be put into the run classpath. Libraries put into the run classpath are available during execution and testing but not in the editor.

    ☒ **A, C**, and **D** are incorrect. Choice **A** is incorrect because adding the libraries to the compile classpath would allow developers to directly import vendor-specific classes, thereby defeating the purpose of coding to JPA interfaces. Choices **C** and **D** are incorrect because these are test targets.

11. While troubleshooting a bug in some code, a developer needs to step into an open source library to figure out what it is doing. How can the developer debug the external library?

A. NetBeans will automatically decompile the external library, allowing the developer to step into it.

B. The external library needs to be compiled with debug flags.

C. The developer needs to add the sources from the open source project to his project and then recompile.

D. The developer should attach the source directory for the open source project to the JAR file in File | Project Properties | Library Or Tools | Libraries depending on the project and library configuration of the project.

☑ **D.** The developer should attach the source directory for the open source project to the JAR file in File | Project Properties | Library or Tools | Libraries depending on the project and library configuration of the project.

☒ **A, B,** and **C** are incorrect. **A** is incorrect because NetBeans does not decompile source code. **B** is incorrect because debug symbols have nothing to do with viewing the source. While **C** might technically work, it would completely defeat the library management tools in NetBeans.

Developing with the JDK

12. An old project requires JDK 1.3 to compile and run. NetBeans 6.8 is being used and was installed with JDK 1.6. How can the old project be compiled and run?

A. Download and install JDK 1.3. Update the `PATH` and `JAVA_HOME` environment variables to point to 1.3.

B. Download and use NetBeans 3.1 and open the project.

C. NetBeans cannot be used with a JDK other than 1.6.

D. Download and install JDK 1.3. In NetBeans, select Tools | Java Platforms and register the 1.3 JDK. In Project Properties for the project, select the 1.3 JDK.

☑ **D.** Download and install JDK 1.3. In NetBeans, select Tools | Java Platforms and register the 1.3 JDK. In Project Properties for the project, select the 1.3 JDK. These steps are the same for all JDKs.

☒ **A, B,** and **C** are incorrect. **A** is incorrect because NetBeans does not consult the operation system path. **B** is incorrect because NetBeans is not tied to supporting only specific versions of Java. **C** is incorrect because NetBeans can most certainly be used with other versions of the JDK.

13. Which of the following SDKs cannot be registered as a Java Platform?

A. JRE 6

B. JDK 1.3

C. Java ME 3.0

D. JRockit JDK 3.0

☑ **A.** A JRE cannot be configured as a Java Platform because it is meant for running Java applications and lacks compiler tools.

☒ **B, C,** and **D** are incorrect. Any JDK, even non-Sun JDKs, can be configured as a Java Platform in NetBeans.

2

Builds and Controls

CERTIFICATION OBJECTIVES

-     Understanding Free-Form Projects
-     Using Version Control Systems
-     Working with Build Files and Processes

-     Configuring the JDK into the Project
- ✓   Two-Minute Drill
- Q&A   Self Test

T his chapter covers free-form projects, version control system support, Ant integration, and project-specific JDK configuration, which are crucial for using NetBeans on a typical project. The free-form project support enables NetBeans to be adapted to just about any project. Version control systems manage the revision history for projects and provide the necessary infrastructure for multiple developers to work concurrently on a project. NetBeans uses Ant as its build system, and knowledge of how these build files work is critical as a project grows in size and complexity. Lastly, NetBeans supports multiple JDKs, thereby allowing each project to use a different JDK if necessary. These four exam topics cover important infrastructure aspects of the IDE that are crucial to daily workflow.

CERTIFICATION OBJECTIVE

Understanding Free-Form Projects

Exam Objective 2.1   Describe the characteristics and uses of a free-form project.

NetBeans includes numerous standard project templates to simplify the creation of new applications. These templates are configured with library dependencies, possess a predefined layout, and include an Ant build file. The Ant build file is integrated with NetBeans' execution, debugging, testing, and profiling features. These templates and their associated wizards enable developers to quickly and easily start new applications with minimal effort. Project templates are selected from File | New Project. Example project templates include Java Application, Java Desktop Application, Web Application, EJB Module, and Enterprise Application Client. However, it is often necessary to create a new NetBeans project from an existing project that has its own code structure and build files. To facilitate importing such projects, NetBeans includes two versatile free-form project templates: Java Free-Form Project and Web Free-Form Application.

The free-form project allows NetBeans to work with just about any Java project that uses Ant for building. Besides using the project's Ant build file, NetBeans does not require that a free-form project conform to a predefined file layout placement of the source files or of the location of external libraries. NetBeans delegates all build, execution, and Javadoc operations to the project's Ant file. Thus, clicking Run | Run Main Project invokes the target in the project's Ant file that launches the application. NetBeans requires the location of source and test files and external libraries necessary to enable code completion and syntax checking.

The two free-form project templates are very similar. Both leverage the project's existing Ant script and allow the source and test file locations, libraries, and output to be configured. The Web Free-Form Application template is an extension of the Java Free-Form Project template and requires the location of web resources (XHTML/HTML files) as well as of the container libraries (`servlet.jar`). The IDE delegates all project-related actions, including server deployment, to the project's Ant script.

The following topics describe how to build and use NetBeans' free-form project templates:

- Creating a Project
- Editing Project Properties
- Integrating JUnit
- Profiling
- Debugging

Creating a Project

To create a new Java free-form project, choose File | New Project and select Java Free-Form Project. The dialog box depicted in Figure 2-1 appears. The free-form project wizard collects the basic project information necessary to get the project started. Configuring additional actions for profiling and testing individual files must be configured afterwards. Not all of the fields in the wizard are required—fields can be edited subsequently via File | Project Properties, which is covered in the next section.

This section uses the MusicCoach application throughout. This application can be downloaded from http://www.cuprak.net/MusicCoach.

Free-Form Project, Step 1

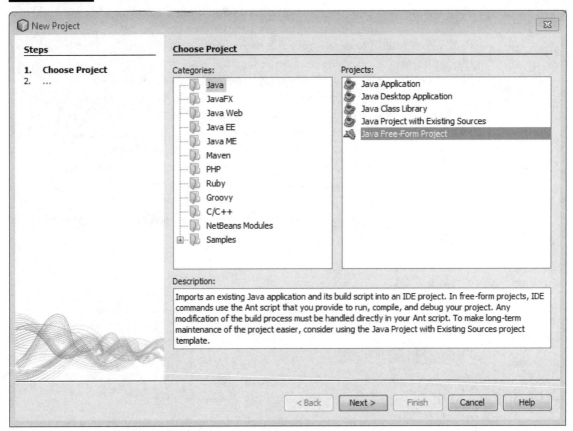

The next step, shown in Figure 2-2, is to select the root directory of the project. This is the directory where all of the project files are stored. NetBeans automatically searches for a `build.xml` file to use as the build for the project. This screen also prompts for the name of the project and the directory where the NetBeans project folder will be created. The NetBeans project folder can be placed anywhere on the system. By default, NetBeans populates the Project Name using the name of the directory and places the NetBeans project folder under the project root selected above it.

FIGURE 2-2   Free-Form Project, Step 2

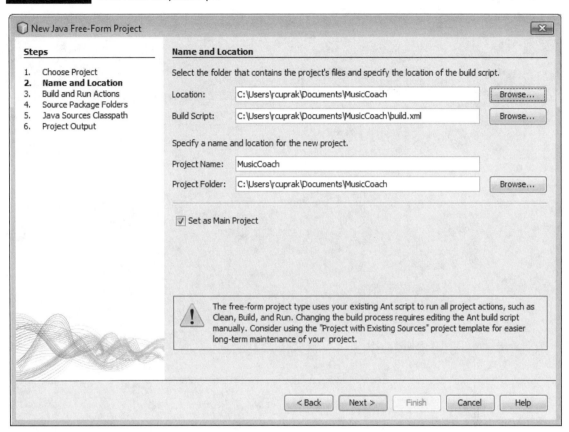

NetBeans drills into the Ant build file to configure the predefined actions. The wizard, shown in Figure 2-3, makes its best attempt at mapping targets in the Ant file to project actions. However, these should be double-checked because NetBeans is just guessing. The target name either can be selected from the list of targets detected in the Ant file or can be typed. Targets can be typed because Ant scripts can be dynamic with import statements and conditional logic. NetBeans may not be able to resolve all Ant file imports until runtime, when Ant variables are evaluated. It is not necessary to populate the actions—this can be done afterwards via File | Project Properties.

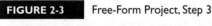

FIGURE 2-3   Free-Form Project, Step 3

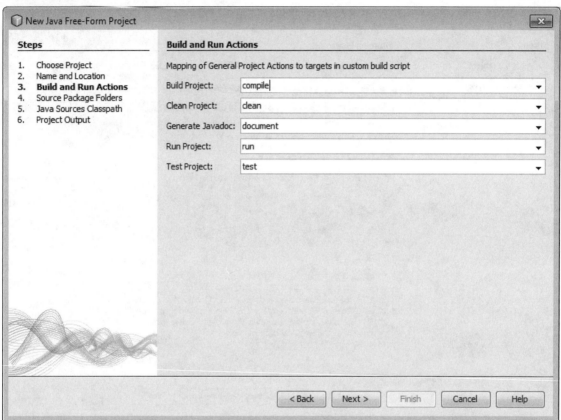

In Step 4, the wizard prompts for the source and test packages as depicted in Figure 2-4. NetBeans again attempts to guess which folders are for each by using common naming patterns—`src`, `test-src`, `test`, and so on. Multiple source code roots can be configured. Choosing Includes/Excludes configures patterns that, respectively, either include or exclude files. By default, NetBeans includes all files under the source directories. The source level and file encoding are also configured. Source level affects editor features such as code completion and syntax checking. For instance, if source level 1.3 is selected, Java 5 classes such as `BlockingQueue` and language features such as generics are unavailable.

The wizard panel in Figure 2-4 configures the project file encoding. By default, UTF-8 is selected. This setting controls how the IDE interprets character encodings beyond the ASCII character set. Newly created files use this encoding. When NetBeans opens a file, it attempts to use the file encoding declared within the file, project declaration, or the encoding that is being used by the IDE.

on the job

The Firefox web browser (www.mozilla.com) can be used to determine the encoding of a file. Open the file in the web browser: File | Open File. You can see the encoding by choosing View | Character Encoding. The encoding of the file has a checkmark next to it.

In the next step, shown in Figure 2-5, the Java sources are configured for the IDE. These classpaths are used to support code completion because the IDE delegates all compilation and execution to the project's Ant file.

FIGURE 2-4   Free-Form Project, Step 4

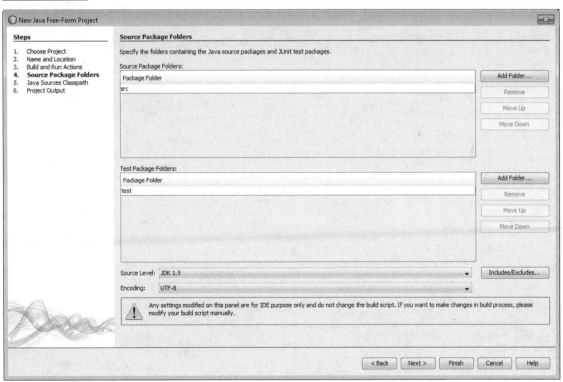

The classpath functionality available to a free-form project has significant limitations compared with a standard project. These limitations include:

- **Source for the libraries cannot be attached.**
- **Javadoc for the libraries cannot be added.**
- **JAR files cannot be pulled from global libraries.**
- **A free-form project cannot depend upon another project.**

The exam may also contrast the free-form project with a "Java Project with Existing Sources." The standard project template and wizard are for instances where the project does not already have an Ant build file or where its Ant file can be easily replaced with the one provided by NetBeans.

FIGURE 2-5   Free-Form Project, Step 5

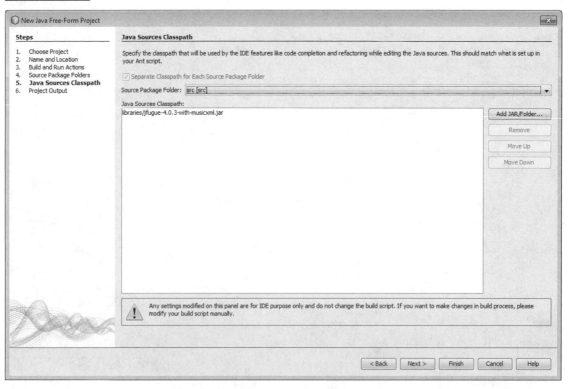

In the last step in the wizard, the output directories for source and test are specified in addition to the output path for Javadoc. This is shown in Figure 2-6. The output JARs are needed to support the debugger and if this project is to be used by another NetBeans standard project. A NetBeans standard project is one that uses an IDE-generated Ant script.

The project is very similar to a Java free-form project. The new project wizard is essentially the same with the exception of two new steps: Web Source and Web Sources Classpath. These two additional steps configure web resources and their dependencies. NetBeans uses this information to provide better coding support of the web.xml, faces-config.xml, and code completion, as well as to provide syntax checking in web source files (XHTML/JSP/and so on).

FIGURE 2-6   Free-Form Project, Step 6

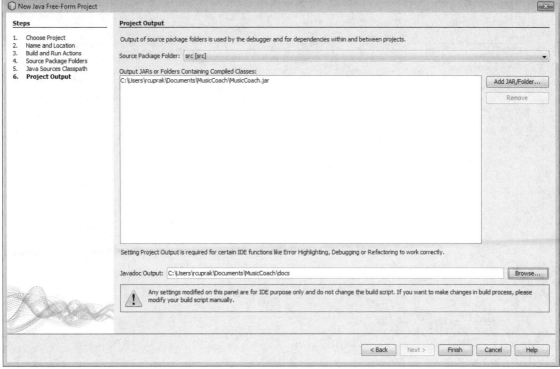

The Web Sources step, shown in Figure 2-7, prompts for several important pieces of information including:

- **Web Pages Folder**   Location of JSP/XHTML/HTML pages and graphics
- **WEB-INF Content**   Location of standard Java web application settings including `web.xml`
- **Context Path**   Deployment path of the application—for instance, a wiki might be deployed to http://www.cuprak.net/wiki with "wiki" being the context path
- **Java EE Version**   The version of the Java EE specification being used by the application

FIGURE 2-7   Web Sources

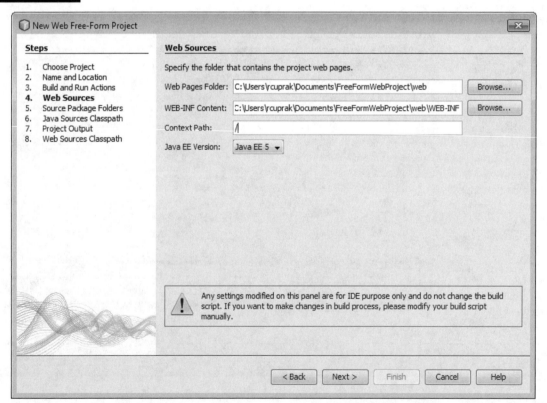

The last step in a free-form web application, depicted in Figure 2-8, prompts for the Web Sources Classpath. This classpath typically includes classes that are used in the JSP/XHTML pages, such as tag libs. If the Servlet API/JSP classes have not already been added to the classpath, they should be added here. As with the Java Sources Classpath, these settings are only used by the IDE to provide its code completion and refactoring features and do not impact how your application is built.

Editing Project Properties

The project settings from the wizard are populated into `nbproject/project.xml`. After a project has been created, you have two ways to edit the settings. The settings can be edited either directly in the `nbproject/project.xml` file or

FIGURE 2-8   Web Sources Classpath

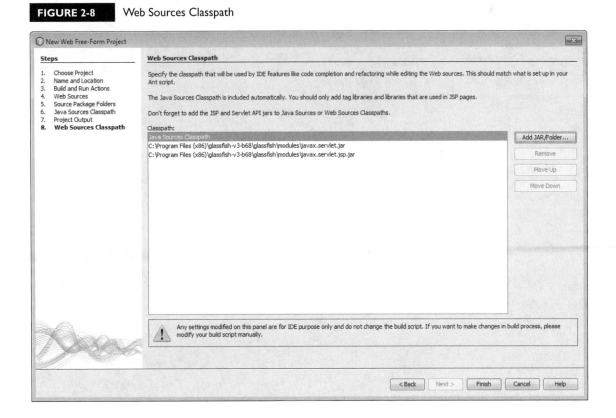

via File | Project Properties, which is shown in Figure 2-9. Manual changes to the XML file should only be used as a last resort. If the Project Properties window is opened and closed after changes to `project.xml` have been made, the changes to `project.xml` are lost. The Free-Form Project Properties dialog box, shown in Figure 2-9, has six panels that mirror the free-form project wizard (see Table 2-1). The Build And Run tab has an additional table not present in the wizard. By using this table, you can add additional context menus. The content of the label column is used as the name of the menu item. Right-clicking the project root in the Projects or Files window accesses custom menu items.

FIGURE 2-9   Build And Run settings

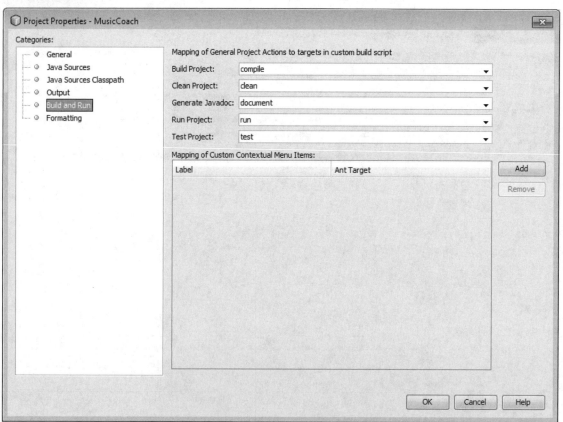

TABLE 2-1	Free-Form Project Properties	
Figure	**Panel Title**	**Notes**
Figure 2-2	General	Lists project location and the build file being used. Fields are informational and non-editable.
Figure 2-4	Java Sources	Configures source and test source directories.
Figure 2-5	Java Sources Classpath	Configures the classpath.
Figure 2-6	Output	Specifies the project output—needed by the debugger and dependent projects.
Figure 2-3	Build And Run	Maps the NetBeans actions to targets in the project's Ant script.
Chapter 7	Formatting	Configures project-specific code formatting.

As mentioned previously, Ant target/action mappings are stored in the file `nbproject/project.xml`. Some changes, such as using multiple Ant files, require direct editing of this file. For example, let's say that we added a custom context menu to populate the database; however, our load script was stored in a separate Ant file. To incorporate this script, you would need to edit the `project.xml` file directly, as shown next.

Two sections are of primary interest for the Ant integration: `ide-actions` and `context-menu` elements. Following is a sample `project.xml` file. The `ide-actions` element maps defined IDE actions to targets in the project's Ant file. The following predefined actions are available for mapping:

- **debug**   Debugs a project
- **build**   Builds a project
- **run**   Runs a project
- **test**   Runs tests for a project
- **run.single**   Runs the currently selected file
- **debug.single**   Debugs the currently selected file
- **compile.single**   Compiles the currently selected file
- **test.single**   Runs the test file for the currently selected file
- **debug.test.single**   Runs the test file for the currently selected file in the debugger
- **debug.fix**   Runs the Apply Code Changes command on the currently selected file

```
<project xmlns="http://www.netbeans.org/ns/project/1">
  <type>org.netbeans.modules.ant.freeform</type>
    <configuration>
      <general-data xmlns="http://www.netbeans.org/ns/freeform-project/1">
        ...
        <ide-actions>
          <action name="build">
            <target>compile</target>
          </action>
          <!-More Actions for running/debugging etc.-->
        </ide-actions>
        <view>
          <items>
            ...
          </items>
          <context-menu>
            <ide-action name="build"/>
            <ide-action name="rebuild"/>
              <ide-action name="clean"/>
              <ide-action name="javadoc"/>
              <ide-action name="run"/>
              <ide-action name="test"/>
              <action>
                <script>database.xml</script>
                <label>Populate Database</label>
                <target>load</target>
              </action>
            </context-menu>
          </view>
        <subprojects/>
      </general-data>
      ...
  </configuration>
</project>
```

In the context-menu element, new menu items can be added and mapped. In the preceding example, the load target in the Ant script database.xml is mapped to a custom Populate Database menu. This menu appears below the Test menu item in the context menu.

on the **Job**

Saving project.xml causes NetBeans to reload the file and repopulate the menus. If the menus are not repopulated, then the file has an error. If NetBeans is restarted and project.xml contains an error, then the project will not be opened by the IDE.

Integrating JUnit

JUnit integration with a free-form project is straightforward and requires only minor changes to the project's Ant script (build.xml). The following code shows a simple target with the JUnit tasks configured appropriately. The two changes necessary for the JUnit integration are highlighted in bold. These two changes print the output to standard out, which NetBeans then scrapes and parses.

```
<target name="test" depends="compile-test">
  <junit haltonerror="false" haltonfailure="false" showoutput="true">
    <formatter usefile="false" type="brief" />
      <classpath>
        <pathelement location="output"/>
        <fileset dir="libraries">
          <include name="**/**"/>
        </fileset>
      </classpath>
    <test name="net.cuprak.MusicCoachTest"/>
  </junit>
</target>
```

The NetBeans test action is mapped to the test target in the project's Ant script in the free-form project wizard. It can be altered or reconfigured afterwards via project properties. Right-clicking the root of the project in the Projects window and choosing Test runs the tests.

Profiling

Although profiling is covered in Chapter 10, profiling a free-form project requires some additional setup. The free-form project wizard does not generate the necessary configuration for profiling either a project or a file. Instead, the IDE will prompt for the relevant Ant targets when the Profile | Profile Main Project or Profile | Profile menus are chosen. The targets for profiling should closely mirror the run targets and differ only in having an additional task and parameters to Java. The one exception is a free-form web project as the web container. Tomcat, for example, is launched with profile parameters. A free-form web project thus requires no modifications to the `build.xml` script.

The following code listing is a simple target for profiling the project. It was derived from the run target with the changes necessary for the Profiler highlighted in bold. No other changes were necessary—NetBeans takes care of adding the nbprofile direct task to the classpath.

```xml
<target name="profile" depends="dist">
  <nbprofiledirect>
    <classpath>
      <pathelement location="libraries/jfugue-4.0.3-with-musicxml.jar"/>
        <pathelement location="MusicCoach.jar"/>
    </classpath>
  </nbprofiledirect>
  <java classname="net.cuprak.MusicCoach">
    <jvmarg value="${profiler.info.jvmargs.agent}"/>
    <classpath>
      <pathelement location="libraries/jfugue-4.0.3-with-musicxml.jar"/>
      <pathelement location="MusicCoach.jar"/>
    </classpath>
  </java>
</target>
```

Profiling a single file requires only a minor change to the previous code listing. NetBeans automatically populates the profile.class Ant property. This property contains the name of the class that was selected for profiling. The following code listing reflects this change:

```xml
<target name="profile" depends="dist">
  <nbprofiledirect>
    <classpath>
      <pathelement location="libraries/jfugue-4.0.3-with-musicxml.jar"/>
      <pathelement location="MusicCoach.jar"/>
    </classpath>
  </nbprofiledirect>
  <java classname="${profile.class}">
    <jvmarg value="${profiler.info.jvmargs.agent}"/>
    <classpath>
      <pathelement location="libraries/jfugue-4.0.3-with-musicxml.jar"/>
      <pathelement location="MusicCoach.jar"/>
    </classpath>
  </java>
</target>
```

Debugging

As in the case of profiling, debugging also requires some additional work for a free-form project. Since NetBeans is not responsible for compiling or executing, hooks must be added or a build file generated. Adding a hook to an existing debug target in the project's Ant script requires editing `project.xml` to map the debug action to the target. Generating a build file will result in NetBeans using the information it has about the project to create a build file, `nbproject/ide-targets.xml`. This option may not be feasible if the project has a complicated and unique build process.

The first time that Debug | Debug Main Project or Debug | Debug File is chosen, the dialog box in Figure 2-10 appears. If a custom Ant target is going to be used, choose Cancel and then set up the `project.xml` file. If the generated-file approach works, choosing Generate will create the `ide-targets.xml` file if it doesn't already exist.

Mapping an existing Ant debug target to the NetBeans debug action requires editing the `nbproject/project.xml` file. The following code snippet documents the addition:

```
<ide-actions>
  <action name="debug">
    <target>debug</target>
  </action>
</ide-actions>
```

FIGURE 2-10

Configuring
debug setup

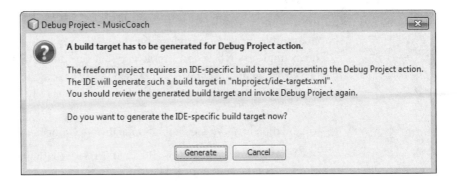

The Ant tasks should start the NetBeans debugger and also pass a couple of important debugger-related settings to the JVM. When compiling the code, the debug flag should be set to true, otherwise NetBeans is unable to set breakpoints. Following is a simple debug target:

```
<target name="debug">
  <nbjpdastart addressproperty="jpda.address" name="MusicCoach"
transport="dt_socket">
    <classpath>
      <pathelement location="libraries/jfugue-4.0.3-with-musicxml.jar"/>
      <pathelement location="MusicCoach.jar"/>
    </classpath>
  </nbjpdastart>
  <java classname="net.cuprak.MusicCoach" fork="true">
    <jvmarg value="-Xdebug"/>
    <jvmarg value="-Xrunjdwp:transport=dt_socket,address=${jpda.address}"/>
    <classpath>
      <pathelement location="libraries/jfugue-4.0.3-with-musicxml.jar"/>
      <pathelement location="MusicCoach.jar"/>
    </classpath>
  </java>
</target>
```

EXERCISE 2-1

Creating a Free-Form Project

In this exercise, you will create a free-form project from an existing code base. A simple example project is provided on the website for the book.

The example code base is a simple application that plays musical notes using JFugue (www.jfugue.org). The project also includes some unit tests that play several scales. The application can be downloaded from http://www.cuprack.net/MusicCoach.

1. Download the MusicCoach application to your hard drive.

2. Run the Ant file contained in the project to generate the output JAR file.

3. Choose File | New Project.

4. Select Java Free-Form Project and click Next.

5. Click the Browse button next to the Location text field. Select the MusicCoach directory on your local hard drive. NetBeans will pre-populate the rest of the fields on the screen. Click Next.

6. In Build And Run Actions, the common NetBeans actions are mapped to Ant targets on this screen. NetBeans does a good job guessing, so no additional work is required.

7. In Source Package Folders, configure the source and test packages. Click Add Folder for each browse to `src` and `test`, respectively. Set the Source Level to 1.5 if it isn't already. Click Next.

8. Java Sources Classpath configures compilation, execution, and testing of the classpath. Add the JFugue JAR file under the `lib` directory to both the `src` and `test` classpaths. The JUnit JAR file in `lib` should be added to just the test classpath. Click Next.

9. In Project Output, select `MusicCoach.jar` from the `dist` directory for `src` and `MusicCoach-test.jar` for `test`. Click Finish.

CERTIFICATION OBJECTIVE

Using Version Control Systems

Exam Objective 2.2   Demonstrate the ability to work with version control systems and the IDE, in order to determine the following: what VCSs are available, which ones you need an external client for, how to pull sources out of a repository, view changes, and check them back in.

Version control systems (VCSs) are an indispensible development tool. They enable multiple developers to concurrently share, edit, and merge files. VCSs track change history, providing traceability. With traceability, file revisions can be retrieved and compared. File comparison is augmented with metadata, including commit comments, modification dates, and the identity of the responsible or offending developer. Building on traceability, VCSs also support tagging and branching. Tagging and branching enable multiple software releases to be tracked and maintained. With tagging, a specific release can be uniquely labeled and thus be easily retrieved. A *branch* is a parallel line of development.

For instance, in many development organizations a branch for the current release and upcoming release coexist and undergo parallel development with frequent merges. Disruptive development, such as major refactoring operations or expansive feature additions, is often done on its own branch.

Best practices surrounding the use of version control systems are a topic unto themselves. Many different version control systems—both commercial and open source—are on the market today. Each version control system tackles the problem of revision control with slight differences depending upon the workflow issues that drove their evolution. Version control systems come in two flavors, client/server and distributed. Several of the major version control systems widely used today include:

- Subversion (http://subversion.tigris.org/)
- CVS (http://www.nongnu.org/cvs/)
- Perforce (http://www.perforce.com/)
- Git (http://git-scm.com/)
- Mercurial (http://mercurial.selenic.com/)
- Rational ClearCase (http://www-01.ibm.com/software/awdtools/clearcase/)

NetBeans is currently preconfigured with support for three version control systems: Subversion, CVS, and Mercurial. NetBeans also has its own built-in version control system for tracking changes between commits, providing a sort of undo/redo support on steroids. The first two version control systems, Subversion and CVS, are the traditional client/server version control systems.

Subversion and CVS are very similar in terms of their operations. Mercurial is a distributed VCS, similar to the more widely used Git VCS. Other version control systems, such as Perforce and ClearCase, are available via the Plugin Manager.

on the job

Additional version control systems can be added to NetBeans via the Plugin Manager. The Rational ClearCase VCS can be downloaded from http://versioncontrol.netbeans.org/clearcase/. A plugin for Git is available at http://nbgit.org/. A third-party plugin for Perforce can be downloaded from http://www.wonderly.org/netbeans/.

The exam focuses on the basic operations common to all of the version control systems. When studying for the exam, you do not need to become an expert on each of the version control systems. This means that if you currently use Subversion, you do not need to become an expert on merging or sharing in Mercurial. For the exam, you will need to know how to:

- Configure version control support in NetBeans
- Checkout a project from version control
- Checkin changes
- Update files
- View differences/history

Version control operations in NetBeans are conveniently located throughout the IDE. Many operations, such as refactoring, will invoke version control operations.

Once a project is associated with a version control system, or checked out from a repository, the context menus in the Projects and Files windows will contain a submenu with the relevant version control operations. Right-clicking a tab for a file also yields the same version control context menu. A versioning window, available by choosing Window | Versioning | <Version Control System>, displays local and remotely changed files.

The main menu through which most developers initially interact with version control support in NetBeans has undergone significant changes starting in NetBeans 6.7—the Versioning menu was renamed to Team. The submenus for CVS, Subversion, Mercurial, and Local History are still present; however, several new menu items were added:

- **Find Issues** Searches the configured issue tracking system for open issues. The issue tracker must be configured first.
- **Report An Issue** Reports an issue to the issue tracking system.
- **Create Build Job** Creates a new job in Hudson, a continuous-integration server.

The contents of the Team/Versioning menu will change if you have a versioned project opened. Operations for that version control system are populated into the Team/Versioning menu. For instance, if you are working with a Subversion-based project, the Subversion operations will precede the submenus for the other version control systems.

Regardless of the NetBeans version, the Versioning or Team menu will contain four submenus covered on the exam: CVS, Mercurial, Subversion, and Local History. The submenus are shown in Table 2-2.

TABLE 2-2   Version Control Submenus

CVS	Mercurial	Subversion	Local History
Checkout...	Initialize Project	Checkout...	Show Local History
Import into Repository...		Import into Repository...	Revert Deleted
Change CVS Root...	Status	Relocate...	Revert to...
	Diff		
Update Project with Dependencies	Update...	Update Project with Dependencies	
Show Changes	Commit...	Show Changes	
Diff		Diff	
Update	Export Diff...	Update	
Commit...	Export Uncommitted Changes...	Commit...	
	Import Patches...		
Export Diff Patch...		Export Diff Patch...	
Apply Diff Patch...	Clone Other...	Apply Diff Patch...	
	Fetch		
Tag...	Share ▸	Copy to...	
Branches ▸	Merge ▸	Switch to...	
		Merge to...	
Show Annotations	Show History		
View Revision...	Show ▸	Show Annotations	
Search History...		Search History...	
	Revert...		
Revert Modifications	Recover ▸	Revert Modifications...	
Resolve Conflicts...		Resolve Conflicts...	
Ignore	Properties...	Ignore	
Exclude from Commit		Svn Properties	

Depending upon the version control system used, additional configuration and software installation may be necessary. The path to the Mercurial and/or Subversion executables must be configured in Tools | Options | Miscellaneous | Versioning. NetBeans uses the native executables to support these version control systems. Consult Chapter 1 for more information on configuring these paths.

The version control support in NetBeans is a large and complicated topic. Most developers probably use only one version control system on a daily basis. Becoming familiar with the support for three version control systems can be very challenging. To simplify studying, common infrastructure functionality is covered first, before diving into the specific version control systems. Exercises explain how to set up a repository for each version control system. The following topics will be covered:

- Visual Feedback
- File Diff Utility
- CVS
- Subversion
- Mercurial

Visual Feedback

Version control support is integrated throughout the NetBeans IDE and especially in the refactoring tools. Once version control support is enabled for a project, NetBeans will perform the relevant file system operations whenever an add, delete, move, or rename operation is performed. The status of the files in a project is communicated via color-coding with the following convention:

- Red marks a file as having conflicts.
- Green marks a new file or a file that is unknown to the version control system.
- Blue marks files that have local changes.
- Gray marks files that are being ignored by the editor.

The color-coding is visible on files in both the Projects and Files windows. The text on editor tabs is also colorized.

In addition to color-coding, NetBeans uses color-coded icons as shown in Figure 2-11. Folders containing either changes or conflicts possess a tiny cylinder badge on the lower right. The cylinder is red if the directory contains a conflict. It is blue if the directory contains either altered files or files scheduled for addition. Using the color-coded cylinders or directories, it is easy to drill down into packages or directories containing changes or conflicts.

FIGURE 2-11

Version control
directory icons

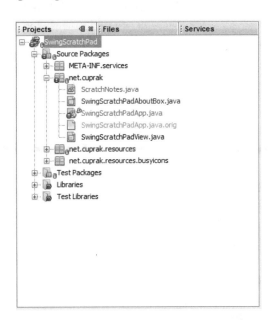

File Diff Utility

Before diving into each individual version control system, it is important to understand the diff utility. The file diff utility in NetBeans is a powerful tool for comparing files. The current revision of a file can also be edited with all of NetBeans' editor features. The diff tool is customized for each of the supported version control systems. The customizations take the form of buttons that invoke custom logic for operations such as merging, committing, refreshing changes, and so on. As in its use by version control support, the diff tool can be used to compare any two files by simply selecting the files in either the Projects or Files window and selecting Tools | Diff from the right-click context menu.

The diff utility is actually two separate utilities, a diff engine for doing the actual comparison and a visualization tool. The engine can be replaced with the Unix diff engine if desired: Tools | Options | Miscellaneous | Diff. Configuration of the diff tool is covered in Chapter 1. The visualization tool graphically compares two files' color-coded additions and deletions, and provides buttons for navigating the differences.

An example diff appears in Figure 2-12.

FIGURE 2-12   Diff utility

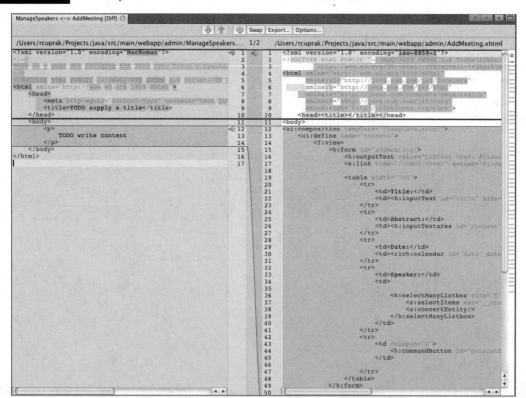

The generic diff utility has six buttons across the top of the window:

⬇	Jumps to the next difference between the two files.
⬆	Jumps to the previous difference between the two files.
🔄	Refreshes the diff.
Swap	Switches the two files so that the one on the right is now on the left.
Export	Exports a Unified Diff file. The patch utility (NetBeans or Unix patch) can then apply the differences.
Options	Opens the Options dialog box to the Diff settings.

The diff utility highlights text using the following color scheme:

- Blue highlighting indicates that content has changed since the earlier revision.
- Green highlighting indicates new content that has been inserted/appended.
- Red highlighting indicates lines/text that has been removed since the previous revision.

The Diff Viewer also places icons on the area between the two files for manipulating the contents of the current revision. The icons can remove a change, insert a single change, or insert all of the changes from a file. The icons are as follows:

⇒》	Inserts the highlighted text in the current revision
⇛》	Reverts the status of the file to the previous state
✖	Removes the highlighted change from the current revision

The exam will frequently ask questions about the meaning of an icon or what the color-coding is conveying. **Make sure to commit the color scheme to memory and to be familiar with the icons.**

CVS

Concurrent Versions System (CVS) is one of the three version control systems supported by NetBeans. NetBeans support of CVS has a long history; it was the first version control system supported by NetBeans. CVS integration runs deep, and unlike either the Subversion or Mercurial integration, the CVS implementation does not require the installation of native binaries.

Although CVS is still used today, developers have been migrating to newer version control systems such as Subversion and Mercurial. Subversion was written to solve many of the CVS technical shortcomings and presents a nearly seamless migration path. Command-line tools for CVS and Subversion are nearly identical. As a result, support for CVS and Subversion in NetBeans is very similar. This simplifies studying for the exam. This section points out differences between the two.

The following topics will be covered in this section:

- Importing Projects
- Checking Out a Project
- Changing a Project's Root
- Showing Changes
- Updating
- Committing
- Tagging and Branching
- Show Annotations
- Viewing Revisions
- Searching History
- Reverting
- Resolving Conflicts

Importing Projects

You import a new project into CVS by choosing Team | CVS | Import Into Repository to launch the CVS import wizard shown in Figure 2-13. Before you select the menu, the project being imported must already be open in NetBeans. The project cannot already be associated with one of the other version control systems.

The first panel of the import wizard prompts for the CVS repository connection parameters including the CVS Root and the Password. The value entered for the CVS root depends upon the configuration of the CVS repository. The next section, which covers checking out a project, discusses the format of the CVS root string in more depth. Click the Next button, and NetBeans verifies the connection to the repository.

FIGURE 2-13   CVS Import, Step 1

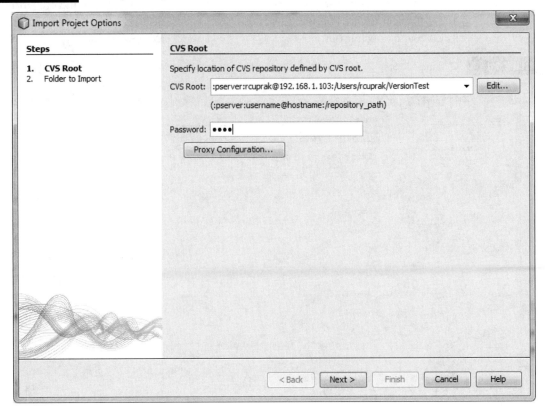

The second step of the wizard, shown in Figure 2-14, prompts for the following parameters:

- **Folder To Import**   Limited to a folder within the project
- **Import Message**   Message describing the reason for the import
- **Repository Folder**   Destination within the repository
- **Checkout After Import**   Project becomes a working copy after the import

If Checkout After Import is not selected, the current project in NetBeans will not be under version control. The project must be subsequently checked out.

Checking Out a Project

Projects are checked out of CVS by choosing Team | CVS | Checkout. Checking out from CVS is a two-step process. First, you enter the server address and credentials, and a connection is established with the CVS server. Second, you choose a directory in CVS and check it out.

FIGURE 2-14   CVS Import, Step 2

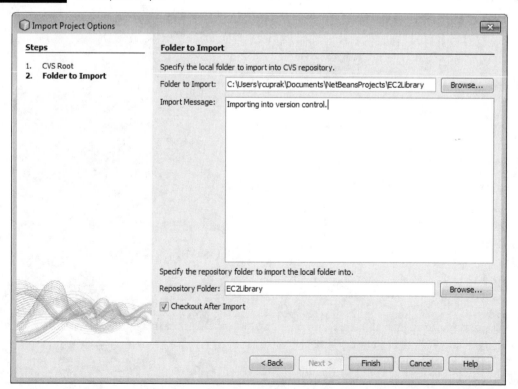

The first dialog box in the checkout CVS wizard, Figure 2-15, prompts for the CVS server settings and credentials. The CVS Root is the connection string used to establish communication with the repository. For your convenience, NetBeans maintains a list of previous CVS roots. The dialog box also prompts for the Password. Proxy server settings can be configured by clicking the Proxy Configuration button. The following CVS root types are supported by NetBeans:

- `pserver` Connection string format:
  `:pserver:username@hostname:/repository_path`
- `ext` Connection string format:
  `:ext:username@hostname:/repository_path`
- `fork` Connection string format:
  `:fork:/repository_path`
- `local` Connection string format:
  `:local:/repository_path`

FIGURE 2-15 CVS Checkout—server settings

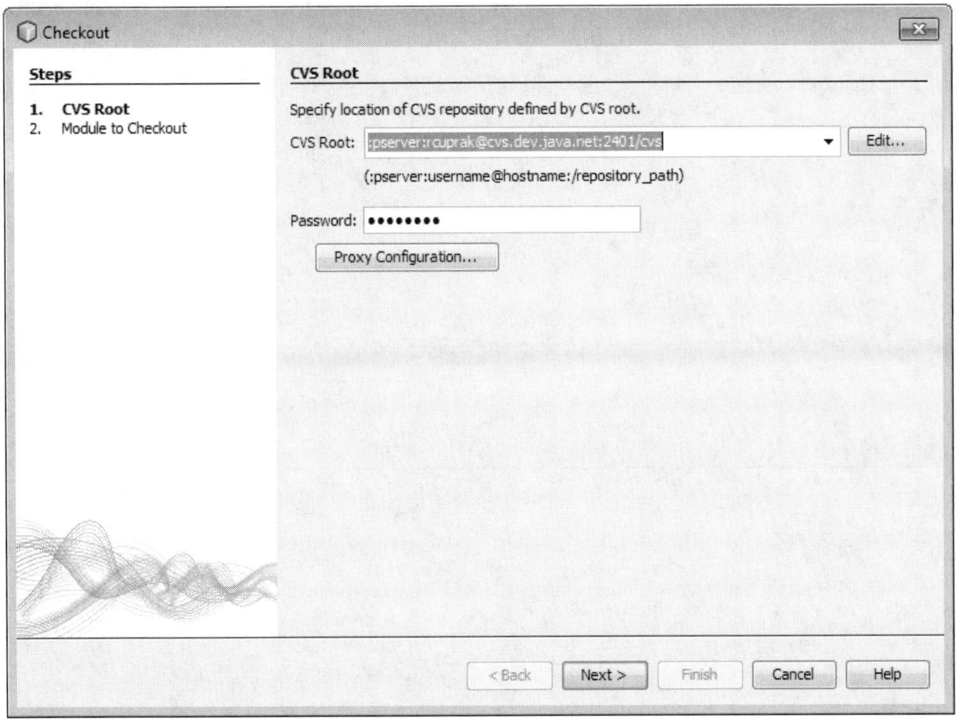

After successfully connecting to the CVS repository, the next step is to pick the Module, Branch, and Local Folder, as shown in Figure 2-16. By clicking the Browse buttons, you can browse for the repository. Once the files are checked out, NetBeans will scan for projects. If one or more projects are detected, NetBeans will ask if they should be opened. If no project is detected, NetBeans will prompt for creating a new project.

FIGURE 2-16   CVS Checkout—selecting a project

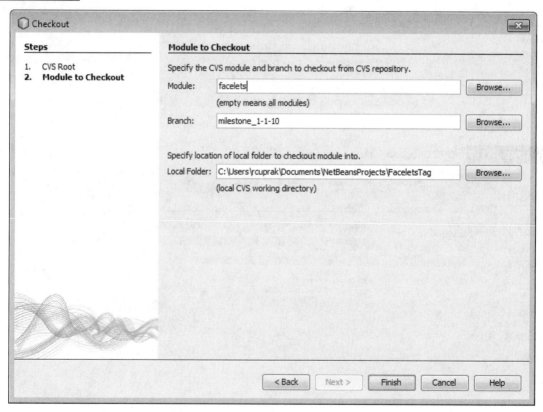

Change CVS Root

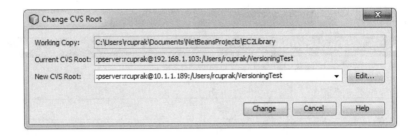

Changing a Project's Root

NetBeans makes it easy to change a project's CVS Root in the event that the hostname of the repository or its path changes. Typically, this happens if the CVS repository is moved to a newer machine or is hosted on a machine with an address that frequently changes. Changing the CVS Root can be done by choosing Team | CVS | Change CVS Root. The dialog box in Figure 2-17 appears. The connection type to the server must stay the same; for example, it cannot switch from `pserver` to `ext`.

Showing Changes

Current changes can be viewed by choosing Team | CVS | Show Changes. Choosing Show Changes opens the CVS window shown in Figure 2-18. This window lists both local and remote file changes. Seven icons are at the top (see Table 2-3).

CVS Show Changes

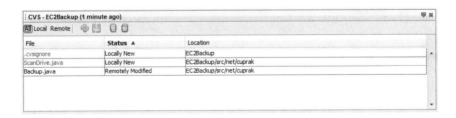

TABLE 2-3	CVS Change Operations

Icon	Description
All	Displays both local and remote changes.
Local	Displays only local changes.
Remote	Displays remote changes.
	Refreshes the list and scans for changes both locally and on the server.
	Diff All—opens the diff viewer, shown in Figure 2-19, to view all of the changes that have been made. Clicking any file will compare it with the revision on the server.
	Update All—pulls down all updates from CVS.
	Commit All—commits all changes to version control.

FIGURE 2-19	CVS Diff All

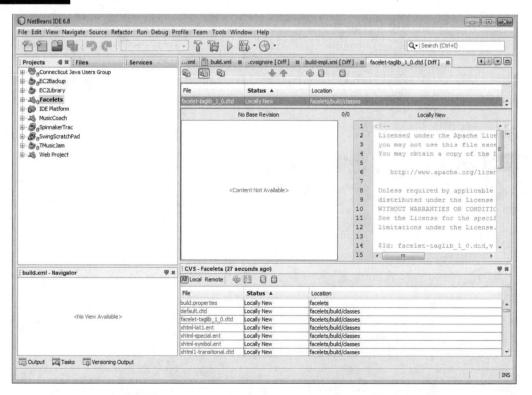

Right-clicking a change row will display a context menu with the following operations:

- **Open** Opens the file in the source editor.
- **Diff** Opens the file in the diff tool.
- **Update** Updates just the selected file.
- **Commit** Commits the selected file.
- **Conflict Resolved** Marks a file as resolved. Choose this when the file conflicts have been manually fixed outside of the NetBeans diff tool.
- **Show Annotations** Displays the commit message, author, date, and revision.
- **Search History** Displays a list of the revisions for a file and provides a user interface for searching those revisions.
- **Exclude From Commit** Defers committing a file. The file will appear with a strike-though line in the list. Choosing Commit All will not commit the file.
- **Revert Modifications** Reverts to the selected file(s).
- **Ignore** Informs the version control system that the file should be ignored.

These same operations are available when viewing changes with Subversion.

Updating

A project is updated by selecting Team | CVS | Update or Team | CVS | Update Project With Dependencies. The latter will also update and retrieve the latest revisions for any project that the current project depends upon. Individual files can also be updated through the use of context menus in the Projects and Files windows. The update operation may result in files being merged, possibly resulting in a conflict.

Committing

You can use one of several different paths to commit code changes to the CVS repository:

- Submit an individual file from the Projects or Files window via the context menu CVS | Commit.
- Submit a group of files from the Projects or Files window by selecting them and then using the CVS context menu.
- Submit an entire project from the Projects or Files window using the CVS context menu or by clicking the root and choosing Team | CVS | Commit.
- Click the Commit All button in CVS Show Changes (Figure 2-18).

Regardless of the approach taken, the dialog box in Figure 2-20 appears. This dialog box lists the files that are uploaded to the server and prompts you for a descriptive comment. If the files are not up to date, NetBeans will display an error message and abort the operation. An update must then be performed and any conflicts resolved.

You can also exclude files from the commit by choosing Team | CVS | Exclude From Commit.

Tagging and Branching

Tagging and branching are two common CVS operations. Tagging is typically used to mark a specific version of the software—such as for a release or QA build. This enables that exact version to be checked out in the future. Branching is performed when development tasks need to be isolated. For example, a branch might be

FIGURE 2-20 CVS Commit dialog box

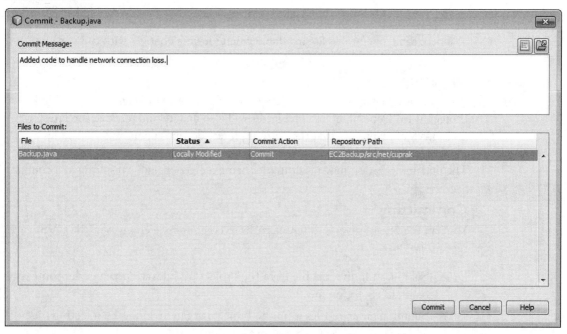

created for a client so that client modifications can continue in isolation from main feature development. Unlike either Mercurial or Subversion, CVS has explicit tag and branch commands. NetBeans exposes these commands via Team | CVS | Tag and Team | CVS | Branches. The Branches submenu has operations for creating a branch, switching to a branch, or merging from a branch. Choosing Team | CVS | Tag displays the dialog box in Figure 2-21. You can use this dialog box to tag a file or a folder. This dialog box prompts for the name of the tag and has a Browse button for selecting a tag from the repository to add that file to that tag.

In addition, the dialog box has three checkboxes:

■ **Avoid Tagging Locally Modified Files**   Ensures that you do not tag files that have not yet been committed

■ **Move Existing Tag**   Moves the tag and attaches it to the current revision in the working directory

■ **Delete Tag**   Deletes the tag from the selected file

You perform the branch operation by selecting Team | CVS | Branch. This displays the dialog box in Figure 2-22, which prompts for a Branch Name and optionally a Tag Name to denote the starting state of the new branch. If the Switch To This Branch Afterwards checkbox is selected, then the working copy is switched over to the branch afterwards.

The other submenus off of Team | CVS | Branches enable you to switch between branches and to perform merges. Merging is beyond the scope of the material covered on the exam.

CVS Tag

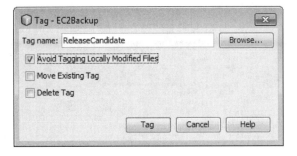

FIGURE 2-22

CVS Branch

Show Annotations

The Show Annotations feature pulls the revisions from version control and labels each line/edit in a file with the responsible developer, as shown in Figure 2-23. This feature is invoked via Team | CVS | Show Annotations. Hovering over a developer's ID shows the revision number and comment. This is an invaluable tool

FIGURE 2-23   CVS Show Annotations

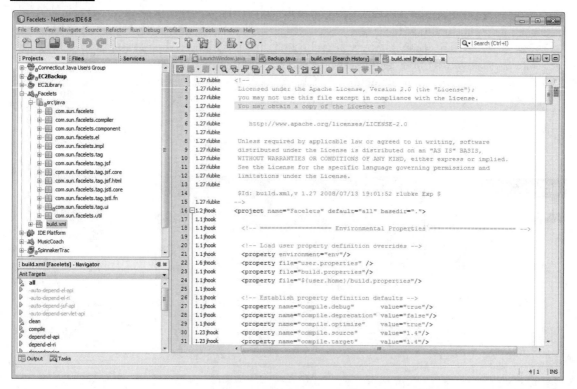

for examining the history of a file and understanding which developer is responsible for which edit.

Viewing Revisions

Individual revisions can be retrieved and viewed via Team | CVS | View Revision or via the context menu CVS | View Revision. This displays the dialog box shown in Figure 2-24. The current head or a specific tag or branch can be retrieved and viewed within the editor. The revision retrieved has the @ symbol appended to its name along with the revision/tag. The file retrieved does not overwrite the current instance in the working directory.

Searching History

To search the history of a file, invoke Team | CVS | Search History, or right-click a file and choose CVS | Search History. NetBeans will open a tab, Figure 2-25, with all of the revisions listed. You can view the listed revisions either as a Summary or as a Diff. Using the summary view, it is easy to quickly see who edited the file and when edits were performed. The diff view is a more detailed view for understanding at a granular level each change made between revisions.

The top panel, above the list of revisions, filters the revision history entries. The history can be filtered according to:

- Message contents
- Username of the developer
- Start and stop dates

CVS View
Revision

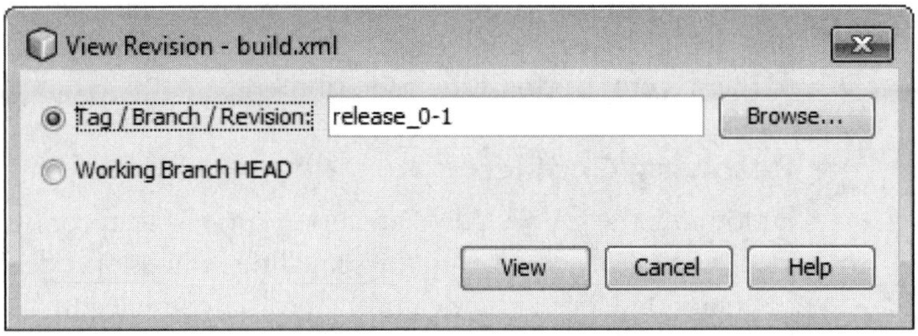

FIGURE 2-25 CVS Search History

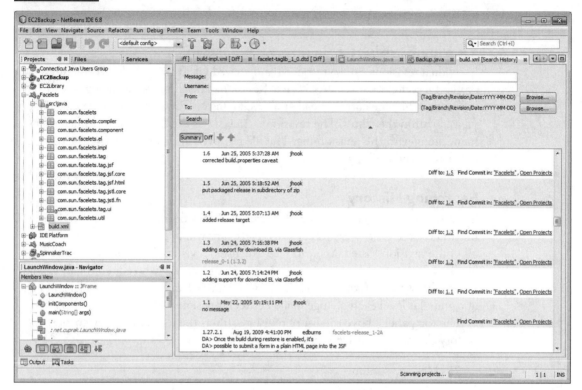

Reverting

Changes to a file are reverted from either the Team menu or context menu by choosing CVS | Revert Modifications. NetBeans will prompt for confirmation that the file or files should be reverted. Unlike Subversion or Mercurial, CVS requires a connection to the server to perform the operation.

Resolving Conflicts

Performing the CVS Update operation can result in conflicts if two developers made competing changes to the same line or lines of code. Before the files can be committed, or in many cases the project compiled, the competing edits must be resolved. When a file contains a conflict, a red exclamation mark is added to the file, and the filename appears in red as depicted in Figure 2-26. In addition, an exclamation mark is added to each folder or directory in the Projects or Files window.

NetBeans provides two approaches to resolving conflicts:

- Manually via editing the text directly (Figure 2-26)
- Graphically using the resolver (Figure 2-27)

The NetBeans Conflicts Resolver displays both revisions side by side and the merged content below them (see Figure 2-27). Conflicts are highlighted in red. Buttons and icons can be used to jump to the next conflict, accept the changes, or to accept the changes and move to the next conflict. After each change, the coloring will change to denote that the conflict has been resolved.

The approach taken largely depends upon the developer's preference. Using the NetBeans Conflicts Resolver, invoked via Team | CVS | Resolve Conflicts, code changes can be individually accepted or rejected, with NetBeans removing the conflict annotations added by CVS. Manually editing the file is a bit trickier and requires understanding the CVS markup (see Figure 2-26). With CVS markup, the

FIGURE 2-26   CVS Resolving conflicts

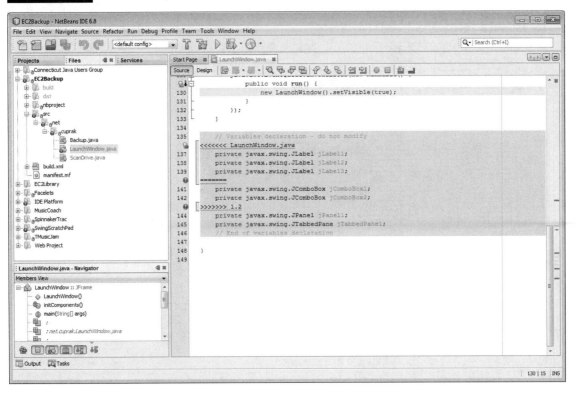

conflicting edits are separated with =======. Preceding the separator, the local code modifications are displayed along with <<<<<<< <File Name>, which marks the start of the conflict. The end of the revision pulled from the repository is terminated with >>>>>>> <revision number>. NetBeans automatically detects when the conflicts have been resolved. Resolved files appear in the standard blue used to mark files with local changes.

Subversion

Subversion (SVN) is a traditional client/server revision control system developed to replace CVS. It is an open source project hosted at Tigris.org (http://subversion. tigris.org) and has recently been accepted as an Apache project (www.apache.org). Subversion was initially developed to be a compelling replacement for CVS and to fix many of the shortcomings that had plagued CVS users. Given this stated design objective, the SVN commands were kept similar to those of CVS. The SVN user experience in NetBeans is very similar to that of CVS.

FIGURE 2-27   CVS Conflicts Resolver

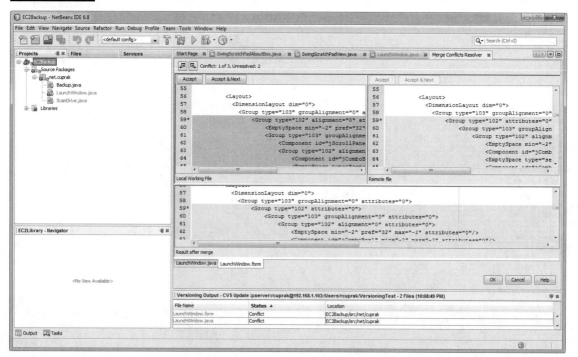

This section covers Subversion operations as they relate to NetBeans. Subversion is a large and complicated version control system. Entire books have been written on it. Some operations, such as add, remove, and rename, are not covered because they are discussed in the chapter on refactoring. SVN merging is not covered because that is beyond the scope of the exam. The upcoming sections will cover the following topics:

- Configuring Subversion
- Importing Projects
- Checking Out Projects
- Project Relocation
- Showing Changes
- Updating
- Committing Changes
- Resolving Conflicts
- Configuring SVN Properties
- Branching, Tagging, and Copying

Configuring Subversion

Unlike the CVS integration, the Subversion implementation in NetBeans requires the native SVN executables. If Subversion is not installed, the first time an SVN operation is performed, NetBeans will display the dialog box shown in Figure 2-28.

The binaries can either be downloaded and installed automatically via the Update Center or manually installed. Manually downloading the Subversion binaries is a good choice if you are also going to use Subversion from the command line.

on the **job**

NetBeans 6.8 requires Subversion 1.5 or greater. If you are using another Subversion client that is an older version, be very careful. New Subversion clients automatically upgrade a working copy. For instance, if you are using both NetBeans and Eclipse on a project and Eclipse is using Subversion 1.4, the NetBeans 1.5 Subversion client will upgrade the project. This will break the Subversion integration in Eclipse unless you upgrade. If you download and install Subversion 1.6 and run update, you will break the NetBeans Subversion support.

FIGURE 2-28 Subversion binaries

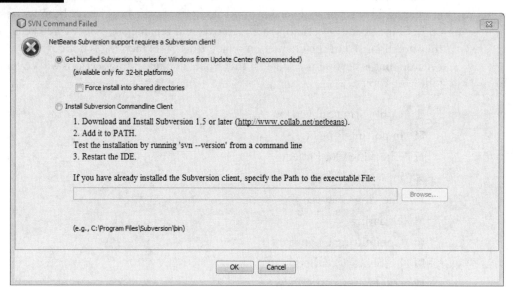

On Windows it may be necessary to install additional software for accessing remote Subversion repositories. If the remote repository is accessed via an ssh tunnel (svn+ssh), plink must be downloaded from the PuTTY website (http://www.chiark.greenend.org.uk/~sgtatham/putty/) and installed. PuTTY is a client secure shell (SSH) implementation. The plink executable provides command-line access to the backend. Depending upon Windows security settings, it is a good idea to run plink from the command prompt, cmd.exe, first. This verifies that the plink application was downloaded correctly, is compatible with the Windows version, and clears any security constraints for Internet downloaded applications. Secure shell implementations are preinstalled on Solaris, Linux, and Mac OS X—no additional setup is required on these platforms.

Importing Projects

A new project is imported into Subversion by choosing Team | Subversion | Import
Into Repository. This will display the Import dialog box in Figure 2-29 for Windows.
The Tunnel Command is necessary only if secure shell (ssh) is being used to
connect to the server. The Repository URL is the remote address and path of the
Subversion repository. A terminal window may flash briefly if ssh is being used.

FIGURE 2-29   Subversion Import, Step 1

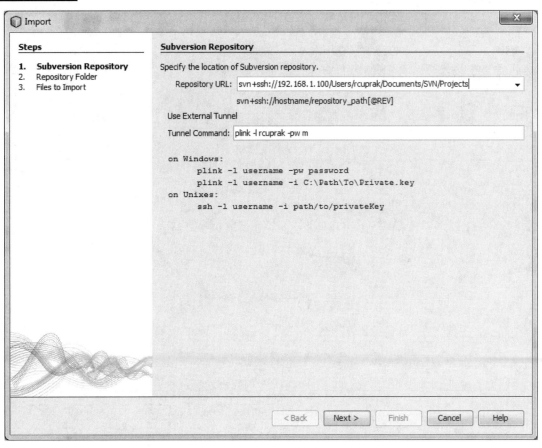

The next step for importing a project is to specify the folder name, pick the location within Subversion, and to enter a commit comment as shown in Figure 2-30. Clicking the Browse button displays a dialog box similar to a file browser, depicted in Figure 2-31. If you are following the standard Subversion layout with a trunk, tags, and branch directories, you must use the Into A New Folder button to create the required folders.

Subversion Import, Step 2

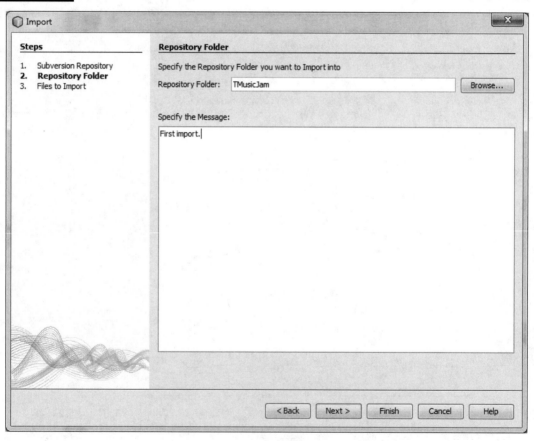

FIGURE 2-31   Subversion Import: repository browser

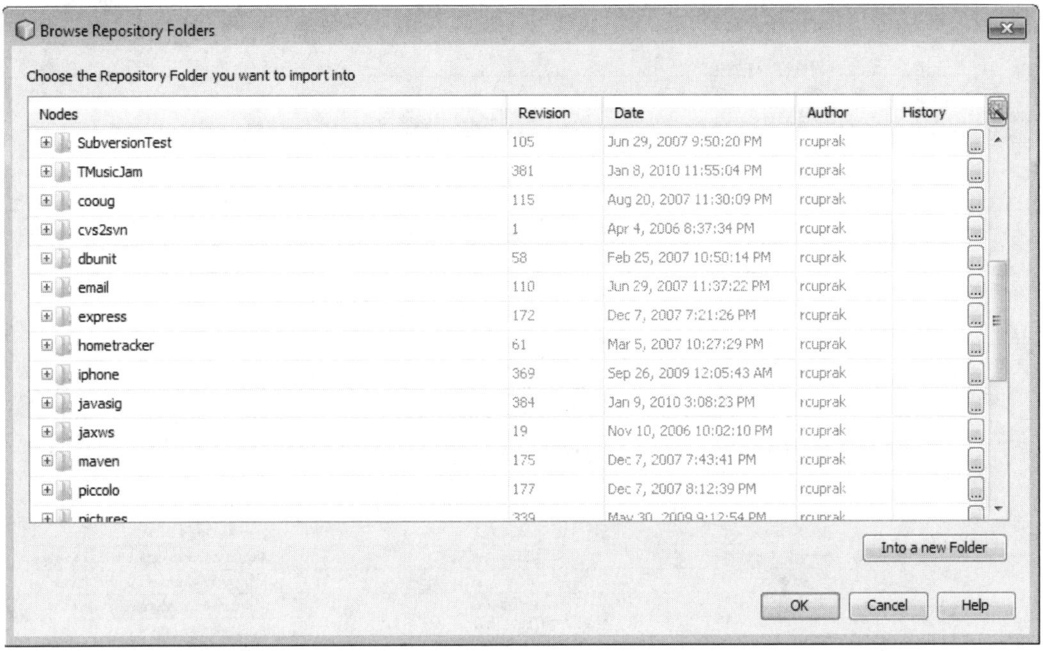

Clicking the Finish button displays a confirmation screen (see Figure 2-32). This final step gives you control over the files being added to version control. An import action for each file can be set:

- Add As Text
- Add As Binary
- Add As Directory
- Exclude From Commit

Adding a file as text or binary dictates the MIME type that is used. Directories can either be added or excluded. Once the Finish button is clicked, the files are added and committed to version control. The current project will become a working copy.

FIGURE 2-32 Subversion Import: Confirmation

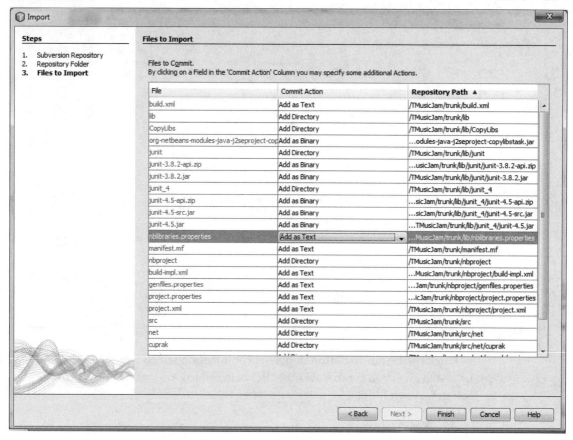

Checking Out Projects

Projects are checked out by choosing Team | Subversion | Checkout. In Windows, the displayed dialog box is the same one shown in Figure 2-29, except for the window title. Other platforms may vary and also query for a Certificate File, Passphrase fields, and Proxy Configuration.

In the subsequent dialog box shown in Figure 2-33, the Subversion Repository Folder, Repository Revision, and Local Folder can be selected. If a folder name differing from the folder name in Subversion is desired, select Skip <*Directory*> And Checkout Only Its Content, and specify a Local Folder to store the project. It is not

FIGURE 2-33 Subversion Checkout

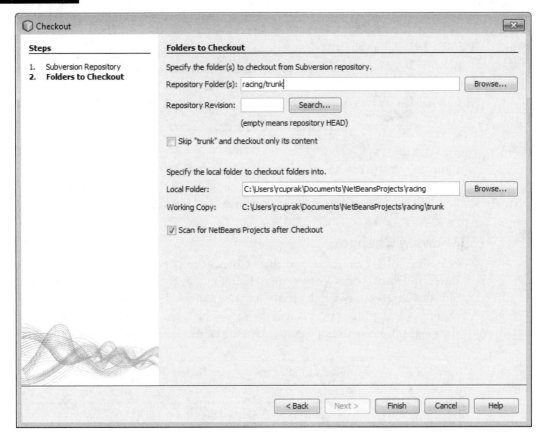

required that the directory being checked out, or any of its subdirectories, contain a NetBeans project. NetBeans will prompt after the checkout to create a project; creating a project is optional. If the checked-out directory contains a NetBeans project, NetBeans will open the project in the IDE.

Project Relocation

The current NetBeans project can be "relocated" by choosing Team | Subversion | Relocate. An example of project relocation is shown in Figure 2-34. Relocating enables changing the URL to the repository. Under the hood, NetBeans is running `svn switch -relocate` with the old and new paths. This is extremely useful

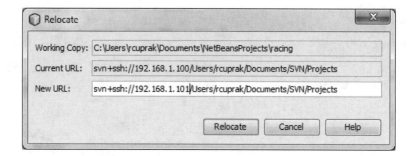

FIGURE 2-34

Relocate

if the Subversion repository is hosted on a machine with a dynamic address. Each repository has a Universally Unique Identifier (UUID), a unique identifier, so it isn't possible to switch to a completely unrelated Subversion repository.

Showing Changes

Selecting Team | Subversion | Show Changes will open the Subversion window shown in Figure 2-35. Opening this window causes NetBeans to check with the Subversion repository for changed files. The window lists local and remote file changes. Operations appear across the top of the table. This interface is basically the same as CVS with just slightly differing icons. Available operations include:

	Shows both local and remote changes. Remote changes are changes that are pulled down on the next update.
	Shows only locally modified files.
	Shows only remotely modified files.
	Refreshes the status of the files. Checks the file system and also the Subversion repository.
	Retrieves changes and opens the diff tool.
	Updates the entire project from version control.
	Commits all changes to version control.

FIGURE 2-35   Show Changes

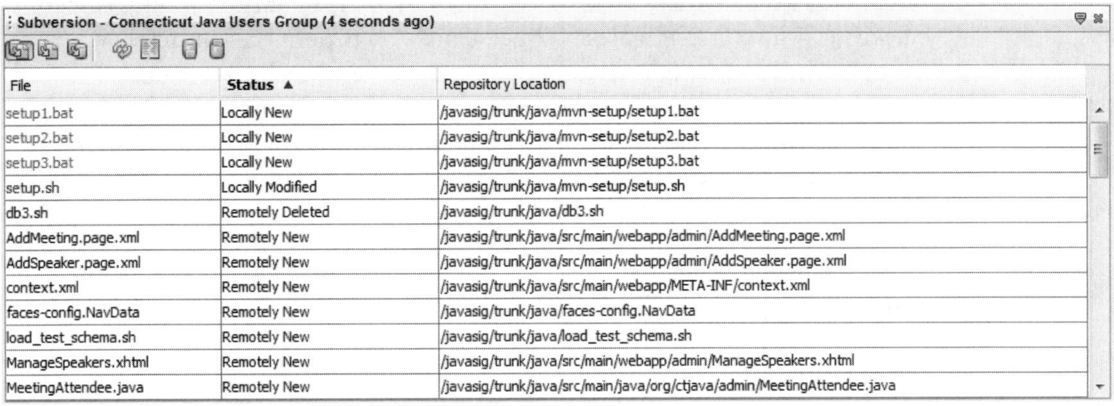

File	Status ▲	Repository Location
setup1.bat	Locally New	/javasig/trunk/java/mvn-setup/setup1.bat
setup2.bat	Locally New	/javasig/trunk/java/mvn-setup/setup2.bat
setup3.bat	Locally New	/javasig/trunk/java/mvn-setup/setup3.bat
setup.sh	Locally Modified	/javasig/trunk/java/mvn-setup/setup.sh
db3.sh	Remotely Deleted	/javasig/trunk/java/db3.sh
AddMeeting.page.xml	Remotely New	/javasig/trunk/java/src/main/webapp/admin/AddMeeting.page.xml
AddSpeaker.page.xml	Remotely New	/javasig/trunk/java/src/main/webapp/admin/AddSpeaker.page.xml
context.xml	Remotely New	/javasig/trunk/java/src/main/webapp/META-INF/context.xml
faces-config.NavData	Remotely New	/javasig/trunk/java/faces-config.NavData
load_test_schema.sh	Remotely New	/javasig/trunk/java/load_test_schema.sh
ManageSpeakers.xhtml	Remotely New	/javasig/trunk/java/src/main/webapp/admin/ManageSpeakers.xhtml
MeetingAttendee.java	Remotely New	/javasig/trunk/java/src/main/java/org/ctjava/admin/MeetingAttendee.java

Right-clicking a change row will display a context menu with the following operations:

- **Open**   Opens the file in the source editor.
- **Diff**   Opens the file in the diff tool.
- **Update**   Updates just the selected file.
- **Commit**   Commits the selected file.
- **Conflict Resolved**   Marks a file as resolved. Choose when the file conflicts have been manually fixed outside of the NetBeans diff tool.
- **Show Annotations**   Displays the commit message, author, date, and revision.
- **Search History**   Displays a list of the revisions for a file and provides a user interface for searching those revisions.
- **Exclude From Commit**   Defers committing a file. The file will appear with a strike-through in the list. Choosing Commit All will not commit the file.
- **Revert Modifications**   Reverts to the selected file(s).
- **Ignore**   Informs the version control system that the file should be ignored.

These operations are essentially the same across all version control systems covered on the exam.

Searching History

To search the history of a file, invoke Team | Subversion | Search History, or right-click on a file and choose Subversion | Search History. The search functionality has the same capabilities as the CVS search support. NetBeans will open a tab depicted in Figure 2-36 with the revisions listed in chronological order. The listed revisions can be either summarized or viewed as a diff. Using the summary view it is easy to quickly see who edited the file and when edits were performed. The diff view is a more detailed view for understanding at a granular level each change made between revisions.

The top panel, above the list of revisions, filters the revision history entries. The history can be filtered according to:

- Message contents
- Username of the developer
- Start and stop dates

Updating

Updating is a simple task with the Subversion integration. Select the project root in either the Projects or Files windows, and choose Team | Subversion | Update

FIGURE 2-36   Search History

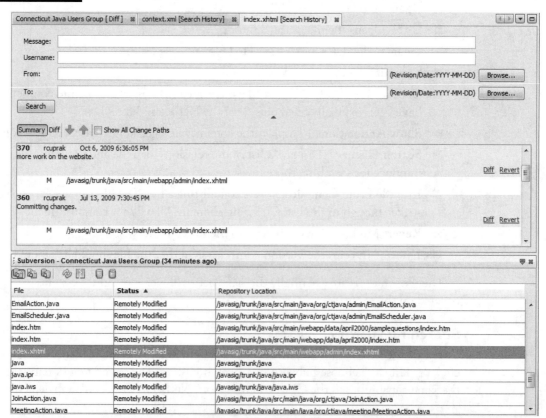

to pull down the latest file changes from Subversion. If you want only certain directories to be updated, right-clicking and choosing Subversion | Update will update only files under the selected directory. To view changes before they are applied, choose Team | Subversion | Show Changes to see what updates are going to be downloaded from the server.

NetBeans projects can depend upon other NetBeans projects. Choosing Team | Subversion | Update Project With Dependencies not only will execute an update on the current project, but also will invoke update on parent projects. Projects that depend upon this project will not be updated, however.

Committing Changes

Committing a file to Subversion can be done practically anywhere in the application where you can right-click a file. The Commit dialog box is shown in Figure 2-37. A file can be committed from the Projects or Files window, or by right-clicking its editor tab and choosing Subversion | Commit.

Single or multiple files can be selected. It is a good idea to provide a comment for the commit describing the changes that were made to the file. The files to be committed appear in the list following the commit comment. Although not shown in the figure, spinning open the Update Issue group enables tying the commit to an issue.

FIGURE 2-37

Commit

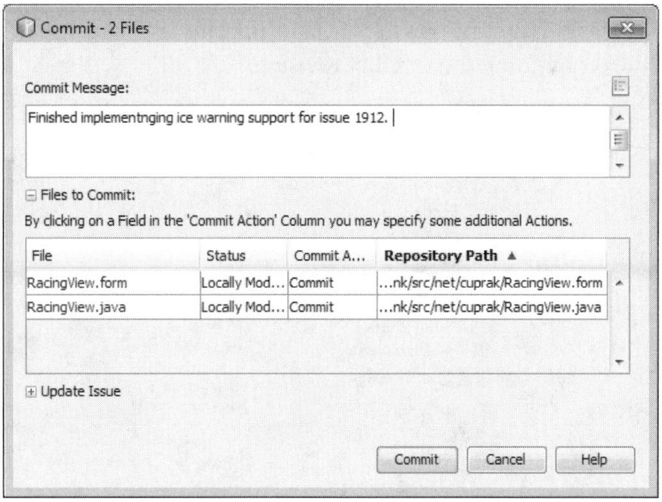

Resolving Conflicts

Invariably conflicts arise when working on files. Suppose two developers edit the same file and also the same block of code concurrently. While Subversion will try its best to merge the files, it isn't always successful. When Subversion is unsuccessful, the name will appear red, and a red badge will appear on its parent folders and also on the project node. Three gray files will also appear in the Files window. Three files are created:

- The original file before any changes were made. This file has the oldest revision number.
- Your changes file has the .mine file extension.
- The other developer's changes file has the newest revision number.

You have two options when resolving a merge conflict:

- Use the NetBeans graphical utility to select one set of changes.
- Manually edit the file.

Figure 2-38 is an example of conflicts in setup.sh. In the figure, the red badge appears on the folder (here, mvn-setup) containing the conflict and on all of the parent folders (in this figure, Connecticut Java Users Group). The name of the file with the conflicts appears in red (setup.sh). The three other files appear below it. Note that setup1.bat appears gray because it is an ignored file as do the files containing the conflict revisions.

FIGURE 2-38

Conflicts

Right-clicking the file and choosing Resolve Conflicts opens the tab appearing in Figure 2-39. Three panels are on this tab. The left panel is the local working copy. The panel at right contains the remote copy. The panel on the bottom contains the final merged changes. The conflicts are highlighted in red. Using this interface, you can select which changes you want to keep for each conflict. The icons 🔲 🔳 navigate between the conflicts. Clicking the Accept button accepts the changes in the panel below it. Clicking the Accept & Next button accepts the changes and moves to the next conflict. Accepted changes will appear green, whereas rejected changes will appear blue. Once the conflicts are resolved, click OK to apply the changes. The three files containing the different revisions are removed.

Double-clicking `setup.bat` opens it in a tab that displays the raw output from Subversion shown in Figure 2-40. The green highlighting along the left side marks material added to the file.

FIGURE 2-39   NetBeans Conflicts Resolver

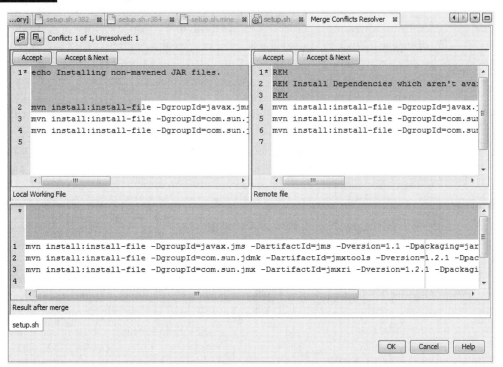

FIGURE 2-40

Conflict file
content

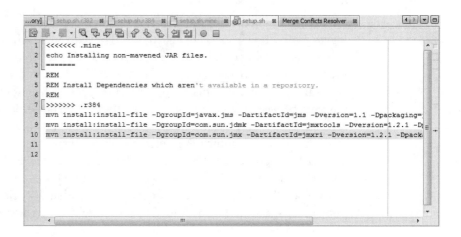

Configuring SVN Properties

Subversion supports metadata on files and directories. The metadata is a list of properties and values. Both the property and value are free-form text. SVN properties are versioned. You can add new properties—for instance, add a description field for image files—or use built-in properties. One common built-in property is `svn:needs-lock`, which is used to enable SVN locking. SVN locking limits a file to being edited by only one developer at a time. NetBeans does not currently honor SVN locking.

Figure 2-41 is the Svn Properties dialog box displayed when selecting a file and choosing Team | Subversion | Svn Properties. Once a property name and value are entered, the Add button becomes enabled, allowing the property to be saved.

If SVN properties are being edited on a directory, the Recursively checkbox is enabled. Selecting Recursively will apply the property to all subdirectories and files. Selecting the property and choosing Remove can remove a property.

Branching, Tagging, and Copying

Subversion does not have explicit operations for tagging or branching like CVS. Instead it uses copying; to branch or tag, a directory is copied to a new location with a descriptive name. Unlike CVS, Subversion supports versioning of directories. The refactoring tools inside NetBeans automatically leverage Subversion's copying support whenever a package is moved or a file is copied to another location. To copy a file or directory, right-click and choose Subversion | Copy To or Team | Subversion | Copy To. NetBeans displays the dialog box in Figure 2-42.

FIGURE 2-41

Svn Properties

FIGURE 2-42   Copy

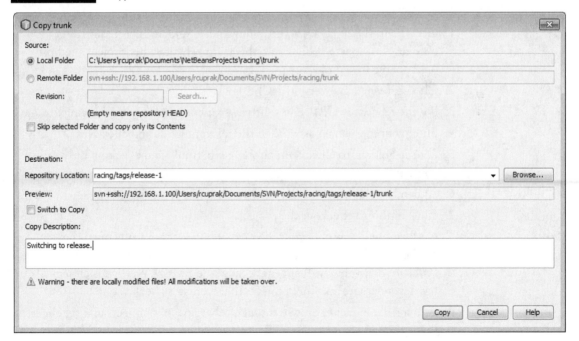

When copying a file/directory in Subversion, you select the source and the destination. The source can either be a local or remote directory/file. If the file/directory is remote, a revision number can be selected. If no revision number is selected, HEAD is assumed. Clicking the Browse button displays the NetBeans Subversion file browser that can be used to select the destination. The destination can also be manually typed. It is considered a good practice to enter a reason for the copy.

Once the Copy button is clicked, the copy is performed and committed to Subversion. If the goal is to also switch the project (local working copy), then Switch To Copy should be selected.

EXERCISE 2-2

Checking Out a Subversion Project

In this exercise, you are going to checkout a project from the Subversion repository on java.net. The SwingX library is an excellent source of Swing components and is used in the next chapter on Java SE Desktop Applications.

To checkout a project from the Subversion repository on java.net:

1. Get a login ID for java.net (http://java.net). A login ID is required for checking out source code from Subversion. The java.net project site hosts open source Java projects.
2. Choose Team | Subversion | Checkout.
3. For the repository URL, enter: https://swingx.dev.java.net/svn/swingx/trunk
4. Enter your username/password in the relevant fields and click Next.
5. For the Folders To Checkout, check "Skip 'trunk' and checkout only its content."
6. Append /**SwingX** to the end of the path in the Local Folder.
7. Click Finish to checkout the project.

   NetBeans will now checkout the project and automatically open the NetBeans project provided by the SwingX team. Note, the Reference Problems dialog box will appear because the SwingX NetBeans project file has dependencies on other projects that were not checked out.
8. As a further exercise, browse through other java.net projects and try checking them out.

Mercurial

Mercurial is an open-source distributed version control system. Unlike with either Subversion or CVS, the entire repository is duplicated on each machine. Each developer has a clone of the repository and is thus effectively working off a fork. As a result, there are some fairly significant workflow differences between Mercurial and CVS or Subversion. First, unlike CVS or Subversion, Mercurial has no checkout operation. The analogous operation is *cloning*, where you clone the parent repository. Second, when you commit files, you are checking them back in to your copy of the repository. Changes can be pushed or pulled to another repository. Changes can be pushed or pulled to any clone—not just the repository that was cloned. Thus, working with Mercurial is similar to always working on your own branch in CVS or Subversion.

The typical Mercurial workflow is depicted in Figure 2-43. Both the working directory and local repository reside on the local machine, typically under the same directory root. Files are edited in the working directory and committed to the local repository. From the local repository, changes can be pushed or pulled to other shared repositories. An example of a shared repository is the NetBeans project (http://hg.netbeans.org/main). The local repository contains the complete revision history. Subversion keeps only the original files (last update) in the .svn directory, whereas CVS has only working copies. Many operations that require a remote connection in either CVS or Subversion are local operations with Mercurial.

Mercurial is used by many large projects including NetBeans, OpenJDK, OpenSolaris, and Mozilla. Using the Mercurial support in NetBeans, it is possible to clone the NetBeans source tree and to begin modifying the IDE.

Since you are working with your own copy of the repository, you can commit your changes. With CVS and Subversion this would not be possible unless you were involved with the project and had commit permissions.

FIGURE 2-43

Mercurial workflow
(http://wiki
.netbeans.org/
HgNetBeansSources)

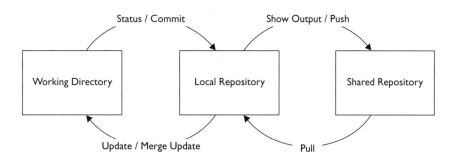

The following topics will be covered in this section:

- Configuring Mercurial
- Initializing a New Project
- Cloning
- Committing Changes
- Updating
- Reverting Changes
- Showing Changes

Configuring Mercurial

The Mercurial support in NetBeans requires the native Mercurial binaries. These can be downloaded from the Mercurial website (http://mercurial.selenic.com/), which provides installers for all of the major platforms including Windows, Solaris, Mac OS X, and Linux. Graphical installers are provided for Windows and Mac OS X; package utilities are used for the other platforms. Mercurial does require Python, which is a separate install.

Once Mercurial is installed and added to the PATH environment variable, NetBeans should auto-detect its presence, and no further setup is required. The Windows installer for Mercurial can optionally set up the PATH environment variable. The path to Mercurial binaries can also be configured in the options dialog box, Tools | Options | Miscellaneous | Versioning. If the path for some reason is not set, the Mercurial executable is named `hg.exe`, and the typical path to it is `C:\Program Files (x86)\Mercurial`.

Initializing a New Project

Initializing a new project is analogous to importing a project in either Subversion or CVS. To initialize a project, select the top-level node of the project in the Projects window and choose Team | Mercurial | Initialize Project. This will display the dialog box shown in Figure 2-44. This dialog box is prompting for the local Mercurial repository directory. If the default values are accepted, the Mercurial repository directory, `.hg`, is placed in the project directory. After initializing the project, the files should be committed by choosing Team | Mercurial | Commit.

FIGURE 2-44

Initializing
Mercurial project

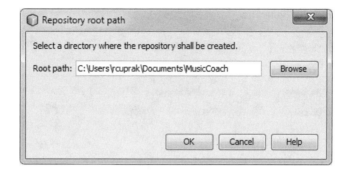

Cloning

Cloning an external repository is equivalent to checking out a project in the
Subversion or CVS version control systems. Cloned projects can originate either
from a remote repository or from an existing NetBeans project that is being stored in
a Mercurial repository and is opened in the IDE. Cloning an existing IDE project is
a painless technique to create a branch that is instantly available. You can clone an
existing project by choosing Team | Mercurial | Clone – [Project Name]. NetBeans
will prompt for the source repository, name, and destination.

Cloning a remote project is more involved than cloning a local project. To clone
a remote project, choose Team | Mercurial | Clone Other. This displays the dialog
box in Figure 2-45. The first step to cloning a repository is to specify the Repository
URL along with a User name and Password if required. The valid URL formats are

- ```local/filesystem/path[#revision]```
- ```file://local/filesystem/path[#revision]```
- ```http://[user[:pass]@host[:port]/[path][#revision]```
- ```https://[user[:pass]@host[:port]/[path][#revision]```
- ```ssh://[user[:pass]@host[:port]/[path][#revision]```

The next panel in the wizard, shown in Figure 2-46, defines the pull and push
paths. The *pull* path defines the repository path to pull changes from when choosing
Mercurial | Share Pull from default. The *push* path is the path to which changes are
pushed when selecting Team | Mercurial | Share | Push to default.

FIGURE 2-45   Mercurial Clone, Step 1

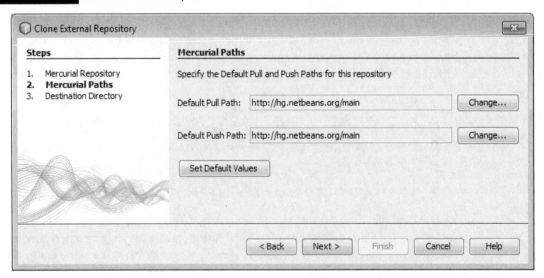

FIGURE 2-46   Mercurial Clone, Step 2

The last step in the cloning process, shown in Figure 2-47, prompts for the Parent Directory where the cloned project is to be placed. A Clone Name also is required. NetBeans can optionally scan the repository and open any NetBeans projects.

Committing Changes

A big difference between CVS and Subversion versus Mercurial is in the commit process. Under both the context menu and main Mercurial menu is a Commit menu item. The two menus also have Push To Default and Push Other menu items. The workflow is shown in Figure 2-43. Changes are first committed to the local repository. Committing creates a new changeset. Once changes are committed to the local repository, they can then be pushed to the original repository used to clone this repository or to another repository. You can also share changes by having other developers pull from the repository.

The Commit dialog box depicted in Figure 2-48 is similar to the commit dialog boxes of both Subversion and CVS. It lists the files to be committed along with a comment and can optionally update the issue tracker. The Push Dialog, shown in Figure 2-49, is invoked via Team | Mercurial | Share | Push To Other. It will prompt for the remote server and credentials.

FIGURE 2-47   Mercurial Clone, Step 3

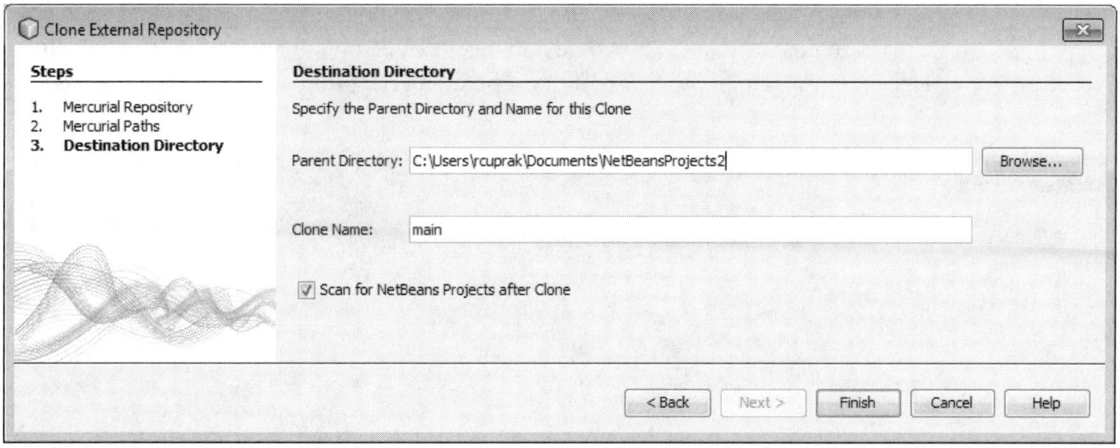

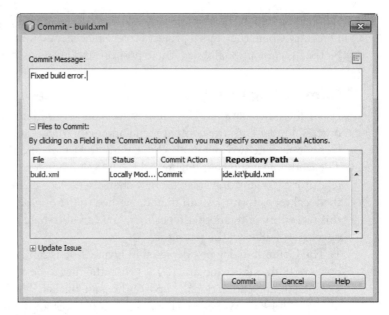

FIGURE 2-48

Mercurial
Commit

Updating

Updating in Mercurial involves pulling changesets from another repository. The changes are pulled from the remote repository into the current repository. An update must then be performed to synchronize the working directory with the local repository. NetBeans automatically performs the update when a pull is performed. This is analogous to a CVS update. Changes can be pulled from either the default repository or from another repository. The menu operations involved are invoked

FIGURE 2-49

Mercurial Push
Dialog

from Team | Mercurial | Share | Pull From Default or Pull From Other. The Mercurial update command can be invoked separately via Team | Mercurial Update.

Related to updating is fetch: Team | Mercurial | Fetch. This pulls changes from the shared repository, updates the local working directory, merges the changes, and if successful, commits the changes back to the local repository. This simplifies the workflow by combining several Mercurial commands.

Reverting Changes

Reverting files in Mercurial is similar to reverting in Subversion and CVS. Choose Team | Mercurial | Revert to revert a file. This will display the Revert Modifications dialog box shown in Figure 2-50. Using this dialog box, you can select the revision. Selecting a revision displays information about it including the commit message, author, and date. Additionally, the file can be backed up.

Showing Changes

Changes can be viewed by choosing Team | Mercurial | Status. This will open the Mercurial status window shown in Figure 2-51. This window lists the pending changes. The interface is basically the same as in CVS (look back at Figure 2-18), except there is no filtering for local and remote changes.

FIGURE 2-50

Mercurial Revert

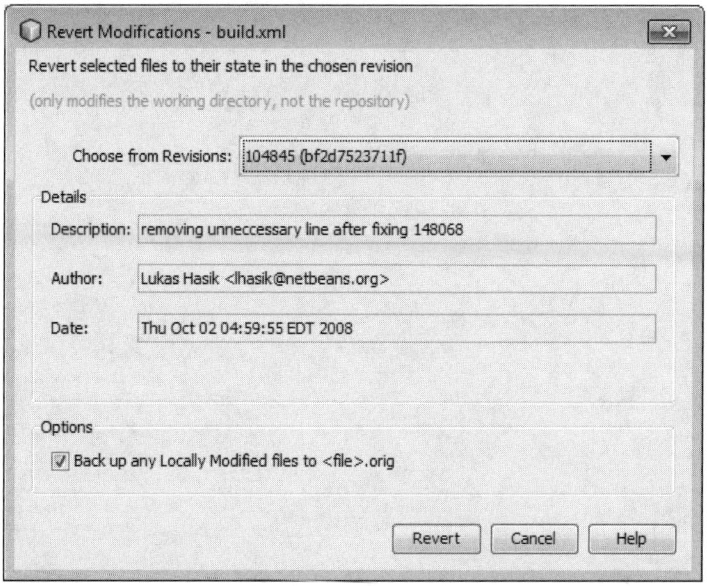

Right-clicking a change row will display a context menu with the following operations:

- **Open** Opens the file in the source editor.
- **Diff** Opens the file in the diff tool.
- **Update** Updates just the selected file.
- **Commit** Commits the selected file to the local repository.
- **Mark As Resolved** Marks a file as resolved. Choose when the file conflicts have been manually fixed outside of the NetBeans diff tool.
- **Show Annotations** Displays the commit message, author, date, and revision.
- **Revert Modifications** Reverts to the selected file(s).
- **Exclude From Commit** Defers committing a file. The file will appear with a strike-through in the list. Choosing Commit All will not commit the file.

FIGURE 2-51 Mercurial status

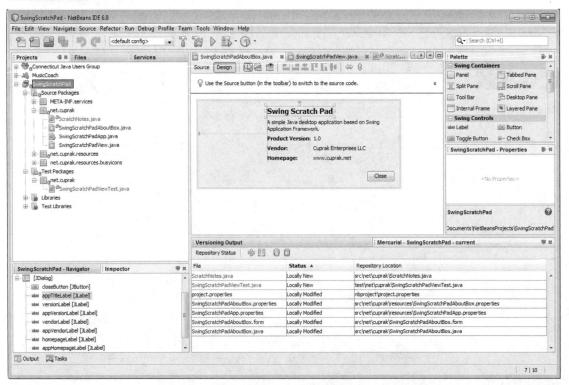

EXERCISE 2-3

Creating a Mercurial Project and Cloning

In this exercise, you create a new project and import the project into a Mercurial repository. You then clone the project and experiment with pushing and pulling.

1. Create a new Java Desktop Application by choosing File | New Project | Java Desktop Application.

2. Create a couple of source code files, and drop some widgets onto the main panel.

3. Import the project into a Mercurial repository by choosing Team | Mercurial | Initialize Project.

4. Accept the root path suggested by the IDE.

5. Commit your changes by choosing Team | Mercurial | Commit. Enter a comment and select Commit.

6. Clone the project. Choose Team | Clone [Project Name].

7. Accept the suggested defaults. The Clone Name field specifies the name of the new clone. Choose Clone to clone the project. NetBeans will open the clone in a new project.

8. In the original project, make some additional changes to the main panel, and commit to the Mercurial repository.

9. Select the cloned project in the Projects window. Choose Team | Mercurial | Share | Pull From Default.

10. Confirm that the code changes were pulled from the original project.

11. Experiment with making conflicting changes.

Local History

Version control systems such as CVS, Mercurial, Subversion, Perforce, and so on are great for tracking code history and maintaining an audit trail. Code history, when combined with a diff tool, is an indispensible means for understanding where changes have been made. Changes can easily be reverted with a click of a button, allowing developers to experiment with making complex code changes without bad consequences. In many ways a version control system is a powerful undo/redo system—one that can be used throughout the day. Changes to code are constantly being made, evaluated, and rolled backed. Version control systems have one major weakness; it is the responsibility of the developer to commit changes. Many times changes cannot be committed for a period of time—the feature might be incomplete, buggy, or the developer might take an extended vacation. NetBeans bridges these shortcomings with its Local History system.

The Local History version control system integration in NetBeans is not a full-fledged version control system. It cannot be used to share changes between developers, so it isn't a replacement for CVS, Subversion, or Mercurial. Unlike full-fledged version control systems, Local History lacks an explicit commit. Instead, it tracks all changes, no matter how small, over a period of time each time you save a file. By default, it tracks changes for seven days and is configurable in Tools | Options | Miscellaneous | Versioning | Local History. The time limit mitigates the footprint of the history on disk. Most of the history consists of routine changes/ experimentation with no value. For example, adding a temporary debug statement and then fixing the formatting of that statement is not a useful edit that anyone would care about in six months. Local History is the undo/redo support with the façade of the version control system integration.

The local history submenu, Team | Local History, has three menu items:

- **Show Local History** Views changes made to the current file.
- **Revert Deleted** Recovers a deleted file.
- **Revert To** Reverts to a previous editing state.

The Show Local History menu opens a new tab in NetBeans showing the history of the current file. This is shown in Figure 2-52. The top panel of the tab contains a list of the revisions ordered by timestamp along with a label. The bottom panel is a file diff with the selected row revision on the left and the current revision on the right. The following actions can be performed:

- **Labeling** A revision can be labeled by clicking a label cell and entering text.
- **Filtering** Right-clicking the label column displays a context menu for filtering the labels.
- **Reverting** Right-click a revision and select Revert From History to revert the file to the selected revision.
- **Deleting** Right-click a revision and select Delete From History to purge a revision.

FIGURE 2-52   Show Local History

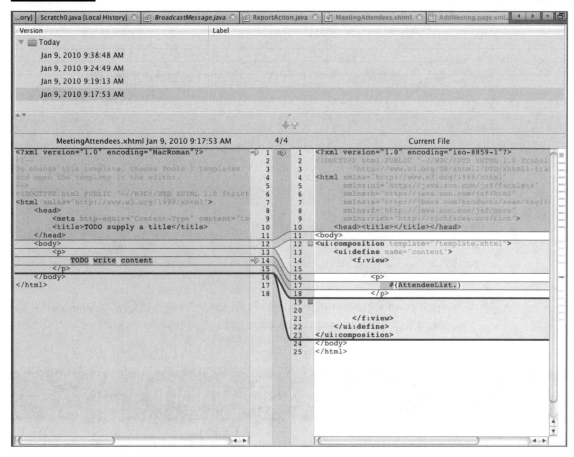

The Revert Deleted menu reverts deleted files/directories. Although Revert Deleted is available from the Team | Local History menu, it is more intuitive to right-click the directory containing the deleted item. Revert Deleted will undelete all files and directories in the local history. Most importantly, this functionality is only available to files created and deleted in NetBeans. If the file is created and deleted outside of NetBeans, this functionality may not work.

The Revert To menu displays the dialog box shown in Figure 2-53 for the current file containing the list of local revisions. The file can be reverted by selecting a revision from the list and clicking Revert. If it turns out that the operation was undesirable, it can always be undone by digging back into the local history. Note: reverting creates a new revision, which means that undoing a revert operation requires reverting back to a previous reversion.

FIGURE 2-53 Local history revert

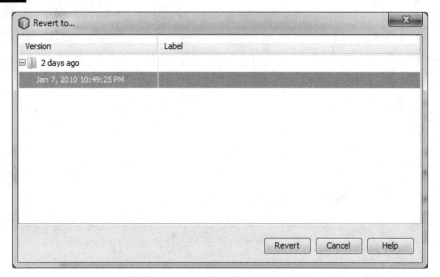

Version control support in NetBeans is an expansive topic. The Scenario & Solution will quickly test what you've learned.

SCENARIO & SOLUTION

You create a new source code file and implement a complex algorithm. Accidently, you delete it before committing it to version control. You want to recover the file.	Use the Local History feature.
You are using MS Windows and need to connect to a Subversion repository via `ssh`.	If needed, install Subversion command-line tools and plink, a command-line interface to the PuTTy `ssh` tool in Windows.
You would like to checkout files from a CVS repository.	No additional applications are needed because CVS is built into NetBeans.
You are starting a new project in which development will be distributed. You would like each developer working on his or her own branch.	Use the Mercurial Distributed Version Control System, which is installed in NetBeans.
You are editing a file and want to see how it differs from what is in CVS/SVN.	On the Subversion menu, choose the Show Changes menu option.

Experimenting with Local History

In this exercise, you will repeatedly edit a file and then selectively revert your changes.

1. Open a scratch Java Application project for experimenting. This is a project that contains nothing valuable and that you can delete after this exercise.
2. Switch to the Files window.
3. Open the `nbproject` directory.
4. Double-click `project.properties` to edit it.
5. Randomly change the values of a couple of properties throughout the file.
6. Save the file.
7. Remove some properties from the file.
8. Save the file.
9. Add a couple of new properties to the file.
10. Right-click the file's tab and select Local History | Show Local History.
11. Click each one of the revisions to compare with the current revision.
12. Add or remove content in the current file.

CERTIFICATION OBJECTIVE

Working with Build Files and Processes

Exam Objective 2.3   Describe the ways in which you can change the build process for a standard project, such as configuring project properties and modifying the project's Ant build script.

NetBeans 6.8 supports two build systems: Ant (ant.apache.org) and Maven (maven.apache.org). Both are open source and Apache projects. Ant is a cross-platform general-purpose build tool. It uses an XML file format and can easily be extended with plugins. You can think of it as Java's Make. Maven is also a build tool, but takes a more expansive view of the build process. It tracks and manages the dependency graph of a project. For instance, a specific version of Hibernate has a multitude of dependencies—those dependencies in turn depend on other projects ad infinitum. Maven also has predefined life cycles and project layouts. Contrasting the build systems, Ant is free form whereas Maven is highly structured.

NetBeans provides excellent support for both build systems. The certification exam, which targets NetBeans 6.1, focuses exclusively on Apache Ant. NetBeans has had excellent Ant integration for many years—it is the build system used by the IDE in its standard projects. Early on, the NetBeans team realized the value of Ant over a proprietary build system, and a conscious decision was made not to reinvent the wheel. The NetBeans Ant support makes it easy for developers to customize the build process. In the previous section, we examined the NetBeans free-form project support. The free-form project support enables NetBeans to easily work with existing projects without forcing a re-architecting to make the project IDE compatible. In this section, we review the structure and extension points of the Ant files used by NetBeans standard projects.

To facilitate development, NetBeans ships with numerous predefined project templates. These are instantiated through project wizards via File | New Project. The Java projects groups, specifically Java, Java Web, Java EE, and NetBeans Modules, all use Ant as their build system. With the exception of the Java Free-Form Project and Web Free-Form Application, NetBeans provides a predefined set of Ant build scripts. The IDE is prewired for these Ant scripts—meaning that the run action is preconfigured to invoke the Ant target, and so on. Additionally, the classpath can be manipulated in the editor, and no changes to the build system are required. The goal, as is the case with Maven, is to simplify the development process and let the developer focus on writing code and not a build system.

on the job

One caveat regarding the project templates—Ant is used for Java projects; however, NetBeans supports many other technologies including PHP, Ruby, and C++. These other project types do not use Ant as their build system. They use the build system typically used by those technologies. For instance, the C++ projects use the make utility.

Chapter 1 covered the basic configuration of the Ant integration, including configuring Ant version, classpath, verbosity, and properties. This section splits up and covers the following topics:

- Project Structure
- Running Targets
- Customizing Ant Scripts

Project Structure

Integral to understanding the build process and how to customize it is understanding the structure of a standard NetBeans project. A standard NetBeans project refers to a template that "offers the highest integration with the IDE's support of certain technologies" to quote the online documentation. A standard project template can be thought of as an application skeleton; the infrastructure code is in place, and there is a defined layout. The developer can just begin writing code and click Run. The developer is not worried about constructing the classpath for execution or the parameters necessary to launch the application for debugging or profiling. The IDE controls the project layout and maintains the classpath at a granular level—compile, run, compile test, run test. As a result, the IDE is able to simplify the development process. Unlike the free-form project, the menus are prebound. Individual unit tests can be run without diving into `project.xml`.

NetBeans includes numerous project templates. Depending upon the plugins activated, the File | New Project dialog box can be filled. However, NetBeans has only four types of standard Java projects:

- Java SE Applications
- Java Web
- Java EE Applications
- NetBeans Modules

While each of the project types is slightly different in terms of layout and build targets, they all share a common set of files and directories:

- **src** Contains the source files for the project.
- **test** Contains the test files for the project.
- **build.xml** Contains customized build changes. This file is invoked by the IDE. It imports `build-impl.xml`.
- **dist** Contains the output of the build.
- **nbproject** NetBeans project directory—contains metadata for the project.
  - **project.properties** Config settings for the project. These properties are shared between users.
  - **genfiles.properties** Tracks changes in IDE-generated files. *Never* edit this file.

- **build-impl.xml** Contains the core build targets, which can be overridden in build.xml. This file should *never* be edited.
- **private** Directory contains settings for only the current user. This directory should *not* be checked in to version control.
  - **private.properties** Properties for the current user/local machine.

The main Ant build script for a project is build.xml. For a new project, this file is empty—targets are imported from build-impl.xml. The build-impl.xml should never be modified. While the IDE does not prevent you from editing this file, the IDE might overwrite this file. Right-clicking build.xml and choosing Run Target or Debug Target runs targets in this file. Targets in build-impl.xml can also be directly run in the same manner. Menus such as Run | Run Main Project and Debug | Debug Main Project are mapped to targets in build.xml.

When an Ant target is executed, either through a menu or via a context menu, NetBeans will automatically display an Output window as shown in Figure 2-54. The

FIGURE 2-54 Ant Output window

Output window enables you to view standard out and standard error from the Ant script. Application output will also appear in this window.

Running Targets

You can invoke Ant targets multiple ways from within NetBeans. Targets such as `run` can be explicitly invoked via the context menu on the Ant file or by invoking an IDE action such as Run | Run Main Project from a menu. Ant targets can also be invoked from the command line. From the command line, typing **ant** will cause the `build.xml` file to be loaded and the default target to be executed. The default target will compile the project's sources, generate the Javadoc, and finally run the unit tests.

The Ant scripts generated by NetBeans do not require a NetBeans installation on the computer for the basic operations such as compiling, running, and testing. However, certain targets pertaining to debugging and profiling require NetBeans because they are useless without the IDE. Targets that require the IDE are development related and are not part of the basic build/deploy/test life cycle. The ability to use the scripts independently of the IDE was a conscious design decision. This allows a project to standardize on a single build solution. Building is not segregated into "building in the IDE" or "building by the official project scripts." All maintenance of the project, such as management of external libraries, can therefore take place in the IDE.

The Ant targets that can be executed from the command line vary depending upon the project type. Table 2-4 lists targets that can be executed from the command line for Java SE and Java Web projects. Java Web and EJB applications possess targets for deploying to servers. The Ant files generated by NetBeans follow a standard naming pattern for their targets. Targets prefixed with a dash (–) should not be invoked directly. These targets are part of a larger sequence of targets. Targets without a dash can often be run independently as long as they don't tie in to a specific IDE feature such as debugging a single file or profiling.

TABLE 2-4

Targets

Java SE	Java Web
clean	clean
compile	clean-ear
compile-test	compile
default	compile-jsps
jar	compile-test
javadoc	default
run-applet	dist
run	dist-ear
test	do-dist
test-report	do-ear-dist
	Javadoc
	run
	run-deploy
	run-main
	run-test-with-main
	run-undeploy
	run-test-with-main
	run-undeploy
	test
	verify

Customizing Ant Scripts

The NetBeans Ant scripts generated by the project wizards contain hooks for adding custom extensions and behaviors. The hooks allow the build process to be customized for the particular project. Each project has its own sets of requirements outside the functionality implemented in code. Some common tasks that require changes to the build system include:

- Obfuscating generated byte code
- Digitally signing output
- Calculating unit test coverage
- Launching a third-party installer application to generate an installer

■ Generating Java sources from an XML file prior to invoking the compiler

■ Starting a server on a remote box prior to running unit tests

■ Incrementing a build number and storing the result back into version control

However, editing the project's build file should only be done when it is appropriate and the functionality is not already available in NetBeans. For instance, editing the `build.xml` file to inject a new library to the compile step would be a bad idea. First, NetBeans already provides a mechanism for managing libraries, and secondly, code completion for the library would not be available in the editor. When evaluating whether a change to the build system is necessary, first check to see if NetBeans already has an easier and intuitive way to accomplish the same thing.

NetBeans provides clear and well-documented hooks for adding customizations to the build file. The customization can participate in the IDE build cycle or extend it for use in integration build servers such as Hudson, CruiseControl, and so on. Four approaches may be taken when customizing a project's build:

■ Implement pre-/post-targets to perform tasks either before or after a specific life-cycle stage like compile, run, test, and so on.

■ Override an existing Ant target to completely replace its functionality.

■ Change settings passed to the compiler/debugger/and so on, in `project .properties`.

■ Add new targets to the build file for project-specific tasks.

When a project is generated, a `build.xml` file is placed at the root of the project directory. This file is initially empty. However, it imports `nbproject/build-impl.xml`, which has nearly 100 targets. These targets perform operations ranging from cleaning the output directories to compiling and generating Javadoc. NetBeans binds to the targets in `build-impl.xml`. Customization should be made to the `build.xml`. As mentioned previously, `nbproject/build-impl.xml` should not be altered.

NetBeans provides hooks for inserting operations into the build process. These hooks are listed in Table 2-5. The hooks are divided into five sections: initialization, compilation, JUnit compilation, jar, and clean. With these hooks you can perform operations before and after the main action; for example, `-pre-compile` and `-post-compile`. These hooks are empty targets in the `build-impl.xml` file. Other targets can be overridden, but care must be taken to maintain expected functionality.

TABLE 2-5 | Build Hooks

Section	Override Hook (Empty)	Description
Initialization	-pre-init	Invoked before project initialization
	-post-init	Invoked after project initialization
Compilation	-pre-compile	Invoked before source is compiled
	-post-compile	Invoked after source is compiled
	-pre-compile-single	Invoked before a single file is compiled
	-post-compile-single	Invoked after a single file is compiled
JUnit Compilation	-pre-compile-test	Invoked prior to the tests being compiled
	-post-compile-test	Invoked after tests are compiled
	-pre-compile-test-single	Invoked before a single test is compiled
	-post-compile-test-single	Invoked after a single test is compiled
Jar	-pre-jar	Invoked before a JAR file is generated
	-post-jar	Invoked after a JAR file is generated
Clean	-post-clean	Invoked after the clean operation

on the job

Troubleshooting Ant script files can be very challenging. Many developers tackle build problems with copious echo statements that are used for tracking variable values and execution progress. However, the NetBeans debugger can debug Ant scripts. Its powerful debugger allows you to see what is going on in the script and to step through it.

Custom properties to be used by the build script can be stored in two locations—either in `project.properties` or in `nbproject/private/private.properties`. The only difference between these two files is that `private.properties` is user specific and is not checked in to version control. That makes this file ideal for storing settings specific to a user or machine. The `project.properties` file stores lots of settings for the build including the classpath, parameters passed to `javac`, and so on. This is where settings from File | Project Properties are stored.

EXERCISE 2-5

Creating a Free-Form Project

In this exercise, you will customize `build.xml` and add properties to both `project.properties` and `private.properties`.

1. Create a new Java Application by choosing File | New Project | Java Application.
2. Switch to the Files window, and double-click `build.xml` under the project.
3. Add the following content to `build.xml`:

```xml
<target name="-pre-init">
    <echo message="hi from -pre-init"/>
</target>
<target name="-post-init">
    <echo message="hi from -post-init"/>
    <echo message="${private.properties.message}"/>
    <echo message="${project.properties.message}"/>
</target>
<target name="-pre-compile">
    <echo message="hi from -pre-compile"/>
</target>
<target name="-post-compile">
    <echo message="hi from -post-compile"/>
</target>
<target name="-pre-compile-single">
    <echo message="hi from -pre-compile-single"/>
</target>
<target name="-post-compile-single">
    <echo message="hi from post-compile-single"/>
</target>
<target name="-pre-compile-test">
    <echo message="hi from -pre-compile-test"/>
</target>
<target name="-post-compile-test">
    <echo message="hi from -post-compile-test"/>
</target>
<target name="-pre-compile-test-single">
    <echo message="hi from -pre-compile-test-single"/>
```

```
    </target>
    <target name="-post-compile-test-single">
        <echo message="hi from -post-compile-test-single"/>
    </target>
    <target name="-pre-jar">
        <echo message="hi from -pre-jar"/>
    </target>
    <target name="-post-jar">
        <echo message="hi from -post-jar"/>
    </target>
    <target name="-post-clean">
        <echo message="hi from -post-clean"/>
    </target>
```

4. Add the following line to `project.properties`:
   `project.properties.message=Hi from project properties`

5. Add the following line to `private.properties`:
   `private.properties.message=Hi from private properties!`

6. Right-click `build.xml` and choose Run Target | default.

7. What happens if the contents of `-post-init` and `-pre-init` are swapped?

8. In what order are the targets executed?

9. Set a breakpoint in `-post-init`, and step through the build process.

CERTIFICATION OBJECTIVE

Configuring the JDK into the Project

Exam Objective 2.4   Configure your project to compile against and run on a specific version of the JDK.

The last section of Chapter 1 covered the steps necessary to add or remove JDKs in NetBeans. This section will cover the steps necessary to make a project compile and run against a specific version of the JDK. As mentioned in Chapter 1, each project can be configured with its own JDK. Projects are independent of the JDK/JRE being used to run NetBeans. This is very important, because Java applications often must support older JRE versions or bugs fixed in legacy applications still in production.

The JDK for a project is configured in the Project Properties dialog box shown in Figure 2-55. This dialog box is displayed by choosing File | Project Properties | Libraries. The JDK is chosen from the Java Platform drop-down list. Clicking the Manage Platforms button brings up the configuration screens described in Chapter 1. This JDK selection determines three things:

- JRE used to run/debug/profile
- JRE used for code completion/syntax checking
- JRE used to execute unit tests

The JDK set on a project affects the source/binary level for a project. This is set on File | Project Properties | Sources. An example of this operation is depicted in Figure 2-56. The source/binary level can never be greater than the source/binary level of the JDK. For example, if JDK 1.3 is selected for a project, the source level

FIGURE 2-55   Project Properties: Libraries

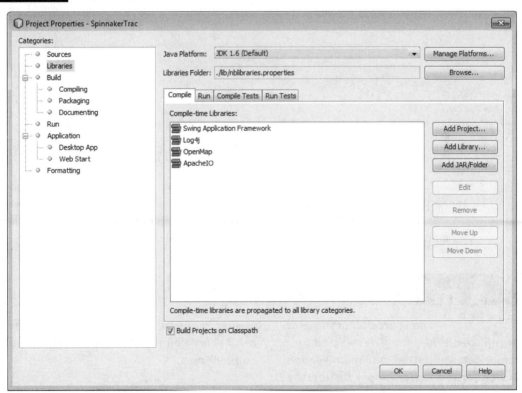

FIGURE 2-56   Project Properties: Sources

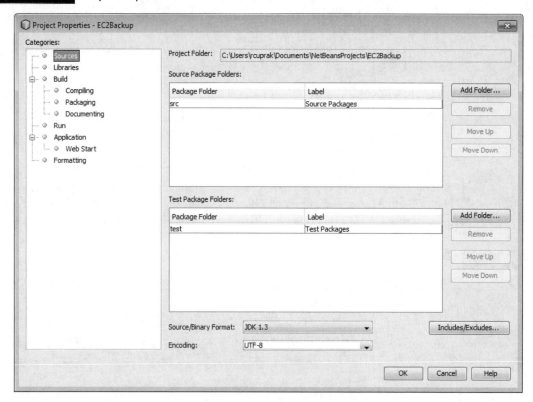

cannot be 1.5. When changing the JDK, NetBeans will automatically warn you and change the source/binary level if necessary.

Changing the JDK raises an interesting issue: how is the code actually compiled? Surprisingly, the selected JDK's `javac` is not used for compilation. Instead, it is the `javac` of the JDK being used to run Ant that is employed. The source/binary level controls the byte code that is emitted by the compiler.

e x a m

ⓦ a t c h   *The source/binary level is not reflexive. While the JDK selected for a project determines the maximum version allowed for the source/binary setting, the*   *reverse is not true. A JDK version of 1.6 and a 1.3 source/binary is a valid configuration combination.*

EXERCISE 2-6

Back in Time to an Older JDK

In this exercise, you create a new project using JDK 1.6 and then switch the project over to JDK 1.3 to see the effect. This exercise assumes that you are running Java 6.

1. Download and install JDK 1.3 from java.sun.com. Finding JDK 1.3 might be a challenge, but it is still available.

2. Launch NetBeans and create a new Java Application: File | New Project | Java Application.

3. In the main method of the application add the following code:
   ```
   System.out.println("Java version: " +
   System.getProperty("java.version"));
   ```

4. Run the application and verify that it prints *1.6*.

5. Choose File | Project Properties | Libraries.

6. Click Manage Platforms and configure JDK 1.3 as in Chapter 1. Click Close when you're done.

7. Select JDK 1.3 for the project. NetBeans will immediately warn that it is changing the source/binary level to 1.3. Click OK to accept the changes.

8. Run the project again and verify that it now prints *1.3*.

CERTIFICATION SUMMARY

This chapter covered four important feature sets of NetBeans—free-form project, version control, Ant build files, and per-project JDK configuration. By studying this chapter, you are now able to:

1. Create a new NetBeans project using the free-form template.

2. Name the supported version control systems and perform the following tasks:
   - Import a project to a repository.
   - Checkout a project from a repository.
   - Update a file or files.
   - Commit changes to a repository.
   - Resolve merge conflicts and view file/directory history.
   - View the current status of the project.

3. Alter and extend the build process.

4. Change the JDK for a project and understand the interplay between source level and the JDK.

These are important IDE skills to master, and you will interact with these core features of the IDE on a daily basis. At this point, you should be an expert on creating projects and maintaining projects as well as versioning them. The stage is set for building applications in the next chapter.

✓ TWO-MINUTE DRILL

Understanding Free-Form Projects

- ❑ The free-form template enables NetBeans to work with just about any Java project regardless of layout.
- ❑ There are two types of free-form projects:
  - ❑ Java Free-Form Project
  - ❑ Web Free-Form Application
- ❑ The project's Ant build file is leveraged and integrated into menus.
- ❑ The classpath property is used for code editing and syntax checking—not for compiling or execution.
- ❑ A Web Free-Form project requires additional configuration for web sources and web configuration files.
- ❑ The `nbproject/project.xml` file contains project settings including the mapping of IDE actions to Ant targets. NetBeans can generate an `nbproject/ide-targets.xml` file to support debugging.
- ❑ JUnit integration requires simple changes to the Ant target so that the output does not go to a file.
- ❑ The Profiler and Debug IDE actions require custom Ant targets that are specific to NetBeans.

Using Version Control Systems

- ❑ Three version control systems are supported by default: Subversion, Mercurial, and CVS.
- ❑ Additional version control systems can be installed via the Plugin Manager.
- ❑ NetBeans requires the binary executables be installed and configured in Tools | Options | Miscellaneous | Versioning for Subversion and Mercurial.
- ❑ Version control operations are accessed via the Team menu.
- ❑ Version control operations are available via the context menu (right-click menu) for files in the Projects and Files windows as well as on the editor tab titles.
- ❑ Local history takes a snapshot of a file every time it is saved.
- ❑ Local history records add/delete operations performed by the editor.

Working with Build Files and Processes

❑ Changes and additions to the build process are made to the `build.xml` file at the root of the project.

❑ `nbproject/build-impl.xml` contains the core infrastructure Ant targets and should never be edited.

❑ `build.xml` imports `nbproject/build-impl.xml`.

❑ `nbproject/project.xml` is the main project file and can be edited, but those edits are overwritten by the project properties editor.

❑ `nbproject/project.properties` contains properties used to configure the Ant script. While this file can be edited, it rarely needs to be.

❑ `nbproject/private` contains settings for the current user and should not be added to version control.

❑ Ant targets are invoked either from the menus/context menus (Run | Run Main Project, and so on) or by choosing Run Target/Debug Target.

❑ `private/project.properties` contains local Ant file parameters.

❑ NetBeans provides empty targets to facilitate hooking into the build system. Review Table 2-5.

❑ `build.xml` can be run from the command line outside of the IDE.

❑ Targets names prefixed with a dash (–) are part of a build sequence and should not be run independently.

Configuring the JDK into the Project

❑ Each project can be associated with a different JDK.

❑ JDK settings for a project are configured by File | Project Properties | Libraries.

❑ The source/binary level in File | Project Properties | Sources controls the byte code emitted.

❑ The source/binary level maximum value is determined by the JDK selected for a project.

❑ The actual JDK used for compiling a project is the one used to launch Ant.

❑ The source/binary level controls the value passed into the `–source` parameter of `javac`.

SELF TEST

The following questions will help you measure your understanding of the material presented in this chapter. Read all the choices carefully because there might be more than one correct answer. Choose all correct answers for each question.

Understanding Free-Form Projects

1. A NetBeans project needs to be created for an existing code base that possesses its own unique code structure and Ant build file. Which project template should be used?
   A. Java Application
   B. Java Desktop Application
   C. Java Project With Existing Sources
   D. Java Free-Form Project

2. In a free-form project, which of the following settings cannot be configured in the IDE?
   A. Java Development Kit (JDK)
   B. Multiple source roots
   C. JUnit integration
   D. Source code for external libraries

3. What is the difference between the "Java Free-Form Project" and a "Java Project With Existing Sources"?
   A. There are no differences between the two project types.
   B. Java Free-Form Project uses its own Ant build file, not one provided by NetBeans.
   C. Java Project With Existing Sources uses its own Ant build file, not one provided by NetBeans.
   D. NetBeans generates a custom Ant file for a Java Free-Form Project.

4. A project team has made the decision to switch from another IDE to NetBeans. The project is large and complicated, with its own Ant build file and Eclipse project file. Which is the most expedient and supported path to get up and running with NetBeans?
   A. Create a new NetBeans project using the Java Application project template. Reorganize the existing sources to match the layout required by the new project.
   B. Use the Java Free-Form Project template.
   C. Choose File | Open Project and select the project's Ant script. NetBeans will then analyze the Ant script and create a NetBeans free-form project.
   D. Create a `pom.xml` file (Maven) for the project, and use the Maven project support in NetBeans.

Using Version Control Systems

5. Which version control systems does NetBeans support?

   A. Subversion

   B. Mercurial

   C. CVS

   D. All of the above

6. NetBeans requires native executables for which of the following version control systems?

   A. CVS, Subversion

   B. Subversion, Mercurial

   C. CVS, Mercurial

   D. None

7. When a new Java class is added to a project, what happens regarding version control integration?

   A. The class is automatically scheduled for addition (svn add/cvs add) and appears colored green in the Projects window.

   B. The new class wizard prompts for whether the class should be added to version control. If Yes is chosen, the class is scheduled for addition, and the file icon appears red in the Projects window.

   C. Nothing.

   D. The filename is colored red in the Projects window until the add operation is invoked by right-clicking the file.

8. When checking out a directory from version control, must the directory contain a NetBeans project?

   A. No, but a subfolder must contain a NetBeans project.

   B. Yes, the directory must contain a NetBeans project.

   C. No, NetBeans prompts for creating a project after the checkout.

9. A Subversion update is performed resulting in a conflict. How can this conflict be resolved?

   A. Right-click the file and select Subversion | Resolve Conflicts. Use the graphical Conflicts Resolver to merge the file.

   B. Double-click the file and manually fix the conflicts.

   C. Right-click the file and select Subversion | Merge Changes. Use the graphical merge utility to resolve the conflicts.

   D. A and B

Working with Build Files and Processes

10. A NetBeans project is being added to a Perforce repository using a separate Perforce utility outside of NetBeans. Which files or directories should not be added to the repository?

    A. `nbproject/private`

    B. `build.xml`

    C. `nbproject/build-impl.xml`

    D. `nbproject/project.xml`

11. A job for a NetBeans project is being set up on a continuous integration server. The continuous integration server will checkout the project frequently from version control and do a test build. What Ant script should the continuous integration server use to build the project?

    A. `nbproject/build.xml`

    B. `nbproject/build-impl.xml`

    C. `nbproject/project.xml`

    D. `build.xml`

12. Prior to packaging, a code obfuscator needs to be run on the classes. Which Ant target should be added to `build.xml` and include this logic?

    A. `-post-init`

    B. `-pre-compile`

    C. `compile`

    D. `-post-compile`

13. A web project has added a target to the project's Ant file to deploy the web application to a remote QA environment. The QA environment requires unique credentials for each developer. Where should these credentials be stored?

    A. `project.xml`

    B. `nbproject/project.properties`

    C. `nbproject/private/private.properties`

    D. `build.xml`

Configuring the JDK into the Project

14. NetBeans is launched using JDK 1.6. The JDK for a project is set to 1.3 with a source level of 1.2. Which JDK instance is used to run Ant?

    A. 1.3

    B. 1.4

    C. 1.5

    D. 1.6

15. The source/binary setting in Project Properties controls what aspect of the project?

    A. JDK used to run the project.

    B. Byte code emitted by the compiler.

    C. `javac` implementation used to compile the code.

    D. Both A and C.

SELF TEST ANSWERS

Understanding Free-Form Projects

1. A NetBeans project needs to be created for an existing code base that possesses its own unique code structure and Ant build file. Which project template should be used?

A. Java Application

B. Java Desktop Application

C. Java Project With Existing Sources

D. Java Free-Form Project

☑ **D.** Java Free-Form Project—this project type leverages an existing Ant file and source code layout.

☒ **A, B**, and **C** are incorrect. **A** is incorrect because the source code of the project would have to be reorganized. **B** is incorrect because the source code of the project would have to be reorganized. **C** is incorrect because the Java Project With Existing Sources uses an existing tree but uses a NetBeans generated build script.

2. In a free-form project, which of the following settings cannot be configured in the IDE?

A. Java Development Kit (JDK)

B. Multiple source roots

C. JUnit integration

D. Source code for external libraries

☑ **A.** The JDK used by Ant is the one that is used by the project.

☒ **B, C**, and **D** are incorrect. **B** is incorrect because multiple source roots can be configured. **C** is incorrect because JUnit with custom Ant files is supported. **D** is incorrect because source code can be configured for external libraries in a free-form project.

3. What is the difference between the "Java Free-Form Project" and a "Java Project With Existing Sources"?

A. There are no differences between the two project types.

B. Java Free-Form Project uses its own Ant build file, not one provided by NetBeans.

C. Java Project With Existing Sources uses its own Ant build file, not one provided by NetBeans.

D. NetBeans generates a custom Ant file for a Java Free-Form Project.

☑ **B.** Java Free-Form Projects use the project's existing `build.xml` file—not one provided by NetBeans.

☒ **A, C,** and **D** are incorrect. **A** is incorrect because there are differences between these project templates. Specifically NetBeans generates an Ant build file for a "project with existing sources." **C** is incorrect because NetBeans provides a `build.xml` file for a project with sources. **D** is incorrect because NetBeans generates an Ant file for a project with existing sources and not for a free-form project.

4. A project team has made the decision to switch from another IDE to NetBeans. The project is large and complicated, with its own Ant build file and Eclipse project file. Which is the most expedient and supported path to get up and running with NetBeans?

A. Create a new NetBeans project using the Java Application project template. Reorganize the existing sources to match the layout required by the new project.

B. Use the Java Free-Form Project template.

C. Choose File | Open Project and select the project's Ant script. NetBeans will then analyze the Ant script and create a NetBeans free-form project.

D. Create a `pom.xml` file (Maven) for the project, and use the Maven project support in NetBeans.

☑ **B** is correct since the project uses a custom layout and its own Ant script.

☒ **A, C,** and **D** are incorrect. **A** is incorrect because reorganizing the source code is a lot of work and complicates tracing file history in version control. **C** is incorrect because NetBeans does not reverse engineer a project from its Ant script. **D** is incorrect because this is more work than **A** because it requires tracking down all of the dependencies and possibly restructuring the project.

Using Version Control Systems

5. Which version control systems does NetBeans support?

A. Subversion

B. Mercurial

C. CVS

D. All of the above

☑ **D.** All of the version control systems listed are supported by NetBeans out of the box.

☒ **A, B,** and **C** are incorrect because not just one but all are supported.

6. NetBeans requires native executables for which of the following version control systems?

A. CVS, Subversion

B. Subversion, Mercurial

C. CVS, Mercurial

D. None

☑ **B.** NetBeans requires the native executables for Mercurial and Subversion.

☒ **A, C,** and **D** are incorrect. **A** is incorrect because NetBeans does not use the native CVS binaries. **C** is incorrect for the same reason as **A**; CVS libraries are not required. **D** is incorrect because NetBeans requires the executables for both Subversion and Mercurial.

7. When a new Java class is added to a project, what happens regarding version control integration?

A. The class is automatically scheduled for addition (svn add/cvs add) and appears colored green in the Projects window.

B. The new class wizard prompts for whether the class should be added to version control. If Yes is chosen, the class is scheduled for addition, and the file icon appears red in the Projects window.

C. Nothing.

D. The filename is colored red in the Projects window until the add operation is invoked by right-clicking the file.

☑ **A.** NetBeans automatically schedules the file for addition to version control. New files scheduled for addition are colored green in the Projects window.

☒ **B, C,** and **D** are incorrect. **B** is incorrect because NetBeans does not prompt for whether the file should be added to Subversion. Also, files scheduled for addition are colored green and not red. **C** is incorrect because files are automatically added to version control. **D** is incorrect; the user does not have to do anything to get a new file added to version control.

8. When checking out a directory from version control, must the directory contain a NetBeans project?

A. No, but a subfolder must contain a NetBeans project.

B. Yes, the directory must contain a NetBeans project.

C. No, NetBeans prompts for creating a project after the checkout.

☑ **C.** NetBeans does not require that a directory being checked out, nor any of its subdirectories, possess a NetBeans project. NetBeans will prompt to create a project afterwards; however, that is optional.

☒ **A** and **B** are incorrect because NetBeans does not require the presence of a NetBeans project.

9. A Subversion update is performed resulting in a conflict. How can this conflict be resolved?

   A. Right-click the file and select Subversion | Resolve Conflicts. Use the graphical Conflicts Resolver to merge the file.

   B. Double-click the file and manually fix the conflicts.

   C. Right-click the file and select Subversion | Merge Changes. Use the graphical merge utility to resolve the conflicts.

   D. A and B

   ☑ **D.** Both **A** and **B** are methods used to resolve conflicts.

   ☒ **A** and **B** and **C** are incorrect. **A** is incorrect because this method will resolve conflicts. **B** is incorrect because this method will resolve conflicts. **C** is incorrect because merging deals with integrating changes between folders/brances.

Working with Build Files and Processes

10. A NetBeans project is being added to a Perforce repository using a separate Perforce utility outside of NetBeans. Which files or directories should not be added to the repository?

    A. `nbproject/private`

    B. `build.xml`

    C. `nbproject/build-impl.xml`

    D. `nbproject/project.xml`

    ☑ **A.** The `private` directory contains files for the current user/local machine. This is where settings that are not to be shared are stored.

    ☒ **B, C,** and **D** are incorrect. **B** is incorrect because `build.xml` is the Ant file for the project. **C** is incorrect because `build-impl.xml` is used by `build.xml` and provides most of the target definitions. **D** is incorrect because `project.xml` defines the project.

11. A job for a NetBeans project is being set up on a continuous integration server. The continuous integration server will checkout the project frequently from version control and do a test build. What Ant script should the continuous integration server use to build the project?

    A. `nbproject/build.xml`

    B. `nbproject/build-impl.xml`

    C. `nbproject/project.xml`

    D. `build.xml`

    ☑ **D.** The `build.xml` file in the project directory is the one that is used to build the project.

    ☒ **A, B,** and **C** are incorrect. **A** is incorrect because `nbproject/build.xml` does not exist. **B** is incorrect because `build-impl.xml` does contain the targets used to build the project, but they are often overridden in `build.xml`. **C** is incorrect; `project.xml` is the project file.

12. Prior to packaging, a code obfuscator needs to be run on the classes. Which Ant target should be added to `build.xml` and include this logic?

A. `-post-init`

B. `-pre-compile`

C. `compile`

D. `-post-compile`

☑ **D.** Obfuscation is performed after the compile.

☒ **A** and **B** are incorrect because `-post-init` is invoked before the project has been compiled. **C** is incorrect because overriding the compile would require a significant amount of work for no benefit.

13. A web project has added a target to the project's Ant file to deploy the web application to a remote QA environment. The QA environment requires unique credentials for each developer. Where should these credentials be stored?

A. `project.xml`

B. `nbproject/project.properties`

C. `nbproject/private/private.properties`

D. `build.xml`

☑ **C** is the correct answer. `nbproject/private/private.properties` does not get checked into version control and is used to pass properties into the `build.xml` script.

☒ **A**, **B**, and **D** are incorrect. **A** is incorrect because `project.xml` does not store properties for the build process. **B** is incorrect because `nbproject/project.properties` is shared among developers. **D** is incorrect because `build.xml` is shared among developers.

Configuring the JDK into the Project

14. NetBeans is launched using JDK 1.6. The JDK for a project is set to 1.3 with a source level of 1.2. Which JDK instance is used to run Ant?

A. 1.3

B. 1.4

C. 1.5

D. 1.6

☑ **D** is the correct answer because the implementation is being provided and run under the JDK being used to run NetBeans.

☒ **A**, **B**, and **C** are incorrect because the JDK set for a project does not control the JDK used to launch an Ant file.

15. The source/binary setting in Project Properties controls what aspect of the project?

A. JDK used to run the project.

B. Byte code emitted by the compiler.

C. `javac` implementation used to compile the code.

D. Both A and C.

☑ **B.** Source/Binary setting is used to formulate the `-source` flag passed to the compiler.

☒ **A, C,** and **D** are incorrect. **A** is incorrect because the source/binary level does not control which JDK is used. **C** is incorrect because specific `javac` executables are not tracked or used by NetBeans. **D** is incorrect because **A** and **C** are both incorrect.

3

Java SE Desktop Applications

CERTIFICATION OBJECTIVES

- Creating Desktop Applications from Existing Sources

- Managing Classpaths for Compilation and Debugging

- Creating Forms with the GUI Builder

- Packaging and Distributing Java Desktop Projects

✓ Two-Minute Drill

Q&A Self Test

Although web applications have been in vogue since the dot-com boom in the late 1990s, desktop applications are just as important as ever. Java initially rose to prominence through its applet technology that provided a rich GUI experience in the web browser. This was long before Google reinvented the Web and set a higher bar for usability. Java's desktop capabilities have continued to grow and mature over the years. Highly sophisticated desktop applications have been written on the Java platform ranging from Geographical Information Systems (GIS) software packages to imaging packages for biotech and everything in between. NetBeans enhances Java desktop application development by providing an integrated set of tools for developing and deploying robust and feature-rich Java desktop applications.

Java Standard Edition (SE) desktop applications are built using Java's rich Swing/AWT class library. They can be distributed as applets, via Java Web Start (JNLP), as double-clickable JAR archives, or installed using third-party installers and launchers. NetBeans expedites desktop application development through its graphical Swing/AWT GUI editor, support for Beans Bindings (JSR 295), Swing Application Framework (JSR 296), and packaging/build support. It is, in every sense of the phrase, an integrated development environment. It leverages Java extensions, which are freely available, open source, and standards based. The certification exam will test your proficiency with creating, building, and deploying Java desktop applications using NetBeans.

CERTIFICATION OBJECTIVE

Creating Desktop Applications from Existing Sources

Exam Objective 3.1   Demonstrate the ability to create NetBeans projects from the source code of an existing Java SE program.

NetBeans provides numerous built-in project types to expedite development. Each project category, Java, Java Web, and Java EE, includes project templates for creating new NetBeans projects from existing sources. Creating a project from existing sources enables existing projects to be imported into NetBeans. Typically projects being imported using this mechanism were either defined in other IDEs, predate NetBeans, or were developed with a custom layout. Another possibility is that the project was created using NetBeans, but the NetBeans project files are not available. These projects are indispensable when trying to understand and debug external libraries or applications.

The exam objective discussed in this section focuses on Java Standard Edition (SE) programs. Java SE programs refer to applets, desktop, or command-line applications. A Java SE program could also be a custom server application that does not depend upon the Java EE APIs or that is an API library. A Java SE application requires only the JRE and not one of the specialized runtime environments such as Java ME or Java EE. Although this chapter focuses heavily upon GUI applications, it is important to remember that creating a Java SE project from existing sources does not automatically imply a GUI application. This project type could be used to import code for a test framework like JUnit or an application container like Spring.

This project type is similar to the free-form project discussed in Chapter 2. Both the free form project type covered in Chapter 2 and the project type from existing sources discussed in this chapter are used for creating projects from existing sources. The primary difference between the two centers on the level of NetBeans integration provided. A free-form project (see Chapter 2) uses the project's build script (`build.xml`). This places the onus for managing the maintenance and debugging of the build process upon the developer. If a new dependency is added to the build, the NetBeans project must be updated manually. Debugger and profiler integration requires additional effort. In addition, a free-form project cannot depend upon another NetBeans project. A Java SE project created from existing sources is a standard NetBeans project. In a standard project, NetBeans manages the build and external dependencies. Source code for external dependencies as well as Javadoc can be added. This greatly simplifies the development experience, enabling NetBeans to automate and standardize project maintenance and execution.

A four-step wizard drives the process of creating a new Java SE project with existing sources:

- Choose Project
- Name And Location
- Existing Sources
- Includes & Excludes

The wizard does not configure external libraries, and thus library configuration must be performed post–project creation. Since most projects have external dependencies, most projects will probably not compile successfully once the wizard is dismissed. Configuring libraries for Java SE projects with existing sources is covered in Exam Objective 3.3 and tackled in the next section.

The example application used throughout this chapter is Jmol and is available from http://jmol.sourceforge.net. The exercise at the end of this section takes you through the process of checking out the project and completing the wizard. Jmol is an open source application that renders the 3-D structures of proteins.

Step 1: Choose Project

To create a new "Java Project with Existing Sources," choose File | New Project. This opens the first step in the wizard, shown in Figure 3-1. Under Categories select Java and select Java Project With Existing Sources from the Projects list box on the right. Click Next to move to the next step in the wizard.

Step 2: Name And Location

The next step in the New Project wizard asks for basic project setup information. It is shown in Figure 3-2 and configures the following:

- ■ **Project Name** Name of the project that will appear in the Projects window.
- ■ **Project Folder** Location where the NetBeans project file information should be stored. This is where the nbproject directory will be placed along with the build script.
- ■ **Build Script Name** Name of the NetBeans build script to be created.
- ■ **Use Dedicated Folder For Storing Libraries** Enables the storing of libraries in a central location. Facilitates the sharing of projects between users.
- ■ **Libraries Folder** Location of the libraries—needed if the project is to be shared.
- ■ **Set as Main Project** Sets this project as the main project at the conclusion of the wizard.

The project folder is used to store the build script and nbproject directory. If Use Dedicated Folder For Storing Libraries is selected, then project libraries are stored in a dedicated directory. This directory can be shared by placing it under version control. The default settings, when checked, put the libraries into a lib directory under the project folder.

The Build Script Name option enables the name of the script to be customized. This option is not for choosing a build script. NetBeans generates its standard build script. If the project already has a build script and tighter NetBeans integration is not desired, then a free-form project should be used instead.

on the job

If you are sharing among a group of developers, the project folder should contain the sources for the project. If the project folder does not contain the sources and is in a "random" location on the hard drive, correctly replicating project paths on different computers might become challenging.

FIGURE 3-1

Step 1: Choose
Project

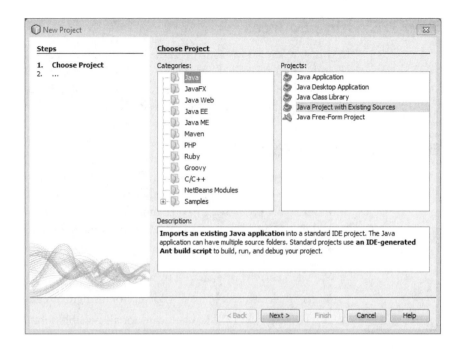

FIGURE 3-2

Step 2: Name
And Location

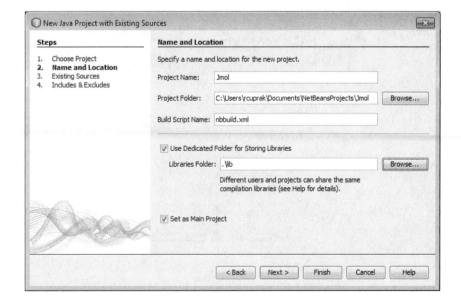

Step 3: Existing Sources

In this step, shown in Figure 3-3, the source and test packages are selected for the project. The Add Folder button displays a file browser for choosing directories. Multiple directories can be configured. Configuration of test sources is optional. The selected directories do not necessarily have to appear below the project folder.

Step 4: Includes & Excludes

The last step in the wizard, shown in Figure 3-4, configures the packages/folders that are to be either included or excluded. This enables precise control over what classes or resources are processed by NetBeans. Thus, if a project is being created to work on a small part of a code base, only the files pertinent to the task need to be included. Rules for the patterns include:

- Each pattern is separated by a comma.
- A single asterisk (*) is a wildcard for a single directory.
- Two asterisks (**) is a wildcard for all possible subfolders.

FIGURE 3-3

Step 3: Existing
Sources

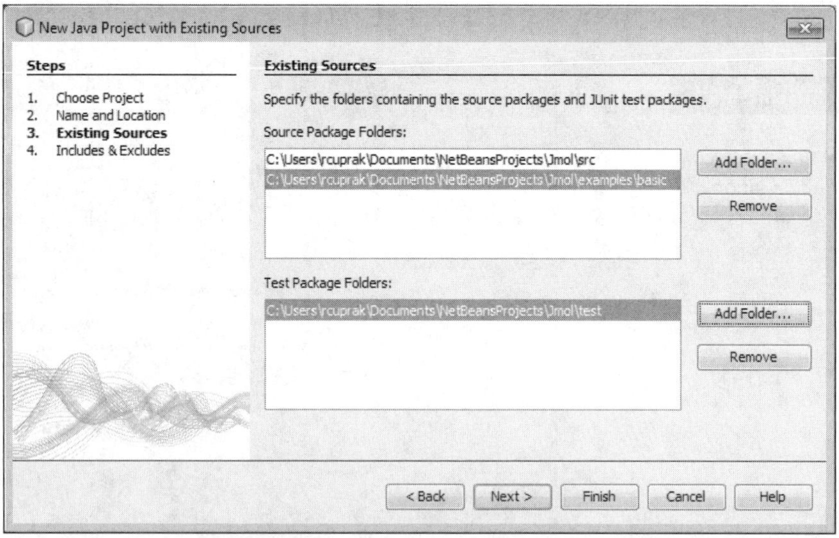

The following file structure is used in Table 3-1 to illustrate the effects of different patterns:

```
C:\USERS\RCUPRAK\DOCUMENTS\DATABASESCAN\SRC
    └──net
        └──cuprak
            ├──experiment
            │      Experiment.java
            │      experiment.properties
            │
            ├──load
            │      LoadFile.java
            │
            └──run
            │   TestPlacement.java
            │   TestScan.java
            │
            └──simulator
                   TestSimulator.java


C:\Users\rcuprak\Documents\DatabaseScan>
```

One important caveat with the example above is that `**.java` will not match all Java files; to match all Java files, the directory wildcard must be used: `**/*.java`.

After clicking the Finish button, the project is opened in NetBeans. Since the classpath has not been configured yet, the project does not compile. NetBeans automatically detects the version control system being used by the project.

TABLE 3-1   Include Patterns

Pattern	Files Included
net/cuprak/**.properties	net/cuprak/experiment/experiment.properties
net/cuprak/**.properties, **/*.java	net/cuprak/experiment/Experiment.java net/cuprak/experiment/experiment.properties net/cuprak/load/LoadFile.java net/cuprak/run/TestPlacement.java net/cuprak/run/TestScan.java net/cuprak/run/simulator/TestSimulator.java
net/cuprak/run/**	net/cuprak/run/TestPlacement.java net/cuprak/run/TestScan.java net/cuprak/run/simulator/TestSimulator.java

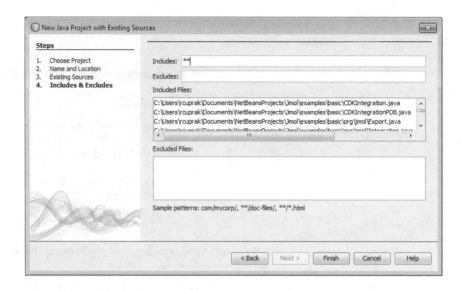

FIGURE 3-4

Step 4: Includes
& Excludes

e⟩x⟩a⟩m

ⓦatch   *The Java Free-Form Project   build script, and libraries are used only
and Java Project With Existing Sources both   for code completion. A Java Project With
enable NetBeans projects to be created   Existing Sources is a standard project with
for existing code bases. As mentioned, the   the IDE managing the classpaths.
free-form project uses the project's existing*

EXERCISE 3-1

Creating a Java Program with Existing Sources

In this exercise, you checkout the open source project Jmol from version control and
create a new Java SE project from existing sources. This open source project was the
source of the screenshots throughout this section.

Jmol (http://jmol.sourceforge.net/) is an open source viewer for chemical
structures. It renders molecules in 3-D and supports real-time manipulation. The
application is written entirely in Java. While the sources come with a build script,
the application does not include a NetBeans project. The objective of this exercise
is to checkout the project and set it up in NetBeans. This exercise also helps to
reinforce your version control skills from Chapter 2. In Exercise 3-2 you configure
the classpath for the application, thereby enabling you to run the project.

1. Choose Team | Subversion | Checkout.

2. Enter the following Repository URL:

   `https://jmold.svn.sourceforge.net/svnroot/jmol/trunk/Jmol`

3. Click Next and pick a local folder to checkout the project into. Accept the defaults for the other options. Make sure the Scan For NetBeans Projects After Checkout option is selected.

4. Click Finish. NetBeans now checks out the project from Subversion.

5. After the checkout is complete, NetBeans asks, "Do you want to create an IDE project from the checked-out sources?" Select the Create Project button.

6. The New Project wizard in Figure 3-1 is displayed. Select Java under Categories and pick Java Project With Existing Sources from the Projects list box. Click Next.

7. On the next screen, Name And Location, shown in Figure 3-2:

   a. Change Project Name to **Jmol**.

   b. For Project Folder, select the Jmol directory created by the Subversion checkout.

   c. Ensure that Use Dedicated Folder For Storing Libraries is checked. Choose the `jars` directory under the `Jmol` directory.

   d. Click the Next button.

8. On the Existing Sources screen, shown in Figure 3-3, make the following selections:

   a. Click the Add Folder button for the Source Package Folders box and select the `src` directory.

   b. Click the Add Folder button for the Test Package Folders box and select the `test` directory.

   c. Click the Next button.

9. On the Includes & Excludes screen, type `**` in the Includes field so that everything in `source` and `test` is included in the project.

10. Click Finish.

At this point the project does not compile. In Exercise 3-2 you will configure the classpath and run the project.

Managing Classpaths for Compilation and Debugging

Exam Objective 3.2 Describe how to manage the classpath of a Java SE project, including maintaining a separate classpath for compiling and debugging.

This objective covers managing the classpath for all standard Java SE projects. Specifically this section covers the classpath management for compilation and execution. Although the objective specifically mentions maintaining a classpath for debugging, NetBeans does not possess an explicit debug classpath that is different from the run classpath. At this time it isn't feasible to set a different classpath for Run Main Project versus Debug Main Project. Having two separate classpaths for running and execution would create significant project maintenance problems. Furthermore most external libraries don't ship with two versions, with one having debug symbols.

Most of the content for this objective was already covered in Chapter 1 as a part of Exam Objective 1.4. That section covered how to configure a global repository of libraries to be shared among multiple projects and also how to manage library dependencies for a project. This section reviews that information and puts it in the context of the Java SE projects. Comparisons also are made with the other NetBeans project types.

Java SE projects are a specific project category that depends only upon the Java SE APIs and runs on the Java Standard Edition. NetBeans provides excellent classpath management support that is tightly integrated into the IDE and also the build process. This tight integration enables a developer to focus upon writing code without the distraction of implementing a build system to manage the classpath. While writing a build script to compile a project is easy, challenges arise once a project must be debugged.

Java SE projects are created by choosing File | New Project | Java and one of the five Java SE project templates:

- Java Application
- Java Desktop Application
- Java Class Library
- Java Project With Existing Sources
- Java Free-Form Project

For these project templates NetBeans manages and leverages the classpath to provide code assistance in the form of syntax checking and auto-completion and also builds the classpath for compiling, testing, and execution. This section covers the following topics:

- Understanding Classpath Types
- Editing Java SE Project Classpaths
- Understanding Project Classpath Differences
- Configuring Classpath Variables

Understanding Classpath Types

As discussed in Chapter 1, NetBeans supports multiple classpaths for a project. These classpaths are listed again in Table 3-2. Multiple classpaths enforce isolation within a project so that unit test libraries are not accidently used in business logic or implementation classes used instead of interfaces. For example, if `junit.jar` is added to the compile test classpath, classes under the source directory are unable to import or use the `@Test` annotation. Adding JUnit annotations to source files, not test source files, would result in a build failure.

The relationships between the classpaths are illustrated in Figure 3-5. In this figure we can see a clear inheritance. Sources and test sources refer to the respective source and test source root directories that get compiled. As mentioned previously in the first section, a project may have multiple source and test roots. The compile classpath includes the sources and any other dependencies such as JAR files and class directories required to compile the project. The run classpath includes the compilation output along with implementation classes. For example, the JPA interfaces would be added to the compile classpath, whereas the implementation, such as Hibernate or TopLink, would be added to the runtime classpath.

The compile test class depends upon the compile classpath and also the source directories containing the test sources. The compile test classpath also includes any libraries used in the test sources such as JUnit, TestNG, and so on. The run test classpath uses the output from compilation of both the sources and test sources as

TABLE 3-2	
Classpath Types	

Classpath	Description
Compile	Classpath used for compiling as well as importing and auto-completion
Compile test	Classpath used for compiling test sources
Run	Classpath used for running a project
Run test	Classpath used for running unit tests

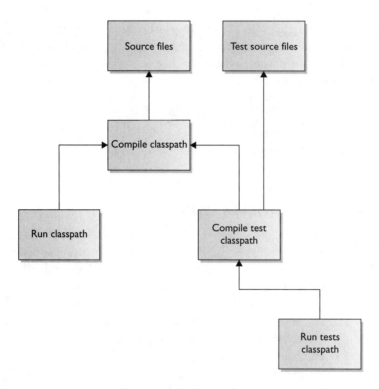

well as the library dependencies of both compile and test compile. The classpath should closely mirror the runtime classpath. In many cases the run and run test classpath should be identical.

Editing Java SE Project Classpaths

The classpath for a project can be edited by right-clicking the project in the Projects window and selecting Properties | Libraries. Alternatively, right-clicking the Libraries node in the Projects window displays a specialized context menu for editing the classpath. The options on this context menu include Add Project, Add Library, Add JAR/Folder, and Properties. The Properties option displays the Project Properties dialog box with the Libraries category preselected. Classpath additions added from this context menu are appended to the compile classpath. The Libraries node in NetBeans displays only the compile classpath.

The Project Properties dialog box with the Libraries category selected is shown in Figure 3-6. Note that this figure has library dependencies required by the Jmol project covered in Exercises 3-1 and 3-2. The following classpath-related items are configured on this panel:

- **Java Platform**   The JDK libraries to be used for the project.
- **Libraries Folder**   Location where libraries are stored to facilitate project sharing.
- **Classpaths**   Classpaths for Compile, Run, Compile Tests, and Run Tests.
- **Build Projects On Classpath**   Builds projects that this project depends upon.

The Java Platform and Libraries Folder settings were covered in Chapter 1. The Java Platform determines what Java platform classes are available to the project. The libraries folder is a central location for storing project libraries so they may be easily shared among multiple developers.

The tabbed pane with the four classpaths is the target of this objective. On the first two tabs the compile and run/debug classpaths are configured. The last two tabs configure the test classpaths that will be covered in Chapter 9. Along the side of the tabbed pane are seven buttons:

- **Add Project**   Adds another project as a dependency.
- **Add Library**   Adds a library, configured in the Library Manager, to the project.
- **Add JAR/Folder**   Adds a JAR or folder of classes to the project.

FIGURE 3-6

Project
Properties:
Classpath

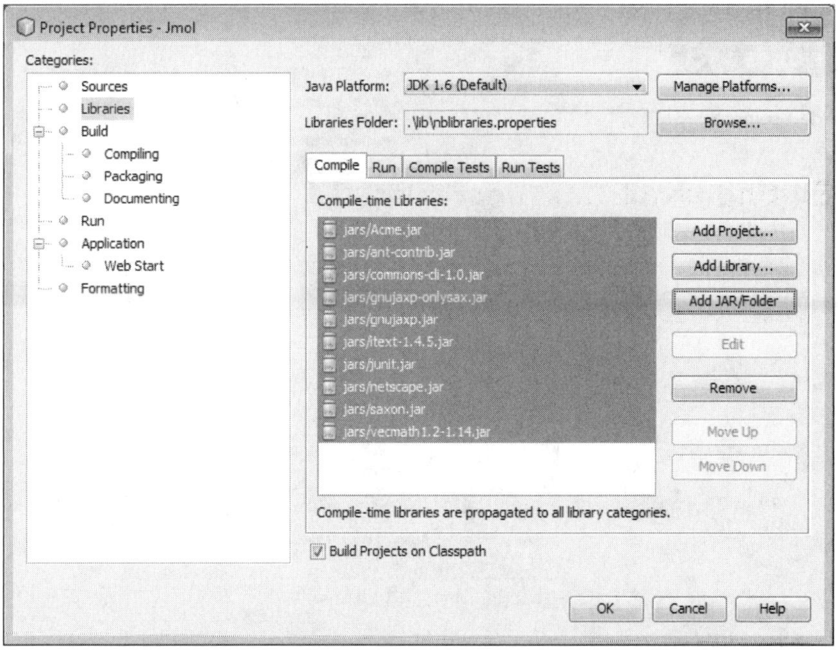

- ■ **Edit**   Edits an entry in the classpath.
- ■ **Remove**   Removes a classpath entry.
- ■ **Move Up**   Moves a dependency up in ordering.
- ■ **Move Down**   Moves a dependency down in ordering.

The first button, Add Project, adds another project as a dependency. Selecting this button displays the dialog box shown in Figure 3-7. Selecting another project does not open that project in NetBeans. Instead, the output of the project is added as a dependency. Dependencies from the subproject are not automatically added. In the case of Figure 3-7, the DatabaseUtility.jar project depends upon log4j. For the Jmol project to compile successfully, log4j must explicitly be added to the compile classpath.

The Add Library button displays the dialog box shown in Figure 3-8, which adds libraries to the current project. The libraries that appear in this dialog box have already been imported into the project and are possibly being used in one of the classpaths. To import a new library, select Import to display a list of all the global libraries. Consult the section on the Library Manager in Chapter 1 for more information on how to configure global libraries. You can also choose the Create button to make a new project-specific library.

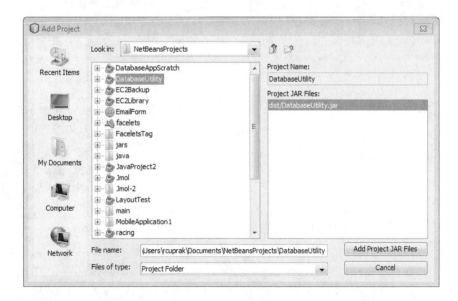

FIGURE 3-8

Add Library

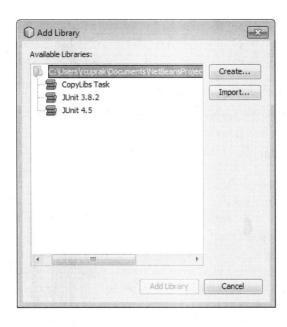

If a libraries folder has been configured for a project, libraries added to the project are placed in that directory. This facilitates sharing of the project between developers. If the default folder name is accepted when creating the Java SE project, NetBeans creates a `lib` directory under the project folder. Figure 3-9 shows the contents of the directory for a simple project. This project has five dependencies. The `log4j-1.2.15.jar` file was added as a JAR dependency. `CopyLibs`, `junit`, `junit_4`, and `PostgreSQLDriver` are all libraries. The `nblibraries.properties` file is the configuration file for the libraries.

FIGURE 3-9

Libraries layout

```
C:\USERS\RCUPRAK\DOCUMENTS\NETBEANSPROJECTS\DATABASEUTILITY\LIB
    log4j-1.2.15.jar
    nblibraries.properties

    CopyLibs
        org-netbeans-modules-java-j2seproject-copylibstask.jar

    junit
        junit-3.8.2-api.zip
        junit-3.8.2.jar

    junit_4
        junit-4.5-api.zip
        junit-4.5-src.jar
        junit-4.5.jar

    PostgreSQLDriver
        postgresql-8.3-603.jdbc3.jar
```

Selecting the Add JAR/Folder button displays the dialog box shown in Figure 3-10. In this dialog box a JAR file can be selected and added to a project. When adding a JAR file to the classpath, there are several options for handling the paths:

- **Relative Path**   Relative path from the project folder to the JAR/folder.
- **Path From Variable**   Variable is specified that is used to resolve the path.
- **Copy To Libraries Folder**   Copies the JAR/folder to the `lib` directory.
- **Absolute Path**   An absolute path is used to reference the JAR/folder.

The Path From Variable and Copy To Libraries Folder options both facilitate sharing of the project between developers. Relative Path can be used if the JAR/folder is already under the project folder. Absolute Path hard-codes the path, thus making the project machine-specific.

The Edit button, shown in Figure 3-6, opens a dialog box for manipulating the library. Which dialog box opens will vary depending upon whether the classpath entry is a JAR/folder or a library. References to other projects cannot be edited. Figure 3-11 shows the Edit Jar Reference dialog box for a JAR/folder dependency. The Javadoc and Sources for the dependency can be optionally specified.

Figure 3-12 shows the Customize Library dialog box for a library. A library can contain multiple JAR files as well as multiple source and Javadoc directories.

Buttons are also present in the dialog box for ordering the classpath entries. The order of the entries controls the sequence in which dependencies are resolved.

FIGURE 3-10

Add JAR/Folder

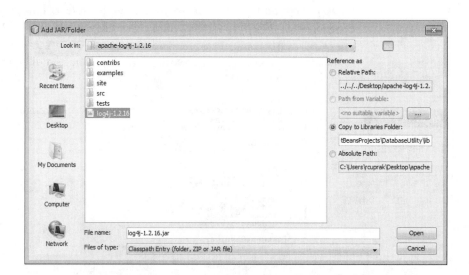

FIGURE 3-11

Edit JAR
dependency

exam
ⓦatch   *Memorize the different
classpaths that can be configured for a
project. Also remember that the order
in which dependencies are resolved
is dependent on the order of the
dependencies in the classpath. There*

*are four types of classpaths and four ways
in which a path to a dependency can be
specified. Experiment with all of them, and
try moving the project around to see what
types of error occur when paths are broken.*

FIGURE 3-12

Edit library
dependency

Understanding Project Classpath Differences

For the exam it is important to understand how configuring the classpath for a Java SE project differs between Java SE projects and also other project types. Big differences exist between Java SE projects and Java Web and EJB project types. There are two types of variances—classpaths available and libraries that are pre-populated onto the classpath. Pre-populated classpaths help to bootstrap-develop for specific project types. For example, the Java Desktop Application project type comes in two variants, with one including the necessary JPA libraries and JDBC drivers for creating a database-backed desktop application. Often the biggest hurdle to starting a project is getting the initial set of dependencies on the classpath and configured.

All of the Java SE project types, with the exception of the Java Free-Form Project, have the same set of four classpaths: Compile, Run, Compile Tests, and Run Tests. The Java Free-Form project, discussed in Chapter 2, is significantly different. As mentioned previously, the classpath for a free-form project is used to support only editor functionality such as syntax checking and auto-completion. The other Java SE project types vary only in the libraries that are configured. Differences between these project types are highlighted in Table 3-3.

NetBeans supports many different project types including Java EE, Java Web, Java ME, and JavaFX. For Java EE and Java Web these projects lack the runtime classpath because they are packaged and deployed to application servers. JavaFX projects have only one classpath for dependencies. Java ME projects are significantly different and possess only a single classpath.

TABLE 3-3   Java SE Initial Classpath Differences

Java SE Project	Compile Classpath	Compile Test Classpath
Java Application	None	JUnit 3.8.2 JUnit 4.5
Java Desktop Application Basic	Swing Application Framework Swing Layout Extensions	
Java Desktop Application Database	Swing Application Framework Swing Layout Extensions Beans Binding TopLink Essentials	
Java Project With Existing Sources	None	
Java Class Library	None	

on the **Job**

Troubleshooting classpath problems can be extremely challenging. The system property, `java.class.path`, can be retrieved to see the contents of the classpath. The JVM `-verbose` flag can also be very useful. NetBeans will not check the classpath to see if you have conflicting dependencies. For example, NetBeans will not detect if two libraries use incompatible versions of an XML parser. A Maven-based project would help handle and better manage a project with numerous dependencies.

Configuring Classpath Variables

Starting with version 6.1, NetBeans began supporting path variables. Path variables are configured in the IDE by choosing Tools | Variables. This displays the Manage Variables dialog box, shown in Figure 3-13. These variables are used to abstract the location of resources. This is very useful when it is necessary for resource locations to vary between machines. This obviously isn't possible with either relative or absolute paths. Copying the resources into a project, while solving the problem, forces a particular project setup.

In Figure 3-14 a variable path is used to add the log4j JAR file to a Java SE project. These path variables can be accessed and manipulated from the `build.xml` script via the property `var.JAR_LIBRARIES`.

When the project is moved to another machine or opened in a NetBeans instance that does not yet have the variable defined, NetBeans warns of an unresolved dependency. Right-clicking the project and choosing Resolve Reference Problems prompts you to define the unknown variable.

FIGURE 3-13

Setting path variables

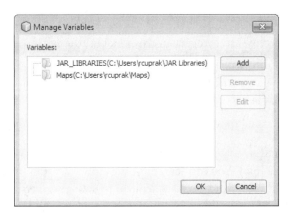

FIGURE 3-14

Adding a
resource using
variable paths

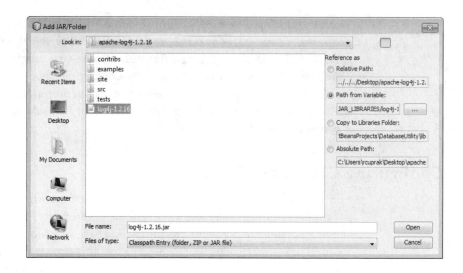

EXERCISE 3-2

Managing the Classpath

In this exercise, you populate the classpath of the project you created in Exercise 3-1. Once the classpath is configured, the project will successfully compile.

1. Right-click the project in the Projects window and choose Properties.
2. Select the Libraries category.
3. Choose Add JAR/Folder.
4. Browse to the Jmol project, and select all of the JAR files under the `jars` directory.
5. Click the Run category in the panel on the left.
6. Click Browse, and NetBeans scans the project for all classes containing a main method. Choose `org.openscience.jmol.app.Jmol` from the list of classes.
7. Close the Properties window.

Choosing Run | Run Main Project or Debug | Debug Main Project compiles and launches Jmol. You can search for files to view using Jmol at www.rcsb.org/pdb. Search for "flu" or "cold" to see chemical structures related to these diseases. Click the download link and then open the file inside of Jmol.

Creating Forms with the GUI Builder

Exam Objective 3.3   Demonstrate knowledge of the NetBeans GUI Builder and the ability to lay out and hook up basic forms using it.

Building user-friendly interfaces for rich client applications is neither trivial nor easy. To simplify Java GUI development, NetBeans includes the powerful NetBeans GUI Builder graphical layout tool for constructing Swing/AWT GUIs. It is a feature-rich tool that addresses many of the challenges of constructing a robust user interface. These challenges include drawing the screen, creating resizable screens leveraging Java layouts, internationalization, and data binding. Such challenges often confound Java developers. Building layouts in Java often requires copious amounts of redundant code to specify layout constraints and copy values between the data model and the screen. Visualizing the effects of constraints is tricky enough when initially coding a screen. However, reorganizing an existing screen with dozens of controls can be downright impossible without a sketch enumerating the overarching design. Internationalization, storing text and warning messages in resource bundles, is often overlooked, especially if the application isn't initially destined for multiple regions, despite the fact that resource bundles help ensure text consistency across an application. Data binding is often solved in an ad hoc manner and is hard to do correctly.

At the heart of the NetBeans GUI Builder is a WYSIWYG (what you see is what you get) editor. With this editor, components can be dropped on a screen and rearranged. Layout manager constraints, including GridBag, can be visually edited and previewed. NetBeans generates the source code; depending on the layout chosen, no additional libraries are required at runtime. NetBeans also introduces two additional layouts, Free Design and Absolute Layout, to expedite development.

Data binding is the shuttling of values between the screen and the data model. It is a tricky problem to solve because the Swing components vary considerably, and the hooks are not uniform. Here, NetBeans takes a novel approach by integrating Beans Binding (JSR 295) into the IDE. While this requires an additional library at runtime, its value and usefulness cannot be overstated.

GUI internationalization takes two forms: designing a GUI that adapts dynamically as label text changes, and actually pulling the labels from resource bundles. The GUI editor and its support of visually editing constraints tackle the former. The latter, resource bundles, NetBeans supports by automatically synchronizing labels with the resource files. NetBeans also handles escaping of the resource bundles. This means that you can type in i18n characters (for example, Chinese, German, or Korean characters), and NetBeans escapes them properly without having to use the `native2ascii` utility.

NetBeans takes GUI development a step further with templates for creating an application and database-backed screens. Application templates come with prewired menus and a content pane. The database-backed screens tie the Beans Binding support directly to fields within the database. Thus, CRUD (Create Read Update Delete) operations can be implemented quickly.

This objective is split into the following topics:

- Touring the Editor
- Creating Forms and Adding Components
- Working with Layouts
- Navigating Generated Code
- Generating Event Listeners
- Understanding Beans Binding
- Understanding Internationalization Support

Touring the Editor

If you have ever worked with Microsoft Visual Basic or Interface Builder on Mac OS X, then the NetBeans GUI Editor, formerly known as Matisse, will be very familiar. The editor is a graphical tool for dragging GUI widgets onto a panel, arranging them, and binding them to the data model. It contains a component palette, properties panel, and the panel for visually arranging components. While the NetBeans GUI Builder may resemble other editors, it is Java specific and contains additional tools for internationalizing and managing layouts. The NetBeans GUI Builder follows and promotes Java best practices for GUI development.

This section provides an overview of the nuts and bolts of the editor. The following topics are discussed:

- Opening the NetBeans GUI Editor
- Understanding Project Dependencies
- Navigating the Editor

Opening the NetBeans GUI Editor

To understand how to open the NetBeans GUI Builder, a brief overview of how the builder generates the UI is necessary. The NetBeans GUI Builder takes the approach of generating Java code. As a result, the NetBeans GUI Builder requires a controlled environment with specific hooks. When a Swing control is repositioned on a panel, NetBeans regenerates the code with the requisite constraint or parameter changes. NetBeans generates its code in specific blocks that cannot be edited; code blocks will be covered shortly. What this means is that in order to edit a user interface visually, NetBeans must have initially created the GUI.

To create a new user interface that is editable by NetBeans, choose File | New File. The categories Swing GUI Forms and AWT GUI Forms contain different starting templates for GUIs. Table 3-4 lists the contents of both categories. AWT is the original GUI technology that shipped with Java in 1995. Unless you have a specific reason for using AWT, create new graphical interfaces using Swing. Since Java version 1.2, Swing has been standard and includes a much larger toolkit of GUI components. AWT uses native widgets and takes the lowest common denominator approach.

When NetBeans creates a new form, a couple of things happen under the hood:

- A new class is created for the form.
- An XML file, with the same name as the form and the file extension `.form`, is created.

The XML file is used internally by the editor and is completely hidden in both the Projects and Files windows in NetBeans. If the XML form file is missing, NetBeans treats the form as a regular Java class, and the GUI cannot be edited with NetBeans. Listing 3-1 contains the contents of a form file. Since this file is for internal use by the IDE, its contents won't be discussed here. Many of the elements, however, are self-documenting.

TABLE 3-4 GUI File Templates	**AWT GUI Forms**	**Swing GUI Forms**
	Applet Form	JApplet Form
	Dialog Form	JDialog
	Frame Form	JFrame Form, JInternal Frame Form
	Panel Form	JPanel Form
		Bean Form
		Application Sample Form
		MDI Application Sample Form
		Master/Detail Sample Form
		OK / Cancel Dialog Sample Form

NetBeans will automatically check the XML form file info version control. If you are using Subversion with file locking, both the Java form class and the XML form file must be locked together. Since NetBeans does not support the file-locking attribute and hides the XML form file, this must be done outside of the editor.

LISTING 3-1: Example `.form` (JFrame)

```xml
<?xml version="1.0" encoding="UTF-8" ?>
<Form version="1.5" maxVersion="1.7"
type="org.netbeans.modules.form.forminfo.JFrameFormInfo">
  <Properties>
    <Property name="defaultCloseOperation" type="int"
      value="3"/>
    <Property name="name" type="java.lang.String" value="Form"
      noResource="true"/>
  </Properties>
  <SyntheticProperties>
    <SyntheticProperty name="formSizePolicy" type="int"
      value="1"/>
  </SyntheticProperties>
  <AuxValues>
    <AuxValue name="FormSettings_autoResourcing"
      type="java.lang.Integer" value="2"/>
    <AuxValue name="FormSettings_autoSetComponentName"
      type="java.lang.Boolean" value="true"/>
    <AuxValue name="FormSettings_generateFQN"
      type="java.lang.Boolean" value="true"/>
    <AuxValue name="FormSettings_generateMnemonicsCode"
      type="java.lang.Boolean" value="false"/>
    <AuxValue name="FormSettings_i18nAutoMode"
      type="java.lang.Boolean" value="false"/>
    <AuxValue name="FormSettings_layoutCodeTarget"
      type="java.lang.Integer" value="2"/>
    <AuxValue name="FormSettings_listenerGenerationStyle"
      type="java.lang.Integer" value="0"/>
    <AuxValue name="FormSettings_variablesLocal"
      type="java.lang.Boolean" value="false"/>
    <AuxValue name="FormSettings_variablesModifier"
      type="java.lang.Integer" value="2"/>
  </AuxValues>
  <Layout>
    <DimensionLayout dim="0">
      <Group type="103" groupAlignment="0" attributes="0">
        <EmptySpace min="0" pref="400" max="32767"
          attributes="0"/>
      </Group>
    </DimensionLayout>
    <DimensionLayout dim="1">
```

```
    <Group type="103" groupAlignment="0" attributes="0">
      <EmptySpace min="0" pref="300" max="32767"
         attributes="0"/>
    </Group>
  </DimensionLayout>
</Layout>
</Form>
```

The previous discussion assumed that a Java project was already open in NetBeans. The NetBeans GUI Builder isn't tied to a particular Java project type. This means that a form can be created and added to a web project or an EJB project. You can even run the form by right-clicking and selecting Run. Adding a form to a non-Java desktop project can be useful when testing utility methods or troubleshooting code. However, it probably is a better idea to write unit tests.

NetBean provides a template for creating a GUI application. To create a new project using this template, choose File | New Project. Choose the Java category and select Java Desktop Application. The next step in the wizard is shown in Figure 3-15. On this panel a decision must be made under Choose Application Shell as to whether the project will use a Java Persistence API provider and hence pull data from a database. If Basic Application is chosen, the project is immediately created and opened. A Database Application requires additional configuration.

FIGURE 3-15

New Java
Desktop
Application:
Name And
Location

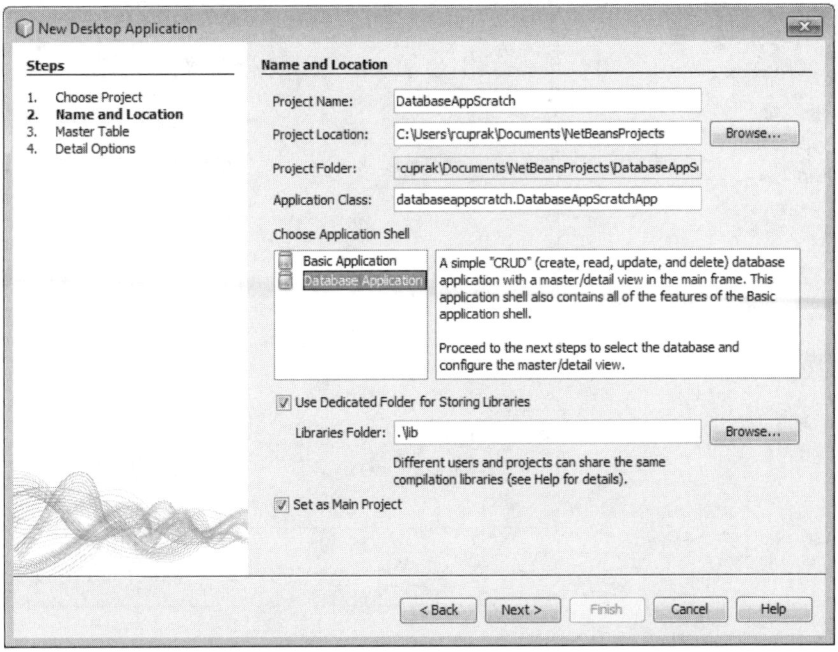

If a database GUI application is chosen, the wizard continues with two additional steps that will result in an application shell with a master/detail user interface for a database table. To create this shell, the wizard prompts for the database connection and also for the columns that are to appear in the master table and that are used for editing an entry. At the conclusion of the wizard, NetBeans generates a user interface for performing basic CRUD operations (Create Read Update Delete).

In Figure 3-16 the Database Connection is chosen along with a table from that database. Selecting a database displays a list of available columns. The connection to the database must be configured prior to creating the project.

In the next step, shown in Figure 3-17, the detail columns are chosen. These are the columns that the user can edit.

After the application concludes, the editor opens with a basic user interface, as shown in Figure 3-18. It must be stressed that this is a starting point for creating a new application. NetBeans has done the hard work of setting up the JPA configuration files, adding the necessary dependencies, and creating an initial form. With this in place you can continue with development.

FIGURE 3-16

Java Database Desktop Application: Step 1

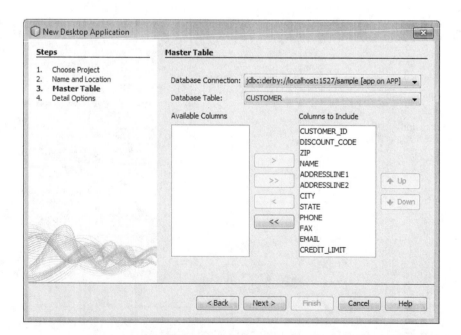

Java Database
Desktop
Application:
Step 2

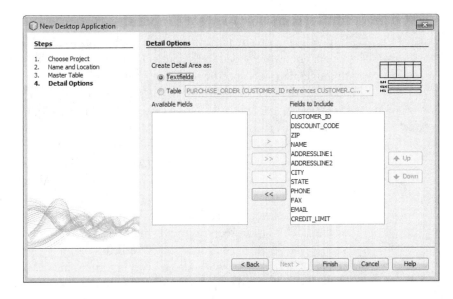

Java Database Desktop Application: master/detail interface

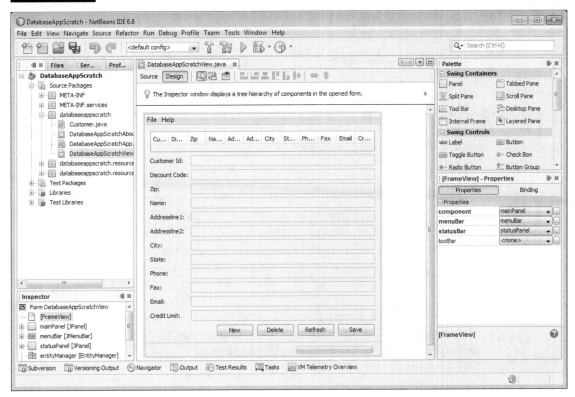

Understanding Project Dependencies

Depending upon the project type and the layouts used, additional external library dependencies are added to the project. The libraries added are minimal and used to implement very specific features. These library dependencies are automatically added to the project regardless of the project type. Thus, if you create a Java Web Application and then add a form, NetBeans adds the required supporting JARs without any manual intervention. JAR files are added to support the two additional layouts, data binding, and also to support new Java Desktop Applications.

NetBeans may add two additional JARs for Absolute Layout and Group Layout. The Absolute Layout is an absolute positioning layout. The Absolute Layout requires the Absolute Layout library that contains the JAR file `AbsoluteLayout.jar`. Group Layout is the layout being used under the hood when the Free Design layout has been selected. This layout requires the Swing Layout Extensions library that contains the `swing-layout-1.0.4.jar` file (NetBeans 6.8) if deploying or running the JRE 5 or older. Group Layout was added to the platform in Java 6. Both of these libraries can be viewed and added to a project regardless of whether the NetBeans GUI Builder is being used. These libraries can be viewed via Tools | Libraries.

exam

ⓦatch

As of Java SE 6, Group Layout is now part of the JRE. In Chapter 1 the Layout Generation Style setting was discussed. This setting determines whether the Swing Layout Extensions library is included. If the Java Platform is set to JDK 1.6 and the Source/Binary Format is set to JDK 5, the project compiles and might even start on JRE 5; however, at some point the Java 5 JVM attempts to load the `GroupLayout` class and fails.

To reduce the amount of redundant code that a developer must write to shuttle values between the GUI controls and the data model, NetBeans includes Beans Binding (JSR 295). As soon as a property of a control is bound, NetBeans adds the Beans Binding library to the project. This library includes just one JAR file—`beansbinding-1.2.1.jar`. This library can also be used independently of the NetBeans GUI Editor.

on the job

In March 2009 the Better Beans Binding Project was founded to expand development. More information on the project can be found at http://kenai .com/projects/betterbeansbinding/pages/Home.

Form-based applications created with the Java Desktop Application project template depend upon several different libraries. Library dependencies vary depending upon whether the project is database based and hence includes JPA. At the minimum, form-based applications include the Swing Application Framework library that contains two JAR files: `appframework-1.0.3.jar` and `swing-worker-1.1.jar`. The Swing Application Framework, JSR 296, is a standard framework for developing Java applications. More information on it can be found at https://appframework.dev.java.net.

If the Java Desktop Application is database based, two additional libraries are added from the TopLink Essentials library. These JAR files include `toplink-essentials.jar` and `toplink-essentials-agent.jar`. A database driver JAR file also is added. The TopLink Essentials JPA implementation is used. Switching to another JPA provider, such as Hibernate, requires manually updating configuration files and adding the requisite libraries. More information on TopLink can be found at www.oracle.com/technology/products/ias/toplink/jpa/index.html.

To summarize, Table 3-5 lists the JAR files that are needed when using the NetBeans GUI Editor and a Java Desktop Application project.

Navigating the Editor

The NetBeans GUI Builder comprises several windows that can be rearranged or detached. The main edit window is where a GUI is built graphically. Figure 3-19 shows the NetBeans GUI Editor editing `AddBoat.java`. The default window

TABLE 3-5   NetBeans GUI Editor JAR Dependencies

JAR File	Library	Description
`swing-layout-1.0.4.jar`	Swing Layout Extensions	Group Layout required when Free Design is selected as the layout
`AbsoluteLayout.jar`	Absolute Layout	An absolute positioning layout
`beansbinding-1.2.1.jar`	Beans Binding	Binding framework for wiring components to the data model
`appframework-1.0.3.jar` `swing-worker-1.1.jar`	Swing Application Framework	Underpinnings of a Java Desktop Application
`toplink-essentials.jar` `toplink-essentials-agent.jar`	TopLink Essentials	JPA implementation used in a Java Desktop Application that is backed by a database

FIGURE 3-19   NetBeans GUI Builder

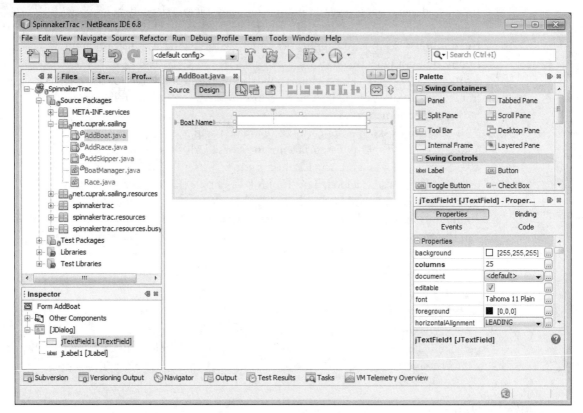

layout includes a Palette window and Properties window on the right. The window on the lower left is the Inspector. These three windows and the main editor window compose the NetBeans GUI Editor. Components are dragged from the palette onto the form with component properties being edited in the Properties window. The Inspector providing a visualization of the component tree.

The three supporting windows and the main editor are interconnected. Selecting a component in the Inspector window selects it on the form and also causes the Properties window to update. Selecting a component on the form changes the selection on the Inspector and Properties windows. Changing a property, such as Font color for a `JLabel`, on the Properties window changes how the component is rendered in the editor. Each of these three windows will now be discussed individually.

Understanding the Editor Window   The main NetBeans GUI Editor window is composed of a drawing panel and a toolbar. Components are dragged and placed on the main editor window. What happens to a component once it is placed on the editor window is contingent on the layout and is covered in the section on layouts. Across the top of the editor window is the toolbar. The toolbar actions are documented in Table 3-6. Most of the toolbar actions are tied to the Free Design layout, which enables developers to design screens without having to fiddle with layouts.

The NetBeans GUI Editor has two modes: Design and Source. It initially opens in the Design mode, which is the visual mode where components can be dragged and dropped onto the editor window. In the other mode, Source, the generated source can be viewed and edited with some restrictions. The section "Navigating Generated Code" later in this chapter will explain in more detail the guard blocks.

| **TABLE 3-6** | NetBeans GUI Editor Toolbar |

Icon	Layout	Function
Source	All	Switches to the Source view. In this view, only code not responsible for rendering the screen can be edited. NetBeans provides hooks for customizing the generated code.
Design	All	Switches to the Design view. In this view, components can be visually dragged and arranged on the screen.
	All	Selection mode—the mouse can select and move components around.
	All	Connection mode—the first click selects the source component. Second click selects the destination component.
	All	Preview Design—previews the form.
	Free Design	Align left—aligns the components on the left border. Leftmost component is used.
	Free Design	Align right—aligns the components on the right. Rightmost component is used.
	Free Design	Center horizontally—centers the components horizontally. Centers on the widest component.
	Free Design	Align along the top—aligns components on their top border. Topmost component is used.
	Free Design	Align along the bottom—aligns components on their bottom. Bottommost component is used.
	Free Design	Center vertically—centers the components vertically. Centers on the widest component.
	Free Design	Change horizontal resize behavior—enables horizontal resizing for the component.
	Free Design	Change vertical resize behavior—enables vertical resizing for the component.

Within the Design mode, the mouse pointer can operate in two modes: Selection and Connection. These modes are toggled in the toolbar. Selection mode is the default mode. In this mode components can be visually manipulated and arranged. In the Connection mode, component events and actions can be bound together. When binding, the first component selected is the event source, and the second is the listener or target. For example, JCheckbox (source) can be wired to JTextField (target) such that when JCheckbox is selected, JTextField becomes editable. In the Connection mode, once the two components are selected, a wizard appears to guide you through the process. This is an extremely powerful feature and will be discussed further in the section "Understanding Beans Binding" along with Exercise 3-5.

The other icons in the toolbar pertain to the alignment of components in the Free Design layout. These toolbar icons require two or more components to be selected. For these actions to be enabled, all of the selected components must be in the same container. For example, one component cannot be in JPanel1 and another component in JPanel2. The actions performed by these icons are self-explanatory.

Right-clicking the root panel of a form displays a context menu. The root panel of a form is the form itself—this can be a JPanel, JFrame, JDialog, or some other container. This context menu is shorter than the context menu for a component or a container. The context menu has the following entries:

- **Preview Design** Switches Look & Feel used to preview the layout.
- **Bind** Displays bind options that are available and can be bound.
- **Set Layout** Sets the layout for the container.
- **Customize Layout** Opens the GridBagLayout Customizer. Only enabled if GridBag is selected as the layout.
- **Add From Palette** Adds a component from the palette.
- **Design This Container** Opens the container in a new editor window.
- **Set Default Size** Resizes the component to its preferred size.
- **Change Order** Changes the order in which the components are instantiated.
- **Copy** Copies the selected component(s) to the clipboard.
- **Paste** Pastes the clipboard onto the container. Behavior will vary depending upon the layout of the container.
- **Customize Code** Displays the Code Customizer for a component.
- **Properties** Displays the property editor in a modal dialog box.

Understanding the Palette   The Palette window contains the components that can be dragged onto a form. The components are grouped into seven categories by default. Right-clicking the window displays a context menu for customizing the palette. The default categories are:

- **Swing Containers**   Includes Java containers such Tabbed Pane, Scroll Pane, and Panel (aka `JPanel`).
- **Swing Controls**   Includes all of the built-in Swing controls such as `JLabel`, `JSlider`, and `JTextField`.
- **Swing Menus**   Includes menu bars, menus, and menu separators.
- **Swing Windows**   Includes Dialogs, Frame, Color Chooser, File Chooser, and Option Pane.
- **AWT**   Includes built-in AWT controls such as Label, Checkbox, and Text Field.
- **Beans**   Contains one item, Choose Bean, which opens a wizard for creating a new bean.
- **Java Persistence**   These beans are used to hook a form up to a JPA provider.

on the
job

Mixing Swing and AWT components should be avoided if possible. AWT components are termed "heavyweight," while Swing components are "lightweight." AWT components use the native platform controls and thus do not support transparency and are limited to being rectangular. Z-ordering issues arise because Swing widgets cannot sit on top of AWT components such as scroll panes.

Most of the component categories are self-explanatory with the exception of the Java Persistence category. The entries under this category are not visual components that appear on a form. Instead the contents of this category are elements that you can add to a form for enabling database integration. You would use these components if you were creating a form that displayed the contents of a database table in a Swing table. The entries under Java Persistence include:

- **Entity Manager**   Manages the state and life cycle of entities within the persistence context. If a database application is chosen, NetBeans configures an EntityManager.
- **Query**   JPA Query using EJB-QL and is dependent upon the Entity Manager. EJB-QL is the Enterprise JavaBeans Query Language.
- **Query Result**   A list (`java.util.List`) that contains the results of a query.

Understanding the Properties Window   The Properties window edits
the properties of the current selection in the editor window. The properties for a
component are constructed either through introspection or from a `BeanInfo`
object. The Properties window is divided into four categories:

- **Properties**   Displays properties, such as background color, font, and number
  of columns for the selected component. Values entered in here are literals and
  are not dynamically evaluated expressions.
- **Binding**   Contains many of the same properties from the Properties tab.
  However, the properties can be bound using expressions that are evaluated
  at runtime. For example, instead of hard-coding background color on the
  Properties tab, it could instead be bound to a `getBackgroundColor()`
  method on a Java Bean.
- **Events**   On the Events tab, listeners can be registered to receive events.
  Only events supported by the component are listed.
- **Code**   Controls the generation of code by the NetBeans GUI Editor.

If no cell has focus, typing will display a find sheet that can be used to quickly
locate properties.

Understanding the Inspector   The Inspector window displays the object graph
of the main editor window. At the root of the graph is a form such as `JDialog`,
`JFrame`, or `JPanel`. Clicking an entry in the component tree selects the component
on the main editor window. Controls can be rearranged by dragging—a blue indicator
will flag the insertion point. Right-clicking a component displays the same context
menu as in the main editor.

The component name can be set by double-clicking an entry in the tree. The
name entered will be used in code generation. Figure 3-20 shows an example where
the components have been given descriptive names.

FIGURE 3-20

Inspector window

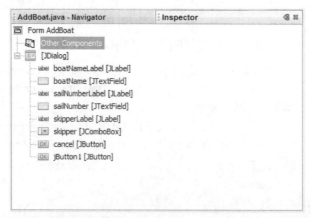

Creating Forms and Adding Components

New forms are created in the NetBeans GUI Editor by choosing File | New File and selecting either Swing GUI Forms or AWT GUI Forms. Table 3-7 lists the forms that are available for each category.

Once the form has been created, controls can be dragged onto it from the component palette. Right-clicking and choosing Add From Palette also adds components.

Working with Layouts

Java layouts are a powerful abstraction for defining the layout and behavior of Java user interfaces. Layout managers determine the size and position of the controls within a container. They take into account the control's preferred size, minimum size, maximum size, and the available screen real estate. Forms are not static even if their definitions are fixed. Java applications can run on a multitude of devices where

TABLE 3-7   Form Types

Form	Description
Swing GUI Forms	
JDialog	Creates a form that extends `javax.swing.JDialog`.
JFrame	Creates a form that extends `javax.swing.JFrame`.
JInternalFrame	Creates a form that extends `javax.swing.JInternalFrame`.
JPanel Form	Creates a form that extends `javax.swing.JPanel`.
JApplet Form	Creates a form that extends `javax.swing.JApplet`.
Bean Form	Creates a new form based on a JavaBeans component.
Application Sample Form	Creates a skeleton application with a menu bar and a main method.
MDI Application Sample Form	Creates a new application with a main method as well as menus. The content area of the `JFrame` is a `JDesktopPane`.
Master / Detail Sample Form	Creates a CRUD (Create Read Update Delete) form that edits a database table.
OK / Cancel Dialog Sample Form	Creates a simple dialog form.
AWT GUI Forms	
Applet Form	Creates a form that extends `java.applet.Applet`.
Dialog Form	Creates a form that extends `java.awt.Dialog`.
Frame Form	Creates a form that extends `java.awt.Frame`.
Panel Form	Creates a form that extends `java.awt.Panel`.

the font and control dimensions vary considerably. Even if an application is only targeting Windows, differences exist between versions of Windows such as Windows XP and Vista. Users also have a habit of customizing appearance settings. Changing the locale and presentation language affects the visual layout as well. Using a layout manager, the size and position of the controls are controlled by the layout's constraints.

Layout managers also tackle the problem of dynamic resizing. A good user interface permits users to resize frames and dialog boxes to suit their needs. A layout manager defines how changes in a form's dimensions are allocated. For example, when resizing a form, you would expect the text fields to grow while labels remain fixed.

Although layout managers enable the creation of adaptable user interfaces, coding them can be challenging as well as time-consuming. Each layout manager has a different set of constraints to learn and has varying strengths and weaknesses. Constructing a user interface often involves using at least two layouts with some nesting of panels to achieve the desired effect and resize behavior. As we've seen, NetBeans expedites GUI development by enabling you to visualize the layout and tweak it without coding. Depending on the layout manager chosen, you may not even have to edit any constraints.

NetBeans supports most of the Java layout managers with the exception of `OverlayLayout` and `SpringLayout`. It supports the following layouts:

- **Free Design** This is actually Group Layout. Group Layout was added to Java SE 6 and is available in a stand-alone JAR file for pre–Java 6 applications. It was originally developed for the NetBeans GUI Builder. This layout handles horizontal and vertical arrangement separately.

- **Absolute Layout** An absolute positioning layout manager, it is really no different than passing in null as the layout. Developers are discouraged from using it because NetBeans supports this layout only for historical reasons.

- **Border Layout** Divides the container into five regions: north, south, east, west, and center.

- **Box Layout** A layout manager in which components are stacked either vertically or horizontally like boxes.

- **Card Layout** Each component is placed on a card, and only one card in the stack of cards is visible at a time.

- **Flow Layout** Arranges components in a line.

- **GridBag Layout** Arranges components in a grid. Supports a rich set of constraints with support for spanning cells and controlling space, alignment, and padding.

- ■ **Grid Layout**   This layout arranges the components in a grid.
- ■ **Null Layout**   Results in no layout manager being used. Null is passed into a container's `setLayout()` method. Each control must have its coordinates set as well as its dimensions.

To set the layout for a container, right-click the container and select Set Layout. Right-clicking the container in the Inspector can also set the layout. Each panel on a form can have a different layout. By default, NetBeans sets the Free Design layout as the default when a new form is created. Free Design, Null, and Absolute layouts are essentially free form—you can drag components anywhere on the screen. Of these three, only Free Design is a true layout that adapts to look-and-feel changes as well as screen-resizing events. For all other layout managers, the constraints must be manually edited in the Properties window. However, the GridBagLayout Customizer, available through the context menu on a container, is a visual editor for `GridBagConstraints`.

on the **Job**   *Control properties can impact how a control renders and appears in a layout. For instance, if a JTextField has no content and the number of columns (characters) hasn't been configured, then it will shrink to showing only one character. Additionally, to keep a JTextField from dramatically shrinking to one character when a screen is resized smaller, you'll want to set the minimum size using the preferred size after the screen has been packed. For other controls such as JTextArea, you'll want to configure the number of rows and columns.*

As Free Design and GridBag receive preferential treatment, these will be covered individually.

Free Design

The NetBeans GUI Editor Free Design, which is the Group Layout, is the default layout for new forms. When using this layout, controls can be dragged out onto the screen and positioned as well as aligned without manipulating properties on the Properties window. When placing a component in the form, dashed lines appear and disappear depending upon its proximity to other components. These dashed lines are guides for consistently spacing and aligning components. These guidelines are shown in Table 3-8. Often more than one dashed guideline appears. Note that there is a small preferred distance between two components and a medium preferred distance between two components.

TABLE 3-8	Free Design Guidelines	
Baseline	jLabel2	A dashed line appears when two adjacent components are being positioned so that the text baselines line up, that is, y coordinates match. The baseline of the text in the `JTextField` should line up with the `JLabel` text—not the bottom borders of both components.
Edge	Item 1 Item 2 Item 3 Item 4 Item 5	Dashed lines appear whenever parallel edges of two adjacent components are near each other. This simplifies the task of aligning or resizing a component so that its top, bottom, right, or left edge matches that of an adjacent component.

TABLE 3-8	Free Design Guidelines *(continued)*	
Indentation		A vertical dashed guideline appears when the bottom of two vertically stacked components is offset to the right. This ensures consistent indentation among components.
Inset		Vertical and horizontal dashed lines appear whenever a component nears the border of its container. This ensures uniform padding.
Offset		A vertical dashed line indicates an offset from the adjacent component. This ensures that components are spaced consistently.

In addition to guidelines, anchors are also present to indicate common alignments. An example of this is shown in Figure 3-21. In this example, the text field is indented from the left edge of the checkbox. The checkbox's top and left edges are anchored to the top and left edges of the container. Right-clicking the component and choosing Anchor changes these anchors. Four anchor options are presented: Right, Left, Top, and Bottom.

FIGURE 3-21

Anchors

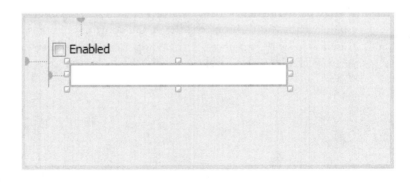

The resize behavior of a component is controlled either from the toolbar or by right-clicking the component and choosing Auto Resizing. Two options are available: Horizontal and Vertical. If resizing is enabled, additional space is apportioned to components that have auto-resizing. The toolbar icons were documented earlier in this chapter.

The dimensions of two or more components can be synchronized. Selecting multiple components and choosing Same Size synchronizes the dimensions. Either width and height or just one or the other can be selected.

The earlier section, "Navigating the Editor," documents the other toolbar icons that can be used for aligning multiple components on the screen.

GridBag

The GridBag layout manager is one of the most powerful layout managers in Java. While the other layouts, except Free Design, require you to edit the constraints in the Properties window, NetBeans provides the GridBagLayout Customizer. The customizer is shown in Figure 3-22. Right-clicking the container and choosing Customize Layout opens it.

The screen is arranged with two panels: on the left is the constraints editor, while on the right is a visual representation. In the visual representation, gray blocks represent the controls; the actual controls are not drawn. The blocks are identified by their names—if the component names have not been set, then it can be challenging to understand which blocks represent which components.

FIGURE 3-22   GridBagLayout Customizer

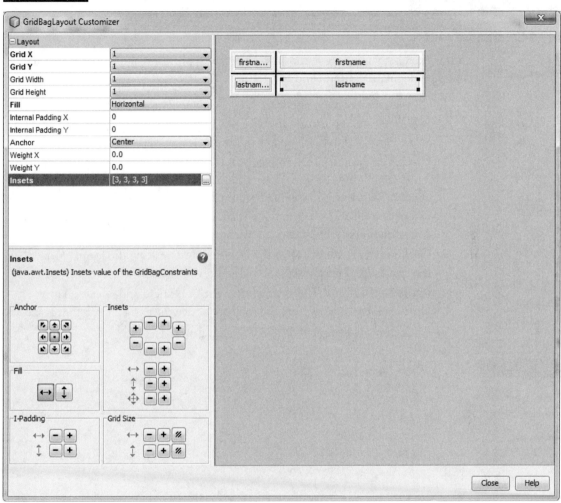

EXERCISE 3-3

Free Design Layout

In this exercise, you create a new Java Desktop Application and add a form to it. You then populate the form and test resizing.

1. Create a new desktop application by choosing File | New Project and select Java Desktop Application from the Java category. Choose Basic Application as the Application Shell and click Finish.

2. Create the form depicted in Figure 3-23. To quickly add the same component multiple times to the form, select the component on the palette, and then click the editor window while holding down the SHIFT key. You need to release the SHIFT key before the last add, otherwise the editor adds the component and then queues another one.

3. Click Preview Design to test the layout and try resizing the form. Notice that the text fields do not resize. Close the preview.

4. In the NetBeans GUI Builder, choose each text field and select Change Horizontal Resizability from the toolbar. Notice the extra anchor that is added.

5. Click Preview Design and try resizing it again.

FIGURE 3-23

Form layout
exercise

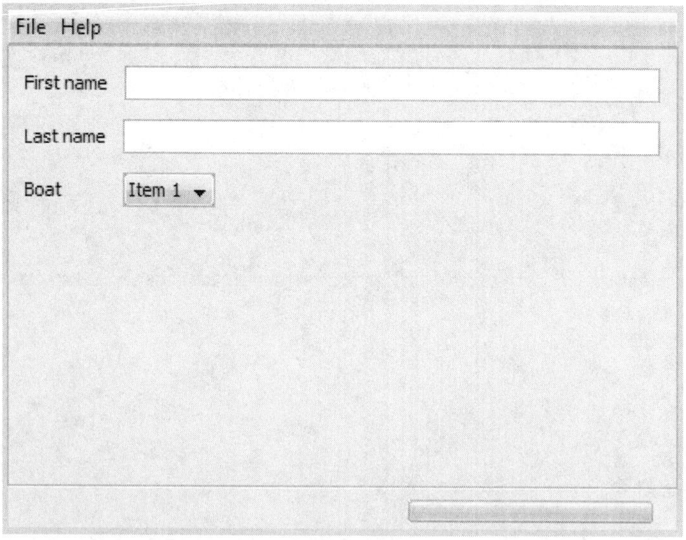

EXERCISE 3-4

Free Design Layout Using GridBag Layout

In this exercise, you use GridBag Layout to create the same user interface you created in Exercise 3-3.

1. Create a new desktop application by choosing File | New Project, and select Java Desktop Application from the Java category. Choose Basic Applications as the Application Shell and click Finish.

2. Switch layout managers to GridBagLayout by right-clicking on the form and choosing Set Layout | GridBagLayout.

3. Drag out all of the components needed to recreate the UI in Figure 3-23 that you just created using the Free Design layout.

4. Right-click the form and choose Customize Layout.

5. Use the GridBagLayout Customizer to replicate the component arrangement in Figure 3-23. Note that if you haven't worked with GridBag Layout before, this may take some time.

6. Click Preview Design to test the form.

Navigating Generated Code

The NetBeans GUI Builder generates code to render the user interface. Each time something is changed in the layout of the screen, NetBeans regenerates the source code. As mentioned earlier, NetBeans stores layout information in an XML file with the extension of `.form`. Not all of the Java code in the Java class backing the form is regenerated, just specific blocks of code. These are clearly delineated with comments.

NetBeans generates two blocks of code. The first block of code is the `initComponents` method. This method initializes the components and populates the form. It is invoked from the form's constructor. The second block of code declares the member variables for the components. Member variable declaration is optional; most of the components such as `JLabel` probably will be added to the container once and never referenced again. NetBeans locks both of these blocks and prevents you from editing them. However, you can view the code, and there is support for customizing much of the generated code. The "locked" code has a dark gray background color. A code snippet is shown in Figure 3-24.

Problems can arise during development if two developers are editing the same form. Even if there are no conflicts, especially with the .form *file, the merge may still cause unexpected behavior.*

FIGURE 3-24   Form source code with guarded code

```
package net.cuprak.sailing;

public class AddSkipper extends javax.swing.JPanel {

    public AddSkipper() {
        initComponents();
    }

    /** This method is called from within the constructor to
     * initialize the form.
     * WARNING: Do NOT modify this code. The content of this method is
     * always regenerated by the Form Editor.
     */
    @SuppressWarnings("unchecked")
    // <editor-fold defaultstate="collapsed" desc="Generated Code">
    private void initComponents() {
        java.awt.GridBagConstraints gridBagConstraints;

        firstnameLabel = new javax.swing.JLabel();
        firstname = new javax.swing.JTextField();

        setName("Form"); // NOI18N
        setLayout(new java.awt.GridBagLayout());
        org.jdesktop.application.ResourceMap resourceMap = org.jdesktop.application.Application.
        firstnameLabel.setText(resourceMap.getString("firstnameLabel.text")); // NOI18N
        firstnameLabel.setName("firstnameLabel"); // NOI18N
        gridBagConstraints = new java.awt.GridBagConstraints();
        gridBagConstraints.gridx = 0;
        gridBagConstraints.gridy = 0;
        gridBagConstraints.insets = new java.awt.Insets(3, 3, 3, 3);
        add(firstnameLabel, gridBagConstraints);

        firstname.setColumns(25);
        firstname.setText(resourceMap.getString("firstname.text")); // NOI18N
        firstname.setName("firstname"); // NOI18N
        gridBagConstraints = new java.awt.GridBagConstraints();
        gridBagConstraints.gridx = 1;
        gridBagConstraints.gridy = 0;
        gridBagConstraints.fill = java.awt.GridBagConstraints.HORIZONTAL;
        gridBagConstraints.weightx = 1.0;
        gridBagConstraints.insets = new java.awt.Insets(3, 3, 3, 3);
        add(firstname, gridBagConstraints);
    }// </editor-fold>

    // Variables declaration - do not modify
    private javax.swing.JTextField firstname;
    private javax.swing.JLabel firstnameLabel;
    // End of variables declaration
```

Although NetBeans is generating the layout code and instantiating the components, it provides numerous hooks for customizing and controlling the generated code. These hooks range from modifiers to code snippets that NetBeans inserts for you. The following is a rundown of these hooks:

- **Variable name**   Name of the variable for a specific component.
- **Variable modifiers**   Standard Java access modifier: default, `public`, `private`, and `protected` as well as `static`, `final`, `volatile`, and `transient` to be used for a class member variable declaration.
- **Type parameters**   Type parameters for components that support generics.
- **Use local variable**   Swing component is local to `initComponents`, and a member variable for the class is not created.
- **Custom creation code**   Code snippet for instantiating the component. For example, creating the component using a specific constructor.
- **Pre-creation code**   Code snippet that will be evaluated prior to the creation of the component.
- **Post-creation code**   Code that will execute immediately following component instantiation.
- **Pre-init code**   Code that is executed before bean properties are set.
- **Post-init code**   Code that is executed after bean properties are set.
- **Post-listeners code**   Code that is executed after listeners are executed.
- **Pre-adding code**   Code that is executed before the component is added to the parent container.
- **Post-adding code**   Code that is executed immediately after the component is added to the parent container.
- **After-all-set-code**   Code that is executed after the component's setup is complete.
- **Pre-declaration code**   Code that executes prior to the declaration of the variable for the component.
- **Post-declaration code**   Code that executes after the declaration of the variable for the component.
- **Code generation**   Two options are available—this component can either be created from generated code, or it can be serialized out and read back in at runtime.
- **Serialize to**   Name of the file to serialize the component.

To understand where each of the code blocks fits in, the following listing was
created by adding comments to these properties with the name of the property:

```
private void initComponents() {
  java.awt.GridBagConstraints gridBagConstraints;
  firstnameLabel = new javax.swing.JLabel();
  // Pre-creation code
  firstname = new javax.swing.JTextField();
  // Post-creation code
  setName("Form"); // NOI18N
  setLayout(new java.awt.GridBagLayout());
  org.jdesktop.application.ResourceMap resourceMap =
    org.jdesktop.application.Application.getInstance(
    spinnakertrac.SpinnakerTracApp.class).getContext().
    getResourceMap(AddSkipper.class);
  firstnameLabel.setText(resourceMap.getString(
    "firstnameLabel.text")); // NOI18N
  firstnameLabel.setName("firstnameLabel"); // NOI18N
  gridBagConstraints = new java.awt.GridBagConstraints();
  gridBagConstraints.gridx = 0;
  gridBagConstraints.gridy = 0;
  gridBagConstraints.insets = new java.awt.Insets(3, 3, 3, 3);
  add(firstnameLabel, gridBagConstraints);
  // Pre-init code
  firstname.setColumns(25);
  firstname.setText(resourceMap.getString("firstname.text"));
  firstname.setName("firstname"); // NOI18N
  // Post-init code
  // Post-listeners code
  // Pre-adding code
  add(firstname, new java.awt.GridBagConstraints());
  // Post-adding code
  // After-all-set code
}// </editor-fold>
```

There are two approaches to customizing the code. The first approach is to use
the Code Customizer. The Code Customizer is shown in Figure 3-25. Right-clicking
a component in either the editor or Inspector and choosing Customize Code
from the menu displays this dialog box. The main content area contains the code

FIGURE 3-25   Code Customizer

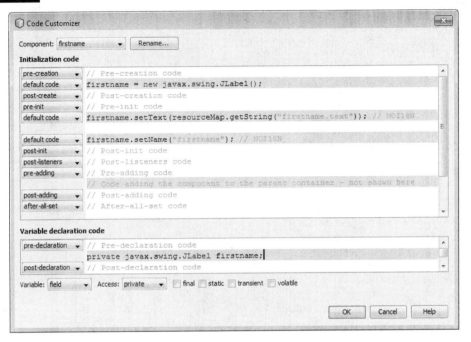

that is generated, interspersed with your custom code. Lines appearing in gray are generated, although they can be edited by choosing Custom from the combo box. Note, auto-completion is available in this dialog box. Any member variables or methods you may have added to the class are available.

The second approach to customizing the generated code is through the Properties window. Selecting the component in either the editor or Inspector and choosing Binding in the Properties window displays the list of properties in Figure 3-26. The only options available on this property panel but not in the Code Customizer pertain to generating serialized code, that is, generating a binary representation of the component.

Since the Properties window has limited real estate, clicking the ellipsis (...) button for custom code displays the code editor shown in Figure 3-27. This code editor supports auto-completion.

FIGURE 3-26

Code properties

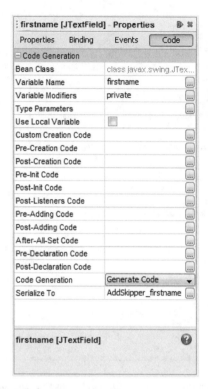

Generating Event Listeners

Each Swing or AWT component broadcasts numerous events to listeners. Examples of listeners that can be registered on many components include `ActionListener`, `FocusListener`, `KeyListener`, and `MouseListener` to name a few. Each component can have a slightly different set of listeners. The NetBeans GUI Editor provides a convenient UI for registering and generating code that responds to these events.

There are two ways to register a listener on a component in either the editor or Inspector window. The first is to right-click a component, select Events, and

FIGURE 3-27

Adding code

```
firstname.setDocument(new MyDocument());
```

Action	Hierarchy	MouseMotion
Ancestor	HierarchyBounds	MouseWheel
Change	InputMethod	PropertyChange
Component	Item	VetoableChange
Container	Key	
Focus	Mouse	

TABLE 3-9

JButton Events

then select the event of interest. The events are grouped into categories to simplify navigation. The event categories for JButton are shown in Table 3-9. The other way is through the Properties window on the Events tab. The Properties window for JButton is shown in Figure 3-28. If the listener is defined in the Properties window, it will use the name provided as the basis for the method. When using the context menu approach, the method name is generated using the name of the component and event. To change the name of the method, click the ellipsis button to the right of the name in the Properties window.

FIGURE 3-28

JButton **Events** property window

Events	
actionPerformed	save
ancestorAdded	<none>
ancestorMoved	<none>
ancestorMoved	<none>
ancestorRemoved	<none>
ancestorResized	<none>
caretPositionChanged	<none>
componentAdded	<none>
componentHidden	<none>
componentMoved	<none>
componentRemoved	<none>
componentResized	<none>
componentShown	<none>
focusGained	<none>
focusLost	<none>
hierarchyChanged	<none>
inputMethodTextChanged	<none>
itemStateChanged	<none>
keyPressed	<none>
keyReleased	<none>
keyTyped	<none>
mouseClicked	<none>
mouseDragged	<none>
mouseEntered	<none>
mouseExited	<none>
mouseMoved	<none>
mousePressed	<none>
mouseReleased	<none>
mouseWheelMoved	<none>
propertyChange	<none>
stateChanged	<none>
vetoableChange	<none>

Regardless of the approach used, the code will be generated in the form class. NetBeans immediately switches over to the Source view so that you may edit the generated code. The method name can only be changed through the Properties window. The parameter types and names cannot be changed. Content added to the method is preserved even as components are rearranged on the form. However, if a component is deleted, its listener methods are also deleted. If a component is copied and pasted, its methods also are copied and pasted, albeit with different names.

The listener code generated depends upon configuration parameters set on the form. To access the form's configuration parameters, select the root node in the Inspector window. This displays a Properties window with the same content as Figure 3-29. The Listener Generation Style has the following choices: Anonymous Inner Classes, One Inner Class, and Main Class. The default setting is Anonymous Inner Classes. The default setting for new forms is configured in Tools | Options | Miscellaneous | GUI Builder. This was discussed in Chapter 1.

FIGURE 3-29	
Form properties	

Form AddBoat - Properties	
Code Generation	
Variables Modifier	private
Local Variables	☐
Generate Full Classnames	☑
Generate Mnemonics Code	☐
Listener Generation Style	Anonymous Inner Classes
Layout Generation Style	Standard Java 6 code
Resources and Internationalization	
Set Component Names	☑
Automatic Resource Managem	All Resources
Design Locale	default language

Choosing Anonymous Inner Classes results in the following code being generated for an `ActionListener` on a Save button:

```
private void initComponents() {
  ...
  saveButton.addActionListener(new java.awt.event.ActionListener() {
    public void actionPerformed(java.awt.event.ActionEvent evt) {
      save(evt);
    }
  });
  ...
}
private void save(java.awt.event.ActionEvent evt) {
  // TODO add your handling code here:
}
```

Choosing One Inner Class results in the following code for the same scenario:

```
private void initComponents() {
  ...
  saveButton.addActionListener(formListener);
  ...
}
private class FormListener implements java.awt.event.ActionListener,
javax.swing.event.AncestorListener {
  FormListener() {}
  public void actionPerformed(java.awt.event.ActionEvent evt) {
    if (evt.getSource() == saveButton) {
      RaceForm.this.save(evt);
    }
  }
}
private void save(java.awt.event.ActionEvent evt) {
  // TODO add your handling code here:
}
```

Choosing Main Class results in the following code:

```
private void initComponents() {
  ...
  saveButton.addActionListener(this);
  ...
}
public void actionPerformed(java.awt.event.ActionEvent evt) {
  if (evt.getSource() == saveButton) {
    RaceForm.this.save(evt);
  }
}
private void save(java.awt.event.ActionEvent evt) {
  // TODO add your handling code here:
}
```

Understanding Beans Binding

The NetBeans GUI Builder goes a step beyond generating code for laying out components. NetBeans also integrates with Beans Binding (JSR 295). Beans Binding is a framework for synchronizing properties. It focuses on supporting Swing components and binding Swing components to the data model or to other Swing components. If you have developed applications using Java Server Faces (JSF), this concept should sound familiar. In JSF, the Java Server Faces Expression Language is used to bind JSF components to your beans. You do not have to write code that calls the equivalent get Text()/setText() of a JTextField on a JSF TextField.

Beans Binding is extremely powerful and saves a significant amount of time. Consider the situation where you are writing a calculator that adds or subtracts two values, as shown in Figure 3-30. If you were coding this without Beans Binding, then

Calculator
binding example

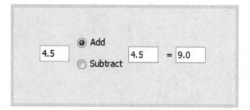

the code would be sprinkled with `getText()`/`setText()`. Most importantly, you would also have to register listeners to detect when a value has changed or a radio button was selected. Thus, the simple calculator ends up requiring copious amounts of code. To run this example and see the code differences, visit http://www.cuprak .net/BeansBindingCalculator.

To use Beans Binding, your data model and controls need to fire `PropertyChangeEvents`. To create a new data model that fires `PropertyChangeEvents`, create a new bean by choosing File | New File | JavaBeans Object | JavaBeans Component. Doing that generates an initial skeleton object. The skeleton object is a regular Java object with a `PropertyChangeSupport` instance and several methods for managing listeners. A sample property is included to show how things work. This is standard JavaBeans programming. The following listing shows a typical implementation for the `Race` class in the SpinnakerTrac application:

```java
import java.beans.*;
import java.io.Serializable;
import java.util.Date;

public class Race implements Serializable {
  public static final String PROP_COURSE_PROPERTY =
    "courseProperty";
  public static final String PROP_DATE_PROPERTY = "dateProperty";
  private String course;
  private Date date;
  private PropertyChangeSupport propertySupport;
  public Race() {
     propertySupport = new PropertyChangeSupport(this);
  }
  public String getCourse() {
    return course;
  }
  public void setCourse(String course) {
    String oldValue = this.course;
    this.course = course;
    propertySupport.firePropertyChange(PROP_COURSE_PROPERTY,
      oldValue, course);
  }
```

```
public Date getDate() {
  return date;
}
public void setDate(Date date) {
  Date oldValue = this.date;
  this.date = date;
  propertySupport.firePropertyChange(PROP_DATE_PROPERTY,
    oldValue, course);
}
public void addPropertyChangeListener(PropertyChangeListener
  listener) {
  propertySupport.addPropertyChangeListener(listener);
}
public void removePropertyChangeListener(
  PropertyChangeListener listener) {
  propertySupport.removePropertyChangeListener(listener);
}
}
```

To bind a form to the Race bean instance, the `Race` class is dragged from the Projects window onto the form. While nothing appears on the form, a new node is created under the form node in the Inspector window for the form. In the generated code for the form, a new member variable of type Race is created. Controls on the form can now be bound to the Race object instance. This is done by either right-clicking and then choosing Bind, or by using the Properties window Binding tab. When the property on the Swing control is selected, the Bind dialog box is displayed. This is shown in Figure 3-31. In Figure 3-31, the text property of a

FIGURE 3-31

Text field binding

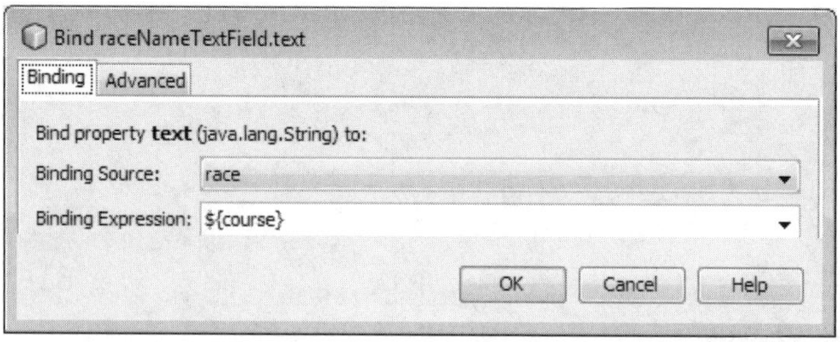

JTextField is being bound to the course property on the Race class. When the application is run, text typed into the text field is automatically pushed to the course property as the user types.

Beans Binding and JavaBeans

In this exercise, you create a bean with a String and Boolean property. A UI for this bean is created and bound to the bean.

1. Create a new Java Desktop Application by using File | New Project and selecting Java Desktop Application from the Java category.

2. Create a new bean, named Car, by choosing File | New File and selecting JavaBeans Component from the JavaBeans Object category.

3. Paste the following content into the bean, noting the use of PropertyChangeEvents:

```java
public class Car implements Serializable {
  public static final String MANUFACTURER_PROPERTY =
    "ManufacturerProperty";
  public static final String RUNS_ON_DIESEL_PROPERTY =
    "RunsOnDiesel";
  private String manufacturer;
  private boolean runsOnDiesel;
  private PropertyChangeSupport propertySupport;
  public Car() {
    propertySupport = new PropertyChangeSupport(this);
  }
  public String getManufacturer() {
    return manufacturer;
  }
  public void setManufacturer(String value) {
    String oldValue = manufacturer;
```

```
        this.manufacturer = value;
        propertySupport.firePropertyChange(
          MANUFACTURER_PROPERTY, oldValue, manufacturer);
        System.out.println("Manufacturer: " + manufacturer);
      }
    public boolean isRunsOnDiesel() {
        return runsOnDiesel;
      }
    public void setRunsOnDiesel(boolean value) {
        boolean oldValue = runsOnDiesel;
        this.runsOnDiesel = value;
        propertySupport.firePropertyChange(
          RUNS_ON_DIESEL_PROPERTY, oldValue, runsOnDiesel);
        System.out.println("Runs on diesel " + value);
      }
    public void addPropertyChangeListener(
        PropertyChangeListener listener) {
        propertySupport.addPropertyChangeListener(listener);
      }
    public void removePropertyChangeListener(
        PropertyChangeListener listener) {
        propertySupport.removePropertyChangeListener(listener);
      }
  }
```

4. Create a new `JFrame` form by choosing File | New File and selecting
   `JFrame` from the Swing GUI Forms category. Name the dialog box
   `AddCar`.

5. Drag the Car bean from the Projects window onto the `AddCar` form. In the
   Inspector window, a node "car1" should be added to Other Components.

6. Drag a Text Field and Check Box onto the `AddCar` form from the Swing
   Controls category in the Palette window.

7. Right-click the Text Field and choose Bind | Text. In the Bind dialog box that
   appears, select the Binding Source as "car1" and select `manufacturer` from

the Binding Expression drop-down list. NetBeans inserts `${manufacturer}` into the field.

8. The Text Field dramatically shrinks; in the Properties window set the number of columns to 25.

9. Right-click the Check Box and choose Bind | Selected. Set the Binding Source as "car1" and select `runsOnDiesel` for the Binding Expression. NetBeans sets the Binding Expression to `${runsOnDiesel}`.

10. Run the form by right-clicking and selecting Run File.

11. Notice that as you type, the Car bean will be automatically updated and the current contents dumped into the Output window.

12. To experiment further, add an additional field that also changes the manufacturer property, and watch both of them update in synchrony.

To bind the `JTextField` and `Race` class in this example, NetBeans generated the following Beans Binding code:

```
bindingGroup = new BindingGroup();
Binding binding =Bindings.createAutoBinding(
  AutoBinding.UpdateStrategy.READ_WRITE, race,
  ELProperty.create("${course}"), raceNameTextField,
  BeanProperty.create("text"));
bindingGroup.addBinding(binding);
bindingGroup.bind();
```

The literal `${course}` is a Beans Binding Expression (EL) that is evaluated at runtime.

Since many Swing controls do not conform to the Java Beans Specification, Beans Bindings provides special adapters to fire synthetic properties. These are listed in Table 3-10.

TABLE 3-10	Beans Binding Synthetic Properties

Property	Read/Write	Description
`java.swing.AbstractButton, javax.swing.JButton, javax.swing.JMenuItem, javax.swing.JToggleButton`		
`selected`	Read/Write	The selected state of the button.
`javax.swing.JComboBox`		
`selectedItem`	Read/Write	The selected item.
`javax.swing.JSpinner`		
`value`	Read/Write	Current value of the spinner.
`javax.swing.JSlider`		
`value`	Read	Current value of the slider.
`value_IGNORE_ADJUSTING`		Fired with the final value of the slider—not fired continuously as the user drags.
`javax.swing.JList`		
`selectedElement`	Read	Selected element in the list.
`selectedElements`		Selected elements in the list.
`selectedElements_IGNORE_ADJUSTING`		Selected element—not fired while selection is being changed.
`selectedElements_IGNORE_ADJUSTING`		Selected elements—not fired while the selection is being changed.
`javax.swing.JTable`		
`selectedElement`	Read	Selected element in the table.
`selectedElements`		Selected elements in the table.
`selectedElement_IGNORE_ADJUSTING`		Selected element in the table—not fired while the value is changing.
`selectedElements_IGNORE_ADJUSTING`		Selected elements in the table—not fired while the values are changing.
`javax.swing.JTextComponent, JEditorPane, JTextArea, JTextField`		
`text`	Read	Current text—fired as the user types.
`text_ON_FOCUS_LOST`		Current text—fired after focus has been lost.
`text_ON_ACTION_OR_FOCUS_LOST`		Current text—fired after focus or action event.

Beans Binding and Swing Components

In this exercise, you wire a `JCheckBox` to the enabled state of a `JTextField`. When the checkbox is selected, the `JTextField` will be read-only.

1. Create a new `JFrame` form in the NetBeans GUI Editor.

2. Drag a Check Box and Text Field onto the form from Swing Controls.

3. Right-click the Check Box and choose Bind | Selected. This opens the Bind dialog box.

4. Select the Text Field in the Binding Source drop-down list.

5. In the Binding Expression drop-down list, select Enabled Boolean. The expression `${enabled}` appears in the box.

6. Choose OK to close the dialog box.

7. Right-click the `JFrame` form in the Projects window and choose Run File. Notice how the checkbox affects the enabled state of the Text Field.

Understanding Internationalization Support

Creating a screen that resizes correctly is only the first step in creating an application that can be localized. The next step is storing the text, font, graphics, and color data in a resource bundle. To simplify the task and promote good GUI development from the start, NetBeans automatically stores these resources in a bundle. By default, a resource bundle is created for each new form created in the IDE. The resource bundle is named after the form.

In Figure 3-32, the `net.cuprak.sailing.resources` package contains the resource bundles for the forms. NetBeans created the `resources` package. An additional locale for China was added and appears with the `_zh_CN.properties` extension. This was added by right-clicking the `AddBoat.properties` file and choosing Add | Locale. Chinese text was then directly entered into the editor, and NetBeans populated the properties file with `boatNameLabel.text=\u5E06\` `u8239\u8CFD for boatNameLabel.text=` 帆船赛

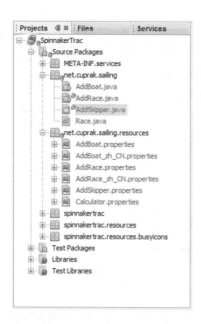

FIGURE 3-32

Resource bundles

Packaging and Distributing Java Desktop Projects

Exam Objective 3.4   Demonstrate the ability to package and distribute a built Java Desktop project for use by another user.

An application that only runs in the IDE isn't too useful unless the target audience is only the developer that wrote it. At some point, an application must be released to a nondeveloper who doesn't have NetBeans installed and who would prefer not to use the command line. Packaging and distributing an application presents many unique challenges including providing a mechanism to distribute and launch an application, resolving application dependencies, and handling application upgrades. An application isn't useful unless it can be deployed to an end user.

Java provides several different solutions for deploying desktop applications. These solutions vary in complexity and end-user experience. The deployment methods supported for Java desktop applications by NetBeans include:

- Executable JAR (double-clickable)
- Java Web Start

NetBeans doesn't produce an installer/launcher combination. There is no support for bundling the output of a project along with its classpath dependencies into a distribution that includes a JRE and native launcher. The two solutions discussed in this section assume that the JVM has already been installed on the end user's computer.

Creating an Executable JAR

NetBeans packages the output of a Java SE project into a single JAR file. This JAR file includes the compiled code of the project along with any resources such as property files or graphics. A separate directory stores external dependencies used on the runtime classpath. These dependencies are linked via the manifest in the project's JAR file. This JAR file can then be run either from the command line or by double-clicking it in the file browser. In both cases, a Java virtual machine must be installed on the computer.

on the job *One important caveat regarding double-clickable JAR files: there is no way to control JVM settings such as heap space or garbage collection. This means that a double-clickable JAR file must run within the constraints of the default JVM settings.*

The target JAR file uses the project name and is placed in the dist directory under the project's root. A lib directory is also placed in the dist directory. The lib directory contains the project dependencies that are copied to this location. NetBeans automatically sets the Main-Class attribute in the META-INF/MANIFEST.MF and populates the Class-Path property with the project's runtime classpath. The layout of this directory is shown in Figure 3-33. Listing 3-1 is an example manifest from a database-backed Java SE application.

LISTING 3-1:   MANIFEST.MF

```
Manifest-Version: 1.0
Ant-Version: Apache Ant 1.7.1
X-COMMENT: Main-Class will be added automatically by build
Class-Path: lib/appframework-1.0.3.jar lib/swing-worker-1.1.jar
lib/beansbinding-1.2.1.jar lib/toplink-essentials.jar
lib/toplink-essentials-agent.jar lib/postgresql-8.3-603.jdbc3.jar
lib/swing-layout-1.0.4.jar
Created-By: 14.3-b01-101 (Apple Inc.)
Main-Class: net.cuprak.sailing.SpinnakerTracApp
```

FIGURE 3-33

The `dist`
directory

```
C:\USERS\RCUPRAK\PROJECTS\SPINNAKERTRACDB\DIST
    README.TXT
    SpinnakerTracDB.jar
    lib
        appframework-1.0.3.jar
        beansbinding-1.2.1.jar
        postgresql-8.3-603.jdbc3.jar
        swing-layout-1.0.4.jar
        swing-worker-1.1.jar
        toplink-essentials-agent.jar
        toplink-essentials.jar
```

The `Main-Class` attribute is pulled from the current run configuration. This is configured in Project Properties. Project Properties is displayed by choosing File | Project Properties or by right-clicking the project in the Projects window and choosing Properties. Configuration of the main class is shown in Figure 3-34. Multiple configurations can be created and deleted. The configuration selected in the Configuration drop-down list is used for the `Main-Class` attribute. The other settings on this screen are used by NetBeans to launch the application, but are not included in the output. If these settings are necessary, a launcher such as a bat or shell script needs to be written to invoke the application.

on the job

If deployment via Java Web Start is not feasible and a turnkey solution is desired, use a third-party installer. A third-party installer can bundle the application into a native launcher with the JVM. This ensures that your application is isolated from other programs on the system and from JVM versions. There are many good commercial packages as well as open source solutions including Install4j (http://www.ej-technologies.com/) and IzPack (http://izpack.org/). For Mac OS X, Apple provides Package Maker and Jar Bundler. In either case, the output in the `dist` directory is a good starting point for feeding an installer.

FIGURE 3-34

Project
Properties: Run

Project Properties - SpinnakerTracDB

Categories:
- Sources
- Libraries
- Build
  - Compiling
  - Packaging
  - Documenting
- Run
- Application
  - Desktop App
  - Web Start
- Formatting

Configuration: <default config>   New...   Delete

Main Class: net.cuprak.sailing.SpinnakerTracApp   Browse...

Arguments:

Working Directory: Browse...

VM Options:

(e.g. -Xms10m)

☐ Run with Java Web Start

OK   Cancel   Help

The Packaging category, also in Project Properties and shown in Figure 3-35, configures a few additional parameters including:

- What files are to be excluded from the JAR file
- Whether the JAR file is to be compressed
- Whether to build the JAR file after compiling

By default, NetBeans excludes Java sources and the form data files used by the graphical editor. The same file pattern is used for exclusions as discussed in the first part of this chapter. Compressing a JAR file speeds up the file downloads. Deselecting the Build JAR After Compiling option stops NetBeans from generating the JAR file.

As mentioned previously, there are two ways to launch a JAR file:

- Double-click the JAR file.
- Run it from the command line using `java -jar <JAR name>`.

Running the application from the command line, `cmd.exe` on Windows, for example, is useful when debugging because standard out and standard error appear in the console window automatically.

To run the output on another machine, copy the `dist` directory to the other computer. This can be accomplished by zipping up the directory. A more elegant solution, Java Web Start, is discussed next.

FIGURE 3-35

Project
Properties:
Packaging

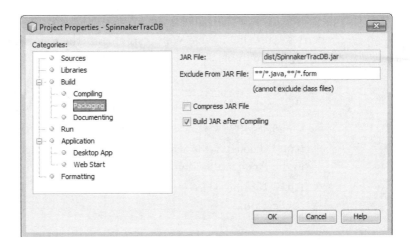

Deploying via Java Web Start

Java Web Start (JWS) is one of the deployment options available for Java SE applications. Java Web Start is a network-based solution for deploying Java applications via the web browser. Unlike applets that run inside of a web browser, JWS applications run as independent applications that can be launched from shortcuts on the desktop. Initially launching an application via JWS requires a network connection unless it is being served up locally. JWS applications can be lazily downloaded and also cached on machines for offline use. Caching also increases performance. In addition, applications deployed via JWS can be easily updated. Java Web Start is a powerful deployment tool.

Java Web Start is enabled on the Web Start node under the Application category in Project Properties. Project Properties is displayed by either choosing File | Properties or right-clicking the project in the Projects window and choosing Properties. Choosing Enable Web Start enables the rest of the controls on the screen, as shown in Figure 3-36. The parameters on this screen are:

- **Codebase**   Represents the location of the application. Three options can be chosen: Local Execution, Web Application Deployment, and User Defined.
- **Codebase Preview**   Read-only field showing what code base will be used.
- **Icon**   The icon that will be displayed while the application is being loaded, in the Application Manager, and on the desktop.
- **Allow Offline**   Deselect if a network connection is not necessary for the application.

FIGURE 3-36

Java Web Start
properties

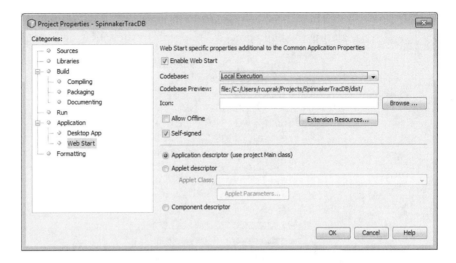

- **Self-Signed** When this checkbox is selected, NetBeans generates a certificate and signs the JAR files. If no certificate is provided and the application is not signed, the application is unable to access resources on the local machine. A user receives a warning that an application is self-signed.

- **Application Descriptor** Results in the `application-desc` pointing to the application's `main` class specified on the Run panel in Project Properties.

- **Applet Descriptor** Enables the deployment of an applet. The drop-down list enables selecting the Applet class. Clicking the Applet Parameters button configures applet parameters such as width and height.

- **Component Descriptor** The application is deployed as a library for use by another Java application.

Once the Enable Web Start checkbox is selected, two new files are added to the project:

- `master-application.jnlp` Template JNLP file, which will be populated by the build.

- `preview-application.html` Template HTML file for launching the application.

After the project is built, the `dist` directory contains a `launch.html` file and a `launch.jnlp` file that were created from the two template files. If an icon is selected, the build process copies the icon into the `dist` directory automatically.

The `master-application.jnlp` file is a stub file that NetBeans populates during the build process. It appears in the following listing:

```
<jnlp spec="1.0+" codebase="${jnlp.codebase}"
  href="launch.jnlp">
 <information>
 <title>${APPLICATION.TITLE}</title>
  <vendor>${APPLICATION.VENDOR}</vendor>
  <homepage href="${APPLICATION.HOMEPAGE}"/>
  <description>${APPLICATION.DESC}</description>
  <description kind="short">
    ${APPLICATION.DESC.SHORT}
  </description>
  <!--${JNLP.ICONS}-->
  <!--${JNLP.OFFLINE.ALLOWED}-->
 </information>
 <!--${JNLP.SECURITY}-->
 <resources>
  <!--${JNLP.RESOURCES.RUNTIME}-->
  <!--${JNLP.RESOURCES.MAIN.JAR}-->
  <!--${JNLP.RESOURCES.JARS}-->
  <!--${JNLP.RESOURCES.EXTENSIONS}-->
 </resources>
 <application-desc main-class="${jnlp.main.class}">
  <!--${JNLP.APPLICATION.ARGS}-->
 </application-desc>
</jnlp>
```

For the SpinnakerTrac project, the `launch.jnlp` file is created and populated in the following listing. Prior to building, the `main` class must be selected in the Run category in Project Properties. Note that the runtime classpath is used in generating the JAR elements.

```
<?xml version="1.0" encoding="UTF-8" standalone="no"?>
 <jnlp codebase=
  "file:/Users/rcuprak/NetBeansProjects/SpinnakerTracDB/dist/"
  href="launch.jnlp" spec="1.0+">
 <information>
  <title>Database Application Example</title>
  <vendor>Sun Microsystems Inc.</vendor>
  <homepage href="http://appframework.dev.java.net"/>
  <description>
    An empty application shell to be used as a basis
    for Swing applications working with databases
  </description>
```

```
  <description kind="short">
    Database Application Example
  </description>
  <icon href="icon.png" kind="default"/>
 </information>
 <security>
  <all-permissions/>
 </security>
 <resources>
  <j2se version="1.5+"/>
  <jar eager="true" href="SpinnakerTracDB.jar" main="true"/>
  <jar href="lib/appframework-1.0.3.jar"/>
  <jar href="lib/swing-worker-1.1.jar"/>
  <jar href="lib/beansbinding-1.2.1.jar"/>
  <jar href="lib/toplink-essentials.jar"/>
  <jar href="lib/toplink-essentials-agent.jar"/>
  <jar href="lib/postgresql-8.3-603.jdbc3.jar"/>
  <jar href="lib/swing-layout-1.0.4.jar"/>
 </resources>
 <application-desc main-class="net.cuprak.sailing.TestA">
 </application-desc>
</jnlp>
```

The title, vendor, description, and home page properties are configured in the Application category in Project Properties. A splash screen for the application can also be configured on this panel. This screen is shown in Figure 3-37.

The Scenario & Solution solidifies your understanding of how the contents of a JNLP file are generated for a project when Java Web Start support is enabled.

FIGURE 3-37

Application information

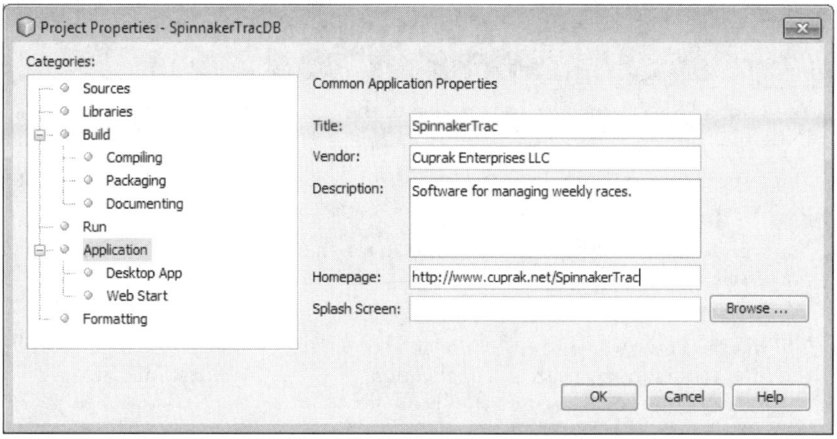

Configuring the build to use a keystore with a signed certificate requires editing `nbproject/private/private.properties` and adding the following properties:

```
jnlp.signjar.keystore=<keystore location>
jnlp.signjar.storepass=<keystore password>
jnlp.signjar.keypass=<key password>
jnlp.signjar.alias=<alias>
```

These properties can also be stored in `nbproject/project.properties`, but this isn't a good solution because this file is checked into version control and thus would reveal the keystore/key password to others.

Selecting Run With Java Web Start in the Run category of Project Properties tests Java Web Start deployment. This setting is shown in Figure 3-38. This provides a quick and easy way to test deployment of the application locally.

on the job

If you receive errors about mismatching certificates, check the JAR dependencies of the project. Some open source and commercial JAR libraries are signed. If this is the case, create a JNLP file for the library with a component descriptor.

Once the application is built, the contents of the `dist` directory can be uploaded to a server for others to run the application.

SCENARIO & SOLUTION

You want a JAR dependency to be added to the JNLP file.	Add it to either the compile or runtime classpaths in the Project Properties dialog box.
You want the main method of a specific class to be used when launching the application.	Set it from either the Run category in Project Properties or from Run	Set Project Configuration.
You wish to use your own keystore by specifying the properties such that the passwords aren't exposed to other developers.	Use `nbproject/private/private .properties`.
You want to know where to customize and configure the title, vendor, home page, and application description value populated into the JNLP file.	They are configured in Project Properties in the Application Category.

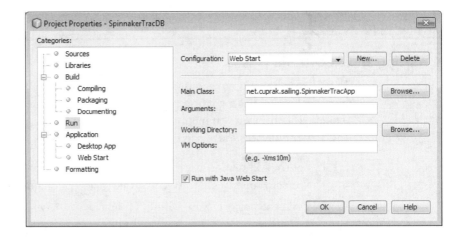

FIGURE 3-38

Project
Properties:
Run With Java
Web Start

EXERCISE 3-7

Using Java Web Start

In this exercise, you create a Java SE project and run it using Java Web Start.

1. Create a new Java Desktop Application by choosing File | New Project | Java | Java Desktop Application. Click Next.

2. Give the project a name and choose Basic Application as the application shell. Enter a package and class name for the main class, for example, `net.cuprak.sailing.SailTrackerApp`. SailTrackerApp will contain Java's `main` method. Click Finish.

3. Right-click the project name in the Projects window. Choose Properties to edit the project.

4. Under Application, select the Web Start category.

5. Select the Enable Web Start checkbox.

6. Click the Run category.

7. Select the Run With Java Web Start checkbox and choose Self-Signed.

8. Click OK to close the dialog box.

9. Choose Run | Run Main Project to launch the application using Java Web Start.

EXERCISE 3-8:

Creating an Executable JAR

In this exercise, you run the Jmol application you created in the first two exercises by both double-clicking it and running it from the command line. Success in this exercise is contingent on having Java properly installed and configured on the `PATH`. Consult http://java.sun.com for more information.

1. Set the Main Class to `org.openscience.jmol.app.Jmol` via File | Project Properties | Run. Click OK to accept changes.

2. Build the project: Run | Build Project.

3. Copy the `dist` directory to another location on the computer or on another computer with Java installed, preferably the same or a new version of the JRE.

4. In the file browser, double-click the `Jmol.jar` file to run it.

5. To run Jmol from the command line, launch `Cmd.exe` via Run on Windows. Change to the `dist` directory. Run Jmol by typing `java -jar Jmol.jar`

CERTIFICATION SUMMARY

This chapter covered four topics related to Java SE and desktop application development using NetBeans. You are now able to:

■ Create a new NetBeans project using existing sources.

■ Manage compilation and debugging classpaths of Java SE projects.

■ Create complex user interfaces using the NetBeans GUI Builder.

■ Deploy applications either as a double-clickable JAR file or via Java Web Start.

The Project With Existing Sources template is very similar to the Java Free-Form Project discussed in Chapter 2. However, unlike the Java Free-Form Project, Java Project With Existing Sources is built with the NetBeans-provided build script. NetBeans also manages project dependencies.

Managing classpaths for compilation and debugging is a project management feature NetBeans supports for Java Standard Projects. Java Standard Projects use the NetBeans build scripts such as Java Project With Existing Sources. NetBeans partitions the libraries into compile, run, compile tests, and run tests classpaths. Libraries can be stored with a project or can be referenced by a variable or pulled from a NetBeans library.

The NetBeans GUI Builder is a powerful editor for rapidly building Swing or AWT user interfaces. It supports most of the layout managers. Items are dragged out from the palette and onto the screen. Component properties are edited in the Properties window. The Inspector window displays the Swing component hierarchy. Unlike other editors, it can bind controls to Java Beans. The NetBeans GUI Builder also stores all localizable items, such as text and colors, in resource bundles automatically.

The last section of this chapter covered the deployment of Java applications. NetBeans supports either double-clickable JAR files or Java Web Start. For double-clickable JAR files, compiled code as well as a project's dependencies are copied to the `dist` directory. The `dist` directory can be zipped and transferred to another machine. The project's JAR file can then be double-clicked or run from the command line. Java Web Start can be configured in Project Properties under the Web Start category. The application can be self-signed, not signed, or a valid certificate can be used. NetBeans takes care of creating the JNLP file.

✓ # TWO-MINUTE DRILL

Creating Desktop Applications from Existing Sources

❑ Java Project With Existing Sources is a standard NetBeans project.

❑ Standard NetBeans projects use the NetBeans-generated build script.

❑ Java Project With Existing Sources is one of two types of projects for creating a new NetBeans project from an existing code base; the other project type is the Java Free-Form Project.

❑ Specific files/directories can be included or excluded from the project.

❑ A central directory for sharing libraries can be configured.

❑ The New Project wizard does not configure the classpath; the classpath must be configured post–project creation.

❑ The project directory does not necessarily have to contain the project sources.

Managing Classpaths for Compilation and Debugging

❑ Classpath can be configured by right-clicking the project and choosing Properties or by choosing File | Project Properties.

❑ Classpath entries can be added in the Projects window by right-clicking the Libraries node.

❑ Classpath entries can include references to other projects, JAR folders, or libraries.

❑ The run classpath inherits from the compile classpath.

❑ Interfaces belong on the compile classpath.

❑ Interface implementations belong on the runtime classpath.

❑ The four classpaths for a Java SE project are compile, run, compile tests, and run tests.

❑ Dependencies can be added to a project by using Relative, Absolute, or Path Variables, or can be copied to a library directory.

❑ Path variables are used to abstract the path.

❑ Java EE and Java Web projects lack a runtime classpath.

❑ Java SE projects are pre-populated with library dependencies.

❑ The Free-Form web project has only one classpath for supporting the Java editor (code completion, syntax checking, and so on).

❑ Multiple source and test roots can be configured for the project.

Creating Forms with the GUI Builder

❑ The NetBeans GUI Builder has four windows: Editor, Inspector, Palette, and Properties.

❑ Components are dragged from the Palette window onto the main Editor window.

❑ Properties for components including binding expressions, events, and custom code are managed on the Properties window.

❑ New forms are created by choosing File | New File and selecting a form under Swing GUI Forms or AWT GUI Forms.

❑ The NetBeans GUI Builder only works for forms created by NetBeans.

❑ The NetBeans GUI Builder supports the following layouts: Free Design, Absolute, Border, Box, Card, Flow, GridBag, Grid, and Null.

❑ The Free Design layout is the default layout for new forms.

❑ NetBeans GUI Editor opens in the Design mode for a new form.

❑ The Free Design layout is `javax.swing.GroupLayout` that was added in Java SE 6.

❑ The Swing Layout Extensions Library is required for projects targeting pre–Java 6 environments. Depending upon configuration, NetBeans will add this library. This library includes the JAR file `swing-layout-1.0.4.jar`.

❑ When using the Free Design layout, the toolbar icons for alignment and resizing become enabled.

❑ For the Free Design layout, NetBeans provides the following guides: Baseline, Edge, Indentation, Inset, and Offset.

❑ For the Free Design layout, anchors are represented by half-circles and show which components are bound to other components and container edges.

❑ GridBagLayout Customizer is used to graphically manipulate `GridBagConstraints` for a container.

❑ GridBagLayout Customizer is displayed by right-clicking and choosing Customize Layout.

❑ NetBeans populates a form in the `initComponent` method of a form.

❑ NetBeans GUI Builder–generated code cannot be edited.

❑ Practically all aspects of the generated code can be customized including creation, pre-creation, post-creation, pre-init, post-init, post-listeners, pre-adding, post-adding, after-all-set, pre-declaration, and post-declaration.

❏ NetBeans can generate event listeners. Event listeners can be created using the Events tab in the Properties window or by right-clicking a component and choosing Event.

❏ Beans Binding, JSR 295, is used for binding components to other components and also to the data model.

❏ NetBeans automatically adds `beansbinding-1.2.1.jar` to a project the first time that property is bound in a form.

❏ To bind one component to another component, switch to the Connection mode and select two components. An editor then appears for configuring the binding.

❏ For a bean to work with Beans Binding, the bean should fire `PropertyChangeEvents`.

❏ A bean can be added to a form by dragging it from the Projects window onto the NetBeans GUI Builder editor. The bean must be compiled before this is done.

❏ NetBeans automatically stores all text, fonts, colors, and graphics in resource bundles.

❏ By default, a resource bundle is created for each form.

Packaging and Distributing Java Desktop Projects

❏ Java desktop projects can be distributed as either a zip archive containing an executable JAR file or via Java Web Start.

❏ The `dist` directory can be zipped up and copied to another machine. Double-clicking the project's JAR file under `dist` or invoking it from the command line via `java -jar <project JAR>` launches the application.

❏ The application's runtime classpath is copied into `dist/lib`.

❏ NetBeans automatically populates the `MANIFEST.MF` file with the `Main-Class` and `Class-Path` properties.

❏ To enable Java Web Start, choose File | Project Properties | Web Start. Select Enable Java Web Start.

❏ The main class for both Java Web Start and the project's manifest is pulled from the current Run Configuration.

❏ The Run Configuration is set in Project Properties in the Run category. It can also be set via Run | Set Project Configuration.

❑ To specify the certificate to be used to sign the JARs, properties (discussed in the chapter) must be added in either `private.properties` or `project.properties`.

❑ To run a project using Java Web Start, on the Run category in Project Properties choose Run With Java Web Start.

❑ The files `master-application.jnlp` and `preview-application.html` are used to generate `launch.jnlp` and `launch.html` in the `dist` directory.

SELF TEST

The following questions will help you measure your understanding of the material presented in this chapter. Read all the choices carefully because there might be more than one correct answer. Choose all correct answers for each question.

Creating Desktop Applications from Existing Sources

1. With respect to the Java Project With Existing Sources template, which statement is false?
   A. NetBeans prompts for the existing Ant script that will be used to build the project.
   B. The project directory does not have to contain the project sources.
   C. Specific classes/files can be excluded from the project.
   D. The name of the build script can be selected.

2. Which pattern is invalid and will not include any files?
   A. `/**`
   B. `**/*.properties`
   C. `*.java`
   D. `org/junit`

3. True or False? Java Project With Existing Sources can contain multiple source directories?
   A. True
   B. False

4. What project setting is not configured in the Java Project With Existing Sources wizard step?
   A. Build script name
   B. Source directory(s)
   C. Path exclusions
   D. Classpath

Managing Classpaths for Compilation and Debugging

5. Which of the following is not a Java SE classpath type?
   A. Compile
   B. Run
   C. Debug
   D. Compile tests

6. Right-clicking the Libraries node of a project in the Projects window and choosing Add Project will add a project dependency. To what classpath will this dependency be added?

   A. Compile

   B. Runtime

   C. Compile tests

   D. Run tests

7. You have three projects, A, B, and C. Project A depends upon B, and B depends upon C. Project A does not use any of the APIs or classes in C. What should the compile and runtime classpath of Project A look like?

   A. Compile A; Runtime B

   B. Compile B; Runtime C

   C. Compile B; Runtime A

   D. Compile B

   E. Compile A

8. A developer is going to check a project into a version control system that will be shared by all the members of the team. The team stores all JAR libraries in a central version control repository so that the artifacts can be used by multiple projects. Each developer checks this artifact repository out and into a separate location on his or her machine. How should the paths to the dependencies be specified?

   A. Relative path

   B. Absolute path

   C. Variable

   D. Configure a libraries folder

Creating Forms with the GUI Builder

9. Which of the following layouts is not supported by NetBeans?

   A. Group Layout

   B. Free Design

   C. Card Layout

   D. Spring Layout

10. When creating a new form, in what mode does the form initially open?

   A. Source mode

   B. Design mode

   C. Connection mode

   D. Preview

11. An existing form is modified with a new constructor that takes additional parameters. However, when this constructor is first used, the form appears blank. What method should be invoked from the constructor so that the form is populated?

A. `initComponents()`

B. `super()`

C. `doLayout()`

D. `repaint()`

E. `pack()`

12. A `JTextField` and a `JLabel` are being placed on the same line in a form using the Free Design layout. Which guides should be used to align them?

A. Inset

B. Offset

C. Baseline

D. A and B

E. B and C

13. True or False? An existing application is imported into NetBeans using the Java Project With Existing Sources wizard. The application has an existing Swing GUI. This GUI can be edited with the NetBeans GUI Builder.

A. True

B. False

Packaging and Distributing Java Desktop Projects

14. For a Java SE application, which of the following distribution methods does NetBeans support?

A. Executable JAR

B. Java Web Start

C. WAR

D. EAR

E. Choices A and B

15. The contents of which directory are zipped up for distribution?

A. `lib`

B. `bin`

C. `build`

D. `dist`

16. How is Java Web Start distribution enabled for a Java SE project within NetBeans?

    A. Select Enable Java Web Start under the Web Start category in Project Properties.

    B. Select Deploy Using Java Web Start under the Packaging category in Project Properties.

    C. Java SE projects are deployed using Java Web Start by default.

    D. Select Deploy Using Java Web Start under the Run category in Project Properties.

17. NetBeans copies and performs substitutions on which files for Java Web Start?

    A. `launch.jnlp` and `launch.html`

    B. `master-application.jnlp` and `preview-application.html`

    C. `launch.jnlp` and `preview-application.html`

    D. `master-application.jnlp` and `launch.html`

SELF TEST ANSWERS

Creating Desktop Applications from Existing Sources

1. With respect to the Java Project With Existing Sources template, which statement is false?
   A. NetBeans prompts for the existing Ant script that will be used to build the project.
   B. The project directory does not have to contain the project sources.
   C. Specific classes/files can be excluded from the project.
   D. The name of the build script can be selected.

   ☑ **A.** Java Project With Existing Sources prompts for the name of the build script; however, the build script is created by NetBeans. Free-form projects prompt for an existing build script.

   ☒ **B, C,** and **D** are incorrect. **B** is incorrect because the project directory does not have to contain the project sources. A directory anywhere else on the machine can be chosen. **C** is incorrect because files can be included or excluded. **D** is incorrect because the name of the build script can be selected.

2. Which pattern is invalid and will not include any files?
   A. `/**`
   B. `**/*.properties`
   C. `*.java`
   D. `org/junit`

   ☑ **A.** The pattern `/**` will not produce any match. Patterns do not start with a slash.

   ☒ **B, C, D** are incorrect. **B** is incorrect because `**/*.properties` will match all properties files. **C** is incorrect because all files with the `.java` extension in the root directory will be matched. **D** is incorrect because files under `org/junit` will be matched.

3. True or False? Java Project With Existing Sources can contain multiple source directories?
   A. True
   B. False

   ☑ **True.** A project can contain multiple source roots.

4. What project setting is not configured in the Java Project With Existing Sources wizard step?
   A. Build script name
   B. Source directory(s)

    C. Path exclusions

    D. Classpath

    ☑ D. The classpath is not configured in the wizard.

    ☒ A, B, and C are incorrect. A is incorrect because the "Build script name" is configured in this step. B is incorrect because the "Source directory(s)" are configured in this set. C is incorrect because "Path exclusions" are configured in this step.

Managing Classpaths for Compilation and Debugging

5. Which of the following is not a Java SE classpath type?

    A. Compile

    B. Run

    C. Debug

    D. Compile tests

    ☑ C. There is no debug classpath.

    ☒ A, B, and D are incorrect. A is incorrect because compile is a Java SE classpath. B is incorrect because run is a Java SE classpath. D is incorrect because compile tests is a Java SE classpath.

6. Right-clicking the Libraries node of a project in the Projects window and choosing Add Project will add a project dependency. To what classpath will this dependency be added?

    A. Compile

    B. Runtime

    C. Compile tests

    D. Run tests

    ☑ A. Dependencies added via the context menu are appended to the compile classpath.

    ☒ B, C, and D are incorrect. B is incorrect because the project dependency will not be added to the runtime classpath. C is incorrect because the project will not be added to the compile tests classpath. D is incorrect because the project dependency will not be added to the run tests classpath.

7. You have three projects, A, B, and C. Project A depends upon B, and B depends upon C. Project A does not use any of the APIs or classes in C. What should the compile and runtime classpath of Project A look like?

   A. Compile A; Runtime B

   B. Compile B; Runtime C

   C. Compile B; Runtime A

   D. Compile B

   E. Compile A

> ☑ **B.** Project B is required for compiling while Project B requires Project C at runtime.
>
> ☒ **A, C**, and **D** are incorrect. **A** is incorrect because Project B needs to be on the compile classpath, and having it on the runtime classpath won't allow the compiler to resolve Project A's dependencies on Project B. **C** is incorrect because Project C needs to be on the runtime classpath. **D** is incorrect because Project C is required on the runtime classpath. **E** is incorrect because neither Project B nor Project C is added as a dependency.

8. A developer is going to check a project into a version control system that will be shared by all the members of the team. The team stores all JAR libraries in a central version control repository so that the artifacts can be used by multiple projects. Each developer checks this artifact repository out and into a separate location on his or her machine. How should the paths to the dependencies be specified?

   A. Relative path

   B. Absolute path

   C. Variable

   D. Configure a libraries folder

> ☑ **C.** A variable, defined in Tools | Variables, would allow the team to checkout the external libraries anywhere on their computer.
>
> ☒ **A, B**, and **D** are incorrect. **A** is incorrect because developers can checkout the external dependencies to any location on their computer. Relative paths would not work in this situation. **B** is incorrect because absolute paths are computer specific. **D** is incorrect because the libraries are centrally stored, and a libraries folder would have the same problem as a relative path.

Creating Forms with the GUI Builder

9. Which of the following layouts is not supported by NetBeans?

A. Group Layout

B. Free Design

C. Card Layout

D. Spring Layout

☑ **D.** Spring Layout is not supported by NetBeans.

☒ **A, B,** and **C** are incorrect. **A** is incorrect because NetBeans supports Group Layout. **B** is incorrect because NetBeans supports Free Design. **C** is incorrect because NetBeans supports Card Layout.

10. When creating a new form, in what mode does the form initially open?

A. Source mode

B. Design mode

C. Connection mode

D. Preview

☑ **B.** The editor opens in Design mode, enabling you to immediately begin populating the form.

☒ **A, C,** and **D** are incorrect. **A** is incorrect because the editor opens in Design mode. **C** is incorrect because Select mode is the default for the cursor. **D** is incorrect because Preview is not a mode, and thus the editor does not open in it.

11. An existing form is modified with a new constructor that takes additional parameters. However, when this constructor is first used, the form appears blank. What method should be invoked from the constructor so that the form is populated?

A. `initComponents()`

B. `super()`

C. `doLayout()`

D. `repaint()`

E. `pack()`

☑ **A.** The `initComponents` method does the actual work of creating the user interface.

☒ **B, C, D,** and **E** are incorrect. **B** is incorrect because a constructor of the `super` class does not call `initComponents`. **C** is incorrect because `doLayout` is a Swing method involved in the component layout. **D** is incorrect because `repaint` causes the screen to redraw. **E** is incorrect because `pack()` positions and sizes components already added.

12. A `JTextField` and a `JLabel` are being placed on the same line in a form using the Free Design layout. Which guides should be used to align them?

A. Inset

B. Offset

C. Baseline

D. A and B

E. B and C

☑ **E.** is correct. An offset would help ensure that the components are properly spaced, and a baseline would ensure that the text baselines match.

☒ **A, B, C,** and **D** are incorrect. **A** is incorrect because insets are for spacing a component within its parent container. **B** is incorrect because you would also use a baseline. **C** is incorrect because you would also use an offset. **D** is incorrect because you would not use an inset.

13. True or False? An existing application is imported into NetBeans using the Java Project With Existing Sources wizard. The application has an existing Swing GUI. This GUI can be edited with the NetBeans GUI Builder.

A. True

B. False

☑ **False.** NetBeans generates the source code to render a user interface. It cannot reverse-engineer code with an unknown structure.

Packaging and Distributing Java Desktop Projects

14. For a Java SE application, which of the following distribution methods does NetBeans support?

A. Executable JAR

B. Java Web Start

C. WAR

D. EAR

E. Choices A and B

☑ **E.** NetBeans support generates an executable JAR file and also the artifacts required for Java Web Start.

☒ **A, B, C,** and **D** are incorrect. **A** is incorrect because NetBeans also generates artifacts for Java Web Start. **B** is incorrect because NetBeans also generates artifacts for an executable JAR file. **C** is incorrect because NetBeans does not build a WAR file for a Java SE application. **D** is incorrect because NetBeans does not build an EAR file for a Java SE application.

15. The contents of which directory are zipped up for distribution?

    A. `lib`

    B. `bin`

    C. `build`

    D. `dist`

    ☑ **D.** The `dist` directory contains the generated project JAR file and also the external library dependencies.

    ☒ **A, B,** and **C** are incorrect. **A** is incorrect because the `lib` directory, under `dist`, only contains the external library dependencies and not the compiled code for the project. **B** is incorrect because there is no `bin` directory. **C** is incorrect because `build` contains only the compile code for the project.

16. How is Java Web Start distribution enabled for a Java SE project within NetBeans?

    A. Select Enable Java Web Start under the Web Start category in Project Properties.

    B. Select Deploy Using Java Web Start under the Packaging category in Project Properties.

    C. Java SE projects are deployed using Java Web Start by default.

    D. Select Deploy Using Java Web Start under the Run category in Project Properties.

    ☑ **A.** Java Web Start is enabled on the Web Start panel in Project Properties.

    ☒ **B, C,** and **D** are incorrect. **B** is incorrect because there is no such setting in the Package category of Project Properties. **C** is incorrect because Java Web Start is not the default deployment strategy. **D** is incorrect because the Run category has a Run With Java Web Start checkbox that is used for testing and using Java Web Start from the IDE.

17. NetBeans copies and performs substitutions on which files for Java Web Start?

    A. `launch.jnlp` and `launch.html`

    B. `master-application.jnlp` and `preview-application.html`

    C. `launch.jnlp` and `preview-application.html`

    D. `master-application.jnlp` and `launch.html`

    ☑ **B.** These are the template files used to generate `launch.jnlp` and `launch.html`.

    ☒ **A, C,** and **D** are incorrect. **A** is incorrect because these are the output files. **C** is incorrect because `preview-application.html` is an output file. **D** is incorrect because `launch.html` is an output file.

Part II

NetBeans IDE Development Support

CHAPTERS

4   Java EE Web Applications

5   Database Connectivity

6   Source Editor

7   Refactoring Support

4

Java EE Web Applications

CERTIFICATION OBJECTIVES

- Creating Web Applications from Existing Sources

- Adding and Using NetBeans-Available Web Frameworks

- Understanding the Visual Web JSF Framework

- Working with Server Instances

- Building and Deploying Web Applications

✓ Two-Minute Drill

Q&A Self Test

NetBeans supports the development of web applications through various means including project import support, web framework support, application/web server integration, and build/deployment support. In essence, NetBeans provides support through the entire software development process, giving few reasons to ever leave the comfort of your IDE. The exam targets common tasks that are performed when developing web applications such as container/server setup, project importing, and web application creation. Objective 1.3, "Working with Server Instances," covers registering and interfacing with application servers. Objective 4.2, "Understanding the Visual Web JSF Framework," delves into the web application framework support in the IDE.

Objective 4.1, "Creating Web Applications from Existing Sources," covers importing and configuring of existing non-NetBeans IDE projects.

Mastering these objectives will prepare you well for the exam and will assist you in web application development throughout your career.

Being familiar with the software development life cycle is important. Knowing about the NetBeans-related tools and resources at your disposal is equally beneficial. Objective 4.3, "Adding and Using NetBeans-Available Web Frameworks," assists you in deciding on the best architecture to use. Objective 4.5, "Building and Deploying Web Applications," assists you in the build and end-state deployment processes. Objective 4.4, "Using the HTTP Server-Side Monitor," assists you in testing and tuning the application. Note that Objective 4.4 is covered in Chapter 8.

Working through this chapter will get you comfortable with all exam-related web development and support questions. Be prepared, as setting up application servers and learning web frameworks can be time-consuming. For the scope of the exam, having general knowledge of frameworks, application servers, and web-related processes should suffice. When learning (or refreshing your knowledge) about web-related technologies, for the scope of the exam, manage your time and focus.

CERTIFICATION OBJECTIVE

Creating Web Applications from Existing Sources

Exam Objective 4.1   Describe how to create a NetBeans project from the source code of an existing web application.

Creating a NetBeans project from the source code of an existing web application is similar to creating a NetBeans project from the source code of an existing Java application, as covered in Chapter 3. The main differences relate to the settings necessary for web applications, both in content and directory structures.

A four-step wizard drives the process for creating a new web application with existing sources. We will examine each step:

- Choose Project
- Name And Location
- Server And Settings
- Existing Sources And Libraries

Step 1: Choose Project

To create a new Web Application With Existing Sources, choose File | New Project (CTRL-SHIFT-N). This opens the first step in the wizard, shown in Figure 4-1. Under Categories select Java Web, and from the Projects list box on the right, choose Web Application With Existing Sources. Click Next to move to the next step in the wizard.

FIGURE 4-1

Step 1: Choose Project

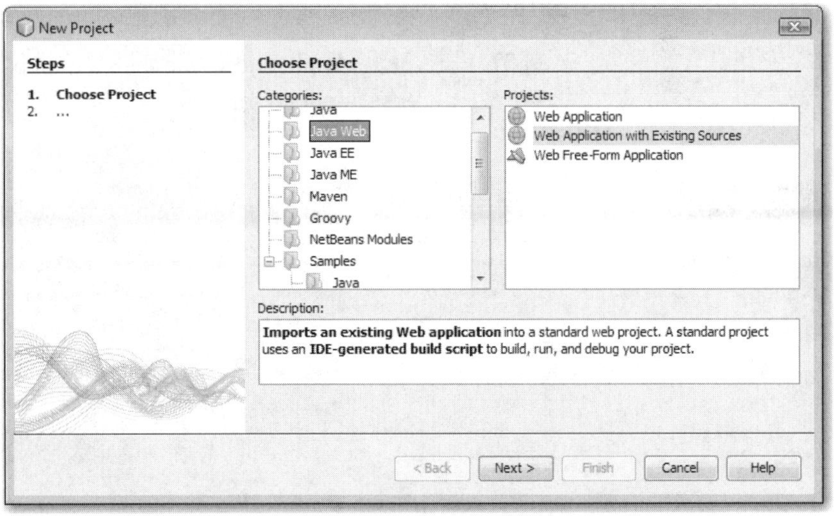

Step 2: Name And Location

The next step in the New Project wizard asks for basic project setup information. It is shown in Figure 4-2 and configures the following:

- **Location**   Name of the folder that contains the source code for the web application.
- **Project Name**   Name of the project that will appear in the Projects window.
- **Project Folder**   Location where the NetBeans project file information will be stored. This is where the `nbproject` directory is placed along with the build script.
- **Use Dedicated Folder For Storing Libraries**   Enables the storing of libraries in a central location. Facilitates the sharing of projects between users.
- **Libraries Folder**   Location of the libraries—needed if the project is to be shared.
- **Set As Main Project**   Sets this project as the main project at the conclusion of the wizard.

Step 3: Server And Settings

In this step, shown in Figure 4-3, you have the ability to set properties for server-related settings.

- **Add To Enterprise Application**   Enables the web project to be added to an existing enterprise application.

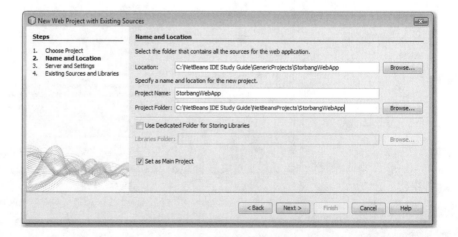

FIGURE 4-2

Step 2: Name And Location

FIGURE 4-3

Step 3: Server
And Settings

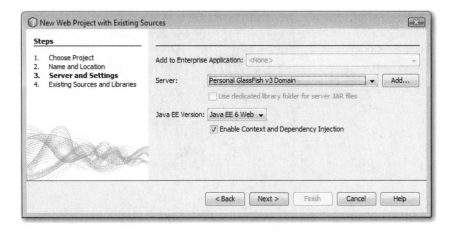

- **Server**   Specifies the target server to be used with the web project. Only registered servers may be selected. The Add button allows you to register a new server.
- **Use Dedicated Library Folder For Server JAR Files**   Is only enabled if the same selection was made in the previous step.
- **Java EE Version**   Specifies the Java EE level for your web application. Options are Java EE 6 Web, Java EE 5, and J2EE 1.4. The levels must match the compliancy of the application server.

If you need to review settings in a previous step, select the Back button. Providing that you don't change the project type in step 1, your settings are preserved for when you return to the step you were on.

Step 4: Existing Sources And Libraries

In this step, shown in Figure 4-4, web folders and the source and test package folders are selected for the project. Browse and Add Folder buttons display file browsers for choosing directories. Multiple directories can be configured for source and test package folders. Configuration of test sources is optional.

- **Web Pages Folder**   Specifies the location of the project's web pages.
- **WEB-INF Content**   Specifies the location of the project's WEB-INF content.
- **Libraries Folder**   Specifies the location of the project's class library deficiencies.
- **Sources Package Folders**   Specifies the location of source directories.
- **Test Package Folders**   Specifies the location of test directories.

FIGURE 4-4

Step 4: Existing
Sources And
Libraries

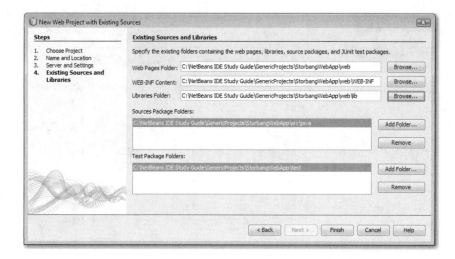

After you click the Finish button, the project is created on your computer and opened in NetBeans. The folder specified in Step 2's Location property determines where the web pages, Java sources, and libraries are situated.

The Projects And Files windows display the logical and file structure of the project. Many of these settings can be modified in the Project Properties dialog box after the project has been created.

EXERCISE 4-1

Creating a Web Program with Existing Sources

In this exercise, you create a web application from existing sources.

1. Prepare a simple web application. If you do not have one available, consider using a sample web application for this exercise such as ServletExamples. Note that before it can be used to create a new project with existing sources, the IDE has to be restarted after the sample project is created. If you want to use the same folder as the project folder, you also have to delete build.xml and the build directory (if it exists).

2. Use the New Projects wizard to create a Web Application With Existing Sources from your base or modified sample application.

3. Run the application to ensure that it works.

Adding and Using NetBeans-Available Web Frameworks

Exam Objective 4.3   Demonstrate knowledge of which web frameworks are available in the NetBeans IDE and how they are added to and used in a web application.

Web frameworks provide a well-defined structure for developers to build dynamic web applications, services, and websites. Web frameworks primarily consist of a class library and related configuration files. Popular frameworks are available in NetBeans as global libraries that can be added to your projects. When you're creating a new web application, NetBeans prompts for the web application to be used and adds the required libraries and configuration files to the project automatically. Frameworks with wizard support include Spring (Spring Framework and Spring Web MVC (Model-View-Controller)), Struts, and JavaServer Faces, as shown in Table 4-1. NetBeans Visual Web JavaServer Faces is included in NetBeans 6.1 and is detailed in the next objective. There is no limit on frameworks that can be used in the IDE. Frameworks that are not available in the core installation can be added to the global libraries or directly to a project's libraries folder. However, the downloaded frameworks will not have wizard support for the setting up of configuration files, special directory structures, or features. Some frameworks that are installed as plugins/modules may have additional tooling support such as the extended drag and drop features of NetBeans Visual Web JSF Framework.

| TABLE 4-1 | NetBeans-Available Web Frameworks and Web-Supporting Modules |

Web Support	Availability in NetBeans 6.8	Availability in NetBeans 6.7	Availability in NetBeans 6.5	Availability in NetBeans 6.1
Spring	2.5	2.5	2.5	2.5
Struts	1.3.8	1.3.8	1.2.9	1.2.9
JavaServer Faces	Yes	Yes	Yes	Yes
Visual Web JSF	n/a	Plugin Manager	Plugin Manager	Yes
Visual Web ICEfaces	n/a	Plugin Portal	Plugin Portal	n/a
RichFaces Palette	Plugin Portal	Plugin Portal	Plugin Portal	Plugin Portal

Adding Web Frameworks

Web Frameworks can be added to a new project through the New Project wizard (File | New Project) or to an existing project from the Project Properties dialog box via the panel associated with the Frameworks node.

When you're using the New Project wizard, a Web Application project needs to be selected after choosing to the Java Web category. The wizard is a four-step process. Step 1 defines the project as a Web Application, as shown in Figure 4-5. Step 2 defines the project's name and location, as shown in Figure 4-6. In step 2, you may also define a dedicated library folder for storing your libraries. Step 3 is for establishing server-related settings, as represented in Figure 4-7. Step 4 is the step we are most concerned with, because it provides selection and configuration of the web frameworks we wish to have included in our application. Frameworks are available by selection of their checkbox in the Frameworks list box, as shown in Figure 4-8. When the desired framework is selected, tabbed panels with various configuration options show. Upon your selecting the Finish button, your project is set up with all of the necessary libraries, folders, wizards, and configuration files relative to your selected frameworks.

on the
Job

Grails is an open-source web application framework based on the Groovy language. Grails is added to a project though the New Project wizard with Groovy as the Categories type and Grails Application as the Projects type. A Grails project is not necessary in order to use Groovy. You can create Groovy Classes and Scripts through the New File wizard.

FIGURE 4-5

New Project:
Choose Project
step

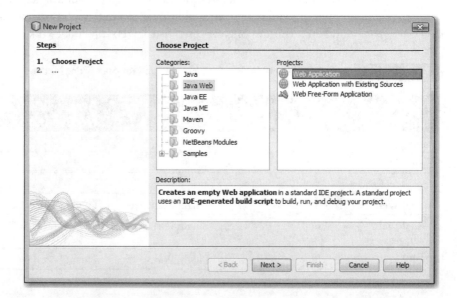

FIGURE 4-6

New Project:
Name And
Location step

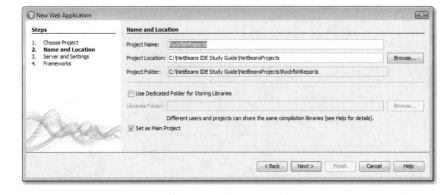

FIGURE 4-7

New Project:
Server And
Settings step

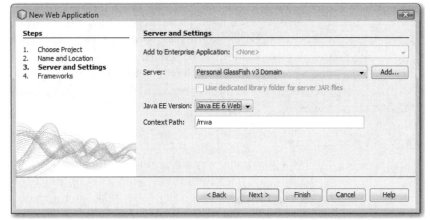

FIGURE 4-8

New Project:
Frameworks step

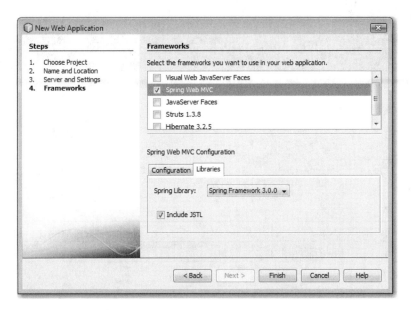

Let's take a look at some of the files that are added to a web application when Spring, Struts, and JavaServer Faces projects are established. We show this analysis in Table 4-2 and Figure 4-9.

Figure 4-9 shows the libraries that are added when using the New Project wizard to add web frameworks. Note that the Tomcat libraries and JDK are not part of the web frameworks. Also note that the JSF libraries are included with GlassFish v3, so if that is your configured server, they do not appear separately. The left Libraries tree is within a Spring web application, the center one is within a Struts web application, and the one on the right is within a JavaServer Faces web application.

Understanding Web Frameworks

By now you should have a basic understanding of the available web frameworks in the NetBeans IDE and the files associated with them. However, if you haven't used the frameworks in the past, you may want to have a general idea of what they are and what they do. The following subsections explore Struts, Spring, and JavaServer Faces from a high level in regard to the general knowledge that may be needed for the exam.

Struts

Struts is a web framework maintained by the Apache Software Foundation (struts .apache.org). It is a web-based Model-View-Controller (MVC) framework primarily focused on the presentation tier. In an MVC architecture, the model contains the

| TABLE 4-2 | Web Framework Additions to NetBeans Web Application Projects |

	Basic Web Application	Spring 2.5 Framework	Struts 1.3.8 Framework	JSF 2.0 Framework
Welcome page	`index.jsp`	`redirect.jsp`, `jsp/index.jsp`	`index.jsp`, `welcomeStruts.jsp`	`welcomeJSF .jsp` or `index .xhtml` (Facelets setting)
Config files	Application server dependent	`web.xml`, `applicationContext .xml`, `dispatcher-servlet.xml`	`web.xml`, `struts-config.xml`, `tiles-defs.xml`, `validation.xml`, `validator-rules .xml`	`web.xml`
Source packages	None	None	`com.myapp.struts`	None
Libraries	See Figure 4-9.			

FIGURE 4-9   Web framework libraries

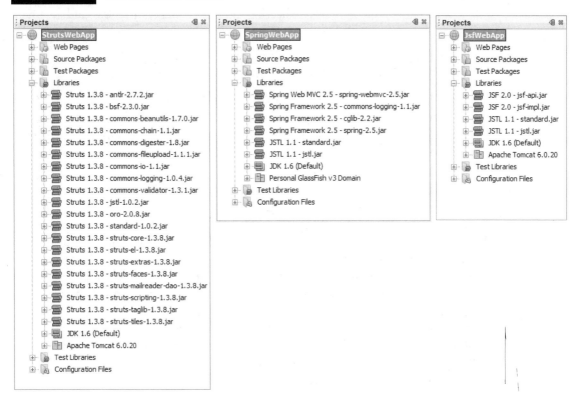

business logic, the view is responsible for displaying the results back to the user, and the controller handles all of the requests from the user and selects the appropriate view to return.

In Struts, JSP implements the view layer, and the `ActionServlet` acts as the controller. Consider reviewing the "Introduction to the Struts Web Framework" tutorial at the following URL: http://netbeans.org/kb/docs/web/quickstart-webapps-struts.html.

on the job

The Forums at JavaRanch include Application Frameworks Forums (www.coderanch.com/forums/c/14/Application-Frameworks) for discussion on Struts, Spring, GWT, Flex, and other frameworks, as well as a forum on various implementations of the JSF specification (http://www.coderanch.com/forums/f-82/JSF).

Wizard-Generated Struts Files   Struts-related file types can be generated by choosing File | New File. Upon selecting the Struts category in the wizard, relative to a context Struts application, the following File Type options are available:

- **Struts Action**   Creates a new Struts action class that extends the `Action`. The default name is `NewStrutsAction`.
- **Struts Action Form Bean**   Creates a new form bean that extends `ActionForm`. The default name is `NewStrutsActionForm`. Completing the wizard generates the desired file type with the appropriate template and data.

Spring

Spring is a web framework maintained by Spring Source (www.springsource.com). Spring contains a web-based MVC framework as one of its components. A primary goal of the Spring Framework is encouraging the development of applications with Plain Old Java Objects (POJOs). Spring implements the Inversion of Control (IoC) principle. The IoC principle is an abstract principle where program flow is not centrally controlled, thus being considered inverted. The Spring IoC Container manages beans that form the backbone of the application. For specific details on the IoC Container, reference the following online documentation: http://static .springsource.org/spring/docs/2.0.x/reference/beans.html. Also, consider reviewing the "Introduction to the Spring Framework" tutorial at the following URL: http:// netbeans.org/kb/docs/web/quickstart-webapps-spring.html.

Wizard-Generated Spring Files   The most apparent and useful feature that comes along with setting up a project with the Spring Framework is the numerous Spring-related file types that can be generated with the New File wizard. Upon selecting the Spring Framework category in the wizard, relative to a context Spring application, the following File Type options are available:

- **Spring XML Configuration File**   Creates a new Spring XML configuration file.
- **Abstract Controller**   Creates a Spring Web MVC controller that extends `AbstractController`. The default name is `NewAbstractController`.
- **Simple Form Controller**   Creates a Spring Web MVC controller that extends `SimpleFormController`. The default name is `NewSimpleFormController`.

Completing the wizard generates the desired file type with the appropriate template and data.

e x a m

If asked about supported (default) frameworks, don't be thrown off on legacy frameworks that were once packaged with NetBeans such as Tapestry *or plugins that can be obtained through the NetBeans Plugin Portal. Spring, Struts, JSF, and Visual Web JSF frameworks are the primary APIs you should be concerned with.*

JavaServer Faces

JavaServer Faces is Java's standard web framework. It was developed through the Java Community Process (http://jcp.org/). JSF's main features include an API for representing user interface components and managing their state, event handling, server-side validation, data conversion, page navigation, internationalization, and accessibility. The framework is based on the specifications detailed in JSR-252 (JavaServer Faces 1.2) and JSR-314 (JavaServer Faces 2.0). NetBeans supports both of these versions. Consider reviewing the "JSF 2.0 Support in NetBeans IDE 6.8" tutorial at the following URL: http://netbeans.org/kb/docs/web/jsf20-support.html.

Wizard-Generated JSF Files   JSF-related file types can be generated with the New File wizard. Upon selecting the JavaServer Faces category in the wizard, relative to a context JSF application, the following File Type options are available:

- **JSF Page**   Creates a new Facelets file or JSP file (JSP fragment). The default name is `newjsf`.
- **JSF Managed Bean**   Creates a new managed bean class. The default name is `NewJSFManagedBean`.
- **JSF Faces Configuration**   Creates a new JSF configuration file. The default name is `faces-config.xml`.
- **JSF Composite Component**   Creates Facelets composite components. The default name is `out.html`.
- **JSF Pages From Entity Classes**   Creates a set of JSF pages, JSF controller and converter classes, JSF utility classes, a default style sheet and JavaScript file, and `faces-config.xml` entries. Also has the capability to create a set of JPA controller classes and related classes.
- **Facelets Template**   Creates a new Facelets template. The default name is `newTemplate.xhtml`.
- **Facelets Template Client**   Creates a new Facelets template client. The default name is `newTemplate.xhtml`.

Completing the wizard generates the desired file type with the appropriate template and data.

EXERCISE 4-2

Making Use of JavaServer Faces Libraries

The following exercise tests your critical thinking skills in regard to JSF libraries.

1. Validate that GlassFish was installed along with the NetBeans installation. You can perform this check in the Services window.

2. Create a new JSF JPA sample application.

3. The JSF libraries (`jsf-api.jar` and `jsf-impl.jar`) are not shown at the base of the libraries folder. Where are they and why are they there? Note that the files would be at the base when a project is set up with Tomcat as the target server.

CERTIFICATION OBJECTIVE

Understanding the Visual Web JSF Framework

Exam Objective 4.2   Distinguish between a visual web application and a web application.

Before you crack your knuckles and get ready to dive into the Visual Web JSF Framework and its supporting Woodstock component set, know this…they are end-of-life. This does not mean that they won't be supported again, but in regard to NetBeans 6.8, they are off the map. Off the map because the JSF world has moved to Facelets so the Visual Web JSF framework represents an outdated way to create web applications. With Facelets, you can use a tool like Dreamweaver to create the pages. Thus, with Facelets, artists can create the user interface and the programmer is left to building the back end.

So when reviewing this chapter, do so only as *read-only*; that is, read the material in the chapter without exercising it in the IDE. If you do feel adventurous, though, make sure you are using NetBeans 6.1 when working with the Visual Web JSF Framework. Don't bother using a different version of the IDE, because you may be dealing with missing or untested components. With all this being said, let's begin.

A basic web application project may have the developer performing GUI-related scripting in source code editors and validating the expected functionality (for example, web pages) through web browsers and other resources at deployment time. However, visual web frameworks are supported by visual web editors, also known as WYSIWYG (What You See Is What You Get) editors. Supported visual web frameworks also have the ability to drag and drop components from palette windows into the WYSIWYG editor or source files (component is converted to text). Additional file wizards and other visually supporting features are also available with these frameworks.

For the scope of the exam, you will primarily need to be concerned with the visual web frameworks and how they relate to the JavaServer Faces technology. Let's briefly talk about JSF again. JavaServer Faces is a Java-based web framework designed to ease the development of user interfaces. Its underlying architecture is a request-driven MVC web framework. JSF has a standard component API for user interface components, a decoupled rendering model, a request-processing life cycle, and tools for managing beans, page navigation, and value binding. Configuration files such as `faces-config.xml` are utilized by the framework. JSF's latest specification is defined in JSR-314 (http://jcp.org/en/jsr/detail?id=314). Many implementations of the JSF specification meet and extend the framework. Popular implementations include Oracle ADF Faces and Apache MyFaces.

Available visual JSF-related frameworks include the RichFaces Palette, Visual Web ICEfaces Framework, and the NetBeans Visual Web JSF (VWJ) Framework. Note that the RichFaces Palette is currently not loaded with features, and Visual Web ICEfaces was not prevalent in the exam version of the IDE. We will briefly discuss the latter two frameworks so you understand the concept of a visual web application. We also take a look at Deployment Descriptor Visual Editors.

- Visual Web Frameworks
- Deployment Descriptor Visual Editors

Visual Web Frameworks

NetBeans primary visual web frameworks include the Visual Web ICEfaces and Visual Web JSF frameworks. We'll discuss both.

Visual Web ICEfaces

Visual Web ICEfaces is an IDE-integrated collection of visual aids and tools that makes working with the ICEfaces components easy and efficient. ICEfaces is an open source AJAX framework that extends the core functionality of the JSF API.

ICEfaces both extends base components and implements new ones. The Visual Web ICEfaces toolset provides various features such as ICEfaces Facelet templates, code completion, and dragging of ICEfaces components from the Palette window into ICEfaces source files (where the component is automatically converted to text at the insertion point).

Installing Visual Web ICEfaces   Visual Web ICEfaces has plugins available at the NetBeans Plugin Portal (http://plugins.netbeans.org/PluginPortal/). The downloaded ZIP file includes both an ICEfaces Project Integration plugin and an ICEfaces Run-Time Libraries plugin. Both are needed and different downloads are available for NetBeans 6.5.1 and 6.7. Selecting the downloaded plugins (.nbm files) for installation results in the screen shown in Figure 4-10.

Using ICEfaces Components   When creating a new project (CTRL-SHIFT-N), select support for ICEfaces in the last step. This enables the Visual Web ICEfaces features. One of the most visible features is ICEfaces support for drag and drop component functionality. ICEfaces components are shown in the Palette window, as represented in Figure 4-11.

FIGURE 4-10

Visual Web
ICEfaces plugins
installation

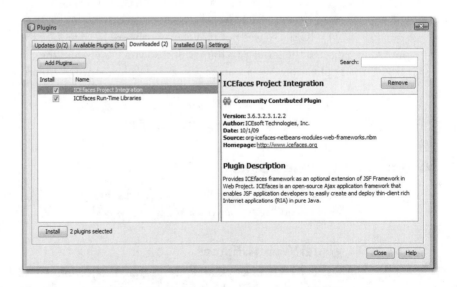

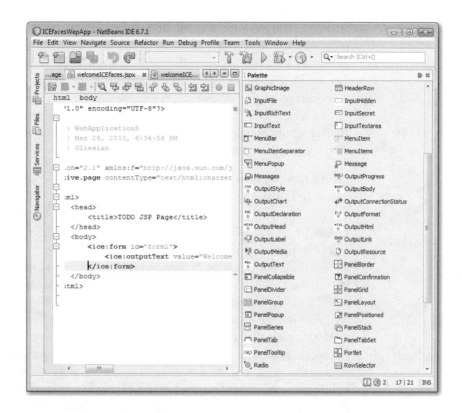

FIGURE 4-11

ICEfaces
components
in the Palette
window

e x a m

ⓦ a t c h   *The deeper the understanding you have of JavaServer Faces, the better you understand the visual frameworks supporting them. That is, learn JSF. Read an online tutorial on JSF or for more in-depth knowledge, consider picking up* **Core JavaServer Faces, Second Edition,** *by David Geary and Cay Horstmann (Prentice Hall PTR, 2007).*

Visual Web JSF Applications

Visual Web JSF is an IDE-integrated collection of visual aids and tools that assist with working with Woodstock components, configuration files, and other JSF elements. Woodstock is an open source framework that makes use of AJAX. Woodstock extends the core functionality of the JSF API by both extending the base components and implementing new ones. Note that Woodstock components are end-of-life. As such, you can find migration matrixes online to move to different frameworks. The Woodstock to Oracle ADF Faces migration matrix can be found at this URL: www.oracle.com/technology/products/adf/adffaces/woodstock2adfMatix .html. The Woodstock to ICEfaces migration matrix can be found at this URL: www.icefaces.org/main/resources/woodstock-icefaces-mapping.iface.

The Visual Web JSF toolset provides various features that integrate with existing NetBeans functionality such as additional file templates, code completion, drag and drop functionality, and a properties editor as part of the Palette window.

Using NetBeans Visual Web JSF   The Visual Web JSF Framework is available by default in NetBeans 6.1 and is available through the Plugin Manager in NetBeans 6.5 and 6.7. The framework is not readily available in NetBeans 6.8. However, NetBeans includes the Visual Web JSF plugins in NetBeans 6.9 Milestone 1 as part of their build process verification efforts. Be aware that these plugins are not currently being tested and are not planned for the final release of 6.9. Figure 4-12 shows the plugins available in NetBeans 6.9 Milestone 1. As mentioned earlier in the chapter, there is no need to actually use the NetBeans Visual Web JSF to prepare for the exam. But if you feel that you must, use the framework in the exam targeted at NetBeans 6.1.

NetBeans Visual Web JSF is well-liked, and users (on previous NetBeans versions) continue to ask for it to be supported. Unfortunately, the NetBeans team does not have an unlimited amount of resources, and they must prioritize their efforts based on current technology needs, important bug fixes, and tasks related to their core vision / "mission statement." Keep in mind, though, that the NetBeans team is flexible and will adjust their focus if the demand is there.

Using Visual Web JSF Components   When creating a new project, select support for Visual Web JavaServer Faces in the last step. This enables the Visual

FIGURE 4-12

Visual Web
JSF Plugins for
NetBeans 6.9
Milestone 1

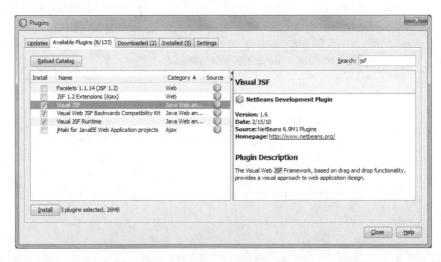

Web JSF features in your new project. Visual Web JSF has support for drag and drop component functionality. The component library in the Visual Web JSF is Woodstock. Woodstock components are shown in the Palette window in Figure 4-13. Components can be dragged from the palette directly into the various editors mapped against the JSP/JSF files. When a JSP-based web page is opened for editing in a Visual Web JSF application, this palette is opened by default, along with the Visual Designer for the file. The file has three editing modes: Visual Designer (Design button), JSP Editor (JSP button), and the Java Source Code Editor (Java button), as shown in the top of the editor in Figure 4-13:

- **Visual Designer** Invoked via the Design button, allows for the visual editing of JSP/JSF components.
- **JSP Editor** Invoked via the JSP button, switches to an editor so that the source code can be edited manually.
- **Java Source Code Editor** Invoked via the Java button, supports editing of the JSP/JSF backing bean through the basic Java source code editor.

FIGURE 4-13   Visual Web JSF components

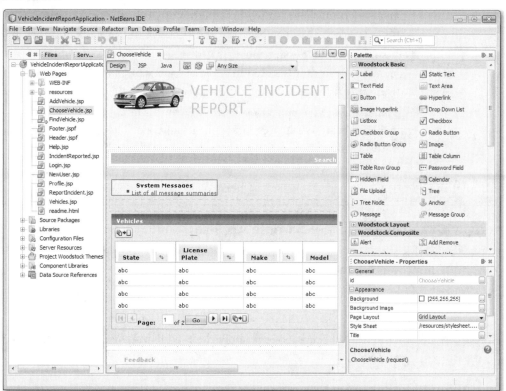

The Properties window (CTRL-SHIFT-7) and the Inspector window also provide configuration and inspection support of the JSP/JSF files.

Component tags vary based on framework and user preference. Traditionally, basic JSF uses an h: for basic components, ICEfaces uses ice:, and Visual Web JSF uses webuijsf:. Respective examples are `<h:outputText value="text"/>`, `<ice:outputText value="text"/>`, *and* `<webuijsf:staticText value="text"/>`.

Wizard-Generated Visual Web JSF Files   Visual JSF-related file types can be generated with the New File wizard. Upon selecting the JavaServer Faces category in the wizard, relative to a context Visual Web JSF application, the following File Type options are available:

- **Visual Web JSF Page**   This template creates a new blank web page. Design the page by dragging components from the palette.
- **Visual Web JSF Page Fragment**   This template creates a new blank web page. Design the page by dragging components from the palette.
- **Visual Web JSF Request Bean**   With this template, you can create a new managed bean that is stored in request scope. The managed bean is added to the `managed-beans.xml` file and is visible in the application outline.
- **Visual Web JSF Session Bean**   With this template, you can create a new managed bean that is stored in session scope. The managed bean is added to the `managed-beans.xml` file and is visible in the application outline.
- **Visual Web JSF Application Bean**   With this template, you can create a new managed bean that is stored in application scope. The managed bean is added to the `managed-beans.xml` file and is visible in the application outline.

EXERCISE 4-3

Working with a Visual Web JSF Sample Application

In this exercise, you add a simple component to an existing JSF page using drag and drop features of the Visual Web JSF Framework.

1. Open the Vehicle Incident Report sample application.
2. Open the `FindVehicles.jsp` file in Design view.
3. Drag the Label component under the Find button, and change the text to **TEST**.

4. Run the application and validate that the web page is displayed with the new label, TEST.

5. Bonus: Add a component type (of your choice) to a page that needs business logic to be added or modified in the backing bean. Make all necessary middle-tier changes. Ensure that the component has all the necessary attributes in place. Run the application and verify the desired functionality.

Deployment Descriptor Visual Editors

Visual editors exist for support of basic deployment descriptors. Deployment descriptors are XML-based files that provide configuration settings for components in web applications, such as Servlets and JavaServer Pages. The Deployment Descriptor Visual Editors are not a feature specific to the Visual Web JSF Framework. It is a core feature installed with the NetBeans Java Bundle. Deployment Descriptor Visual Editors provide form components that allow you to edit and view the content of the descriptors. Since deployment descriptors are XML-based files, the concept of tying in the visual editor to the files is rather simple. When content in the descriptor is modified, the associated elements in the XML file are updated accordingly. Web applications have three primary types of deployment descriptors: `web.xml`, `sun-web.xml`, and `context.xml`. The visual editor for `web.xml` is shown in Figure 4-14 and corresponds to the partial code listing that follows.

- **sun-web.xml**   Deployment descriptor for the GlassFish application server.
- **context.xml**   Deployment descriptor for the Apache Tomcat web server.
- **web.xml**   General deployment description for web applications.

```xml
<?xml version="1.0" encoding="UTF-8"?>
<web-app version="2.5" xmlns="http://java.sun.com/xml/ns/javaee"
xmlns:xsi="http://www.w3.org/2001/XMLSchema-instance" xsi:
schemaLocation="http://java.sun.com/xml/ns/javaee
http://java.sun.com/xml/ns/javaee/web-app_2_5.xsd">
...
  <welcome-file-list>
    <welcome-file>index.html</welcome-file>
    <welcome-file>welcome.faces</welcome-file>
  </welcome-file-list>
  <error-page>
    <error-code>400</error-code>
    <location>/errorpages/BadRequest.faces</location>
  </error-page>
```

```
<error-page>
  <error-code>401</error-code>
  <location>/errorpages/Unauthorized.faces</location>
</error-page>
<error-page>
  <error-code>403</error-code>
  <location>/errorpages/Forbidden.faces</location>
</error-page>
<error-page>
  <error-code>404</error-code>
  <location>/errorpages/NotFound.faces</location>
</error-page>
<error-page>
  <error-code>500</error-code>
  <location>/errorpages/ServerError.faces</location>
</error-page>
...
</web-app>
```

on the **Job**

JSF's `faces-config.xml` configuration file is supported with a specialized editor with two modes: PageFlow and XML. In PageFlow mode, the user can visually configure page navigation with assistance from the Properties window. In XML mode, the user accesses the XML editor with extended popup menu support. The right-click popup menu includes JavaServer Faces | Add Navigation Rule, Add Navigation Case, and Add Managed Bean.

FIGURE 4-14

The `web.xml` Deployment Descriptor Visual Editor

| web.xml | | | | | | | |
| General | Servlets | Filters | **Pages** | References | Security | XML | Welcome Files |

Welcome Files

Welcome Files: `index.html, welcome.faces`   Browse...
Use comma(,) to separate multiple welcome files.

Go To Source(s)

Error Pages

Error Page Location	Error Code	Exception Type
/errorpages/BadRequest.faces	400	
/errorpages/Unauthorized.faces	401	
/errorpages/Forbidden.faces	403	
/errorpages/NotFound.faces	404	
/errorpages/ServerError.faces	500	

Add...   Edit...   Remove

JSP Property Groups   Add JSP Property Group...

CERTIFICATION OBJECTIVE

Working with Server Instances

Exam Objective 1.3   Demonstrate the ability to work with servers in the IDE, such as registering new server instances and stopping and starting servers.

Web applications depend on application or web servers for development and deployment. Application servers implement all of the necessary Java Specification Request (JSR) specifications and thus provide a full Java EE compliant application stack. Web servers need to meet two primary specifications for compliancy, the Servlet specification and the JavaServer Pages specification. Table 4-3 lists current servers that work with the NetBeans 6.8 Milestone 1 IDE. An up-to-date list of supported servers can be found at http://wiki.netbeans.org/servers.

After a plugin is installed, NetBeans provides interfaces that allow for many integration features with the server including general registration of the server

TABLE 4-3   Various NetBeans 6.8–Supported Application and Web Servers

Server Name	Server Type	Supported Server Versions*	Server Plugin Availability
Apache Tomcat	Web	5.0, 5.5, 6.0	Installed
JBoss	Application	4.0.4, 4.0.5, 4.*x*	Installed
Oracle WebLogic	Application	9.*x*, 10.*x*	Installed
Oracle GlassFish Server	Application	1, 2.*x*, 3, 3 Prelude	Installed
Sun Java System Application Server (Sun GlassFish Enterprise Server)	Application	8.2	Installed
Apache Geronimo	Application	2	Plugin Manager
Oracle OC4J	Application	10g	Plugin Manager
Sun Java System Web Server	Web	7.0	Plugin Manager
OW2 JOnAS	Application	4.7.*x*, 4.8.*x*	NetBeans Plugin Portal
Jetty	Web	6, 7, 8	Under development

instance and various server interfacing features such as menu item access to the admin console, debug mode, and server log. We'll touch on these features:

- Registration
- IDE/Server Integration

Registration

To make use of these features, the application server must be registered. NetBeans has server-support plugins installed by default for several servers. Other servers are supported by plugins that must be downloaded from the Plugin Portal or obtained first through the Plugin Manager. You can register server instances for servers that already have their modules/plugins installed. Registration is done by completing the Add Server Instance wizard. The Add Server Instance wizard can be invoked by selecting the Add Server menu item from a right-click of the Servers node in the Services window. The Add Server Instance wizard can also be invoked from the Add Server button in the Servers window, which is opened by selecting Tools | Server. The Add Server Instance wizard includes a three-step process, with the first step being selection of the desired server, as shown in Figure 4-15. Note that the server must be installed on your computer for registration to be successful.

The second step in registering a server is specifying the location of the server. Figure 4-16 shows Step 2, where the edit box accepts the location of the server.

The last step in registering a server is providing the properties related to the server instance. Typical components are included in Step 3 for local instances, the

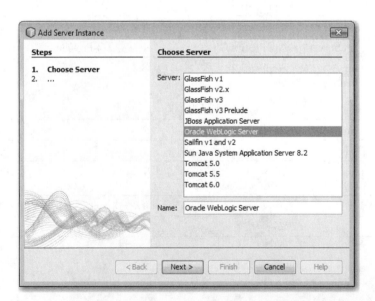

FIGURE 4-15

Add Server
Instance dialog
box: Step 1,
Choose Server

Add Server
Instance dialog
box: Step 2,
Server Location

domain path, the host ID, port number, username, and the password. Step 3 is shown in Figure 4-17.

Add Server
Instance dialog
box: Step
3, Instance
Properties

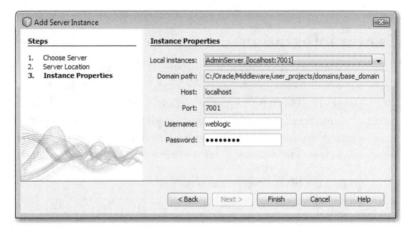

Selecting Finish adds a node for the server under the Servers node in the Services window, as shown in Figure 4-18. In addition, all related server functions would be added to the IDE.

Oracle WebLogic
Server node

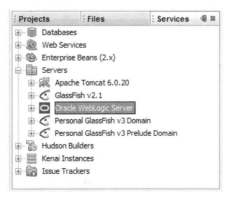

EXERCISE 4-4

Integrating an Application Server with a NetBeans Server Plugin

The following exercise tests your ability to download and install a server, retrieve and install its server-support plugin, and register the server.

1. Install an application server of your choice such as Oracle WebLogic Server from www.oracle.com/technology/products/weblogic.

2. If necessary, get the plugin from the NetBeans Plugin Manager and/or Plugin Portal.

3. Register the plugin with the Add Server Instance wizard.

IDE/Server Integration

Once a server instance is registered, you can use various means to control the application or web server. You can find features throughout the many dialog boxes of the IDE that provide reference or configuration related to the registered server instance. The most direct and apparent interface is the popup menu of the server node in the Services window, which provides for various means to interface with the server. The following items are present in the popup menu:

- **Start**   Starts the server.
- **Start In Debug Mode**   Starts the server in debug mode.
- **Start In Profile Mode**   Starts the server in profile mode.
- **Restart**   Restarts the server.
- **Stop**   Stops the server.
- **Refresh**   Refreshes the status of the server (started or stopped).
- **Remove**   Removes the server instance from the IDE.
- **View Admin Console**   Opens the server's administration console in the target web browser.
- **View Server Log**   Opens the server's log file in a window in the bottom right of the IDE.
- **View Update Center**   Opens the update center, if applicable. The update center for GlassFish is shown in Figure 4-19.
- **Properties**   Opens the Servers dialog box (Tools | Servers). This dialog box allows for viewing and/or modifying server properties.

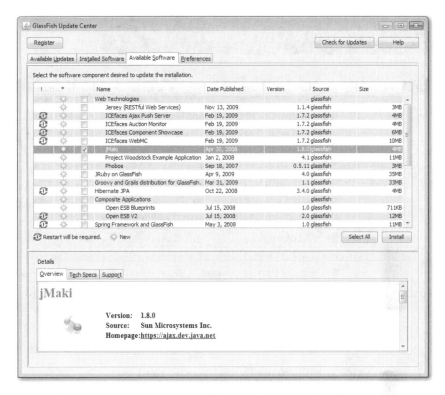

FIGURE 4-19

GlassFish Update Center

The GlassFish Update Center is very useful in keeping the GlassFish application server up to date with desired features. The Scenario & Solution explores usage of various configuration components in the GlassFish Update Center dialog box.

SCENARIO & SOLUTION

You wish to view the technical details of a software component.	Select the Tech Specs tab in the Details pane, where you can find information on technical details, features, and requirements.
You wish to register your version of GlassFish.	Click the Register button at the upper left and complete the registration form.
You wish to know if the software component you want to install warrants an IDE restart.	Look for the Restart Will Be Required icon in the first column, next to the row of your desired software component.
You wish for your update center connection to go over a proxy.	Click the Preferences tab, select the Connect Through A Proxy Server checkbox, and make the necessary updates to the components.

Building and Deploying Web Applications

Exam Objective 5.5   Demonstrate a knowledge of basic tasks related to building and deploying web applications to a server, such as changing the target server and undeploying an application.

Monitoring the output log from an application build process is similar to watching your bowling ball approach the pins. You anticipate a successful build or "strike." However, knocking down all ten pins or performing an error-free build isn't always the case. In both scenarios, the sense of accomplishment or failure is often experienced with an utmost reserved expression. This section covers many of those tasks that bring on suspense, such as when you compile, begin the run process, or invoke your deployed application. For this objective, we examine common development tasks, build settings configurations, and the basic deployment processes. This coverage should prepare you adequately for the building and deploying web applications exam objective.

■ Common Development Tasks
■ Configuring Build Settings
■ Deployment Processes

Common Development Tasks

Common tasks related to web application development include cleaning, building, running, and deploying the application. Table 4-4 details many of the common approaches to invoke these tasks.

Each of these tasks is bound to XML targets (actions) defined in the `build.xml` file, more specifically, the `build-impl.xml` file that `build.xml` imports. Let's take a look at some of the typical targets that are associated with the commands in Table 4-5. Note that project, build, and run configurations can affect the usage of these actions. You can see the Ant targets called by looking in the output window when running a command.

You can expand the `build.xml` file node in the Files window to show all of the targets. You can run individual targets by right-clicking the `build.xml` file node and selecting Run Target | [target_name], as shown in Figure 4-20. Note that targets with a description property set appear in the main list; otherwise, they appear under Other Targets.

TABLE 4-4   Common Development Tasks

Action	Popup Menu	Run Menu	Shortcut	Toolbar Icon
Run the web application	Run	Run Main Project	F6	
Build the web application	Build	Build Main Project	F11	
Clean and build the web application	Clean and Build	Clean and Build Main Project	SHIFT-F11	
Clean the web application	Clean	None	None	None
Deploy the web application	Deploy	None	None	None
Repeat the build/run process	None	Repeat Build/Run	None	None
Stop the build/run process	None	Stop Build/Run	None	None

TABLE 4-5   Typical XML Targets Against Development Processes

XML Target	Clean	Clean and Build	Run	Build	Deploy
init:	X	X	X	X	X
undeploy-clean:	X	X			
deps-clean:	X	X			
check-clean:	X	X			
clean:	X	X			
init:		X			
deps-module-jar:		X	X	X	X
deps-ear-jar:		X	X	X	X
deps-jar:		X	X	X	X
library-inclusion-archive:		X	X	X	X
library-inclusion-in-manifest:		X	X	X	X
compile:		X	X	X	X
compile-jsps:		X	X	X	X
do-dist:		X		X	
dist:		X		X	
run-deploy:			X		X
run-display-browser:			X		
run:			X		

FIGURE 4-20   Runnable `build.xml` targets

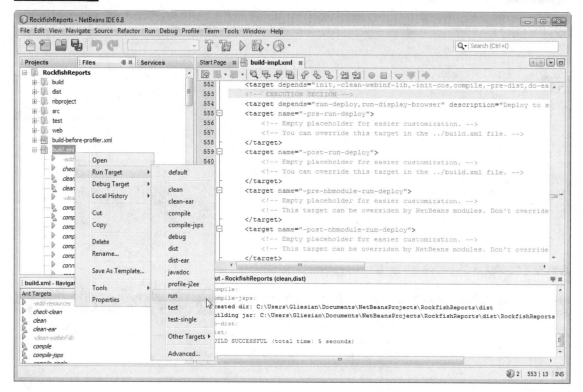

You can also run individual targets directly under the `build.xml` node by right-clicking the target and selecting Run Target. Targets that cannot be run from the Files window appear gray. Runnable targets have an orange triangle next to the blue triangle.

Configuring Build Settings

Build and Run properties are configurable in the Project Properties dialog box. You can get to this dialog box by right-clicking the project name in the Projects or Files window and selecting the Properties menu item.

Three panels provide configuration settings of the build process. These panels are associated with the Build node and are associated with subnodes labeled Compiling, Packaging, and Documenting. We'll take a look at each panel.

Compiling Panel for Build Processes

The Compiling panel in the Project Properties dialog box, as shown in Figure 4-21, configures compilation settings. The panel is displayed after selecting the Compiling node under the Build node. The following items are configurable in the panel:

- **Generate Debugging Info**   Generates debugging information during compilation. Reference the session establishment section in Chapter 9 for more details on this setting.
- **Report Uses Of Deprecated APIs**   Reports use of deprecated APIs during compilation.
- **Additional Compiler Options**   Additional compiler options to be specified in a space-separated list.
- **Test Compile All JSP Files During Builds**   Compiles JavaServer Pages files during the build process.

FIGURE 4-21

Project Properties: Build/Compiling

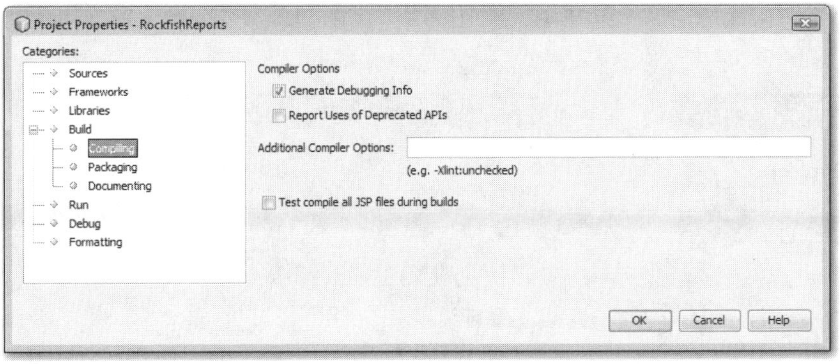

Packaging Panel for Build Processes

The Packaging panel in the Project Properties dialog box, as shown in Figure 4-22, configures settings related to packaging processes. The panel is displayed after selecting the Packaging node under the Build node. The following items are configurable in the panel:

- **WAR File**   The name of the WAR file. It should end with `.war`.
- **Exclude From WAR File**   Files to be excluded from the WAR file. Double asterisks filter the directories recursively (for example, `**/*.java`).
- **Compress WAR File**   Compresses the WAR file.
- **WAR Content**   Supports adding projects, libraries, and files/folders to the WAR file as well as their individual removal.

Documenting Panel for Build Processes

The Documenting panel in the Project Properties dialog box, as shown in Figure 4-23, configures settings related to Javadoc documentation. The panel is displayed after selecting the Documenting node under the Build node. The panel provides for the addition of Javadoc options through visual components as represented in Table 4-6. For clarity, Javadoc is a Java API documentation generator. It's invoked via the `javadoc` command.

FIGURE 4-22

Project
Properties:
Build/Packaging

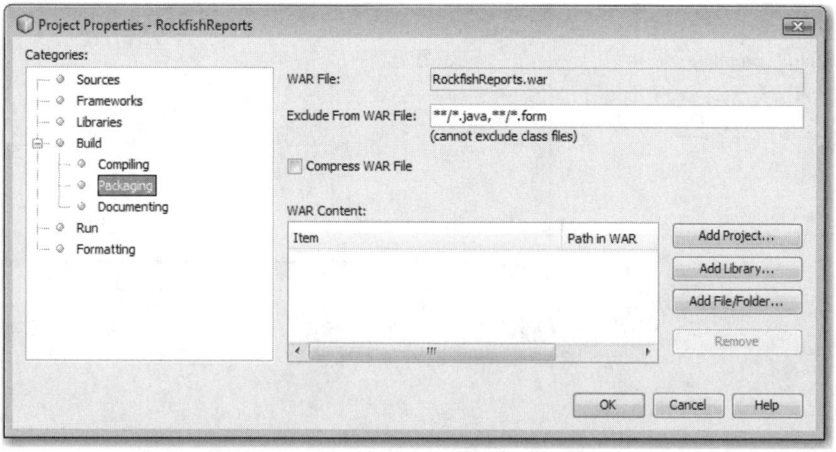

FIGURE 4-23

Project
Properties:
Build/Documenting

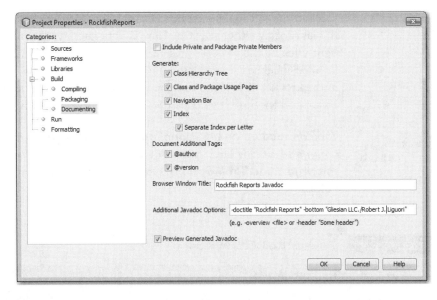

TABLE 4-6   Javadoc Settings

Panel Component	javadoc Option	Description
Include Private And Package Private Members checkbox	`-private`	Generates documentation for all classes and members.
Generate Class Hierarchy Tree checkbox	`Default. -notree` (to exclude)	Includes the class/interface hierarchy pages.
Generate Class And Package Usage Pages checkbox		
Generate Navigation Bar checkbox	`Default. -nonavbar` (to exclude)	Includes the navigation bar.
Generate Index checkbox	`Default -noindex` (to exclude)	Includes the index.
Generate Index, Separate Index Per Letter checkbox	`-splitindex`, (`-noindex` cannot also be specified)	Includes the index and splits it alphabetically.
Document Additional Tags: @author checkbox	`-author`	Includes the @author text in applicable docs.
Document Additional Tags: @version checkbox	`-version`	Includes the @version text in applicable docs.
Browser Window Title edit box	`-windowtitle "TITLE"`	Displays the specified string in the browser window title bar.
Additional Javadoc Options edit box	Reference online Javadoc documentation	Provides for additional or replacement options. These options take precedence over component settings.

After the settings are applied via selection of the OK button, you can generate the Javadoc by either selecting Run | Generate Javadoc from the main menu or right-clicking the project and selecting Generate Javadoc. If the Preview Generated Javadoc checkbox was selected in the Project Properties window, the Javadoc opens in the browser after it has been generated, as shown in Figure 4-24. You may call the Javadoc Index Search with SHFIT-F1 or context search with ALT-F1.

You can read up on additional options (that is, flags) for the Javadoc command, at this URL: http://java.sun.com/javase/6/docs/technotes/tools/ solaris/javadoc.html#options. Note that this documentation is specific to Solaris.

FIGURE 4-24 Generated Javadoc documentation

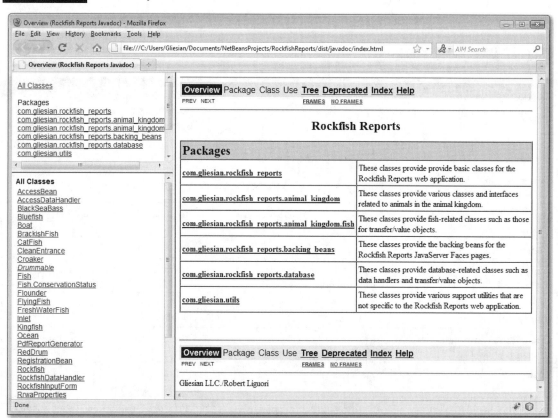

Run Panel for Run Processes

The Run panel in the Project Properties dialog box, as shown in Figure 4-25, configures settings related to Run processes. The following items are configurable in the panel:

- **Server**   The target server of the web application
- **Java EE Version**   The Java Enterprise Edition version (for example, J2EE 1.4, Java EE 5, Java EE 6)
- **Context Path**   The URL namespace of an application
- **Display Browser On Run**   Determines if a browser is displayed at runtime
- **Relative URL**   The URL relative to the context path
- **Deploy On Save**   Determines if the file changes are redeployed upon being saved
- **VM Options**   Virtual machine options used for running main classes and unit tests

Deployment Processes

The NetBeans IDE provides support for deploying and undeploying web applications. We'll examine the processes for both.

Deploying Web Applications

Deployment to Apache Tomcat and GlassFish application servers is automatic, as the context WAR file is placed in the appropriate autodeploy directly at deployment time (for example, right-click the project node and select Deploy). For other application

FIGURE 4-25

Project
Properties: Run

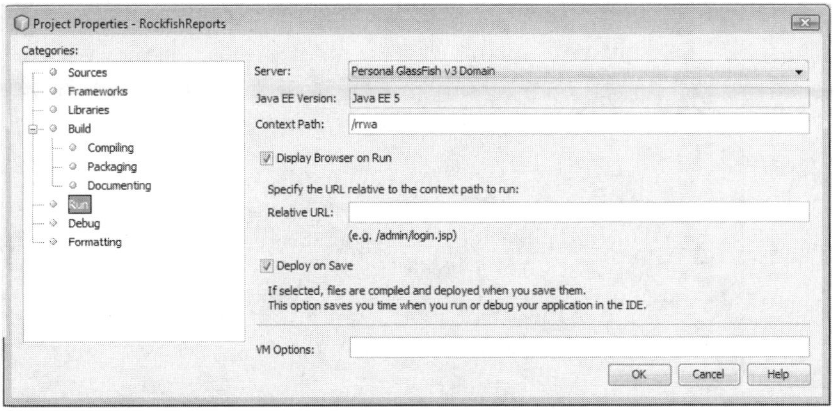

servers that are hosted outside of the IDE or that lack the appropriate integration support, the WAR file needs to be manually deployed. Practically all application servers include a console management interface that is accessible through a web browser. The application consoles have the ability to deploy local or remote WAR files. Figure 4-26 shows the Application Server console for GlassFish. As you can see in the figure, there is support for deploying other types of applications in addition to WAR files, such as Enterprise Applications, Custom MBeans, and Java Business Integration (JBI) Service Assemblies.

on the
job

One of the first things you should do when working with an application server is to explore the web console and understand its deployment processes. You'll also need to investigate application-specific configuration files, such as those used in JBoss and Glassfish.

FIGURE 4-26   GlassFish Application Server console

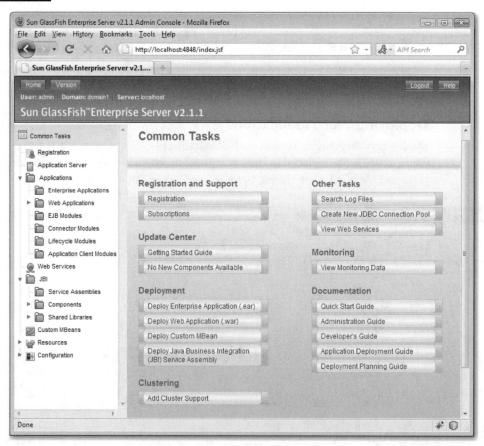

Undeploying Web Applications

Undeploying applications is easy. All application web consoles provide an easy means to undeploy applications, as shown in Figure 4-27. It's often as simple as selecting the application you want undeployed and clicking an Undeploy button. Note that this process removes the WAR file from the autodeploy directory. A safer way to keep the application but make it unavailable is to disable it, which can also be done with a button in the web console.

NetBeans' goal is to make your life easy. If you can keep from leaving the IDE to perform a task, you'll be able to save some time and a little bit of energy. So, for integrated/registered application servers such as GlassFish, there is undeployment support as well. And it's really easy; you just need to know where to look. To undeploy a web application with the IDE, go to the Services window, open the node of your application server, find the web application in the subsequent subnodes, and right-click it. A popup menu opens with an Undeploy menu item, as shown in Figure 4-28. Click and the app is gone.

FIGURE 4-27   Undeployment via GlassFish Application Server console

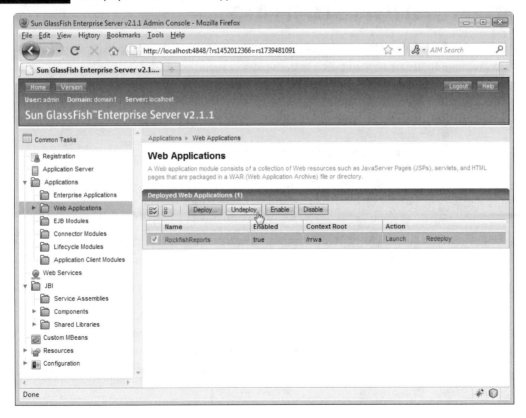

FIGURE 4-28

Undeployment
via the Services
window

CERTIFICATION SUMMARY

This chapter focused on objectives related to Java EE web applications. There are actually six related objectives, but the one on the HTTP server-side monitor is covered in a separate chapter. The remaining five objectives deal with creating web apps from existing sources, understanding NetBeans-available web frameworks, using the visual web frameworks, building/deploying web applications, and working with server instances.

From a high level, we learned the following:

■ Creating a web application from existing sources is done through the New Project wizard. The wizard provides a four-step process that results in a new application with NetBeans-specific folders, properties, and build files.

■ NetBeans-available web frameworks are added to projects through the New Project wizard. Frameworks include JSF, Spring, and Struts as well as Visual Web JSF or Visual Web ICEfaces if their modules are installed. Hibernate also can be added for convenience.

■ The Visual Web JSF Framework adds visual features such as a visual web editor, a visual page navigation editor, palette support of Woodstock components, and more. The Visual Web JSF Framework is not supported in recent versions of NetBeans. Woodstock is a set of JSF components that has

reached end-of-life in favor of other framework components such as those of
Oracle ADF and ICEfaces.

■ Registering server instances for installed servers adds various features that
support the target server, including console invocation and the binding
of server commands to NetBeans menu items (that is, start and stop
commands).

After completing this chapter, you will be more familiar with web frameworks and
will have gained the necessary experience to score well on web framework–related
questions on the exam.

✓ # TWO-MINUTE DRILL

Creating Web Applications from Existing Sources

❑ The New Project wizard (CTRL-SHIFT-N) and choosing Web Application with Existing Sources under the Java Web category creates new web applications from existing sources.

❑ Creating a web application from existing sources is a four-step process with settings made in the following dialog boxes: Choose Project, Name And Location, Server And Settings, Existing Sources And Libraries.

❑ The Choose Project dialog/step allows for the selection of the project type (for example, Web Application With Existing Sources) from the Java Web category.

❑ The Name And Location dialog/step configures the project's location, name, and folder location. Establishing dedicated folders and the main project setting is also done in this step.

❑ The Server And Settings dialog/step configures the target server, Java EE version, and context path. Adding the project to open enterprise projects and enabling dedicated folders is also done in this step.

❑ The Existing Sources And Libraries dialog/step configures the location of the existing web page folders, WEB-INF content, libraries, source, and test packages.

Adding and Using NetBeans-Available Web Frameworks

❑ Readily available NetBeans IDE web frameworks include Spring, Struts, and JavaServer Faces.

❑ Web framework libraries, directories, and configuration files are added to a new project when the desired framework is selected in the New Projects wizard.

❑ Spring is a web framework with a myriad of features supporting the middle tier. Spring contains a web-based MVC framework.

❑ Struts is a web-based MVC framework primarily supporting the presentation tier.

❑ JavaServer Faces is a web framework with various features including an API for representing user interface components and managing their state.

Understanding the Visual Web JSF Framework

❑ The visual web framework may provide file templates, code completion, and drag and drop support.

❑ The NetBeans Visual Web JSF Framework is available in NetBeans 6.1 directly and in 6.5 and 6.7 through the Plugin Manager.

❑ The Visual Web JSF Framework includes a PageFlow Editor for the `faces-config.xml` configuration file.

❑ The Visual Web JSF Framework includes a Visual Designer for visually editing web files.

❑ The Visual Web JSF Framework includes a JSP Editor for visually editing JavaServer Pages files.

❑ The Visual Web JSF Framework includes a component properties editor as part of the Palette window.

❑ Woodstock is a JSF component library as part of the Visual Web JSF Framework. Woodstock is end-of-life. Users are encouraged to migrate to similar frameworks/component-sets such as Oracle ADF Faces or ICEfaces.

❑ Various frameworks implement the JSF specification, both meeting and extending the API (that is, Oracle ADF Faces, RichFaces, ICEfaces, and Apache MyFaces).

❑ ICEfaces is an open source AJAX framework that extends the JSF API.

❑ ICEfaces is available through the online Plugin Portal for NetBeans 6.5.1 and 6.7. The module that includes visual web support can be considered the Visual Web ICEfaces framework.

❑ The RichFaces Palette is a visual tool that provides drag and drop assistance to RichFaces components.

Working with Server Instances

❑ The Add Server Instance wizard registers servers that are installed locally on the computer. It is a three-step process: Choose Server, Server Location, and Instance Properties.

❑ Selecting Tools | Servers opens the Properties dialog box for all of the registered servers.

❑ Selecting Tools | Servers followed by clicking the Add Server button opens the Add Server Instance wizard.

❏ Right-clicking the Servers node in the Services window and selecting Add Server opens the Add Server Instance wizard.

❏ Right-clicking a registered server opens a dialog box with the following menu items: Start, Start In Debug Mode, Start In Profile Mode, Restart, Stop, Refresh, Remove, View Admin Console, View Server Log, View Update Center, and Properties.

Building and Deploying Web Applications

❏ The NetBeans IDE provides support for cleaning, building, running, and deploying web applications.

❏ The web application build processes are tied to Ant's `build.xml` file.

❏ The `build.xml` file points to the `build-impl.xml` file.

❏ The `build.xml` file can be opened and examined in the Files window.

❏ Individual targets of the build file can be executed.

❏ The Project Properties dialog box provides configuration means for compiling, packaging, and documenting.

❏ The Project Properties dialog box provides configuration means for a web application's run processes.

❏ Application servers have web consoles that can deploy and undeploy web applications.

❏ Web applications can be deployed in the Projects window relative to the popup menu Deploy commands of the project node.

❏ Web applications can be undeployed in the Services window relative to the popup menu's Undeploy command for each web application node.

SELF TEST

The following questions will help you measure your understanding of the material presented in this chapter. Read all the choices carefully because there might be more than one correct answer. Choose all correct answers for each question.

Creating Web Applications from Existing Sources

1. Within the New Web Project With Existing Sources wizard, which dialog page has the Set As Main Project checkbox?

   A. 1. Choose Project

   B. 2. Name And Location

   C. 3. Server And Settings

   D. 4. Existing Sources And Libraries

   E. None of the above

2. True or False? The settings in Step 2 (Name And Location) of the New Web Project With Existing Sources wizard are the same as the settings in New Java Project With Existing Sources wizard.

   A. True

   B. False

Adding and Using NetBeans-Available Web Frameworks

3. In the last step of the New Project wizard for creating web applications, which framework is a persistence framework and hence not a web framework?

   A. Java ServerFaces

   B. Struts

   C. Spring

   D. Hibernate

4. Which web framework makes use of the following three files as part of its framework: `tiles-defs.xml`, `validation.xml`, `validator-rules.xml`?

   A. Spring

   B. Struts

   C. Tapestry

   D. JavaServer Faces

Understanding the Visual Web JSF Framework

5. Which item is not a Woodstock basic component? Note that these components were indirectly referenced by links to the ADF Faces and ICEfaces migration matrix URLs.

A. Text Area

B. Hyperlink

C. Dial

D. Tree

6. What tag pair corresponds to a table column in the Visual Web JSF Framework?

A. `<webuijsf:tablecolumn></webuijsf:tablecolumn>`

B. `<webui:tablecolumn></webui:tablecolumn>`

C. `<ice:tablecolumn></ice:tablecolumn>`

D. `<ice:column></ice:column>`

7. Considering the following Illustration, what JSF `configuration` file is being displayed in the PageFlow Editor?

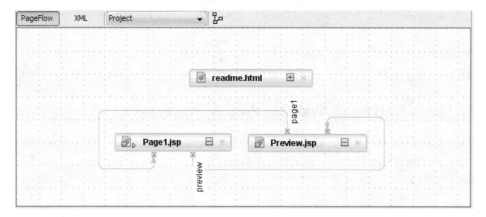

A. `sun-web.xml`

B. `faces-config.xml`

C. `web.xml`

D. `web-config.xml`

Working with Server Instances

8. How is the GlassFish Update Center opened?

   A. In the Services window, right-click the Servers node, and select the View Update Center menu item.

   B. In the Services window, expand the Servers node, right-click the GlassFish node, and select the View Update Center menu item.

   C. In the Servers window, expand the Services node, right-click the GlassFish node, and select the View Update Center menu item.

   D. There is no GlassFish Update Center.

9. Server support plugins are available/installed for which application and/or web servers by default? That is, the plugin does not need to be obtained through the Plugin Manager or Plugin Portal.

   A. Apache Tomcat

   B. Sun GlassFish

   C. Oracle OC4J

   D. OW2 JOnAS

Building and Deploying Web Applications

10. What format is used in the Exclude From WAR File edit box found in the Build/Packaging node of the Project Properties dialog box to exclude all Java source files for the target WAR file?

    A. `*.java`

    B. `*/**.java`

    C. `*all*.java`

    D. `**/*.java`

11. When running a web application, how can you ensure that the web browser is displayed when an application is deployed?

    A. Select the Display Browser On Run checkbox associated with the Run node in the Project Properties dialog box.

    B. Select the Display Browser On Run checkbox associated with the Build/Packaging node in the Project Properties dialog box.

    C. Ensure the web browser is open on your desktop, because the application will only run in the browser if it's already open.

    D. Click the Display Browser On Run icon in the Run toolbar.

SELF TEST ANSWERS

Creating Web Applications from Existing Sources

1. Within the New Web Project With Existing Sources wizard, which dialog page has the Set As Main Project checkbox?
   A. 1. Choose Project
   B. 2. Name And Location
   C. 3. Server And Settings
   D. 4. Existing Sources And Libraries
   E. None of the above

   ☑ **B.** The Name And Location dialog page (that is, the second step) has the Set As Main Project checkbox available.

   ☒ **A, C,** and **D** are incorrect. **A** is incorrect because the Set As Main Project checkbox is not on the Choose Project dialog page. **C** is incorrect because the Set As Main Project checkbox is not on the Server And Settings dialog page. **D** is incorrect because the Set As Main Project checkbox is not on the Existing Sources And Libraries dialog page. **E** is incorrect because "None of the above" is not correct.

2. True or False? The settings in Step 2 (Name And Location) of the New Web Project With Existing Sources wizard are the same as the settings in New Java Project With Existing Sources wizard.
   A. True
   B. False

   ☑ **False.** The settings in Step 2 (Name And Location) of the New Web Project With Existing Sources and Step 2 (Name And Location) of the New Java Project With Existing Sources wizards are not the same. The New Java Project With Existing Sources wizard has a Build Script Name component that the New Java Project With Existing Sources wizard does not have.

Adding and Using NetBeans-Available Web Frameworks

3. In the last step of the New Project wizard for creating web applications, which framework is a persistence framework and hence not a web framework?
   A. Java ServerFaces
   B. Struts

C. Spring

D. Hibernate

☑ **D.** The Hibernate (persistence) framework is selectable to be set up in the New Project wizard when creating web applications.

☒ **A, B,** and **C** are incorrect. **A** is incorrect because JavaServer Faces is a web framework. **B** is incorrect because Struts is a web framework. **C** is incorrect because Spring is a web framework.

4. Which web framework makes use of the following three files as part of its framework: `tiles-defs.xml`, `validation.xml`, `validator-rules.xml`?

A. Spring

B. Struts

C. Tapestry

D. JavaServer Faces

☑ **B.** The Struts web framework makes use of the following files, amongst others: `tiles-defs.xml`, `validation.xml`, `validator-rules.xml`.

☒ **A, C,** and **D are** incorrect. **A** is incorrect because Spring does not make use of the following files as part of its core architecture: `tiles-defs.xml`, `validation.xml`, `validator-rules.xml`. **C** is incorrect because Tapestry does not make use of the following files as part of its core architecture: `tiles-defs.xml`, `validation.xml`, `validator-rules.xml`. **D** is incorrect because JavaServer Faces does not make use of the following files as part of its core architecture: `tiles-defs.xml`, `validation.xml`, `validator-rules.xml`.

Understanding the Visual Web JSF Framework

5. Which item is not a Woodstock basic component? Note that these components were indirectly referenced by links to the ADF Faces and ICEfaces migration matrix URLs.

A. Text Area

B. Hyperlink

C. Dial

D. Tree

☑ **C.** Dial is not a Woodstock basic component.

☒ **A, B,** and **D** are incorrect. **A** is incorrect because Text Area is a Woodstock basic component. **B** is incorrect because Hyperlink is a Woodstock basic component. **D** is incorrect because Tree is a Woodstock basic component.

6. What tag pair corresponds to a table column in the Visual Web JSF Framework?

   A. `<webuijsf:tablecolumn></webuijsf:tablecolumn>`

   B. `<webui:tablecolumn></webui:tablecolumn>`

   C. `<ice:tablecolumn></ice:tablecolumn>`

   D. `<ice:column></ice:column>`

   ☑ **A.** `<webuijsf:tablecolumn></webuijsf:tablecolumn>` are the tags used for table columns in the Visual Web JSF Framework.

   ☒ **B, C,** and **D** are incorrect. **B** is incorrect because the `webui:tablecolumn` tags are invalid. **C** is incorrect because the `ice:table` column tags are invalid. **D** is incorrect because `ice:column` is the ICEfaces equivalent of `webuijsf:tablecolumn`.

7. Considering the following Illustration, what JSF `configuration` file is being displayed in the PageFlow Editor?

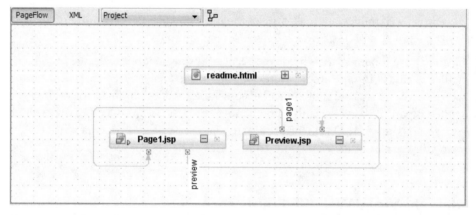

   A. `sun-web.xml`

   B. `faces-config.xml`

   C. `web.xml`

   D. `web-config.xml`

   ☑ **B.** The `faces-config.xml` file is shown with the PageFlow Editor.

   ☒ **A, C,** and **D** are incorrect. **A** is incorrect because the `sun-web.xml` file is not displayed in the illustration. **C** is incorrect because the `web.xml` file is not displayed in the illustration. **D** is incorrect because the `web-config.xml` file is not displayed in the illustration, nor is it a valid file.

Working with Server Instances

8. How is the GlassFish Update Center opened?

   A. In the Services window, right-click the Servers node, and select the View Update Center menu item.

   B. In the Services window, expand the Servers node, right-click the GlassFish node, and select the View Update Center menu item.

   C. In the Servers window, expand the Services node, right-click the GlassFish node, and select the View Update Center menu item.

   D. There is no GlassFish Update Center.

   ☑ **B.** In the Services window, expand the Servers node, right-click the GlassFish node, and select the View Update Center menu item to invoke the GlassFish Update Center.

   ☒ **A, C,** and **D** are incorrect. **A** is incorrect because there is no View Update Center menu item directly associated with the Servers node. You must right-click the application server's node to get this menu item. **C** is incorrect because there is no Servers window or Services node. There's a Services window and a Servers node. **D** is incorrect because a GlassFish Update Center does exist.

9. Server support plugins are available/installed for which application and/or web servers by default? That is, the plugin does not need to be obtained through the Plugin Manager or Plugin Portal.

   A. Apache Tomcat

   B. Sun GlassFish

   C. Oracle OC4J

   D. OW2 JOnAS

   ☑ **A** and **B.** Server support plugins are available for Apache Tomcat web server and Sun GlassFish application server by default.

   ☒ **C** and **D** are incorrect. **C** is incorrect because Oracle OC4J is available through the Plugin Manager and not by default. **D** is incorrect because OW2 JOnAS is available through the Plugin Portal and not by default.

Building and Deploying Web Applications

10. What format is used in the Exclude From WAR File edit box found in the Build/Packaging node of the Project Properties dialog box to exclude all Java source files for the target WAR file?

    A. `*.java`

    B. `*/**.java`

    C. `*all*.java`

    D. `**/*.java`

> ☑ **D.** The `**/*.java` format is used in the Exclude From WAR File edit box found in the Build/Packaging node of the Project Properties dialog box to exclude all Java source files for the target WAR file.
>
> ☒ **A, B,** and **C** are incorrect. **A** is incorrect because `*.java` does not ensure exclusion of all Java source files from the target WAR file. **B** is incorrect because `*/**.java` does not ensure exclusion of all Java source files from the target WAR file. **C** is incorrect because `*all*.java` does not ensure exclusion of all Java source files from the target WAR file.

11. When running a web application, how can you ensure that the web browser is displayed when an application is deployed?

    A. Select the Display Browser On Run checkbox associated with the Run node in the Project Properties dialog box.

    B. Select the Display Browser On Run checkbox associated with the Build/Packaging node in the Project Properties dialog box.

    C. Ensure the web browser is open on your desktop, because the application will only run in the browser if it's already open.

    D. Click the Display Browser On Run icon in the Run toolbar.

> ☑ **A.** When running a web application, you can ensure that the web browser is displayed at runtime by selecting the Display Browser On Run checkbox associated with the Run node in the Project Properties dialog box.
>
> ☒ **B, C,** and **D** are incorrect. **B** is incorrect because there is no Display Browser On Run checkbox associated with the Build/Packaging node in the Project Properties dialog box. **C** is incorrect because the web browser does not need to be currently open in order for the browser to be displayed at runtime. **D** is incorrect because there is no Display Browser On Run icon.

5

Database Connectivity

CERTIFICATION OBJECTIVES

- Working with Databases in the IDE

✓ Two-Minute Drill

Q&A Self Test

Relational databases are major components of many business systems. To maintain the databases, database vendors provide tools to assist in the design, development, implementation, and administration of databases within their business systems. Many of these tools provide visual support, as does MySQL Workbench in the designing of tables. For database administrators, these tools are often a must. However, for application developers, a lighter tool base usually suffices. The NetBeans Database Explorer supplies such primary support. Through the Database Explorer, users can perform various basic tasks such as registering JDBC (Java Database Connectivity) database drivers, connecting to databases, managing tables and views, performing SQL commands, and saving schemas.

The exam primarily focuses on using the Database Explorer, SQL Editor, and associated functionality. Therefore, this chapter will prepare you to use these tools. As a developer, you will find that with the use of these resources, you may not need to use administrative consoles outside of the IDE for database-related activities. Once you have completed this chapter, you will have all the knowledge needed to score well on questions related to working with the Database Explorer.

CERTIFICATION OBJECTIVE

Working with Databases in the IDE

Exam Objective 1.5   Demonstrate knowledge of working with databases in the IDE, including registering new database connections and tables running SQL scripts.

In the Services window of the IDE is a Databases node. This node and all its subnodes are considered the Database Explorer, as shown in Figure 5-1. The Services window also contains Web Services, Servers, Hudson Builders, Kenai Instances, and Issue Trackers nodes, but they do not directly relate to the database module and are not covered in this chapter. Actually, the only other node covered on the exam is the Servers tab, and it is covered in Chapter 4.

FIGURE 5-1

Services window

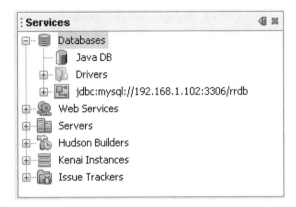

exam
ⓦatch
The java.net hosted development site and community will be subsuming the Kenai project because they are similar in nature. Also note that the integration of kenai.com with NetBeans was initially done in version 6.7 of the IDE, so Kenai will not be referenced on the exam.

The Database Explorer is the primary module of the NetBeans IDE that provides support for working with databases. Figure 5-2 provides a quick look at the different databases that will interface with the Database Explorer throughout this chapter.

The IDE provides other means for database support as well, such as capturing database schemas in XML format through the New File wizard (Persistence | Database Schema). You can view captured schemas in the Projects window. To meet the objective of working with databases in the IDE, the Database Explorer and SQL Editor of the IDE are covered in detail throughout this chapter. As such, we will look at the following IDE elements:

- Database Explorer
- Database Support Components

FIGURE 5-2   Database Explorer databases used in this chapter

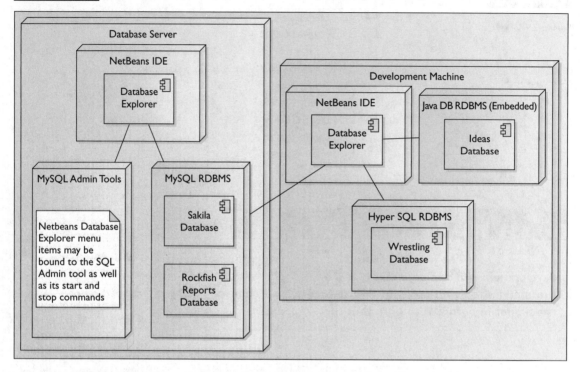

Database Explorer

The Database Explorer allows you to interface with databases through the IDE. This section discusses the various means of establishing database connections with the Database Explorer including registering JDBC drivers, connecting to databases, and viewing current connections. The Database Explorer also interfaces closely with database support components such as the SQL Editor and Table Viewer. These items are detailed in the next section:

- JDBC Driver Registrations
- JDBC-Supported Database Connections
- Java DB Connections

JDBC Driver Registrations

Registering JDBC drivers allows the IDE to connect to databases from within the IDE. NetBeans 6.8 comes with a few drivers already registered: Java DB (Embedded), Java DB (Network), JDBC-ODBC (Open Database Connectivity) bridge, MySQL (Connector/J driver), and PostgreSQL. These registered drivers are listed under the Drivers node in the Database Explorer. The Drivers node is the place for adding, removing, and configuring JDBC drivers.

Creating a Driver Registration   If you need a driver that is not registered, you can perform the registration by right-clicking the Drivers node and selecting New Drivers. A New JDBC Driver window (see Figure 5-3) opens. Fill in the Driver File(s), Driver Class, and Name boxes. An example of registering the Mckoi SQL JDBC database driver is shown in Figure 5-3. You can obtain the driver from the Mckoi website: www.mckoi.com/.

FIGURE 5-3

Registering the
Mckoi JDBC
driver

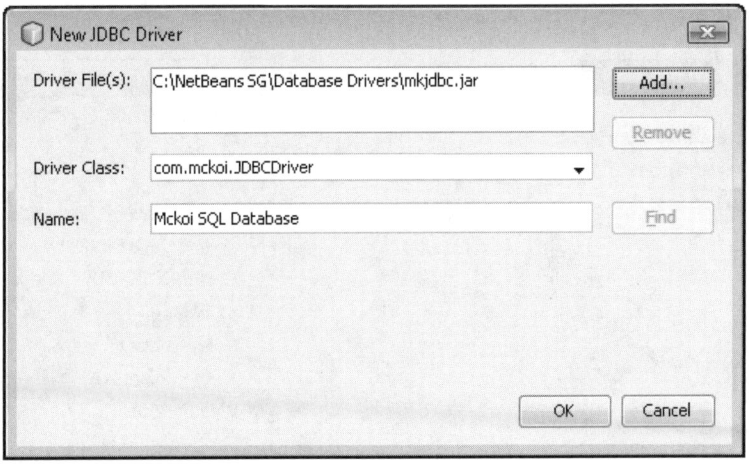

Registering a driver simply creates a template to be used later when establishing a connection. The registry is saved in an XML file in `.netbeans/[version]/config/Databases/JDBCDrivers`. The `com_mckoi_JDBCDriver.xml` file is shown here:

```
<?xml version='1.0'?>
<!DOCTYPE driver PUBLIC '-//NetBeans//DTD JDBC Driver 1.1//EN'
'http://www.netbeans.org/dtds/jdbc-driver-1_1.dtd'>
<driver>
 <name value='Mckoi SQL Database'/>
 <display-name value='Mckoi SQL Database'/>
 <class value='com.mckoi.JDBCDriver'/>
 <urls>
  <url value='file:/C:/NetBeans%20SG/Database%20Drivers/mkjdbc.jar'/>
 </urls>
</driver>
```

Removing a Driver Registration   Removing driver registrations is easy; just right-click the registered driver and select Delete, as shown in Figure 5-4.

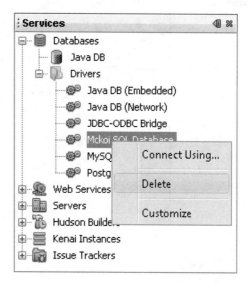

FIGURE 5-4

Deleting driver registrations

Configuring a Driver Registration   Driver registration settings can be configured by right-clicking the driver name and selecting the Customize menu item. The same New JDBC Driver window opens as when you created the initial registration. Make the desired changes and select OK.

Registering a JDBC Driver

In this exercise, you register a JDBC driver with the IDE. The HyperSQL database driver is used with this exercise, but you can use a different driver and database. Table 2 in the bonus appendix entitled NetBeans Database Integration on the CD can help you select a different database driver if desired.

1. Retrieve the `hsqldb.jar` file from the HyperSQL download site: http://sourceforge.net/projects/hsqldb/files/. Note: The file is currently included in the HyperSQL Database Engine project ZIP file (that is, `hsqldb-[version].zip`).

2. In the Database Explorer, select Drivers | New Driver. The New JDBC Driver dialog box appears.

3. Add the driver file you downloaded to the Driver File(s) box. For the HyperSQL database, find this file at `hsqldb\lib\hsqldb.jar`.

4. Select the driver's entry class from the Driver Class drop-down list. It should be `org.hsqldb.jdbcDriver`.

5. Enter **HSQLDB** for the driver's name and click OK.

6. Verify that the HSQLDB driver is located in the driver list under the Drivers node.

7. Bonus: Install the HyperSQL database, create a wrestling-themed database, and connect to it.

INSIDE THE EXAM

Deep Database Integration

If you create a Java Desktop Application, you can select a Database Application that creates a basic CRUD (Create, Read, Update, Delete) form (Swing) for editing a database. Additional screens can be added for other tables with Master/Detail Sample Form. This database functionality is much more than just a light viewer for running queries or changing table structures. NetBeans can introspect database tables for both web and Swing forms, and so on. The database integration runs deep in the IDE and adds significant value to development.

For instance, if you are creating a new class, several templates leverage this integration:

- **Swing GUI Forms** Master/Detail Sample Form
- **Persistence** Entity Class, Entity Class from Database, JPA Controller Classes from Entity Classes, Persistence Unit, Database Schema
- **Hibernate** Hibernate Configuration wizard, Hibernate Mapping wizard, Hibernate Mapping Files and POJOs from Database, `HibernateUtil .java`

JDBC-Supported Database Connections

The Database Explorer can connect to JDBC-supported databases in the IDE when the appropriate database driver is registered. You first need to create a database connection; then you can work with that connection to perform various tasks.

Creating a Database Connection The New Database Connection dialog box lets you create a new connection to a database. You can invoke this dialog box either by right-clicking the Databases node and selecting New Connection, or by right-clicking a driver registration node under the Drivers node and selecting Connect Using. The JDBC URL for different drivers may have various formats. Because the JDBC URL format is well defined for Java DB, PostgreSQL, and MySQL drivers, the wizard provides a Data Input Mode of Field Entry for establishing these connections, as shown in Figure 5-5. Note that when the Show JDBC URL checkbox is selected, the URL is adjusted as the fields are added. If you do not know the JDBC URL or field attributes for a specific connection, get it from the vendor. The basic JDBC URL is in the format `jdbc:[DATABASE_ID]://[IP_ADDRESS]:[PORT]/[DATABASE_NAME]`.

FIGURE 5-5

New Database
Connection
dialog box

Using a Connection to a Database   Different icons are used to show whether databases are connected, as shown in Figure 5-6. These icons appear next to databases in the Database Explorer.

Right-clicking the Database node displays six menu items. These menu items let you execute commands and set properties for database connections:

- **Connect**   Connects a database to the IDE
- **Disconnect**   Disconnects a database from the IDE
- **Execute Command**   Opens the SQL Editor for the context connection
- **Refresh**   Refreshes information in subnodes of the connection
- **Delete**   Deletes a disconnected database
- **Properties**   Opens a table displaying properties of the database

FIGURE 5-6

Database
connection status
icons

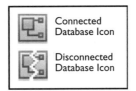

Subnodes of the database connections let you interact with database tables, views, and procedures. These subnodes and their features are covered later in the chapter.

The latest version of the API is JDBC 4.0. The Scenario & Solution details its latest features, which may provide functionality missing from earlier drivers.

Java DB Connections

The Java DB database server is an open source implementation of the Apache Derby database that is supported by Oracle. It is 100 percent Java, CDC, SQL, and JDBC compliant. It is fully transactional and secure. Java DB has a small footprint of approximately 2.5MB. It is available in both embedded and traditional server modes. The NetBeans Database Explorer has the ability to connect and interface with the Java DB database.

SCENARIO & SOLUTION

You wish to know the primary features new to the JDBC 4.0 API.	SQL exception handling and connection management enhancements, auto-loading of the JDBC driver class, support for RowID SAL type, DataSet implementation of SQL using Annotations, and SQL support.
You wish to know the primary features new to the JDBC 3.0 API.	Reusability of prepared statements by connection pools, new `BOOLEAN` data type, parameter calling to `CallableStatement`, data altering capability in Blob and Clob.
You wish to know the primary features new to the JDBC 2.1 API.	Ability to scroll forward and backward in a result set, perform updates to database tables using Java methods, work with time zones in Data, Time, and Timestamp values. The API also preserves the precision of `BigDecimal` values, uses SQL3 data types as column values, and can use multiple SQL statements in batch.
You wish to know the primary features new to the JDBC 2.0 API.	Use of the DataSource interface for making a connection, use of JNDI to specify and obtain database connections, use of pooled connections, distributed transactions, and handling/passing data using RowSets.
You wish to know the primary features new to the JDBC 1.2 API.	Use of updatable ResultSets and pass-through schedulers.

Enabling the Java DB Database Server   The Java DB database server is automatically registered with the IDE. This is because it is bundled with the JDK, and NetBeans knows to look for its presence. In addition to automatic registration, a Java DB node is available immediately under the Databases node of the Database Explorer. The Java DB node has four context-menu items that can be seen after right-clicking: Start Server, Stop Server, Create Database, and Properties. To use a preexisting installation of Java DB or Apache Derby, update the installation and database locations in the Java DB Properties dialog box invoked by the Properties menu item.

Creating a Java DB Connection   Connecting to an existing Java DB can be done by right-clicking the Databases node and selecting New Connection. Two driver name options are related to the Java DB database: Embedded and Network. The embedded driver is used when the application accesses the database from only one JVM. The network driver is used when the database needs to be accessed from various JVMs over a network.

The Java DB URL format is

```
jdbc:derby://[IP_ADDRESS]:[PORT]/[DATABASE_NAME]
```

To create a new Java DB database, right-click the Java DB node and select Create Database. From the Create Java DB Database dialog box, you need to specify only the database name, username, and password. When creating a Java DB database with the name "Ideas," the following URL automatically is established:

```
jdbc:derby://localhost:1527/Ideas
```

Right-clicking the Java DB Databases node displays the same menu items as other database connections do: Connect, Disconnect, Execute Command, Refresh, Delete, and Properties.

Database Support Components

The SQL Editor provides a direct means of sending commands to the JDBC-supported database. The SQL Editor has various toolbars and a Table Viewer. It directs status output to the Output window and also receives commands from

INSIDE THE EXAM

MySQL Server Integration

When the NetBeans IDE detects a MySQL server running or installed on the local machine, a MySQL Server node appears under the Databases node of the Database Explorer. If you don't have MySQL on your machine, you won't see the MySQL Server node.

Right-clicking the MySQL Server node brings up nine menu items: Create Database, Start, Stop, Connect, Disconnect, Delete, Refresh, Run Administration Tool, and Properties.

The Create Database menu item lets you create a new database or set up a sample database. The *Properties* menu item lets you bind the appropriate SQL Server commands to the *Start*, *Stop*, and *Run Administration Tool* menu items. The *Connect* and *Disconnect* menu items respectively connect and disconnect the IDE from the MySQL database server. The *Delete* menu item removes the MySQL Server node. The *Refresh* menu item refreshes the list of databases on the server.

the Database Explorer. The SQL Editor and related components are shown in Figure 5-7. The MySQL Sakila sample database (see the bonus appendix entitled NetBeans Database Integration on the CD) is used for screenshots throughout this chapter. This section discusses each database-support component.

- SQL Editor
- Table Viewer
- Output Window
- Database Explorer Integration

SQL Editor

The SQL Editor executes commands against registered and connected JDBC-supported databases. The SQL Editor has a Connection combo box at its top left that lets you set which database is associated with the editor. The toolbar associated with the SQL Editor is separated into six sections. Each section provides value-added features to the SQL Editor. The Scenario & Solution explores these features.

FIGURE 5-7   NetBeans SQL Editor

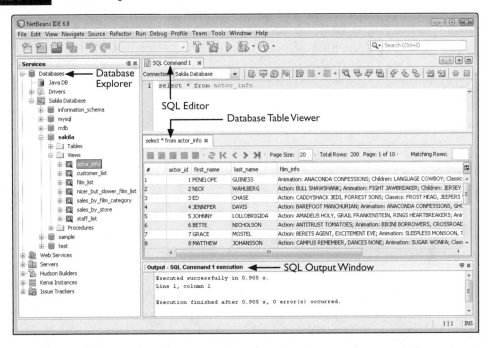

SCENARIO & SOLUTION

You need to execute SQL, select the connection in the Services window, view the SQL commands history, or keep the prior tabs.	You may select from the Run SQL, Select Connection In Services, SQL History, and Keep Prior Tabs toolbar buttons.
You need to navigate between a history of your edits or between files.	You may select from the Last Edit, Back, and Forward toolbar buttons.
You need to find selected words and traverse between occurrences of the selection.	You may select from the Find Selection, Find Previous Occurrence, Find Next Occurrence, and Toggle Highlight Search toolbar buttons.
You need to traverse between or set bookmarks.	You may select from the Previous Bookmark, Next Bookmark, and Toggle Bookmark toolbar buttons.
You need to shift lines.	You may select from the Shift Line Left and Shift Line Right toolbar buttons.
You need to create a macro.	You may select from the Start Macro Recording and Stop Macro Recording toolbar buttons.

In addition to the previously mentioned SQL Editor features from the toolbars, the SQL Editor has many of the same features as other NetBeans IDE source editors, such as line numbers, current line marker, bookmarking, comment support, and document cloning. These features are shown in Figure 5-8.

FIGURE 5-8   SQL Editor features

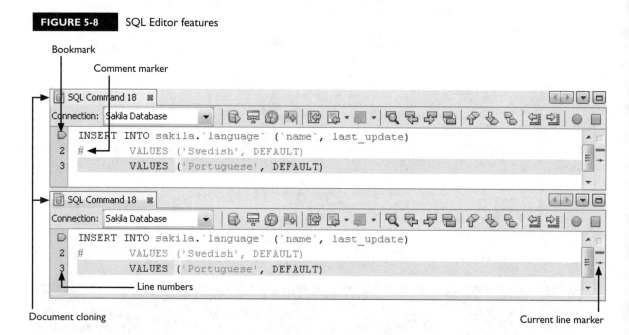

Bookmark

Comment marker

Document cloning

Line numbers

Current line marker

The features listed in the Scenario & Solution section are intuitive, and your best bet is to try each one at least a couple of times. The SQL History dialog box displays a nice presentation of the history of recent SQL commands, as shown in Figure 5-9.

FIGURE 5-9

SQL History

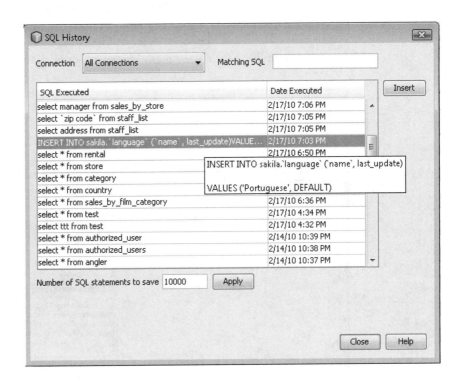

![EXERCISE 5-2]

Interfacing with the Sakila Database Through the Database Explorer

In this exercise, you use the Database Explorer to perform various tasks on the MySQL Sakila sample database. You need to have MySQL installed and be connected to the Sakila database. You can install the Sakila sample database from the plugin located in the Plugin Manager, as shown next:

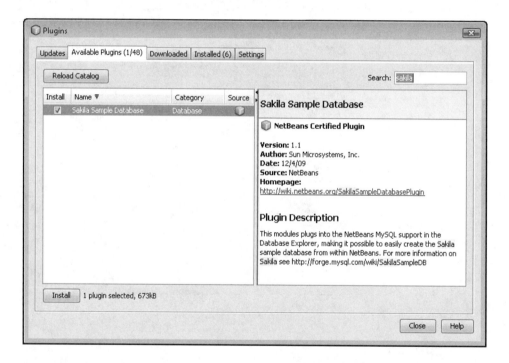

A six-minute NetBeans screencast on database improvements implemented since NetBeans IDE 6.5 can be found here: http://netbeans.org/kb/docs/ide/database-improvements-screencast.html.

Let's now perform some actions on the database:

1. Modify and save the last name of an actor/actress in the actor table. This can be done by using the table and toolbar buttons without directly entering SQL into the editor.

2. Insert a new member of the staff into the staff table. This can be done by using the table and toolbar buttons without directly entering SQL into the editor.

3. View the contents of the film table.

4. Execute the nicer_but_slower_film_list view.

5. Grab the table definition of the rental table.

6. Create a new table, delete it, and recreate it.

Table Viewer

The SQL Table Viewer displays tables (for example, ResultSets) returned by SQL commands. Figure 5-10 displays the customer_list view of the Sakila database in the Table Viewer.

The Table Viewer has various features:

■ **Record manipulation** Toolbar buttons to insert and delete records, commit changes, and cancel records are available. There is also a button for truncating the table. These buttons are enabled only for modifiable records and/or tables.

■ **Pagination** The table is paginated based on an input value for the page size. The Page Size corresponds to the number of records displayed on a page. There are icons to refresh the page, go to the first page, go to the previous page, go to the next page, and go to the last page. The total number of rows (records) is displayed. The current page relative to the total pages is displayed.

FIGURE 5-10   Sakila customer_list view

select * from customer_li... ✕

| | Page Size: 500 | Total Rows: 599 Page: 1 of 30 | Matching Rows: | Argen |

#	ID	name	address	zip code	phone	city	country	notes	SID
1	359	WILLIE MARKHAM	1623 Kingstown Drive	91299	296394569728	Almirante Brown	Argentina	active	2
2	560	JORDAN ARCHULETA	1229 Varanasi (Benares) Manor	40195	817740355461	Avellaneda	Argentina	active	1
3	322	JASON MORRISSEY	1427 A Corua (La Corua) Place	85799	972574862516	Baha Blanca	Argentina	active	1
4	24	KIMBERLY LEE	96 Tafuna Way	99865	934730187245	Crdoba	Argentina	active	2
5	445	MICHEAL FORMAN	203 Tambaram Street	73942	411549550611	Escobar	Argentina	active	1
6	530	DARRYL ASHCRAFT	166 Jinchang Street	86760	717566026669	Ezeiza	Argentina	active	2
7	89	JULIA FLORES	1926 El Alto Avenue	75543	846225459260	La Plata	Argentina	active	1
8	107	FLORENCE WOODS	1532 Dzerzinsk Way	9599	330838016880	Merlo	Argentina	active	1
9	585	PERRY SWAFFORD	773 Dallas Manor	12664	914466027044	Quilmes	Argentina	active	1
10	243	LYDIA BURKE	1483 Pathankot Street	37288	686015532180	San Miguel de Tucumn	Argentina	active	1
11	331	ERIC ROBERT	430 Kumbakonam Drive	28814	105470691550	Santa F	Argentina	active	1
12	405	LEONARD SCHOFIELD	88 Nagaon Manor	86868	779461480495	Tandil	Argentina	active	1

■ **Matching rows filter**   The table has a character-string filter based on the selected input in the Matching Rows edit box. Only the records with matching strings will be displayed.

■ **Column sorting**   Records are sorted by table columns when clicking the column title names. Sorting is based on the current page size view and not the entire set of data.

The record manipulation features are also available along with other self-describing commands when you right-click to open the context menu. This is shown in Figure 5-11.

Output Window

SQL Command Execution windows are opened in the Output window with information related to the commands executed from the SQL Editor Input window. They are always in pairs, with a reference number starting at 1. For example, the SQL Command 5 window corresponds with the SQL Command 5 Execution window, as shown in Figure 5-12. The next set of windows includes the number 6, and so forth. The SQL Command Execution window displays the positive and negative results of the SQL Editor commands.

FIGURE 5-11

Table Viewer
context menu

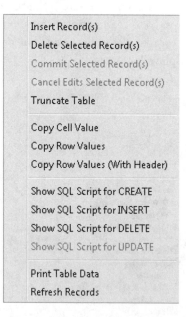

FIGURE 5-12   Output window

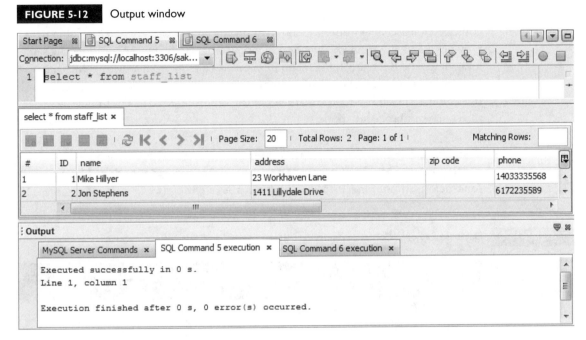

Right-clicking the Output window reveals a context menu with the following items: Copy, Paste, Find, Find Next, Find Previous, Filter, Wrap Text, Larger Font, Smaller Font, Choose Font, Save As, Clear, and Close.

Database debug mode can be enabled or disabled by right-clicking the Databases node and selecting the appropriate menu item (Enable Debug or Disable Debug). Debug mode lists SQL statements in the Output window that are not displayed in the SQL Editor window. For example, creating or deleting tables from a database node in the Services window shows corresponding SQL statements in the Output window, but only when the debug mode is enabled.

Database Explorer Integration

Every integrated database has Tables, Views, and Procedures nodes in the Database Explorer. Right-clicking the node opens a context menu with the following commands:

- **Tables node**   Create Table, Recreate Table, Execute Command, Refresh
- **Views node**   Create View, Execute Command, Refresh
- **Procedures node**   Execute Command, Refresh

The Execute Command menu item invokes the SQL Editor relative to the context database. The Refresh menu item updates the node. The Create Table item provides a dialog box for the creation of a new table, and Create View does the same for a view. The Recreate Table menu item creates a table from a `.grab` file that was captured through the relative menu item of the actual table node. Table 5-1 shows this command (Grab Structure) and all of the others relative to right-clicking a table, view, or procedure node.

on the job

Consider using LiquiBase (www.liquibase.org) for database change management. LiquiBase is an open source, database-independent library for tracking, managing, and applying database changes.

TABLE 5-1   Database Explorer Context Menus

Context Menu Item Command	Tables Node	Views Node	Procedures Node	Command Description
View Data	Yes	Yes		Views records in the Table Viewer, shows command in SQL Editor, shows execution notes in Output window
Execute Command	Yes	Yes	Yes	Opens SQL Editor relative to context database
Add Column	Yes			Opens Add Column dialog box to append column to table
Refresh	Yes			Refreshes node
Delete	Yes	Yes		Deletes node, shows execution notes in Output window
Grab Structure	Yes			Saves table structure to a file named `[filename].grab`
Recreate Table	Yes			Creates a table from a `.grab` file
Properties	Yes	Yes	Yes	Shows element properties

CERTIFICATION SUMMARY

This chapter covered the NetBeans Database Explorer. Its only database-related certification objective requires familiarity with driver registration and working with database tables as well as other features of database integration. All of these features are accessed through the Database Explorer.

The first half of this chapter covered topics related to database connectivity. These topics included JDBC driver registration, establishing JDBC-supported and Java DB database connections, as well as integration with MySQL utilities. Again, all of this was done through the Database Explorer.

We moved on to discuss working with the databases once a connection is established. We used the SQL Editor to execute SQL commands. We explored interfacing with databases and the SQL Editor through tables, views, and procedures.

You should now be able to connect to, interact with, and capture details about databases, all while working with the Database Explorer and SQL Editor.

TWO-MINUTE DRILL

Working with Databases in the IDE

❑ The Database Explorer contains features such as establishing and viewing database connections, adding database drivers, interacting with database structures, working with SQL statements, and migrating schemas.

❑ Java DB is a database with a small footprint supported by Oracle. It is bundled with the JDK. Java DB drivers are automatically registered in the Database Explorer.

❑ MySQL is an open source relational database. A MySQL node is automatically established in the Database Explorer if the IDE detects its installation.

❑ The IDE can register any JDBC driver via the New JDBC Driver dialog box.

❑ Java DB, MySQL, PostgreSQL, and JDBC-ODBC bridge JDBC drivers are registered by default in the core IDE.

❑ Each table node has subnodes for Tables, Views, and Procedures.

❑ The IDE provides means to create, recreate, view, modify, and delete tables.

❑ Table definitions can be saved. This is done by right-clicking the table and selecting Grab Structure.

❑ The IDE can capture database schemas through the New File wizard. The Persistence Category and Database Schema must be selected in the wizard along with the database URL. The database must also be running at the time of the capture.

❑ The SQL Editor executes commands against a connected database.

❑ Commands in the SQL Editor can be run by pressing CTRL-SHIFT-E.

❑ The SQL Editor primary toolbar has four buttons. These buttons can execute SQL commands, select connections in the Services window, list SQL history, and keep prior tabs open.

❑ Database debug mode can be enabled to list various SQL statements in the Output window.

SELF TEST

The following questions will help you measure your understanding of the material presented in this chapter. Read all the choices carefully because there might be more than one correct answer. Choose all correct answers for each question.

Working with Databases in the IDE

1. What is the root node of the Database Explorer in the Services window?

   A. Databases

   B. Drivers

   C. Java DB

   D. Database Explorer

2. Consider the following illustration. How is the New JDBC Driver dialog box invoked?

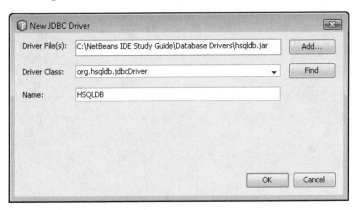

   A. Right-click the Databases node and choose New Driver.

   B. Right-click the Drivers node and choose New Driver.

   C. Choose Tools | JDBC Drivers | New Driver.

   D. Press CTRL-ALT-D.

3. If NetBeans detects an installation of MySQL on the local machine, a MySQL node will appear under the Databases node that provides additional MySQL support.

   A. True

   B. False

4. When the Database Explorer's debug mode is enabled, the various SQL statements can be viewed in which window?
   A. Services
   B. Databases
   C. Test Results
   D. Output

5. When grabbing a table structure (that is, right-click [table] | Grab Structure), what is the file extension applied to the file that is created with the table definition?
   A. `.grab`
   B. `.table`
   C. `.tbx`
   D. `.structure`

6. Three nodes exist for each database node in the Database Explorer. Select the three that apply.
   A. Tables
   B. Views
   C. Procedures
   D. Stored Procedures

7. In the SQL History dialog box, what is the maximum number of SQL statements that can be saved?
   A. 10
   B. 100
   C. 10,000
   D. 1,000,000

8. What are the tooltips associated with the icons in the SQL Editor's toolbar? Select all that apply.
   A. Run SQL
   B. Select Connection In Services
   C. SQL History
   D. SQL Diff
   E. Keep Prior Tabs

9. Consider the following illustration. When adding a column to a table, what constraints can be applied? Select all that apply.

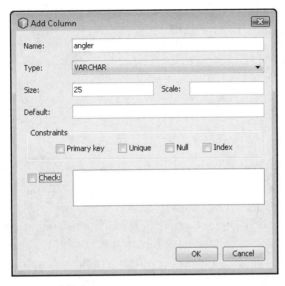

A. Primary Key, Unique, and Index

B. Unique, Null, and Index

C. Null

D. Primary Key, Unique, Null, and Index

10. Captured database schemas are visible in what window?

A. Projects

B. Tasks

C. Output

D. Navigator

11. Captured database schemas are saved in what file format?

A. Binary format

B. Dataset format

C. Serialized file format

D. XML format

SELF TEST ANSWERS

Working with Databases in the IDE

1. What is the root node of the Database Explorer in the Services window?

A. Databases

B. Drivers

C. Java DB

D. Database Explorer

☑ **A.** Databases is the base node of the Database Explorer in the Services window.

☒ **B, C,** and **D** are incorrect. **B** is incorrect because Drivers is not the base node of the Database Explorer. Drivers is a folder under the Databases node. **C** is incorrect because Java DB is not the base node of the Database Explorer. Java DB is a database node under the Databases node. **D** is incorrect because Database Explorer is not a node.

2. Consider the following illustration. How is the New JDBC Driver dialog box invoked?

A. Right-click the Databases node and choose New Driver.

B. Right-click the Drivers node and choose New Driver.

C. Choose Tools | JDBC Drivers | New Driver.

D. Press CTRL-ALT-D.

☑ **B.** The New JDBC Driver dialog box is invoked by right-clicking the Drivers node and choosing New Driver.

☒ **A, C,** and **D** are incorrect. **A** is incorrect because no New Driver menu item is associated with the Databases node. **C** is incorrect because there is no Tools | JDBC Drivers menu item. **D** is incorrect because CTRL-ALT-D does not open the New JDBC Driver dialog box.

3. If NetBeans detects an installation of MySQL on the local machine, a MySQL node will appear under the Databases node that provides additional MySQL support.

A. True

B. False

☑ **A.** This is a true statement. If NetBeans detects an installation of MySQL on the local machine, a MySQL node will appear under the Databases node, that provides additional MySQL support.

4. When the Database Explorer's debug mode is enabled, the various SQL statements can be viewed in which window?
- A. Services
- B. Databases
- C. Test Results
- D. Output

☑ **D.** The Output window displays the log of various SQL statements when the Database Explorer's debug mode is enabled.

☒ **A, B,** and **C** are incorrect. **A** is incorrect because the Services window does not display the log of SQL statements. **B** is incorrect because there is no Databases window. **C** is incorrect because the Test Results window does not display the log of SQL statements.

5. When grabbing a table structure (that is, right-click [table] | Grab Structure), what is the file extension applied to the file that is created with the table definition?
- A. `.grab`
- B. `.table`
- C. `.tbx`
- D. `.structure`

☑ **A.** The file extension `.grab` is used for table definition files.

☒ **B, C,** and **D** are incorrect. **B** is incorrect because the `.table` file extension is not used for table definition files. **C** is incorrect because the `.tbx` file extension is not used for table definition files. **D** is incorrect because the `.structure` file extension is not used for table definition files.

6. Three nodes exist for each database node in the Database Explorer. Select the three that apply.
- A. Tables
- B. Views
- C. Procedures
- D. Stored Procedures

☑ **A, B,** and **C.** Each database node has subnodes for Tables, Views, and Procedures.

☒ **D** is incorrect because the node used for stored procedures is called Procedures and not Stored Procedures.

7. In the SQL History dialog box, what is the maximum number of SQL statements that can be saved?
   A. 10
   B. 100
   C. 10,000
   D. 1,000,000

   ☑ **C.** The maximum number of SQL statements that can be saved (as configurable in the SQL History dialog box) is 10,000.

   ☒ **A, B,** and **D** are incorrect. **A** is incorrect because 10 is not the maximum number of SQL statements that can be saved. **B** is incorrect because 100 is not the maximum number of SQL statements that can be saved. **D** is incorrect because 1,000,000 is not the maximum number of SQL statements that can be saved.

8. What are the tooltips associated with the icons in the SQL Editor's toolbar? Select all that apply.
   A. Run SQL
   B. Select Connection In Services
   C. SQL History
   D. SQL Diff
   E. Keep Prior Tabs

   ☑ **A, B, C,** and **E.** Four icons exist in the SQL Editor's primary toolbar. The associated tooltips are Run SQL, Select Connection In Services, SQL History, and Keep Prior Tabs.

   ☒ **D** is incorrect because no icon has a SQL Diff tooltip.

9. Consider the following illustration. When adding a column to a table, what constraints can be applied? Select all that apply.
   A. Primary Key, Unique, and Index
   B. Unique, Null, and Index
   C. Null
   D. Primary Key, Unique, Null, and Index

   ☑ **A, B,** and **C.** Valid checkboxes that can be selected together include (**A**) Primary Key, Unique, and Index; (**B**) Unique, Null, and Index; and (**C**) Null.

   ☒ **D** is incorrect because the dialog box will not allow the Primary Key checkbox to be selected along with the Null checkbox.

10. Captured database schemas are visible in what window?

    A. Projects

    B. Tasks

    C. Output

    D. Navigator

    ☑ **A.** Captured database schemas are visible in the Projects window.

    ☒ **B, C,** and **D** are incorrect. **B** is incorrect because captured database schemas are not visible in the Tasks window. **C** is incorrect because captured database schemas are not visible in the Output window. **D** is incorrect because captured database schemas are not visible in the Navigator window.

11. Captured database schemas are saved in what file format?

    A. Binary format

    B. Dataset format

    C. Serialized file format

    D. XML format

    ☑ **D.** Captured database schemas are saved in XML format.

    ☒ **A, B,** and **C** are incorrect. **A** is incorrect because captured database schemas are not saved in binary format. **B** is incorrect because captured database schemas are not saved in dataset format. **C** is incorrect because captured database schemas are not saved in serialized file format.

6
Source Editor

CERTIFICATION OBJECTIVES

- Modifying Behavior of the Source Editor
- Understanding Error Highlighting and Correction
- Using Editor Hints

- Generating Code
✓ Two-Minute Drill
Q&A Self Test

Toom oday's source code editors have enhanced features that allow for quick and efficient development and editing, especially with the Java language. The NetBeans Source Editor is no exception and has risen to the top of well-liked editors. Its popularity is due to its numerous features, many of which are integrated with the core IDE. Since developers spend most of their time in the Source Editor, features such as build integration and ease-of-use are important. Throughout this chapter, we'll explore many of the features of the NetBeans IDE Source Editor

It's important to note that the Source Editor is actually a collection of editors. Some of the more popular editors are shown in Table 6-1. Each editor is invoked and specialized relative to file types. The certification exam focuses on the Java editor.

This chapter helps prepare you for the exam by covering configuration of the Source Editor and three of the editor's primary features:

- IDE diagnostic messages and correction
- Editor hints; how they are displayed and invoked
- Code generation by use of code completion and code templates

Once you complete the chapter, you'll be familiar enough with the Source Editor to score well on the exam-related questions and to use the editor more effectively for your on-the-job needs.

TABLE 6-1   NetBeans Source Editors

Language Editor	Filename Extensions	6.8 Installation Bundle
C++	`.c, .cpp`	C++ bundle
Groovy	`.groovy`	Java bundle
HTML	`.html`	Java bundle
XHTML	`.xhtml`	Java bundle
Java	`.java`	Java, Java SE, JavaFX bundles
JavaServer Pages	`.jsp`	Java bundle
JavaServer Faces	`.jsf`	Java bundle
JavaFX	`.fx`	JavaFX bundle
PHP	`.php`	PHP bundle
Java Properties	`.properties`	Java and Java SE bundles
Ruby	`.rb, .rbx`	Ruby bundle
XML	`.xml`	Most bundles

CERTIFICATION OBJECTIVE

Modifying Behavior of the Source Editor

Exam Objective 5.2   Describe how to use the Options window to change the default appearance and behavior of the Source Editor.

The appearance and general behavior of the Source Editor are configurable through the Options window. You can open the Options window by selecting Tools | Options from the main menu bar. For Mac OS X, you can open the Options window by selecting NetBeans | Preferences. When the Options window (for the Java bundle) opens, you see a set of at least five panel selectors (icons) at the top, with the first selector, General, available by default, as depicted in Figure 6-1. The remaining icons are Editor, Fonts & Colors, Keymap, and Miscellaneous. Icons vary depending upon installed bundles.

Clicking each icon displays different configuration options in the main portion of the dialog box—the main window below the icons. The General and Miscellaneous panels, covered in Chapter 1, are related to general configurations. This section/ objective focuses on the three remaining icons/panels (Editor, Fonts & Colors, and Keymap) and associated configurations.

- ■ Editor Panel Configurations
- ■ Fonts & Colors Panel Configurations
- ■ Keymap Panel Configurations

Editor Panel Configurations

The Editor panel of the Options window provides several tabbed panels that allow for the configuration of the Source Editor and/or specific editors (for example, the Java source editor). When specific editors can be configured through a tabbed panel,

FIGURE 6-1

Panel selectors
in the Options
window

General   Editor   Fonts & Colors   Keymap   Miscellaneous

a Language combo box at the top of the panel allows for the selection of the desired setting controls. Upon selection of the language from the combo box, the panel controls and contents change. The Editor panel includes the following tabs:

- General
- Formatting
- Code Completion
- Code Templates
- Hints
- Mark Occurrences
- Macros

General Tab

The General panel allows for configuration of code folding and camel case behavior, as shown in Figure 6-2.

FIGURE 6-2

General tab

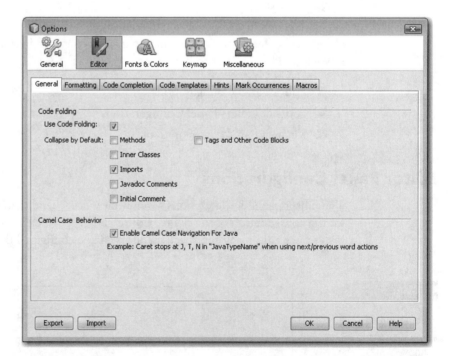

Code Folding   Code folding is a Source Editor feature that selectively hides specialized text blocks such as Java imports and Javadoc comments. Code folding can be entirely enabled by the selection of the Use Code Folding checkbox in the General panel. When it's enabled, a selectable code-folding graphic in the editor allows you to collapse or expand foldable elements. When the feature is disabled, the graphics are not present. The code-folding graphic is a box with an enclosed plus sign or minus sign relative to the information being shown or hidden, along with a line that extends to the end of the block. Figure 6-3 shows code folding for the comment and method of `toString()` and shows code expansion for the comment and method of `finalize()`. Code folding is available for methods, inner classes, imports, Javadoc comments, the initial comment, tags, and other code blocks.

on the job

*The shortcut CTRL-SHIFT-MINUS **collapses all code folds. The shortcut** CTRL-SHIFT-PLUS **expands all code folds.***

Camel Case Navigation   Camel case navigation is enabled by default in the Source Editor. With camel case navigation enabled, the cursor stops at the first word, and at all the nonconsecutive uppercase letters in words in an identifier when using next (CTRL-RIGHT) and previous (CTRL-LEFT) word actions. When camel case navigation is disabled, the word actions will skip over camel case characters in identifiers. When an identifier includes camel case characters but begins with a lowercase character, it is considered lower camel-case convention.

FIGURE 6-3

Code folding

```
[+]   /**...*/
      @Override
[+]   public String toString() [{...}]

[-]   /**
       * Functionality performed when this object is garbage collected.
       *
       * @throws java.lang.Throwable Causes f nalization to halt
       */
      @Override
[-]   protected void finalize() throws Throwable {
          rrwaLogger.fine("Finalized Rockfish");
      }
```

In camel case navigation, the cursor will stop before the letters A, I, O, O, and E in `ArrayIndexOutOfBoundsException`, when traversing to the right. The cursor will also stop before the "t" and "S" in `toString` when moving to the right. With camel case navigation disabled, all camel case characters will be ignored when traversing to the right, except the first character of the identifier. For example, for the identifier `RockfishReports`, the cursor will start before the first "R" and then move on to the next element in the source code, without stopping before the second "R."

Formatting Tab

In the Formatting panel, the following TAB key behaviors are configurable for all languages. For the Java language, the following items are configurable:

- Tabs and indents
- Alignment
- Brace placement
- Code wrapping
- Blank lines
- Coding spacing

Figure 6-4 shows the Tabs And Indents panel for configuration with the Java source editor. As configuration changes are made, the source code example in the Preview area changes accordingly. Java formatting changes are self-explanatory upon viewing the panels related to the different categories. Take a few minutes to step through them all.

Code Completion Tab

In the Code Completion panel, the editor behavior that assists the user in automatically or manually completing partially inserted code is configurable. Checkboxes are provided for global settings when selecting All Languages from the Language combo box at the top of the Code Completion tab. The self-explanatory text accompanying these checkboxes includes the following:

- Auto Popup Completion Window
- Auto Popup Documentation Window

FIGURE 6-4

Formatting tab

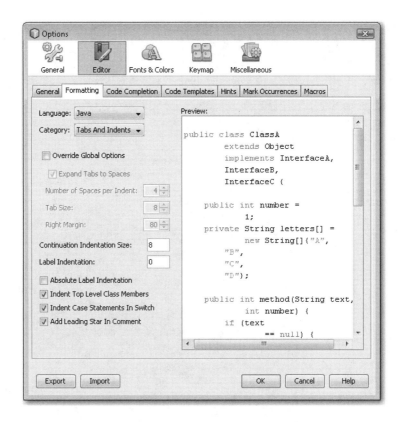

- Display Documentation Next To Completion
- Insert Single Proposal Automatically
- Case Sensitive Code Completion
- Show Deprecated Members In Code Completion
- Insert Closing Brackets Automatically

When selecting Java from the Language combo box, you can define triggers and related settings for code completion, as shown in Figure 6-5. Code completion is covered in detail later in this chapter.

FIGURE 6-5

Code
Completion tab

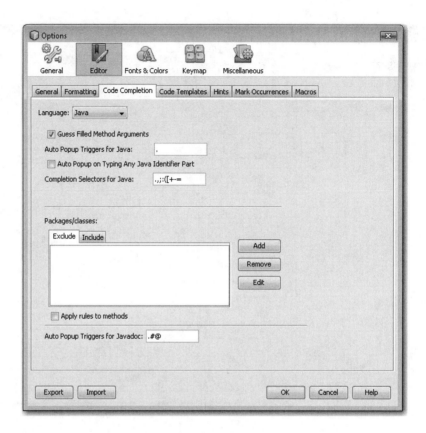

Code Templates Tab

The Code Templates panel, shown in Figure 6-6, manages code templates. Code templates consist of three parts:

- **Abbreviation** The character sequence that is typed causes the "expanded text" to be substituted.
- **Expanded Text** Text to be inserted when the abbreviation is typed. Expanded text may use special code template syntax to specify how the code template behaves. Code templates are covered later in this chapter.
- **Description** Description of the abbreviation/expanded text.

The Expand Template On combo box defines the keystroke(s) used to invoke code completion. Options include Space, Shift-Space, Tab, or Enter. The Tab key is set by default to invoke code completion. See the bonus appendix entitled NetBeans Code Templates on the CD for commonly used Java-related NetBeans Code Templates.

Code
Templates tab

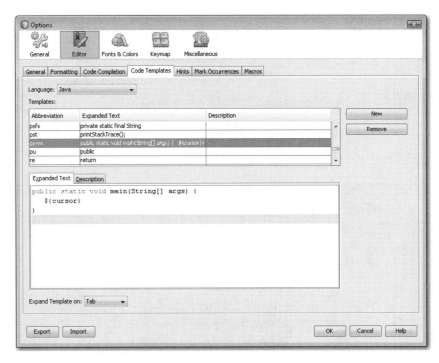

Hints Tab

The Hints panel, as shown in Figure 6-7, customizes hints and tips that help you as you work in the Source Editor. The Hints panel has settings for Apache Maven POM files, Java, and JavaScript files.

Mark Occurrences Tab

The Mark Occurrences panel, shown in Figure 6-8, enables you to specify which occurrences of Java keywords are marked when the cursor is on one of their instances. The only language currently supported for marking occurrences in the Java NetBeans bundle is Java.

Macros Tab

The Macros panel enables you to customize and create Source Editor macros and to set shortcuts for them, as shown in Figure 6-9. Clicking the New button allows you to set the name of a new macro through a dialog box and thereafter to set the macro code through the Macro Code text area. Creating a macro by using Edit | Start Macro Recording and Edit | Stop Macro Recording places a new recorded macro into the list. The details of creating and running macros are outside the scope of the exam.

FIGURE 6-7

Hints tab

FIGURE 6-8

Mark
Occurrences tab

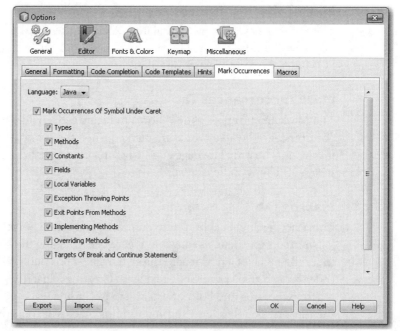

FIGURE 6-9

Macros tab

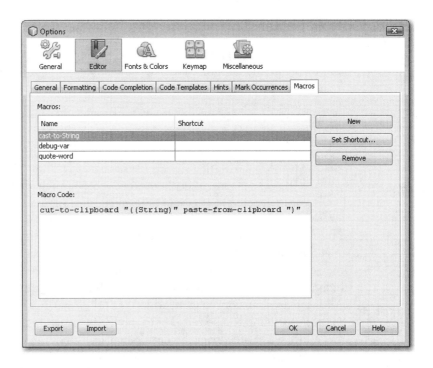

on the
job

Anonymous usage data can be sent to the NetBeans team to aid them in analyzing the most commonly used features of the IDE. This collected data includes IDE configuration information, project type information, and information on the use of web application frameworks, JDBC drivers, version control systems, servers, and productivity features (for example, the debugger). To enable this sharing of data, simply select the Usage Statistics checkbox in the Options window associated with the General icon. Even though information about passwords, class names, and source code is not collected, you may want to check with your boss and/or configuration management team before enabling this feature.

exam
watch

Remember that the exam targets NetBeans 6.1. This chapter uses NetBeans 6.8, which has many changes *within the Options window including new features, layout restructuring, and refined functionality.*

Fonts & Colors Panel Configurations

The Fonts & Colors panel of the Options window provides several tabbed panels that configure the display of attributes including highlighting and coloring. Tabs included in the Fonts & Colors panel are as follows:

- Syntax
- Highlighting
- Annotations
- Diff

Syntax Tab

The Syntax panel controls the configuration of syntax attributes for the Language selections listed in Table 6-2 as well as for the All Languages selection. All categories associated with the All Languages selection are considered parent settings. Individual language selection category elements that share the same name as an All Languages category element will inherit their settings by selecting Inherited in the corresponding combo box. For example, if you define the Background color for the Whitespace category of the Java Language as Inherited, it uses the Whitespace category background setting applied in the All Languages section. Syntax attributes that can be configured are fonts, foreground colors, background colors, as well as effects and their colors.

Figure 6-10 shows the Keyword category attributes for the Java language being inherited from the All Languages configuration. The Preview section displays examples of the category and updates when the attributes are changed. Once selected in the category list, the element shows a blinking underline three times in the Preview section for each occurrence. For example, the Keyword selection will have a blinking underline (three blinks) for all keywords in the sample code.

TABLE 6-2   Language Categories for Syntax Attributes

DTD	Cascading Style Sheets	Diff File
Expression Language	Externally Parsed Entity	HTML
JSON	Java	JavaScript
JavaScript Comments	JavaScript Strings	Plain Text
Properties	SQL	Tag File
XHTML	XML	Yaml

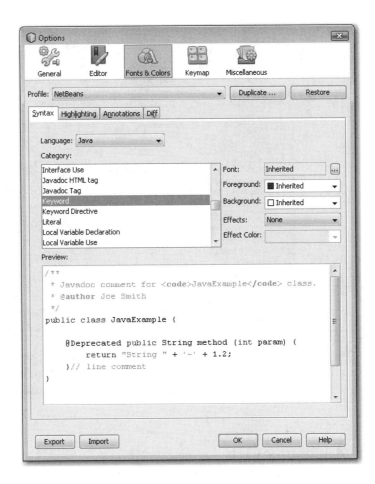

FIGURE 6-10

Syntax tab

Highlighting Tab

The Highlighting panel has controls for setting the foreground and background colors of many IDE elements, as shown in Figure 6-11.

on the job

For those of you who are color blind, keep an eye on the proposed color-blindness profile request opened up in the issues database: https://netbeans.org/bugzilla/show_bug.cgi?id=179638.

FIGURE 6-11

Highlighting tab

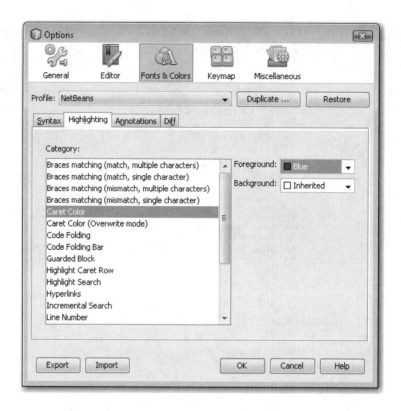

Annotations Tab

The Annotations panel lets you set foreground, background, and underlining attributes of elements related to annotation categories. For example, if a condition exists relative to a category such as a source code error, that line of source code would have the defined attributes as configured for the related category. Figure 6-12 shows the Annotations tab in the Fonts & Colors panel.

Diff Tab

The Diff panel enables you to set the background colors of highlighted elements of the diff tool, as shown in Figure 6-13. The background color can be modified for added, removed, and changed text, applied and unapplied text while merging, unresolved conflicts, as well as deleted and changed text in the sidebar.

FIGURE 6-12

Annotations tab

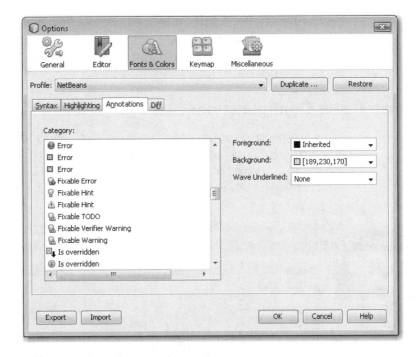

FIGURE 6-13

Diff tab

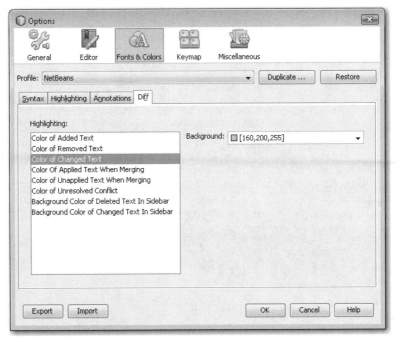

To illustrate color highlighting in the diff tool, we show (in Figure 6-14) the tool diffing Local History changes of the Rockfish class. To do this, right-click the Rockfish.java source file in the Projects window, and then choose Local History | Show Local History.

Keymap Panel Configurations

The Keymap panel configures keyboard shortcuts. Shortcuts are keystroke combinations that perform defined actions (for example, CTRL-R is the shortcut for the defined Renamed action). Groupings of shortcuts relate to profiles. NetBeans IDE 6.8 provides five profiles: Eclipse, Emacs, Idea, NetBeans, and NetBeans 5.5.

FIGURE 6-14   Highlighting illustrated by diffing Local History

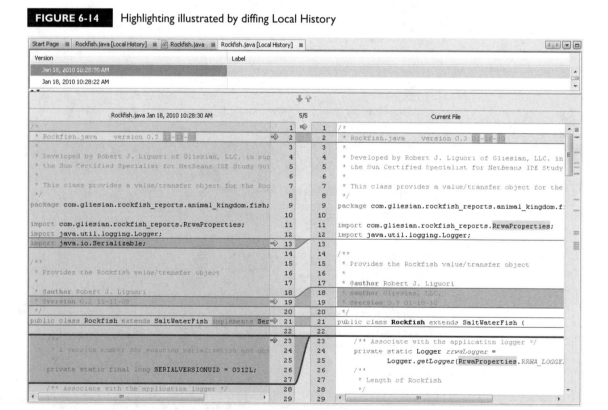

Figure 6-15 shows the Profile combo box in the Keymap panel. Each action has a defined shortcut and category. The ellipsis button next to the shortcut opens a popup with three options: Edit, Reset To Default, and Clear. If a shortcut already exists, a fourth option is included called Add Alternative. A detailed list of many shortcuts included in NetBeans 6.1 is available in Appendix C.

Profiles can be managed by selecting the Manage Profiles button. A dialog box opens, allowing for the duplication, default restoration, deletion, exportation, and importation of Keymap profiles.

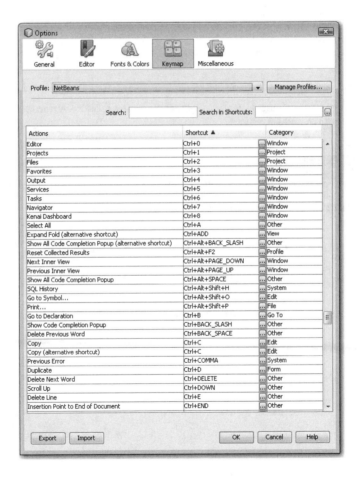

As we have seen, many features of the NetBeans IDE are configurable through the Options window. The Scenario & Solution explores the common items that are configured through Tools | Options.

SCENARIO & SOLUTION

You need to configure code folding, camel case behavior, formatting, code completion, code template, editor hints, symbol occurrences, and macros.	Go to Tools	Options, Editor panel.
You need to configure fonts and colors of the following features: syntax, highlighting, annotations, and diffs.	Go to Tools	Options, Fonts & Colors panel.
You need to configure keymap settings.	Go to Tools	Options, Keymap panel.
You need to configure miscellaneous features such as issue tracking, profiling, and version.	Go to Tools	Options, Miscellaneous panel.

EXERCISE 6-1

Changing Behavior of the Source Editor

This exercise changes the general behavior of features related to the Source Editor and/or IDE through configurations in the Options window.

1. From the Options window, change the background color for Java language source code lines that are in error.

2. From the Options window, change the number of spaces per indent, tab size, and right margin settings for Java files only.

3. From the Options window, deselect the Insert Closing Brackets Automatically feature.

4. From the Options window, change the background colors of all highlighting elements for the Diff feature.

5. From the Options window, change the Keymap profile.

6. From the Options window, deselect the Snapping Floating Windows feature.

7. From the Options window, add a Tasks pattern.

8. Export your new Options configurations to a ZIP file.

Understanding Error Highlighting and Correction

Exam Objective 5.3   Describe the ways the IDE highlights errors in source code and the tools the IDE offers for correcting those errors.

The NetBeans IDE highlights errors in the source code by displaying diagnostic indicators. These indicators can be in the form of icons/glyphs, source code element highlighting/underlining, marks, and messages. These various indicators are present in various locations such as next to Projects window nodes and files, within the left margin of the Source Editor window, throughout the error stripe on the right of the Source Editor window, in the Source Editor relative to the specific element in question, and in the Output window. This section details these means of error highlighting relative to the IDE:

- Projects Window Diagnostic Icons
- Source Editor Left Margin Annotation Diagnostic Glyphs
- Source Editor Diagnostic Highlighting
- Error Stripe Diagnostic Marks
- Output Window Diagnostic Messages

Projects Window Diagnostic Icons

Diagnostic icons are displayed in the Projects window next to files with errors or warnings. Files with issues including errors and warnings have a wrench icon next to the filename in the Projects window as well as next to the filename in the tab within the Source Editor. In addition, files with errors have an error marker (exclamation mark on octagon) overlaid on the file type icon. This error marker propagates upward to all nodes relative to the file (that is, to package folders). Figure 6-16 demonstrates error and warning icons being represented in the Projects window.

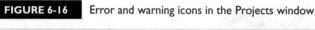

FIGURE 6-16   Error and warning icons in the Projects window

Source Editor Left Margin Annotation Diagnostic Glyphs

Annotation glyphs (see Figure 6-17) appear in the left margin of the Source Editor to present the user with information regarding the related source code line(s). Glyphs exist for many conditions including errors, override indicators, bookmarks, and debugging breakpoints. A segmented down arrow is presented next to an indicator if more than one glyph is associated with the line. Clicking the multiple annotations indicator cycles through the glyph display. Hovering over glyphs provides popup descriptions of the condition.

on the **Job**

Consider taking the time to commit to memory the different types of glyphs that can be seen in the glyph gutter and in other places in the IDE. A listing related to functional categories is shown in the Options window under the Annotations tab associated with the Fonts & Colors panel.

Source Editor Diagnostic Highlighting

When errors and warnings are discovered by the IDE or compiler, the elements under question will be underlined. Various elements can be configured to be underlined when certain conditions occur. Optionally, the Wave Underlined effect can be modified to just an underline, a strike-through, or no effect at all. The color of the underline as well as the foreground and background colors of the text can also be modified. This configuration is performed in the Options window under the Syntax tab of the Fonts & Colors panel. Figure 6-18 shows the entire statement being underlined due to the absence of the line terminator (semicolon).

FIGURE 6-17   Annotation glyphs in the left margin

```
Start Page  |  Rockfish.java  |

135
136        // THIS SCREENSHOT DEMONSTRATES GLYPHS IN THE LEFT MARGIN
137
           /**
139         * Overrides the toString methods, returning a string representing the
140         * rockfish object.
141         */
           @Override
143        public String toString() {
               String returnValue = "[" + this.length + "; " + this.weight + "; ";
145            return returnValue;
146        }
147
148        /**
149         * Functionalty performed when this object is garbage collected.
150         *
151         * @throws java.lang.Throwable Causes finalization to halt
152         */
           @Override
154        protected void finalize() throws Throwable {
               rrwaLogger.fine("Finalized Rockfish");
156        }
157
158    }
       }
160    // THIS SCREENSHOT DEMONSTRATES GLYPHS IN THE LEFT MARGIN
```

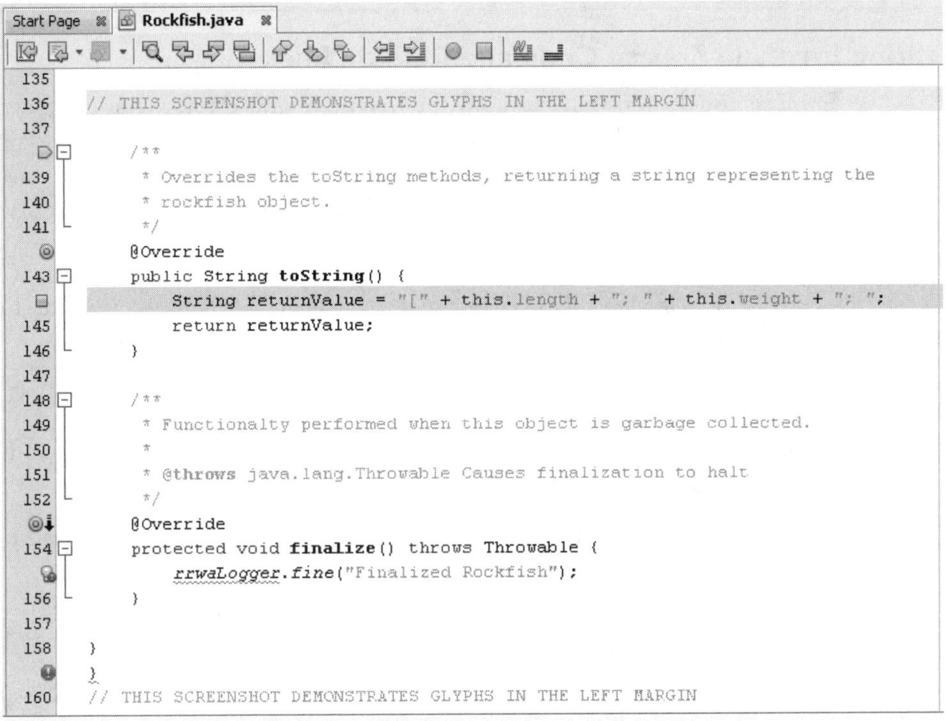

FIGURE 6-18

Error underlining

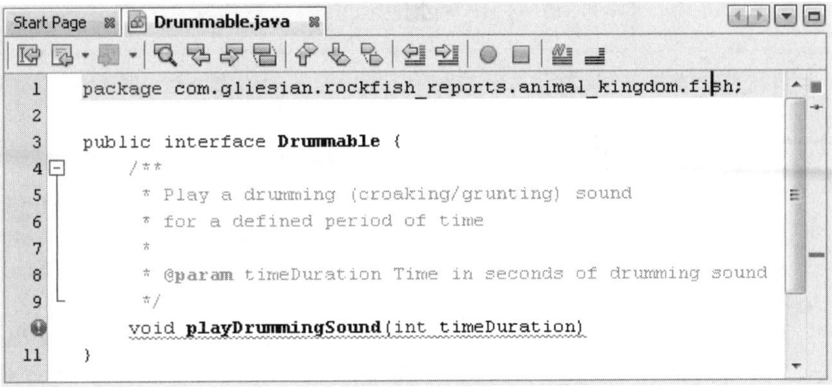

```
Start Page  |  Drummable.java  |

1      package com.gliesian.rockfish_reports.animal_kingdom.fish;
2
3      public interface Drummable {
4          /**
5           * Play a drumming (croaking/grunting) sound
6           * for a defined period of time
7           *
8           * @param timeDuration Time in seconds of drumming sound
9           */
           void playDrummingSound(int timeDuration)
11     }
```

Highlighting Errors in Source Code and Related Files

This exercise demonstrates the way the IDE highlights errors in various types of files including Java, JSP, HTML, XML, and Ant. Doing the legwork yourself to produce the errors is slightly outside of the scope of the exam. However, findings ways to generate various errors helps you better understand the associated highlighting features. Let's generate some errors!

1. Setup: Create or include source files for Java, JSP, HTML, XML, and Ant. In many cases of this exercise, you can consider using NetBeans sample projects because they have most of the elements you need (for example, JSP Examples project).

2. Generate three errors in the Java source file, and observe if and how the errors are highlighted.

3. Generate three errors in the JavaServer Pages source file, and observe if and how the errors are highlighted.

4. Generate three errors in the HTML source file, and observe if and how the errors are highlighted.

5. Generate three errors in the XML source file, and observe if and how the errors are highlighted.

6. Generate three errors in the Ant source file, and observe if and how the errors are highlighted.

Error Stripe Diagnostic Marks

Diagnostic marks are seen in the error stripe to the right of the Source Editor in relation to various conditions of the source code, as seen in Figure 6-19.

Table 6-3 details the colors of error marks and their meanings. These colors are not configurable.

Hovering over the error mark reveals the meaning of the mark in a tooltip (for example, Bookmark). For errors, the tooltip shows a brief explanation of the problem (for example, "';' expected, cannot find symbol," and so on).

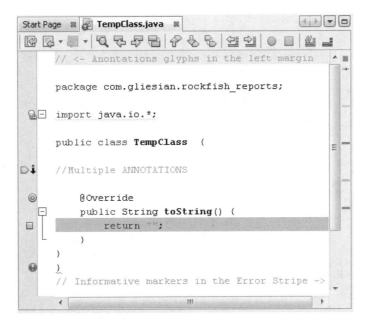

FIGURE 6-19

Error marks in
the error stripe

When you hover over the box at the top of the error stripe with your cursor, a tooltip says how many errors and warnings exist for the opened file in the Source Editor. A green box indicates no errors or warnings. An orange box means warnings but no errors. A red box means either errors, or errors and warnings.

Output Window Diagnostic Messages

The Output window displays information, warnings, and error messages about the build and compilation processes. When errors are found, they may be linked to the source code via a hyperlink. Clicking the link opens the file in the Source Editor and brings the cursor to the line in question. Figure 6-20 displays the Output window at the bottom of the IDE with error messages.

TABLE 6-3

Error Marks:
Colors and
Meanings

Error Mark Color	Error Mark Meaning
Thin black line with solid centered square	Current line
Dark gray	Bookmark
Pink	Line breakpoint
Orange	Warning (e.g., Unused import)
Red	Error (e.g., "';' expected, cannot find symbol," etc.)

FIGURE 6-20   Output window with error messages

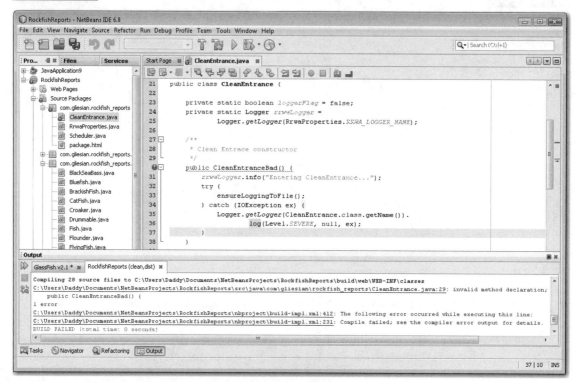

CERTIFICATION OBJECTIVE

Using Editor Hints

Exam Objective 5.4   Demonstrate the ability to use editor hints, such as implementing all the methods for an implemented interface.

An illuminated light bulb is often used to represent a new idea. In NetBeans, you may have noticed a bulb appearing in the left margin of lines containing an error—for instance, if you have typed a class, but the class has not yet been imported. The light bulb not only flags errors and warnings, but also draws your attention to editor hints that may be invoked to help in code remediation. Hovering the cursor over the light bulb pops up a tooltip displaying text with a brief description of the problem. Clicking the light bulb or pressing ALT-ENTER while being on the associated line also shows the tooltip popup as well as another popup window with editor hints (suggested corrective actions). Selecting the editor hints performs the corrective action. This section discusses some of the solutions that can be generated from selected editor hints. Corrective actions covered are listed relative to the following hint types:

- Class Importing Hints
- Missing Methods, Fields, and Variable Hints
- Inherited Methods Implementation Hints

Class Importing Hints

Class importing hints are provided for errors related to the existence or absence of necessary import statements. An annotation glyph appears as a light bulb if an import statement exists for a class that isn't being used or if a class is being used without a corresponding import.

Unused Import Statement Removal

Import statements that include a class name, static member, or wildcard with no references in the source code are not needed. These statements are flagged with light bulb glyphs in the left margin. The glyphs can be clicked to display editor hints. When there is only one unused import, the Remove Unused Imports editor hint is displayed. When there are multiple unused imports, the Remove All Unused Imports editor hint also appears, as shown in Figure 6-21.

You can automatically remove all unused import statements by pressing CTRL-SHIFT-I from within the Source Editor.

FIGURE 6-21

Import statement additions

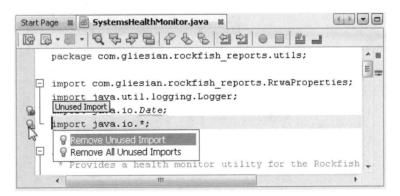

```
Start Page  ☒ |🗋 SystemsHealthMonitor.java ☒|

package com.gliesian.rockfish_reports.utils;

import com.gliesian.rockfish_reports.RrwaProperties;
import java.util.logging.Logger;
  Unused Import  a.io.Date;
import java.io.*;
    💡 Remove Unused Import
    💡 Remove All Unused Imports
    * Provides a health monitor utility for the Rockfish
```

Adding Import Statements

When you use classes from other packages, they must have corresponding import statements in your source code. If they do not have the imports, the statements with the classes depending on the imports are flagged with light bulb glyphs in the left margin. Clicking the glyphs displays the editor hints. Hints include "Add import for [package].[class_name]" and "Create class [class_name] in package [package]."

CTRL-SHIFT-I in this context opens a Fix All Imports dialog box. Figure 6-22 shows the dialog box when no import statement is present for the Timer class that is being used in the source code for this example. Pressing ALT-SHIFT-I performs fast import correction for a highlighted class.

on the job

NetBeans makes heavy use of tooltips. If you need a quick hint as to what a problem is or what a button does, just hover the mouse over the item, and wait to see if a tooltip comes up. These tips come in handy with the glyph gutter annotations and the markers in the error stripe.

Missing Methods, Fields, and Variable Hints

Editor hints are available for missing methods, fields, and variables.

Missing Methods

Suppose you call a method named `generateReport()` that does not exist. The IDE presents the light bulb in the left margin. Clicking the glyph shows the editor

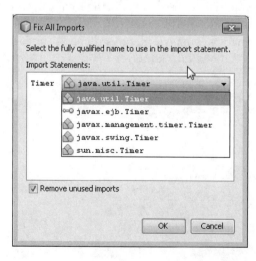

FIGURE 6-22

Fix All Imports dialog box

hint, "Create Method `generateReport()` in [package_name].[class_name]."
Invoking this hint generates the method with filler information:

```
private void generateReport() {
   throw new UnsupportedOperationException("Not yet implemented");
}
```

Missing Fields and Variable Hints

When Java identifiers are present but not declared, editor hints provide several
means of correction. Figure 6-23 shows the use of the identifier `test` that does
not have a declaration. Editor hints exist to declare the identifier as a field, method
parameter, or local variable.

When the "Create Field test in com.gliesian.rockfish_reports.animal_kingdom
.fish.CatFish" editor hint is selected, the field declaration is added for `test`:

```
package com.gliesian.rockfish_reports.animal_kingdom.fish;
public class CatFish extends BrackishFish {
   private int test;
   public void testMethod() {
      int value = test;
   }
}
```

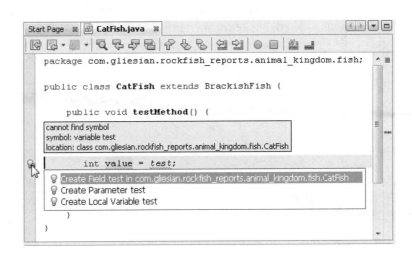

FIGURE 6-23

Editor hints
for undeclared
identifier

When the Create Parameter test editor hint is selected, the method signature changes with `test` added as a parameter:

```
package com.gliesian.rockfish_reports.animal_kingdom.fish;
public class CatFish extends BrackishFish {
  public void testMethod(int test) {
    int value = test;
  }
}
```

When the "Create Local Variable test" editor hint is selected, the method includes a local declaration for the `test` variable:

```
package com.gliesian.rockfish_reports.animal_kingdom.fish;
public class CatFish extends BrackishFish {
  public void testMethod() {
    int test;
    int value = test;
  }
}
```

on the **job**

Consider adding your own editor hints to the IDE. The NetBeans Java Hint Module Tutorial provides instructions as to how to create Java hints: http://platform.netbeans.org/tutorials/nbm-java-hint.html.

Inherited Methods Implementation Hints

When you change the signature of a class to implement an interface, an editor hint is provided to create the methods for you.

As an example, consider the signature `public class Kingfish extends SaltWaterFish {}` being changed to `public class Kingfish extends SaltWaterFish implements Drummable {}`. Selecting the editor hint, "Implement all abstract methods" adds the following code in the `SaltWaterFish` class:

```
public void playDrummingSound(int timeDuration) {
  throw new UnsupportedOperationException("Not supported yet.");
}
```

EXERCISE 6-3

Inserting a Cast from an Editor Hint

This exercise is designed to use an editor hint to automate the creation of a cast.

1. Create a simple Java application (for example, HelloWorld).

2. Create a condition where a cast needs to be inserted.

3. Example:

```
Exception e = new Exception();
NullPointerExceptionnpe = e;
```

4. Select the light bulb editor hint for insertion of a cast.

5. The code should now compile successfully.

EXERCISE 6-4

Producing Annotation Glyph Icons in the Left Margin

This exercise produces glyph icons by introducing coding mishaps. This exercise is intentionally challenging because you need to figure out how to create the errors in order to become very familiar with the annotation glyphs under various conditions. Also, by doing this exercise, you witness various ways the NetBeans IDE behaves based on your interactions with the Source Editor.

1. Create a simple Java application (for example, HelloWorld).

2. Introduce code that produces an Error icon with the tooltip, "Class, interface, or enum expected."

3. Introduce code that produces an Error icon with the tooltip, "Illegal start of type."

4. Introduce code that produces an Error icon with the tooltip, "'{' expected."

5. Introduce code that produces a Fixable Error icon with the tooltip, "cannot find symbol."

6. Introduce code that produces a Fixable Error icon with the tooltip, "Illegal character: \[XX]."

7. Introduce code that produces a Fixable Warning icon with the tooltip, "Field hides another field."

8. Introduce code that produces a Fixable Warning icon with the tooltip, "Unused Import."

CERTIFICATION OBJECTIVE

Generating Code

Exam Objective 5.5 Demonstrate the ability to use live code templates such as automatic generation of constructors, try/catch loops, and getters and setters.

NetBeans provides tools to enhance the productivity of software developers. These tools include code completion, code templates, and live code templates. Code completion assists developers in filling in source code that they would have had to commit to memory or have researched from API documentation (for example, a method name of a class). Code templates allow for the expansion of text from a defined abbreviation using a defined shortcut. Live code templates are the same as simple code templates, except they include "live" editable fields upon code text expansion. We will look at the details of each of these individually.

- Code Completion
- Code Templates
- Live Code Templates

Code Completion

Code completion is automatic or prompted generation of code based on partial code, triggers, and popup command selections.

Code Completion Usage

Code completion can be used to complete Java elements such as package, method, and class names, method/constructor signatures and parameters, and closing brackets. Take, for example, the source code input of `import jav` followed by CTRL-SPACE. A code completion list box displays with "`jav`" being used as the beginning part of available package names (that is, `java` and `javax`). Select `javax` from the list and press Enter or the period key. All available package elements are listed. In this case there are over 30 elements. Select `crypto` from the list box and press Enter or the period key. You now see all available classes. The first class is highlighted by default in the displayed list box, with a second popup being opened with the associated Javadoc documentation. Press the semicolon key, and

TABLE 6-4   Means to Open the Code Completion Popup List Box

Action	Event
CTRL-SPACE, CTRL-BACKSLASH	Opens code completion box listing elements for the class and imported items
Leading characters of an expression followed by CTRL-SPACE-BACKSLASH	Opens code completion box relative to the leading characters
Identifier and period followed by a pause	Opens code completion box relative to the identifier
CTRL-SPACE-SPACE, CTRL-ALT-BACKSLASH, CTRL-ALT-SPACE	Opens code completion box listing elements for the class and all items relative to the class path (e.g., packaged classes)
Uppercase character string followed by CTRL-SPACE	Opens code completion box list that includes all classes with matching camel-case characters (e.g., ASH lists `AdaptStateHelper` and `AnySeqHelper`)

the associated class is added to the import statement, followed by a semicolon. This was a common-use case of code completion.

There are many ways to open code completion popups to help you with development, as detailed in Table 6-4.

Once the code completion popup box has been opened, you have several ways to work with the elements presented in the list box, as shown in Table 6-5.

Code completion is also supported by a code generation popup window. The popup is available by pressing ALT-INSERT. Menu options open various dialog boxes that include functionality for the generation of constructors, getters and setters, `equals` and `hashCode` methods, and properties.

TABLE 6-5   Code Completion List Box Stimuli

Code Completion List Box Stimuli	Resultant Action
Press HOME, END, UP, DOWN, PAGE UP, or PAGE DOWN.	Performs list box navigation
Press the comma key.	Performs code completion ending with a comma
Press ENTER.	Performs code completion
Press ESC.	Exits code completion popup
Press the semicolon key.	Performs code completion ending with a semicolon

Code Templates

Code templates in their simplest form expand abbreviations into expanded text. This expansion is performed with the assistance of a defined keystroke sequence, also known as an expander in this context. The expander may be SPACE, SHIFT-SPACE, TAB, or ENTER. The most commonly used expander shortcut is the TAB key. The expander is configurable in the Code Templates tab of the Options window and Editor panel. Code templates actually consist of three parts: an abbreviation, expanded text, and a description. Code templates can be created, modified, or deleted within the Code Templates tab. Code templates are grouped by languages. The most commonly used code templates of the Java programming language are presented in the bonus appendix entitled NetBeans Code Templates on the CD.

The expanded text may use special code template syntax to affect how the code template behaves.

Code Template Usage

Let's take a look at some commonly used code templates and their benefits. If you don't use these already, you will probably start as soon as you put this book down.

St-TAB (type **St** and press TAB) expands to `String`. The benefit here is speed. `String` is represented almost as fast as you thought to type it.

twn-TAB expands to `throw new`. As you can see, the abbreviation can expand to multiple words.

Psfb-TAB expands to `public static final boolean`. That's a savings of 22 keystrokes. Tally that up over the course of your career.

Special Code Templates Syntax

Special Code Templates Syntax allows for additional features besides just replacing an abbreviation with a longer piece of text such as cursor placement. Because of the special syntax, `${cursor}`, as shown in Appendix D, the cursor automatically goes between the quotes upon expansion.

sout-TAB expands to `System.out.println("[[CURSOR_GOES_HERE]]");`. The clear benefit here is convenience, because you do not need to backspace and position the cursor between the quotes.

pvsm-TAB expands to the following code, creating the entire `main` method with cursor placement:

```
public static void main(String[] args) {
    [[CURSOR_GOES_HERE]]
}
```

The other two special syntax constructs that are used heavily in "live" code templates are ${selection} and ${param_name [arg]}. Using ${selection} defines the position for pasting the content of the editor selection. Parameter constructs are the basis of editable fields. Reference the bonus appendix entitled NetBeans Code Templates on the CD for examples of these constructs.

on the
job

NetBeans provides functionality for file templates. You can either create your own file templates, or use those provided by NetBeans. You will probably find yourself doing both. File templates are similar to code templates with the main difference being that file templates are relative to a file type, and code templates are representative of lines of code.

exam

watch   *Code templates can only be expanded by what is configured in the Editor | Code Templates tab of the Options window. Expansion options include SPACE,*   *SHIFT-SPACE, TAB, or ENTER. You are almost guaranteed to see a question related to the expansion of code templates on the exam.*

EXERCISE 6-5

Creating a HelloWorld Project in 30 Seconds

This exercise lets you create a HelloWorld project, modify the main file, perform formatting, and run the application, all in 30 seconds or less. At the same time, you are using different NetBeans IDE features you have learned and some new ones. Ready, set, go!

1. Press CTRL-SHIFT-N to initiate the New Project wizard.
2. Use the arrow keys to select Java Category from the Categories list.
3. Press TAB.
4. Use the arrow keys to select Java Application Project from the Projects list.
5. Press ENTER to invoke the focused Next button.
6. Input **HelloWorld** for the Project Name field in the New Java Application window of the wizard.
7. Ensure the Create Main Class and Set As Main Project checkboxes are selected.

8. Press ENTER. The project is created and the `Main.java` class opens in the Source Editor.

9. Press CTRL-G, input **18** into the edit box, and press ENTER. The cursor goes to the TODO line we are replacing.

10. Press CTRL-E to delete the TODO line.

11. Type **sout** and press TAB. "sout" is expanded to `System.out.println("");` with the cursor between the quotes. Note: TAB is the default expander.

12. Type **Hello, World!** between the quotes.

13. Press CTRL-A to select all the text.

14. Press ALT-SHIFT-F to format the selected text.

15. Press F6 to run the project.

16. Verify `Hello, World!` is printed to the Output window.

17. Take a breather and congratulate yourself.

Live Code Templates

Live code templates are the same as code templates, but include "live" editable fields upon expansion. While constructor-related, try/catch loops, and getters and setters functionality can be related to live code templates as mentioned in the objective, their features are more prevalent in other areas of the IDE such as within code insertion popups, basic code templates, and refactoring commands. Actual live code templates that use special code syntax to give them "live" editable capabilities include those represented in Table 6-6. Items in box brackets are representative of "live" editable fields. These box brackets are for use in the table and are not seen in the actual templates. Editing the field and pressing ENTER changes the value and associated fields. Pressing TAB traverses to the next editable field. Pressing ESC exits the code template.

Live Code Template Usage

Just like regular code templates, live code templates are created from expanding abbreviations. The main difference for live code templates is the use of code constructs that place the template into a live state with editable fields. The presence of parameter constructs can create live code templates. The general format for parameter constructs is simple with the inclusion of hints and values:

```
${param_name hint=value hint=value ...}
```

TABLE 6-6   Various Live Code Templates

Live Code Templates for Conditional Statements	
iff	`if ([exp]) {` `}`

ifelse	`if ([exp]) {`
	`}else{`
	`}`

inst	`if ([args] instanceof [Object]) {`
	`    Object [object] = (Object) args;`
	`}`

Code Templates for Iteration Statements	

forc	`for (Iterator [it] = [col].iterator(); it.hasNext();)`
	`{`
	`    [Object] [object] = it.next();`
	`}`

fore	`for (String [string] : [args]) {` `}`

fori	`for (int [i] = 0; i < [args].length; i++) {`
	`    [String] [string] = args[i];`
	`}`

forl	`for (int [i] = 0; i < [lst].size(); i++) {`
	`    [Object] [object] = lst.get(i);`
	`}`

forv	`for (int [[i] = 0; i < [vct].size(); i++) {`
	`    [Object] [object] = vct.elementAt(i);`
	`}`

whilexp	`while ([exp]) {` `}`
dowhile	`do {` `} while ([exp]);`

whileit	`while ([it].hasNext()) {`
	`    [Object] [object] = it.next();`
	`}`

whilen	`while ([en].hasMoreElements()) {`
	`    [Object] [object] = en.nextElement();`
	`}`

Live Code Templates for System Messages	
soutv	`System.out.println("[args] = " + args);`

Available hints include `default`, `editable`, `instanceof`, `array`, `iterable`, `type`, `iterableElementType`, `leftSideType`, `rightSideType`, `cast`, and `newVarName`. Knowing the exact details of these hints is outside the scope of the exam, but you can find out more within the IDE's help system.

As a general example, the live code template syntax for a basic assertion statement would be as follows:

```
assert (${EXP instanceof="boolean" default="exp"}) : ${STRING
instanceof="java.lang.String" default="string"};
```

Once expanded, the live code template would be created with the EXP field editable with the cursor:

```
assert ([exp]) : [string];
```

Pressing TAB allows the string field to be edited. Press ENTER to leave the live code template once you are done.

Remember to use the `-ea` switch in your project configuration to enable assertions.

There are a few ways to invoke code generation from the Source Editor detailed in the Scenario & Solution.

SCENARIO & SOLUTION

You wish to generate code such as constructors, getters and setters, `equals` and `hashCode` methods, and properties.	Inside the Source Editor, right-click, select Insert Code or press ALT-INSERT, and then select the desired code generation action from the popup menu.
You wish to generate code such as getters and setters, variable declarations, and extracted interfaces in a safe manner.	Inside the Source Editor, right-click Refactor, and then select the desired code.
You wish to expand abbreviations into expanded text or to use abbreviations in association with smart templates.	Input the desired abbreviation and invoke the code template by the defined expand template keystroke (SPACE, SHIFT-SPACE, TAB, or ENTER).
You wish to open a popup to assist with code completion.	Press CTRL-SPACE from within the Source Editor.
You wish to open a popup to assist with code completion for elements associated with the classpath.	Press CTRL-SPACE-SPACE, CTRL-ALT-BACKSLASH, or CTRL-ALT-SPACE from within the Source Editor.

EXERCISE 6-6

Writing Descriptions for Code Templates

As of NetBeans 6.8, the descriptions for Java Code Templates elements have yet to be completed. The absence of the information provides the perfect opportunity to complete the descriptions yourself. Once they're completed, you should be a code templates expert with polished Java fundamental skills (for example, better keyword and statements understanding).

1. In the Options window, click the Editor icon, and select the Code Templates tab.
2. Ensure that the first Templates table row is selected for the En code template abbreviation.
3. Select the Description tab and provide a description for En. (For example, "An Enumeration class allows for the creation of enumeration types containing a fixed set of constants as fields.")
4. Provide a description for each abbreviation.

CERTIFICATION SUMMARY

This chapter refined your expertise with the Source Editor. In doing so, we noted that the Source Editor is actually a collection of various editors. We also stated that the exam primarily focuses on the Java source editor. We moved on to provide ample coverage of the four Source Editor–related objectives. The objectives covered Source Editor configurations, error highlighting and correction, editor hints, and code generation.

In regard to configurations, we covered the settings features in the Editor, Fonts & Colors, and Keymap panels of the Options window. The exam may ask for specific information provided in these panels, so ensure you review the features as detailed in this chapter.

We then discussed the various ways the IDE highlights diagnostics in relationship to the Source Editor including Projects window icons, left margin annotation glyphs, Source Editor highlighting, error stripe marks, and Output window messages. Being able to visualize these different types of diagnostics helps you at test time.

We covered editor hints, when they are available, and how they can be invoked. Being comfortable with editor hints not only helps you on the exam, but also helps you greatly on the job with your productivity.

We covered the many ways that code can be generated in the Source Editor. We covered code completion, code templates, and live code templates. Generating code saves development teams time and money. Since code generation is such an important feature, you can likely expect at least a couple of related questions on the exam.

Completing this chapter, you have gained all of the knowledge needed to score well on questions related to the Source Editor.

✓

TWO-MINUTE DRILL

Modifying Behavior of the Source Editor

❏ The Source Editor is conceptualized as a collection of editors.

❏ The editors provided by NetBeans include HTML, Java, JSP, and XML source editors.

❏ The exam focuses on the Java editor. It is integrated with key IDE components such as the GUI Builder, the compiler, and the debugger.

❏ The Options window provides configuration options to change the default appearance and behavior of the IDE.

❏ The General panel in the Options window provides for selection of the default web browser, proxy settings configuration, and activation of Usage Statistics.

❏ The Editor panel in the Options window provides for configuration of code folding, camel case behavior, source code formatting, code completion, code templates, hints, the marking of occurrences, and macros.

❏ The Fonts & Colors panel in the Options window provides for configuration of language syntax attributes, IDE component (for example, status bar) highlighting, annotation glyphs coloring, and background coloring of the diff tool components.

❏ The Keymap panel in the Options window allows for the selection and management of Keymap Profiles.

Understanding Error Highlighting and Correction

❏ The NetBeans IDE produces various diagnostics in the form of icons, glyphs, highlighting, marks, and messages.

❏ The Projects window displays icons next to various nodes in regard to existence of warnings, errors, and information diagnostics. The icon is generally the same as the icon under normal conditions, with an added symbol such as a wrench or an exclamation mark.

❏ The left margin of the Source Editor includes annotation diagnostic glyphs for errors, warnings, and fixable problems.

❏ The Source Editor includes diagnostic highlighting of errors by the use of underlining.

❏ The error stripe at the right of the Source Editor includes diagnostic marks as well as marks correlating to bookmarks and comments for the todo list.

❏ The Output window produces warning and error messages upon building the project. Errors have hyperlinks to the problems in the source code.

Using Editor Hints

❑ Light bulbs are displayed in the left margin of the Source Editor relative to fixable warnings and errors. Hovering over the light bulb opens a popup detailing the issue at hand.

❑ Editor hints are invokable commands associated with fixable problems flagged by source code warnings and errors.

❑ Editor hints are listed by selecting ALT-ENTER relative to the fixable code or by clicking the associated light bulb in the left margin. Clicking the desired editor hint invokes it.

Generating Code

❑ Code completion consists of mechanisms that assist the user in automatically or manually completing partially inserted code.

❑ Code completion popup windows can be invoked by pressing CTRL-SPACE.

❑ Code completion popup windows associated with the entire classpath can be invoked by pressing CTRL-SPACE-SPACE, CTRL-ALT-BACKSLASH, or CTRL-ALT-SPACE.

❑ A code generation popup is available when pressing ALT-INSERT that allows you to automate code such as constructors, getters and setters, `equals`, and `hashCode` methods and properties.

❑ Code templates consist of abbreviations designed to be expanded into fuller text upon a designated keystroke selection.

❑ Code templates can be expanded by pressing SPACE, SHIFT-SPACE, TAB, or ENTER as defined in the Code Templates tab of the Editor panel in the Options window.

❑ Code templates can use special code templates syntax to affect how the code template behaves.

❑ Live code templates are code templates that include editable fields within the "live" expanded text. Tabbing traverses the editable fields highlighted in blue. The ESC key terminates the editing mode.

SELF TEST

The following questions will help you measure your understanding of the material presented in this chapter. Read all the choices carefully because there might be more than one correct answer. Choose all correct answers for each question.

Modifying Behavior of the Source Editor

1. Code folding is configurable under the General tab under which panel selection?
   A. Tools | Options, General panel
   B. Tools | Options, Editor panel
   C. Tools | Options, Keymap panel
   D. Tools | Options, Miscellaneous panel

2. Checkboxes are provided in the Options window for which Code Completion features? Select all that apply.
   A. Auto Popup Completion Window
   B. Insert Single Proposals Automatically
   C. Case Sensitive Code Completion
   D. Auto Comment Spellchecker
   E. Auto Popup Documentation Window

3. If camel case navigation for Java is enabled through the Options window, the caret stops at which characters in SaltWaterFish when using Next (CTRL-RIGHT) / Previous (CTRL-LEFT) word actions?
   A. The caret only stops at the first character S.
   B. The caret stops at all nonconsecutive capital letters; S, W, and F.
   C. The caret stops at the first and last camel-case characters, S and F.
   D. The caret does not stop at any characters.

4. Which macros are supplied by NetBeans by default as listed in the Options window? Select all that apply.
   A. cast-to-String
   B. debug-var
   C. quote-word
   D. select-invalid-identifier

Understanding Error Highlighting and Correction

5. Which Fonts & Colors profile associated with the Options window has the color black associated with default color used for the left margin, default line colors, and so on?
   A. Earth
   B. NetBeans 5.5
   C. Norway Today
   D. City Lights
   E. None of the above

6. What language categories exist for Syntax coloring configuration? Select all that apply.
   A. DTD
   B. HTML
   C. JOVIAL
   D. JSP
   E. XML

7. What attributes are configurable for diff tool items being highlighted?
   A. Background colors
   B. Foreground colors
   C. Background and foreground colors
   D. None of the above

Using Editor Hints

8. What editor hints are listed for an unused import statement when pressing ALT-ENTER? Select all that apply.
   A. Remove Unused Import
   B. Generate Import Related Code
   C. Refactor Imports
   D. All of the above

9. Which statement will result in a light bulb with the editor hint "possible loss of precision required: short found: int"?
   A. `int x = 1; short y = 2; int z = x + y;`
   B. `int x = 1; short y = 2; short z = x + y;`
   C. `short x = 1; short y = 2; short z = (short) (x + y);`
   D. `int x = 1; int y = 2; int z = x + y;`

10. If there are multiple statements on one line with errors that have fixable hints, what is seen in the left margin?

    A. A light bulb accompanied by an exclamation mark in a red octagon.

    B. Three layered light bulbs accompanied by an exclamation mark in a red octagon.

    C. Two separate light bulbs accompanied by an exclamation mark in a red octagon.

    D. The word "Mult" in a red octagon.

11. Which corrective actions can be performed from editor hints?

    A. Initializing variables

    B. Inserting method parameters

    C. Inserting casts

    D. Managing missing and unused import statements

    E. All of the above

Generating Code

12. Consider the following illustration:

How would this Generate Getters And Setters dialog box be invoked?

    A. In the Source Editor, right-click to open popup, and then choose Refactor | Encapsulate Fields.

    B. Select the menu option Source | Insert Code | Getter And Setter.

    C. In the Source Editor, right-click to open popup, and then choose Insert Code | Getter And Setter.

    D. B and C.

    E. All of the above.

SELF TEST ANSWERS

Modifying Behavior of the Source Editor

1. Code folding is configurable under the General tab under which panel selection?
   A. Tools | Options, General panel
   B. Tools | Options, Editor panel
   C. Tools | Options, Keymap panel
   D. Tools | Options, Miscellaneous panel

   ☑ **B.** Code folding is configurable on the General tab under the Tools | Options, Editor panel selection.

   ☒ **A, C,** and **D** are incorrect. **A** is incorrect because code folding is not configurable relative to the Tools | Options, General panel selection. **C** is incorrect because code folding is not configurable relative to the Tools | Options, Keymap panel selection. **D** is incorrect because code folding is not configurable relative to the Tools | Options, Miscellaneous panel selection.

2. Checkboxes are provided in the Options window for which Code Completion features? Select all that apply.
   A. Auto Popup Completion Window
   B. Insert Single Proposals Automatically
   C. Case Sensitive Code Completion
   D. Auto Comment Spellchecker
   E. Auto Popup Documentation Window

   ☑ **A, B, C,** and **E.** Checkboxes are provided in the Options window for the following Code Completion features: Auto Popup Completion Window, Insert Single Proposals Automatically, Case Sensitive Code Completion, Auto Popup Documentation Window.

   ☒ **D** is incorrect because there is no Auto Comment Spellchecker checkbox.

3. If camel case navigation for Java is enabled through the Options window, the caret stops at which characters in SaltWaterFish when using Next (CTRL-RIGHT) / Previous (CTRL-LEFT) word actions?
   A. The caret only stops at the first character S.
   B. The caret stops at all nonconsecutive capital letters; S, W, and F.
   C. The caret stops at the first and last camel-case characters, S and F.
   D. The caret does not stop at any characters.

☑ **B.** If camel case navigation for Java is enabled through the Options window, the caret stops at all nonconsecutive capital letters in `SaltWaterFish` when using Next (CTRL-RIGHT) / Previous (CTRL-LEFT) word actions. The letters are S, W, and F.

☒ **A, C, and D** are incorrect. **A** is incorrect because the caret stops on S, W, and F. **C** is incorrect because the caret stops on S, W, and F. **D** is incorrect because the caret stops on S, W, and F.

4. Which macros are supplied by NetBeans by default as listed in the Options window? Select all that apply.
   A. cast-to-String
   B. debug-var
   C. quote-word
   D. select-invalid-identifier

   ☑ **A, B, and C.** The macros cast-to-String, debug-var, and quote-word are supplied by default in the Options window.

   ☒ **D** is incorrect because select-invalid-identifier is not a supplied macro.

Understanding Error Highlighting and Correction

5. Which Fonts & Colors profile associated with the Options window has the color black associated with default color used for the left margin, default line colors, and so on?
   A. Earth
   B. NetBeans 5.5
   C. Norway Today
   D. City Lights
   E. None of the above

   ☑ **D.** The City Lights profile has black associated with the default line color, left margin, and other elements.

   ☒ **A, B, C, and E** are incorrect. **A** is incorrect because the Earth profile has white associated with the default color. **B** is incorrect because the NetBeans 5.5 profile has white associated with the default color. **C** is incorrect because the Norway Today profile has a darker color [18,30,49] associated with the default color, but it is not black. **E** is incorrect because "None of the above" is an incorrect answer.

6. What language categories exist for Syntax coloring configuration? Select all that apply.

 A. DTD

 B. HTML

 C. JOVIAL

 D. JSP

 E. XML

 ☑ **A, B, D,** and **E.** Syntax color configuration is available for the following categories/languages among others: DTD, HTML, JSP, and XML.

 ☒ **C** is incorrect because JOVIAL is not available as a category for syntax color configuration.

7. What attributes are configurable for diff tool items being highlighted?

 A. Background colors

 B. Foreground colors

 C. Background and foreground colors

 D. None of the above

 ☑ **A.** Background colors can be configured for the diff tool items being highlighted.

 ☒ **B, C,** and **D** are incorrect. **B** is incorrect because foreground colors are not configurable for diff tool items being highlighted. **C** is incorrect because foreground colors are not configurable for diff tool items being highlighted, but background colors are configurable. **D** is incorrect because the answer is not "None of the above."

Using Editor Hints

8. What editor hints are listed for an unused import statement when pressing ALT-ENTER? Select all that apply.

 A. Remove Unused Import

 B. Generate Import Related Code

 C. Refactor Imports

 D. All of the above

 ☑ **A.** The only editor hint provided for unused imports when pressing ALT-ENTER is "Remove Unused Import."

 ☒ **B, C,** and **D** are incorrect. **B** is incorrect because there is no "Generate Import Related Code" editor hint. **C** is incorrect because there is no "Refactor Imports" editor hint. **D** is incorrect because only answer **A** is correct, not "All of the above."

9. Which statement will result in a light bulb with the editor hint "possible loss of precision required: short found: int"?

A. `int x = 1; short y = 2; int z = x + y;`
B. `int x = 1; short y = 2; short z = x + y;`
C. `short x = 1; short y = 2; short z = (short) (x + y);`
D. `int x = 1; int y = 2; int z = x + y;`

  ☑ **B.** Variables x and y are implicitly casted to integers; therefore their sum does not fit into a short.

  ☒ **A, C,** and **D** are incorrect. **A** is incorrect because the statements are technically correct and will not cause a light bulb to be displayed. **C** is incorrect because the statements are technically correct and will not cause a light bulb to be displayed. **D** is incorrect because the statements are technically correct and will not cause a light bulb to be displayed.

10. If there are multiple statements on one line with errors that have fixable hints, what is seen in the left margin?

A. A light bulb accompanied by an exclamation mark in a red octagon.
B. Three layered light bulbs accompanied by an exclamation mark in a red octagon.
C. Two separate light bulbs accompanied by an exclamation mark in a red octagon.
D. The word "Mult" in a red octagon.

  ☑ **A.** When multiple statements are on one line with errors, only one light bulb accompanied by an exclamation mark in a red octagon is displayed.

  ☒ **B, C,** and **D** are incorrect. **B** is incorrect because there is no glyph with multiple light bulbs. **C** is incorrect because there can be only one glyph displayed at a time. **D** is incorrect because there is no glyph with the word "Mult" in a red octagon.

11. Which corrective actions can be performed from editor hints?

A. Initializing variables
B. Inserting method parameters
C. Inserting casts
D. Managing missing and unused import statements
E. All of the above

  ☑ **E.** All of the listed corrective actions can be performed from editor hints including initializing variables, inserting method parameters, inserting casts, and managing missing and unused import statement.

Generating Code

12.   Consider the following illustration:

How would this Generate Getters And Setters dialog box be invoked?

A.   In the Source Editor, right-click to open popup, and then choose Refactor | Encapsulate Fields.

B.   Select the menu option Source | Insert Code | Getter And Setter.

C.   In the Source Editor, right-click to open popup, and then choose Insert Code | Getter And Setter.

D.   B and C.

E.   All of the above.

    ☑   **D. D** is correct because both answer **B** and **C** are valid. The Generate Getters And Setters dialog box can be invoked by first opening the appropriate source file and then selecting Source | Insert Code | Getter And Setter and by right-clicking the source file | Insert Code | Getter And Setter.

    ☒   **A, B** (alone), **C** (alone), and **E** are incorrect. **A** is incorrect because the Generate Getters And Setters dialog box cannot be opened by right-clicking the Source Editor and selecting Refactor | Encapsulate Fields. Note that this was a tricky test question because you can encapsulate fields using the Refactor menu; it's just that the dialog box is different. **B** and **C** are incorrect individually, as they both allow means to open the Generate Getters And Setters dialog box as represented in answer **D. E** is incorrect because "All of the above" answers are not correct.

7

Refactoring Support

CERTIFICATION OBJECTIVES

- Refactoring Source Code
- Two-Minute Drill

Q&A   Self Test

The NetBeans Refactoring module supports the performance of high-level code transformations. These transformations, better known as refactoring processes, change the internal structure of the code without changing its external behavior. Refactoring improves the quality of your software product without changing its functionality.

There are many reasons for refactoring code. Refactoring is the process of reorganizing, renaming, and restructuring code so that the code is easier to read and maintain. It is an integral part of day-to-day development activities. Refactoring does not change functionality or features. It is important to note that while automated refactoring features of code development environments are popular, they sometimes impart undesirable changes that can change the existing code functionality; care and caution must be practiced when using these tools.

Examples of refactoring include renaming classes or fields, encapsulating fields, and changing method signatures. Periodic refactoring is important for the long-term health and viability of any project. The benefits of refactoring are listed in Figure 7-1.

FIGURE 7-1   The benefits of refactoring

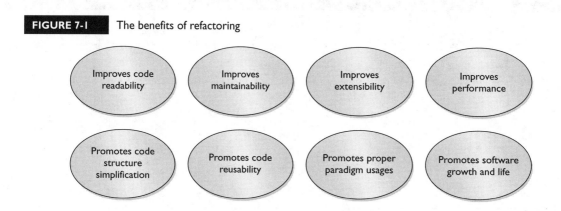

Consider showing Figure 7-1 to your boss and/or coworkers to spark a discussion on adopting periodic refactoring activities. Couple this with reports from software quality tools, and it'll be a quick sell.

The importance and popularity of refactoring has been recognized for some time now and has been captured in many books and websites. One such book is *Refactoring: Improving the Design of Existing Code*, by Martin Fowler et al (Addison Wesley, 1999). Author Martin Fowler also hosts a website on refactoring: http://www.refactoring.com. Both his website and book contain a catalog of common refactorings. The catalog is periodically updated on his website: http://refactoring .com/catalog/. Many of the detailed refactorings have been adopted by today's IDEs such as IntelliJ IDEA, Eclipse IDE, JDeveloper IDE, and the NetBeans IDE. Danny Dig also maintains a refactoring-related website (http://refactoring.info) with an emphasis on providing links to workshops, articles, and papers on refactoring.

The exam focuses on how to use the different refactorings provided by the NetBeans IDE. Therefore, this chapter discusses the basic refactoring architecture applied by NetBeans and the IDE's refactoring commands, how to configure the processes, and how to invoke them.

NetBeans Refactoring Architecture

NetBeans architecture supports a Refactoring API on which the Refactoring module has been implemented. The API can be referenced at the NetBeans API website covering Javadoc documentation on all NetBeans APIs: http://bits.netbeans.org/dev/javadoc/. You may find this link beneficial if you are interested in contributing and improving the module, or if you are just interested in seeing the underpinnings of the API.

Remember that refactoring does not change the functionality of the code, improve performance, or fix bugs (for example, threading issues). The process does not improve system qualities such as flexibility, security, capacity, or availability. Refactoring simply improves the structure of the code. And as you've seen in the introduction and will now see in detailed examples, refactoring is an important part of the development process.

All the refactoring operations are consistent throughout the IDE for each Java element. A series of selections and validations must occur before a refactoring operation is performed. Figure 7-2 details the general flow of a NetBeans IDE refactoring process.

FIGURE 7-2   Basic NetBeans refactoring process flow

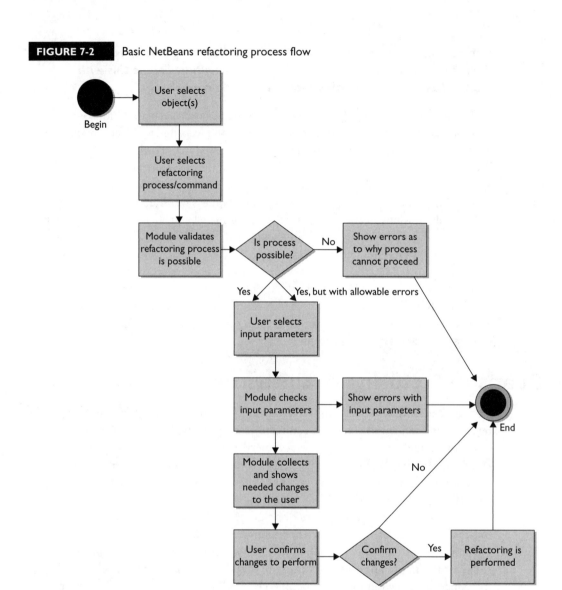

Understanding the NetBeans Refactoring Process

Each refactoring process follows the same primary flow. In this exercise, you map a NetBeans refactoring with the basic flow.

1. Review and become familiar with Figure 7-2, which shows the basic NetBeans refactoring process flow.

2. Choose any NetBeans refactoring process/command (for example, Rename or Safely Delete).

3. Create a new flow control diagram based on your selected refactoring command and on the basic refactoring process outline provided in Figure 7-2.

CERTIFICATION OBJECTIVE

Refactoring Source Code

Exam Objective 5.1   Describe the purpose and uses of refactoring and demonstrate the ability to perform basic refactoring on Java source code.

NetBeans IDE refactorings are logically grouped into five categories represented in Table 7-1. The refactoring categories are best practices, simplification, generalization, organizational, and management. Thinking in terms of these categories helps you create a mental map of the operations. These groupings are repeated throughout this chapter to help you memorize the refactorings. These groupings are not standards; they were designed specifically for use in this book.

TABLE 7-1	Refactoring Descriptions

Menu Option	Description
Best Practices Refactorings	
Find Usages	Not a complete refactoring, but identifies where certain elements exist that could help to determine whether to perform refactoring.
Rename	Renames packages, classes, interfaces, methods, and fields and all references to them from any source code files in the project.
Move	Moves a class or interface to another package. All references in the project source code files are updated accordingly.
Copy	Copies a class or interface to the same or another package.
Safely Delete	Verifies that code elements are not referenced before deleting them.
Simplification Refactorings	
Change Method Parameters	Changes the method signature including its visibility modifier.
Generalization and Realization Refactorings	
Pull Up	Moves methods and fields to an existing superclass.
Push Down	Moves inner classes, methods, and fields to all immediate subclasses.
Extract Interface	Creates a new interface from public nonstatic methods in a class or interface, and updates the extracting class or interface so it is inherited.
Extract Superclass	Creates a new superclass and updates the extracting class so it is inherited.
Use Supertype Where Possible	Changes the type to a supertype for code that references the selected class.
Organizational Refactorings	
Move Inner To Outer Level	Moves an inner class up one level. If the inner class is a top-level inner class, it is made into an outer class with its own source code file. If the inner class is nested within another inner class, method, or variable, it is moved up to be within the same level of that scope.
Convert Anonymous To Inner	Converts an anonymous class to an inner class.
Introduce Variable	Introduces a new statement for a variable from an existing block of code. The existing block of code is replaced with a call to the new statement.
Introduce Constant	Introduces a new statement for a constant from an existing block of code. The existing block of code is replaced with a call to the new statement.
Introduce Field	Introduces a new statement for a field from an existing block of code. The existing block of code is replaced with a call to the new statement.
Introduce Method	Introduces a new method from an existing block of code. The existing block of code is replaced with a call to the method.
Encapsulate Fields	Generates accessor (getters) and mutator (setters) methods with an option to allow referencing code to use the new methods.

| TABLE 7-1 | Refactoring Descriptions *(continued)* |

Refactoring Management	
Undo	Undoes refactorings based on the order in which they were most recently performed.
Redo	Redoes refactorings based on the order in which they were recently undone.

The main refactorings that the IDE supports are structured around key Java elements including packages, classes, interfaces, methods, fields, and inner classes. Table 7-2 shows you what you can do in regard to refactoring with each element. The information in Table 7-2 is explored further in the Scenario & Solution.

| TABLE 7-2 | Refactorings and Java Elements |

Refactoring Command	Java-Related Element
Rename	Packages, classes, interfaces, methods, and fields
Move	Classes and interfaces
Copy	Classes and interfaces
Safely Delete	Packages, classes, interfaces, methods, and fields
Change Method Parameters	Methods
Pull Up	Methods and fields
Push Down	Methods, fields, and inner classes
Extract Interface	Public nonstatic methods
Extract Superclass	Methods and fields
Use Supertype Where Possible	Classes
Move Inner To Outer Level	Inner classes
Convert Anonymous To Inner (NetBeans 6.1), Convert Anonymous To Member (NetBeans 6.8)	Anonymous inner classes
Introduce Variable	Primitive literals, String objects
Introduce Constant	Primitive literals, String objects
Introduce Field	Primitive literals, String objects
Introduce Method	Blocks of code
Encapsulate Fields	Fields

SCENARIO & SOLUTION

You wish to perform refactoring operations on a class.	Use Rename, Move, Copy, Safely Delete, or Use Supertype Where Possible.
You wish to perform refactoring operations on a field. What commands are available?	Use Rename, Safely Delete, Pull Up, Push Down, Extract Superclass, or Encapsulate Fields.
You wish to perform refactoring operations in regard to unnesting inner classes.	Use Move Inner To Outer Level or Convert Anonymous To Inner.
You wish to perform refactoring operations on primitive literals.	Use Introduce Variable, Introduce Constant, Introduce Field, or Introduce Method.
You wish to perform refactoring operations on packages.	Use Rename or Safely Delete.

We shall now explore (with the exam-targeted version of NetBeans, 6.1) each refactoring as detailed in Table 7-1 and Table 7-2. We look at each refactoring within the following categorized sections:

- Best Practices Refactorings
- Simplification Refactorings
- Generalization and Realization Refactorings
- Organizational Refactorings
- Refactoring Management

Best Practices Refactorings

Proper packaging, application of naming conventions, and clearance of unused code are all examples of best practices when it comes to coding software applications. Basic refactorings such as Rename, Move, and Safely Delete directly support these operations. You may find yourself turning to these features when you inherit code that has not met best practices. Consider reviewing *The Elements of Java Style* by Rogue Wave Software (Cambridge University Press, 2000) for more details of proper Java style and practices. This section explores the following refactoring commands to ensure the use and adoption of best practices:

- Find Usages
- Rename

- Move
- Copy
- Safely Delete

Find Usages

The Find Usages command does not perform refactoring. Instead it can be used as a research tool to see if refactoring is needed. Have you inherited Java code where several instance variables have been misspelled or have used camel case and underscores interchangeably? Or you might have run into code that extensively uses public variables. This may also make you cringe, wondering what other surprises await in lieu of best practices. The Find Usages command could come to your rescue to quickly expose where these misnamed variables are used.

Many developers use the Find Usages command when trying to understand how an application has been constructed. In Figure 7-3, the Find Usages dialog box is used to find all usages of the class Rockfish. The Search In Comments checkbox displays any comments where the string is represented. You may also decide to find only usages based on all or direct subtypes. The scope of the search can be one or all projects.

After the user selects the Find button from the Find Usages dialog box, the search is performed, and all usages are displayed in the Usages window, as shown in Figure 7-4. Let's first look at the glyph gutter on the left. These icons are shared by the Refactoring window that we will cover later. The turning arrows update the data. The facing-arrows glyph expands and collapses all of the nodes in the tree. The next two glyphs show the logical and physical views, respectively. The up arrow glyph moves the selection to the previous occurrence. The down arrow moves the selection to the next occurrence.

FIGURE 7-3

Find Usages
dialog box

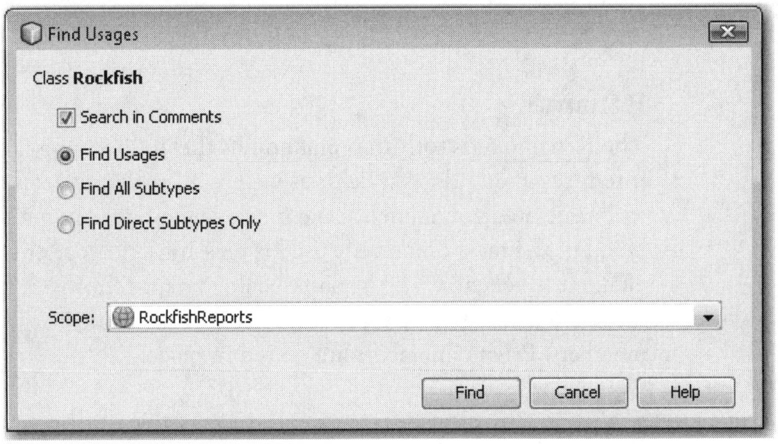

FIGURE 7-4   Usages window within the project

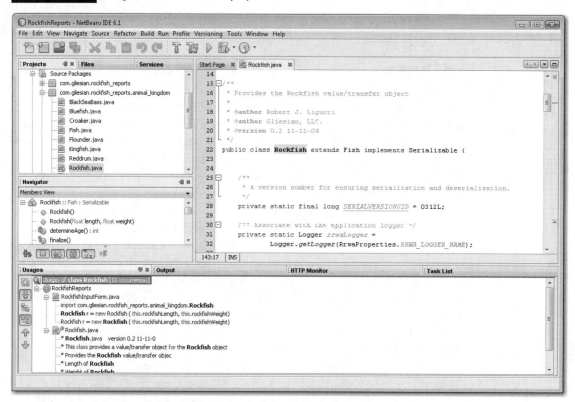

The body of the Usages window shows all of the usages of the selected elements. Among other things, elements that can be searched include packages, classes, methods, and fields.

Rename

The Rename refactoring command has the ability to rename packages, classes, interfaces, methods, and fields as well as all references to them in the source code and associated comments. You can use several ways to get to the refactoring dialog box, but the most commonly used is pressing CTRL-R after selecting the desired element to refactor. The Rename dialog box, as shown in Figure 7-5, provides a means to define the newly desired name. The dialog box only appears for public members. Private members are edited in place.

FIGURE 7-5

Rename Class
refactoring
dialog box

All refactoring of public entities allows you to preview the change first by selecting the Preview dialog box in the initial refactoring dialog box. Figure 7-6 shows all occurrences of changes that occur if the class name Fish is changed to SaltWaterFish. The second and third sections detail the changes by providing a diff of the files. The glyph gutter and refactoring usages list are very similar to those provided with the Find Usages command. The Do Refactoring button moves forward with the refactoring. The Cancel button terminates the refactoring.

on the Job

Software quality tools such as FindBugs, Checkstyle, and PMD expose many coding deficiencies that can be improved upon through refactoring. Poorly named fields and absent encapsulation are just a couple of items that can be identified. All three of these tools can be incorporated into the IDE via plugins obtained through the online NetBeans Plugin Portal.

FIGURE 7-6   Refactoring window within the project

Move

The Move refactoring command allows the developer to move classes or interfaces from one package to another. For example, Figure 7-7 represents the desired move within a UML diagram.

Here, we wish to move all classes and interfaces except the `Tagable.java` and `package.html` files. To do so, the files can be selected and the Move refactoring menu option can be invoked upon them, or the files can be selected and dragged into the desired package. Either way, the Move Classes dialog box is opened, as shown in Figure 7-8. But how the moving is done produces different results. When moving the files by dragging to a new location in the Projects window, the checkbox option

FIGURE 7-7   Move refactoring represented with UML

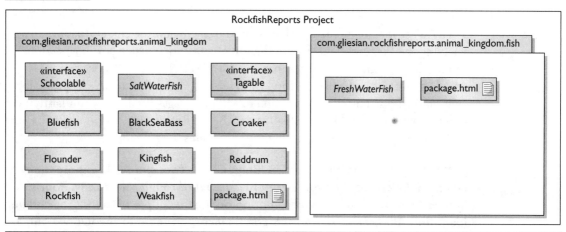

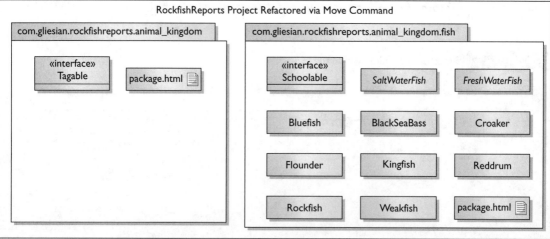

FIGURE 7-8

Move refactoring
dialog box

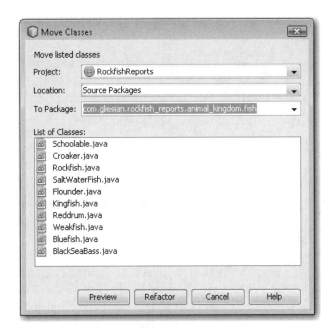

FIGURE 7-8

Move refactoring
dialog box

Move Without Refactoring also appears in the same Move refactoring dialog box. If this option is selected, source code references will not be updated.

Copy

The copy refactoring copies classes or interfaces either within or between packages, directories or projects. When you copy locally, the filename, class name, constructors, and related elements are updated. When you copy to another package, the same changes are made, but you have the option to keep the same name. Figure 7-9 shows a Copy dialog box where one class is copied from the `com.gliesian` `.rockfish_reports.animal_kingdom.fish` package within the Rockfish Reports web project to the `com.gliesian.fish_migration_simulator` `.fish` package within the FishMigrationSimulator project.

Many refactoring operations also apply to other source code files such as HTML pages, JavaServer Pages, properties files, and XML files.

Safely Delete

Safely Delete checks for references prior to deleting the file. Most developers have come across code they were pretty certain wasn't used anymore. They would yank out the code and recompile only to find that it was indeed still used in other files. Safely Delete fixes this problem by taking out the guesswork in just a couple of clicks.

FIGURE 7-9

Copy refactoring
dialog box

Figure 7-10 shows a very basic inheritance pattern where the class
CatFish extends the abstract class BrackishFish. If the developer
deletes BrackishFish, the code breaks because CatFish depends on it.

Let's assume our project has several classes representing fish, and at first
glance they look like they may be inheriting only from SaltWaterFish and
FreshWaterFish, so we could get rid of BrackishFish. Let's not make this
assumption; instead perform a Safely Delete check on BrackishFish. In the
dialog box shown in Figure 7-11 we would click Preview to view any potential
dependencies.

FIGURE 7-10

Inheritance
shown with UML

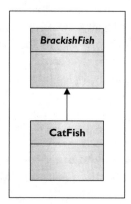

FIGURE 7-11

Safe Delete refactoring dialog box

Safe Delete
Search for usages and delete BrackishFish.
Search In Comments
Preview
Refactor
Cancel
Help

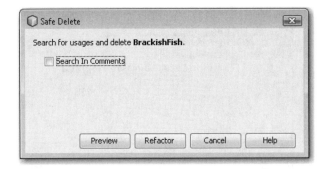

As you can see in Figure 7-12, there were dependencies, so they came back as errors. NetBeans allows the user to perform refactorings with warnings, but not with errors. Your next step would be to click the Show Usages button to view the dependencies.

The Usages window in Figure 7-13 that appears after you select Show Usages in the Safe Delete dialog box shows the warning and errors. The window also provides a Rerun Safe Delete button that can be clicked after you perform additional changes to your project.

FIGURE 7-12

Safe Delete error and warning dialog box

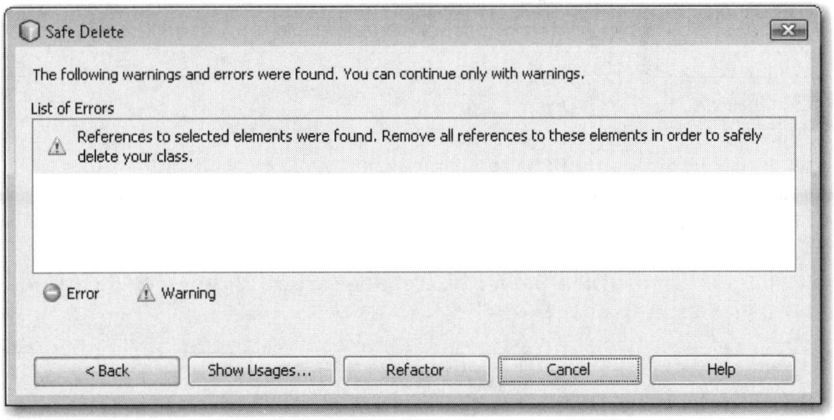

Safe Delete
The following warnings and errors were found. You can continue only with warnings.
List of Errors
References to selected elements were found. Remove all references to these elements in order to safely delete your class.
Error
Warning
< Back
Show Usages...
Refactor
Cancel
Help

FIGURE 7-13

Usages window
for Safe Delete

Simplification Refactorings

Sometimes when we code, we make things more complex than they need to be.
Changing the number and even ordering of parameters can greatly simplify the
structure and improve readability, usability, and understanding. As such, we examine
the Change Method Parameters refactoring in this section.

Change Method Parameters

The Change Method Parameters refactoring command is synonymous to changing
a method's signature. Let's take a look at the following code, where we want to pass
the expiration period in as a parameter to the `scheduleAccountExpiration`
`Reminders` method:

```java
public class Scheduler {
  // Scheduler Constructor
  public Scheduler() {
    scheduleAccountExpirationReminders();
  }
  // Schedule the Outstanding Signature Reminder
  private void scheduleAccountExpirationReminders() {
    DateFormat dfm = new SimpleDateFormat("yyyy-MM-dd HH:mm:ss");
    Date date = null;
    try {
      dfm.setTimeZone(TimeZone.getTimeZone("GMT-5:00"));
      // Starts interval on a Monday
      date = dfm.parse("2010-01-04 07:00:00");
    } catch (ParseException ex) {
      Logger.getLogger(Scheduler.class.getName()).log(Level.SEVERE, null, ex);
    }
    long expirationPeriod = (604800 * 1000); // One week
    Timer t = new Timer();
    t.schedule(new AccountNotificationTask(), date, expirationPeriod);
  }
```

```
// Notification Task
static class AccountNotificationTask extends TimerTask {
  public void run() {
    ...
  }
 }
}
```

To get to the Change Method Parameters dialog box, invoke the Change Method Parameters refactoring command while the method is selected. Once the dialog box is open, you have the options to add parameters, remove unused methods, change the order of parameters, and change the visibility modifier for the method, as shown in Figure 7-14.

For this specific example, we need to make three changes. The first two are done by the refactoring itself.

First, the parameter name and type are added to the method signature:

```
private void scheduleAccountExpirationReminders(double expirationPeriod) {
  ...
}
```

Second, the default argument we selected is filled in for the first parameter by calling scheduleAccountExpirationReminders methods:

```
scheduleAccountExpirationReminders(604800000);
```

And last, for this specific example, we want to comment out the following line:

```
// long expirationPeriod = (604800 * 1000); // One week
```

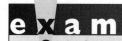

*Varargs (variable arguments) can only be used in the final argument position. Within the Change Method Parameters dialog box, if you attempt to add a new parameter in the last argument position or move the vararg argument away from the last position with the Move Up button, the Refactor button is disabled, so the change is not allowed, and an error message is displayed. Here is a valid vararg signature example:**

```
public static void format (String pattern, Object... arguments) {}.
```

Generalization and Realization Refactorings

Generalization exists when a specialized class inherits elements of a more general class. Realization exists when a class implements an interface. NetBeans provides refactoring support of these principles with five refactoring commands:

- Pull Up
- Push Down
- Extract Interface
- Extract Superclass
- Use Supertype Where Possible

Pull Up

The Pull Up refactoring command supports the movement of methods and/or fields to a class's existing superclass. Consider the class `SaltWaterFish`. Two fields and two methods are related to the conservation status of saltwater fish. The superclass of `SaltWaterFish` is `Fish`. Also, `Fish` has other subclasses such as `FreshWaterFish` and `BrackishFish` that could make use of the conservation status functionality. It would make sense to move the conservation-related fields and methods up to the `Fish` class.

```
package com.gliesian.rockfish_reports.animal_kingdom.fish;
public abstract class SaltWaterFish extends Fish {
  public enum ConservationStatus {
    NO_RISK, LOW_RISK, THREATENED, EXTINCT
  }
  private ConservationStatus conserveStatus = ConservationStatus.NO_RISK;
  public ConservationStatus getConserveStatus() {
    return conserveStatus;
  }
```

```
public void setConserveStatus(ConservationStatus conserveStatus) {
   this.conserveStatus = conserveStatus;
  }
}
```

All classes that extend `Fish` inherit the `Fish` class's attributes and operations. Figure 7-15 shows the benefit of Pull Up refactoring in this scenario. The conservation-related functionality is made available to all `Fish` subclasses after the Pull Up refactoring is completed.

FIGURE 7-15 Pull Up refactoring shown with UML

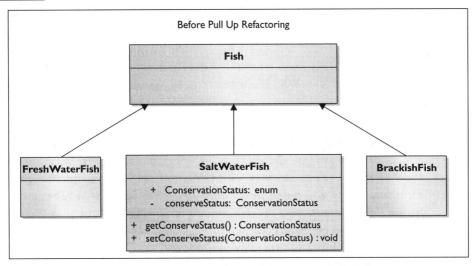

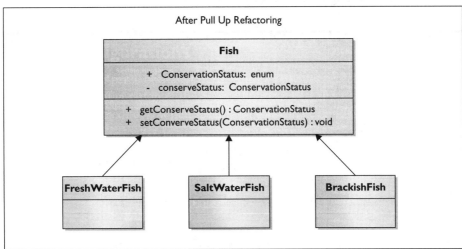

To perform the refactoring, open the Pull Up refactoring dialog box, and select all of the desired fields and methods, as shown in Figure 7-16.

After the Pull Up refactoring has been completed, the conservation-related functionality will have been moved from the `SaltWaterFish` class to the `Fish` class:

```
package com.gliesian.rockfish_reports.animal_kingdom.fish;
public class Fish {
  public enum ConservationStatus {
    NO_RISK, LOW_RISK, THREATENED, EXTINCT
  }
  private ConservationStatus conserveStatus = ConservationStatus.NO_RISK;
  public ConservationStatus getConserveStatus() {
    return conserveStatus;
  }
  public void setConserveStatus(ConservationStatus conserveStatus) {
    this.conserveStatus = conserveStatus;
  }
}
```

on the **job**

Just because refactoring can be quick and easy to perform with the NetBeans IDE, doesn't mean you should rush into performing code refinements. Consider drawing out your refactorings with UML and analyzing what changes you wish to make, before you make them. Take your new design to a team member for review, because you may receive recommendations for better refactorings. You may even receive reasons (for example, political or technical) not to refactor certain code. Note that excessive refactoring can pollute the version control system, making it hard to track changes.

FIGURE 7-16

Pull Up
dialog box

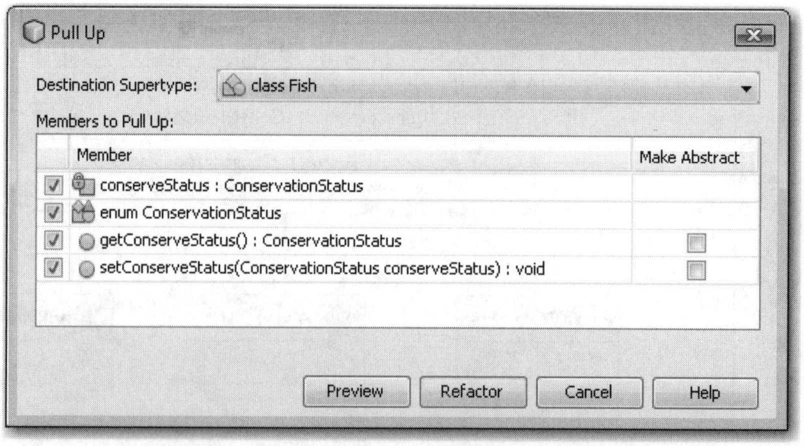

Pull Up		
Destination Supertype: class Fish		▾

Members to Pull Up:

	Member	Make Abstract
☑	conserveStatus : ConservationStatus	
☑	enum ConservationStatus	
☑	getConserveStatus() : ConservationStatus	☐
☑	setConserveStatus(ConservationStatus conserveStatus) : void	☐

Preview   Refactor   Cancel   Help

Push Down

The Push Down refactoring command moves inner classes, methods, and fields to selected immediate subclasses.

For example, let's look at the `SaltWaterFish` class. The instance variable `totalNumberOfStripes` does not apply to all fish, because all fish do not have stripes.

```
package com.gliesian.rockfish_reports.animal_kingdom.fish;
public abstract class SaltWaterFish extends Fish {
  public int totalNumberOfStripes = 14;
}
```

We wish to push down this variable into subclasses of fish objects that do have stripes such as the rockfish, aka Striper. To do this, we must invoke the Push Down command that brings us to the Push Down dialog box, as shown in Figure 7-17.

By default, the Push Down refactoring pushes down the selected element into all of the subclasses. However, if you preview the refactoring, you can individually deselect refactorings, as shown in Figure 7-18.

Extract Interface

The Extract Interface refactoring command creates a new interface from public nonstatic methods in a class or interface and updates the extracting class or interface so it inherits from the newly created interface.

Programming to an interface helps to decouple implementation from use. Many saltwater fish make a drumming sound. Fish that croak or grunt like this include croakers, red drum, and weakfish. Our project currently only supports playing sounds for the croaker fish in the `Croaker` class. We have special requirements for using

FIGURE 7-17

Push Down
dialog box

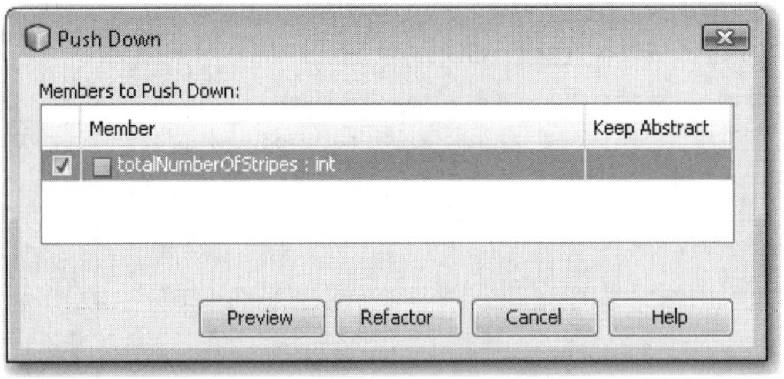

FIGURE 7-18   Push Down preview refactoring window

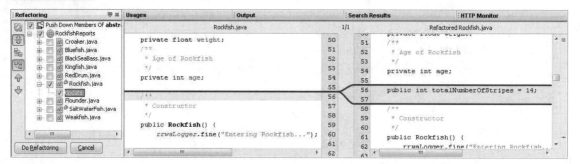

different file types and playback mechanisms depending on the type of fish, so we wanted to program to an interface for the `playDrummingSound` method.

```
package com.gliesian.rockfish_reports.animal_kingdom.fish;
public class Croaker extends SaltWaterFish {
  /**
   * Play a drumming (croaking/grunting) sound
   * for a defined period of time
   *
   * @param timeDuration Time in seconds of drumming sound
   */
  public void playDrummingSound(int timeDuration){
// TODO
  }
}
```

Figure 7-19 shows that once the `playDrummingSound` method signature is extracted into the interface, it is available to all classes after they implement that interface.

FIGURE 7-19   Extract Interface refactoring shown with UML

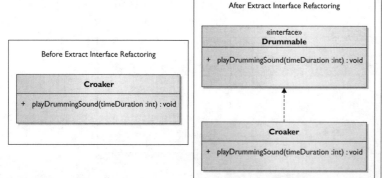
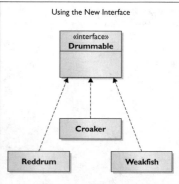

The Extract Interface dialog box is rather straightforward, as shown in Figure 7-20. You have the option of selecting the members you want extracted into the new interface as well as of defining the name of the new interface.

Extract Superclass

The Extract Superclass refactoring command creates a new superclass with the selected members and sets the original class to inherit from the newly created class.

Consider the class Sailfin. A sailfin is a flying fish. The Sailfin class has the method flyAboveWater that could be used by other objects that represented flying fishes.

```
package com.gliesian.rockfish_reports.animal_kingdom.fish;
public class Sailfin {
  public void flyAboveWater (int distanceInInches) {
    }
}
```

When you select the flyAboveWater method and invoke the Extract Superclass command, the Extract Superclass dialog box opens, as shown in Figure 7-21.

After the desired methods have been selected, the name of the new superclass has been stipulated, and the Refactor button has been clicked, a new superclass is created with the specified methods and/or fields. In this case the flyAboveWater

FIGURE 7-20

Extract Interface
dialog box

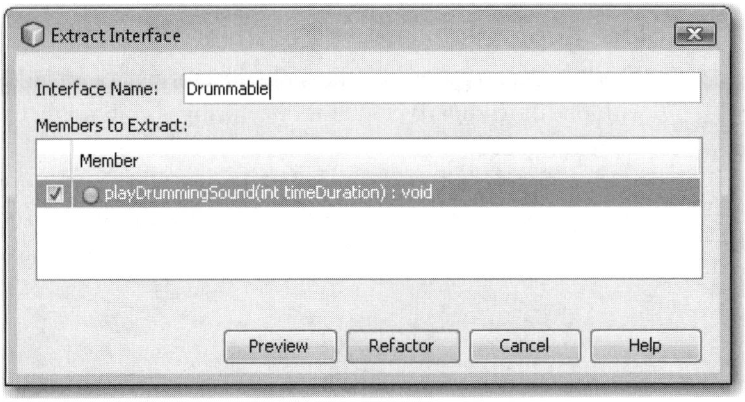

FIGURE 7-21

Extract Superclass
dialog box

method has been moved to the new `FlyingFish` superclass, and the `Sailfin` class has been modified to extend the `FlyingFish` class.

```
package com.gliesian.rockfish_reports.animal_kingdom.fish;
  public class Sailfin extends FlyingFish {
}

package com.gliesian.rockfish_reports.animal_kingdom.fish;
public class FlyingFish {
  public void flyAboveWater(int distanceInInches) {
  }
}
```

Use Supertype Where Possible

The Use Supertype Where Possible refactoring command is used to replace a type with one of its supertypes. This refactoring is commonly used when polymorphism is being leveraged.

Consider the following code for class `PdfReportGenerator`. We plan for the rockfish reference to be instantiated against a supertype such as was done for the black sea bass. Our desired refactoring is depicted in Figure 7-22. You could simply

FIGURE 7-22

Use Supertype
Where Possible
refactoring shown
with UML

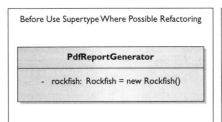 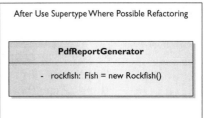

just replace the word `Rockfish` with `Fish`; however, running the Use Supertype
Where Possible command shows all of the acceptable supertypes that may be used in
its related dialog box, as shown in Figure 7-23.

```
package com.gliesian.rockfish_reports.utils;
import com.gliesian.rockfish_reports.animal_kingdom.fish.Fish;
import com.gliesian.rockfish_reports.animal_kingdom.fish.BlackSeaBass;
import com.gliesian.rockfish_reports.animal_kingdom.fish.Rockfish;
import java.util.ArrayList;
public class PdfReportGenerator {
    ArrayList<Fish> fish = new ArrayList<Fish>();
    private Fish blackSeaBass = new BlackSeaBass();
    private Rockfish rockfish = new Rockfish();
}
```

After the refactoring is performed, the affected statement looks like this:

```
Fish rockfish = new Rockfish();
```

FIGURE 7-23

Use Supertype
Where Possible
dialog box

Organizational Refactorings

As developers, we tend to have expectations of where and how code should be structured and organized. When you have to work with projects that are delivered to you, you may find illogical coding situations. With refactoring, you can quickly put things where they belong. NetBeans IDE has seven refactorings that support better organization.

- Move Inner To Outer
- Convert Anonymous To Inner
- Introduce Variable
- Introduce Constant
- Introduce Field
- Introduce Method
- Encapsulate Fields

Move Inner To Outer

The Move Inner To Outer refactoring command moves an inner class up one level. If the inner class is a top-level inner class, it is made into an outer class with its own source code file. If the inner class is nested within another inner class, method, or variable, it is moved up to be within the same level of that scope.

Consider the following inner and outer classes:

```
// Outer Class
public class Ocean {
  //Inner class
  public class Inlet {
    public void retrieveTideInformation(){
      System.out.println("Tide Information");
    }
  }
}
```

Select the inner class and invoke the Move Inner To Outer refactoring. The Move Inner To Outer dialog box displays, as in Figure 7-24.

The Move Inner To Outer dialog box prompts you for the class name and provides a checkbox for the declaration field of the current outer class. If the

Move Inner To
Outer refactoring
dialog box

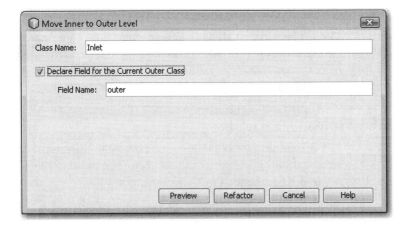

checkbox is selected and the Refactor button is clicked, the inner class is removed
from the source code, and a new file named `Inlet.java` is created with the
following content:

```
package com.gliesian.rockfish_reports.utils;
public class Inlet {
  Ocean outer;
  public Inlet(Ocean outer) {
    super();
    this.outer = outer;
  }
  public void retrieveTideInformation() {
     System.out.println("Tide Information");
  }
}
```

If the checkbox is not selected and the Refactor button is clicked, the inner class
is removed from the source code and a new file named `Inlet.java` is created with
the following content:

```
package com.gliesian.rockfish_reports.utils;
public class Inlet {
  public void retrieveTideInformation() {
    System.out.println("Tide Information");
  }
}
```

Convert Anonymous To Inner

The Convert Anonymous To Inner refactoring command converts an anonymous class to an inner class. In NetBeans 6.8, the refactoring has been modified to Convert Anonymous To Member. Since this refactoring is not on the exam and it is still in development, we forego coverage.

Introduce Variable

The Introduce Variable refactoring command introduces a new statement for a local variable from an existing block of code. The existing block of code is replaced with a call to the new statement.

For the following code example, we introduce variable statements for the two integer primitives:

```
public void tallyTotalFish() {
  int totalFish = 2 + 10;
  System.out.println("totalFish");
}
```

Select the value 2 and invoke the Introduce Variable command. The Introduce Variable dialog box displays, as shown in Figure 7-25. Adding a name, selecting the Declare Final checkbox, and selecting OK updates the source as shown next. Note that a variable statement was added for the 10 value as well, with similar steps.

```
public void tallyTotalFish() {
  final int rockfishCount = 2;
  final int bluefishCount = 10;
    int totalFish = rockfish + bluefish;
    System.out.println("totalFish");
}
```

FIGURE 7-25

Introduce Variable
dialog box

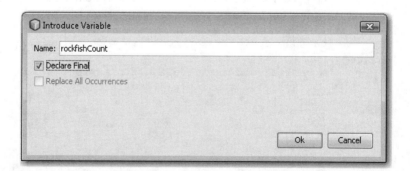

Introduce Constant

The Introduce Constant refactoring command introduces a new statement for a constant from an existing block of code. The existing block of code is replaced with a call to the new statement.

Consider the following block of code, where we include the version name of our application ("rrwa-0.1") in the object's toString method. This version string is an ideal candidate to represent as a constant.

```
/**
* Overrides the toString methods, returning a string representing the
* RrwaProperties object.
*/
  @Override
  public String toString() {
  String returnValue = "[" + "rrwa-0.1" +  "]";
  return returnValue;
}
```

To introduce a new constant for this string, simply highlight the complete string including quotation marks with your mouse, and invoke the Introduce Constant command. The Introduce Constant dialog box displays, as seen in Figure 7-26.

In the dialog box, give the new constant a name and a visibility modifier. Select the OK button, and the following constant string is generated in your source code:

```
public static final String RRWA_VERSION_ID = "rrwa-0.1";
```

Also notice that the original string is now replaced with a reference to the constant identifier, RRWA_VERSION_ID.

```
public String toString() {
   String returnValue = "[" + RRWA_VERSION_ID + "]";
   return returnValue;
}
```

FIGURE 7-26

Introduce Constant dialog box

Introduce Field

The Introduce Field refactoring command introduces a new statement for a field from an existing block of code. The existing block of code is replaced with a call to the new statement.

To use this refactoring, you select a block of code and then choose the Introduce Field command, the Introduce Field dialog box opens, as shown in Figure 7-27.

When you introduce a field or instance variable, you have the options of selecting the name, visibility modifier, and whether it should be final. If there is more than one occurrence, the Replace All Occurrences checkbox is active and shows you how many occurrences in parentheses. A really nice feature of this refactoring is the ability to select where you want the new field to be initialized. Radio button selections for this initialization allow you to select between the current method and the field scope, or within the constructor(s).

Introduce Method

The Introduce Method refactoring command introduces a new method from an existing block of code. The existing block of code is replaced with a call to the method.

FIGURE 7-27

Introduce Field
dialog box

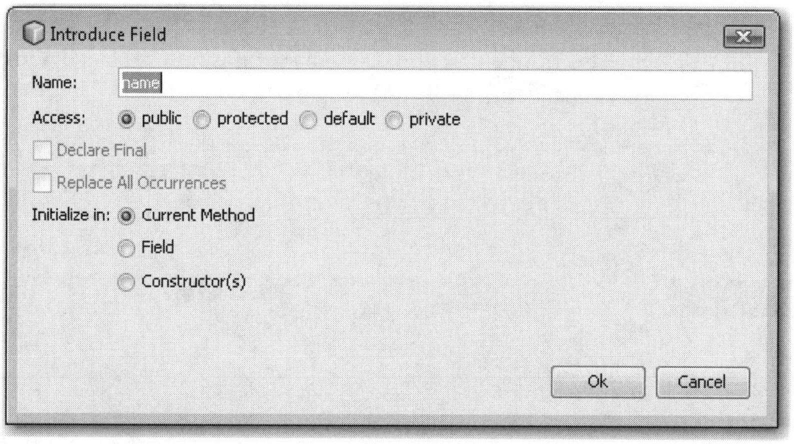

Consider the following code example, where we wish to remove all of the print statements from a constructor to a new method:

```java
public SystemsHealthMonitor () {
  rrwaLogger.fine("Entering SystemsHealthMonitor...");

  System.out.println("============================" );
  System.out.println("Rockfish Reports Monitoring" );
  System.out.println("============================" );
  System.out.println("Uptime:" + this.uptime);
  System.out.println("Database connection:" + this.dbStatus);
  System.out.println("SMTP Server connection:" + this.smtpServerStatus);
}
```

To introduce a method, select the block of code you wish to move, and then invoke the Introduce Method command. A dialog box opens, as shown in Figure 7-28. Select a name for the new method and for the visibility modifier.

After the OK button is selected, the method is created in the same source file, the selected block of code is moved into the new method, and a call to the method is created at the initial location of the block.

```java
public SystemsHealthMonitor () {
  rrwaLogger.fine("Entering SystemsHealthMonitor...");
  printSystemsStatus();
}

    public void printSystemsStatus() {
        System.out.println("============================");
        System.out.println("Rockfish Reports Monitoring");
        System.out.println("============================");
        System.out.println("Uptime:" + this.uptime);
        System.out.println("Database connection:" + this.dbStatus);
        System.out.println("SMTP Server connection:" + this.smtpServerStatus);
    }
```

FIGURE 7-28

Introduce Method
dialog box

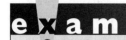

w a t c h

While the Introduction and other refactoring features have basically the same intent among varying IDEs, their implementations may vary slightly. If you have used the refactoring features on JDeveloper, Eclipse, or IntelliJ IDEA, make sure you don't confuse the refactoring features between IDEs. Differences include command-naming differences, refactoring menu organization, feature availability, and the means of invoking the refactorings.

Encapsulate Fields

The Encapsulate Fields refactoring command hides your instance variables by allowing you to mark them private and to generate associated public accessor (getter) and mutator (setter) methods through the dialog box components. Keep in mind that there is little reason to create getter and setter methods by hand when the IDE does it for you, quickly and error free.

Consider the `numberOfStripesPerSide` instance variable in the `Rockfish` class. Since this instance variable is marked as public, it is not well hidden and is therefore not encapsulated. Note that rockfish typically have seven or eight stripes running down each side.

```
package com.gliesian.rockfish_reports.animal_kingdom.fish;
public class Rockfish extends SaltWaterFish {
   ...
   public int numberOfStripesPerSide = 7;
   ...
}
```

We will go through a short exercise to encapsulate the field, as shown in UML in Figure 7-29.

FIGURE 7-29   Encapsulate Fields refactoring shown with UML

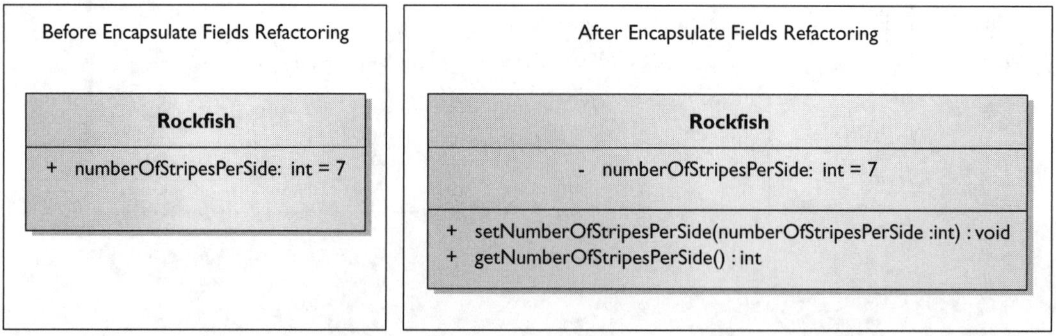

Before Encapsulate Fields Refactoring
Rockfish
+ numberOfStripesPerSide: int = 7

After Encapsulate Fields Refactoring
Rockfish
- numberOfStripesPerSide: int = 7
+ setNumberOfStripesPerSide(numberOfStripesPerSide :int) : void + getNumberOfStripesPerSide() : int

Encapsulate Fields
dialog box

To encapsulate the `numberOfStripesPerSide` field, we select the identifier and invoke the Encapsulate Fields refactoring command. The Encapsulate Fields dialog box for 6.1 NetBeans opens, as shown in Figure 7-30. Note that the NetBeans 6.8 Encapsulate Fields dialog box has additional fields (Insert Point, Sort By, and Javadoc) and additional buttons (Select All, Select None, Select Getters, and Select Setters).

Selecting the checkboxes associated with the getter and setter methods for the `numberOfStripesPerSide` field, adjusting the visibility modifiers, and selecting the Refactor button modifies the code as represented in the following listing:

```
package com.gliesian.rockfish_reports.animal_kingdom.fish;
public class Rockfish extends SaltWaterFish {
  ...
  private int numberOfStripesPerSide = 7;
  public int getNumberOfStripesPerSide() {
    return numberOfStripesPerSide;
  }
  public void setNumberOfStripesPerSide(int numberOfStripesPerSide) {
    this.numberOfStripesPerSide = numberOfStripesPerSide;
  }
  ...
}
```

Refactoring Management

History and metadata surrounding each refactoring operation is recorded. Because of this, previous refactoring operations can be undone or redone, providing they are on top of the history stack, as is depicted in Figure 7-31.

Let's take a closer look at the Refactor Undo and Refactor Redo commands.

Refactoring Management activity stack

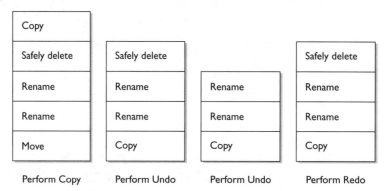

Refactoring Undo and Refactoring Redo

Once you perform a refactoring command, that command and all previous refactorings that occurred can be undone in a LIFO (last in, first out) order. Once you undo a refactoring command, that command can be redone prior to any additional refactoring changes occurring.

exam
ⓦatch

In NetBeans 6.1, the standard Edit | Undo and Edit | Redo commands are not the same as the Refactor | Undo [refactoring] and Refactor | Redo [refactoring] commands, as the former commands do not have refactoring support. In Eclipse Galileo the standard commands are overloaded with refactoring features. Other IDEs overload the standard Edit | Undo and Edit | Redo operations as well. NetBeans is currently pursuing this overloading approach under issue ID: https://netbeans.org/bugzilla/show_bug.cgi?id=48427.

Becoming Familiar with the Refactoring Catalog

Martin Fowler has written a book on refactoring and also maintains an updated catalog of common refactorings online: http://refactoring.com/catalog/. This exercise allows you to compare the refactoring features in the NetBeans IDE to those detailed in the catalog.

1. Create a list of NetBeans IDE refactoring capabilities.

2. Map NetBeans refactoring capabilities against those provided in the online catalog: http://refactoring.com/catalog/.

3. Review the remaining refactoring processes in the catalog that do not map to NetBeans implemented features. Are there any unimplemented features that NetBeans could integrate into their IDE?

4. Are there any common refactoring processes that you know of that are not in the catalog that NetBeans could integrate into their IDE?

5. If you have answers for either step 3 or 4 where you have identified a value-added refactoring that could be added to NetBeans, consider checking in the NetBeans IDE issue database to see if they are already pursuing that refactoring; if not, open up a new issue.

CERTIFICATION SUMMARY

This chapter discussed refactoring as it relates to the NetBeans IDE. We learned that refactoring is the process of changing the structure of source code, which improves our code relative to desired system qualities. We also learned that the NetBeans IDE supports several refactoring processes. These processes have a common defined flow that involves validating that the desired process is possible, checking user-defined input parameters for errors, and confirming the desired changes with the user. For concept-understanding purposes, all of the refactorings were grouped into five main categories: best practices refactorings, simplification refactorings, generalization and realization refactorings, organizational refactorings, and refactoring management. For each refactoring, we described the various configuration options and showed the details in screenshots and coding examples. To do well on the exam, you should be able to understand the purpose of each refactoring, know how to invoke it, configure it, review its intent, and how to confirm its operation.

✓ TWO-MINUTE DRILL

Refactoring Source Code

❑ Refactoring is the process of changing the internal structure of your code without changing its external behavior.

❑ Fixing bugs and improving the functionality of your code is not considered refactoring.

❑ Refactoring operations reside under their own top-level Refactor menu.

❑ Open the refactoring menu by right-clicking a Java source file in the source editor window, followed by clicking the Refactor menu option.

❑ Open the refactoring menu by right-clicking an attribute or operation in the Members View window associated with a Java source file, followed by a single click.

❑ The Find Usages command identifies where certain elements are referenced and can help identify candidates for refactoring.

❑ The Rename refactoring command renames packages, classes, interfaces, methods, and fields, and all references to them from any source code files in the project.

❑ The Move refactoring command moves a class or interface to another package. All references in the project source code files are updated accordingly.

❑ The Copy refactoring command copies a class or interface within the same package, another package, or another project.

❑ The Safely Delete refactoring command safely deletes code elements without references to them.

❑ The Change Method Parameters refactoring command changes the method signature including its visibility modifier.

❑ The Pull Up refactoring command moves methods and fields to an existing superclass.

❑ The Push Down refactoring command moves inner classes, methods, and fields to all immediate subclasses.

❏ The Extract Interface refactoring command creates a new interface from public nonstatic methods in a class or interface, and updates the extracting class or interface to inherit from the new interface.

❏ The Extract Superclass refactoring command creates a new superclass and updates the extracting class so it is inherited.

❏ The Use Supertype Where Possible refactoring command changes the type to a supertype for code that references the selected class.

❏ The Move Inner To Outer Level refactoring command moves an inner class up one level. If the inner class is a top-level inner class, it is made into an outer class with its own source code file. If the inner class is nested within another inner class, method, or variable, it is moved up to be within the same level of that scope.

❏ The Convert Anonymous To Inner refactoring command converts an anonymous class to an inner class.

❏ The Introduce Variable refactoring command introduces a new statement for a variable from an existing block of code. The existing block of code is replaced with a call to the new statement.

❏ The Introduce Constant refactoring command introduces a new statement for a constant from an existing block of code. The existing block of code is replaced with a call to the new statement.

❏ The Introduce Field refactoring command introduces a new statement for a field from an existing block of code. The existing block of code is replaced with a call to the new statement.

❏ The Introduce Method refactoring command introduces a new method from an existing block of code. The existing block of code is replaced with a call to the method.

❏ The Encapsulate Fields refactoring command generates accessor (getters) and mutator (setters) methods with an option to allow referencing code to use the new methods.

❏ The Undo refactoring command undoes refactorings based on the order in which they were most recently performed.

❏ The Redo refactoring command redoes refactoring based on the order in which they were recently undone.

SELF TEST

The following questions will help you measure your understanding of the material presented in this chapter. Read all the choices carefully because there might be more than one correct answer. Choose all correct answers for each question.

Refactoring Source Code

1. Which refactoring features are supported by NetBeans 6.1? Select all that apply.
   A. Introduction of variables, constants, and fields
   B. Generation of accessor and mutator methods
   C. Application of generics
   D. Extraction of methods and/or fields into superclasses

2. After selecting a refactoring command, what buttons are represented in a dialog box?
   A. Preview button, Refactor button, Cancel button, Help button
   B. Review button, Refactor button, Cancel button, Help button
   C. Diff button, Refactor button, Cancel button, Help button
   D. Diff button, Refactor button, Cancel button

3. The dialog box associated with Rename refactoring includes a checkbox with what accompanying text?
   A. Force Rename Refactoring
   B. Record Rename Refactoring
   C. Update Javadoc Comments
   D. Apply Rename On Comments

4. Which is not considered a refactoring process?
   A. Changing method signatures
   B. Fixing bugs
   C. Moving classes
   D. Extracting methods into a new superclass

5. Consider the following illustration. Again, this is from NetBeans 6.1, and NetBeans 6.8 differs slightly. Which action invokes the given refactoring menu?

A. Clicking the Refactor menu bar

B. Right-clicking a Java source file in the source editor window and selecting Refactor

C. Right-clicking a Java source file in the project window and selecting Refactor

D. Right-clicking an attribute or operation in the Members View window associated with a Java source file and selecting Refactor

E. All of the above

6. What keyboard shortcut invokes Rename refactoring? Select all that apply.

A. CTRL-R

B. SHIFT-R

C. CTRL-SHIFT-R

D. CTRL-ALT-R

E. All of the above

7. In the Change Method Parameters dialog box, which feature does not exist?

A. The ability to change the access modifier

B. The ability to rename the method

C. The ability to reorder the parameters via Move Up and Move Down buttons

D. The ability to preview the refactoring

Rename...	Ctrl +R
Move...	
Copy...	
Safe Delete...	
Change Method Parameters...	
Pull Up...	
Push Down...	
Extract Interface...	
Extract Superclass...	
Use Supertype Where Possible...	
Move Inner to Outer Level...	
Convert Anonymous to Inner	
Introduce Variable...	
Introduce Constant...	
Introduce Field...	
Introduce Method...	
Encapsulate Fields...	
Undo	
Redo	

8. Given the following tooltips, match them with the Refactoring window's annotation glyphs:

    A. Show logical view

    B. Show physical view

    C. Collapse all nodes in the tree

    D. Expand all nodes in the tree

    E. Next occurrence—Ctrl + Period

    F. Previous occurrence—Ctrl + Comma

    G. Refresh the refactoring data

TABLE 7-3	Annotation Glyph	Annotation Glyph Tool Tip
Refactoring Window Annotation Glyphs	🔁	
	⬍	
	⬇	
	🔳	
	🔲	
	⬆	
	⬇	

9. Which statement is not true in regard to the Find Usages command?

    A. The gutter icons are the same for the Usages window and the Refactoring window.

    B. The Find Usages dialog box has a checkbox labeled Search In Comments.

    C. The Find Usages dialog box has a Scope combo box that allows for the selection of searching across all open projects or the current project.

    D. The shortcut for Find Usages is ALT-F6.

10. When you create a new class by using the Extract Superclass command, which statement is true?

    A. The new superclass is placed into the top-level package without exception.

    B. The new superclass is placed into the same package from which the class was extracted.

    C. The Extract Superclass command provides an option via a drop-down combo box listing targeted packages to be placed in.

    D. The Extract Superclass command provides an option via an edit box and Browse button in order to target packages to be placed in.

11. Which system qualities can be improved with refactoring? Select all that apply.

- A. Readability
- B. Maintainability
- C. Validity
- D. Extensibility
- E. Performance
- F. Security

12. Which two refactoring commands support unnesting classes?

- A. Move Inner To Outer Level
- B. Unnest Inner Class
- C. Move Anonymous Class To Inner
- D. Convert Anonymous To Inner

13. Considering the following declaration, which statements can be created when the Introduce Variable command is used on the `'A'` character literal to create a new variable named `newCharacter`? Select all that apply.

```
Character c = 'A';
```

- A. `char newCharacter = 'A';`
- B. `final char newCharacter = 'A';`
- C. `Character newCharacter = 'A';`
- D. `final Character newCharacter = 'A';`
- E. All of the above

14. Bonus: After you highlight a primitive literal in your source code, a light bulb appears in the gutter bar. What editor hints are present when clicking the light bulb? Select all that apply.

- A. Surround with /* selection */
- B. Introduce Variable…
- C. Introduce Constant…
- D. Introduce Field…
- E. Introduce Method…
- F. All of the above

SELF TEST ANSWERS

Refactoring Source Code

1. Which refactoring features are supported by NetBeans 6.1? Select all that apply.
   A. Introduction of variables, constants, and fields
   B. Generation of accessor and mutator methods
   C. Application of generics
   D. Extraction of methods and/or fields into superclasses

   ☑ **A, B,** and **D** are correct. The introduction of variables, constants, and fields is supported. The generation of accessor and mutator methods is supported. The extraction of methods and fields into superclasses is supported.

   ☒ **C** is incorrect because generics refactoring is not supported in NetBeans 6.1.

2. After selecting a refactoring command, what buttons are represented in a dialog box?
   A. Preview button, Refactor button, Cancel button, Help button
   B. Review button, Refactor button, Cancel button, Help button
   C. Diff button, Refactor button, Cancel button, Help button
   D. Diff button, Refactor button, Cancel button

   ☑ **A.** After selecting a refactoring command, the Preview button, Refactor button, Cancel button, and Help button are available in a dialog box.

   ☒ **B, C,** and **D** are incorrect. **B** is incorrect because there is no Review button. **C** is incorrect because there is no Diff button. **D** is incorrect because there is no Diff button, and there is a Help button that is not listed.

3. The dialog box associated with Rename refactoring includes a checkbox with what accompanying text?
   A. Force Rename Refactoring
   B. Record Rename Refactoring
   C. Update Javadoc Comments
   D. Apply Rename On Comments

   ☑ **D.** Apply Rename On Comments is included next to a checkbox associated with the Rename refactoring dialog box.

   ☒ **A, B,** and **C** are incorrect. **A** is incorrect because Force Rename Refactoring is not an option. **B** is incorrect because Record Rename Refactoring is not an option. **C** is incorrect because Update Javadoc Comments is not an option.

4. Which is not considered a refactoring process?

A. Changing method signatures

B. Fixing bugs

C. Moving classes

D. Extracting methods into a new superclass

☑   **B.** While correcting bugs and fine-tuning functionality is highly beneficial to your code and overall project, it is not considered a refactoring process. Refactoring has to do with improving the structure of code, not its functionality.

☒   **A, C,** and **D** are incorrect. **A** is incorrect because changing method signatures by modifying the number of parameters is considered a refactoring process. **C** is incorrect because moving classes to more suitable packages is considered a refactoring process. **D** is incorrect because extracting methods into new or existing superclasses is a common refactoring process.

5. Consider the following illustration. Again, this is from NetBeans 6.1, and NetBeans 6.8 differs slightly. Which action invokes the given refactoring menu?

Rename...	Ctrl+R
Move...	
Copy...	
Safe Delete...	
Change Method Parameters...	
Pull Up...	
Push Down...	
Extract Interface...	
Extract Superclass...	
Use Supertype Where Possible...	
Move Inner to Outer Level...	
Convert Anonymous to Inner	
Introduce Variable...	
Introduce Constant...	
Introduce Field...	
Introduce Method...	
Encapsulate Fields...	
Undo	
Redo	

A. Clicking the Refactor menu bar

B. Right-clicking a Java source file in the source editor window and selecting Refactor

C. Right-clicking a Java source file in the project window and selecting Refactor

D. Right-clicking an attribute or operation in the Members View window associated with a Java source file and selecting Refactor

E. All of the above

☑   **E.** All of the above, because all of the listed steps invoke the refactoring menu. In some instances when a certain refactoring is not allowed, it is shown in the menu, but is disabled as indicated by lighter-colored text.

6. What keyboard shortcut invokes Rename refactoring? Select all that apply.
   A. CTRL-R
   B. SHIFT-R
   C. CTRL-SHIFT-R
   D. CTRL-ALT-R
   E. All of the above

   ☑ **A.** The keyboard shortcut CTRL-R invokes Rename refactoring. Rename refactoring can be done on packages, classes, interfaces, methods, and fields.

   ☒ **B, C,** and **D** are incorrect because they do not invoke the Rename refactoring.

7. In the Change Method Parameters dialog box, which feature does not exist?
   A. The ability to change the access modifier
   B. The ability to rename the method
   C. The ability to reorder the parameters via Move Up and Move Down buttons
   D. The ability to preview the refactoring

   ☑ **B.** The Change Method Parameters dialog box does not allow for the modification of the method's name.

   ☒ **A, C,** and **D** are incorrect because they are all available features within the Change Method Parameters dialog box. This refactoring allows for the changing of the method's access modifier, the reordering of the parameters, and for previewing the refactoring. Other features are also included.

8. Given the following tooltips, match them with the Refactoring window's annotation glyphs:
   A. Show logical view
   B. Show physical view
   C. Collapse all nodes in the tree
   D. Expand all nodes in the tree
   E. Next occurrence—Ctrl + Period
   F. Previous occurrence—Ctrl + Comma
   G. Refresh the refactoring data

TABLE 7-4	Annotation Glyph	Annotation Glyph Tool Tip
Refactoring Window Annotation Glyphs	(glyph)	
	(glyph)	
	(glyph)	
	(glyph)	
	(glyph)	
	(glyph)	
	(glyph)	

☑ Table 7-5 details the Refactoring window's annotation glyphs and matching tooltips.

TABLE 7-5	Annotation Glyph	Annotation Glyph Tool Tip
Refactoring Window Annotation Glyphs; Answers	(glyph)	**G.** Refresh the refactoring data
	(glyph)	**D.** Expand all nodes in the tree
	(glyph)	**C.** Collapse all nodes in the tree
	(glyph)	**A.** Show logical view
	(glyph)	**B.** Show physical view
	(glyph)	**F.** Previous occurrence—Ctrl + Comma
	(glyph)	**E.** Next occurrence—Ctrl + Period

9. Which statement is not true in regard to the Find Usages command?

   A. The gutter icons are the same for the Usages window and the Refactoring window.

   B. The Find Usages dialog box has a checkbox labeled Search In Comments.

   C. The Find Usages dialog box has a Scope combo box that allows for the selection of searching across all open projects or the current project.

   D. The shortcut for Find Usages is ALT-F6.

   ☑ **D.** The correct shortcut for the Find Usages command is ALT-F7. The Test Project command is ALT-F6.

   ☒ **A, B,** and **C** are incorrect because they all represent true statements about the Find Usages command. **A** is an incorrect answer because "The gutter icons are the same for the Usages window and the Refactoring window" is a true statement. **B** is an incorrect answer because "The Find Usages dialog box has a checkbox labeled Search In Comments is a true statement. **C** is an incorrect answer because "The Find Usages dialog box has a Scope combo box that allows for the selection of searching across all open projects or the current project" is a true statement.

10. When you create a new class by using the Extract Superclass command, which statement is true?

   A. The new superclass is placed into the top-level package without exception.

   B. The new superclass is placed into the same package from which the class was extracted.

   C. The Extract Superclass command provides an option via a drop-down combo box listing targeted packages to be placed in.

   D. The Extract Superclass command provides an option via an edit box and Browse button in order to target packages to be placed in.

   ☑ **B.** The new superclass is placed into the same package as the class was extracted from.

   ☒ **A, C,** and **D** are incorrect. **A** is an incorrect because the superclass is not placed in the top-level package by default. **C** and **D** are incorrect answers because no visual components support the placement of the superclass into a desired package outside of the one used when it was created.

11. Which system qualities can be improved with refactoring? Select all that apply.

   A. Readability

   B. Maintainability

   C. Validity

   D. Extensibility

   E. Performance

   F. Security

☑ **A, B, D,** and **E.** Refactoring can improve the readability, maintainability, extensibility, and performance of code.

☒ **C** and **F** are incorrect. **C** is incorrect because refactoring does not improve validity, the ability to validate results of a system or user input. **F** is incorrect because refactoring does not improve security, the ability to ensure information assurance.

12. Which two refactoring commands support unnesting classes?

    A. Move Inner To Outer Level

    B. Unnest Inner Class

    C. Move Anonymous Class To Inner

    D. Convert Anonymous To Inner

☑ **A** and **D.** Unnesting refactoring commands include Move Inner To Outer Level and Convert Anonymous To Inner.

☒ **B** and **C** are incorrect. **B** is incorrect because there is no Unnest Inner Class command. **C** is incorrect because there is no Move Anonymous Class To Inner command.

13. Considering the following declaration, which statements can be created when the Introduce Variable command is used on the `'A'` character literal to create a new variable named `newCharacter`? Select all that apply.

```
Character c = 'A';
```

    A. `char newCharacter = 'A';`

    B. `final char newCharacter = 'A';`

    C. `Character newCharacter = 'A';`

    D. `final Character newCharacter = 'A';`

    E. All of the above

☑ **A** and **B.** The Introduce Variable command on a primitive `char` literal creates primitive `char` declarations.

☒ **C** and **D** are incorrect. **C** and **D** are incorrect because Character wrapper classes cannot be created from using the Introduce Variable command on primitive `char` literals.

14. Bonus: After you highlight a primitive literal in your source code, a light bulb appears in the gutter bar. What editor hints are present when clicking the light bulb? Select all that apply.

A. Surround with /* selection */

B. Introduce Variable...

C. Introduce Constant...

D. Introduce Field...

E. Introduce Method...

F. All of the above

☑ **F.** All of the above. All of the listed commands are available from clicking the gutter bar light bulb.

☒ **A, B, C, D,** and **E** are incorrect because the correct answer is "All of the above." **A** Surround with /* selection */, **B** Introduce Variable..., **C** Introduce Constant..., **D** Introduce Field..., and **E** Introduce Method are all listed when clicking the gutter bar light bulb.

Part III

NetBeans IDE Application Tools

CHAPTERS

8   HTTP Server-Side Monitor

9   Local and Remote Debugging

10   Testing and Profiling

8

HTTP Server-Side Monitor

CERTIFICATION OBJECTIVES

- Using the HTTP Server-Side Monitor
- Two-Minute Drill

Q&A   Self Test

N etBeans includes the HTTP Server-Side Monitor (HSSM), a powerful tool for monitoring and debugging HTTP traffic. This tool has a variety of uses ranging from troubleshooting web services and analyzing Ajax calls to monitoring and capturing server traffic. This chapter requires a working knowledge of the HyperText Transfer Protocol (HTTP) standard. HTTP is an application layer protocol used in distributed information systems. The initial version HTTP 1.0 was released in 1996 and is not an official Internet standard. However, you can read up on its specification RFC 1945 at http://ftp.ics.uci.edu/pub/ietf/http/rfc1945.html. HTTP 1.1, which was released in 1999, is the current standard. HTTP 1.1 was developed by the Network Working Group of the Internet Engineering Task Force (IETF). You can read up on the HTTP 1.1 specification RFC 2616 at http://www.w3.org/Protocols/rfc2616/rfc2616.html. Throughout the chapter we reference parts of the specification, but the primary focus is on using the HSSM.

If you have done Servlet programming, you are familiar with the doGet and doPost methods. To capture the exact parameters that are passed to these methods, you would need to dump them to standard out, route the parameters through a logging API, or wait to see where the data ends up in your application. With the HSSM, these extra logging steps are not necessary because the monitor captures all GET and POST messages for you and allows you to view and analyze the information very easily. If you are not smiling now, you should be, because the HSSM makes software developers' lives a lot easier when they need it the most.

This chapter more than prepares you for the types of questions you will find on the exam relative to the monitor. Not only will the preparation from this chapter allow you to score well on the exam, but you will have found a new HTTP monitoring tool that you can use quite frequently at work, if you are not using it already.

CERTIFICATION OBJECTIVE

Using the HTTP Server-Side Monitor

Exam Objective 4.4   Describe how to monitor HTTP requests when running a web application.

Viewing the HTTP request messages and their responses can be invaluable when analyzing system activity. Thankfully, monitoring HTTP request messages is as simple as viewing records in the HSSM. To properly prepare you for exam-related questions on the HSSM, this stand-alone section of the chapter gives you a refresher on some elements of the HTTP standard, instructions for configuring the HSSM, and in-depth pointers enabling you to fully exploit this powerful tool.

- The HyperText Transfer Protocol Standard
- HTTP Server-Side Monitor Setup
- HTTP Server-Side Monitor Usage

The HyperText Transfer Protocol Standard

The HyperText Transfer Protocol is an Application layer protocol for distributed computing. The Application layer is part of the Internet Protocol Suite as defined by the Internet STD, RFC 1122 specification. The other layers include the Transport layer, Internet layer, and the Link layer. Figure 8-1 represents the HTTP Stack relative to the Internet Protocol Suite.

HTTP typically makes use of the TCP Transport layer, but may use other transport protocols such as UDP. Being an application protocol, HTTP communicates via sessions, transactional sequences of network request-responses. HTTP request messages consist of a request line (for example, GET statement), headers, an empty line, and an optional message body. HTTP responses include a status line (that is, status code message), a general message, and the requested resource in the body that may be application data or an error message.

The following sections provide a quick look at some of the additional elements making up the HTTP standard including HTTP request methods, HTTP headers, and HTTP status codes.

FIGURE 8-1

HTTP Stack

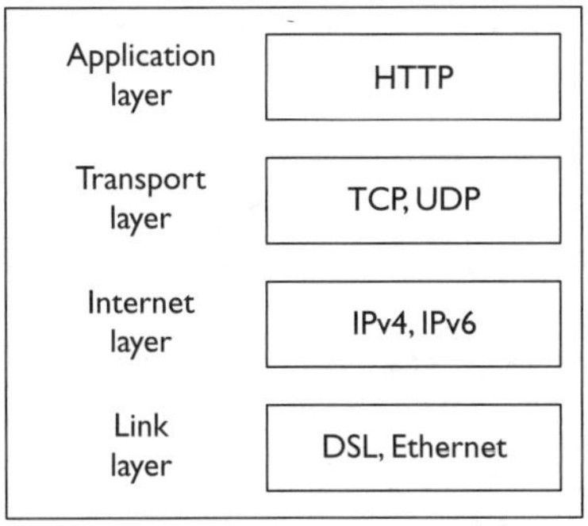

HTTP Request Methods

The HTTP standard defines methods for actions to be performed on identified resources. The resource may correspond to data or a file (for example, requesting an image). Table 8-1 defines the eight HTTP request methods.

HTTP Headers

HTTP headers make up the main part of an HTTP request. The headers define characteristics of the data that is being served. Table 8-2 provides a list of HTTP headers. To learn more, go to Wikipedia: http://en.wikipedia.org/wiki/List_of_HTTP_headers.

HTTP Response Status Codes

There are numerous HTTP response status codes. They are broken into five categories: Informational, Success, Redirection, Client Error, and Server Error. Each category starts with a number from 1 to 5, respectively, and each code must be three digits. Multiple standards have contributed to the list of HTTP response status codes, but we are concerned only with those derived from the original HTTP/1.0 and HTTP/1.1 specifications. These codes are shown in Table 8-3.

- ■ **RFC 1945**   Hypertext Transfer Protocol—HTTP/1.0
- ■ **RFC 2616**   Hypertext Transfer Protocol—HTTP/1.1

TABLE 8-1   HTTP Request Methods and Descriptions

Request Method	Description
HEAD	Requests a representation of the specified resource without the response body
GET	Requests a representation of the specified resource
POST	Submits data to be processed to the identified resource
PUT	Uploads a representation of the specified resource
DELETE	Removes the specified resource
TRACE	Returns the received request
OPTIONS	Returns the methods that the server supports
CONNECT	Converts the request connection to a transparent TCP/IP tunnel

TABLE 8-2   HTTP Headers

Accept	Content-Type	Max-Forwards
Accept-Charset	Date	Pragma
Accept-Encoding	Expect	Proxy-Authorization
Accept-Language	From	Range
Accept-Ranges	Host	Referer
Authorization	If-Match	TE
Cache-Control	If-Modified-Since	Upgrade
Connection	If-None-Match	User-Agent
Cookie	If-Range	Via
Content-Length	If-Unmodified-Since	Warn

TABLE 8-3   HTTP/1.0 and HTTP/1.1 Response Status Codes

Status Code Number	Status Code Name	Status Code Origin
Informational Status Codes		
100	Continue	HTTP/1.1
101	Switching Protocols	HTTP/1.1
Success Status Codes		
200	OK	HTTP/1.0
201	Created	HTTP/1.0
202	Accepted	HTTP/1.0
203	Non-Authoritative Information	HTTP/1.1
204	No Content	HTTP/1.0
205	Reset Content	HTTP/1.1
206	Partial Content	HTTP/1.1
Redirection Status Codes		
300	Multiple Choices	HTTP/1.1
301	Moved Permanently	HTTP/1.0
302	Found	HTTP/1.0
303	See Other	HTTP/1.1
304	Not Modified	HTTP/1.0
305	Use Proxy	HTTP/1.1
306	Switch Proxy	HTTP/1.1

| TABLE 8-3 | HTTP/1.0 and HTTP/1.1 Response Status Codes *(continued)* |

Status Code Number	Status Code Name	Status Code Origin
307	Temporary Redirect	HTTP/1.1
Client Error Status Codes		
400	Bad Request	HTTP/1.1
401	Unauthorized	HTTP/1.0
402	Payment Required	HTTP/1.1
403	Forbidden	HTTP/1.0
404	Not Found	HTTP/1.0
405	Method Not Allowed	HTTP/1.1
406	Not Acceptable	HTTP/1.1
407	Proxy Authentication Required	HTTP/1.1
408	Request Timeout	HTTP/1.1
409	Conflict	HTTP/1.1
410	Gone	HTTP/1.1
411	Length Required	HTTP/1.1
412	Precondition Failed	HTTP/1.1
413	Request Entity Too Large	HTTP/1.1
414	Request-URI Too Long	HTTP/1.1
415	Unsupported Media Type	HTTP/1.1
416	Requested Range Not Satisfiable	HTTP/1.1
417	Expectation Failed	HTTP/1.1
Server Error Status Codes		
500	Internal Server Error	HTTP/1.0
501	Not Implemented	HTTP/1.0
502	Bad Gateway	HTTP/1.0
503	Service Unavailable	HTTP/1.0
504	Gateway Timeout	HTTP/1.1
505	HTTP Version Not Supported	HTTP/1.1
506	Variant Also Negotiates	HTTP/1.0
507	Insufficient Storage	HTTP/1.0
509	Bandwidth Limit Exceeded	HTTP/1.0
510	Not Extended	HTTP/1.0

Additional HTTP status codes are listed at Wikipedia: http://en.wikipedia
.org/wiki/List_of_HTTP_status_codes. These codes are primarily derived from
the following RFCs:

- **RFC 2295** Transparent Content Negotiation in HTTP
- **RFC 2518** HTTP Extensions for Distributed Authoring—WEBDAV
- **RFC 2774** An HTTP Extension Framework
- **RFC 2817** Upgrading to TLS Within HTTP/1.1
- **RFC 4918** HTTP Extensions for Web Distributed Authoring and
  Versioning (WebDAV)

HTTP Server-Side Monitor Setup

For the most part, setting up the HTTP Server-Side Monitor is easy. It starts
automatically for the Tomcat Web Server
and is enabled by a checkbox in GlassFish's
server properties dialog box. However, using
the HSSM with servers started outside of
the IDE requires a little work the first time
around. We will explore the setup steps
of each.

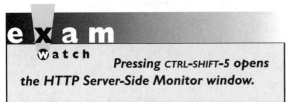

Pressing *CTRL-SHIFT-5 opens
the HTTP Server-Side Monitor window.*

- HSSM Setup and the Tomcat Web Server
- HSSM Setup and the GlassFish Application Server
- HSSM Setup and Servers Started Outside of the IDE

HSSM Setup and the Tomcat Web Server

The HSSM is automatically enabled and displayed when your application is
deployed to the Tomcat Web Server. Let's do just that and deploy a sample
application to Tomcat. Set up the sample project named "JSP Examples (J2EE 1.4)."
Right-click the project name in the Projects window and select Properties. In the
Properties dialog box, select the Run node and ensure the Server setting is Apache
Tomcat. Select OK. Now run the application. The HSSM automatically displays in
the lower-right corner of the IDE, as shown in Figure 8-2.

| FIGURE 8-2 | The HTTP Server-Side Monitor |

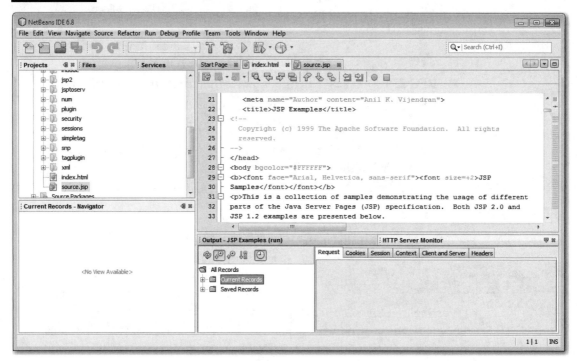

When you ran the sample application, the `index.html` file was loaded into the web browser, as shown in Figure 8-3. We will use this application later in the chapter as the stimulus for HTTP request messages that we will monitor in the HSSM.

HSSM Setup and the GlassFish Application Server

Configuring HSSM for GlassFish is also easy. The GlassFish application server, Sun Java System Application Server (SJSAS), and any other application server or web server registered with the IDE may have included the option to support configuration of the HSSM. This configuration option is controlled by an Enable HTTP Monitor checkbox in the Server properties dialog box. When you select the checkbox, an HTTP Monitor Effect confirmation dialog box opens with the following message, "Deploying apps with HTTP monitoring enabled eliminates the ability to cache static content for those web applications." When you deselect the checkbox, a Disabling HTTP Monitor confirmation dialog box opens with the message, "To completely disable HTTP monitoring, you may need to undeploy all web applications that have been deployed since it was enabled."

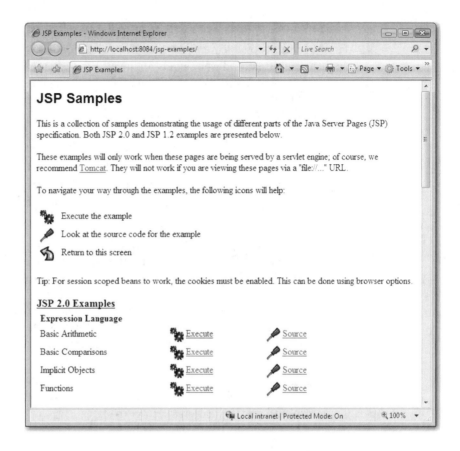

FIGURE 8-3

JSP Examples
(J2EE 1.4) sample
application

When the checkbox is selected, the HSSM displays output after the first HTTP request message is processed. The Properties dialog box is opened by either selecting Tools | Servers and the applicable application server node in the Servers list, or by going to the Services window (CTRL-5), and right-clicking Properties on a server's node.

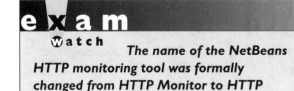

The name of the NetBeans HTTP monitoring tool was formally changed from HTTP Monitor to HTTP **Server-Side Monitor in NetBeans 6.5. Since the exam targets NetBeans 6.1, you see it referred to as "HTTP Monitor."**

HSSM Setup and Servers Started Outside of the IDE

HSSM setup is possible for servers launched independently of the IDE. Many application servers and web servers are Java EE compliant, as shown in the third table of Chapter 4. Because of this compliance, they can be adapted for use with the HSSM.

The following steps set up HSSM for an external server:

1. In the `WEB-INF/lib` directory add the HSSM-related JAR files: `org-netbeans-modules-schema2beans.jar` and `org-netbeans-modules-web-httpmonitor.jar`. These JAR files deploy with your application. You can find the files located in the NetBeans IDE installation directory.

2. In the `WEB-INF/web.xml` deployment descriptor file, add a filter declaration. This filter associates the HSSM module with the necessary HTTP request messages and associated functionality.

Note that the filter declaration may differ depending on the Servlet API version. There is little room for error when setting up a filter, so check with the latest NetBeans documentation when doing so. In short, you need to supply the filter class name (`org.netbeans.modules.web.monitor.server.MonitorFilter`), initialization parameter name (`netbeans.monitor.ide`), and parameter values specifying the IP address of the host(s), NetBeans version(s), and the application server port(s).

EXERCISE 8-1

Monitoring HTTP Requests Against GlassFish

The Calculator sample project consists of two projects, a calculator web server and a Servlet client. The client allows two numbers to be entered into a web page and forwarded to the calculator web service. The web service adds the numbers together and returns a result. The client renders the results to a new web page.

In this exercise, you set up the Calculator sample project so you can monitor the HTTP request messages being sent from the client application to the server application. In addition, you modify the values of the HTTP request through the HSSM, send the new request, and view the results in the web browser.

1. Set up the Calculator sample project. Select File | New Project. From the Categories list, choose the Web Services category from the Samples node. From the Projects list, select the Calculator project. Select Next and Finish.

2. Ensure configuration for the monitor is enabled. Select Tools | Servers. Select GlassFish v 2.1 or 3 in the Servers list. Ensure the Enable HTTP Monitor checkbox is selected.

3. Ensure GlassFish v 2.1 or 3 is associated with the project. Right-click the CalculatorApp node and select Properties. Select Run in the Project Properties window. Ensure the Server is set to GlassFish v 2.1 or 3.

4. Build and Run the CalculatorApp application.

5. Build and Run the CalculatorClientApp application. Make sure you have an association to the `org.me.calculator` package from the CalculatorApp project.

6. From the launched web page (that is, http://localhost:8080/CalculatorClientApp/), enter two numbers and select the Get Result button. A new web page displays the result.

7. In the HSSM, find and save the Get ClientServlet record.

8. Right-click the Get ClientServlet saved record, and select Edit and Replay. Supply new input values.

9. Send the new HTTP request from the monitor tool. The result displays in your web browser.

HTTP Server-Side Monitor Usage

Using the HTTP Server-Side Monitor is relatively easy. Once the monitor is set up, it's just a matter of opening the window and working with the support components. The HSSM is divided into two panels where these components reside. The left panel is primarily responsible for management of the records. Components of the left panel include a toolbar and a node structure of All Records, Current Records, and Save Records. Toolbar and node behavior will be discussed shortly in the "Managing HSSM Records" section. The right panel is primarily for viewing/analyzing HSSM records and is discussed in detail in the "Analyzing HSSM Records" sections. One of the most useful features of the monitor is the ability to edit and replay records in order to send new HTTP request messages.

- Managing HSSM Records
- Analyzing HSSM Records
- Replaying HSSM Records

Managing HSSM Records

Managing HSSM records is primarily done from the left panel of the HSSM. Deploy the JSP Examples (J2EE 1.4) sample application to the Tomcat Web Server or to the GlassFish Application Server, and you see a monitor window similar to that shown in Figure 8-4. Note that the tab for the HTTP Monitor window is on the far right, but it can be easily dragged to the left side as was done in Figure 8-5. In this section we focus on the left panel of the figure. We informally call this panel the HSSM Records Management panel. For GlassFish v3, brackets need to be removed from the project name, otherwise the application fails to deploy.

FIGURE 8-4   HTTP Server-Side Monitor against GlassFish Application Server

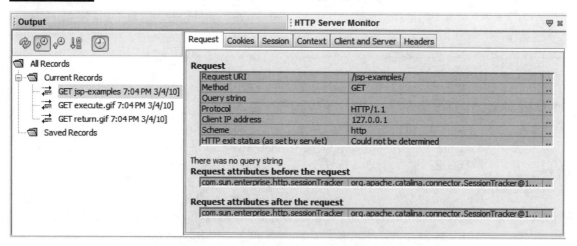

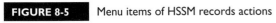

FIGURE 8-5   Menu items of HSSM records actions

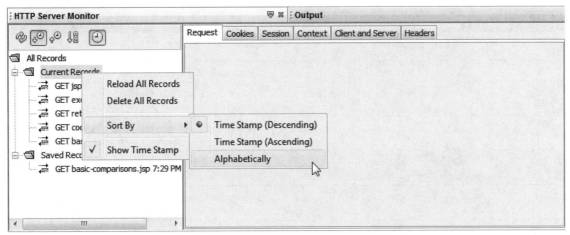

The HSSM Records Management panel is reserved for the record nodes and a supporting toolbar. The root node is the All Records node with subnodes of Current Records and Saved Records. The All Records node always shows the two subnodes. The subnodes can be expanded to display record nodes when the given node has one or more existing records.

Nodes have supporting popup menus that are available by right-clicking. The All Records, Current Records, and Saved Records nodes all have the same popup menus, as shown in Figure 8-5.

Menu items for these nodes share the same features of the toolbar, also shown in the figure. The functionality is self-explanatory, but we detail the features anyway in Table 8-4.

You may have noticed icons in the previous figures next to each HSSM record. These icons represent the type of HTTP request message. Icons for HTTP request messages that include the GET method have bidirectional arrows with a yellow centered rectangle. Icons for HTTP request messages that include the POST message have bidirectional arrows with a green centered square. Under normal conditions (that is, when processing of requests is successful), the icons display as previously described and as shown in Figure 8-6.

TABLE 8-4	Actions for Managing HSSM Records

Toolbar Icon	Menu Item Text	Action
![icon]	Reload All Records	Reloads all of the records
N/A	Delete All Records	Deletes all of the records
![icon]	Sort By | Time Stamp (Descending)	Sorts records by timestamps in descending order for both current and saved records by nodes
![icon]	Sort By | Time Stamp (Ascending)	Sorts records by timestamps in ascending order for both current and saved records by nodes
![icon]	Sort By | Alphabetically	Sorts records by timestamps in alphabetical order for both current and saved records by nodes
![icon]	Show Time Stamp	Shows the timestamps of the HTTP request messages next to the respective records

However, when HTTP response messages respond with other types of information, the method icons are marked with a badge. The badge or rather, miniature icon, represents a specific status code or group of status codes, as documented in Table 8-5.

For more information on status codes included in HTTP response messages reference the Status Code Definition web page of the HTTP standard on the www.w3.org website: http://www.w3.org/Protocols/rfc2616/rfc2616-sec10.html.

FIGURE 8-6

HTTP request
method icons

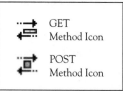

GET
Method Icon

POST
Method Icon

TABLE 8-5	Badge Icons Related to HTTP Response Messages

Layered Badge	Status Codes	Description
Information badge: white *i* in blue octagon	1xx Informational	Responses are provisional, each with a status line, optional headers, and empty line terminator. Note that HTTP/1.0 has no 1xx responses.
None	2xx Success	Responses because the server successfully received, understood, accepted, and processed the request.
Warning badge: exclamation point in yellow octagon	3xx Redirection	Responses with outstanding actions needed by the client.
Error badge: white X in red octagon	4xx Client Error; only the 400 status code currently uses this badge	Responses due to client-related errors.
None	5xx Server Error	Responses due to server-related errors.

The last things to mention about the HSSM Records Management panel are the popup menus. These are launched by right-clicking a current or saved record. Records under the Current Records node have four menu items: Save, Replay, Edit and Replay, and Delete. Menu items are the same for records under the Saved Records node, but without the Save, because the record is already saved. The Save action moves records under the Current Records node to the Saved Records node. The Delete action deletes the record. The Replay and Edit And Replay actions are discussed in the "Replaying HSSM Records" section.

Analyzing HSSM Records

HSSM record nodes are recorded in the HSSM Records Management panel on the left side of the tool. On the right side of the tool is a panel that includes a series of tabbed windows for the display of information relative to each HSSM record (that is, HTTP request/response information). Each window has one or more tables providing information about the records. We informally call this right panel of the monitoring tool the HSSM Record View panel. The tabbed windows that are available in this panel are Request, Cookies, Session, Context, Client And Server, and Headers.

We look at these tables relative to a remote HTTP GET method request from the JSP Examples application. The GET message is sent after the Submit Query button is selected with the desired input field (for example, NetBeans IDE Rocks!), as shown in Figure 8-7. Unlike in the other examples, this call is performed from a remote machine on the LAN under test. In this example, the IP address for the remote client is 192.168.1.103, and the server IP address is 192.168.1.101.

As a simple exercise, look for this data in the upcoming tables.

Let's take a look at the data in each of the tabbed windows.

Request Tab The Request tab of the HSSM Record View panel, as shown in Figure 8-8, displays HTTP request information in a Request table and optionally a Parameters table for existing parameters. In the Request table, key/value pairs are included for the Request URI, HTTP Request Method, Query String parameters, HTTP Protocol, Client IP Address, the Scheme, and the HTTP Exit Status (for example, status code information). Parameter data is represented in the Parameters table.

FIGURE 8-7   Functions execution example in the JSP Examples sample application

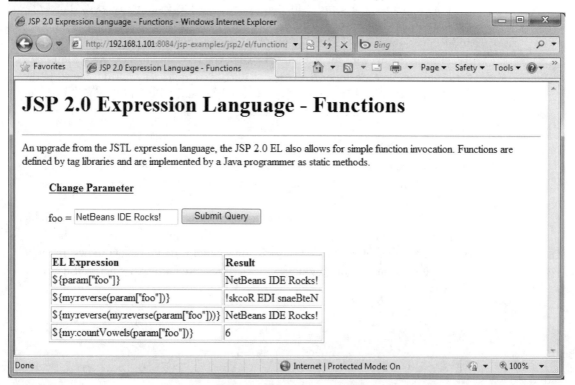

FIGURE 8-8   Request tab of the HSSM

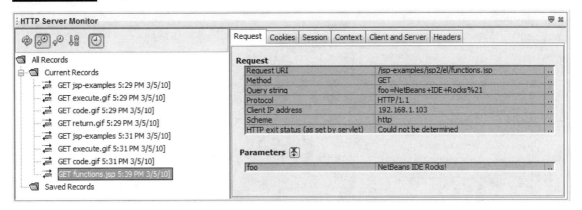

Cookies Tab   The Cookies tab of the HSSM Record View panel, as shown in Figure 8-9, displays incoming and outgoing cookie information. If there is no cookie information, the table is not displayed. Instead you see the text "No incoming cookies" and/or "No outgoing cookies."

Session Tab   The Session tab of the HSSM Record View panel, as shown in Figure 8-10, displays general session information. If the session is new, the following text is displayed: "The session was created as a result of this request." If the session already existed, the following text is displayed: "The session existed before this request." Session attributes, if available, are detailed as they existed after the current request. Session attributes, if available, are detailed as they existed before the request if the session was previously established. The Session Properties table includes information about the session ID, when it was created, when it was last accessed, and the setting of the maximum inactivity interval.

FIGURE 8-9   Cookies tab of the HSSM

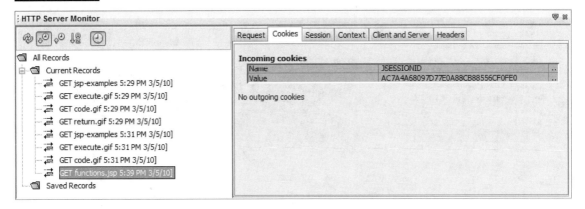

FIGURE 8-10   Session tab of the HSSM

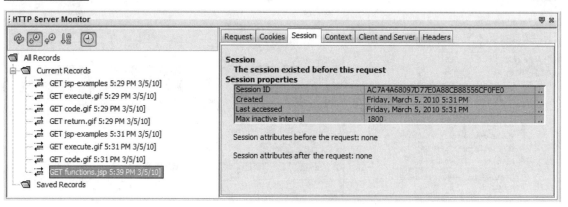

Context Tab   The Context tab of the HSSM Record View panel, as shown in Figure 8-11, displays information about Servlet context, context attributes, and initialization parameters. As with the tables in the other tabs, they appear only when there is information to be displayed. Otherwise the table entry is replaced with explanatory text in the figure, as shown in the figure about initialization parameters.

Client And Server Tab   The Client And Server tab of the HSSM Record View panel, as shown in Figure 8-12, displays information relative to the client and server machines communicating via the HTTP session. The information is shown in both Client and Server tables. Client information includes data on the HTTP protocol,

FIGURE 8-11   Context tab of the HSSM

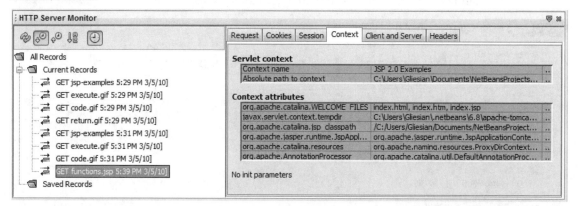

FIGURE 8-12   Client And Server tab of the HSSM

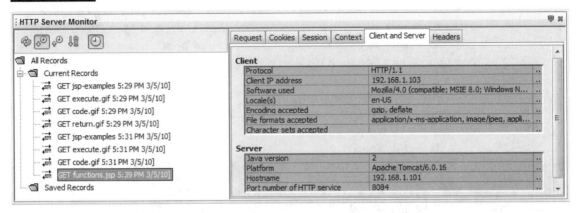

the client IP address, the software used (for example, browser), locales, encoding attributes, acceptable file formats, and acceptable character sets. Server information includes data about the Java version, platform (for example, server), hostname, and the port number of the HTTP service.

Headers Tab   The Headers tab of the HSSM Record View panel, as shown in Figure 8-13, displays information in regard to HTTP request headers. Many of the values are too large to see in their entirety within the table cell. Clicking the ellipses on the right opens a View Value dialog box, where the entire value of a given cell can be viewed. This ellipsis functionality applies to all tables.

FIGURE 8-13   Headers tab of the HSSM

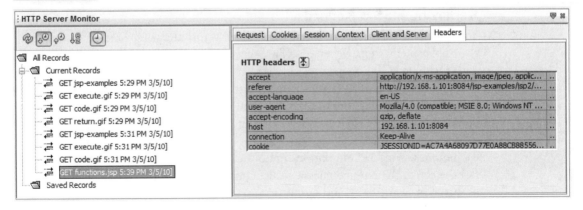

Wireshark is a free network protocol analyzer: www.wireshark.org. If you need to go deeper than what the HTTP Server-Side Monitor provides, consider using Wireshark. Wireshark works for Windows, Unix, and Mac OS X. Consult IT policies prior to downloading this and similar applications, because some companies may flag such tools as a violation of corporate security policies.

As discussed, viewing and analyzing HTTP session information is one of the most important and often-used features of the HSSM. The Scenario & Solution details the available tables in each window and when you need to see that information.

SCENARIO & SOLUTION

You need to view the general HTTP request information including supplied parameters.	View the Request and Parameters tables in the Request window.
You need to view incoming and information about cookies.	View the Incoming Cookies and Outgoing Cookies tables in the Cookies window.
You need to view session information including properties and state both before and after the request.	View the Session Properties, Session Attributes Before The Request, and Session Attributes After The Request tables in the Session window.
You need to view context and initialization parameters.	View the Servlet Context, Context Attributes, and Init Parameters tables in the Context tab/window.
You need to view client (e.g., IP address) and server (e.g., application server) information.	View the Client and Server tables in the Client And Server window.
You need to view HTTP header names and values.	View the HTTP Headers table in the Headers window.

Replaying HSSM Records

To replay an HTTP request, simply right-click a current or saved record and select the Replay menu item. When a replay occurs, a new HTTP request message is sent with the same HTTP request parameters.

All current and saved records can be edited and replayed. Right-click the desired record and select the Edit And Replay.. menu item. The Edit And Replay dialog box opens. In the Edit And Replay dialog box are five tabbed windows: Query, Request, Cookies, Server, and Headers. Let's take a look at the content and functionality of each of these windows in relationship to the GET-method HSSM record produced from selecting the Numberguess execute command in the JSP Examples main page, as shown in Figure 8-14, and submitting an initial guess of 312.

In the HSSM Record Management panel, we need to right-click the "GET numguess.jsp" record so the Edit And Replay dialog box will appear. The following

FIGURE 8-14

JSP Examples
sample project
Numberguess
execute
command

subsections detail each tabbed panel in the dialog box. Many tables are displayed with values. The values can be modified by clicking the table cell and making the adjustment, or by clicking the ellipsis and making the changes in the associated Edit And Replay dialog box. The Edit And Replay dialog box comes in handy for lengthy text because the edit box provided in the dialog box is much larger than what the table cell provides. For each tab, selecting Send HTTP Request sends a new HTTP request with all of the data from all of the tables in the Edit And Replay dialog box. The tabbed panels that are available are Query, Request, Cookies, Server, and Headers.

Query Tab   The Query tab of the Edit And Replay dialog box, as shown in Figure 8-15, allows for the modification, addition, and removal of query parameters. New rows are added for each new parameter name/value pair, even if the parameter name is the same as an existing one. Query name/value rows can be sorted alphabetically from A to Z or from Z to A, or can be shown in their natural state by use of the sorting button.

FIGURE 8-15

Query tab of
Edit And Replay
dialog box

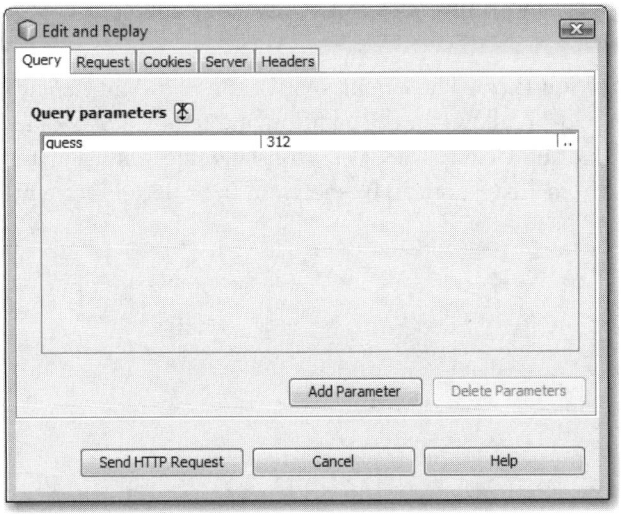

Request tab of
Edit And Replay
dialog box

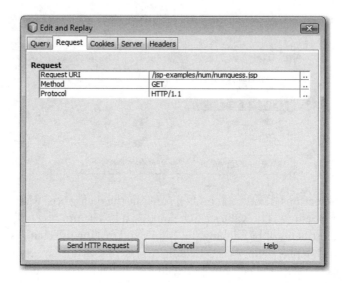

Request Tab The Request tab of the Edit And Replay dialog box, as shown in Figure 8-16, allows for the modification of the request URI, HTTP method, and protocol values.

The request URI is the URI/URL where the request is coming from (for example, the web page). The protocol value can be also changed, but caution needs to be taken here because falling back from HTTP/1.1 to HTTP/1.0 does not support all of the HTTPS Request attributes that may be in the HSSM record such as HTTP headers. The HTTP method can be changed by clicking the value cell. A combo box opens with the GET, POST, and PUT methods to select from.

Cookies Tab The Cookies tab of the Edit And Replay dialog box, as shown in Figure 8-17, allows for the addition and removal of cookies by selecting the Add Cookie and Delete Cookies buttons. Cookies can be sorted alphabetically from A to Z or from Z to A, or can be shown in their natural state by use of the sorting button.

Cookies tab of
Edit And Replay
dialog box

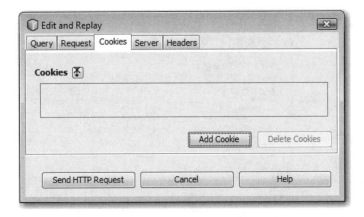

Server Tab   The Server tab of the Edit And Replay dialog box, as shown in
Figure 8-18, allows for the modification of the server hostname and HTTP service
port number.

Headers Tab   The Headers tab of the Edit And Replay dialog box, as shown in
Figure 8-19, allows for the modification and removal of HTTP headers of HTTP
request messages. When adding a header that already exists in a row, the header

Server tab of
Edit And Replay
dialog box

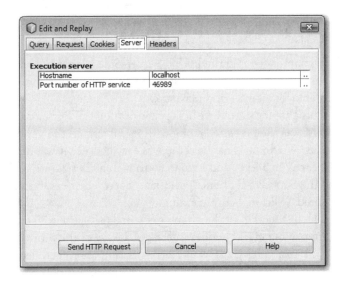

Headers tab of
Edit And Replay
dialog box

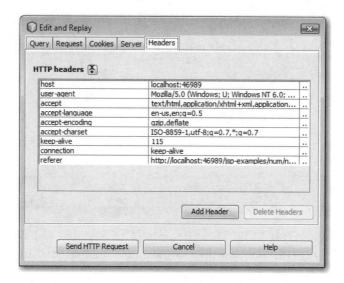

name is shared, but the value is appended to the existing value separated by a
comma. Headers can be sorted alphabetically from A to Z or from Z to A, or be
shown in their natural state by use of the sorting button.

CERTIFICATION SUMMARY

This chapter covered the HTTP Server-Side Monitor. The monitor, also referred to
in this chapter as HSSM, captures HTTP request/response information and makes it
available for analysis and playback.

This chapter started with a review of the HTTP standard. The configuration of
HSSM was then covered along with its support in the various web and application
servers. We found that the setup was easy because it was automatically done with the
Tomcat Web Server and is enabled though a configuration checkbox for GlassFish
and the Sun Java System Application Server. Servers started outside of the IDE
required additional configuration.

The last section of the chapter covered using the tool for capturing, viewing,
and replaying HTTP request messages. Usage of the tool was explained while using
the JSP Examples (J2EE 1.4) NetBeans sample project. Features were discussed
such as saving, editing, and playing back messages. Upon exercising the HSSM
with the sample project, you have gained the knowledge necessary to score well on
the monitor-related questions of the exam and to leverage HSSM to troubleshoot
everyday issues.

✓ TWO-MINUTE DRILL

Using the HTTP Server-Side Monitor

- ❏ The formal name of the monitoring tool has changed in recent versions from "HTTP Monitor" to "HTTP Server-Side Monitor."
- ❏ The shortcut to display the HTTP Server-Side Monitor is CTRL-SHIFT-5.
- ❏ The HTTP Server-Side Monitor's main features are Save, Edit, Refresh, Sort, Replay, and Delete HTTP request records.
- ❏ The HTTP Server-Side Monitor is enabled and displayed automatically when an application is deployed to the Tomcat Web Server.
- ❏ The HTTP Server-Side Monitor must be enabled for supported application servers (for example, GlassFish and SJSAS) through the server's configuration settings. This is done via selecting an Enable HTTP Monitor checkbox in the Properties dialog box for the given application server.
- ❏ Servers outside of the IDE can enable the HTTP Server-Side Monitor with the inclusion of the following two JARS in the WEB-INF/lib folder: org-netBeans-modules-web-httpmonitor.jar and org-netbeans-modules-schema2beans.jar and a filter declaration in the WEB-INF/web.xml file.
- ❏ The HTTP Server-Side Monitor is divided into right and left panels.
- ❏ The left panel of the monitor displays current and saved records. The records can be sorted alphabetically or by timestamp. The records may include status badges on top of their associated icons.
- ❏ The right panel of the monitor displays HTTP request and related information through various tables with multiple tabs/windows. The tabs are Request, Cookies, Session, Context, Client And Server, and Headers.
- ❏ Records can be modified by right-clicking the record and selecting the Edit And Replay command.
- ❏ Selecting the ellipsis button in the tables of the Edit And Replay dialog box opens context-sensitive dialog boxes for the editing of request messages.
- ❏ Records can be played back by right-clicking the record and selecting the Replay command.

SELF TEST

The following questions help you measure your understanding of the material presented in this chapter. Read all the choices carefully because there might be more than one correct answer. Choose all correct answers for each question.

Using the HTTP Server-Side Monitor

1. What was the original name of the HTTP Server-Side Monitor?
   A. HTTP Monitor
   B. HTTP M&C
   C. HTTP Sniffer
   D. HTTP Server Monitor

2. What is the shortcut to open the HTTP Server-Side Monitor window?
   A. F5
   B. CTRL-F5
   C. SHIFT-5
   D. CTRL-SHIFT-5

3. Within the left side of the HTTP Server-Side Monitor is a panel with Records nodes. Under the root All Records node, what nodes are available?
   A. Saved Records
   B. Current Records and Saved Records
   C. Current Records, Saved Records, and Sample Records
   D. Saved Records, Rejected Records, and Sample Records

4. True or False? When a right-click is performed on an element in the Saved Records node, a popup menu is displayed with three menu items, Replay, Edit And Replay, and Delete.
   A. True
   B. False

5. In each table of the HTTP Server-Side Monitor window associated with HTTP requests, the cells in the last column include an abbreviated ellipsis (..). When clicking this cell, what is displayed relative to the record?
   A. The Edit And Replay dialog box is displayed.
   B. A Delete Record Confirmation dialog box is displayed.
   C. A View Value dialog box is displayed.
   D. The help system launches based on the context of the table information.

6. Through the toolbar and the popup menu of the All Records node, the current and saved records in the HTTP Server-Side Monitor can be sorted. Select all sorting algorithms that apply.

A. By timestamp, ascending.

B. By timestamp, descending.

C. Alphabetically, A–Z

D. Alphabetically, Z–A

7. When editing a Headers table within a saved HTTP request record, an Add Header button adds a new header (name/value pair). If you attempt to add a new header when the same header name already exists in the table, how is the new header information handled?

A. The header information is not allowed since the header name already exists in the table.

B. The header information is added to the table as a new record.

C. The header information shares the header name on the same row and adds the value to the Value cell prefaced by a comma.

D. The header information replaces the old header value with the new header value.

8. Along with a filter declaration, what modules need to be included in the `WEB-INF/lib` directory of remote servers (external to the IDE) to allow interfacing of the HTTP Server-Side Monitor? Select all that apply.

A. `org-netbeans-modules-schema2beans.jar`

B. `org-netbeans-modules-db-mysql-sakila.jar`

C. `org-netbeans-modules-httpmonitor.jar`

D. `org-netbeans-modules-j2ee-ejbjarproject.jar`

9. What windows/tabs are included in the Edit And Replay dialog box for editing saved records?

A. Query, Request, and Headers tabs

B. Query, Request, Cookies, Server, and Headers tabs

C. Request, Cookies, Session, Context, Client And Server, and Headers tabs

D. Query, Request, Cookies, Session, Context, Client And Server, and Headers tabs

10. In the HTTP Server-Side Monitor record list, each record has an associated icon. Badges may be included on top of these icons relative to the type of HTTP status code returned. Warning badges are associated with what type of status codes?

A. 1xx Information status codes

B. 2xx Success status codes

C. 3xx Redirection status codes

D. 4xx Client Error status codes

E. 5xx Server Error status codes

11. True or false? The HTTP Server-Side Monitor can reference outgoing cookies but not incoming cookies.

    A. True

    B. False

12. Consider the following illustration from NetBeans 6.7.1. What text goes next to the undefined checkbox in the Servers dialog box when configuring the connection for the GlassFish 2.1 application server?

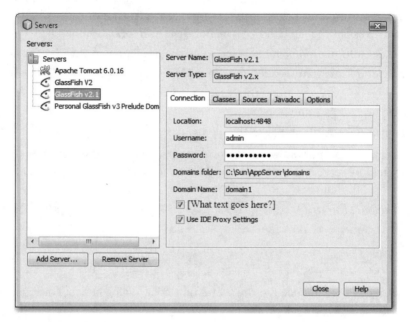

    A. Disable HTTP Monitor

    B. Enable HTTP Monitor

    C. Disable HTTP Monitor Filtering

    D. Enable HTTP Monitor Filtering

SELF TEST ANSWERS

Using the HTTP Server-Side Monitor

1. What was the original name of the HTTP Server-Side Monitor?
   A. HTTP Monitor
   B. HTTP M&C
   C. HTTP Sniffer
   D. HTTP Server Monitor

   ☑ **A.** The original name of the HTTP Server-Side Monitor was HTTP Monitor.

   ☒ **B, C,** and **D** are incorrect. **B** is incorrect because the monitor was never called the HTTP M&C. **C** is incorrect because the monitor was never called the HTTP Sniffer. **D** is incorrect because the monitor was not originally called the HTTP Server Monitor, but you may see it referenced as such as a semi-abbreviation of the HTTP Server-Side Monitor.

2. What is the shortcut to open the HTTP Server-Side Monitor window?
   A. F5
   B. CTRL-F5
   C. SHIFT-5
   D. CTRL-SHIFT-5

   ☑ **D.** The shortcut used to open the HTTP Server-Side Monitor window is CTRL-SHIFT-5.

   ☒ **A, B,** and **C** are incorrect. **A** is incorrect because F5 is used to continue the debugger and not to open the HTTP Server-Side Monitor. **B** is incorrect because CTRL-F5 is used to start debugging the main project and not to open the HTTP Server-Side Monitor. **C** is incorrect because SHIFT-5 is used to finish the debugger session.

3. Within the left side of the HTTP Server-Side Monitor is a panel with Records nodes. Under the root All Records node, what nodes are available?
   A. Saved Records
   B. Current Records and Saved Records
   C. Current Records, Saved Records, and Sample Records
   D. Saved Records, Rejected Records, and Sample Records

   ☑ **B.** Under the All Records node within the left panel of the HTTP Server-Side Monitor are nodes for Current Records and Saved Records.

   ☒ **A, C,** and **D** are incorrect. **A** is incorrect because Saved Records is not the only node available under the All Records node. **C** is incorrect because there is no Sample Records node. **D** is incorrect because there are no Rejected Records or Sample Records nodes.

4. True or False? When a right-click is performed on an element in the Saved Records node, a popup menu is displayed with three menu items, Replay, Edit And Replay, and Delete.
   A. True
   B. False

   ☑ **True.** When an element in the Saved Records node is right-clicked, a popup menu displays with three menu items: Replay, Edit And Replay, and Delete.

5. In each table of the HTTP Server-Side Monitor window associated with HTTP requests, the cells in the last column include an abbreviated ellipsis (..). When clicking this cell, what is displayed relative to the record?
   A. The Edit And Replay dialog box is displayed.
   B. A Delete Record Confirmation dialog box is displayed.
   C. A View Value dialog box is displayed.
   D. The help system launches based on the context of the table information.

   ☑ **C.** A View Value dialog box displays. This option is available to show the full value of the second column because it often has more data than can be displayed in the current table orientation.

   ☒ **A, B,** and **D** are incorrect. **A** is incorrect because clicking the abbreviated ellipsis does not display the Edit And Replay dialog box. **B** is incorrect because clicking the abbreviated ellipsis does not display a Delete Record Confirmation dialog box. **D** is incorrect because clicking the abbreviated ellipsis does not launch the help system.

6. Through the toolbar and the popup menu of the All Records node, the current and saved records in the HTTP Server-Side Monitor can be sorted. Select all sorting algorithms that apply.
   A. By timestamp, ascending.
   B. By timestamp, descending.
   C. Alphabetically, A–Z.
   D. Alphabetically, Z–A.

   ☑ **A, B,** and **C** are correct. Current and saved records can be sorted by timestamp (ascending and descending) and alphabetically (only A–Z).

   ☒ **D** is incorrect because the current and saved records cannot be sorted alphabetically (Z–A).

7. When editing a Headers table within a saved HTTP request record, an Add Header button adds a new header (name/value pair). If you attempt to add a new header when the same header name already exists in the table, how is the new header information handled?

A. The header information is not allowed since the header name already exists in the table.

B. The header information is added to the table as a new record.

C. The header information shares the header name on the same row and adds the value to the Value cell prefaced by a comma.

D. The header information replaces the old header value with the new header value.

☑ **C.** The new header shares the name of the existing header in the table and adds the value to the Value cell prefaced by a comma.

☒ **A, B, and D** are incorrect. **A** is incorrect because new header information is allowed. **B** is incorrect because new header information with the same header name of as existing header name is not be added to a new row. **D** is incorrect because new header information does not replace existing header information.

8. Along with a filter declaration, what modules need to be included in the `WEB-INF/lib` directory of remote servers (external to the IDE) to allow interfacing of the HTTP Server-Side Monitor? Select all that apply.

A. `org-netbeans-modules-schema2beans.jar`

B. `org-netbeans-modules-db-mysql-sakila.jar`

C. `org-netbeans-modules-httpmonitor.jar`

D. `org-netbeans-modules-j2ee-ejbjarproject.jar`

☑ **A and C.** The HTTP Monitor can interface with application servers outside of the IDE when the JAR files `org-netbeans-modules-schema2beans.jar` and `org-netbeans-modules-httpmonitor.jar` are included in the servers' `WEB-INF/lib` directory.

☒ **B and D** are incorrect. **B** is incorrect because the Sakila database support module is not needed for HTTP Monitor integration. **D** is incorrect because the EJB support module is not needed for HTTP Monitor integration.

9. What windows/tabs are included in the Edit And Replay dialog box for editing saved records?

A. Query, Request, and Headers tabs

B. Query, Request, Cookies, Server, and Headers tabs

C. Request, Cookies, Session, Context, Client And Server, and Headers tabs

D. Query, Request, Cookies, Session, Context, Client And Server, and Headers tabs

☑ **B.** The window/tabs included in the Edit And Replay dialog box are Query, Request, Cookies, Server, and Headers.

☒ **A, C, and D** are incorrect. **A** is incorrect because all of the windows/tabs are not listed for the Edit And Replay dialog box. **C** is incorrect because the Edit And Replay dialog box does not have Session and Client And Server tabs. **D** is incorrect because the Edit And Replay dialog box does not have Session, Context, and Client And Server tabs.

10. In the HTTP Server-Side Monitor record list, each record has an associated icon. Badges may be included on top of these icons relative to the type of HTTP status code returned. Warning badges are associated with what type of status codes?

    A. 1xx Information status codes

    B. 2xx Success status codes

    C. 3xx Redirection status codes

    D. 4xx Client Error status codes

    E. 5xx Server Error status codes

    ☑ **C.** In the HTTP Server-Side Monitor record list, warning badges are included relative to 3xx Redirection HTTP status codes being returned.

    ☒ **A, B, D,** and **E** are incorrect. **A** is incorrect because warning icons are not associated in the record list with 1xx Information status codes. **B** is incorrect because warning icons are not associated in the record list with 2xx Success status codes. **D** is incorrect because warning icons are not associated in the record list with 4xx Client Error status codes. **E** is incorrect because warning icons are not associated in the record list with 5xx Server Error status codes.

11. True or false? The HTTP Server-Side Monitor can reference outgoing cookies but not incoming cookies.

    A. True

    B. False

    ☒ **B.** The statement is false. The HTTP Server-Side Monitor can reference both incoming and outgoing cookies.

12. Consider the following illustration from NetBeans 6.7.1. What text goes next to the undefined checkbox in the Servers dialog box when configuring the connection for the GlassFish 2.1 application server?

    A. Disable HTTP Monitor

    B. Enable HTTP Monitor

    C. Disable HTTP Monitor Filtering

D. Enable HTTP Monitor Filtering

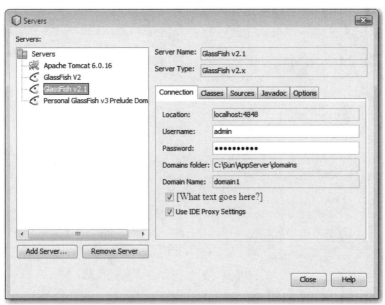

☑ **B.** The missing text is "Enable HTTP Monitor."

☒ **A, C,** and **D** are incorrect. **A** is incorrect because "Disable HTTP Monitor" is not the text displayed. **C** is incorrect because "Disable HTTP Monitor Filtering" is not the text displayed. **D** is incorrect because "Enable HTTP Monitor Filtering" is not the text displayed

9

Local and Remote Debuggers

CERTIFICATION OBJECTIVES

- Debugging Local Applications
- Debugging Remote Applications

✓ Two-Minute Drill

Q&A Self Test

N etBeans debugging support has been strong since its inception, and just about every subsequent build has improved upon it. It's actually difficult to conceptualize, let alone itemize, all of the things that the NetBeans debugger does. Fortunately for the exam, you need to master only the most commonly used debugging features. These features include starting the debugger, setting breakpoints, stepping through code, and using various debugging windows to view and interface with the debugger. We cover these areas against the first objective related to local applications and the debugger. Later in the chapter we discuss the fundamental differences between local and remote debugging and also explain how to debug web applications. After you have completed this chapter, you will have enough knowledge to score well on the debugging-related questions on the exam. You may also find yourself using the debugger more frequently on the job, in place of redirecting analysis data to standard out or log files.

CERTIFICATION OBJECTIVE

Debugging Local Applications

Exam Objective 6.2   Describe how to debug a local (desktop) application, including setting breakpoints and stepping through code.

Debugging local applications is a common activity. If you are debugging your Java applications solely by redirecting messages to standard out, you are missing the benefits of using a true debugger, as described throughout the chapter. With the NetBeans IDE debugger, you can set breakpoints, start the debugger, and view the state of various variables faster than you can pepper your source code with print statements such as `System.out.println("Debug 1")`, `System.out .println("Debug 2")`, and so on. If you are a seasoned developer and have been using the NetBeans IDE debugging features, then this section helps solidify your knowledge for the exam. In the upcoming sections, we cover setting up a session, setting breakpoints, stepping through code, and using the various debugging windows.

- Session Establishment
- Breakpoint Settings
- Code Stepping
- Debugging Support Windows

Session Establishment

Prior to starting a session, the Generate Debugging Info property must be enabled. NetBeans 6.8 documentation specifically states, "If selected, the compiled classes include information necessary for stopping at breakpoints and stepping through the application with the debugger." This setting is selected by default when installing the IDE. So if you've been using the debugger, you may not even know the setting exists. You can find the Generate Debugging Info checkbox in the Project Properties dialog box under the Build | Compiling nodes, as shown in Figure 9-1. This dialog box can be opened by right-clicking your project in either the Projects or Files window. If the button is deselected and you try to use the debugger, you should see an error in the Debugger Console of the Output window.

Starting a debugging session is easy, and you can do it in several ways. The most common way is by clicking the Debug Main Project icon in the Run (View | Toolbars | Run) toolbar. This action, or simply pressing CTRL-F5, executes the program until it reaches a breakpoint, exception, or terminates normally. Another way to start a session is by pressing F7, which maps to the Step Into command. You can also find the Step Into command on the Debug menu in the main menu bar: Debug | Step Into. For reference, Figure 9-2 shows the full Debug menu. Run To Cursor is enabled if the cursor has selected an insertion point in one of the project files. All of these items including stepping are detailed in the upcoming sections. When a session is

FIGURE 9-1   Generate Debugging Info checkbox

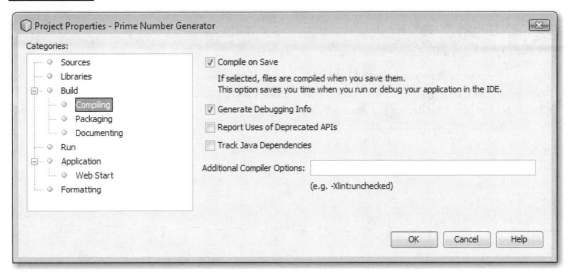

established, information and controls are available in nine related debugging windows: Variables, Watches, Call Stack, Loaded Classes, Breakpoints, Sessions, Threads, Sources, and Debugging. Coverage for these windows is done later in the chapter.

We have discussed several ways of starting up a debugging session. The Scenario & Solution further explores each way and adds a couple more.

SCENARIO & SOLUTION

You wish to execute the program until it reaches a breakpoint, an exception, or it terminates normally.	Right-click the Debug Main Project icon in the Run toolbar, select Debug | Debug Main Project, right-click the Projects window and choose Debug, or press CTRL-F5.
You wish to execute a runnable file or unit test up to the point of the first breakpoint or until execution stops.	Select the runnable file or unit test and Debug | Debug [filename].
You wish to execute the program to the insertion point set by the cursor and then pause the execution of the program.	Right-click the Run To Cursor icon in the Debug toolbar, select Debug | Run to Cursor, or press F4.
You wish to execute the program to the first line in the main method and then pause the execution of the program.	Right-click the Step Into icon in the Debug toolbar, select Debug | Step Into, or press F7.

e x a m

ⓦatch   *NetBeans 6.5 and later versions have debugging menu items under the Debug menu. NetBeans 6.1 and earlier* *versions have debugging menu items under the Run menu.*

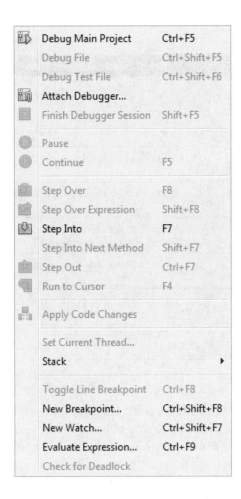

FIGURE 9-2

Debug menu
items

Breakpoint Settings

Breakpoints are marked places in code where execution pauses when the debugger
reaches that point. Breakpoint glyphs reside in the left margin to annotate the type
and location of the breakpoint. Primary breakpoint markers are shown in Table 9-1.
Breakpoint marker settings are persistent and need to be cleared for permanent removal.

TABLE 9-1	Breakpoint Settings	

Breakpoint Glyph	Glyph Body Color	Breakpoint Description
⬛	Pink	Line breakpoint
▽	Gray	Disabled nonline breakpoint
◨	Red	Invalid line breakpoint
⬗	Gray	Disabled conditional line breakpoint
▼	Pink	Nonline breakpoint (i.e., class, exception, method, thread, or field breakpoint)
◧	Pink	Conditional line breakpoint
▽	Red	Invalid nonline breakpoint
⬜	Gray	Disabled line breakpoint

Breakpoints are commonly set and configured through the New Breakpoint dialog box (Debug | New Breakpoint or CTRL-SHIFT-F8). However, they can be set through a variety of means. Let's take a look at setting line breakpoints, for example. You can click in the left margin of the source editor to set a line breakpoint. You can select CTRL-F8 to set a line breakpoint. You can also select Debug | Toggle Line Breakpoint from the main menu to set a line breakpoint.

Line breakpoints have the background of the source line colored the same as the body of the breakpoint glyphs. Nonline breakpoints do not color the background of the source lines. When a breakpoint is reached, a program counter (right-arrow badge) shows on top of the breakpoint glyph. This associated source line has a green background. Figure 9-3 shows the program marker, one enabled line breakpoint, one disabled line breakpoint, and one method breakpoint.

For each breakpoint that is reached, related information is printed in the Debugger Console of the Output window.

Six types of breakpoints can be set: line, class, exception, method, thread, and field. We examine each type in the following sections.

FIGURE 9-3   Breakpoint glyphs in the left margin

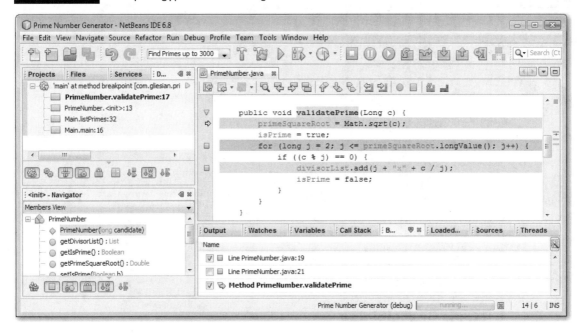

Line Breakpoints

Line breakpoints are available to pause a program on a specified line. A line breakpoint is established through the New Breakpoint dialog box (CTRL-SHIFT-F8) with the Breakpoint Type being Line. Line breakpoints can also be configured by right-clicking the breakpoint glyph in the left margin and selecting Breakpoint | Properties. The Breakpoint Properties dialog box will be displayed, as shown in Figure 9-4. There are three group boxes in the dialog box that allow for additional settings.

■ **Settings group box**   File and line number attributes are defined in this group box.

■ **Conditions group box**   Breakpoints can be tied to Boolean conditions and/or break counts in this group box. Break count options include Equals To, Is Greater Than, and Is Multiple Of for a user-selectable value.

■ **Actions group box**   The Suspend combo box provides three settings for the suspension of threads: No Thread (Continue), Breakpoint Thread, and All Threads. Whenever the breakpoint is hit for any of the selected conditions, the text in the Print Text edit box is directed to the Debugging Console window.

FIGURE 9-4

Breakpoint
Properties dialog
box for a line

Class Breakpoints

Class breakpoints are available to pause program execution when a class is loaded
and/or unloaded from the JVM. A class breakpoint is established through the New
Breakpoint dialog box with the Breakpoint Type being Class, as shown in Figure 9-5.
The three group boxes in the dialog box allow for additional settings:

- **Settings group box** The Class Name edit box designates the class or classes
(for example, `java.util.*`) that will have the breakpoint upon being
loaded to or unloaded from the JVM. The Stop On combo box sets whether
the breakpoint specifically occurs when the class is loaded (Class Load),
unloaded (Class Unload), or both (Class Load Or Unload).

- **Conditions group box** The Exclude Classes checkbox and edit box
components allow for exclusion of classes when an entire package is used with
a wildcard in the Settings Class Name edit box. "The Break When Hit Count"
checkbox components allow for the triggering of the breakpoint when the hit
count of loaded and/or unloaded instances is Equals To, Is Greater Than, or Is
Multiple Of what is defined in the corresponding edit box.

FIGURE 9-5

New Breakpoint
dialog box for
a class

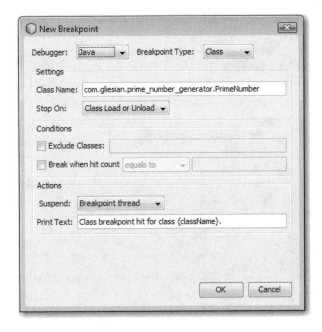

- **Actions group box**   The Suspend combo box provides three settings for the suspension of threads: No Thread (Continue), Breakpoint Thread, and All Threads. Whenever the breakpoint is hit for any of the selected conditions, the text in the Print Text edit box is directed to the Debugger Console window.

Exception Breakpoints

Exception breakpoints are available to pause execution whenever a specified exception is caught, is not handled in the source code, or is encountered (handled or not). An exception breakpoint is established through the New Breakpoint dialog box with the Breakpoint Type being Exception, as shown in Figure 9-6. The three group boxes in the dialog box allow for additional settings:

- **Settings group box**   The Exception Class Name edit box designates the exception(s) that will have the breakpoint upon being caught or uncaught. The Stop On combo box sets whether the breakpoint specifically occurs when the exception is Caught, Uncaught, or Caught Or Uncaught.

FIGURE 9-6

New Breakpoint
dialog box for an
exception

- **Conditions group box**   You can apply filters on classes throwing the exception. Breakpoints can be tied to Boolean conditions and/or to break counts in this group box. Break count options include Equals To, Is Greater Than, and Is Multiple Of for a user-selectable value.

- **Actions group box**   The Actions combo box provides three settings for the suspension of threads: No Thread (Continue), Breakpoint Thread, and All Threads. Whenever the breakpoint is hit for any of the selected conditions, the text in the Print Text edit box is directed to the Debugger Console window.

Method Breakpoints

Method breakpoints are available to pause methods and constructors before they are entered, exited, or both. A method breakpoint is established through the New Breakpoint dialog box with the Breakpoint Type being Method, as shown in Figure 9-7. The three group boxes in the dialog box allow for additional settings:

- **Settings group box** Settings can be established to stop on all methods of an individual class or a specific method. The Stop On combo box options include Method Entry, Method Exit, and Method Entry Or Exit.
- **Conditions group box** Breakpoints can be tied to Boolean conditions and/ or break counts in this group box. Break count options include Equals To, Is Greater Than, and Is Multiple Of for a user-selectable value.
- **Actions group box** The Actions combo box provides three settings for the suspension of threads: No Thread (Continue), Breakpoint Thread, and All Threads. Whenever the breakpoint is hit for any of the selected conditions, the text in the Print Text edit box is directed to the Debugger Console window.

FIGURE 9-7

New Breakpoint dialog box for a method

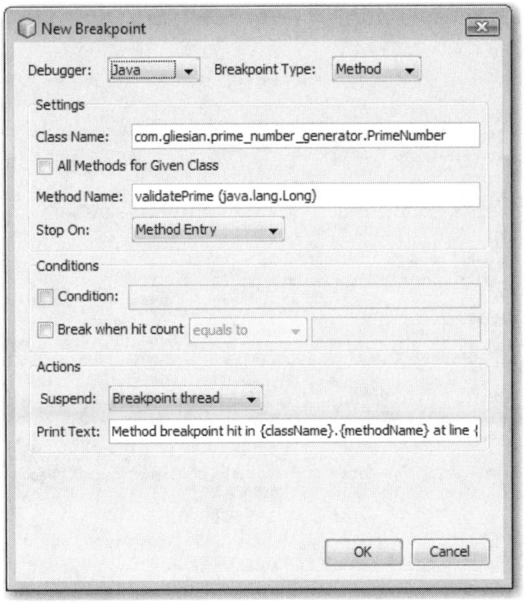

Thread Breakpoints

Thread breakpoints are available to pause execution whenever a thread starts, stops, or both. A thread breakpoint is established through the New Breakpoint dialog box with the Breakpoint Type being Thread, as shown in Figure 9-8. The three group boxes in the dialog box allow for additional settings:

- **Settings group box** The Stop On combo box settings include Thread Start, Thread Death, or Thread Start Or Death.
- **Conditions group box** Breakpoints can be tied to break counts in this group box. Break count options include Equals To, Is Greater Than, and Is Multiple Of for a user-selectable value.
- **Actions group box** The Actions combo box provides three settings for the suspension of threads: No Thread (Continue), Breakpoint Thread, and All Threads. Whenever the breakpoint is hit for any of the selected conditions, the text in the Print Text edit box is directed to the Debugger Console window.

FIGURE 9-8

New Breakpoint dialog box for a thread

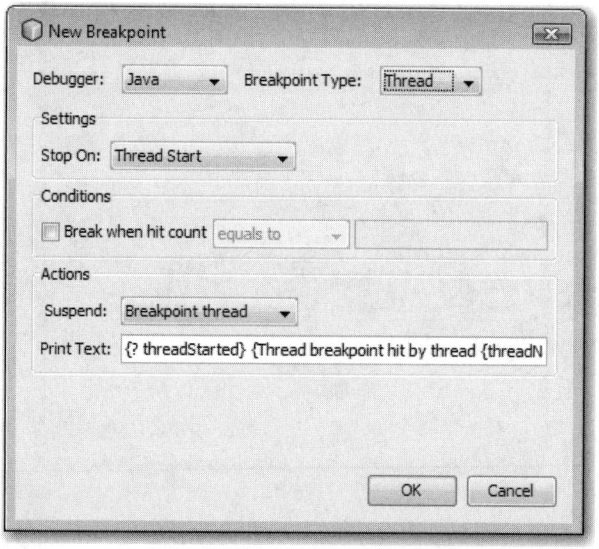

Field Breakpoints

Field breakpoints are available to pause execution on a field in a specified class. A field breakpoint is established through the New Breakpoint dialog box with the Breakpoint Type being Field, as shown in Figure 9-9. The three group boxes in the dialog box allow for additional settings:

- **Settings group box**   The Class Name, Field Name, and Stop On settings may be established in the group box. The Stop On combo box options include Field Access, Field Modification, and Field Access Or Modification.

- **Conditions group box**   Breakpoints can be tied to Boolean conditions and/or break counts in this group box. Break count options include Equals To, Is Greater Than, and Is Multiple Of for a user-selectable value.

- **Actions group box**   The Actions combo box provides three settings for the suspension of threads: No Thread (Continue), Breakpoint Thread, and All Threads. Whenever the breakpoint is hit for any of the selected conditions, the text in the Print Text edit box is directed to the Debugger Console window.

FIGURE 9-9

New Breakpoint
dialog box for
a field

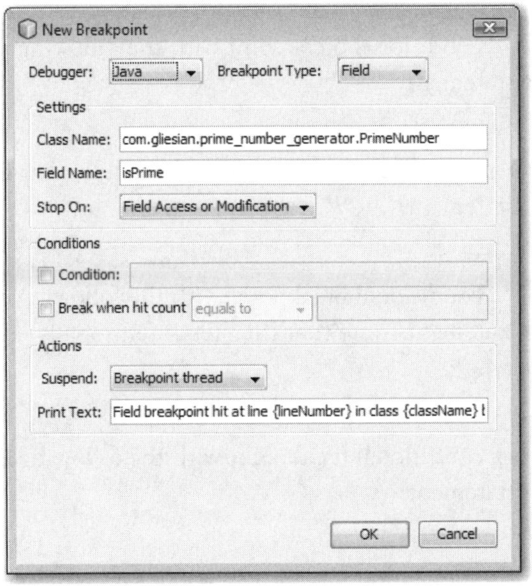

Applying Conditions to Breakpoints

This exercise applies Boolean conditions to breakpoints. That is, if an expression evaluates to true, the condition is hit; otherwise, program execution continues pass the breakpoint. This example uses line breakpoints.

1. Create a simple HelloBreakPoints application with the following source code:

```
package hello_breakpoints;
public class HelloBreakPoints {
 public static void main(String[] args) {
  String s = ""test1"";
  int i = 2;
  boolean b;
  System.out.println(""Hello Breakpoint 1"");
  System.out.println(""Hello Breakpoint 2"");
  System.out.println(""Hello Breakpoint 3"");
  System.out.println(""Hello Breakpoint 4"");
  }
}
```

2. Apply a conditional breakpoint with the following expression to the first print statement:

```
s instanceof String
```

3. Apply a conditional breakpoint with the following expression to the second print statement:

```
i == 2
```

4. Apply a conditional breakpoint with the following expression to the third print statement (note that this step intentionally uses one equals sign; it is not a typo):

```
b = true
```

5. Apply a conditional breakpoint with the following expression to the fourth print statement:

```
true
```

6. Run the application in debug mode and step through each line. Note that the program pauses on each breakpoint as each evaluates to true.

7. Bonus: Steps 2 through 6 have expressions that evaluate to true. Explain why they evaluate to true.

Configuration of various Java debugger settings was added to the Tools | Options window in NetBeans 6.7. The tab is located relative to the Miscellaneous icon. Consult Chapter 1 for additional coverage.

Code Stepping

Stepping through code is fundamentally the most important feature of the debugger. Being able to control where you want to look in your source code at runtime and displaying related data in context to that position is very useful when determining what the code is doing. Code-stepping features allow you to step one line at a time, or in and out of various structural elements. For a quick look at the commands, Table 9-2 details their names and shortcut keys. The following sections detail the functional capabilities of each stepping-related command. The illustrations correspond to the glyphs in the Debug menu off of the main menu and on the Debug toolbar (View | Toolbars | Debug).

TABLE 9-2   Code-Stepping Commands

Stepping Toolbar Glyph	Stepping Command	Stepping Shortcut
	Step Over	F8
	Step Over Expression	SHIFT-F8
	Step Into	F7
N/A	Step Into Next Method	SHIFT-F7
	Step Out	CTRL-F7
	Run To Cursor	F4
	Pause	None
	Continue	F5
	Finish Debugging Session	SHIFT-F5

Step Over

The Step Over command executes the current line. If the current line contains a method or constructor, the entire call is executed without stepping into any of the individual lines. The debugger then moves to the next line. The command is invoked by choosing Debug | Step Over or by pressing F8.

Step Over Expression

The Step Over Expression command executes one method call in an expression. If multiple method calls exist on the line, including chaining, the command steps through the expression and views each value of each method in the Local Variables window. When there are no more method occurrences to be traversed, the debugger moves to the next line. The command is invoked by choosing Debug | Step Over Expression or by pressing SHIFT-F8.

Step Into

The Step Into command executes the current line. If the current line has a method or constructor call, the debugger pauses before executing the first line within the call. If there are multiple methods, the most likely method call is highlighted by default with a boxed line. The command is invoked by choosing Debug | Step Into or by pressing F7. You can start a debugging session with the Step Into command.

Step Into Next Method

The Step Into Next Method command executes one method or constructor call in a line. If multiple method calls are on the line, you can select the desired call with the cursor. The most likely method call is highlighted by default with a boxed line. The command is invoked by choosing Debug | Step Into Next Method or by pressing SHIFT-F8.

Step Out

The Step Out command steps out of the current method by executing all remaining source code lines and entering back into the calling method. If the source line is not part of a method, only one source line is executed. The command is invoked by choosing Debug | Step Out or by pressing CTRL-F7.

Run To Cursor

The Run To Cursor command allows the program execution to continue up to the insertion point placed by the cursor. At the insertion point, the program execution pauses. The command is invoked by choosing Debug | Run To Cursor or by pressing F4. You can start a debugging session with the Run To Cursor command.

Pause

The Pause command suspends all of the threads in the current debugger session. The command is invoked by choosing Debug | Pause. There is no shortcut key for the Pause command.

Continue

The Continue command allows program execution to continue to the next breakpoint, or until the execution is suspended or terminated. The command is invoked by choosing Debug | Continue or by pressing F5.

Debugging Support Windows

Nine debugging support windows exist: Variables, Watches, Call Stack, Loaded Classes, Breakpoints, Sessions, Threads, Sources, and Debugging. The first eight are displayed in the bottom right of the IDE. The last (the Debugging window) is displayed in the upper-left pane. All windows provide information and controls against debugging sessions. Each window is detailed in this section. You will not need to know the fine details of each window for the exam, so they are covered only at a high level in this section. Shortcuts for windows are shown in the Windows | Debugging menu, shown in Figure 9-10. Additional menu items may be included on your Debugging submenu, depending on your version of NetBeans and installed NetBeans bundle.

FIGURE 9-10

Debugging
submenu

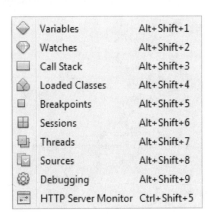

◇	Variables	Alt+Shift+1
▽	Watches	Alt+Shift+2
▢	Call Stack	Alt+Shift+3
◈	Loaded Classes	Alt+Shift+4
▢	Breakpoints	Alt+Shift+5
⊞	Sessions	Alt+Shift+6
▤	Threads	Alt+Shift+7
▣	Sources	Alt+Shift+8
⚙	Debugging	Alt+Shift+9
▦	HTTP Server Monitor	Ctrl+Shift+5

Variables Window

The Variables window, as shown in Figure 9-11, lists the variables in the current call. Right-clicking the empty portion of the Variables window displays a popup menu with the following choices: New Watch, Delete, Delete All, and Edit. Depending on the type of item selected in the list and the table column, the following menu items may be shown in a right-click popup: Display As (Decimal, Hexadecimal, Octal,

FIGURE 9-11   Variables debugging window

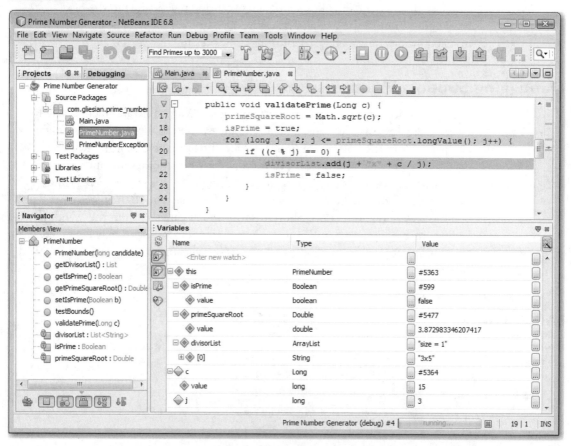

Binary, Character, Time), Created Fixed Watch, Show Only Rows Where, and/or Go To Source). The Variables window (ALT-SHIFT-1) opens in the bottom right of the IDE.

on the

(j)ob

As of NetBeans 6.5, you can evaluate expressions in the Evaluate code window while in a debugging session. The results of your expression against current context elements are shown in the Variables window. The window can be opened by selecting Debug | Evaluate Expression or by pressing CTRL-F9.

Watches Window

The Watches window, as shown in Figure 9-12, lists specified variables and expressions to watch while in a debugging session. Right-clicking the empty portion of the Watches window displays a popup menu with the following choices: New Watch and Delete All. Right-clicking a watch item displays a popup menu that may have the following among other items: Delete Fixed Watch, Show References, and Mark Object. The Watches window (ALT-SHIFT-2) opens in the bottom right of the IDE. A fixed watch is an object that is currently assigned to a variable. A normal watch describes the contents of the variable.

Call Stack Window

The Call Stack window, as shown in Figure 9-13, lists the sequence of calls made during the execution of the current thread while highlighting the current call.

FIGURE 9-12   Watches debugging window

Name	Type	Value	
⊞ c	Long	#65	
◇ c==51	boolean	false	
<Enter new watch>			

FIGURE 9-13 Call Stack window

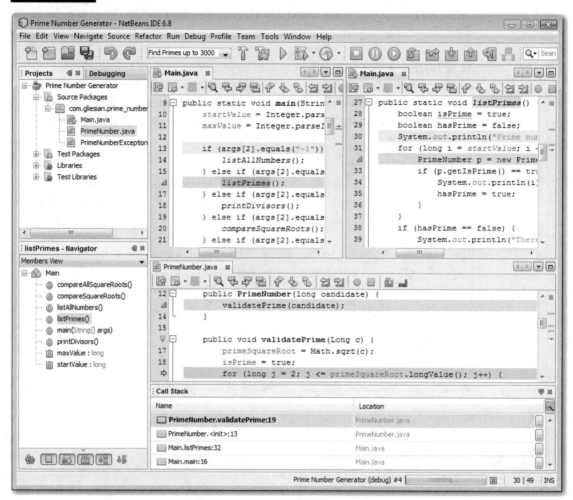

Right-clicking the empty portion of the Call Stack window displays a popup menu with the following choice: Copy Stack. Right-clicking a call displays a popup menu with the following choices: Make Current, Pop To Here, Go To Source, and Copy Stack. The Call Stack window (ALT-SHIFT-3) opens in the bottom right of the IDE.

Loaded Classes Window

The Loaded Classes window, as shown in Figure 9-14, lists the loaded classes for the current debugging session. Right-clicking a loaded class displays a popup menu with the following choices: Show In Instances View, Show Only Subclasses, and Go To Source. The Sources window (ALT-SHIFT-4) opens in the bottom right of the IDE.

FIGURE 9-14 Loaded Classes window

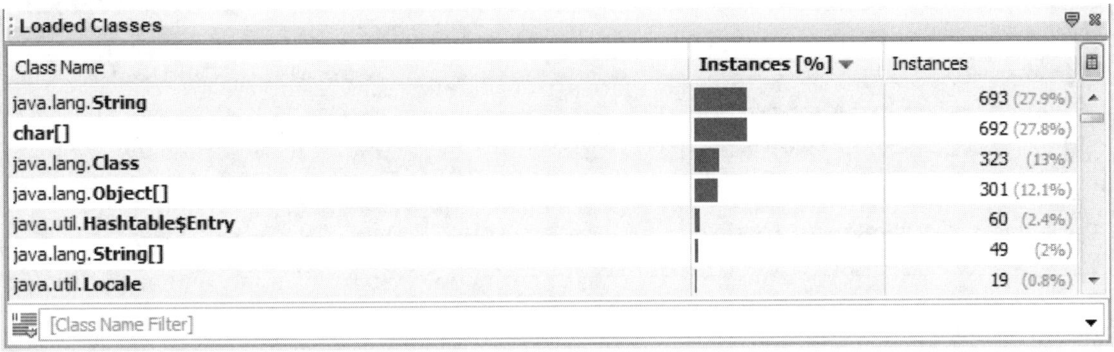

Breakpoints Window

The Breakpoints window, as shown in Figure 9-15, lists all of the project breakpoints. Right-clicking the empty portion of the Breakpoints window displays a popup menu with the following choices: New Breakpoint, Enable All, Disable All, and Delete All. Right-clicking a breakpoint in the list displays a popup menu with the following choices: Go To Source, Disable/Enable, Move Into Group, New Breakpoint, Enable All, Disable All, Delete, Delete All, and Properties. The Breakpoints window (ALT-SHIFT-5) opens in the bottom right of the IDE.

Sessions Window

The Sessions window, as shown in Figure 9-16, lists all running debugging sessions. Session states may be Starting, Running, or Stopped. Right-clicking the empty portion of the Sessions window displays a popup menu that may include the following choice, depending on the column: Finish All. Right-clicking a session in the list displays a popup menu with the following choices: Scope, Language, Make Current, Finish, Finish All, and Show Only Rows Where. Items are enabled or disabled based on context. The Sessions window (ALT-SHIFT-6) opens in the bottom right of the IDE.

FIGURE 9-15

Breakpoints
window

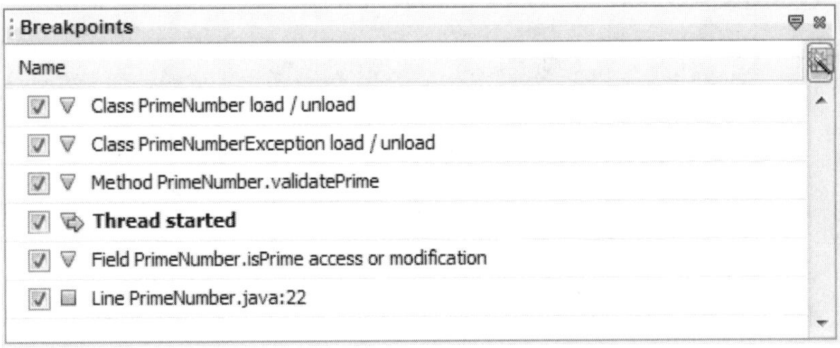

Sessions				
▽ **Name**	State	Language	Host Name	
⊞ com.gliesian.prime_number_generator.Main	Stopped	Java	localhost	
⊞ com.gliesian.prime_number_generator.Main1	Stopped	Java	localhost	
⊞ com.toy.anagrams.ui.Anagrams	Stopped	Java	localhost	
⊞ marsroverviewer.MarsRoverViewerApp	Stopped	Java	localhost	

Threads Window

The Threads window, shown in Figure 9-17, lists all of the threads in the current debugging session. Thread states may be Monitor, Not Started, Running, Sleeping, Unknown, Waiting, or Zombie. Right-clicking a thread in the list displays a popup menu with the following choices: Make Current, Resume/Suspend, Interrupt, and Go To Source. Items are enabled or disabled based on context. The Threads window (ALT-SHIFT-7) opens in the bottom right of the IDE.

Sources Window

The Sources window, as shown in Figure 9-18, lists source code files that may be available to the debugger. Right-clicking the empty portion of the Sources window displays a popup menu with the following choices: Add Source Root, Move Up, Move Down, and Reset Order. The Move Up and Move Down menu items are enabled only when you right-click a source root that can move in that direction. The Sources window (ALT-SHIFT-8) opens in the bottom right of the IDE.

Threads		
Name	State	Suspe...
⊟ 🔲 **system**		☐
⊟ 🔲 **main**		☑
🔲 **main**	Running	☑
⊞ Reference Handler	Waiting	☐
⊞ Finalizer	Waiting	☐
⊞ Signal Dispatcher	Running	☐
⊞ Attach Listener	Running	☐

FIGURE 9-18   Sources window

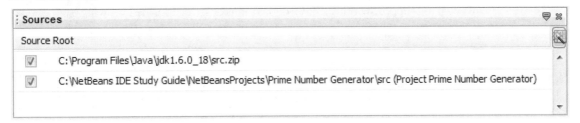

Debugging Window

The Debugging window lists all of the threads in the current debugging session and allows you to view, suspend, and resume the thread. The Debugging window is not in NetBeans 6.1 so is therefore not on the exam.

The Debugging window (ALT-SHIFT-9) opens in the left pane and may be grouped with other open windows such as Projects, Files, and Services.

Figure 9-19 shows the debugging against the Mars Rover Viewer sample application (`MarsRoverViewerApp`).

FIGURE 9-19

Debugging window

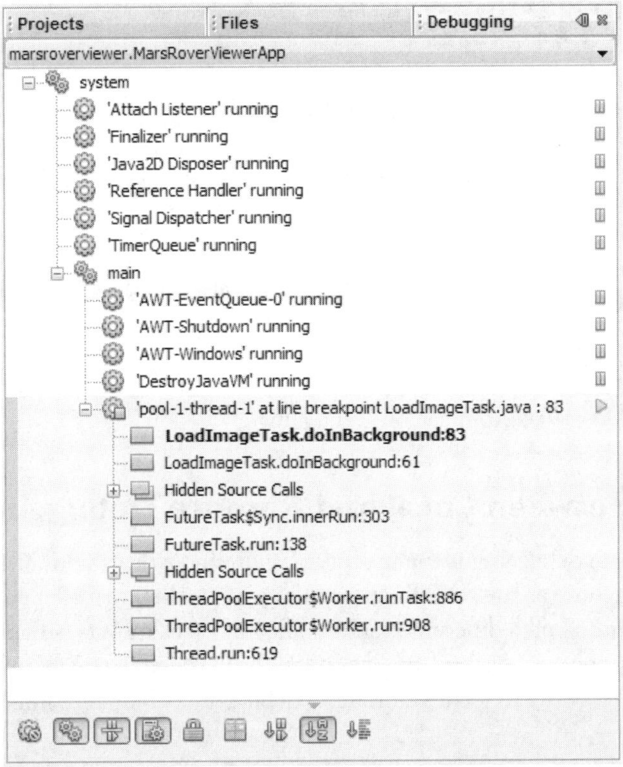

Debugging Support Windows Behavior

Debugging support windows have behavior as described in the following two subsections.

Opening and Closing Windows   Debugging support windows, which open when a debugging session is running, automatically close when all debugging sessions finish. Debugging support windows that are opened when there is no debugging session running stay open until you close them.

Changing Visible Columns in Debugging Windows   All debugging support windows with the exception of the Debugging window have an icon in the upper-right corner that opens a Change Visible Columns dialog box. The dialog box has a checkbox for each column. If the checkbox is selected, the column is displayed. If deselected, the column is not displayed. Mandatory columns are listed, but their checkbox component is disabled because the column cannot be deselected.

CERTIFICATION OBJECTIVE

Debugging Remote Applications

Exam Objective 6.3   Describe the difference between local and remote debugging and describe how to debug a remote web application.

This section touches on the primary differences in debugging and the various means to debug remote and/or web applications.

- Differences Between Local and Remote Debugging
- Web Application Debugging

Differences Between Local and Remote Debugging

Local debugging is the process of analyzing a program that is running on the same machine as the IDE. Remote debugging is the process of analyzing a program that is running on a different machine. Setting breakpoints, stepping through code, setting watches, analyzing variables, and all other debugging features are essentially the same between local and remote debugging. The main difference is the need to attach the debugger when you are debugging remotely. As such, there are three primary steps in starting a remote debugging session:

1. Start the remote application in debugging mode.
2. On the machine where the IDE is running, open the project with the source code.
3. Attach the debugger.

Starting the Remote Application in Debugging Mode

To debug a remote application, the application must be started in debug mode. To do this, you need to pass additional switches and values to the Java interpreter. As there are many JVMs by various vendors, the switches and settings for debugging may vary slightly. Also note that -X[name] options are not standardized and are subject to change or removal. With this being said, you need to find the documentation for your specific JVM to determine exactly what you need to do to set up debugging. Exercising java -h or java -X prints some help information to get you started. Information specific to Sun's Hotspot VM can be found here: http://java.sun.com/products/jpda/doc/conninv.html. For the scope of the exam, you simply need to know that the -Xdebug switch is a common switch that is required when invoking the interpreter.

If you have time, you can go through the exercise of setting up a remote debugging session. However, understanding only the concept of remote debugging is needed. You would probably be better off studying other areas or objectives where you are weak.

Opening the Project in the IDE

The process of opening the project to be used for debugging is straightforward being done in the traditional manner (e.g., CTRL-SHIFT-O). Make sure that you use the source code that matches the remote application that is running.

Attaching the Debugger

Attaching the debugger requires some configuration. For the purpose of the exam, we are most concerned with details of the Java debugger, which is based on the Java Platform Debugger Architecture (JPDA). The JPDA includes the following three-layered APIs:

- **Java Debug Interface (JDI)**   A high-level Java language interface with support for remote debugging.

■ **Java Debug Wire Protocol (JDWP)**   A protocol that defines the format of information and requests transferred between the process being debugged and the debugger front-end.

■ **JVM Tools Interface (JVM TI)**   A low-level native interface that defines the services a Java virtual machine provides for tools such as debuggers and profilers. The JVM TI replaces the legacy JVMPI and JVMDI interfaces.

In addition to the JPDA debugger, other platforms can be attached to the IDE including the Web Page Debugger (JavaScript), Gdb debugger, and Ruby debuggers. Debugger platforms are attached through the Attach dialog box, which is invoked via Debug | Attach Debugger or through the Attach Debugger menu item associated with the Debug Main Project icon in the Run toolbar. Once in the dialog box, you see several ways to attach a debugger. The Scenario & Solution explores ways to attach the JPDA debugger.

SCENARIO & SOLUTION

You desire attachment to debuggee by process-id (pid).	Select the `ProcessAttach` type.
You desire attachment by shared memory to other VMs.	Select the `SharedMemoryAttach` type.
You desire acceptance of shared memory connections that are initiated by other VMs.	Select the `SharedMemoryListen` type.
You desire attachment by socket to other VMs.	Select the `SocketAttach` type.

on the job

Consider adding the FindBugs, Checkstyle, and PMD plugins to your IDE. These software quality tools may expose flaws in your code that may help expedite debugging once they are resolved. Note that these tools are not integrated with the debugger.

Several NetBeans IDE tools and features support debugging local, remote, and web applications. You can monitor HTTP messages with the HTTP Server-Side Monitor, as detailed in Chapter 8. You can test source code with JUnit, as detailed in Chapter 10. You can profile applications as detailed in Chapter 10. A new feature in NetBeans 6.9 is Debugger Attachment History; the last four Debug Attachment configurations are appended to the menu associated with the Debug Main Project icon in the Run toolbar.

Web Application Debugging

When debugging a web application, you can decide to debug server-side code, JavaScript on the client side, or both, as shown in the Project Properties dialog box in Figure 9-20. Server-side debugging allows you to set breakpoints on and to step through the Java code or JSP code. Client-side debugging allows you to set breakpoints on and to step through HTML and JavaScript code. Active debuggers are listed in the Sessions window (ALT-SHIFT-6).

Note that if you try to debug an application on the client side and the browser doesn't have the necessary support to run the NetBeans JavaScript Debugger, a dialog box displays the same information as in Figure 9-20.

FIGURE 9-20

Debug settings
in the Project
Properties
dialog box

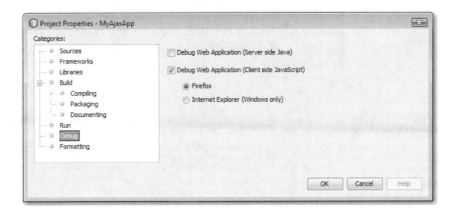

Install Firefox
Add-ons
dialog box

When you decide to debug on the client side with the NetBeans JavaScript
Debugger, both Firefox and Internet Explorer need add-ons to support client-side
debugging. The IDE detects whether necessary add-ons are present and prompts
you to install them if they are not, as shown for Firefox in Figure 9-21. Firefox
automatically installs the `netbeans.firefox.extensions` add-on and the
Firebug add-on. Internet Explorer installs the `netbeans.ie.extension` add-on
and guides you through manual installation of the Active Scripting Debugger
Framework add-on, as shown in Figure 9-22.

on the
job

*Firebug is currently the most popular CSS/HTML/JavaScript debugger.
NetBeans has recognized this and has not tried to replicate its features in
current versions of the IDE. Actually, the NetBeans JavaScript Debugger may
be a thing of the past because its plugin is not included in the initial release
of NetBeans 6.9.*

Install Active
Scripting
Debugger
Framework
dialog box

TABLE 9-3	NetBeans JavaScript Debugger Requirements	
Resource	**Firefox**	**Internet Explorer**
Browser versions	v2.0.0.x and v3	v6 and v7
Browser debugging tool	Firebug v1.2	Active Scripting Debugger Framework v1.0a
Extension support	NetBeans Firefox Extension v0.6	NetBeans IE Extension v0.6

Table 9-3 shows the latest known requirements for using the NetBeans JavaScript Debugger.

You can verify the installation of the add-ons in the Add-ons window of your browser, as shown for Firefox in Figure 9-23. For Firefox, select Tools | Add-ons. For Internet Explorer, select Tools | Manage Add-ons | Enable or Disable Add-ons.

FIGURE 9-23

Firefox Add-ons

EXERCISE 9-2

Debugging Various Files in a Web Application

This exercise has you setting breakpoints in various types of web application files and stepping through those breakpoints.

1. Download the NetBeans 6.5 MyAjaxApp sample application from http://netbeans.org/kb/samples/, and open it in the NetBeans IDE.

2. Ensure server-side and client-side debugging is enabled. You can do this by verifying the checkboxes are selected in the Debug node of the Project Properties window. Select the Debug Web Application (Server Side Java) checkboxes. Select the Debug Web Application (Client Side JavaScript) checkboxes, along with the Firefox radio button.

3. Set breakpoints in the `AutoCompleteServlet.java` Servlet file.

4. Set breakpoints in the `composer.jsp` JavaServer Pages file.

5. Set breakpoints in the `javascript.js` JavaScript file.

6. Start the debugger.

7. In the Sessions window, ensure that the MyAjaxApp and NETBEANS-FIREFOX-DBUGGER-0 sessions are listed.

8. Continue the debugger repeatedly so you stop on each breakpoint.

CERTIFICATION SUMMARY

This chapter contained information related to the Java debugger. The chapter was broken into two primary sections based on the local and remote debugging objectives. The first section detailed session establishment, breakpoint settings, code stepping, and debugging support windows. The information was laid out in a sequential pattern to complement your learning. Since all of the features are used in an integrated way, it behooves you to use the debugger as often as possible leading up to the test to gain the necessary experience. The second section detailed remote debugging. Coverage included steps to attach the remote debugger and setting up the NetBeans JavaScript Debugger tool. If you take the time to actually use the debugger and perform the exercises in the chapter, you will score well on debugger-related questions on the exam.

✓ TWO-MINUTE DRILL

Debugging Local Applications

❑ There are several ways to start a debugging session: Debug | Debug Main Project (CTRL-F5), Debug | Step Into (F7), Debug | Run To Cursor (F4), and by right-clicking the project and choosing Debug.

❑ Individual runnable files including unit tests can be debugged: Select the file, Debug | Debug [filename].

❑ A debugging session can be stopped by choosing Debug | Finish Debugging Session (SHIFT-F5).

❑ Six types of breakpoints can be set: class, exception, method, field, thread, and line.

❑ The shortcut to the New Breakpoint dialog box is CTRL-SHIFT-F8.

❑ Breakpoints can be controlled based on Boolean conditions.

❑ NetBeans provides eight primary session-related commands: Step Over, Step Over Expression, Step Into, Step Into Next Method, Step Out, Run To Cursor, Continue, and Pause.

❑ The Step Over command (F8) allows the debugger to step through lines of code while executing entire routines.

❑ The Step Over Expression command (SHIFT-F8) allows the debugger to step through an expression and view the value of each method call in the expression in the Variables window.

❑ The Step Into command (F7) allows the debugger to step into lines of code individually.

❑ The Step Into Next Method command (SHIFT-F7) allows the debugger to execute singular source lines and to stop before execution of the first statements of methods.

❑ The Step Out command (CTRL-F7) allows the debugger to execute singular source lines and exit out of methods after executing the remaining lines.

❑ The Run To Cursor command executes the debugger up to the insertion point made by the cursor.

❑ The Continue (F5) command resumes the execution of the debugger.

❑ The Pause command suspends the execution of the debugger.

❑ There are nine primary debugging windows: Variables, Watches, Call Stack, Loaded Classes, Breakpoints, Sessions, Threads, Sources, and Debugging.

❑ The Variables window (ALT-SHIFT-1) lists the variables in the current call.

❑ The Watches window (ALT-SHIFT-2) lists specified variables and expressions to watch while in a debugging session.

❑ The Call Stack window (ALT-SHIFT-3) lists the sequence of calls made during the execution of the current thread while highlighting the current call.

❑ The Loaded Classes window (ALT-SHIFT-4) lists the loaded classes for the current debugging session. Right-clicking a class and choosing Show In Instances View opens the Instances window with related information.

❑ The Breakpoints window (ALT-SHIFT-5) lists all of the project breakpoints.

❑ The Sessions window (ALT-SHIFT-6) lists all running debugging sessions.

❑ The Threads window (ALT-SHIFT-7) lists all of the threads in the current debugging session.

❑ The Sources window (ALT-SHIFT-8) lists source code files that may be available to the debugger.

❑ The Debugging window (ALT-SHIFT-9) displays a list of threads in the current debugging session and allows for the suspension and resumption of those threads.

❑ The Debug toolbar is present when sessions are established. The toolbar has icons for Finish Debugger Session, Pause, Continue, Step Over, Step Over Expression, Step Into, Step Out, Run To Cursor, and Apply Code Changes.

Debugging Remote Applications

❑ Remote debugging is the process of debugging applications on remote computers.

❑ Debug | Attach Debugger allows for the attachment of the Java Debugger (JPDA), Web Page Debugger (JavaScript), and various other debuggers.

❑ The JVM TI replaces the JVMPI and JVMDI interfaces.

❑ The -Xdebug switch is used when starting up remote applications such as Tomcat in the debug mode.

❑ The NetBeans JavaScript Debugger depends on Firebug and the NetBeans Firefox Extension when using the Firefox web browser for debugging.

❑ The NetBeans JavaScript Debugger depends on Active Scripting Framework and the NetBeans IE Extension when using the Internet Explorer web browser for debugging.

❑ The NetBeans IDE detects if the web browser that is to be used does not have the necessary add-ons to support debugging and thereafter begins the install process for the necessary add-ons.

SELF TEST

The following questions will help you measure your understanding of the material presented in this chapter. Read all the choices carefully because there might be more than one correct answer. Choose all correct answers for each question.

Debugging Local Applications

1. How is the menu command reached that allows debugger windows to be opened by selecting a window name?

A. Debugging Window | [window_name]

B. Debugger Windows | [window_name]

C. Window | Debugger Windows | [window_name]

D. Window | Debugging | [window_name]

2. How can you add a line breakpoint? Select all that apply.

A. Click in the left margin of the source editor.

B. Press CTRL-F8.

C. Select Debug | Toggle Line Breakpoint from the main menu.

D. All of the above.

3. What types of breakpoints can be added in addition to line breakpoints? Select all that apply.

A. Class breakpoints

B. Exception breakpoints

C. Method breakpoints

D. Field breakpoints

E. Module breakpoints

F. Thread breakpoints

4. True or false. In the Breakpoints window, you can organize breakpoints by groups.

A. True

B. False

5. What is a conditional breakpoint?

A. A breakpoint that is hit only when a Boolean expression evaluates to true.

B. A breakpoint that is hit only when a Boolean expression evaluates to false.

C. A breakpoint that is hit only if the line number and filename are defined in a `conditional.xml` file.

D. A breakpoint that has a dependency to another breakpoint occurring.

6. How do you finish (gracefully stop) a debug session? Select all that apply.

 A. Press SHIFT-F4.

 B. Select Debug | Finish Debugger Session from the main menu.

 C. Click the Finish Debugger Session icon from the Debug toolbar.

 D. Right-click the project within the Projects window and select Finish Debugger Session.

7. Which step command causes the execution of the program to resume until the next breakpoint is reached?

 A. Step Over

 B. Step Into

 C. Resume

 D. Continue

8. The Loaded Classes debugging window has a table with three columns. What are the header names of these columns?

 A. Name, Type, Value

 B. Name, State, Language

 C. Class Name, Loaded, Instances

 D. Class Name, Instances [%], Instances

Debugging Remote Applications

9. Complete the following table to match connector types to functions. Connector types are SocketAttach, SharedMemoryAttach, ProcessAttach, SocketListen, and SharedMemoryListen.

Connector Type	Description
	Accepts shared memory connections initiated by other VMs
	Accepts socket connections initiated by other VMs
	Attaches by shared memory to other VMs
	Attaches by socket to other VMs
	Attaches to debuggee by process-id (pid)

10. Various flags relate to debugging functionality when invoking the Java interpreter. Select all that apply.

A. `-Xdebug`

B. `-Xnoagent`

C. `-Xrunjdwp`

D. `-Xprepare`

11. The JavaScript debugger is capable of installing debugging support add-ons into which browsers? Select all that apply.

A. Firefox

B. SeaMonkey

C. Chrome

D. Internet Explorer

SELF TEST ANSWERS

Debugging Local Applications

1. How is the menu command reached that allows debugger windows to be opened by selecting a window name?

    A. Debugging Window | [window_name]

    B. Debugger Windows | [window_name]

    C. Window | Debugger Windows | [window_name]

    D. Window | Debugging | [window_name]

    ☑ **D.** The menu command that allows debugger windows to be opened by selecting a window name is reached by choosing Window | Debugging | [window_name].

    ☒ **A, B,** and **C** are incorrect. **A** is incorrect because Debugging Window is not a menu bar item. **B** is incorrect because Debugger Windows is not a menu bar item. **C** is incorrect because Debugger Windows is not a menu item under the Window menu bar item.

2. How can you add a line breakpoint? Select all that apply.

    A. Click in the left margin of the source editor.

    B. Press CTRL-F8.

    C. Select Debug | Toggle Line Breakpoint from the main menu.

    D. All of the above.

    ☑ **D.** All of the above is correct because a line breakpoint can be set by clicking the left margin of the source editor relative to the line you want to have a breakpoint set at, pressing CTRL-F8, or selecting Debug | Toggle Line Breakpoint from the main menu.

    ☒ **A, B,** and **C** are incorrect if selected individually, because all the answers are correct.

3. What types of breakpoints can be added in addition to line breakpoints? Select all that apply.

    A. Class breakpoints

    B. Exception breakpoints

    C. Method breakpoints

    D. Field breakpoints

    E. Module breakpoints

    F. Thread breakpoints

    ☑ **A, B, C, D,** and **F.** In addition to line breakpoints, class, exception, method, field, and thread breakpoints may be added.

    ☒ **E** is incorrect. There is no such thing as module breakpoints.

4. True or false. In the Breakpoints window, you can organize breakpoints by groups.

   A. True

   B. False

   ☑ **A. True.** In the Breakpoints window, you can organize breakpoints by groups. Right-click the breakpoint in the Breakpoints window, and select Move Into Group, followed by selection of an existing group or invocation of the New Group dialog box.

5. What is a conditional breakpoint?

   A. A breakpoint that is hit only when a Boolean expression evaluates to true.

   B. A breakpoint that is hit only when a Boolean expression evaluates to false.

   C. A breakpoint that is hit only if the line number and filename are defined in a `conditional.xml` file.

   D. A breakpoint that has a dependency to another breakpoint occurring.

   ☑ **A.** A conditional breakpoint is a breakpoint that is hit only when a Boolean expression evaluates to true.

   ☒ **B, C, and D** are incorrect. **B** is incorrect because conditional breakpoints are hit only when the Boolean expression evaluates to true. **C** is incorrect because there is no such `conditional .xml` file; it was fabricated in an attempt to throw you off. **D** is incorrect because a conditional breakpoint is not a breakpoint dependent on another breakpoint occurring.

6. How do you finish (gracefully stop) a debug session? Select all that apply.

   A. Press SHIFT-F4.

   B. Select Debug | Finish Debugger Session from the main menu.

   C. Click the Finish Debugger Session icon on the Debug toolbar.

   D. Right-click the project within the Projects window and select Finish Debugger Session.

   ☑ **B and C.** A debug session can be stopped in a variety of ways including the selection of Debug | Finish Debugger Session from the main menu or by clicking the Finish Debugger Session icon on the Debug toolbar.

   ☒ **A and D** are incorrect. **A** is incorrect because SHIFT-F4 runs the debugger to the cursor. Pressing SHIFT-F5 stops the session. **D** is incorrect because there is no menu option from the Projects node to end the debugger session.

7. Which step command causes the execution of the program to resume until the next breakpoint is reached?

A. Step Over

B. Step Into

C. Resume

D. Continue

☑ **D.** The Continue step command causes the execution of the program to resume until the next breakpoint is reached.

☒ **A, B,** and **C** are incorrect. **A** is incorrect because Step Over only executes the current line. **B** is incorrect because Step Into only executes the current line. **C** is incorrect because there is no Resume step command.

8. The Loaded Classes debugging window has a table with three columns. What are the header names of these columns?

A. Name, Type, Value

B. Name, State, Language

C. Class Name, Loaded, Instances

D. Class Name, Instances [%], Instances

☑ **D.** The column names of the table in the Loaded Classes window are Class Name, Instances [%], and Instances.

☒ **A, B,** and **C** are incorrect. **A** is incorrect because Name, Type, and Value are not table header names in the Loaded Classes window. They are header names in the Variables and Watches windows. **B** is incorrect because Name, State, and Language are not table header names in the Loaded Classes window. They are header names in the Sessions window. **C** is incorrect because Loaded is not a table header name in the Loaded Classes window.

Debugging Remote Applications

9. Complete the following table to match connector types to functions. Connector types are `SocketAttach`, `SharedMemoryAttach`, `ProcessAttach`, `SocketListen`, and `SharedMemoryListen`.

Connector Type	Description
	Accepts shared memory connections initiated by other VMs
	Accepts socket connections initiated by other VMs
	Attaches by shared memory to other VMs
	Attaches by socket to other VMs
	Attaches to debuggee by process-id (pid)

☑ The following table matches the connector types to functions:

Connector Type	Description
SharedMemoryListen	Accepts shared memory connections initiated by other VMs
SocketListen	Accepts socket connections initiated by other VMs
SharedMemoryAttach	Attaches by shared memory to other VMs
SocketAttach	Attaches by socket to other VMs
ProcessAttach	Attaches to debuggee by process-id (pid)

10. Various flags relate to debugging functionality when invoking the Java interpreter. Select all that apply.

A. -Xdebug

B. -Xnoagent

C. -Xrunjdwp

D. -Xprepare

☑ **A**, **B**, and **C**. The -Xdebug, -Xnoagent, and -Xrunjdwp flags relate to debugging functionality when invoking the Java interpreter.

☒ **D** is incorrect because there is no -Xprepare flag.

11. The JavaScript debugger is capable of installing debugging support add-ons into which browsers? Select all that apply.

A. Firefox

B. SeaMonkey

C. Chrome

D. Internet Explorer

☑ **A** and **D**. The JavaScript debugger is capable of installing debugging support add-ons into Firefox and Internet Explorer.

☒ **B** and **C** are incorrect. **B** is incorrect because the JavaScript debugger is not currently capable of installing debugging support add-ons into the SeaMonkey web browser. **C** is incorrect because the JavaScript debugger is not currently capable of installing debugging support add-ons into the Chrome web browser.

10

Testing and Profiling

CERTIFICATION OBJECTIVES

-    Testing Applications with JUnit
-    Using the NetBeans Profiler

✓   Two-Minute Drill

Q&A   Self Test

Τhis chapter delves into two important topics that that are too often overlooked: unit testing and profiling. Unit tests are used to verify the basic functionality of an application. Profiling is an operation like debugging, except instead of looking at current stack values and tracing execution flow, the profiler monitors performance and provides tools for identifying and measuring CPU and memory use.

To facilitate unit testing, NetBeans supports JUnit and includes wizards for creating new unit tests and test suites. It also provides an integrated user interface for running and debugging the tests. Starting in NetBeans 6.0 NetBeans integrated a profiler into the IDE. The profiler was based on the JFluid research project from SunLabs. With this advanced profiler, profiling can be turned on and off dynamically while an application is running. Thus, large applications where profiling wasn't feasible can now be analyzed. The type of profiling, either CPU or memory, can be changed without restarting the target application. The NetBeans Profiler supports profiling both local and remote Java applications. A NetBeans project is not required in order to profile an application. The profiler can capture data in snapshots for later analysis. For heap snapshots, NetBeans includes HeapWalker and supports searching the heap using the Object Query Language (OQL).

The NetBeans certification exam covers both JUnit testing and profiling desktop applications. Mastering these tools helps you build repeatable processes and takes the mystery out of application performance problems.

CERTIFICATION OBJECTIVE

Testing Applications with JUnit

Exam Objective 6.1   Demonstrate the ability to work with JUnit tests in the IDE, such as creating JUnit tests and interpreting JUnit test output.

Unit testing is the verification of individual code segments that an application comprises. A code segment can be a method, interface, class, or some piece of functionality. The granularity of the tests is up to the developer. The objective is to split an application into pieces and verify the correctness of the pieces. Once unit tests have been written, they can be periodically or regularly rerun to verify bug fixes and to validate core functionality as code evolves. Unit tests thus become the foundation of a regression test suite.

JUnit is the ubiquitous unit test framework for the Java platform and has been a testing mainstay for the past decade. Although JUnit test cases are written using standard Java classes, NetBeans includes custom user interfaces to expedite development and execution as well as to monitor the tests. NetBeans also isolates the source and classpath for unit tests so that test code doesn't pollute the application. Leveraging the support within NetBeans, unit tests can be easily written and frequently run. NetBeans also supports the continuous integration server Hudson (http://hudson-ci.org). Hudson jobs can be kicked off within NetBeans and thus run the entire unit test suite.

The following topics are covered in this section:

- Understanding JUnit Basics and Versions
- Creating JUnit Tests and Suites
- Managing Testing Classpath
- Running JUnit Tests
- Configuring Continuous Integration Support

Understanding JUnit Basics and Versions

The premise of JUnit is fairly simple: write small nuggets of code to test basic units of functionality. The objective is to test the pieces of the application and verify that they work independently. While the application may not work as a whole, at least there is confidence and verification that the basic application building blocks work correctly. Ideally the unit test cases should be written prior to the actual implementation. Verifying that the building blocks work together is the province of integration testing

A unit test in JUnit is a regular Java class with several methods that perform the testing. Methods that prepare the test environment and post process can be optionally implemented. JUnit provides assert methods, different from the Java language asserts, to test conditions and terminate the test upon failure. Listing 10-1 shows a simple unit test from the MusicCoach application. This unit test has two test methods that are marked with the `@Test` annotation. It has two class-level setup and teardown methods and two instance-level setup and teardown methods: `setUpClass`, `tearDownClass`, `setUp`, and `tearDown`, respectively.

LISTING 10-1 TromboneSlurTest.java

```java
public class TromboneSlurTest {
  protected Trombone trombone;
  public static Note A;
  public static Note E;
  public static Note D;
  @BeforeClass
  public static void setUpClass() throws Exception {
    InstrumentFactory.configureInstruments();
    A = new Note(PitchClass.A,1);
    E = new Note(PitchClass.E,1);
    D = new Note(PitchClass.D,1);
  }
  @AfterClass
   public static void tearDownClass() throws Exception {
    A = null;
    E = null;
    D = null;
  }
  @Before
  public void setUp() {
    trombone = new TenorTrombone(false);
  }
  @After
  public void tearDown() {
    trombone = null;
  }
  @Test
  public void testAToE() {
      assertTrue(trombone.isNaturalSlur(new Note[] {A,E}));
  }
  @Test
  public void testAToD() {
      assertFalse(trombone.isNaturalSlur(new Note[] {A,D}));
  }
}
```

Unit tests can then be grouped into test suites that can be run as entire units. Test suites can include other test suites to form a hierarchical structure. Listing 10-2 shows a simple test suite for trombones in the MusicCoach application. It ties the TromboneTest and TromboneSlurTest into one suite.

LISTING 10-2 Test Suite

```java
@RunWith(Suite.class)
@Suite.SuiteClasses({net.cuprak.music.instruments.
  TromboneSlurTest.class,
```

```
        net.cuprak.music.instruments.TromboneTest.class})
    public class TromboneTestSuite {
        @BeforeClass
        public static void setUpClass() throws Exception {
            // Do nothing
        }
        @AfterClass
        public static void tearDownClass() throws Exception {
            // Do nothing

        }
    }
```

Listings 10-1 and 10-2 target JUnit version 4. NetBeans supports two versions of JUnit: JUnit 3.*x* and 4.*x*. In NetBeans 6.8, JUnit 3.8.4 and 4.5 are preconfigured by default. JUnit 4 employs annotations to mark tests and eliminate the need for subclassing and naming conventions. Consequently JUnit 4 requires Java 5. Since there are many legacy applications, JUnit 3 is still supported. An application can make use of both JUnit 3 and JUnit 4 test classes, but a test class cannot mix versions, because tests and setup code will not execute as expected. JUnit 3 test cases must extend `TestCase`, and a test suite must extend `TestSuite`. JUnit 3 also lacks support for `setUpClass` and `tearDownClass`. In-depth discussion of the differences between JUnit 3 and 4 is outside the scope of this book. More information on the subject and links can be found at www.junit.org. JUnit 4 code samples in Listings 10-1 and 10-2 were back-ported to JUnit 3 in Listing 10-3.

LISTING 10-3   JUnit 3 Example

```
    public class TromboneSlurTest3 extends TestCase {
      private Trombone trombone;
      private Note A;
      private static Note E;
      private Note D;
      public void setUp() {
        trombone = new TenorTrombone(false);
        InstrumentFactory.configureInstruments();
        A = new Note(PitchClass.A,1);
        E = new Note(PitchClass.E,1);
        D = new Note(PitchClass.D,1);
      }
      public void tearDown() {
        trombone = null;
        A = null;
        E = null;
        D = null;
      }
```

```
      public void testAToE() {
        assertTrue(trombone.isNaturalSlur(new Note[] {A,E}));
      }
      public void testAToD() {
        assertFalse(trombone.isNaturalSlur(new Note[] {A,D}));
      }
    }

    public class TromboneTestSuite3 {
      public static Test suite() {
        TestSuite suite = new TestSuite();
        suite.addTestSuite(TromboneSlurTest3.class);
        suite.addTestSuite(TromboneTest3.class);
        return suite;
      }
    }
```

Table 10-1 lists the Java annotations available in JUnit 4.5. Many of these annotations were used in the code listings.

TABLE 10-1   Java 4.5 Annotations

Annotation	Target	Description
@After	Static Method	Runs a cleanup instance method after a test has executed
@AfterClass	Static Method	Runs a cleanup method, which must be static, after all tests have completed.
@Before	Method	Runs a setup method prior to running a test
@BeforeClass	Method	Runs a setup method, which must be static, prior to running tests in a class
@Ignore	Class, Method	Causes a test runner to ignore the test
@Parameters	Static Method	Parameters to be injected into the test class' constructor
@RunWith	Class	Configures to run the tests in the class specified with the annotation
@Suite	Class	Configures the list of classes that are a part of the suite
@Test	Method	Marks a public void method as a test, thereby causing it to run

e**x**a**m**
ⓦatch
Know the difference between JUnit 3.x and 4.x. Also, NetBeans asks only once which version of JUnit should be used for a project. To update to a newer version, the new library must be added in Test Libraries of

Project Properties. It also can be edited by right-clicking Test Libraries in the Projects window. This is a major feature of NetBeans' JUnit support and will be touched upon in the exam.

Creating JUnit Tests and Suites

A new JUnit test or test suite is created by choosing File | New File (CTRL-N) and selecting a project template from the JUnit category. The available choices are shown in Figure 10-1. This dialog box can also be opened by right-clicking and choosing New | Other. The New File dialog box presents the following three options:

- **JUnit Test**   Creates an empty JUnit test.
- **Test For Existing Class**   Creates a simple JUnit test case for testing methods of a single class.
- **Test Suite**   Creates a test suite for all tests in a selected Java test package.

FIGURE 10-1

JUnit file templates

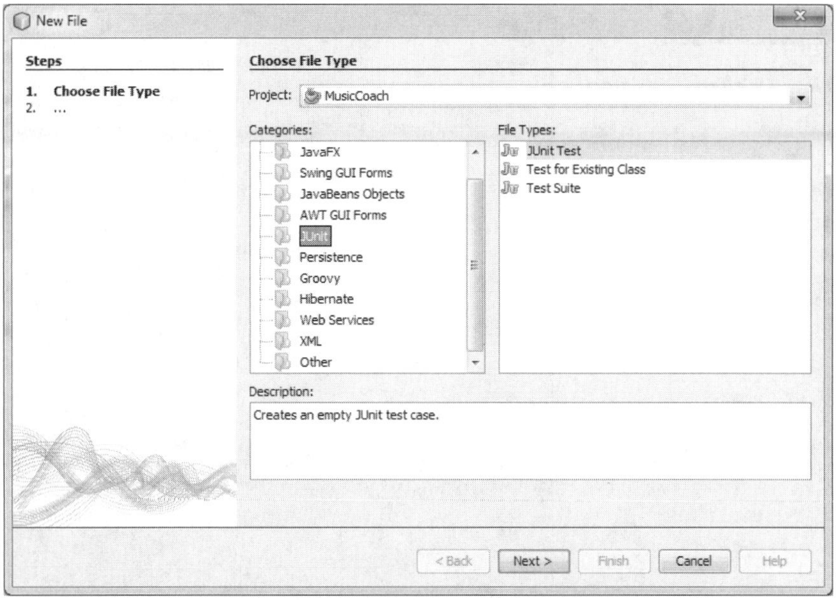

Creating an Empty JUnit Test

Choosing the first option shown in Figure 10-1 and clicking Next displays the panel shown in Figure 10-2. This panel prompts for the basic information necessary to create an empty unit test:

- **Class Name**   The name of the test class to create.
- **Project**   Non-editable field displaying the project to which the new JUnit class is added.
- **Location**   Drop-down list of test source code packages that can be selected.
- **Package**   The package of the new JUnit class. It can be edited or selected.
- **Created File**   Non-editable field displaying the full path to the generated file.
- **Generated Code**   Generates the following types of setup methods:
  - **Test Initializer**   Creates a skeleton public void `setUp()` method.
  - **Test Finalizer**   Creates a skeleton public void `tearDown()` method.
- **Generated Comments**   Only option available is Source Code Hints, which are comments directing you to the code to implement.

Once these options are populated, NetBeans creates a new JUnit skeleton. A project can possess one or more test classpaths, hence the drop-down list for Location.

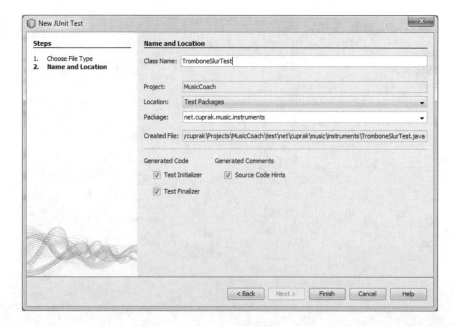

Select JUnit
Version

The first time a JUnit test class is created for a project, NetBeans prompts for the JUnit version to be used. The dialog box that appears is shown in Figure 10-3. NetBeans only asks this question the first time a JUnit test class is created. If JUnit 3 has been chosen, the project can be switched to JUnit 4 by adding the JUnit 4.*x* library to the project in Project Properties.

Creating a JUnit for Existing Class

Choosing the Test For Existing Class option (in the New File dialog box under File Types) displays the panel in Figure 10-4. This New Test For Existing Class dialog box can also be displayed by selecting a class in the Projects window and pressing CTRL-SHIFT-U or right-clicking and choosing Tools | Create JUnit Tests. This panel is used to create JUnit test classes for existing classes and interfaces. NetBeans introspects

New Test For
Existing Class

the class and generates skeleton methods. It is your job to implement each one of these methods. By default, each skeleton test method fails until implemented. This ensures that you do not forget to write a test.

The configuration parameters in this panel include:

- **Class To Test**   The class to be tested.
- **Created Test Class**   The name of the test class to create.
- **Project**   Non-editable field displaying the project to which the new JUnit class is added.
- **Location**   Drop-down list of test source code packages that can be selected.
- **Created File**   Non-editable field displaying the full path to the generated file.
- **Method Access Levels**   Selecting a level causes NetBeans to generate skeleton code for all of the methods matching the access level. Access levels are Public, Protected, and Package Private.
- **Generated Code**   Generates the following types of setup methods:
  - **Test Initializer**   Creates a skeleton public void `setUp()` method.
  - **Test Finalizer**   Creates a skeleton public void `tearDown()` method.
  - **Default Method Bodies**   For skeleton test methods, inserts the following code: `fail("The test case is a prototype.");`
- **Generated Comments**   Selecting either of the following options generates the respective comments:
  - **Javadoc Comments**   Adds Javadoc to the test method. Note that Javadoc is not automatically generated for the setup/teardown methods.
  - **Source Code Hints**   Adds a `TODO` comment in the skeleton test methods.

For JUnit 4, NetBeans automatically generates the following two methods:

```
@BeforeClass
public static void setUpClass()
```

and

```
@AfterClass
public static void tearDownClass()
```

These two methods are respectively executed before any of the tests have been run and after all of the tests have been run. These two methods are created regardless of the settings in Figure 10-4.

Listing 10-4 is a sample JUnit test for an existing class. Accepting the defaults in Figure 10-4 created this class. JUnit 4.*x* was selected as the JUnit version. Test methods are annotated with @Test. NetBeans has attempted to create a reasonable skeleton structure for each test method. Each test method corresponds to a method in the target class. Note the fail (...) invocations in each method that will automatically fail the test.

LISTING 10-4   JUnit Test for Existing Class

```java
//Creating a JUnit for existing code:
public class TromboneTest {
  public TromboneTest() {}
  @BeforeClass
  public static void setUpClass() throws Exception {}
  @AfterClass
  public static void tearDownClass() throws Exception {}
  @Before
  public void setUp() {}
  @After
  public void tearDown() {}
  /**
   * Test of isNaturalSlur method, of class Trombone.
   */
  @Test
  public void testIsNaturalSlur() {
    System.out.println("isNaturalSlur");
    Note[] notes = null;
    Trombone instance = null;
    boolean expResult = false;
    boolean result = instance.isNaturalSlur(notes);
    assertEquals(expResult, result);
    // TODO review the generated test code and
    // remove the default call to fail.
    fail("The test case is a prototype.");
  }
  /**
   * Test of getPositions method, of class Trombone.
   */
  @Test
  public void testGetPositions_Note() {
    System.out.println("getPositions");
    Note note = null;
    Trombone instance = null;
    int[] expResult = null;
    int[] result = instance.getPositions(note);
```

```
      assertEquals(expResult, result);
      // TODO review the generated test code and
      // remove the default call to fail.
      fail("The test case is a prototype.");
    }

    /**
     * Test of getPositions method, of class Trombone.
     */
    @Test
    public void testGetPositions_NoteArr_boolean() {
      System.out.println("getPositions");
      Note[] note = null;
      boolean slur = false;
      Trombone instance = null;
      int[] expResult = null;
      int[] result = instance.getPositions(note, slur);
      assertEquals(expResult, result);
      // TODO review the generated test code and
      // remove the default call to fail.
      fail("The test case is a prototype.");
    }
    /**
      * Test of hasFAttachment method, of class Trombone.
      */
    @Test
    public void testHasFAttachment() {
      System.out.println("hasFAttachment");
      Trombone instance = null;
      boolean expResult = false;
      boolean result = instance.hasFAttachment();
      assertEquals(expResult, result);
      // TODO review the generated test code
      // and remove the default call to fail.
      fail("The test case is a prototype.");
    }
    public class TromboneImpl extends Trombone {
      public TromboneImpl() {
        super(false);
      }
    }
  }
```

Creating a Test Suite

JUnit test suites are used to run a group of tests together. Test suites can include
other test suites. Choosing Test Suite in Figure 10-1 displays the New Test Suite
panel in Figure 10-5. This panel prompts for the basic information necessary to

create the test suite. Listing 10-2 is an example test suite created by NetBeans. By default, NetBeans scans a package looking for unit test cases to be added to the suite. The panel prompts for the following settings before generating the code:

- **Class Name**   Name of the test suite.
- **Project**   Non-editable field displaying the project to which the new JUnit class is added.
- **Location**   Drop-down list of test source code packages that can be selected.
- **Package**   The package where the test suite is stored and also contains the JUnit test classes to be added to the suite.
- **Created File**   Non-editable field displaying the full path to the generated file.
- **Generated Code**   Generates the following types of setup methods:
    - **Test Initializer**   Creates a skeleton public void `setUp()` method.
    - **Test Finalizer**   Creates a skeleton public void `tearDown()` method.
- **Generated Comments**   Generates comments; in the case of a `TestSuite`, only the Source Code Hints option is available. Source code hints add a `TODO` comment in the skeleton methods.

NetBeans can also generate a test suite and unit tests for all the classes in a source package. Right-clicking a package under Source Packages in the Projects window and choosing Create JUnit Tests creates a test suite and JUnits for each class. This is a quick way to generate test skeletons for all of the classes in a package.

FIGURE 10-5

New Test Suite

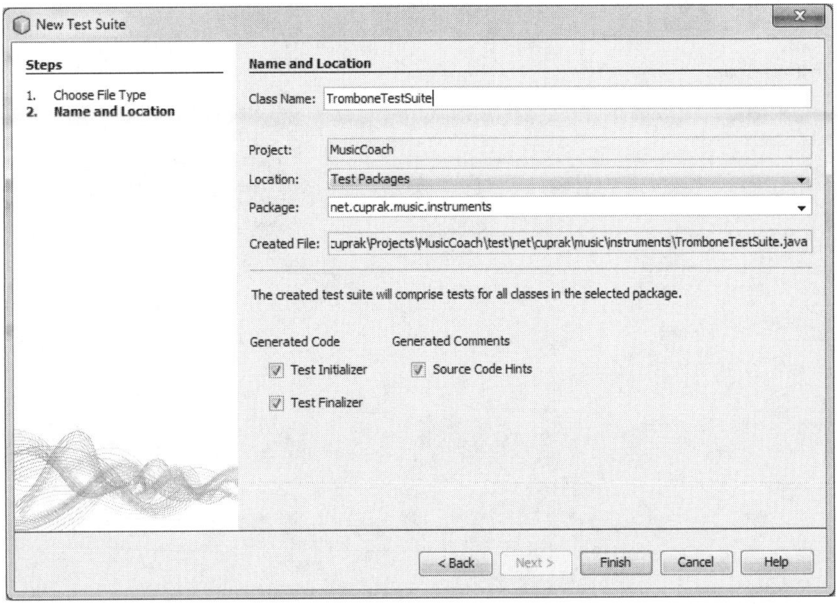

Managing Testing Classpaths

The test classpath for a project is configured in Project Properties for standard projects. A standard project is one that uses the NetBeans-provided build script. Project Properties can be accessed by either right-clicking the project in the Projects window or by choosing File | Project Properties. The dialog box is shown in Figure 10-6. Within Project Properties choose the Libraries category. The Compile Tests and Run Tests tabs configure the classpath for the unit tests. Projects, libraries, and other projects can be added as dependencies. These classpaths extend the compile classpath.

NetBeans maintains two separate classpaths so that references to JUnit or other classes used to support unit testing don't creep into the main source code tree. This enforces a firewall between the application's implementation and its test code. For example, it would be dangerous if mock objects, objects that simulate the behavior of objects in a controlled manner for testing, were inadvertently used in the production deployment.

Running JUnit Tests

JUnit tests and test suites are executed or debugged either in NetBeans or on the command line using the project's Ant script. When testing is initiated, the Tests window opens; this window can be explicitly opened by choosing Window | Output | Test Results. Individual test methods can only be run from this window after all of the test methods have been executed.

FIGURE 10-6

Test classpath

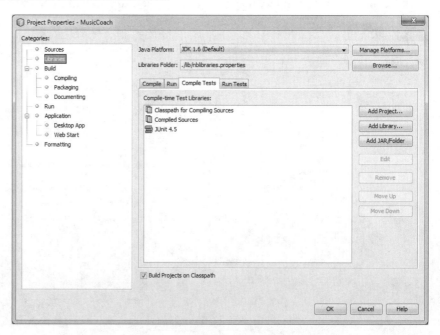

TABLE 10-2	Invocation	Result
	Run | Test File	Runs the unit tests in the current JUnit editor window that is open
Unit Execution Options	SHIFT-F6	
	Run | Test Project	Runs all of the JUnit tests for the project
	CTRL-F6	
	Debug | Debug Test File	Debugs the current test file that is open
	CTRL-SHIFT-F6	

Table 10-2 lists the various methods for running either a single unit test or all of the tests in a project. In addition, right-clicking a JUnit test in the Projects window displays a context menu with Test File and Debug Test File.

When a project is either executed or debugged in NetBeans, the Test Results window shown in Figure 10-7 opens. The window is divided into two panels, with the left side listing the JUnit tests executed and the right side displaying the standard out/error from the tests. A status bar indicates the percentage of tests that have either succeeded or failed. The number of tests that have succeeded and failed

FIGURE 10-7   JUnit test execution

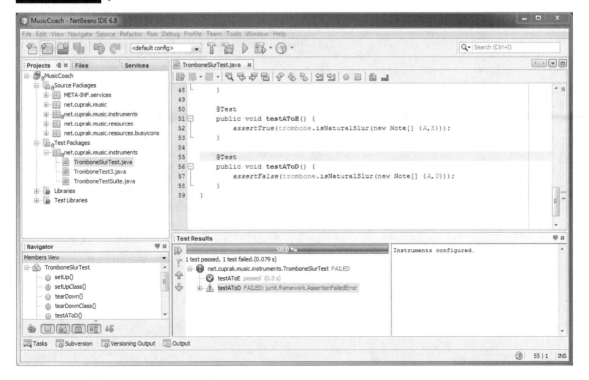

is listed below the status bar. A green "passed" represents a success, whereas a red "FAILED" represents a failure. Double-clicking a test method in the left panel jumps to the code for the test. An individual test can be rerun by right-clicking a test and selecting Run Again. Table 10-3 lists the icons along the left of the window as well as the glyphs on the unit tests denoting their status.

JUnit tests can also be run from the command line. Whether running unit tests in the IDE or on the command line, the Ant script for the project is used. The unit tests can be executed in the project directory by entering `ant test`. This assumes that Ant is already installed. Ant executes the test method in `build.xml`, which is inherited from `nbproject/build-impl.xml`. Executing the test target causes the project to be built. If any unit tests fail, the build script fails execution.

NetBeans automatically outputs XML reports for the unit tests that it runs. These XML files are placed in the directory `build/test/results`. To reformat and generate a human-readable JUnit report, the test-report Ant target can be overridden in `build.xml`. The default implementation in `nbproject/build-`

TABLE 10-3	**Icon**	**Description**
Test Results Window Icons		Reruns the unit tests
		Filter that toggles between showing all results or just failures
		Jumps to the previous failure (CTRL-comma)
		Jumps to the next failure (CTRL-period)
		Icon placed on a JUnit class that has failures
		Icon placed on a JUnit test method that has failed
		Icon placed on a JUnit test method that has succeeded

`impl.xml` contains an empty stub method for this purpose. The following example code, which should be added to `build.xml`, generates an HTML report:

```
<target name="test-report">
  <junitreport todir="${build.test.results.dir}">
    <fileset dir="${build.test.results.dir}">
    <include name="TEST-*.xml"/>
    </fileset>
    <report todir="test-report"/>
  </junitreport>
</target>
```

on the **Job**

The Ant variables used in this snippet were defined in `nbproject/project` ***`.properties`. When you're extending the Ant build, this is a good file to*** ***examine for existing Ant variables.***

EXERCISE 10-1

Running Unit Tests

In this exercise, you are going to run the existing test suite for the Jmol application. In Chapter 3 you checked out Jmol and created a NetBeans project for it. Now you will run it and verify that all of its tests are running.

1. Open the Jmol project you created in Exercise 3-1.

2. Open Test Packages in the Projects window.

3. Open the `org.jmol` node to reveal the `AllTests.java` class.

4. Right-click `AllTests.java` and choose Test File. NetBeans now compiles the project and runs the test suite.

5. The Output window should open displaying the output of the build. If the Test Results window does not open automatically, choose Window | Output | Test Results.

6. Open the `org.jmol.AllTests` node to reveal all of the tests that were run along with their status. All tests should have passed.

7. Notice that the unit tests were written using JUnit 3.

EXERCISE 10-2

Creating a JUnit Test

In this exercise, you create a new JUnit test for an existing Jmol utility class.

1. Open the Jmol project you created in Exercise 3-1.

2. Choose File | New File and select Test For Existing Class from the templates available under the JUnit category. Click Next.

3. Select `org.jmol.util.ArrayUtil` for the Class To Test. You can enter this class directly, or click Browse and search for it.

4. Accept the other defaults and click Finish. The default generates a stub test method for each method in `ArrayUtil.java`.

5. NetBeans should now ask whether the project should use JUnit 3 or 4. Choose JUnit 3 because the other tests were written using JUnit 3, and we want to integrate this new test into the test suite.

6. Open the class `org.jmol.AllTests.java`, and add the following line to the end of the suite method:

   ```
   suite.addTestSuite(org.jmol.util.ArrayUtilTest.class);
   ```

7. Right-click `AllTests.java` in the Projects window and choose Test File. By default, the stub methods created by NetBeans will fail. This is intentional so that you don't forget to implement the methods. Tests should fail until they are implemented.

8. Double-click a failure in the Test Results window to view that stub method.

9. Remove the `assert` and `fail` statements so that the test succeeds.

10. Right-click the failed test in the Test Results window, and choose Run Again to verify that the test now succeeds.

Configuring Continuous Integration Support

NetBeans supports Hudson, which is a continuous integration server. A continuous integration server like Hudson retrieves a project from source control on a regular basis and builds the project as well as runs the unit tests. Good JUnit tests are only useful if you run them regularly. NetBeans facilitates regular JUnit testing by tightly integrating Hudson into the IDE. Projects can be easily added to Hudson, and NetBeans will alert the developer when either the build or JUnits fail. For a large project it often isn't feasible to run all of the JUnits on a developer's desktop machine prior to committing the code. This tight integration with Hudson makes regularly running JUnit tests easy.

Hudson regularly retrieves a project from source control, builds it, and then runs the unit tests. Typically Hudson is configured to watch the version control and kick off a build when code is committed, usually with a time delay. Hudson can also be configured to do regular builds throughout the day or at night. Hudson not only builds the project but also executes the unit tests. Building and testing frequently ensures that bugs are caught early.

Hudson is an open source project and can be downloaded from http://hudson-ci.org. It is a Java web application and is deployed by dropping the WAR file into a Java web application container such as Tomcat or GlassFish. No other configuration is needed to start the application. After it is deployed, permissions can be configured so that not everyone can add, build, or view the results of a build/test. If the Hudson WAR file is dropped into the `webapps` directory of Apache Tomcat, Hudson can be monitored and managed locally at http://localhost:8080/hudson.

on the
job

Continuous integration should involve not only building the code base and running the unit tests but also rebuilding the test environment. For example, database scripts should be run frequently, and the database schema regenerated to ensure that there is a repeatable process in place. Tools such as LiquiBase (www.liquibase.org) can be integrated into the build and test process.

Hudson servers are managed in the Services window under Hudson Builders. An example is shown in Figure 10-8 with a remote Hudson server, MacBook Hudson, configured.

Servers that are already running can be mounted in NetBeans by right-clicking and choosing Add Hudson Instance. This displays the dialog box in Figure 10-9.

FIGURE 10-8

Hudson servers

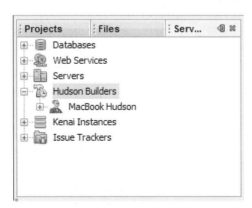

FIGURE 10-9

Add Hudson
Instance

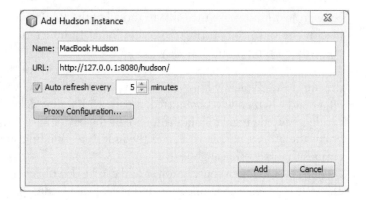

Right-clicking and selecting New Build adds new Hudson jobs. Only applications that are being managed by version control can be added. Once an application is added, the Hudson instance can be opened to display the list of applications, as shown in Figure 10-10. The artifacts from the build can be opened and inspected as well as the JUnit reports.

FIGURE 10-10

Application under
Hudson

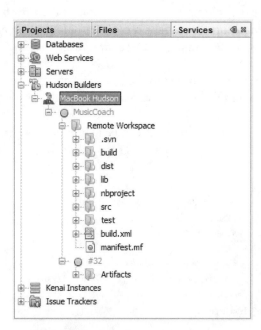

FIGURE 10-11

Hudson popup

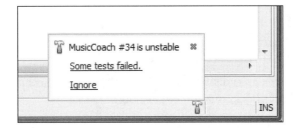

NetBeans checks Hudson at regular intervals for updates on jobs. NetBeans is watching for build failures due to either compilation errors or JUnits. A popup for the MusicCoach application is shown in Figure 10-11. Here we can see a warning that the unit tests have failed. Clicking the link for Some Tests Failed opens the Output window for the JUnit test execution. This is shown in Figure 10-12.

FIGURE 10-12   Hudson JUnit output

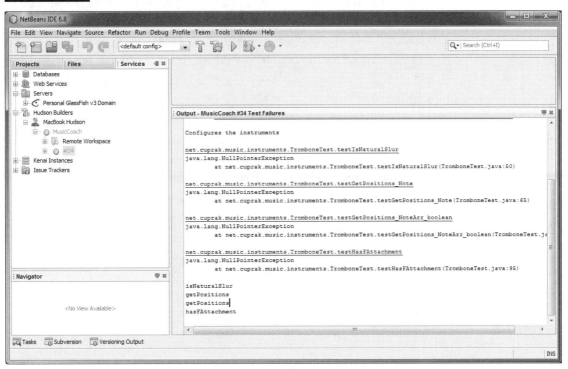

Unit Testing with Hudson

In this exercise, you deploy and configure Hudson. You then create a Hudson job that regularly checks out and builds Jmol.

1. Download the `hudson.war` file from http://hudson-ci.org/.
2. Switch to the Services window in NetBeans.
3. Open the Server node to reveal Personal GlassFish v3 Domain.
4. Right-click Personal GlassFish v3 Domain and choose Start. The GlassFish server starts.
5. Again right-click Personal GlassFish v3 Domain and choose View Admin Console. This opens the web browser to the admin page for GlassFish.
6. In the Admin Console, choose Applications from the Common Tasks tree.
7. In the panel on the right choose Deploy. The panel content swaps out. Click the Browse button for Package File To Be Uploaded To The Server. Browse to and select the `hudson.war` file downloaded previously.
8. Click OK to accept the defaults and deploy the application.
9. Hudson can now be accessed in the web browser at the URL http://localhost:8080/hudson/

   Note that the port may vary depending upon your settings.
10. Switch back to NetBeans and choose Add Hudson Instance. Paste in the URL from Step 9, and pick a descriptive name for your Hudson server. This name is used only inside of NetBeans.
11. To create a new build for the Jmol application, right-click your Hudson instance under Hudson Instances in the Services window.
12. Select the Jmol application and click Create. A Jmol instance is created under your Hudson instance. A web browser launches allowing you to track the progress of the build. It may take a while to build because Hudson checks the sources out of Subversion.
13. Examine the Hudson output looking for the JUnit status and checking for any failures.

Using the NetBeans Profiler

Exam Objective 6.4   Describe the purpose of profiling applications and how to profile a local desktop application in the IDE.

The purpose of profiling is to accurately measure the performance of an application and understand how CPU and memory resources are being consumed. Profiling is similar to debugging in terms of observing and exploring the behavior of an application while it is running and responding to real or simulated input. Debugging is focused on understanding the flow of execution in an application and answering questions such as why a variable changed, why a condition was true, what thread is waiting on the lock, and so on. However, debugging cannot tell you what percentage of a thread's execution time was spent waiting on a lock, how many objects were created, and how much space they are consuming, or whether the application is leaking memory. These types of questions are answered by using a profiler.

Profiling is an extremely important step in the development process. It is often overlooked in the rush to make deadlines, since performance problems, unless egregious, aren't showstoppers for release. Performance problems may not be discovered in QA because the testing is feature driven, and as a result the application isn't run long enough for performance degradation to materialize. Fatal errors such as Java's `java.lang.OutOfMemoryError` are often bandaged by increasing an application's heap without understanding the problem's genesis. Lacking hard profiling data, attribution of performance problems is mere conjecture. Sometimes unfounded blame is placed on Java's virtual machine or Java's garbage collection. Often the blame resides elsewhere. For example, in an image-intensive application the red green blue (RGB) byte-ordering of the images can have a significant performance impact that varies between platforms. Unoptimized SQL statements, completely outside of the control of the Java application, may skew performance.

NetBeans includes an integrated compiler that can be invoked as easily as the debugger. However, unlike a debugger, a profiler is more complicated and requires planning to achieve the best results. A profiler instruments code in order to measure it—byte code is inserted to collect performance statistics. This byte code, however, exacts its own performance penalty, thus changing what is being measured. Given the importance of profiling and the complexity of doing it correctly, the NetBeans certification exam includes a section on profiling. Only profiling of local desktop applications is covered; however, the skills are directly transferable to profiling remote processes and enterprise applications.

The NetBeans Profiler supports three different high-level profiling tasks:

- **Monitor**   This is basic tracking of VM telemetry data including basic memory utilization and thread statistics. This monitoring is available to the CPU and memory tasks.
- **CPU**   Measures and monitors the percentage of time spent in methods and code blocks.
- **Memory**   Measures and monitors object creation, destruction, allocation paths, and supports comparing memory snapshots.

When starting a profiling session, you choose which one of these three tasks you want to perform. The first one, monitoring, provides basic telemetry data. It has minimal impact upon an application and thus is suitable for daily tasks where you want to track some performance data and watch for potential memory and thread leaks. The other two tasks, CPU and memory, are more invasive and can collect copious amounts of data. Given the amount of data these two tasks can generate, a strategy is needed. A strategy entails focusing on discrete features or workflow operations in an application such as opening and closing a molecule in the Jmol application. Both these profiling tasks also capture snapshots. Snapshots capture the current application state for later review, analysis, and comparison. Note that memory and CPU profiling are mutually exclusive.

Since CPU and memory profiling are invasive and can generate copious amounts of data, NetBeans supports profiling points. These are conceptually similar to breakpoints used by the NetBeans Debugger. Profiling points enable you to control and limit the instrumentation. You can define *root methods* that demarcate the start and stop endpoints of a session so that an entire application isn't instrumented. Profiling points can also trigger snapshots, reset collected data, and start a stopwatch.

In addition to the three profiling tasks, NetBeans also supports capturing *heap snapshots*. A heap snapshot is a dump of Java's heap. The heap is where the JVM stores objects created by the Java application. With a heap snapshot, you can see what Java objects have been instantiated and have not yet been garbage collected. NetBeans includes a tool, HeapWalker, for evaluating and querying the heap snapshots. Along with several graphical views, the HeapWalker supports the Object Query Language. With OQL, you can write queries, much like you do in SQL, to ask questions and compute statistics. JavaScript functions can be used, making this an extremely powerful tool. For example, if you are trying to track down a memory leak and know of a document that should no longer be referenced, you can search the heap for the title of the document and then trace the references back.

The following topics are covered in this section:

- Optimizing Java Applications
- Launching the Profiler
- Attaching a Profiler to a Local Application
- Monitoring a Desktop Application
- Understanding CPU Performance
- Using Profiling Points
- Understanding Memory Usage
- Using the HeapWalker

Optimizing Java Applications

Optimizing Java applications not only involves streamlining code, picking efficient algorithms and data types, but also properly configuring the Java virtual machine (JVM). Profiling plays an important role in optimizing the JVM. Optimizing the JVM involves picking appropriate heap and garbage collection settings so that an application runs smoothly and meets its performance objectives. For many applications the default settings are acceptable—others require tweaking and experimentation. Each virtual machine implementation supports different features that can be configured to achieve different performance objectives. While profiling can help find these settings, profiling is also affected by the settings used. The modern JVM from Oracle includes a feature called Ergonomics in which the JVM adapts to its hardware. This must be taken into account when profiling.

Stepping back, Java source code is compiled to byte code and interpreted by the JVM at runtime. This is in contrast to other languages such as C++ and Objective-C, where the code is compiled directly to machine language. When the application is launched, the JVM converts the byte code into machine language using the just-in-time (JIT) compiler. This compiler performs a number of optimizations on-the-fly—such as inlining code and using processor-specific instructions. Objects are instantiated and stored on the heap. The garbage collector manages the heap and reclaims memory used by objects no longer reachable. The choice of the JVM and hence, the JIT, as well as the initial settings for heap and garbage collection, play a critical role in the performance of an application.

Each JVM is launched with an initial heap size and a garbage collector. The garbage collector is responsible for managing the Java heap. Specifically it manages the allocation of memory, ensures that reachable objects are not released, and recovers memory from objects that are no longer reachable. In handling these tasks, the garbage collector must limit fragmentation and compact memory so that new objects can be efficiently instantiated. Since objects have different life cycles, with some objects living a long time, whereas others are being created and destroyed rapidly, different strategies are used. A garbage collector's performance is evaluated on its throughput, overhead, pause time, collection frequency, and promptness. The HotSpot JVM from Oracle includes four garbage collectors:

- **Serial Collector (`-XX:UseSerialGC`)** The garbage collection is done serially with the application pausing for garbage collection. This garbage collector is automatically chosen for non-server-class machines.

- **Parallel Collector (`-XX:+UseParallelGC`)** The garbage collection is done in parallel to take advantage of multiple CPUs on computers. Collection of the young and old generations is done in parallel. This collector is optimal for machines running with multiple CPUs with applications that have pause time constraints.

- **Parallel Compacting Collector (`-XX:+UseParallelOldGC`)** This collector is an extension of the parallel collector, except that it uses a different algorithm for collecting the old generation. This collector is a better choice for applications that have pause time constraints than the parallel collector; however, it is not optimal for shared machines where an application cannot monopolize a thread.

- **Concurrent Mark-Sweep Collector (`-XX:+UseConcMarkSweepGC`)** This is a lower latency collector. It splits the collector into young and old generation collections. Each collection starts with a pause during which objects that are reachable are marked. Then the collector marks objects that are transitively reachable from the previous set. In the final phase, objects that are not reached are swept away. This garbage collector should be used in situations where long garbage collection pauses are unacceptable such as interactive GUI applications.

The Ergonomics feature of the Oracle JVM in Java SE 5 automatically picks the garbage collector and the initial and maximum heap size. This JVM partitions the machine into either server class or client class, depending on hardware resources. The JVM's selection can be overridden by passing in `-client` or `-server`. The server-class constraints are used to determine the class of a machine. Server-class machines possess two or more physical processors and two or more gigabytes of physical memory. This applies to all operating system platforms with the exception of 32-bit editions of Windows. A server-class machine uses the parallel collector, whereas a client machine uses the serial collector. The following heap settings are used:

- **Client**   Initial heap is 4MB and maximum heap is 64MB.
- **Server**   Initial heap is 32MB and maximum heap is 250MB.

The following settings control the heap size:

- **-Xms[bytes]**   Initial size of the heap.
- **-Xmx[bytes]**   Maximum size of the heap.

Numerous other settings control the ratio of free space to the minimum and maximum heap values. These can be found on the Oracle website for the Oracle JVM. Other JVMs have similar documentation.

These settings affect the performance of an application. Setting a maximum heap size too low can result in the error `java.lang.OutOfMemoryError`. Such an error can thus indicate either a memory leak or an improperly sized heap. Using the NetBeans Profiler can help make this clearer.

Launching the Profiler

The NetBeans Profiler has its own dedicated top-level menu in NetBeans. The contents of this menu are listed in Table 10-4 along with the key shortcuts and brief descriptions. This tight integration makes profiling easy and painless. Profiling does not require installing and configuring a separate application, downloading a plugin, or learning new command-line parameters. Application performance characteristics can be probed as easily as an application can be debugged.

The first three menu items are used for initiating a profiling session. Profiling sessions are started for the current main project by invoking Profile | Profile Main Project or for other local and remote processes via Profile | Attach Profiler. The last option, Profile Other, has a submenu whose contents and status depend upon the active window. If the active window is an editor for a unit test, then menus for profiling the test or test suite appear under this menu. If the active window is Projects, the contents vary if a Java package is selected or a unit test or class with a main method is selected. Profiling options are also available when right-clicking a Java class or JUnit test in the Projects window.

The first option, Profile Main Project, profiles the current project. This option uses the current Run configuration in Project Properties. Profiling requires changes to the project build script and calibration of the project's JVM. NetBeans detects whether these steps are necessary and prompts before changes are made.

The Attach Profiler menu option is used to profile an existing Java application. This application does not need to be a project in NetBeans nor do you need the source code for the application. You can profile any Java application—ranging from a NetBeans instance to GlassFish and IBM WebSphere. Attaching a profiler to an existing application is covered in the next section.

TABLE 10-4   Profile Menu

Menu Item	Shortcut	Description
Profile Main Project	ALT-F2	Launches the profiler for the main project.
Attach Profiler		Attaches the profiler to a local or remote process.
Profile Other		Profiles other projects and also includes: Profile File Profile Test For File
Rerun Profiling Session	CTRL-SHIFT-F2	Reexecutes the last profiling session using that session's final configuration settings.
Modify Profiling Session	ALT-SHIFT-F2	Adjusts the settings on the current profiling session. For example, if currently just monitoring, you can switch to analyzing CPU performance.
Stop Profiling Session	SHIFT-F2	Stops the profiling session and quits the application. Menu changes to Detach if profiling an external application.
Reset Collected Results	CTRL-ALT-F2	Resets the collected results for CPU and memory profiling.
Run GC		Runs the garbage collector.
Take Snapshot Of Collected Results	CTRL--F2	Takes a snapshot of either CPU or memory results.
Take Heap Dump		Takes a snapshot of the heap. This can be analyzed afterwards.
Load Snapshot		Loads a memory snapshot into NetBeans for analysis.
Load Heap Dump		Loads a heap dump into NetBeans for analysis.
Compare Memory Snapshots		Compares memory snapshots. Use this to understand how execution runs differ in terms of instantiated objects.
Advanced Commands		Has the following submenu items: Run Profiler Calibration View Command-Line Arguments Display Internal Statistics Unintegrate Profiler From <Project>

Before a project can be profiled, the JVM must be calibrated. Profiling involves adding instrumentation to the byte code of the profiled application. This instrumentation adversely imposes overhead, which must be factored out to collect accurate data. The calibrated data is JVM and machine configuration specific. If changes are made to a machine's hardware configuration such as a faster hard drive or more random access memory (RAM), the JVM calibration should be regenerated. Regenerating calibration data is performed by choosing Profile |

Advanced Commands | Run Profiler Calibration. The first time a profiling is performed, NetBeans automatically prompts to perform calibration.

Pay special attention to calibration on laptop computers. Modern laptops use dynamic frequency scaling to throttle the processor to conserve power and reduce heat output. Throttling the processor thus results in skewed data. Profiling an application must take into account the operating environment, and understanding settings outside of the profiler is imperative. Other applications running the computer can also affect profiling. For example, encoding a video while profiling changes the results.

on the
Job

Profiling code using `System.currentTimeMillis()` is not an accurate technique for collecting performance data. First, retrieving this time requires crossing the boundary from user space into protected space of the operating system. This results in a significant performance penalty. Nesting calls to `System.currentTimeMillis()` would thus skew the results. You can use DTrace on OpenSolaris/Solaris or Mac OS X to see the effect.

NetBeans displays the dialog box in Figure 10-13 the first time an application is profiled. After you click OK the calibration runs, and an option is presented to view the results. The results are shown in Figure 10-14. The results in Figure 10-14 are for a Windows 7 virtual machine running on a MacBook Pro using Parallels. For

FIGURE 10-13

VM calibration
for profiling

FIGURE 10-14

Calibration
results

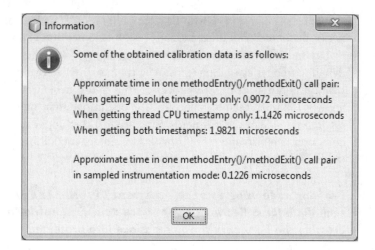

comparison, Table 10-5 lists a comparison between various machines. Differences are also shown for a laptop plugged into a power source and also running on battery.

Calibration data for the profiler is stored under .nbprofiler in a user's home directory. This directory contains a binary with calibration data for each JVM that has been calibrated. The contents of this directory should not be shared across machines because profiling is machine specific.

TABLE 10-5   Calibration Comparisons

Measurement	Windows 7 Virtual Machine PowerBook Pro	Mac OS X PowerBook Pro Power Adapter	Mac OS X PowerBook Pro Battery	Mac OS X Mac Min
Absolute timestamp	0.9071 µs	0.0235 µs	0.1825 µs	0.3025 µs
Thread CPU timestamp	1.1426 µs	4.5225 µs	4.54 µs	5.8975 µs
Both timestamps	1,9821 µs	4.6525 µs	4.66 µs	7.1025 µs
methodEntry()/ methodExit() instrumentation mode	0.1225 µs	0.05 µs	0.0512 µs	0.085 µs

Profiling a project requires changes to the project's Ant files. NetBeans warns before proceeding with the modifications. This dialog box is shown in Figure 10-15. NetBeans makes the following changes to the project:

- Create an `nbproject/profiler-build-impl.xml` script.
- Copy the current `build.xml` to `build-before-profiler.xml` script.
- Create a new `build.xml` script.

New files are scheduled for addition to version control. To revert these changes, choose Profiler | Advanced Commands | Unintegrate Profiler From <Application Name>. The only difference between the original `build.xml` created for a project and the profiler-specific instance is an import statement:

```
<import file="nbproject/profiler-build-impl.xml"/>
```

Attaching a Profiler to a Local Application

The second menu item in Table 10-4 is Attach Profiler. The NetBeans Profiler can be attached to both local and remote Java processes. The Java process being profiled does not need a corresponding project in NetBeans. This means that you can profile any Java application and even ones for which the source code is not available. Thus, if a particular project is not using NetBeans, the NetBeans Profiler can still be utilized. Having the project in NetBeans does bring benefits because it enables

FIGURE 10-15

Enabling profiling

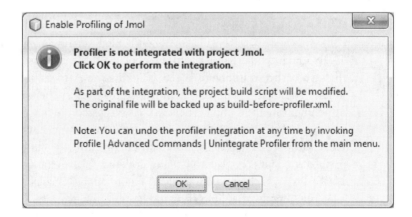

navigation from the profiler output to the source code. Attaching is also useful for profiling long-running applications or applications that have custom start scripts.

NetBeans supports three different attach modes. The attach mode chosen depends upon the location of the application, the JVM version being used, and the profiling statistics to be collected. The three modes include:

- **Local Direct**   In this mode NetBeans launches the Java application so that profiling begins on startup. The application waits for NetBeans to connect to begin profiling.

- **Local Dynamic**   In this mode the profiler can be attached to an application that is already running without restarting it. NetBeans and the application must be on the same computer. Java 6 or greater is required for this to work.

- **Remote Direct**   In this mode applications running on a remote machine can be profiled. NetBeans generates a Remote Pack to be used in launching the application.

To attach to a JVM for profiling, choose Profile | Attach Profiler. This opens the dialog box shown in Figure 10-16. Clicking the Attach button opens the Attach Wizard shown in Figure 10-17. In this step we select the target type as well as the attachment method and invocation. As discussed previously, Dynamic enables the monitoring of applications that are already running, whereas Direct is used to monitor pre-Java 6 or situations where profiling should begin as soon as the application launches. Remote is not covered on the exam and thus is not discussed. NetBeans saves the choices made in Figure 10-17 for subsequent runs. To change the attach mode, the dialog box in Figure 10-16 includes a link for altering the configuration in place of the phrase "No attach settings defined."

FIGURE 10-16

Attach external
application

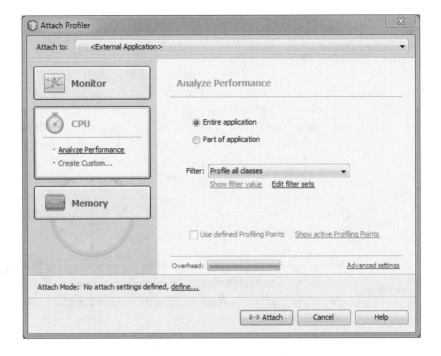

FIGURE 10-16

Attach external
application

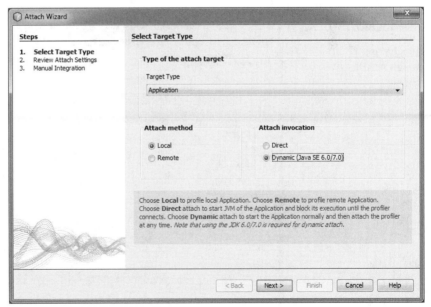

FIGURE 10-17

Attach Wizard:
Select Target Type

After you click Next, NetBeans displays a dialog box for reviewing the settings. An example is shown in Figure 10-18. The contents of this screen vary depending upon the target type.

Clicking Next displays the Manual Integration step in the wizard, shown in Figure 10-19. This screen provides instructions and profiling advice. It also gives you a chance to launch the application and get it to the point where you want to begin profiling. Note, if the project is in NetBeans, you can set explicit profiling points.

Once the application is launched, click Finish to display the dialog box shown in Figure 10-20. This dialog box has a drop-down list of the Java applications running on the computer along with their PID (process identifier). If you have multiple Java processes, you may need to use a platform-specific tool such as the Windows Task Manager to identify the process. Once OK is clicked, NetBeans attaches to the process and begins profiling it.

on the job

When connecting to the local JVM for profiling, NetBeans opens a socket connection to the JVM. On Microsoft Windows a warning may appear: if you do not accept and allow NetBeans to open a connection, then you will not be able to profile.

FIGURE 10-18

Attach Wizard: Review Attach Settings

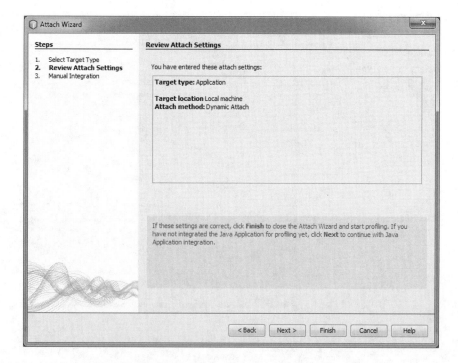

FIGURE 10-19

Attach Wizard:
Manual
Integration

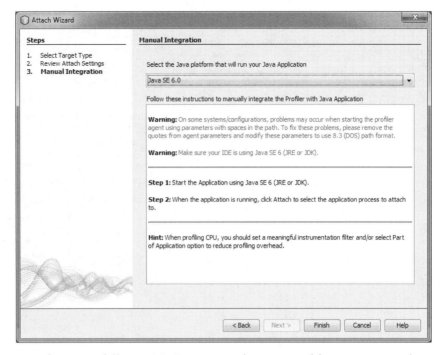

Direct attachment is different. NetBeans provides command-line parameters that you must use to launch the application. These parameters vary depending upon the version of the JVM. Direct attachment is also the only way to connect to pre-Java 6 JVMs. Figure 10-21 shows the dialog box that is displayed after Figure 10-17 if Direct is chosen.

FIGURE 10-20

Select Process
To Attach

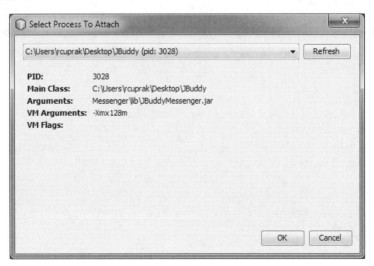

Attach Wizard:
Manual
Integration
(direct)

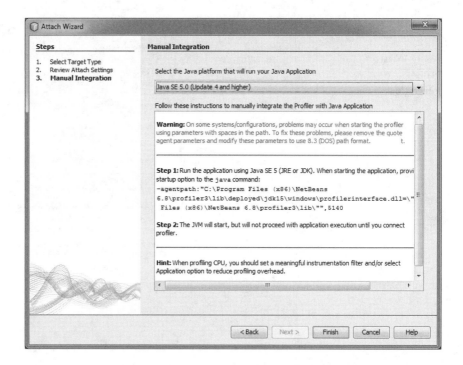

The Scenario & Solution helps you work through when to use each type of attachment mode for the profiler.

SCENARIO & SOLUTION

You want to profile an application that is a NetBeans project.	If the project is the Main project, choose Profile | Profile Main Project. Otherwise, right-click the project and select Profile.
You want to profile an existing Java application that is running Java 6 on the same machine as NetBeans.	Choose Profile | Attach Profiler and choose an Attach Method of Local and an Attach Invocation of Dynamic.
You want to profile an existing Java application that is running Java 5 on the same machine as NetBeans.	Choose Profile | Attach Profiler and choose an Attach Method of Local and an Attach Invocation of Direct. Follow the instructions to manually integrate the Profiler with the Java application.
You want to profile a remote application running on a computer across the hall or around the world.	Choose Profile | Attach Profiler and choose Remote.

EXERCISE 10-4

Attaching the Profiler

In this exercise, you attach a profiler to an existing free commercial Java application. The source for this application is proprietary as well as obfuscated. This demonstrates the power of the NetBeans Profiler. Often you may have to use a profiler to understand how your application is affecting another Java application—for example, if you are using a commercial Java-based queuing system and it keeps running out of Java heap space while you are submitting messages. Java 6 is required for this exercise.

1. Download JBuddy Messenger from www.zionsoftware.com. JBuddy is a free Java-based instant-messaging client. It is a multithreaded Swing application.

2. Expand the downloaded JBuddy application and launch it. For the purposes of this exercise you do not need to log in to any AIM service.

3. In NetBeans, choose Profiler | Attach Profiler. If you have previously attached to another JVM, you need to click the change link for the attach mode; otherwise click Attach.

4. On the wizard panel for Select Target Type, make the following selections and click Next:
   - Target Type: Application
   - Attach Method: Local
   - Attach Invocation: Dynamic

5. On the Review Attach Settings wizard panel, click Finish.

6. In the dialog box for selecting the process, choose the drop-down entry for JBuddy and click OK.

7. The profiler now opens. To stop profiling, choose Profile | Detach. You have the option to either detach or terminate the application.

Monitoring a Desktop Application

The most basic type of profiling in NetBeans is monitoring. With monitoring, NetBeans uses no byte code instrumentation, and thus the impact of profiling is minimal. The information available is not much different than what is available through JConsole, a diagnostic tool included with the JDK. NetBeans uses information available through the Java Management Extension (JMX). Monitoring provides basic insight into an application including memory usage and thread activity. The data available is at a macroscopic level: how much heap space has been consumed and how it has changed over time, how many threads are running, and which threads are running or are in various nonrunning states. Monitoring is a relatively easy way to keep track of application behavior and to catch memory leaks while still in development.

Monitoring tracks and reports memory usage and thread usage over time. Three views are available for this type of monitoring:

- **VM Telemetry Overview**   A window that contains three graphs summarizing application memory usage. This is the default view that is first opened.
- **VM Telemetry**   Opens a window with three tabs that provide a better view and tools for manipulating and exploring the graphs appearing in the VM Telemetry Overview window.
- **Threads**   Opens a window with three tabs. Each tab displays a different view of the same thread data. The first tab includes a time, the second a table with the same data, and the third a pie chart.

Using monitoring, you can see and determine whether an application has a memory or thread leak. If an application has a memory leak, you see heap usage continue to increase over time. A thread leak manifests itself as a steady increase in threads over time. At any point during a profiling session the type of profiling data can be changed. If there appears to be a memory leak or problem with threading, you can choose Profile | Modify Profiling Session to change the data being collected.

Just because the heap continues to fill with objects doesn't mean that you have a memory leak. A high-performance application may be using an object cache to reduce the performance penalty for frequent read operations that are I/O bound. An OutOfMemoryError can also mean that the garbage collector/heap settings haven't been optimized for the application's load.

Monitoring an application is split into the following subsections:

- Starting and Customizing Monitoring
- Understanding Telemetry Overview
- Viewing Threads

Starting and Customizing Monitoring

To monitor an application, choose any one of the first three actions under the Profile menu including Profile Main Project, Attach Profiler, or Profile Other. This displays a dialog box either the same or a similar to Figure 10-22. The boxes in the

FIGURE 10-22

Monitor
Application

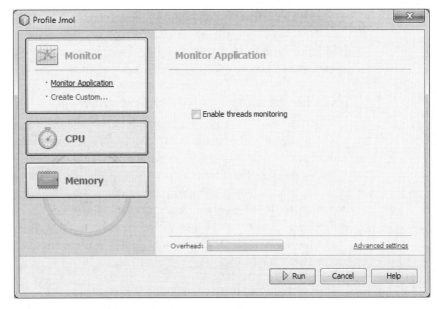

left panel—Monitor, CPU, and Memory—are actually buttons. Clicking the first button, Monitor, displays the basic monitor settings in the panel on the right. With basic settings, only one option is available, Enable Threads Monitoring. If this is checked, the NetBeans Profiler tracks threading performance from the moment the application starts. The Overhead bar toward the bottom of the dialog box graphically depicts the performance impact of this type of monitoring. Clicking Run in the dialog box launches the application and NetBeans begins profiling it.

To edit the Advanced Settings, a custom monitoring configuration must be created. This is accomplished by clicking Create Custom under the Monitor button to display the dialog box in Figure 10-23. A custom configuration can be based upon either the default or another custom configuration.

FIGURE 10-23

New Custom
Configuration

With a custom configuration in place, custom monitor parameters can be set, as shown in Figure 10-24. Custom parameters include Working Directory, Java Platform, and JVM Arguments. In this example the serial garbage collector has been specified to test its impact upon the performance of the application.

Understanding Telemetry Overview

When the NetBeans Profiler launches in the monitoring mode, two new windows appear: Profiler at upper left and VM Telemetry Overview at lower right, as shown in Figure 10-25. (Placement may differ if you have previously used the profiler and rearranged your windows.)

The VM Telemetry window is available regardless of the type of profiling being performed. If it does not appear automatically, it can be displayed via Window | Profiling | Profiling Telemetry Overview. It contains three graphs, each with the X axis representing time. Double-clicking a graph opens the graph in a larger window. The three graphs include:

- **Memory Heap**   This graph displays the available heap versus the used heap. The initial heap size depends upon the initial heap (-Xmsn) and the minimum heap free ratio (-XX:MinHeapFreeRatio) The amount of heap continues to increase until it hits the maximum heap.

- **Memory (GC)**   This graph shows two variables:

  - **Relative Time Spent in GC**   This is the percentage of time spent in garbage collection. Scale is on the right.

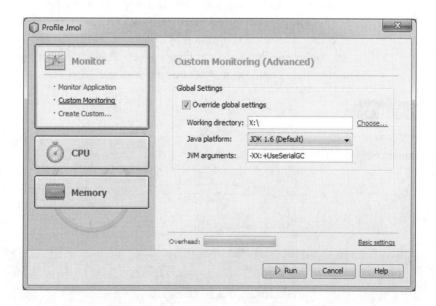

FIGURE 10-24

Custom monitoring configuration

■ **Surviving Generations**   This is a number of generations currently on the heap. Scale is on the left.

■ **Threads / Loaded Classes**   This graph shows two variables:

■ **Threads**   Total number of threads in existence. Scale is on the right.

■ **Loaded Classes**   Total number of classes loaded into the JVM. Scale is on the left.

Double-clicking a graph opens it in a larger window.

The Profiler control panel (window) on the left of Figure 10-25 manages the profiling session. It is organized into six panels that are the same regardless of the type of monitoring being performed. The six panels are:

■ **Controls**   These controls are used to restart/stop the session as well as to change the parameters. The icons are documented in Table 10-6.

FIGURE 10-25   Monitoring

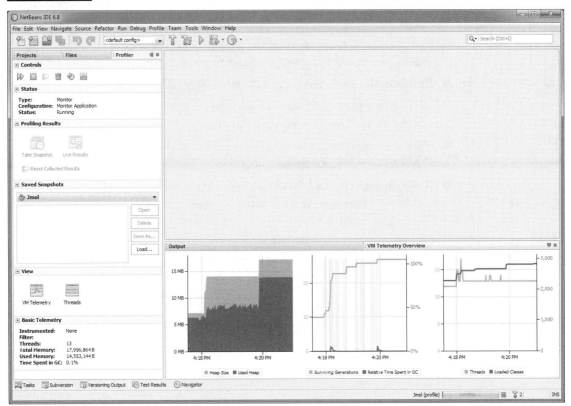

TABLE 10-6	Icon	Description
Profile Controls		Reruns the last profiling session.
		Stops the application that is being profiled.
		Resets the collected results buffer. For use in either CPU or memory profiling.
		Runs the garbage collection in the application being profiled.
		Modifies the profiling session. For example, if doing simple monitoring, you can enable CPU monitoring.
		Displays the telemetry overview.

- **Status**   Displays the status of the session—specifically the type of monitoring being performed along with the name of the configuration.

- **Profiling Results**   Saves either a memory or CPU snapshot.

- **Saved Snapshots**   Lists saved CPU and memory snapshots. These snapshots can be reloaded into the editor for analysis and comparison.

- **View**   Displays either basic telemetry data, as shown in VM Telemetry Overview, or thread information.

- **Basic Telemetry**   Displays basic information about the VM including the number of classes and threads as well as memory usage and a summary of the garbage collection.

Selecting VM Telemetry from the View panel shown in Figure 10-25 opens a window with three tabs. These three tabs correspond to the three graphs on the VM Telemetry Overview window. The larger graphs, shown in Figures 10-26, 10-27, and 10-28, not only are easier to read, but they also track the entire history since

FIGURE 10-26   Memory (Heap)

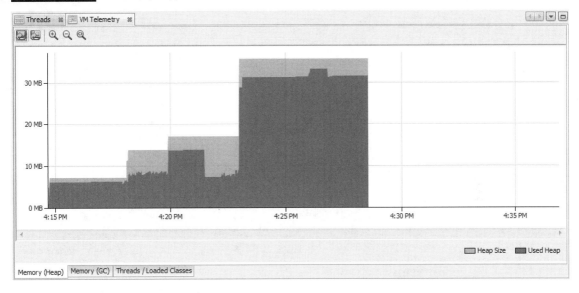

profiling began. In addition, the mouse can be dragged over each graph to get a
precise readout for any time point. Each of the three windows has a set of icons
across the top for performing common actions. These are documented in Table 10-7.

FIGURE 10-27   Memory (GC)

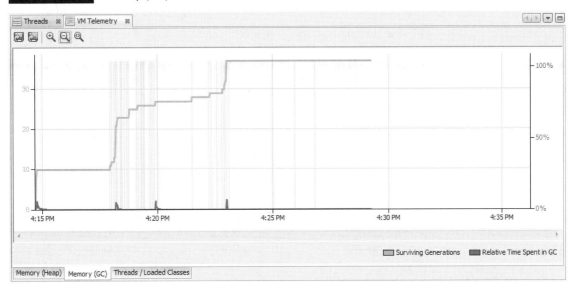

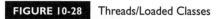

FIGURE 10-28   Threads/Loaded Classes

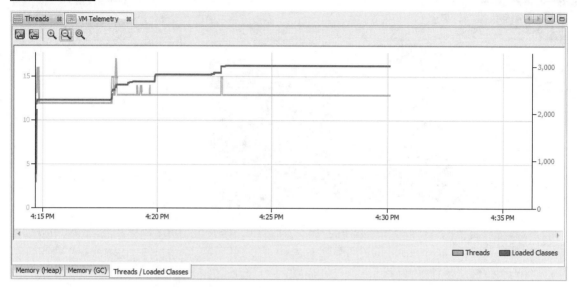

Viewing Threads

Thread telemetry data monitoring must be explicitly enabled. It can be enabled before profiling by choosing Enable Threads Monitoring shown in Figure 10-22. To view the threads, click the Threads icon in the View panel of the Profiler control panel shown in Figure 10-25. This opens a new editor window with the three tabs shown in Figures 10-29, 10-30, and 10-31. If thread monitoring was not enabled prior to running the application, NetBeans prompts for enabling it.

TABLE 10-7

Memory Icons

Toolbar Icon	Description
	Exports the graph as XML, web page, Excel-compatible CSV, or CSV file.
	Saves an image of the current graph to a file.
	Zooms in on the graph.
	Zooms out on the graph.
	Fixes the scale on the graph.

The first thread view, shown in Figure 10-29, is a graphical timeline of the application's threads. Each thread is color-coded to show the state of the thread at a particular moment. The thread states are as follows:

- **Running** The thread is alive and performing tasks.
- **Sleeping** The thread is stopped on a `Thread.sleep()`.
- **Wait** The thread is stopped on a `wait()`.
- **Monitor** The thread has stopped waiting to acquire a lock on a synchronized method.

The second tab, shown in Figure 10-30, summarizes the information from Figure 10-29 in tabular form. In this view the percentage of time each thread spent in the different states is broken out. If an application has been running for a long time, this table provides a quick synopsis.

The Details tab, shown in Figure 10-31, combines the previous two tabs. In this view a color-coded pie chart is displayed along with the timeline for each thread. The threads being displayed can be filtered. An image snapshot can also be saved to disk.

The graphical view is useful if you are trying to understand what is going on in an application and how the execution of threads is being interleaved. If a deadlock is suspected, the debugging tools have the ability to detect deadlocks via Debug | Check For Deadlock.

FIGURE 10-29   Threads Timeline

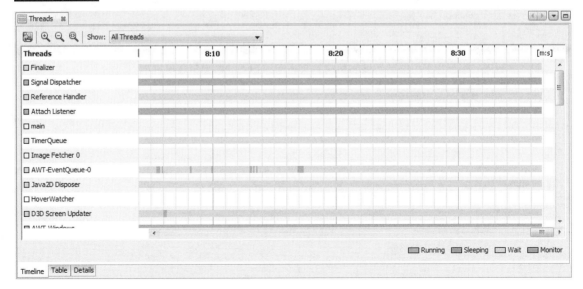

FIGURE 10-30 Threads Table

Thread	Running	Sleeping	Wait	Monitor	Total
Signal Dispatcher	1:59.610 (100.0%)	0.0 (0.0%)	0.0 (0.0%)	0.0 (0.0%)	1:59.610
Attach Listener	1:59.610 (100.0%)	0.0 (0.0%)	0.0 (0.0%)	0.0 (0.0%)	1:59.610
AWT-Windows	1:59.610 (100.0%)	0.0 (0.0%)	0.0 (0.0%)	0.0 (0.0%)	1:59.610
DestroyJavaVM	1:59.610 (100.0%)	0.0 (0.0%)	0.0 (0.0%)	0.0 (0.0%)	1:59.610
AWT-EventQueue-0	7.267 (6.0%)	0.0 (0.0%)	1:52.234 (93.8%)	0.109 (0.0%)	1:59.610
Swing-Shell	0.939 (0.7%)	0.0 (0.0%)	1:58.671 (99.2%)	0.0 (0.0%)	1:59.610
D3D Screen Updater	0.658 (0.5%)	0.0 (0.0%)	1:58.952 (99.4%)	0.0 (0.0%)	1:59.610
Thread-25	0.328 (100.0%)	0.0 (0.0%)	0.0 (0.0%)	0.0 (0.0%)	0.328
Image Fetcher 0	0.109 (2.1%)	0.0 (0.0%)	5.031 (97.8%)	0.0 (0.0%)	5.140
Finalizer	0.0 (0.0%)	0.0 (0.0%)	1:59.610 (100.0%)	0.0 (0.0%)	1:59.610
Reference Handler	0.0 (0.0%)	0.0 (0.0%)	1:59.610 (100.0%)	0.0 (0.0%)	1:59.610
TimerQueue	0.0 (0.0%)	0.0 (0.0%)	1:59.610 (100.0%)	0.0 (0.0%)	1:59.610
Java2D Disposer	0.0 (0.0%)	0.0 (0.0%)	1:59.610 (100.0%)	0.0 (0.0%)	1:59.610
AWT-Shutdown	0.0 (0.0%)	0.0 (0.0%)	1:59.610 (100.0%)	0.0 (0.0%)	1:59.610
Thread-7	0.0 (0.0%)	1:59.610 (100.0%)	0.0 (0.0%)	0.0 (0.0%)	1:59.610
ConsoleReaderThread	0.0 (0.0%)	0.0 (0.0%)	1:59.610 (100.0%)	0.0 (0.0%)	1:59.610
HoverWatcher	0.0 (0.0%)	1:59.610 (100.0%)	0.0 (0.0%)	0.0 (0.0%)	1:59.610

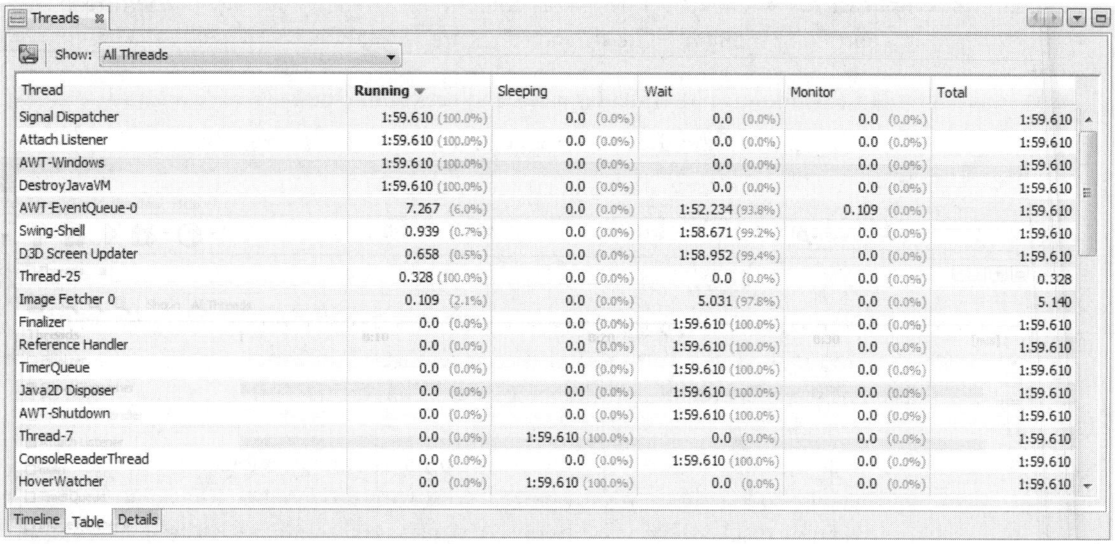

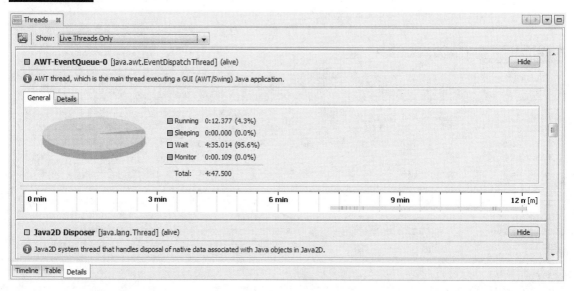

FIGURE 10-31 Threads Details

EXERCISE 10-5

Deadlocking Thread

In this exercise, you troubleshoot a deadlock. The following code creates a classic deadlock situation where each thread is attempting to acquire a lock. In the Threads view these two threads appear red, meaning that they are waiting for a monitor. You then use the debugger to verify the existence of a deadlock.

1. Create a new project by choosing File | New Project.
2. Select Java Application from the Java Category.
3. Pick a Project Name and specify the main class as `net.cuprak` `.example.DeadlockExample`.
4. Click Finish in the wizard, and replace the contents of the `DeadlockExample.java` file with:

```java
package net.cuprak.example;

public class DeadlockExample {
  public Object lock1 = new Object();
  public Object lock2 = new Object();
  private Thread thread1;
  private Thread thread2;

  public DeadlockExample() {
    thread1 = new Thread(new Thread1(),"Deadlocked Thread 1");
    thread2 = new Thread(new Thread2(),"Deadlocked Thread 2");
  }

  public void init() {
    thread1.start();
    thread2.start();
  }

  public class Thread2 implements Runnable {
    public void run() {
      try {
        synchronized (lock1) {
          Thread.sleep(10);
          synchronized (lock2) {}
        }
```

```
      } catch (InterruptedException ex) {
        ex.printStackTrace();
      }
    }
  }

  public class Thread1 implements Runnable {
    public void run() {
      try {
        synchronized (lock2) {
          Thread.sleep(20);
          synchronized (lock1) {}
        }
      } catch (InterruptedException ex) {
        ex.printStackTrace();
      }
    }
  }

  public static void main(String[] args) {
    DeadlockExample main = new DeadlockExample();
    main.init();
  }
}
```

5. Profile the project by either clicking the Profile toolbar icon or choosing Profile | Profile Main Project.

6. In the dialog box that appears (see Figure 10-22) select Monitor and then choose Enable Threads Monitoring.

7. Choose Run to begin profiling.

8. In the Profiler window, choose Threads under View.

9. Verify that "Deadlocked Thread 1" and "Deadlocked Thread 2" appear red and are thus deadlocked.

10. Stop the profiling session by choosing Stop from the Controls section of the Profiler window.

11. Choose Debug | Debug Main Project to start a debug session.

12. After the application has started, choose Debug | Check For Deadlock to verify the deadlock you saw in the Threads view.

Understanding CPU Performance

Analyzing performance involves tracking and understanding the amount of time spent in methods and constructors. To focus optimization activities, you need to know what specific parts of an application are consuming a disproportionate amount of CPU cycles. Without pinpointing the cause of performance problems, proposed solutions are merely conjecture that may only aggravate performance problems. The NetBeans Profiler collects and summarizes performance data, helping guide development planning.

This type of profiling is cumulative and can be reset. This means that at any given point you can clear the history and begin tracking method invocations from scratch. This enables you to determine how CPU resources were utilized between two points. For a file load operation, you would expect most of the time to be spent in I/O methods. To fully leverage this feature, you need profiling points that reset data collection and trigger snapshots. This section focuses on CPU performance profiling; the next section delves into profiler points.

The previous section discussed how to perform basic monitoring of an application. Those views, including VM Telemetry and Threads, are still available when profiling for performance and can be viewed at any time. Profiling an application for performance involves choosing the CPU group when initiating a profile session. When profiling starts, you have only two new views to worry about: Live Results and snapshot views.

Monitoring and collating CPU real-time performance data significantly derogates performance. For an interactive application such as Jmol that has been used in many exercises, the performance penalty is severe if not mitigated through planning and initial configuration of profiling parameters. NetBeans provides several mechanisms to control the scope of collected data including filters, profiling points, and sampling intervals. In addition, NetBeans can exclude code that will skew results such as invocations of `sleep()` and `wait()`.

The following topics are covered:

- Configuring Performance Analysis
- Monitoring Performance
- Capturing Snapshots

Configuring Performance Analysis

Initiating a performance profiling session is no different than initiating a monitoring session, as discussed in the previous section. When the Profile dialog box appears, select CPU, as shown in Figure 10-32. The basic settings are displayed by default. The following settings can be configured:

- **Scope** Either the entire application or just a portion of the application can be profiled. Limiting the scope improves performance. If Part Of Application is selected, a link appears next to it. The link displays a dialog box for selecting the methods to be profiled.

- **Filter** Limits the classes that are to be profiled. The following choices can be made:

  - **Profile All Classes** Profiles all classes in the application including external libraries.

  - **Profile Only Project Classes** Profiles only classes that are a part of the project and are contained in the source directories. A link appears to display the options in this box shown in Figure 10-33.

  - **Quick Filter** Uses the pattern entered in the Set Quick Filter dialog box, as shown in Figure 10-34.

  - **Exclude Java Core Classes** Excludes core Java classes such as `java.lang.String`.

- **Profiling Points** If deselected, then custom profiling points are ignored.

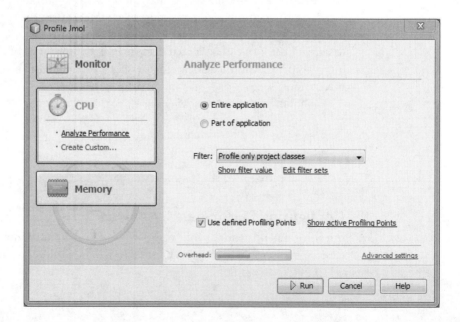

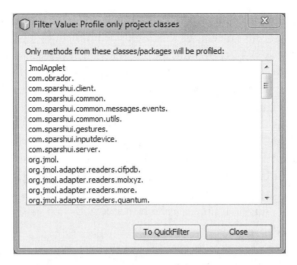

FIGURE 10-33

Profile filter

The profile filter dialog box shown in Figure 10-33 lists the project classes that are profiled when the filter is set to Profile Only Project Classes. Clicking the Show Filter Value link below the Filter drop-down list in Figure 10-32 opens the dialog box in Figure 10-33. The dialog box in Figure 10-33 is helpful for understanding what classes will be profiled. It is also helpful for bootstrapping a Quick Filter by choosing To QuickFilter. When this is done, the filter changes to Quick Filter, and the Set Quick Filter dialog box in Figure 10-34 appears. The Set Quick Filter dialog box is populated with classes from the project.

FIGURE 10-34

Set Quick Filter

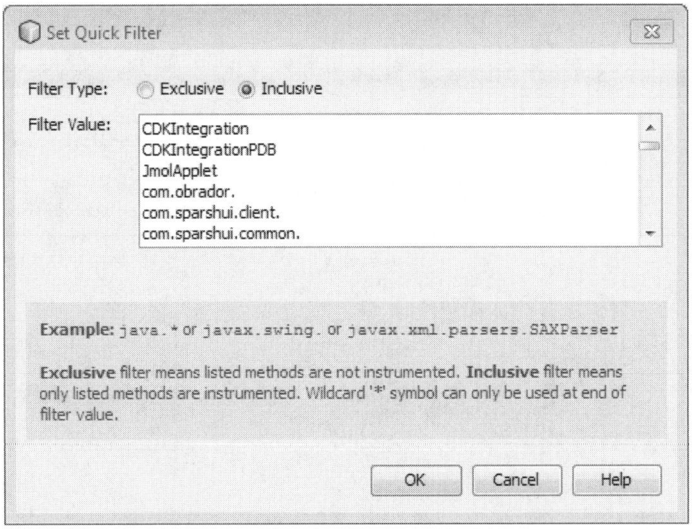

The Set Quick Filter dialog box, shown in Figure 10-34, is an editor that is used to quickly specify the classes that are to be profiled. Full package names must be used. The asterisk enables the specification of all classes within a package.

The filter sets available in the Filter drop-down list in Figure 10-32 are configured by clicking the link Edit Filter Sets below the list. This displays the dialog box shown in Figure 10-35. As can be seen from this screenshot, only the Java Core Classes are defined by default. New sets can be added. Each set makes use of a global library. The filter set can either include or exclude all of the classes in its global libraries. Global libraries are defined and edited by clicking Edit Global Filters.

The Edit Global Filters dialog box is shown in Figure 10-36. NetBeans includes numerous predefined libraries for common application servers and open source packages. Additional libraries can be added and then used in a custom filter set.

FIGURE 10-35

Customize
Filter Sets

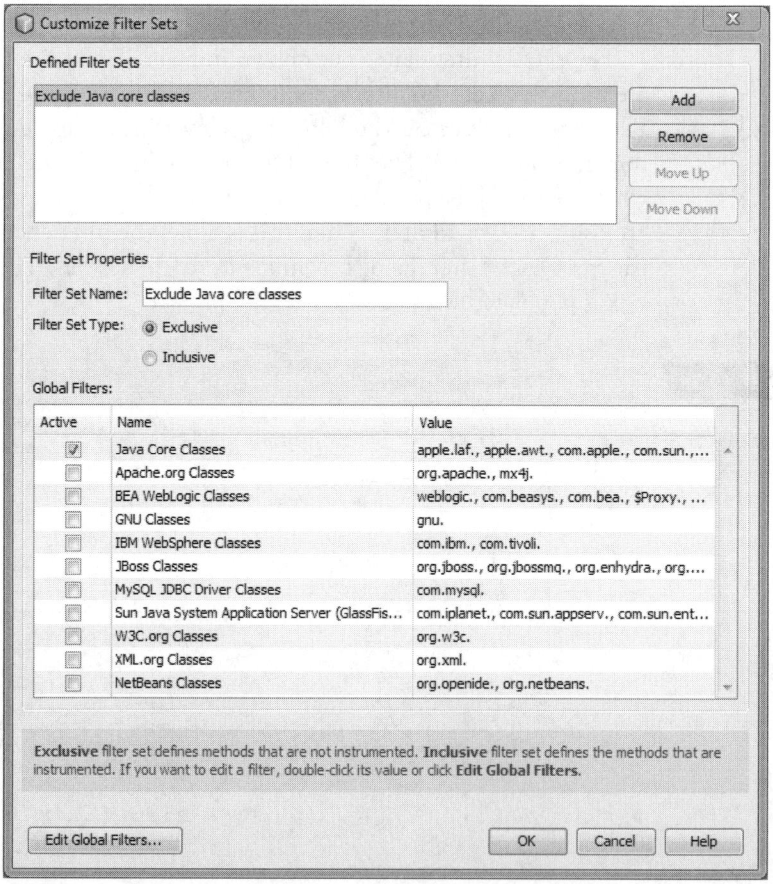

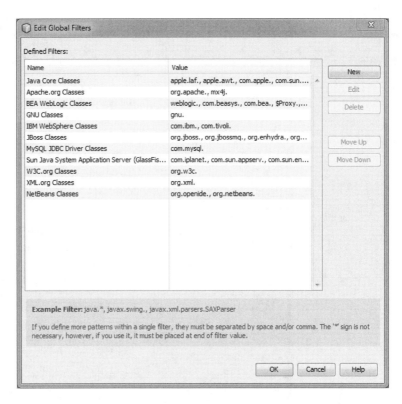

FIGURE 10-36

Edit Global Filters

Advanced configuration settings are configured by first creating a custom configuration by choosing Create Custom under CPU. After the custom configuration is created, choose Advanced Settings in the lower right of the dialog box, as shown in Figure 10-32. The custom settings then appear, as shown in Figure 10-37. The advanced settings are split into three categories: Settings, Threads, and Global Settings. The Settings category configures performance monitoring, whereas the last two categories are part of monitoring and were covered in the previous section. The following parameters are configured under Settings:

- **Method Tracking** You have two choices for this option: "Exact call tree timing" and "Exact call tree, sampled timing." The first option records entry and exit time for each method every time. For the second option, method execution time is recorded only at specific intervals. The number of executions is still recorded.

- **Exclude Time Spent in Thread.sleep() And Object.wait()** Time spent in these methods would skew the results. However, if you are writing a multithreaded application, these can be very useful.

FIGURE 10-37

Advanced settings

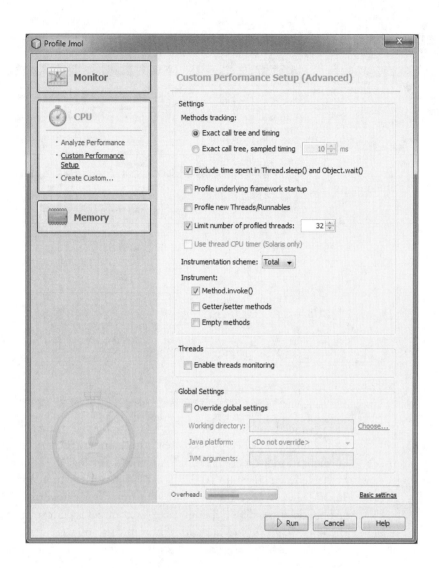

- ■ **Profile Underlying Framework Startup**   Profiles the startup of the JVM.
- ■ **Profile New Threads/Runnables**   This setting is enabled when profiling an entire application. When the setting is selected, instrumentation is added to new threads.
- ■ **Limit Number Of Profiled Threads**   Limits the number of profiled threads. Check the previous setting to profile all threads.

- **Instrumentation Scheme**   Instrumentation schemes determine the sequence in which methods are instrumented for profiling:

  - **Lazy**   This setting is best used when profiling only a part of the application. In Lazy, instrumentation isn't performed until a root method is executed. Then all possible methods from this point are executed. This greatly reduces the scope of instrumentation as well as the performance impact.

  - **Eager**   This is a hybrid approach between Lazy and Total. It analyzes classes as soon as they are loaded for root methods and their dependencies.

  - **Total**   This setting is used for profiling an entire application from the start. All of an application's methods are instrumented as soon as they are loaded.

- **Instrument**   This setting is used to reduce the number of methods instrumented. Setter and getter methods don't often affect performance, nor do empty methods.

It is extremely important to understand these settings and how they impact performance. Adding instrumentation to a method is an expensive operation. Recording the execution time of a method is also very expensive. Elapsed time calculations require using the high-resolution timer specific to the operating system. If an application is call intensive—an interactive graphical application, for example—the impact is substantial and often renders the application barely usable. Minimizing the number of instrumented methods and data points significantly reduces the profiling overhead.

The Scenario & Solution helps you better understand these custom settings.

SCENARIO & SOLUTION

You have an application that is making around 10,000 method calls per second. Which instrumentation should be chosen?	Exact Call Tree, Sampled Timing
You are profiling only a small subset of an application. Which instrumentation scheme should be used?	Lazy
You have setter and getter methods that emit PropertyChangeEvents. These PropertyChangeEvents trigger other calculations and UI updates. Which default setting should be overridden in Advanced Settings?	Instrument Getter/Setter Methods should be checked.
You do not want to exclude time spent in `Object .wait()` from the results. Which setting should be deselected?	Exclude Time Spent In Thread.sleep() And Object.wait().

Monitoring Performance

Once the Run button is clicked in the Profile dialog box, shown in Figure 10-32, the NetBeans Profiler immediately launches the application. If the entire application is being profiled, data collection begins immediately. Otherwise the profiler waits until a profiler point is tripped. When profiling an application, the HotSpot virtual machine dynamically instruments the code. The just-in-time (JIT) compiler dynamically converts Java byte code to machine language. This means that an application being profiled should be "warm" before profiling results are collected.

To see the results while the application is running, click the Live Results icon in the Profiling Results panel of the Profile window. This opens the Live Profiling Results view shown in Figure 10-38. This window contains the following columns:

- **Method** Name of the method being invoked.
- **Self Time [%]** Percentage of the runtime that the method consumed executing.
- **Self Time** Total amount of time the method has executed. Divide by the value in the Invocations column to get an average invocation time.
- **Invocations** The number of times the method has been invoked.

The icons appearing across the top of the table are documented in Table 10-8.

FIGURE 10-38 Live Profiling Results view

Hot Spots - Method	Self time [%] ▼	Self time	Invocations
org.jmol.viewer.Viewer.**render1** (java.awt.Graphics, java.awt.Image, int, int)	■	10795 ms (12.6%)	50
org.jmol.export.dialog.FileChooser.**<init>** ()	■	9188 ms (10.7%)	1
org.jmol.viewer.ActionManager$HoverWatcher.**run** ()	■	6805 ms (7.9%)	3
org.openscience.jmol.app.jmolpanel.MeasurementTable.**<init>** (org.jmol.api.JmolViewer, javax.swing...	■	6250 ms (7.3%)	1
org.jmol.export.dialog.Dialog.**setupUIManager** ()	■	5724 ms (6.7%)	1
org.jmol.viewer.Viewer.**<init>** (java.awt.Component, org.jmol.api.JmolAdapter, String)	■	5695 ms (6.6%)	2
org.jmol.g3d.Platform3D.**allocateBuffers** (int, int, boolean)	■	5049 ms (5.9%)	2
org.openscience.jmol.app.jmolpanel.JmolPanel.**<init>** (org.openscience.jmol.app.JmolApp, org.opens...	■	4353 ms (5.1%)	1
org.openscience.jmol.app.jmolpanel.Splash$WindowListener.**windowActivated** (java.awt.event.Win...	■	3670 ms (4.3%)	3
org.openscience.jmol.app.jmolpanel.JmolPanel.**startJmol** (org.openscience.jmol.app.JmolApp)	▮	3636 ms (4.2%)	1
org.openscience.jmol.app.jmolpanel.Splash.**showSplashScreen** ()	▮	2554 ms (3%)	1
org.jmol.export.history.HistoryFile.**repositionWindow** (String, java.awt.Component, int, int)	▮	2523 ms (2.9%)	3
org.jmol.export.dialog.Dialog.**getOpenFileNameFromDialog** (String, org.jmol.api.JmolViewer, Strin...	▮	1767 ms (2.1%)	1
org.jmol.viewer.RepaintManager.**allocateRenderer** (int, org.jmol.g3d.Graphics3D)	▮	1141 ms (1.3%)	25
org.jmol.api.JmolViewer.**allocateViewer** (java.awt.Component, org.jmol.api.JmolAdapter, String, jav...	▮	838 ms (1%)	2

[Method Name Filter]

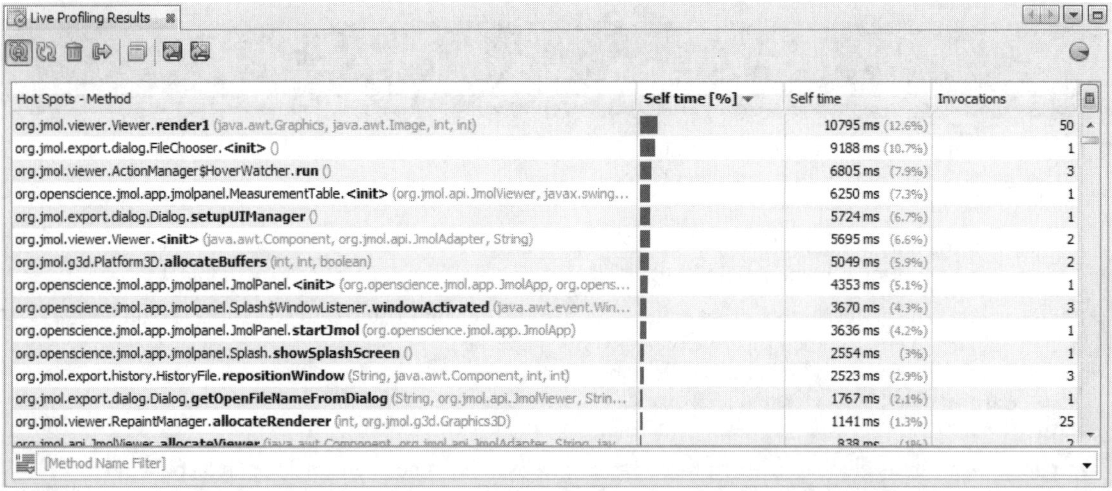

TABLE 10-8	Live Results Icons

Icon	Description
	Toggle button—if selected, results are updated automatically.
	Forces an update of the results. Used when results are not being updated dynamically.
	Runs the garbage collector and updates the results.
	Resets the collected data.
	Takes a snapshot of the collected data.
	Exports the current table to an XML, an HTML, or a CSV file.
	Saves the current view to an image file.

Capturing Snapshots

Snapshots of the profile data are captured by either clicking the icon in the Live Profiling Results window or by clicking the Take Snapshot button in Profiling Results. Additionally, choosing Profile | Take Snapshot Of Collected Results (CTRL-F2) also takes a snapshot. By default, a new snapshot window is created and shown in Figure 10-39. A snapshot window has four tabs:

- **Call Tree**   This tab displays the call tree for the method. The tree can be altered to show methods, classes, or packages.
- **Hot Spots**   This tab is the same view of the data as shown in Figure 10-38.
- **Combined**   This tab combines the Call Tree and Hot Spots views into a split pane.
- **Info**   This tab summarizes configuration settings and root methods.

Right-clicking an entry in Figure 10-39 brings up a context menu with the following entries:

- **Go To Source**   Opens entry in the Java source code file if source is available.

FIGURE 10-39   Snapshot window

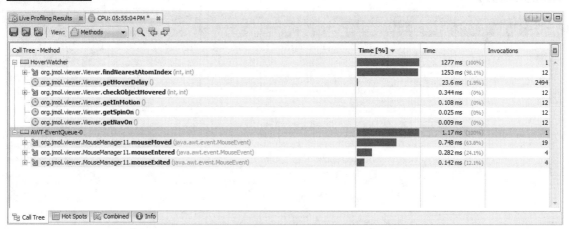

- **Show Subtree**   Shows the subtree for the selection.
- **Show Back Trace**   Shows the back trace for the current selection.
- **Find in Hot Spots**   Switches to the Hot Spots tab and highlights the selected method.
- **Add To Instrumentation Roots**   Adds this method to the instrumentation roots. Instrumentation roots are used to winnow the list of methods being profiled. By using this action, you are adding an additional method to the set that is to trigger profiling.

A captured snapshot is not saved yet. To save the snapshot, click the toolbar icon for Save Snapshot To Project. The snapshot now appears in the Saved Snapshots of the Profile window.

The default behavior when taking a new snapshot is configured in Tools | Options | Miscellaneous | Profiler.   *Review these settings as you go through this chapter.*

Using Profiling Points

Profiling points and root methods are an important feature of the NetBeans Profiler. They are used for both CPU and memory profiling. Conceptually they are very similar to debug breakpoints. When a particular line of code is executed in a debugger, you want to either pause execution to investigate application state or log a message to the console at the breakpoint. With profile points, you want to perform a specific action such as starting a timer, taking a snapshot, or initiating profiling. Profile points are invaluable for large applications where either the overhead of profiling would generate too much data, or the application would be unusable due to the overhead. The following topics will be covered:

- Understanding Profiling Point Basics
- Adding a Profile Root Method
- Selecting Multiple Root Methods
- Inserting a Profile Point

Understanding Profiling Point Basics

Profile points are set in the code and are persisted between editing sessions like breakpoints. To add a profile point to code, you right-click within a Java source code file and choose one of the three options under Profile:

- **Add As Profiling Root Method**   Adds a method as a root method. A root method triggers the profiler to begin collecting data.
- **Select Profiling Root Methods**   Opens a dialog box for selecting multiple root methods within a class.
- **Insert Profiling Point**   Inserts a new profile point.

When a profiling session is started that contains profiling points, the Profiling Points window opens, as shown in Figure 10-40. It lists the profiling points along with the project to which the points belong. If the profiling point has results, the results can be viewed by double-clicking the row. Profiling points can also be added, removed, and disabled. Note, profiling points cannot be added to the application while profiling is in progress.

FIGURE 10-40   Profiling Points window

Scope	Project ▲	Profiling Point	Results
	Jmol	getJmol execution time1:331	1 hit at 18:16:44, report
	Jmol	ExportAction:1,144	No results available

Adding a Profile Root Method

A profile root method triggers the profiler to begin collecting either CPU or memory data when any thread enters the method. All methods below the root method or objects created or destroyed are tracked. This is an easy way to limit profiling to a specific segment or module of an application. When right-clicking and choosing Profile | Add As Profiling Root Method, the cursor should be on a method. For example, in the following code listing you would right-click either `testShowAboutBox` or `println`:

```
public void testShowAboutBox() {
   System.out.println("showAboutBox");
}
```

A dialog box then appears to prompt for the configuration the root method should be added to, as shown in Figure 10-41. Once a root method is set, the configuration switches over to being Part Of Application, as shown in Figure 10-32. A link appears next to the radio button for editing the list of root methods.

Selecting Multiple Root Methods

Choosing Select Profiling Root Methods enables you to select multiple root methods for a class. For example, if a class has 20 methods and you want to make 10 of them root methods, adding them individually would be a laborious process. For this menu item, you may click anywhere in a file. You are first prompted for the configuration to add your root methods to. Then a dialog box appears (example shown in Figure 10-42) for selecting the methods to be made into root methods.

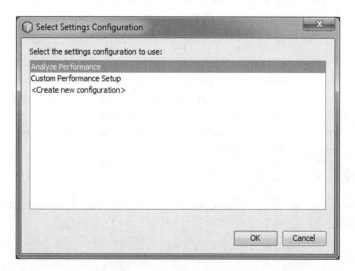

FIGURE 10-41

Select Settings Configuration

FIGURE 10-42

Select Root
Methods

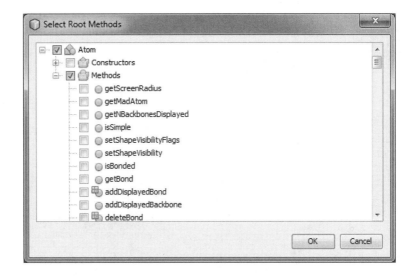

Inserting a Profile Point

Choosing Insert Profiling Point inserts a new profiling point into the code. This
displays the dialog box shown in Figure 10-43. There are five different types of
profile points listed next. Which profile point to select really depends upon the
task at hand.

- **Reset Results**   Resets the profiling results. This is often used to create diffs
  that can then be compared.
- **Stopwatch**   Used to output a timestamp and measure the time differences
  within a method fragment.
- **Take Snapshot**   Takes a snapshot of the current collected results and then
  saves it for further analysis.
- **Timed Take Snapshot**   Takes a snapshot at a specific time. For example,
  this can be used to generate a snapshot if a batch process application fails
  every night in the middle of a run.
- **Triggered Take Snapshot**   Takes a memory snapshot when a constraint such
  as available heap space, surviving generations, used heap space, or allocated
  heap reaches a specific threshold. Only available for memory snapshots.

Reset Results   The Reset Results profiling point clears the statistics that have
been collected. This is useful in combination with the Take Snapshot profile point,
where the objective is to perform a diff. For example, place a Reset Results profile

FIGURE 10-43

New Profiling
Point

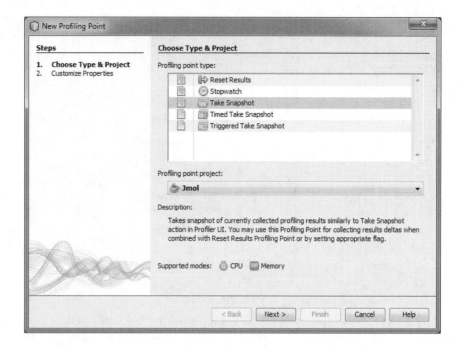

point in code before a file is loaded. After the file is loaded, use a Take Snapshot profile point to capture either memory or CPU statistics. You then know how many objects were created as a part of the open or where CPU resources were spent while loading. Figure 10-44 displays the configuration settings for a new Reset Results profile point. The settings include:

- **Name**   Name of the profile point; includes the line number by default for readability.
- **File**   The file in which the project point belongs.
- **Line**   Line number on which the profile point is to be set along with whether the action should be performed before or after the line executes.

Stopwatch   The Stopwatch profile point enables the recording of a timestamp or the timing of a series of operations. The dialog box for creating a new Stopwatch profile point is shown in Figure 10-45. If Timestamp is selected when the Stopwatch profile point is tripped, the current time is recorded. If the Timestamp And Duration option is selected, then the start time and total execution time are recorded. The File and Line number for the profile point are also specified. The profile point can

FIGURE 10-44

New Profiling
Point: Reset
Results

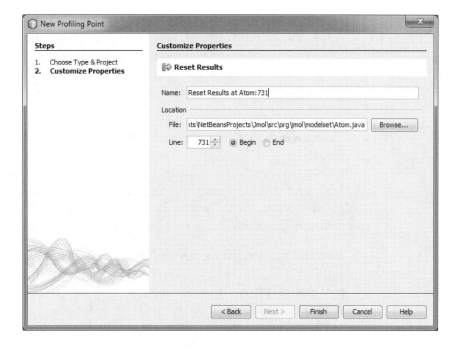

FIGURE 10-44

New Profiling
Point: Reset
Results

FIGURE 10-45

New Profiling
Point: Stopwatch

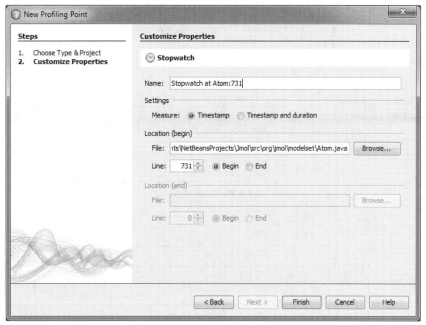

be executed either before the line executes or after it finishes. The end location is only enabled if the duration is being recorded. When you're editing an existing Stopwatch profile point, a button to the right is displayed with the text "Current Line." This button automatically populates the File and Line number boxes with the current cursor position. Stopwatch results are shown in Figure 10-46. Clicking the Report link shown in Figure 10-40 opens the results.

Take Snapshot The Take Snapshot profile point takes either a Profiling Data Snapshot or a Heap Dump. It is configured in the dialog box shown in Figure 10-47. A Profiling Data Snapshot is either a memory or thread snapshot depending upon the type of profiling being performed. Each time the profile point is triggered, a snapshot is generated. The snapshot can be saved either to the project or to a local directory. Optionally data collection can be reset after taking the snapshot.

Timed Take Snapshot A Timed Take Snapshot generates either a profile snapshot or a heap dump at a specific time or repeatedly with a time delay. It is configured using the dialog box shown in Figure 10-48. The type of profile snapshot generated depends upon whether CPU or memory monitoring is being performed. The snapshot or dump can either be saved to the project or to a local directory. Optionally, when the snapshot is taken, collected data can be reset. Unlike previous profile points, this one is not tied to a specific code location; instead it is triggered by an alarm. It can fire just once, or it can fire repeatedly at a predefined interval. This profile point lets long-running processes be monitored easily. For example, this could be used to track the performance of an application as it undergoes load testing over a period of several hours.

FIGURE 10-46

Stopwatch results

getJmol execution time!:331

Type: Stopwatch
Enabled: true
Project: Jmol
Start location: JmolPanel.java, line 331
End location: JmolPanel.java, line 350
Measure: Timestamp and duration
Hits: 1

Data:
1. hit at **18:16:44.833**, duration **206,836.08 μs**

FIGURE 10-47

New Profiling
Point: Take
Snapshot

FIGURE 10-47

New Profiling
Point: Take
Snapshot

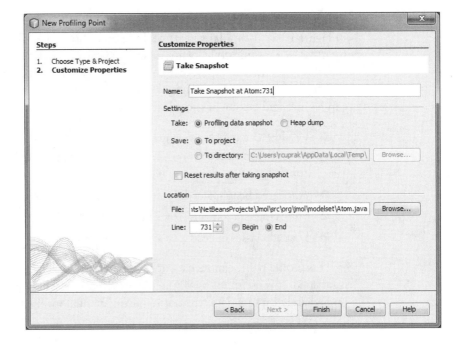

FIGURE 10-48

New Profiling
Point: Timed Take
Snapshot

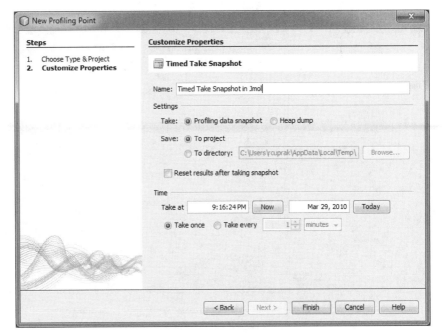

Triggered Take Snapshot   A Triggered Take Snapshot, its configuration shown in Figure 10-49, is similar to a Time Take Snapshot. Like a Timed Take Snapshot it isn't tied to a specific code location, and it also can generate either a CPU or memory snapshot, or a heap dump. It also can reset collected results. Where it differs is with the trigger that causes a snapshot or dump to be generated. A Triggered Take Snapshot can be initiated by one of the following conditions:

- Used heap exceeds a certain percentage of the total heap. For example, a snapshot could be generated when 98 percent of the heap has been consumed.
- Allocated heap exceeds a predefined number of megabytes.
- Surviving generations exceed a specified number.
- Loaded classes exceed a specified number.

This profile point can be executed just once or each time the trigger condition is satisfied. It is useful for hard to replicate situations where you want the profiler to immediately capture data without requiring manual intervention.

FIGURE 10-49

New Profiling Point: Triggered Take Snapshot

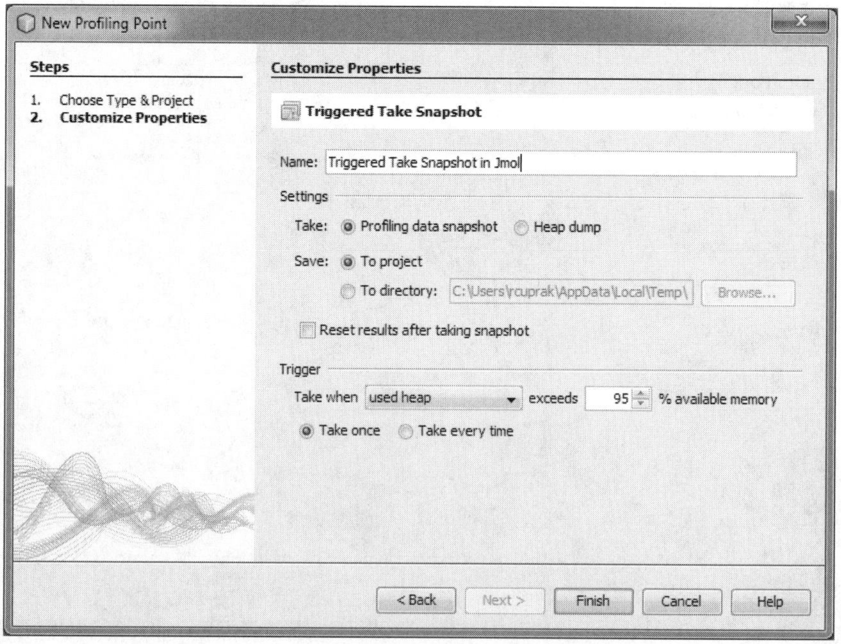

Understanding Memory Usage

Memory profiling is a useful tool for understanding and exploring object creation and longevity. Creating an object and cleaning up after an object take time. When an object is created, space must be allocated on the heap and references tracked. When the object is no longer needed, the garbage collector must verify that the object is not reachable and compact memory to avoid fragmentation. Thus, needless object creation can have a significant impact upon performance that would not be visible from examining thread activity. This type of profiling seeks to answer:

- Between two points in time how many objects were created?
- What objects were created?
- How long did the objects live?
- How many of these objects were reachable at the end?
- How many generations did the objects survive?

These questions can be answered by profiling memory use. The insight gained can then be used to optimize the code and reduce needless object creation. NetBeans facilitates this type of profiling. In addition, NetBeans can optionally track the creator of a class by capturing the stack trace. This is the Record Stack Trace For Allocations setting. This setting makes it possible to find who is instantiating the objects, which is extremely useful when tracking down memory leaks.

The following topics are covered in this section:

- Configuring for Memory Analysis
- Capturing Snapshots
- Viewing Live Results
- Comparing Allocations

Configuring for Memory Analysis

Initiating a memory profiling session is done by choosing Profile | Profile Main Project or Profile | Attach Profiler. You can also initiate a session by clicking the menu item Profile | Profile Other or right-clicking a class with a main method or JUnit test and choosing Profile File. When the Profile dialog box appears, select Memory, as shown in Figure 10-50. The basic settings are displayed by default. The following settings can be configured:

- **Record Object Creation Only**   This setting causes the profiler to track the number of objects instantiated, their type, and bytes allocated.

FIGURE 10-50

Analyze Memory

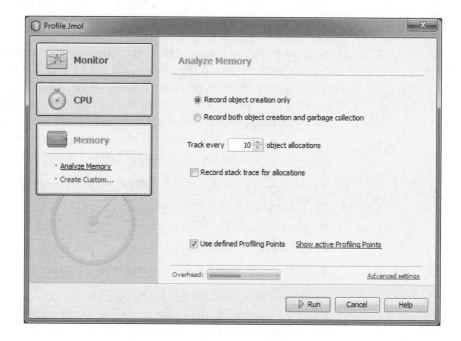

- **Record Both Object Creation And Garbage Collection** This setting causes the profiler to track the number of objects instantiated, their type, bytes allocated, average age, generations, and objects that are live (reachable). Tracking this additional information significantly increases the overhead over the first option.

- **Track Every *n* Object Allocations** This option sets the interval/proportion for stack sampling. This controls the granularity of the data being collected. A value of 1 means that every object allocation is recorded, whereas a value of 10 means that every tenth object is captured. The lower the number the higher the overhead.

- **Record Stack Trace For Allocations** This option causes the profiler to record the stack when an object is created. Using this, you can find out who is instantiating the objects.

- **Use Defined Profiling Points** This enables the use of profiling points.

These settings can have a dramatic impact upon the performance of the application. If a large application is being profiled, there are several ways to reduce the performance penalty:

- Set root methods so that you collect information only on problematic application parts.
- Record only object creations.
- Set a reasonable allocation sampling value. A number too low with a long-running application can generate a tremendous amount of information.
- Record stack traces only when necessary.

The NetBeans Profiler can generate an overwhelming deluge of information. To focus the information generated, use profiling points and reset the collected data so that your analysis is targeted. Java applications generate thousands of objects, so a strategy is needed if the results are to be analyzed and correctly interpreted.

Additional advanced settings are available if a custom configuration is created. The advanced settings are shown in Figure 10-51. The parameters grouped under Settings pertain to memory profiling. The Threads and Global Settings parameters

FIGURE 10-51

Custom memory profile configuration

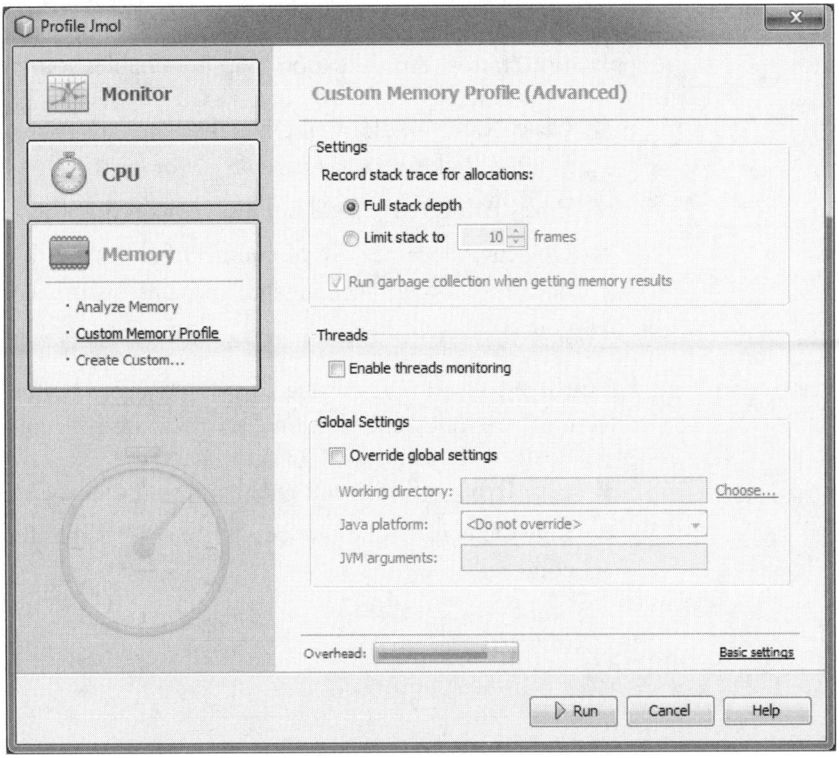

are discussed in the section on monitoring. The custom memory profiling settings are as follows:

- **Record Stack Trace For Allocations** Either the full stack trace or just a subset of the stack trace can be recorded. For example, this is useful when working on a GUI application, because you don't often care about the portion of the stack that invoked the menu item. Also, the more stack frames that are recorded, the bigger the impact upon performance.
- **Run Garbage Collection When Getting Memory Results** This setting gives you a better picture of what objects are actually live (reachable). This does result in a performance penalty.

The first advanced setting is only enabled if stack traces are being collected.

Capturing Snapshots

Snapshots capture allocations made since the last reset. If there have been no resets, either from a profiling point or manually, then the allocation history extends to application startup. An allocation snapshot enables you to see the following:

- **Class Name—Allocated Objects** The type of the object instantiated. Double-clicking a row opens an editor for the class.
- **Bytes Allocated** Total number of bytes that the instances are consuming.
- **Objects Allocated** Total number of objects instantiated. This includes objects that have been created and subsequently collected by the garbage collector.

If garbage collection is included, that is, "Record both object creation and garbage collection," the following additional statistics are collected:

- **Live Bytes** Total number of bytes that the live objects are consuming.
- **Live Objects** Total number of live objects that have not been garbage collected.

- **Avg. Age** Average age of the objects in generations.
- **Generations** The number of different surviving generations that are currently alive on the heap.

Snapshots are captured either manually in NetBeans by clicking Take Snapshot in the Profiling Results group within the Profiler window or by a profiling point. A toolbar button is also present on Live Results for capturing snapshots. A snapshot opens in an editor tab with the timestamp prefixed with the word "Memory." Snapshots created manually are not persisted until they are explicitly saved. An example snapshot is shown in Figure 10-52.

FIGURE 10-52   Memory: Results

Class Name - Allocated Objects	Bytes Allocated ▼		Bytes Allocated		Objects Allocated	
org.jmol.viewer.**ScriptManager**			32 B	(0%)	1	(0%)
org.jmol.viewer.**DataManager**			32 B	(0%)	1	(0%)
org.jmol.viewer.**ActionManager$Mouse**			32 B	(0%)	5	(0%)
org.jmol.viewer.**ActionManager$Gesture**			32 B	(0%)	1	(0%)
org.jmol.util.**TempArray**			32 B	(0%)	1	(0%)
org.jmol.util.**CommandHistory**			32 B	(0%)	1	(0%)
org.jmol.modelset.**TickInfo[]**			32 B	(0%)	2	(0%)
org.jmol.modelset.**Molecule[]**			32 B	(0%)	1	(0%)
org.jmol.modelset.**BoxInfo**			32 B	(0%)	1	(0%)
org.jmol.modelset.**Bond[][][]**			32 B	(0%)	1	(0%)
org.jmol.modelset.**BondIteratorSelected**			32 B	(0%)	2	(0%)
org.jmol.g3d.**Normix3D**			32 B	(0%)	1	(0%)
org.jmol.g3d.**Circle3D**			32 B	(0%)	1	(0%)
org.jmol.atomdata.**RadiusData**			24 B	(0%)	1	(0%)
org.jmol.export.history.**HistoryFile**			24 B	(0%)	1	(0%)
org.jmol.i18n.**GT**			24 B	(0%)	1	(0%)
org.jmol.viewer.**ModelManager**			24 B	(0%)	1	(0%)
org.jmol.viewer.**MouseManager14**			24 B	(0%)	1	(0%)
org.jmol.viewer.**RepaintManager**			24 B	(0%)	1	(0%)
org.jmol.api.**JmolSelectionListener[]**			16 B	(0%)	1	(0%)
org.jmol.console.**ScriptEditor$EditorDocument$MyUndoableEditListener**			16 B	(0%)	1	(0%)
org.jmol.g3d.**Graphics3D$Pixel**			16 B	(0%)	3	(0%)
org.jmol.modelset.**Atom[]**			16 B	(0%)	3	(0%)
org.jmol.modelset.**Group[]**			16 B	(0%)	1	(0%)
org.jmol.modelset.**Model[]**			16 B	(0%)	2	(0%)
org.jmol.util.**Int2IntHash**			16 B	(0%)	1	(0%)
org.jmol.viewer.**ActionManager$HoverWatcher**			16 B	(0%)	1	(0%)

org.jmol

Memory Results   Allocation Stack Traces   Info

FIGURE 10-53 Memory: Allocation Stack Traces

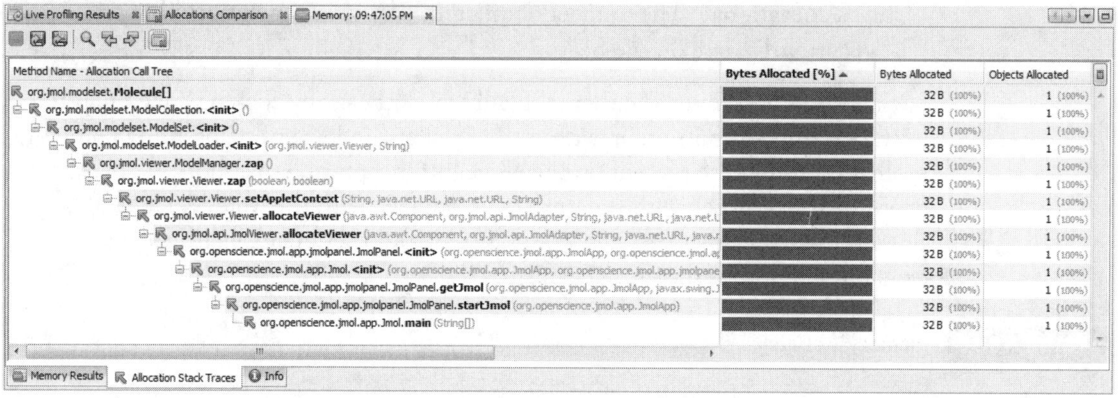

If stack traces are collected while profiling, right-clicking a class in Figure 10-52 and choosing Show Allocation Stack Traces opens the tab shown in Figure 10-53. The tab Allocation Stack Traces lists the different instances and where they were initially created. This is useful for determining who is creating the instances.

Results from Figures 10-52 and 10-53 can be exported for analysis in another application such as Microsoft Excel. A screenshot of the graph or table can be saved for inclusion in reports.

Viewing Live Results

While the application is running, the profiling data can be viewed live. Live Results are displayed by clicking the Live Results icon in the Profiling Results panel of the Profiler window. An example Live Profiling Results view is shown in Figure 10-54. As an application runs, the view dynamically changes. By default, the table is sorted with objects consuming the most heap space at the top. The columns are the same as for the memory snapshots. The available toolbar icons are the same as for the CPU profiling live results in Figure 10-38.

Live Profiling Results

Class Name - Allocated Objects	Bytes Allocated ▾	Bytes Allocated	Objects Allocated
char[]		663,144 B (31.6%)	70,392 (20.7%)
byte[]		380,960 B (18.1%)	1,756 (0.5%)
java.lang.String		185,328 B (8.8%)	73,403 (21.6%)
int[]		52,880 B (2.5%)	2,763 (0.8%)
org.jmol.adapter.smarter.Atom		48,496 B (2.3%)	4,132 (1.2%)
org.jmol.modelset.Atom		38,280 B (1.8%)	4,132 (1.2%)
java.lang.Object[]		35,232 B (1.7%)	7,047 (2.1%)
short[]		34,608 B (1.6%)	197 (0.1%)
sun.java2d.SunGraphics2D		33,800 B (1.6%)	1,589 (0.5%)
java.util.Hashtable$Entry		32,064 B (1.5%)	12,652 (3.7%)
java.lang.StringBuilder		31,904 B (1.5%)	18,809 (5.5%)
java.util.Hashtable$Entry[]		22,040 B (1%)	1,316 (0.4%)
java.lang.Class[]		20,120 B (1%)	9,685 (2.9%)
long[]		17,560 B (0.8%)	616 (0.2%)
sun.java2d.d3d.D3DSurfaceData$D3DWindowSurfaceData[		16,992 B (0.8%)	10,141 (3%)
org.jmol.modelset.Atom[]		16,576 B (0.8%)	17 (0%)
java.awt.Rectangle		15,960 B (0.8%)	6,373 (1.9%)
org.jmol.modelset.Bond[]		14,496 B (0.7%)	6,624 (2%)
org.jmol.bspt.Node		13,776 B (0.7%)	2,772 (0.8%)
org.jmol.modelset.Bond		13,216 B (0.6%)	3,972 (1.2%)
java.lang.Integer		13,152 B (0.6%)	7,869 (2.3%)
java.awt.geom.AffineTransform		11,264 B (0.5%)	1,700 (0.5%)
java.beans.PropertyChangeEvent		10,848 B (0.5%)	3,223 (0.9%)
java.util.concurrent.locks.AbstractQueuedSynchronizer$Node		10,240 B (0.5%)	2,977 (0.9%)
sun.java2d.loops.GraphicsPrimitive[]		9,312 B (0.4%)	51 (0%)
java.lang.String[]		7,944 B (0.4%)	2,635 (0.8%)

[Class Name Filter]

Live Results | History of java.awt.Point

Right-clicking a class in Figure 10-54 and choosing Log Class History switches to the History tab, shown in Figure 10-55. In this view, we can track the number of objects instantiated for a particular class and the number of bytes they are consuming over time. Only one class can be viewed at a time.

FIGURE 10-55 History

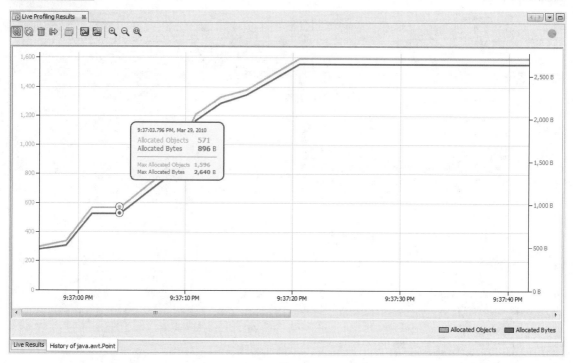

Comparing Allocations

One very handy feature of the NetBeans memory profiler is its ability to compare memory snapshots. Comparing memory snapshots enables you to quickly see what has changed. For example, you could take a snapshot before and after opening a file to see what objects were created. Or you could try two different algorithms for solving a particular problem, generate snapshots, and then compare them to see which one generated more or fewer objects.

Comparing memory snapshots is a powerful feature that can be used to track application memory performance over time. Before embarking on a refactoring job, a snapshot could be captured and then compared afterwards to evaluate the impact on memory utilization. This could also be done when new features are added.

An example memory comparison is shown in Figure 10-56. Here we can see the impact of opening a molecule in Jmol. Increases in objects created are shown as red bars that grow to the right. Decreases are represented as green bars that extend to the left. Profiles are compared by choosing Profile | Compare Memory Snapshots or by clicking the toolbar icon in a memory snapshot for performing a comparison. The memory snapshots compared do not have to be from the same JVM or even from the same application. For example, you could test the impact that upgrading to the latest JVM would have on memory use by comparing a snapshot running on one VM to another. This could also be done when evaluating app servers or other external libraries for inclusion in a project.

FIGURE 10-56   Allocations Comparison

Live Profiling Results ✕	Allocations Comparison ✕			
			Comparison of 09:47:05 PM to 09:49:38 PM	
Class Name - Allocated Objects	Bytes Allocated ▼	Bytes Allocated	Objects Allocated	
org.jmol.adapter.smarter.**Atom**	▉	+48,944 B	+4,132	
org.jmol.modelset.**Atom**	▊	+38,280 B	+4,132	
org.jmol.bspt.**Node**	▏	+14,016 B	+2,772	
org.jmol.modelset.**Bond[]**	▏	+13,280 B	+6,622	
org.jmol.modelset.**Bond**	▏	+13,184 B	+3,972	
org.jmol.bspt.**Leaf**	▏	+7,008 B	+2,773	
org.jmol.symmetry.**SpaceGroup**	▏	+5,544 B	+594	
org.jmol.modelsetbio.**AminoMonomer**	▏	+4,576 B	+484	
org.jmol.symmetry.**SpaceGroup[]**	▏	+2,384 B	+1	
org.jmol.script.**ScriptVariable**	▏	+2,208 B	+645	
org.jmol.modelset.**Group[]**	▏	+2,144 B	+20	
org.jmol.modelset.**Group**	▏	+1,736 B	+263	
org.jmol.modelset.**Bond[][]**	▏	+1,632 B	+20	
org.jmol.modelsetbio.**Monomer[]**	▏	+1,312 B	+3	
org.jmol.adapter.smarter.**Atom[]**	▏	+1,040 B	+6	
org.jmol.adapter.smarter.**Bond[]**	▏	+1,040 B	+1	
org.jmol				

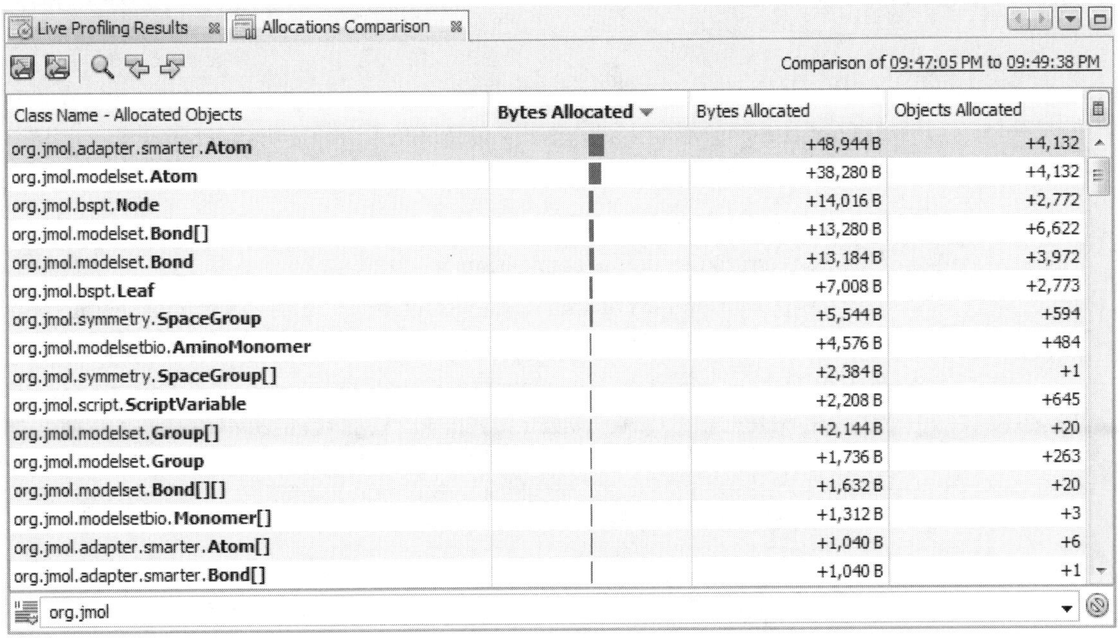

EXERCISE 10-6

Memory Profiling

In this exercise, you evaluate the memory footprints of using a `java.util` `.LinkedList` versus a `java.util.ArrayList`. Although the same number of objects is known ahead of time, we want to see the impact upon the heap of having to repeatedly resize an array.

1. Create a new Java project by choosing File | New Project and selecting Java Application from the Java category.

2. Change the contents of the main method to match this code:

```java
public static void main(String[] args) throws Exception {
  List<String> list = new ArrayList<String>();
  for(int i = 0; i < 10000; i++) {
    list.add("Hello World");
  }
}
```

3. Profile the application by choosing Profile | Profile Main Project.

4. Choose Memory profiling.

5. Change object allocation tracking to 1.

6. Click Run to profile the application.

7. The application runs quickly and exits. NetBeans prompts you for saving the memory snapshot for the session. Accept and save the snapshot to the project.

8. Change the code so that you're using a `LinkedList` instead of an `ArrayList`:

```java
public static void main(String[] args) throws Exception {
  List<String> list = new LinkedList<String>();
  for(int i = 0; i < 10000; i++) {
    list.add("Hello World");
  }
}
```

9. Profile the application again and save the snapshot to the project.

10. When a snapshot is taken, a tab is automatically opened in the IDE. With the last snapshot open, click the toolbar icon "Compare the difference between two comparable memory snapshots" to see the differences.

11. What's different between these two runs?

12. For each memory snapshot, look over the list of objects created.

At the end of this exercise you may be puzzled by the results. Shouldn't 10,000 `Strings` have been created? The JVM is quite intelligent, and it knows that the `String` class is immutable—hence only one instance is created. If you use another object such as a `javax.swing.JFrame`, you would see 10,000 `javax.swing .JFrame` instances. However, that still doesn't explain the number of `Strings` created.

To better understand the number of `Strings` created, you can profile again and choose Record Stack Trace For Allocations to see where they are being instantiated. In the next section you learn how to inspect the content of the Strings.

Using the HeapWalker

The previous section covered memory profiling, which captures comprehensive statistics on the number of objects being created and destroyed as well as who instantiated them. The next question that naturally arises is how you find out what the objects contain. In Exercise 10-5, although we created just one `String`, the memory profile showed numerous instances.

What did the other instances contain? Knowing this bit of information can help trace memory leaks and get a better handle on the contents of the heap. This is where the heap analysis support in NetBeans comes into play.

The NetBeans Profiler can dump the contents of the Java heap to a file. Dumping the contents of a heap to a file is similar to creating a snapshot. In fact, all of the profile points support either generating a snapshot or a heap dump. A heap dump can also be manually generated by choosing Profile | Take Heap Dump. While a memory or CPU profile session is running, a toolbar icon is also present in the Live Results tab. Once the heap is captured, the NetBeans HeapWalker tool can be used for viewing and querying the heap.

Using the HeapWalker does not require that the application be profiled with NetBeans. The NetBeans HeapWalker reads in and analyzes heaps in the HPROF format. A heap dump created outside of NetBeans can be loaded into the HeapWalker by choosing Profile | Load Heap Dump. The following command line generates a heap dump for any running Java process:

```
jmap -dump:format=b,file=snapshot2.jmap <pid>
```

The *pid* is the process identifier that is retrieved from the Task Manager in Windows or via the `ps` command on Unix-based systems. The `jmap` command-line application is included with the JDK. The command-line application `jhat` can also read the heap file and browse it.

To generate a heap dump, choose Profile | Take Heap Dump. This displays the dialog box shown in Figure 10-57. The heap dump can be saved either to the project or to a local directory. Heap dumps saved to the project appear under Saved Snapshots in the Profiler window.

Once a heap dump is generated, NetBeans prompts for whether the heap dump should be opened in the HeapWalker. Opening the heap in the HeapWalker displays the window in Figure 10-58. This window is split into four tabs:

- **Summary** This tab displays basic summary information including:
  - Basic JVM info
  - Environment settings including the operating system and Java version
  - System properties
  - Threads running at the time of the heap dump
- **Classes** This is a list of classes present on the heap. Double-clicking a class opens it on the Instances tab.
- **Instances** This is a list of instances of a class. You can browse the fields for each class, and see who is referencing them. This is useful for figuring out who is holding onto a reference and thus causing a memory leak.
- **OQL Console** This an interactive console for entering Object Query Language (OQL) queries. This enables you to search the heap using SQL-like expressions.

The first tab is shown in Figure 10-58. This tab summarizes the basic information about the JVM. On this tab you can find:

- Total number of classes.
- Total number of class instances contained in the file.

FIGURE 10-57

Choose
Heap Dump
Destination

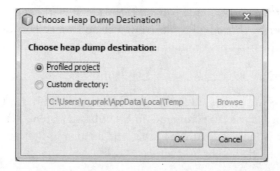

FIGURE 10-58 HeapWalker: Summary tab

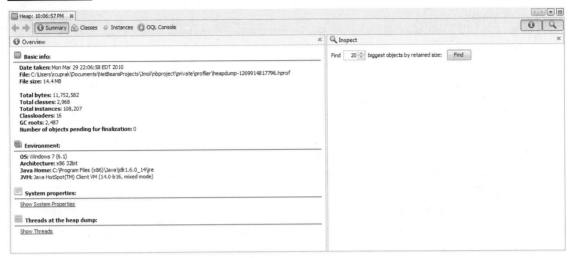

- Number of garbage collection roots.
- Version of the operating system.
- Specific Java installation instance being used.
- Specific Java version being used.
- A dump of system properties, which includes the classpath and parameters passed to the JVM among other things.
- A dump of threads with their current points of execution. Line numbers are available if the code was compiled with debug symbols.

The second tab, shown in Figure 10-59, displays the list of classes that have been loaded. These are not class instances, but classes that were loaded by the JVM and subsequently instantiated or cached. This table includes some useful information including:

- Percent of the heap occupied by a class
- Number of instances created
- Total space occupied by the instances

HeapWalker: Classes tab

Class Name	Instances [%] ▼	Instances		Size	
org.jmol.modelset.**Atom**	I	4132	(3.8%)	363616	(3.1%)
org.jmol.modelset.**Bond**	I	3972	(3.7%)	127104	(1.1%)
org.jmol.modelset.**Bond[]**	I	3875	(3.6%)	78664	(0.7%)
org.jmol.bspt.**Leaf**	I	2773	(2.6%)	55460	(0.5%)
org.jmol.bspt.**Node**	I	2772	(2.6%)	121968	(1%)
org.jmol.script.**Token**			711	(0.7%)	14220	(0.1%)
org.jmol.symmetry.**SpaceGroup**		593	(0.5%)	50405	(0.4%)
org.jmol.modelsetbio.**AminoMonomer**		484	(0.4%)	38720	(0.3%)
org.jmol.g3d.**Rgb16**		266	(0.2%)	5320	(0%)
org.jmol.modelset.**Group**		263	(0.2%)	14465	(0.1%)
org.jmol.modelset.**ModelCollection$Structure**		41	(0%)	1681	(0%)
org.jmol.viewer.**ActionManager$MotionPoint**		40	(0%)	1280	(0%)
org.jmol.modelsetbio.**Sheet**		31	(0%)	2263	(0%)
org.jmol.i18n.**GT$Language**		27	(0%)	459	(0%)
org.jmol.util.**Int2IntHash$Entry**		24	(0%)	480	(0%)
org.jmol.util.**Point3fi**		24	(0%)	960	(0%)
org.jmol.script.**ScriptVariable**		13	(0%)	416	(0%)
org.jmol.modelset.**Bond[][]**		12	(0%)	9696	(0.1%)
org.jmol.viewer.**ActionManager$Mouse**		10	(0%)	320	(0%)
org.jmol.modelsetbio.**Helix**		7	(0%)	427	(0%)

org.jmol

Double-clicking a class in Figure 10-59 switches to the Instances tab shown in Figure 10-60. This tab is split up into three panels:

- **Instances**   A list containing all of the instances of this object type in the heap.
- **Fields**   Selecting an instance brings up a list of its fields that can be browsed. Double-clicking a field switches the view to that instance.
- **References**   Using this view, you can see who is referencing this object. This is extremely useful when troubleshooting memory leaks.

On this tab you can browse specific instances and drill into them. You can see their instance variables and, most importantly, who is maintaining references to them. Knowing who is maintaining references is invaluable when trying to locate a memory leak. For example, you could see an object was still being stored in a `java.util.List` and then drill up to the owner of the list.

FIGURE 10-60   HeapWalker: Instances

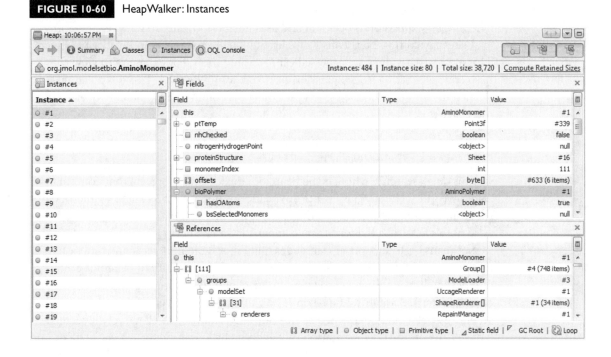

The fourth tab in the HeapWalker is the OQL Console, shown in Figure 10-61. This is one of the most exciting features of the HeapWalker. While the Instances tab is extremely useful, the amount of information can be overwhelming. A given application can have thousands of String instances. The challenge becomes sorting through all of these instances and finding the ones of interest.

The HeapWalker's OQL Console uses the Object Query Language. This language is modeled on SQL and developed by the Object Data Management Group. With this language, the contents of the heap can be filtered, sorted, and analyzed. OQL is also used by the `jhat` tool, which has similar functionality. Documentation OQL queries for `jhat` are applicable to NetBeans. A query has the following form:

```
select <JavaScript expression to select> [ from [instanceof] <class name>
<identifier> [ where <JavaScript boolean expression to filter> ] ]
```

The class name is a fully qualified name, for example, `java.lang.String`. The `where` expression is optional and uses JavaScript. The `select` expression evaluates JavaScript. NetBeans wraps up the Java heap objects in JavaScript objects. This means that values are accessed using dot notation. For example, to view the hash code of a String, the expression `s.hash` would be used. The `s` is a variable defined in the `from` clause—each Java object is bound to a variable. A query best illustrates this:

```
select s.toString() from java.lang.String s
  where s.toString() == "Hello World"
```

This query searches through the heap looking for String objects that contain "Hello World". The `toString()` invocation is not the `toString()` method on the instance you are querying in the heap. It is a JavaScript `toString()` method. Also note the "==", used for String comparison in JavaScript.

NetBeans OQL support also includes numerous built-in objects and functions that can be used in the queries. These objects and built-in functions provide a range of functionality enabling you to query for reachability, to filter, determine the size of objects, compare equality, and so on. The exam will not cover OQL in depth, and an entire book could be devoted to this language and how to effectively leverage it. Consult the online documentation in NetBeans by searching for "OQL." The online documentation lists all of the built-in functions and objects and includes numerous examples.

FIGURE 10-61   HeapWalker: OQL Console

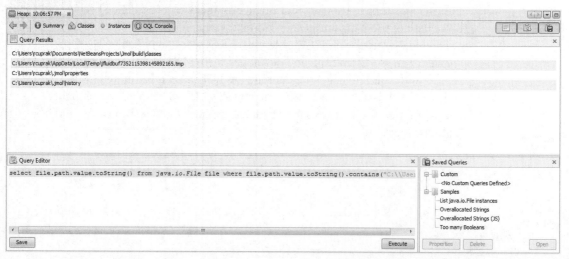

exam

w a t c h   *The OQL queries are not against Java objects. Although the contents of Strings are being queried and you might see examples with methods that exist in Java, these methods are actually JavaScript methods. You cannot invoke String methods to perform evaluations when working with a heap dump. You are accessing the raw properties through a JavaScript wrapper instance. This means that if the property is computed, it isn't available.*

EXERCISE 10-7

Memory Profiling

In this exercise, you search through the Java heap for a particular String instance. This exercise builds on Exercise 10-5. In Exercise 10-5 we expected 10,000 String instances to be created. Memory profiling showed only 34 instances. We determine how many of the String instances contain "Hello World" and count how many instances refer to these instances.

1. Modify the code from Exercise 10-5 with the following addition:

```
public class TestClass {
    public static void main(String[] args) throws Exception {
      List<String> list = new ArrayList<String>();
      for(int i = 0; i < 10000; i++) {
        list.add("Hello World");
      }
      System.out.println("Snap!");
    }
}
```

2. Select the line with `System.out.println("Snap!");` and right-click, choosing Profiling | Insert Profiling Point.

3. Select Take Snapshot and click Next.

4. Select Heap Dump and click Finish.

5. Profile the project by choosing Profile | Profile Main Project.

6. Choose CPU profiling and click run.

7. The application launches and quits. A new heap dump is automatically captured.

8. Open the heap dump from the Saved Snapshots in the Profiler window.

9. Switch to the OQL Console tab.

10. Search for the "Hello World" String by performing the following search:

```
select s.toString() from java.lang.String s
   where s.toString() == "Hello World"
```

11. Notice that there was only one hit. Now issue the following query to determine how many classes refer to this instance:

```
select count(referrers(s)) from java.lang.String s
   where s.toString() == "Hello World"
```

12. Observe that "Hello World" was referred to 10,000 times.

13. To view who is referring to "Hello World", issue the following query:

```
select referrers(s) from java.lang.String s
   where s.toString() == "Hello World"
```

14. To view an entry, click it and the instance opens in the Instances tab.

In Exercise 10-5 the memory dump contained unexpected String instances. Issuing a query to count the number of String instances turns up considerably more this time. The previous memory snapshot did not include the myriad JVM Strings that are created by the JVM.

CERTIFICATION SUMMARY

This chapter covered JUnit integration and the NetBeans Profiler. Both of these features are invaluable tools for testing and verifying application behavior. JUnit is used for testing small granular units of application functionality to verify that that basic functionality works. JUnits form the basis of a regression suite to be executed regularly to confirm expected behavior. Profiling is used to explore the performance aspects of an application at runtime. Using a profiler, you can answer questions such as how many objects are being created, who is creating the objects, how long objects are living, as well as what the CPU and throughput bottlenecks are.

The first section of this chapter covered JUnit. JUnit topics covered included how to create new JUnit tests, run the JUnit tests, and view the results. Importantly, the different versions of JUnit supported by NetBeans were covered along with information on projects mixing versions. The last part of the section briefly discussed NetBeans' Hudson integration, which enables unit tests to be run on a regular basis and monitored within the IDE.

The last half of this chapter covered the NetBeans Profiler. The NetBeans Profiler has three different modes: simple monitoring, CPU analysis, and memory analysis. NetBeans generates a calibration profile that is used to factor out the overhead of the profiler instrumentation. NetBeans can profile any Java application—either from a NetBeans project or running remotely on another machine. Monitoring provides basic telemetry information on the VM including heap usages, number of classes loaded, garbage collection impact, and thread activity. CPU analysis provides in-depth accounting of the time spent in methods. Memory analysis is used for tracking and understanding object creation and destruction. Memory snapshots can be generated, compared, and saved. In both CPU and memory profiling, profiling points can be used to trigger snapshots and reset results. The profiler also includes facilities for generating and reading heaps. A heap snapshot can be loaded into the HeapWalker, and the contents of the heap can be either browsed or searched using OQL.

✓ # TWO-MINUTE DRILL

Testing Applications with JUnit

- ❑ NetBeans supports JUnit 3.*x* and JUnit 4.*x*.
- ❑ NetBeans prompts on the first unit test being created for the JUnit version.
- ❑ NetBeans automatically adds either JUnit 3.*x* or JUnit 4.*x* libraries to the classpath.
- ❑ JUnit 4.*x* requires Java SE 5 or greater.
- ❑ JUnit 4.*x* makes extensive use of annotations.
- ❑ JUnit 3 and JUnit 4 conventions cannot be mixed in the same unit test case.
- ❑ Empty JUnit tests are created by choosing File | New File and selecting JUnit Test from the JUnit category.
- ❑ A JUnit for an existing class can be created by choosing File | New File and selecting Test For Existing Class from the JUnit category.
- ❑ A test suite for an existing class can be created by choosing File | New File and selecting Test Suite.
- ❑ JUnit test classes are placed in a test sources directory.
- ❑ A different classpath is used for unit test compiling and running unit tests.
- ❑ The unit testing classpath is configured in Project Properties on the Compile Tests and Run Tests tabs of the Libraries category.

Using the NetBeans Profiler

- ❑ NetBeans includes a built-in profiler.
- ❑ The profiler measures the performance of a Java application in terms of memory use and threading.
- ❑ A NetBeans project is not required to profile a Java application.
- ❑ Applications to be profiled can be either local or remote.
- ❑ Applications to be profiled can be started outside of NetBeans.
- ❑ The NetBeans Profiler has its own dedicated menu.
- ❑ Profile operations are launched either from the toolbar, by right-clicking a JUnit test or class with a main method, or from the first three options in the Profile menu.

❏ To launch the profiler on the current main project, choose Profile | Profile Main Project.

❏ To attach a profiler to a running application, choose Profile | Attach Profiler.

❏ Calibration is done before running the profiler for the first time.

❏ Calibration should be performed whenever there is a configuration change to a machine.

❏ Calibration and profiling are affected by low power consumption modes on laptops.

❏ Profiling is controlled from the Profiler window in NetBeans.

❏ The Profiler window is divided into six sections: Controls, Status, Profiling Results, Saved Snapshots, View, and Basic Telemetry.

❏ Windows related to the profiler can be reopened from Window | Profiler.

❏ There are three profiling modes: Monitor, Analyze CPU, Analyze Memory.

❏ Monitor mode displays basic VM telemetry information including thread state, memory utilization, and garbage collection.

❏ Telemetry data collected in the monitor mode is available in all the other profiling modes.

❏ CPU and memory profiling are mutually exclusive.

❏ CPU monitoring tracks the amount of time spent in methods and constructors.

❏ Methods profiled can be filtered to reduce the overhead and to target specific blocks of code.

❏ Time spent in `Thread.sleep` and `Object.wait()` can be excluded from profiled results.

❏ The number of threads profiled can be limited.

❏ There are two types of method tracking: "Exact call tree timing" and "Exact call tree, sampled timing."

❏ The three instrumentation schemes are Lazy, Eager, and Total.

❏ Live Results displays collected statistics in real time.

❏ The following profile points are supported: Reset Results, Stopwatch, Take Snapshot, Timed Take Snapshot, Triggered Take Snapshots.

❏ The Reset Results profile point clears either CPU or memory profile data.

❏ The Stopwatch profile point can either print a timestamp or compute the elapsed time between two execution points.

❏ Take Snapshot can capture CPU, memory, or heap snapshots when a specific line of code is executed.

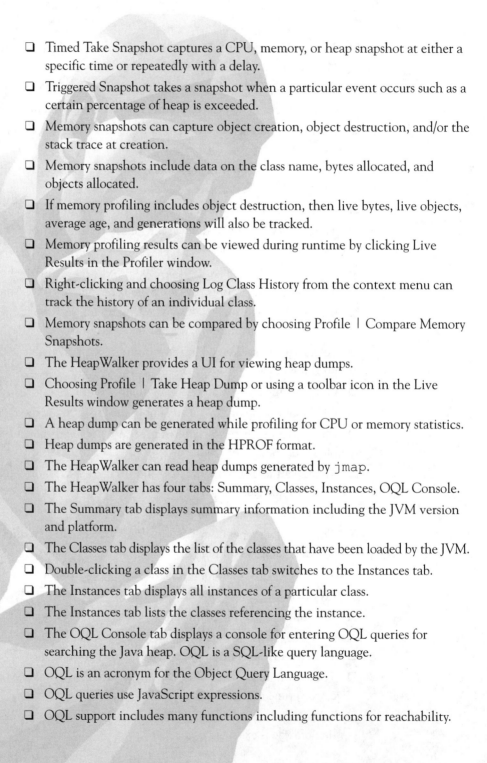

❏ Timed Take Snapshot captures a CPU, memory, or heap snapshot at either a specific time or repeatedly with a delay.

❏ Triggered Snapshot takes a snapshot when a particular event occurs such as a certain percentage of heap is exceeded.

❏ Memory snapshots can capture object creation, object destruction, and/or the stack trace at creation.

❏ Memory snapshots include data on the class name, bytes allocated, and objects allocated.

❏ If memory profiling includes object destruction, then live bytes, live objects, average age, and generations will also be tracked.

❏ Memory profiling results can be viewed during runtime by clicking Live Results in the Profiler window.

❏ Right-clicking and choosing Log Class History from the context menu can track the history of an individual class.

❏ Memory snapshots can be compared by choosing Profile | Compare Memory Snapshots.

❏ The HeapWalker provides a UI for viewing heap dumps.

❏ Choosing Profile | Take Heap Dump or using a toolbar icon in the Live Results window generates a heap dump.

❏ A heap dump can be generated while profiling for CPU or memory statistics.

❏ Heap dumps are generated in the HPROF format.

❏ The HeapWalker can read heap dumps generated by `jmap`.

❏ The HeapWalker has four tabs: Summary, Classes, Instances, OQL Console.

❏ The Summary tab displays summary information including the JVM version and platform.

❏ The Classes tab displays the list of the classes that have been loaded by the JVM.

❏ Double-clicking a class in the Classes tab switches to the Instances tab.

❏ The Instances tab displays all instances of a particular class.

❏ The Instances tab lists the classes referencing the instance.

❏ The OQL Console tab displays a console for entering OQL queries for searching the Java heap. OQL is a SQL-like query language.

❏ OQL is an acronym for the Object Query Language.

❏ OQL queries use JavaScript expressions.

❏ OQL support includes many functions including functions for reachability.

SELF TEST

The following questions will help you measure your understanding of the material presented in this chapter. Read all the choices carefully because there might be more than one correct answer. Choose all correct answers for each question.

Testing Applications with JUnit

1. What key shortcut will test the main project?
   A. CTRL-N
   B. CTRL-M
   C. ALT-F6
   D. F8

2. When does NetBeans prompt for the version of JUnit to be used for a project?
   A. After the first JUnit is added to a project.
   B. When the project is initially created.
   C. NetBeans does not prompt; it is automatically set to the most recent version included with the IDE.
   D. JUnit must be manually added to the classpath.

3. You would like to generate JUnit test classes for each class in a package. You would also like to generate a test suite for all of the tests. How would you go about doing this?
   A. Select the package containing the classes in the Projects window and press CTRL-SHIFT-U.
   B. Select the package containing the classes in the Projects window and right-click, choosing Tools | Create JUnit Tests.
   C. Both A and B.
   D. JUnit tests and test suites must be created individually for each class.

4. Which icon glyph is added to a JUnit test method that fails?

   A.

   B.

   C.

   D.

5. How can an individual unit test method be executed or debugged?

   A. Individual test methods cannot be executed or debugged.

   B. Individual test methods can be executed by performing a right-click in the Navigator window on the method and choosing Debug Test or Run Test.

   C. Right-click the method name in the editor, and choose Debug or Run Test.

   D. Right-click the method in the Test Results window and choose Run Again.

6. NetBeans supports which continuous integration server?

   A. Apache Continuum

   B. Apache Gump

   C. CruiseControl

   D. Hudson

Using the NetBeans Profiler

7. A project has been experiencing performance problems in a production environment requiring regular restarts. To troubleshoot the problem, you open the project in NetBeans to profile it. How do you launch the profiler and application from within NetBeans?

   A. Debug | Profile Main Project

   B. Profile | Profile Main Project

   C. Profile | Attach Profiler

   D. Tools | Profiler Tools

8. A computer that is regularly used for profiling undergoes a major operating system upgrade. What must be done to ensure accurate profiling?

   A. NetBeans must be updated to the latest version.

   B. The JDK must be reinstalled.

   C. The profiler must be calibrated using Profile | Advanced Commands | Run Profiler Calibration.

   D. Nothing needs to be done.

9. Which file is not changed or added when profiling?

   A. `nbproject/build-impl.xml`

   B. `nbproject/profiler-build-mpl.xml`

   C. `build.xml`

   D. `build-before-profiler.xml`

10. True or False? CPU and memory snapshots can be captured concurrently in the same profiling sessions.

    A. True

    B. False

11. You have created a custom configuration for CPU performance profiling. You will only be profiling a small subset of the application. What is the optimal instrumentation scheme?

    A. Lazy

    B. Eager

    C. Total

    D. Aggressive

12. Which icon represents a profiling point in the code?

    A.

    B.

    C.

    D.

13. Which of the following is a valid OQL expression?

    A. `select s from java.lang.String s where s.equals("You Rule!")`

    B. `select s from String s where s = 'You Rule!'`

    C. `select * from java.lang.String s`

    D. `select s from java.lang.String s where s.toString() == "You rule!"`

SELF TEST ANSWERS

Testing Applications with JUnit

1. What key shortcut will test the main project?
   A. CTRL-N
   B. CTRL-M
   C. ALT-F6
   D. F8

   ☑ **C.** The key shortcut ALT-F6 will run the JUnits in the main project.

   ☒ **A, B,** and **D** are incorrect. **A** is incorrect because CTRL-N opens the New File Wizard. **B** is incorrect because CTRL-M performs the Move refactoring action. **D** is incorrect because F8 steps over code in the debugger.

2. When does NetBeans prompt for the version of JUnit to be used for a project?
   A. After the first JUnit is added to a project.
   B. When the project is initially created.
   C. NetBeans does not prompt; it is automatically set to the most recent version included with the IDE.
   D. JUnit must be manually added to the classpath.

   ☑ **A.** NetBeans prompts for the JUnit version to be used for a project after the first JUnit is added to the project.

   ☒ **B, C,** and **D** are incorrect. **B** is incorrect because NetBeans does not prompt for the JUnit version when it first creates a project. **C** is incorrect because NetBeans makes no assumptions about the version of JUnit to be used. **D** is incorrect because NetBeans will add JUnit to the classpath when you create the first unit test.

3. You would like to generate JUnit test classes for each class in a package. You would also like to generate a test suite for all of the tests. How would you go about doing this?
   A. Select the package containing the classes in the Projects window and press CTRL-SHIFT-U.
   B. Select the package containing the classes in the Projects window and right-click, choosing Tools | Create JUnit Tests.
   C. Both A and B.
   D. JUnit tests and test suites must be created individually for each class.

☑ **C.** Both CTRL-SHIFT-U and Tools | Create JUnit Tests on the context menu will create both unit tests and a test suite for a package when a package node is selected in the Projects window.

☒ **A, B,** and **D** are incorrect. **A** is incorrect because the context menu option Tools | Create JUnit Tests will also work. **B** is incorrect because CTRL-SHIFT-U is also correct. **D** is incorrect because unit tests and a test suite can be created for a project by selecting the project and choosing CTRL-SHIFT-U or by right-clicking and choosing Tools | Create JUnit Tests.

4. Which icon glyph is added to a JUnit test method that fails?

A.

B.

C.

D.

☑ **B.** This badge is displayed on unit tests that have failed.

☒ **A, C,** and **D** are incorrect. **A** is incorrect because that icon appears on a unit test, not the individual test methods that have failed. **C** is incorrect because that badge appears on unit tests that have succeeded. **D** is incorrect because that icon is clicked to rerun unit tests.

5. How can an individual unit method be executed or debugged?

A. Individual test methods cannot be executed or debugged.

B. Individual test methods can be executed by performing a right-click in the Navigator window on the method and choosing Debug Test or Run Test.

C. Right-click the method name in the editor, and choose Debug or Run Test.

D. Right-click the method in the Test Results window and choose Run Again.

☑ **D.** Individual unit test methods can only be run once all of the unit tests for a project have been executed. To run an individual unit test method, right-click the test on the method in the Test Results window and choose Run Again.

☒ **A, B,** and **C** are incorrect. **A** is incorrect because individual JUnit test methods can be run only after all of the unit tests for that JUnit class have been executed. **B** is incorrect because individual unit test methods cannot be executed from the Navigator window. **C** is incorrect because there is no context-specific menu in the Editor window for methods.

6. NetBeans supports which continuous integration server?

A. Apache Continuum

B. Apache Gump

C. CruiseControl

D. Hudson

☑ **D.** NetBeans supports the Hudson continuous integration server.

☒ **A, B,** and **C** are incorrect. **A** is incorrect because NetBeans does not support Apache Continuum. **B** is incorrect because NetBeans does not support Apache Gump. **C** is incorrect because NetBeans does not support CruiseControl.

Using the NetBeans Profiler

7. A project has been experiencing performance problems in a production environment requiring regular restarts. To troubleshoot the problem, you open the project in NetBeans to profile it. How do you launch the profiler and application from within NetBeans?

A. Debug | Profile Main Project

B. Profile | Profile Main Project

C. Profile | Attach Profiler

D. Tools | Profiler Tools

☑ **B.** The NetBeans Profiler for the main project is launched using Profile | Profile Main Project.

☒ **A, C,** and **D** are incorrect. **A** is incorrect because Profile Main Project does not appear in the Debug menu. **C** is incorrect because Attach Profiler is used to attach the profiler to a local or remote application that is not launched by NetBeans. **D** is incorrect because Profiler Tools is used to configure profiling for profiling native C++ applications.

8. A computer that is regularly used for profiling undergoes a major operating system upgrade. What must be done to ensure accurate profiling?

A. NetBeans must be updated to the latest version.

B. The JDK must be reinstalled.

C. The profiler must be calibrated using Profile | Advanced Commands | Run Profiler Calibration.

D. Nothing needs to be done.

☑ **C.** Any major changes to a machine require that calibration be rerun to achieve accurate results. This is accomplished via Profile | Advanced Commands | Run Profiler Calibration.

☒ **A, B,** and **D** are incorrect. **A** is incorrect because this is not required and the installation may already be the most recent version. **B** is incorrect because reinstalling the JDK will not affect profiling results, and the JDK installation may already be the most recent. **D** is incorrect because profiler calibration does need to be performed.

9. Which file is not changed or added when profiling?
    A. `nbproject/build-impl.xml`
    B. `nbproject/profiler-build-mpl.xml`
    C. `build.xml`
    D. `build-before-profiler.xml`

    ☑ **A**. The `nbproject/build-impl.xml` file is not changed when the profiler instruments the build files. Instead an `nbproject/profiler-build-impl.xml` file is created.

    ☒ **B, C**, and **D** are incorrect. **B** is incorrect because `nbproject/profiler-build-impl.xml` is created by NetBeans when a project is profiled. **C** is incorrect because this file is backed up and an import to `nbproject/profiler-build-impl.xml` is added. **D** is incorrect because `build-before-profiler.xml` is the copy of the original `build.xml` file.

10. True or False? CPU and memory snapshots can be captured concurrently in the same profiling sessions.
    A. True
    B. False

    ☑ **B**. False. The NetBeans Profiler can either record performance or memory usage but not both concurrently in the same profiling session.

11. You have created a custom configuration for CPU performance profiling. You will only be profiling a small subset of the application. What is the optimal instrumentation scheme?
    A. Lazy
    B. Eager
    C. Total
    D. Aggressive

    ☑ **A**. Since you are profiling only a small subset of the application, you would choose Lazy to reduce the performance impact. Instrumentation schemes determine the order as well as the number of instrumented methods.

    ☒ **B, C**, and **D** are incorrect. **B** is incorrect because Eager would have a negative impact upon performance. The profiler would instrument the methods as soon as a class with a root method was loaded. **C** is incorrect because the profiler would instrument all of the methods of each application class as it is loaded. **D** is incorrect because an Aggressive scheme does not exist.

12.   Which icon represents a profiling point in the code?

    A.

    B.

    C.

    D.

    ☑   **C.** This is the correct icon that represents a profile point in the editor.

    ☒   **A, B,** and **D** are incorrect. **A** is incorrect because it is a suggestion for a code change, for example, to remove unneeded imports. **B** is incorrect because it is a debugger breakpoint. **D** is incorrect because it is the icon representing a syntax error.

13.   Which of the following is a valid OQL expression?

    A.   `select s from java.lang.String s where s.equals("You Rule!")`

    B.   `select s from String s where s = 'You Rule!'`

    C.   `select * from java.lang.String s`

    D.   `select s from java.lang.String s where s.toString() == "You rule!"`

    ☑   **D.** This is the correct answer and represents a valid query using a JavaScript expression.

    ☒   **A, B,** and **C** are incorrect. **A** is incorrect because JavaScript does not have an equals method on its String object. **B** is incorrect because String is not a fully qualified class name and a == is used for String comparison. **C** is incorrect because an asterisk is not a valid JavaScript expression.

Part IV

Appendixes

APPENDIXES

A   NetBeans Versions

B   NetBeans Installations

C   NetBeans Keymap

D   NetBeans Code Templates

E   About the CD

A

NetBeans Versions

NetBeans IDE Versions

NetBeans has a long history in the Java community. It started as a student project in 1996 with its first prerelease in 1997. It was originally known as Xelfi prior to being renamed NetBeans in 1998. From the start it was written completely in Java and ran on all of the supported Java platforms—thus, it was true to the spirit of Java. In late 1999 Sun Microsystems acquired NetBeans. For a brief period NetBeans was renamed to Forte for Java. At the time Sun had also purchased Forte and integrated Forte's tools into NetBeans. In the summer of 2000 Sun open-sourced NetBeans, and netbeans.org went public.

From 2004 to 2007 Sun Microsystems also released and supported commercial variants of NetBeans named Java Studio Creator and Java Studio Enterprise. These targeted corporate and enterprise developers, respectively. Both products were based on NetBeans and were accompanied with support contracts. Java Studio Creator attempted to lower the bar for novice developers. In 2007 Sun migrated customers to NetBeans. NetBeans had continued to evolve and was always a step ahead of the Sun Studio tools.

Here is the NetBeans timeline:

Year	First and Second Quarter Releases	Third and Fourth Quarter Releases
2000	NetBeans is open sourced.	NetBeans 3.1 is released.
2001	NetBeans 3.2 is released.	NetBeans 3.3 is released.
2002	NetBeans 3.4 is released.	No major releases.
2003	NetBeans 3.5 is released.	No major releases.
2004	NetBeans 3.6 is released.	NetBeans 4.0 is released.
2005	NetBeans 4.1 is released.	No major releases.
2006	NetBeans 5.0 is released.	NetBeans 5.5 is released.
2007	NetBeans 5.5.1 is released.	NetBeans 6.0 is released.
2008	NetBeans 6.1 is released.	NetBeans 6.5 is released.
2009	NetBeans 6.7 is released.	NetBeans 6.8 is released.

Each version of NetBeans adds new features and refines old ones. Sun—now Oracle—uses NetBeans to showcase and support new features added to the Java platform. For instance, NetBeans has been the leading environment for JavaFX.

Supported Technologies

This appendix focuses on the feature history of NetBeans 6.x (see Table A-1). Information on older releases and NetBeans press announcements can be found at http://netbeans.org/about/history.html.

Note, Java ME has not been available on all platforms. Also, the Java ME SDK 3.0 replaces Java Wireless Toolkit 2.5.2 and Java Toolkit 1.0 for CDC.

TABLE A-1   Supported Technologies

Technology	NetBeans 6.8	NetBeans 6.7	NetBeans 6.5	NetBeans 6.1
Java EE 6	Supported	n/a	n/a	n/a
Java EE 5	Supported	Supported	Supported	n/a
J2EE 1.4	Supported	Supported	Supported	Supported
Grails	1.1	1.0	1.0	n/a
Groovy	1.6.4	1.5	1.5	n/a
Hibernate	3.2.5	3.2.5	3.2.5	n/a
Java ME	SDK 3.0	SDK 3.0	2.5.2	2.5.2
JavaFX	SDK 1.2.1	SDK 1.2.1	SDK 1.1	n/a
JRuby	1.4	1.2	1.1.4	1.1
PHP	5.3, 5.2, 5.1	5.2	5.2	Early access for PHP
Rails	2.3.4	2.1	2.1	2.0.2
Ruby	1.9, 1.8	1.8	1.8	1.8 prerelease
Spring	2.5	2.5	2.5	2.5
Struts	1.3.8	1.2.9	1.2.9	1.2.9
CVS	1.12.x, 1.11.x	1.12.x, 1.11.x	1.12.x, 1.11.x	1.11.x
Subversion	1.6.x, 1.5.x, 1.4.x	1.5.x, 1.4.x, 1.3.x	1.5.x, 1.4.x, 1.3.x	1.3.x
Mercurial	1.x	1.x	1.0.x	0.94

New Features

This section outlines the new features in each release of NetBeans back to version 6.1. It is important to note that over time the disparate development tools produced by Sun have been migrated to NetBeans to provide for a uniform development experience:

- JFluid is now the NetBeans Profiler.
- Sun Java Studio Mobility is now the Mobility Pack for NetBeans.
- Sun Java Studio Enterprise is now the Enterprise Pack.
- Sun Studio is now the C/C++ pack.
- Sun Java Studio Creator is now the Visual Web Pack. Note that the Visual Web Pack was removed from NetBeans as of version 6.7.

More information on the packs can be found at: http://wiki.netbeans.org/wiki/images/5/53/NetBeansTOI_GreggSporar.pdf.

Since running NetBeans 6.x with every possible plugin and technology dramatically increases the IDE footprint, the Features on Demand initiative was implemented in NetBeans 6.7. This means that a base version of NetBeans can be downloaded—Java SE, for example—and features can be activated as necessary afterwards via the Plugin Manager. Thus, if a Java SE bundle is downloaded and installed, it isn't necessary to download a different version of NetBeans.

To see where NetBeans is going in the future or to check out previous releases: http://netbeans.org/community/releases/roadmap.html.

NetBeans IDE 6.8 New Features

Official release summary: http://netbeans.org/community/releases/68/.

New features of NetBeans IDE 6.8 include support of the following items:

- **C++ profiling**   Improved profiling with Microstate Accounting indicator and I/O usage monitor.
- **GlassFish v3**   Support for the GlassFish version 3 application server: https://glassfish.dev.java.net/.
- **Grails**   Support for Grails 1.1: http://www.grails.org.
- **Groovy**   Support for Groovy 1.6.4: http://groovy.codehaus.org.
- **Java Enterprise Edition 6**   This includes the Java EE 6 web profiles, EJB 3.1, JAX-WS 2.2, and JAXB 2.2 implementations.

- **Java Server Faces 2.0**   Support for JSF 2.0 (JSR 314) and Facelets (https://facelets.dev.java.net/).
- **JavaFX SDK**   SDK was upgraded to 1.2.1.
- **JIRA**   Support for bug tracking: http://www.atlassian.com/software/jira.
- **JRuby**   Support for JRuby 1.4: http://jruby.org.
- **PHP**   Support for PHP 5.3: http://php.net/releases/5_3_0.php.
- **Rails**   Support for Rails 2.3.4.
- **Ruby**   Support for Ruby 1.9: http://www.ruby-lang.org.
- **Struts**   Support for Struts 1.3.8: http://struts.apache.org.
- **Symfony Framework**   Support for the Symfony Open-Source PHP Web Framework: http://www.symfony-project.org.

NetBeans IDE 6.7/6.7.1 New Features

Official release summary: http://netbeans.org/community/releases/67/.

New features of NetBeans IDE 6.7.1 include support of the following items:

- **C++**   Support for code refactoring, profiling (DLight), the Qt library, and macro expansion.
- **Java ME**   Java ME SDK 3.0 was bundled. Support was added for the Java Card Platform 3.0. Improvements were made to the SVG editor.
- **JavaFX**   Live preview was added along with enhanced editor support.
- **JRuby**   Support for JRuby 1.2.
- **Kenai**   Support for integrating with Kenai-hosted projects. Kenai is now end-of-life.
- **Maven**   Support for POM, the creation of plugins, and web services. Library dependency graph viewer was added.
- **PHP**   Support for Selenium and SQL code completion. PHPUnit support was added, and the editor gained SQL code completion.
- **Profiler**   Support for exporting profiler data to CSV, HTML, and XML file formats was added. HeapWalker gained support for OQL queries.

NetBeans IDE 6.5/6.5.1 New Features

Official release summary: http://netbeans.org/community/releases/65/.
New features of NetBeans IDE 6.5.1 include support of the following items:

- **Compile and Deploy** Support for the automatic compilation and deployment on Save for Java and Java EE applications.
- **Database** Improved support including SQL history, SQL completion, and results viewing as well as editing improvements.
- **Grails** Support for Grails 1.0.
- **Groovy** Support for Groovy 1.5.
- **GUI Builder** Support for Nimbus and simple class names.
- **Java Debugger** The debugger was rewritten with a new user interface. Deadlock detection was added with a visual indicator.
- **Java EE 5** Support for all of the APIs implemented against the Java Enterprise Edition 5 specification.
- **Java ME** Support for Java ME including Data Binding, SVG, and Custom Component creation. Code obfuscation was upgraded to ProGuard 4.2 and the test framework to JMUnit 1.1.0.
- **JavaFX** Support for SDK 1.1. Includes support for animation, graphics, and media codecs for rich content application development for desktop and mobile devices.
- **Java SE** Support was added for analyzing Javadoc as well as improved Eclipse project import and synchronization.
- **JavaScript/AJAX** Support for debugging JavaScript was added along with HTTP transaction monitoring. JavaScript Library Manager was enhanced.
- **JUnit** Support for a single test method.
- **PHP** Support for code completion, Xdebug, and web service features.
- **Ruby** Improved JavaScript, AJAX, and Ruby support.

NetBeans IDE 6.1 New Features

Official release summary: http://netbeans.org/community/releases/61/.

New features of NetBeans IDE 6.1 include support of the following items:

- **Axis2** Support for Axis2 web services.
- **Inspect Members and Hierarchy Windows** Inspect Members and Hierarchy actions now work when the caret in the Java Editor is on a Java class for which there is no source available.
- **JavaBeans** Support for JavaBeans including view capability of Java Bean patterns in the Navigator and BeanInfo Editor.
- **Javadoc and Sources Association** Any JAR item on the project classpath can be associated with its Javadoc and sources, too.
- **Javadoc Code Completion** Editing of Javadoc comments is more convenient with code completion.
- **JavaScript** Support for highlighting, refactoring, and code completion was added.
- **Java ME** MIDP emulation support was added for Mac OS X (Update Center). SVN Composer was also added.
- **JSF CRUD Generator** Allows generation of JavaServer Faces CRUD applications from JPA entity classes.
- **MySQL** New support in Database Explorer allowing for registration of MySQL servers, viewing/creating/deleting databases, creating and opening connections to these databases, and launching the administration tool for MySQL.
- **Performance** The IDE now starts 40 percent faster. Memory consumption was reduced.
- **Project Sharing** This is a new feature in Java SE, Java Web, and all Java EE projects to be shared and built unattended. Relative path support was added for dependencies.
- **Spring Framework** Support was added for Spring 2.5 (http://www .springsource.com), which includes Web MVC framework, code completion, and so on.
- **Visual Web JSF** Support for On Demand Binding Attribute in Visual Web JSF projects.

- **Web APIs**   Support for web APIs such as Amazon, Facebook, Google, Twitter, and Zillow were added.
- **Web services**   Support for restful web services was added (JSR 311).
- **Window transparency**   Existing infrastructure has been enhanced to support window transparency (on platforms that provide it).

B

NetBeans
Installations

NetBeans IDE Installations

The NetBeans team has done an excellent job of making installation simple and quick. Official NetBeans installers are available for all of the major operating systems including Solaris, Windows, Mac OS X, and Linux. As NetBeans is written in Java, the only prerequisite is the JDK (Java Development Kit) for Java development and the JRE (Java Runtime Environment) for Ruby, C++, and PHP development. Some JDK bundles from Oracle include NetBeans. Multiple versions of NetBeans can be installed on the same computer.

The NetBeans certification exam targets NetBeans 6.1; however, user interface continuity has been maintained throughout the 6.x release cycle. Choosing to use a more current release of NetBeans, such as 6.8, will not hinder exam preparation. NetBeans 6.8 contains many new enhancements and bug fixes.

If you are still interested in using NetBeans 6.1 for your exam preparation, finding the download page for both NetBeans 6.1 and JDK 5 can be an expedition. To download NetBeans 6.1, select Archive from the download page (http://netbeans .org/downloads), and specify NetBeans version 6.1 with the build type Release. For Java SE 5.0 (http://java.sun.com/javase/downloads) click Previous Releases, and pick JDK 1.5 Update 22.

NetBeans 6.8 still supports JDK 1.5, but future versions will require JDK 1.6 or greater. NetBeans does not impose any JDK/JRE requirements on your project. Although NetBeans 6.8 requires JDK 1.5 or greater, your project can use older versions. Consult Chapter 1 for a more detailed discussion on configuring projects with different JDK versions.

The current download page appears in Figure B-1 (http://netbeans.org/downloads). This figure has seven installers from which to choose. As the download page reveals, NetBeans is much more than a Java IDE. NetBeans supports a variety of additional development languages and frameworks including C/C++, Ruby, PHP, and Groovy. For the purposes of the test, the Java or All installer should be downloaded. The Java SE installer does not include the Java EE features such as editor support for JSP/Facelets files. Selecting the Java installer package does not preclude using C++/Ruby support in the future. Use the Plugin Manager to activate these features via Tools | Plugins. Consult Chapter 1 for a detailed discussion on installing and activating features.

Installing and running NetBeans will require administrative permissions on Mac OS X and Windows, but root access is not needed on Linux. Root access is compulsory if NetBeans is to be installed in a central location and shared among

FIGURE B-1   NetBeans downloads

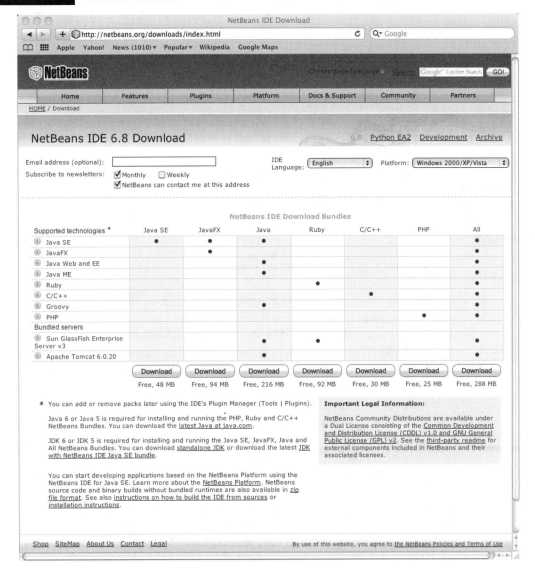

multiple users. After installation, NetBeans does not require write permissions to the installation directory. All files and settings specific to an individual user are stored locally in the user's home directory (this can be configured). The location of a shared directory will vary by operating system and IT environment.

Although the installation steps are roughly the same, each platform-specific installer is different. Official NetBeans installers are available for the following platforms:

- Microsoft Windows (2000/XP/Vista/7)
- Solaris/OpenSolaris
- Mac OS X
- Linux
- OS Independent Zip

Current installers can be downloaded from www.netbeans.org. The following sections document the installation procedure for each platform.

Microsoft Windows

NetBeans for Windows is distributed as a standard Windows installer for Windows 2000, XP, Vista, and Windows 7. While the installer does not require Java to run, a JDK must be preinstalled on the computer for NetBeans. The installer will attempt to auto-detect installed JDKs. For NetBeans 6.8 the current JDK 1.6 should be downloaded and installed from Sun's Java website (java.sun.com). NetBeans 6.8 will also run on JDK 1.5. Oracle provides JDK/NetBeans bundles on the java.sun.com website, although these bundles often include a slightly older point release of NetBeans.

If the goal is to install NetBeans 6.1, the version used on the exam, some additional work may be required. The NetBeans 6.1 installer will not launch unless JDK 1.5 is installed. JDK 5 has been officially discontinued—End of Service Life on November 3, 2009. This means that no more patches/fixes will be forthcoming. Downloading Java 5 requires filling out a form and receiving a download link via e-mail.

After downloading NetBeans and launching the installer, the welcome screen in Figure B-2 is displayed. The list of packs and runtimes displayed will vary depending upon the installer downloaded. Note that the installer will also detect components already installed. The default amount of disk space to be consumed by the installer is displayed at the bottom of the screen.

Clicking the Customize button displays the dialog box shown in Figure B-3. The features that will be installed can be selected or deselected. Tomcat 6 is deselected by default.

FIGURE B-2

Windows
installer welcome

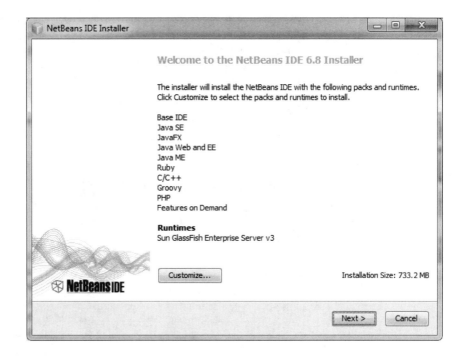

FIGURE B-3

Windows installer
customization

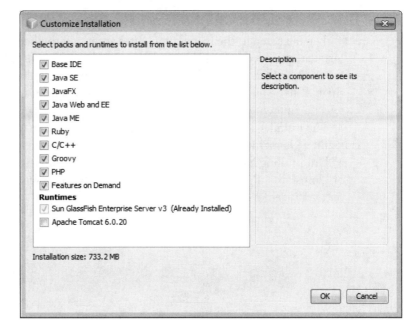

Windows installer
installation
location

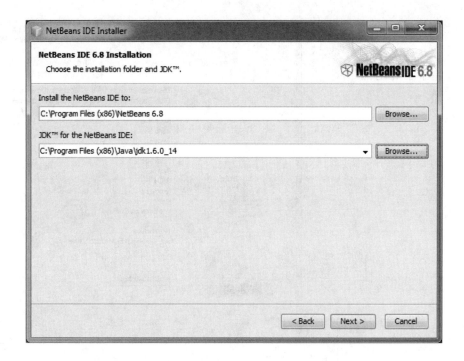

The next step in the installation, after accepting the license, is to choose an
installation directory and also the JDK, as shown in Figure B-4. The default location
for NetBeans 6.8 is under Program Files. The installer will attempt to auto-detect
the JDK to be used. Depending upon the environment, it might be necessary to
select a different JDK.

The installer will create a group under the Start menu/Application menu to
facilitate launching NetBeans.

Uninstalling NetBeans requires going through Add/Remove Programs (XP)
or Uninstall A Program (Windows 7). The uninstaller, shown in Figure B-5, can
optionally remove GlassFish.

FIGURE B-5

Windows
uninstaller

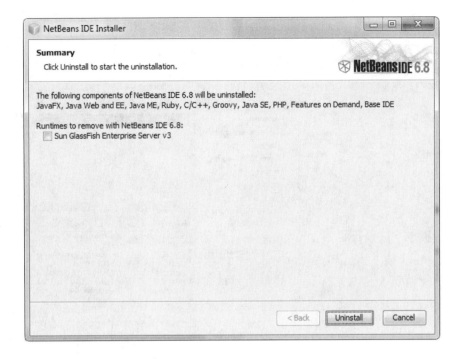

OpenSolaris

OpenSolaris is the open-source branch of the Solaris operating system from Oracle. You have at least two options for installing NetBeans on OpenSolaris: download and install from www.netbeans.org, or via the Package Manager. The Package Manager, shown in Figure B-6, can be accessed via System | Administration | Package Manager. Installing the `java-dev` or `SUNWj6dev` package in the Package Manager is the easier route, because the JDK is installed at the same time. The JDK is also installed by selecting the `netbeans` package. The benefit of installing `java-dev` is that you also get GlassFish and MySQL. Sun Studio Express is also included. With the `java-dev` package, the version of NetBeans installed may not be the most recent version available from the NetBeans website.

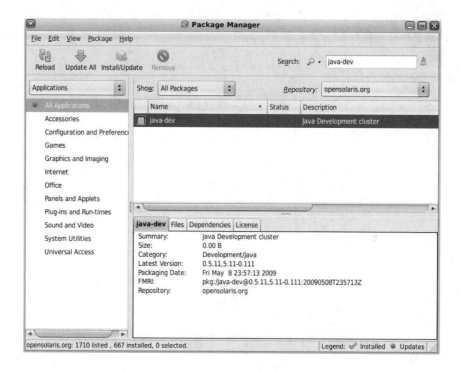

If NetBeans is being installed from the website, the JDK must be installed first. This can be done easily by installing the `java-dev` package via the Package Manager.

The `java-dev` package also includes a version of NetBeans. After the JDK is installed, run the installer from the command line using `sh netbeans-6.8-ml-solaris-x86.sh`.

The installation process is almost the same as with Windows. The panels in the Solaris installer match Figure B-2, Figure B-3, and Figure B-4. The only difference is the installation location, which is `/export/home/<user>/netbeans-6.8` (user's home directory).

NetBeans and the JDK are removed by launching the Package Manager and clicking Remove with the NetBeans/JDK package selected. The Package Manager will go through and remove all installed executables.

Mac OS X

Apple bundles the JRE and JDK with the Mac OS X operating system, meaning that there is no separate download or setup for the JDK. Apple licenses Java from Sun Microsystems and provides their own implementation customized for the Macintosh platform. To run NetBeans 6.8, you need either Mac OS 10.4 (Leopard) or Mac OS 10.5 (Snow Leopard). Consult Apple Technical Note TN2110 (developer.apple .com) for an up-to-date matrix of Java-to–Mac OS X versions.

The NetBeans installer for Mac OS X is distributed on a DMG (disk image) file. When downloading the disk image via Safari, the disk image is automatically mounted and the installer is auto-launched. If the installer does not auto-launch, double-click the `mpkg` file.

The first screen in the installation process, shown in Figure B-7, confirms the version that you are installing. Clicking the Continue button brings up the second screen, a standard license that must be accepted.

On the third step of the installer, shown in Figure B-8, the installation location and features can be customized. By default, the installer will place NetBeans under `/Application/NetBeans`. Installing in this location will require administrative permissions. Installing under `/Applications` will make NetBeans available to all users on the computer.

Electing to customize displays the panel shown in Figure B-9. Each feature to be installed or updated is listed along with the amount of disk space required. By default, both NetBeans and GlassFish will be installed for the All bundle. Tomcat 6 is skipped. GlassFish is installed into `/Applications/NetBeans/ glassfish<version>`. After installation, the NetBeans icon can be dragged onto the Dock to simplify launching.

FIGURE B-7

Mac OS X
installer, Step 1

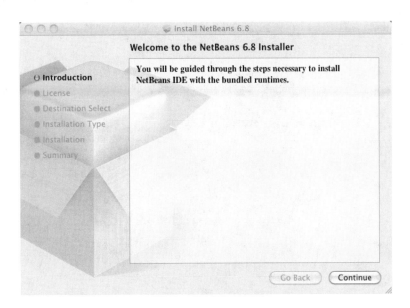

FIGURE B-8

Mac OS X
installer, Step 3

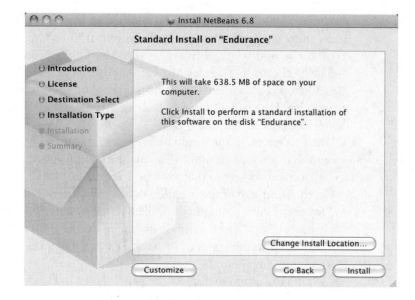

FIGURE B-9

Mac OS X
customizations

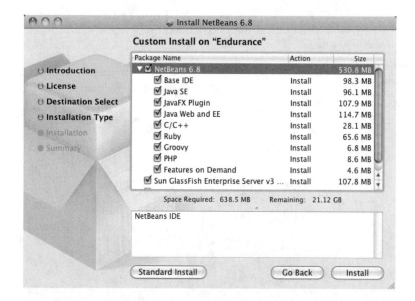

Uninstalling NetBeans is as simple as dragging the NetBeans application icon from `/Applications/NetBeans` to the trash. If your goal is to completely remove all vestiges of NetBeans, the following hidden directories must be deleted from each user's home directory:

- `.nbprofiler`   NetBeans Profiler settings
- `.netbeans`   User directory
- `.netbeans-derby`   Derby database
- `.netbeans-registration`   Registration settings

Linux

The NetBeans team provides a generic installer for Linux distributions such as Red Hat, Ubuntu, Debian, and Slackware. This installer requires a valid JDK to have been installed previously. NetBeans 6.8 requires Java 2 SE 5.0 with JDK 1.5 or Java SE 6 with JDK 1.6. The installer does not need the `JAVA_HOME` environment variable configured; it will scan the system looking for a JDK.

The installer is invoked by executing `sh netbeans-6.8.ml-linux.sh` from the command line. The installer is the same as the Windows installer, with only minor differences in the default paths. NetBeans is installed in the current user's home directory by default.

Uninstalling NetBeans is as simple as deleting the NetBeans directory and deleting the following directories for each NetBeans user:

- `.nbprofiler`   NetBeans Profiler settings
- `.netbeans`   User directory
- `.netbeans-derby`   Derby database
- `.netbeans-registration`   Registration settings

OS Independent Zip

The OS Independent Zip is a ZIP file containing NetBeans minus GlassFish and Tomcat. It does not include any installation scripts; hence, there is no automated checking of the environment for a valid JDK. The ZIP distribution can be used in environments where installers are prohibited or where the developer wants more control over the IDE's setup. For instance, the NetBeans ZIP could be expanded on a shared drive and used by Linux and Windows alike. The `bin` directory contains a shell script, `netbeans`, and a Windows executable, `netbeans.exe`, both of which will launch the IDE. The contents of the ZIP file can be placed anywhere on the system.

C

NetBeans Keymap

NetBeans IDE 6.1 Keymap

The NetBeans IDE has its own configurable Keymap. A keymap is a group of profiles in which each profile is made up of several keyboard shortcuts associated with user-initiated actions. NetBeans includes several profiles from other common editors to ease the transition from other environments such as Eclipse, IntelliJ IDEA, and Emacs. This appendix describes shortcuts from the NetBeans 6.1 profile. Many of these shortcuts are commonly used and may be seen on the exam.

To help with memorization, the shortcuts have been separated into the following sections: File, Code Folding, Navigation, Source, Refactoring, Run, Debugging, Debugging Window, Profiling, Window, Traditional Editor Functions, Miscellaneous, and Help. In addition, a table maps the usage of all shortcuts related to the function keys.

File Shortcuts

Event	Keys
Display the Files window	CTRL-2
Display the New File wizard	CTRL-N
Save	CTRL-S
Save all	CTRL-SHIFT-S
Print preview	CTRL-ALT-SHIFT-P
Display the Find Usages dialog box	ALT-F7
Find next occurrence of the selection	F3
Find previous occurrence of the selection	SHIFT-F3
Find the selection at the cursor	CTRL-F2
Display the Find In Projects dialog box or editor search control depending on context	CTRL-F
Replace selection	CTRL-H
Find selection in projects	CTRL-SHIFT-F
Replace selection in projects	CTRL-SHIFT-H
Toggle search result highlights	ALT-SHIFT-H
Format selection	ALT-SHIFT-F
Paste formatted	CTRL-SHIFT-V
Create a new project	CTRL-SHIFT-N
Open an existing project	CTRL-SHIFT-O

Code Folding Shortcuts

Event	Keys
Expand code folding	CTRL-ADD, CTRL-PLUS
Collapse code folding	CTRL-SUBTRACT, CTRL-MINUS
Expand all code folding	CTRL-SHIFT-ADD, CTRL-SHIFT-PLUS
Collapse all code folding	CTRL-SHIFT-SUBTRACT, CTRL-SHIFT-MINUS

Navigation Shortcuts

Event	Keys
Inspect file members	CTRL-F12
Inspect members	CTRL-SHIFT-F12
Inspect file hierarchy	ALT-F12
Inspect hierarchy	ALT-SHIFT-F12
Go to super implementation	CTRL-SHIFT-P
Go to declaration from type selection	CTRL-B
Go to source from type selection	CTRL-SHIFT-B
Go to type from dialog box selection	CTRL-O
Go to file from dialog box selection	ALT-SHIFT-O
Go to line number	CTRL-G
Go to matching bracket	CTRL-[
Go to last edit location	CTRL-Q
Go to test	CTRL-SHIFT-T
Add bookmark / remove bookmark	CTRL-SHIFT-M
Go to next bookmark	CTRL-SHIFT-PERIOD
Go to previous bookmark	CTRL-SHIFT-COMMA
Go forward	ALT-RIGHT
Go backward	ALT-LEFT
Go to the selection/node in the Projects window	CTRL-SHIFT-1
Go to the selection/node in the Files window	CTRL-SHIFT-2
Go to or add the selection/node in the Favorites window	CTRL-SHIFT-3

Source Shortcuts

Event	Keys
Fix code by suggestion	ALT-ENTER
Fix imports of all classes	CTRL-SHIFT-I
Perform fast import of selected class	ALT-SHIFT-I
Insert/generate code	ALT-INSERT
Select identifier	ALT-SHIFT-J
Insert internationalized string	CTRL-SHIFT-J
Shift the line to the left	ALT-SHIFT-LEFT ARROW
Shift the line to the right	ALT-SHIFT-RIGHT ARROW
Add/remove the comment line	CTRL-SLASH, CTRL-SHIFT-C
Copy selection down one line	CTRL-SHIFT-DOWN ARROW
Copy selection up one line	CTRL-SHIFT-UP ARROW
Move selection down one line	ALT-SHIFT-DOWN ARROW
Move selection up one line	ALT-SHIFT-UP ARROW
Move selection to the left	ALT-SHIFT-LEFT ARROW
Move selection to the right	ALT-SHIFT-RIGHT ARROW
Delete line	CTRL-E
Delete tab	SHIFT-TAB
Delete previous word	CTRL-BACKSPACE
Delete next word	CTRL-DELETE
Delete previous character	BACKSPACE, SHIFT-BACKSPACE

Refactoring Shortcuts

Event	Keys
Perform rename refactoring on a package, class, interface, method, or field.	CTRL-R
Perform move refactoring. This shortcut was introduced in NetBeans 6.8.	CTRL-M
Safe-delete refactoring. This shortcut was introduced in NetBeans 6.8.	ALT-DELETE

Run Shortcuts

Event	Keys
Run main project	F6
Run the selected file	SHIFT-F6
Run the selected file against JUnit test	CTRL-F6
Debug JUnit test file	CTRL-SHIFT-F6
Test project	ALT-F6
Create JUnit 3.x or JUnit 4.x tests	CTRL-SHIFT-U
Compile file/package	F9
Build main project	F11
Clean and build main project	SHIFT-F11
Run SQL	CTRL-SHIFT-E

Debugging Shortcuts

Event	Keys
Start debugging the main project	CTRL-F5
Step out	CTRL-F7
Toggle line breakpoint	CTRL-F8
Evaluate expression	CTRL-F9
Debug the current file	CTRL-SHIFT-F5
Debug JUnit test file	CTRL-SHIFT-F6
Run to the cursor location in the file	F4
Continue the debugger session	F5
Stop the debugger session	SHIFT-F5
Step into	F7
Step into next method	SHIFT-F7
Step over	F8
Step over expression	SHIFT-F8
Step out	CTRL-F7
Display the New Watch dialog box	CTRL-SHIFT-F7
Display the New Breakpoint dialog box	CTRL-SHIFT-F8

Debugging Window Shortcuts

Event	Keys
Display Local Variables window	ALT-SHIFT-1
Display Watches window	ALT-SHIFT-2
Display Call Stack window	ALT-SHIFT-3
Display Loaded Classes window	ALT-SHIFT-4
Display Breakpoints window	ALT-SHIFT-5
Display Sessions window	ALT-SHIFT-6
Display Threads window	ALT-SHIFT-7
Display Sources window	ALT-SHIFT-8

Profiling Shortcuts

Event	Keys
Stop profiling session	SHIFT-F2
Take snapshot of collected results	CTRL-F2
Rerun profiling session	CTRL-SHIFT-F2
Profile main project	ALT-F2
Modify profiling session	ALT-SHIFT-F2
Reset collected results	CTRL-ALT-F2
Toggle profiling point	SHIFT-F9

Window Shortcuts

Event	Keys
Full screen	ALT-SHIFT-ENTER
Display the top-level editor window	CTRL-0
Display the Projects window	CTRL-1
Display the Files window	CTRL-2
Display the Favorites window	CTRL-3
Display the Output window	CTRL-4
Display the Services window	CTRL-5
Display the Task List window	CTRL-6
Display the Navigator window	CTRL-7

Event	Keys
Close the current window	CTRL-F4, CTRL-W
Undock/dock window	ALT-SHIFT-D
Display the Usages window	ALT-SHIFT-U
Next tab	CTRL-PAGE DOWN
Previous tab	CTRL-PAGE UP
Search results	CTRL-SHIFT-0
Display the HTTP Monitor window	CTRL-SHIFT-5
Display the Properties window	CTRL-SHIFT-7
Display the Palette window	CTRL-SHIFT-8
Close all documents	CTRL-SHIFT-F4, CTRL-SHIFT-W
Maximize window	SHIFT-ESC
Document management	SHIFT-F4
Make caller current by going to the calling method	ALT-PAGE DOWN
Make callee current by going to the called method	ALT-PAGE UP

Traditional Editor Functions Shortcuts

Event	Keys
Add semicolon and create new line	CTRL-SHIFT-SEMICOLON
Extend selection backward, primarily by character	CTRL-SHIFT-LEFT ARROW
Extend selection backward, primarily be element	SHIFT-LEFT ARROW
Extend selection down	SHIFT-DOWN ARROW
Extend selection forward, primarily by character	CTRL-SHIFT-RIGHT ARROW
Extend selection forward, primarily by element	SHIFT-RIGHT ARROW
Extend selection to beginning of document	CTRL-SHIFT-HOME
Extend selection to beginning of text on line	SHIFT-HOME
Extend selection to end of document	CTRL-SHIFT-END

Event	Keys
Extend selection to end of line	SHIFT-END
Extend selection to matching bracket for parentheses, braces, and box brackets	CTRL-SHIFT-LEFT BRACE
Extend selection to next page	SHIFT-PAGE DOWN
Extend selection to next word	CTRL-SHIFT-RIGHT ARROW
Extend selection to previous page	SHIFT-PAGE UP
Extend selection up	SHIFT-UP ARROW
Move cursor to the beginning of the document	CTRL-HOME
Move cursor to the end of the document	CTRL-END
Move cursor to the beginning of the text on the line	HOME
Move cursor to the end of the line	END
Move cursor to the matching bracket for parentheses, braces, and box brackets	CTRL-LEFT BRACE
Move cursor to the next word	CTRL-RIGHT ARROW
Move cursor to the previous word	CTRL-LEFT ARROW
Move cursor to top	ALT-SHIFT-PAGE UP
Move cursor to center	ALT-SHIFT-INSERT
Move cursor to bottom	ALT-SHIFT-PAGE DOWN
Scroll up	CTRL-UP ARROW
Scroll down	CTRL-DOWN ARROW
Select all	CTRL-A
Show code completion popup for class and imported items	CTRL-SPACE, CTRL-SHIFT-BACKSLASH
Show code completion popup for class and all items relative to the class path	CTRL-SPACE-SPACE, CTRL-ALT-BACKSLASH, CTRL-ALT-SPACE

Miscellaneous

Event	Keys
Previous error	CTRL-COMMA
Next error	CTRL-PERIOD
Cancel process	CTRL-SHIFT-DELETE
Perform XML transformation	ALT-F6
Check XML file	ALT-F9
Validate XML file	ALT-SHIFT-F9
Convert selection to lowercase	CTRL-U, L
Convert selection to uppercase	CTRL-U, U
Convert case of the selection	CTRL-U, S

Help Shortcuts

Event	Keys
Launch the Help system	F1
Launch the project's generated Javadoc documentation	ALT-F1
Perform Javadoc index search	SHIFT-F1
Show documentation popup	CTRL-SHIFT-SPACE, CTRL-SHIFT-BACKSLASH

Function Key Shortcuts

The following table defines the shortcut actions for function keys, along with function keys that work with other key combinations, relative to the NetBeans 6.8 keymap profile. Note that the only function-key shortcut not shown is Reset Collected Results (CTRL-ALT-F2).

KEY	[DIRECT KEY]	SHIFT-[KEY]	CTRL-[KEY]	CTRL-SHIFT-[KEY]	ALT-[KEY]	ALT-SHIFT-[KEY]
F1	Help	Perform Javadoc index search			Launch relative Javadoc	
F2		Stop profiling session	Take snapshot of collected results	Rerun profiling session	Profile main project	Modify profiling session
F3	Find next selection occurrence	Find previous selection occurrence	Find selection at the cursor			
F4	Run to cursor	Document management	Close the current window	Close all documents		
F5	Continue debugger	Stop debugger session	Debug main project	Debug file		
F6	Run main project	Run the selected file	Run the selected file against JUnit test	Debug JUnit test file	Test project	
F7	Step into	Step into next method	Step out	Display New Watch dialog box	Display Find Usages dialog box	
F8	Step over	Step over expression	Toggle line breakpoint	Display New Breakpoint dialog box		
F9	Compile file/package	Toggle profile point	Evaluate expression		Check XML file	Validate XML file
F10	Menu bar	Popup menu				
F11	Build main project	Clean and build main project				
F12			Inspect file members	Inspect members	Inspect file hierarchy	Inspect hierarchy

Shortcut Reference Documentation

An abbreviated Shortcut document is available by selecting Help | Keyboard Shortcuts Card in the NetBeans IDE. The reference Keymap documentation for NetBeans 6.0, 6.1, and 6.5 can be found at: http://wiki.netbeans.org/ KeymapProfileFor60.

D

NetBeans Code Templates

NetBeans IDE 6.1 Code Templates

NetBeans provides a means to generate text via code templates. Code templates provide abbreviated strings that expand into fuller strings or blocks of code. The expansion occurs when the abbreviation is followed by a user-defined key or key sequence. The keys may be SHIFT, SHIFT-SPACE, TAB, or ENTER, as defined. To edit or view NetBeans' code templates, choose Tools | Options, click Editor, and select the Code Templates tab.

Code template language categories have been provided for many languages. Those provided with the NetBeans 6.1 "Web & Java EE" bundle are shown in Table D-1. Remember that the current version of the exam targets NetBeans 6.1.

Many of the language categories do not yet have content because they have been provided as a means to guide you in organizing your self-created templates in a more maintainable fashion. The category where you put new templates is important because the different categories relate to different file types. For example, you can't use an HTML code template in an HTML file (for instance, [name].html) if you save it in the Java code template language category. Varying categories appear based on module installations and bundle selection. NetBeans 6.8 provides a means to import and export the code templates.

The NetBeans IDE exam is concerned only with Java code templates. Chapter 6 on the Source Editor covers the code templates. This appendix has been included to provide a fuller listing of available Java code templates. Note that future releases

TABLE D-1   NetBeans 6.1 "Web & Java EE" Bundle Code Template Categories

Ant Build Scripts	Manifest File
Bat File	NBS File – NetBeans Scripting
Cascading Style Sheet	Plain Text
DTD – Document Type Definition	Properties
Diff File	SQL – Structured Query Language
Expression Language	Sh File
Externally Parsed Entity	Tag File
HTML – HyperText Markup Language	XML – Extensible Markup Language
JSP – JavaServer Pages	text/languages
Java	text/x-javadoc
JavaScript	

of the IDE may add, remove, or modify code templates for the various language categories including the Java category. Therefore, you should focus on the NetBeans 6.1 Java language code templates for the exam.

Java Code Templates

This section covers the NetBeans 6.1 Java code templates. They have been grouped in this book by relationships to ease the task of memorization. The groupings are as follows:

- Methods and Members
- Primitives
- Interfaces and Classes
- Class Construction Keywords
- Modifier Usages
- Literals
- Exception Handling Elements
- Transfer of Control Statement Elements
- Conditional Statement Elements
- Iteration Statement Elements
- System Messages
- Miscellaneous Elements

Code templates are either expanded to fixed text or are dynamically expanded based on conditions associated with the Special Code Template Syntax. This syntax is best described by documentation produced by NetBeans but is touched on in Chapter 6. You can find the documentation from the IDE Help menu (Help | Help Contents) or by clicking the Help button in the Options window.

Just search for the "Special Code Template Syntax" page. This appendix provides the dynamic code templates for your benefit, but does not explain the syntax because it's outside of the scope of the exam.

Methods and Members

Commonly used operations in Java have code templates associated with their methods. Table D-2 details six methods that can be expanded from short abbreviations. Remember that `length` is commonly used as both a method and an instance

Abbreviation	Expanded Text
psvm	```public static void main(String[] args) { ${cursor} }```
eq	equals
le	length
pst	printStackTrace();
su (6.9)	super
tds	Thread.dumpStack();

variable. For example, the `length()` method is used with the `String` class (for instance, `string.length()`), and the `length` field attribute is associated with arrays (for example, `stringArray.length`). Also, notice that a code template special syntax element is represented here, `${cursor}`. After the `psvm` abbreviation is invoked, the cursor is placed in the body of the `main` method where the syntax has been provided. The `super` code template was added in NetBeans 6.9.

Primitives

Eight primitives are in Java: `boolean`, `char`, `byte`, `short`, `int`, `long`, `double`, and `float`. In NetBeans 6.1, two primitives over five characters in length have code templates, `boolean` and `float`. Code templates for `double` and `short` were added in NetBeans 6.9 Table D-3.

Interfaces and Classes

Commonly used classes and interfaces have code templates as represented in Table D-4. `Enumeration` has a template and is an interface. `Exception`, `Object`, and `String` have templates and are classes.

Abbreviation	Expanded Text
bo	boolean
fl	float
db (6.9)	double
sh (6.9)	short

TABLE D-4

Code Templates for Interfaces and Classes

Abbreviation	Expanded Text
En	Enumeration
Ex	Exception
Ob	Object
St	String

Class Construction Keywords

When creating classes, the code templates in Table D-5 can be used.

Modifier Usages

Access modifiers `public`, `private`, and `protected` have code templates (Table D-6). Various other (non-access) modifiers also have code templates. A useful NetBeans feature is code templates that exist for commonly used combinations of modifiers, as in `Psfs` for `public static final String`. As previously mentioned, code templates come in handy for any keyword over five characters. Code templates for the `native`, `transient`, and `volatile` keywords were added in NetBeans 6.9.

TABLE D-5

Code Templates for Class Construction Keywords

Abbreviation	Expanded Text
cl	class
ex	extends
ie	interface
im	implements
ir	import

TABLE D-6

Code Templates
for Modifier
Usages

Abbreviation	Expanded Text
Psf	public static final
Psfb	public static final boolean
Psfi	public static final int
Psfs	public static final String
ab	abstract
fi	final
na (6.9)	native
pe	protected
pr	private
psf	private static final
psfb	private static final boolean
psfi	private static final int
psfs	private static final String
pu	public
sy	synchronized
tr (6.9)	transient
vo (6.9)	volatile

Literals

There are three reserved Java literals (null, true, and false). Since code templates are not necessary for strings under five characters, only the literal false has a template, as shown in Table D-7.

Exception Handling Elements

Exceptions are related to anomalous conditions that affect the flow of execution of your software. Exception handling in Java makes use of various keywords, as shown with the various code templates in Table D-8. You will also notice that the code template for the trycatch abbreviation has special code template syntax. Remember, for this and the other tables that have special code template syntax, you'll need to reference the NetBeans documentation to fully understand the grammar.

TABLE D-7

Code Templates
for Literals

Abbreviation	Expanded Text
fa	false

TABLE D-8   Code Templates for Exception Handling Elements

Abbreviation	Expanded Text
as (6.8)	`assert`
as (6.9)	`assert ${exp default="true"` `instanceof="boolean"};`
ca	`catch (`
fy	`finally [tab]`

fy (6.9)	`finally {`
	`    ${cursor}`
	`}`

th	`throws`
tw	`throw`
twn	`throw new`

trycatch	`try {`
	`    ${selection}${cursor}`
	`} ${CATCH_STMTS uncaughtExceptionCatchStatements`
	`default="catch (Exception e) {}" editable=false}`

Transfer of Control Statement Elements

Transfer of control statements provides a means to stop or interrupt the normal flow of control. Common keywords used in transfer of control statements are `break`, `continue`, and `return`. The associated code templates are shown in Table D-9. These code templates can be optimized because `break` is always followed by a semicolon, and so is `return`, but with an optional return value. For example, consider the following code template `ret` refinement: `return ${cursor};`. The cursor is placed between the `return` keyword and the semicolon, after the `ret` abbreviation is invoked.

TABLE D-9

Code Templates
for Transfer
of Control
Statement
Elements

Abbreviation	Expanded Text
br	`break`
br (6.8)	`break;`
cn	`continue`
re	`return`

Conditional Statement Elements

Conditional statements are used when you need to determine the direction of flow based on conditions. Table D-10 includes code templates in support of conditional statements.

Iteration Statement Elements

Iteration statements are used when you need to iterate through pieces of code. Table D-11 includes code templates in support of iteration statements.

TABLE D-10   Code Templates for Conditional Statement Elements

Abbreviation	Expanded Text/Code Templates

iff	`if (${EXP instanceof="boolean" default="exp"}) {`
	`   ${selection}${cursor}`
	`}`

ifelse	`if (${EXP instanceof="boolean" default="exp"}) {`
	`   ${selection}${cursor}`
	`} else {`
	`}`

inst	`if (${EXP instanceof="java.lang.Object"`
	`default="exp"} instanceof ${TYPE`
	`default="Object"}) {`
	`   ${TYPE} ${VAR newVarName default="obj"} =`
	`(${TYPE})${EXP};`
	`   ${cursor}`
	`}`

sw	`switch (`

sw (6.9)	`switch (${var instanceof="java.lang.Enum"}) {`
	`   case ${val completionInvoke}:`
	`      ${cursor}`
	`      break;`
	`   default:`
	`      throw new AssertionError();`
	`}`

df	`default:`

TABLE D-11   Code Templates for Iteration Statement Elements

Abbreviation	Expanded Text

`forc`	```for (${IT_TYPE rightSideType type="java.util.Iterator" default="Iterator" editable=false} ${IT newVarName default="it"} = ${COL instanceof="java.util.Collection" default="col"}.iterator(); ${IT}.hasNext();) {```
	 ``` ${TYPE rightSideType default="Object"} ${ELEM newVarName default="elem"} = ${TYPE_CAST cast default="" editable=false}${IT}.next();```
	 ``` ${selection}${cursor}```
	 ```}```

`fore`	```for (${TYPE iterableElementType default="Object" editable=false} ${ELEM newVarName default="elem"} : ${ITER iterable default="col"}) {```
	 ``` ${selection}${cursor}```
	 ```}```

`fori`	```for (int ${IDX newVarName default="idx"} = 0; ${IDX} < ${ARR array default="arr"}.length; ${IDX}++) {```
	 ``` ${TYPE rightSideType default="Object"} ${ELEM newVarName default="elem"} = ${TYPE_CAST cast default="" editable=false}${ARR}[${IDX}];```
	 ``` ${selection}${cursor}```
	 ```}```

`forl`	```for (int ${IDX newVarName default="idx"} = 0; ${IDX} < ${LIST instanceof="java.util.List" default="lst"}.size(); ${IDX}++) {```
	 ``` ${TYPE rightSideType default="Object"} ${ELEM newVarName default="elem"} = ${TYPE_CAST cast default="" editable=false}${LIST}.get(${IDX});```
	 ``` ${selection}${cursor}```
	 ```}```

`forst`	```for (${STR_TOK type="java.util.StringTokenizer" default="StringTokenizer" editable=false} ${TOKENIZER newVarName} = new ${STR_TOK}(${STRING instanceof="java.lang.String"}); ${TOKENIZER}.hasMoreTokens();) {```
	 ``` String ${TOKEN default="token"} = ${TOKENIZER}.nextToken();```
	 ``` ${cursor}```
	 ```}```

`forv`	```for (int ${IDX newVarName default="idx"} = 0; ${IDX} < ${VECTOR instanceof="java.util.Vector" default="vct"}.size(); ${IDX}++) {```
	 ``` ${TYPE rightSideType default="Object"} ${ELEM newVarName default="elem"} = ${TYPE_CAST cast default="" editable=false}${VECTOR}.elementAt(${IDX});```
	 ``` ${selection}${cursor}```
	 ```}```

`wh`	```while (```

`whilexp`	```while (${EXP instanceof="boolean" default="exp"}) {```
	 ``` ${selection}${cursor}```
	 ```}```

TABLE D-11	Code Templates for Iteration Statement Elements *(continued)*

Abbreviation	Expanded Text
| whileit | ```
while(${IT instanceof="java.util.Iterator" default="it"}.hasNext()) {
    ${TYPE rightSideType default="Object"} ${ELEM newVarName default="elem"}
= ${TYPE_CAST cast default="" editable=false} ${IT}.next();
    ${selection}${cursor}
}
``` |
| whilen | ```
while(${ENUM instanceof="java.util.Enumeration"
default="en"}.hasMoreElements()) {
    ${TYPE rightSideType default="Object"} ${ELEM newVarName default="elem"}
= ${TYPE_CAST cast default="" editable=false} ${ENUM}.nextElement();
    ${selection}${cursor}
}
``` |
| dowhile | ```
do {
} while (condition);
``` |

System Messages

System messages provide notifications to the developer/user. If you don't use a logging API, you've probably typed out `System.out.println("[message]");` to produce these messages. Code templates now provide shortcuts for standard error and system messages as detailed in Table D-12.

Miscellaneous Elements

The following NetBeans 6.1 Java code template abbreviations are related to code templates that are well outside of the scope of the exam, so they are not detailed in this appendix: bcom, fcom, iof, jaxbm, jaxbu, newo, and runn. Code templates have the option of having a description associated with them. Look for detailed descriptions being associated with code templates in future versions of the IDE.

TABLE D-12	Code Templates for System Messages

Abbreviation	Expanded Text
serr	`System.err.println("${cursor}");`
sout	`System.out.println("${cursor}");`
soutv	`System.out.println("${EXP instanceof="<any>" default="exp"} = " + ${EXP});`
```

E

About the CD

About the CD

The CD-ROM included with this book comes complete with MasterExam and the electronic version of the book. The software is easy to install on any Windows 2000/XP/Vista/7 computer and must be installed to access the MasterExam feature. You may, however, browse the electronic book directly from the CD without installation. To register for the bonus MasterExam, simply click the Bonus MasterExam link on the main launch page, and follow the directions to the free online registration.

System Requirements

The software requires Windows 2000 or later, Internet Explorer 6.0 or above, and 20MB of hard disk space for full installation. The electronic book requires Adobe Acrobat Reader.

Installing and Running MasterExam

If your computer CD-ROM drive is configured to auto run, the CD-ROM will automatically start up when you insert the disc. From the opening screen, you can install MasterExam by clicking the MasterExam link. This begins the installation process and creates a program group named LearnKey. To run MasterExam, choose Start | All Programs | LearnKey | MasterExam. If the auto-run feature did not launch your CD, browse to the CD, and double-click the LaunchTraining.exe icon.

MasterExam

MasterExam provides you with a simulation of the actual exam. The number of questions, the type of questions, and the time allowed are intended to be an accurate representation of the exam environment. You have the option to take an open-book exam including hints, references, and answers; a closed-book exam; or the timed MasterExam simulation.

When you launch MasterExam, a digital-clock display appears in the bottom-right corner of your screen. The clock continues to count down to zero unless you choose to end the exam before the time expires.

Electronic Book

The entire contents of the *Study Guide* are provided in PDF. Adobe's Acrobat Reader has been included on the CD.

Bonus Appendixes

Three bonus appendixes are also included on the CD: "NetBeans Database Integration," "NetBeans Sample Projects," and "NetBeans Resources."

NetBeans IDE Installation Bundles

Current and archived versions of the NetBeans IDE are available via bundles at the NetBeans download URL: http://netbeans.org/downloads/. The CD includes two links to OS-independent ZIP files containing NetBeans installers. The link entitled "NetBeans 6.1 Web & Java EE OS Independent Zip" links you to the ZIP file download page for the exam-targeted version of the IDE, NetBeans IDE 6.1. The link entitled "NetBeans 6.8 Web & Java EE OS Independent Zip" links you to the most current version of the IDE as of this writing, NetBeans IDE 6.8. Note that the GlassFish and Tomcat bundled servers are not included in the OS-independent installers of the IDE.

The NetBeans IDE 6.1 installation bundle is considered the Web & Java EE bundle. The supporting technologies in this bundle are Base IDE, Java SE, and Web & Java EE. The filename is `netbeans-6.1-200805300101-ml.javaee.zip`.

The NetBeans IDE 6.8 installation bundle is considered the Java bundle. The supporting packs (technologies) in this bundle are Java SE, Java Web and EE, Java ME, and Groovy. The filename is `netbeans-6.8-200912041610-ml-java.zip`.

NetBeans IDE installation instructions are included in Appendix B of this book.

Help

A help file is provided through the help button on the main page in the lower-left corner. An individual help feature is also available through MasterExam.

Removing Installation(s)

MasterExam is installed to your hard drive. For best results removing programs, use the Start | All Programs | LearnKey | Uninstall option to remove MasterExam.

Technical Support

For questions regarding the content of the electronic book or MasterExam, please visit www.mhprofessional.com/techsupport/. For customers outside the 50 United States, e-mail: international_cs@mcgraw-hill.com.

LearnKey Technical Support

For technical problems with the software (installation, operation, removing installations), please visit www.learnkey.com, e-mail techsupport@learnkey.com, or call toll-free: 1-800-482-8244.

Glossary

The following terms have been used this book.

Absolute Layout   A layout provided by NetBeans that positions components on a form using predefined coordinates and dimensions. The layout does not take into account font sizes or container. This layout is added to a project by either selecting Absolute Layout as a form's layout or adding the Absolute Layout library.

absolute path   A path that is the full path to a directory or file from the root directory. For example, `C:\Project\SpinnakerTrac` is an absolute path.

access modifier   Modifiers that define the access privileges of interfaces, classes, methods, constructors, and data members.

Active Scripting Debugger Framework   An Internet Explorer browser add-on that provides a debugging environment that extends any Microsoft ActiveX Scripting Host Application.

AJAX   An acronym for *Asynchronous JavaScript and XML*. A web application model where the client layer interfaces with the server without the need for the associated HTML pages to be reloaded.

annotation glyph margin   The left margin of the source editor that displays annotations glyphs. Glyphs that may appear in this margin include bookmarks, breakpoints, errors, warnings, ToDos, and fixable hints.

annotations   An annotation is syntactic metadata that can be added to a class, method, parameter, variable, and package. An example annotation is `@Test`, which is added to a class to denote it as a JUnit 4 unit test.

anonymous class   A type of inner class that has no name. It is defined in the middle of a method.

Ant   An XML-based build tool for Java. It is similar in concept to Make. Extensions can be easily added via Java classes.

Ant build script   An XML file that is interpreted by Apache Ant. It is used to build and deploy applications. NetBeans provides an IDE-generated Ant build script for all Java standard projects.

Ant targets   An Ant target contains a sequence of Ant tasks to be executed. It is named and may depend upon other Ant targets. It is defined in an Ant build script with the tags `<target></target>`.

Ant tasks   An individual unit of work in an Ant target that is executed. Ant includes a default set of tasks for compiling, copying, and manipulating files.

applet   An application that executes within applications, devices, and, most commonly, web browsers. The execution environment must support the applet programming model.

application server   A software framework that hosts various applications and their environments.

assessor method   A method used to return the value of a private or protected field.

AWT   An acronym for *Abstract Window Toolkit*. A platform-independent API for creating rich user interfaces on the desktop. It includes a widget library along with classes for rendering graphics and drawing windows and dialog boxes. Unlike Swing, it uses the operating system's widgets.

Beans Binding   A Java API defined by JSR 295 for keeping two bean properties in sync. It specifically focuses on Swing components and provides adapters for nonconforming components. The NetBeans GUI Builder uses Beans Binding.

Beans Binding expression   An expression used to bind bean properties together in Beans Binding. The syntax was derived from Java Unified Expression Language (EL).

breakpoint   A marked place in code where execution will pause when reached by the debugger.

Breakpoints window   A debugging-related window that lists all of the project's breakpoints.

build.xml   An Ant build script. See Ant build script.

Call Stack window   A debugger window that lists the sequence of calls made during the execution of the current thread up to the current execution point.

Checkstyle   A development tool that assists programmers with adhering to coding standards. Checkstyle has a NetBeans IDE plugin.

classpath   An argument set that tells the Java Virtual Machine where to look for user-defined classes and packages.

code completion   The process that includes mechanisms for assisting the user in automatically or manually completing partially inserted code.

code folding   A source editor feature that allows for the selective hiding of information such as grouped imports and comments.

code template   A three-part template consisting of an abbreviation, expanded text, and a description. The abbreviation is designed to transform into the expanded text when you press a designated key shortcut. The expanded text may use Special Code Template Syntax to affect how the code template behaves.

Codebase   An optional parameter of the `jnlp` element in the JNLP file used by Java Web Start. It is used for finding resources specified in the JNLP file and also for finding the file itself.

cookie   Mechanism where information is set and retrieved on the client side by the resources of web applications.

CSS   An acronym for *Cascading Style Sheets*. It is a language that describes how a markup language should be rendered. It is often used with HTML and XHTML.

CVS   An acronym for *Concurrent Versions Control System*. A popular version control system that is both open source and free. It tracks changes to files, enabling multiple copies of a file to be concurrently edited and merged. It uses client/server architecture with project history being stored on a centralized server. Command-line access is performed using the `cvs` command-line program.

Cygwin Linux-like environment for Windows making it possible to port software running on POSIX systems (for example, Linux) to Windows.

data dictionary See database schema.

database See RDBMS.

Database Explorer A collection of tools in the IDE enabling users to perform various basic tasks such as registering JDBC database drivers, connecting to databases, managing tables and views, performing SQL commands, and saving schemas.

database schema A catalog consisting of a set of system tables in a database that describes the shape of the database. Also known as a data dictionary.

Debugging window A debugger window that displays a list of threads in the current debugging session and allows for the suspension and resumption of those threads.

dialog box A window that either displays information to a user or prompts for a response.

editor hints Invokable commands associated with fixable problems flagged by source code warnings and errors. You can list editor hints by pressing ALT-ENTER relative to the fixable code or by clicking the associated light bulb in the left margin.

Editor panel A panel in the Options window that configures code folding, camel case behavior, source code formatting, code completion, code templates, hints, the marking of occurrences, and macros.

error stripe The strip to the right of the source editor and scrollbar (if shown). It contains color-coded marks for items such as the current line, errors, warnings, bookmarks, and breakpoints.

Executable JAR A JAR file containing a `manfest.mf` in the `META-INF` directory with the `Main-Class` attribute set to a class with a `public static void main(String args[])` method.

external library   A dependency that is added to a Java project, such as a JAR file, directory of classes, or native library for JNI code. The external library provides functionality that is treated as a black box.

FindBugs   A program that uses static analysis to look for bugs in Java code.

Firebug   A Firefox web browser add-on that allows for the editing, debugging, and monitoring of CSS, HTML, and JavaScript in web pages.

Flow Layout   A layout manager that arranges components either left-to-right or top-to-bottom. Components can also be aligned left, right, center, leading, and trailing. The preferred size of the component is used for determining dimensions.

Fonts & Colors panel   A panel in the Options window that configures language syntax attributes, IDE components highlighting, annotation glyphs coloring, and background coloring of the diff tool components.

frame   A top-level window with a title and border.

Free Design   A layout manager in the NetBeans GUI Builder that uses the Group Layout. Using this layout, components can be dragged from the palette and dropped on the editor. Components can be anchored to other components and also to the parent container.

free-form project   A project that does not use the NetBeans-generated Ant build script. Instead, it uses the project's own Ant build script. The NetBeans project must be configured to invoke actions in the project's build script. A free-form project is not a NetBeans Standard Java Project.

General panel   A panel in the Options window that configures the default web browser, proxy settings configuration, and activation of Usage Statistics.

getter   A simple public method used to return an instance variable.

GIS   An acronym for *Geographical Information System*. A term for systems that integrate, store, analyze, and retrieve spatial data.

Git   A free and open source, distributed version control system.

glyph   A symbol/icon used to denote a diagnostic or informative message.

glyph gutter   See annotation glyph margin.

glyph margin   See annotation glyph margin.

GridBag Layout   A layout manager that arranges components in a grid using the `GridBagConstraints` object to control the layout.

Group Layout   A layout manager used to implement layout designs that are specified when components are moved around a form.

heap   A memory area where objects are stored.

HeapWalker   A tool that is a part of the NetBeans Profiler that analyzes the contents of the Java heap. It is used for investigating memory leaks. It enables a developer to view a list of the loaded classes, instances of the classes, fields of the instances, and references to each instance.

Hibernate   An object/relational mapping library.

HTML   An acronym for *HyperText Markup Language*. A collection of tags used to create hypertext documents (for instance, web pages).

HTTP   An acronym for *HyperText Transfer Protocol*. The protocol used for information exchange on the World Wide Web.

HTTP Server-Side Monitor   An integrated NetBeans IDE analysis and recording tool for HTTP messages.

HTTPS   An acronym for *HyperText Transfer Protocol over SSL*. The protocol used for secure information exchange on the World Wide Web.

Hudson   An open source continuous integration server that checks code out from version control, builds it, and can optionally execute unit tests. Typically, it is configured to build projects on a regular basis—often when code is committed to version control.

IDE   An acronym for *Integrated Development Environment*. A development suite that allows developers to edit, compile, debug, connect to version control systems, collaborate, and do much more, depending on the specific tool. Most modern IDEs have add-in capabilities for various software modules to enhance the IDE's capabilities.

import statement   A statement used in the beginning of a class so that external packages are available within the class.

inner class   A class defined within another class. Various types of inner classes include member classes, local classes, and anonymous classes.

interface   A definition of public methods that must be implemented by a class.

internationalization (i18n)   The process of designing or implementing software so that it can be adapted to different languages and regions without reengineering. This involves storing text, fonts, colors, and graphics in resource bundles and adapting input for locales. It also involves handling date, time, currency, text encoding, and numeric formatting appropriately.

issue tracker   A system for tracking and managing issues such as bugs, feature requests, and customer support problems.

J2EE   An acronym for *Java 2 Platform, Enterprise Edition*. The legacy term for Java EE. See Java EE.

J2ME   An acronym for *Java 2 Platform, Micro Edition*. The legacy term for Java ME. See Java ME.

J2SE   An acronym for *Java 2 Platform, Standard Edition*. The legacy term for Java SE. See Java SE.

JAR   An acronym for *Java Archive*. A JAR file is used to store a collection of Java class files. It is represented by one file with the `.jar` extension in the file system. It may be executable.

Java Bean   A reusable Java component based on a platform-independent reusable component model that has standardized means to access and modify the object state of the bean.

Java DB   A database with a small footprint supported by Sun.

Java Debug Interface (JDI)   A high-level Java language interface with support for remote debugging.

Java Debug Wire Protocol (JDWP)   A protocol that defines the format of information and requests transferred between the process being debugged and the debugger front-end.

Java Editor   A source editor that is integrated with key IDE components such as the GUI Builder, the compiler, and the debugger.

Java EE   An acronym for *Java Platform, Enterprise Edition*. A software development platform that includes a collection of enterprise API specifications for EJBs, servlets, and JSPs. Java EE compliance is reached when an application server (full compliance) or web container (partial compliance) implements the necessary Java EE specifications.

Java ME   An acronym for *Java Platform, Micro Edition*. A software development platform including a collection of APIs designed for embedded devices.

Java Platform Manager   The configuration window in NetBeans for adding and removing Java Development Kits to be used in development. This window is used to configure the JDKs available to projects. A project can use only JDKs already defined in the Java Platform Manager.

Java SE   An acronym for *Java Platform, Standard Edition*. A software development platform including a collection of APIs designed for client application development.

Java SE project   A project that contains a main method and depends only on the Java Standard Edition. NetBeans includes support for creating five different types of Java SE projects including Java Application, Java Desktop Application, Java Class Library, Java Project with Existing Sources, and Java Free-Form Project. A Java SE Project possesses a runtime classpath.

Java Unified Expression Language (EL) A unified expression language that combines the JSP and JSF expression languages. It is a special-purpose language where execution is deferred until runtime. It is typically used in web applications to bind controls in the JSF/JSP forms to the data model.

Java Web Start A deployment technology for the Java platform that enables Java applications to be deployed over the network. Deployment is specified in a JNLP file. This deployment method requires that a JVM be installed, and if deployment is performed using a web browser, the browser plugin must be installed. Applications can subsequently be launched from the desktop.

Javadoc A tool that produces HTML documentation from extracted comments of Java source code.

JavaScript A scripting language that is most often used in conjunction with HTML. JavaScript has no connection to Java.

JConsole A monitoring and management tool that is a part of the JDK. It supports local or remote applications monitoring. It tracks CPU as well as memory usage.

JDBC An acronym for *Java Database Connectivity*. A database-connectivity API providing independent connectivity between the Java programming language and various data sources—for example, databases.

JDK An acronym for *Java Development Kit*. A bundled set of development utilities for compiling, debugging, and interpreting Java applications. The Java Runtime Environment (JRE) is included in the JDK.

jhat A Java heap analysis tool.

JMX A standard Java API that is used for managing and monitoring applications as well as services. It was developed through JSR 3.

JNLP An acronym for *Java Network Launching Protocol*. A technology enabling Java applications to be distributed via the web browser and run inside a secure sandbox.

JPQL   An acronym for *Java Persistence Query Language*. An API used for searching and retrieving persisted application data.

JRE   An acronym for *Java Runtime Environment*. An environment that is used to run Java applications. It contains basic client and server JVMs, core classes, and supporting files.

JRuby   A pure Java implementation of the Ruby interpreter.

JSF   An acronym for the *JavaServer Faces* API. A presentation layer web technology for the Java platform, designed as a component framework for building web user interfaces.

JSP   An acronym for the *JavaServer Pages* API. A dynamic web content solution that uses template data and custom elements to expedite and ease the development of the presentation layer. JavaServer Pages are compiled to servlets before the page content is rendered.

JSTL   An acronym for *JavaServer Pages Standard Tag Library*. An extended library of JavaServer Pages tag functions.

JTA   An acronym for *Java Transaction API*. A technology that allows applications and Java EE servers to access transactions.

JUnit   A testing framework for testing individual units of source code. It specifically tests Java code. NetBeans supports JUnit versions 3 and 4.

JVM   An acronym for *Java virtual machine*. The platform-independent environment where the Java interpreter executes.

JVM Tools Interface (JVM TI)   A low-level native interface that defines the services a Java virtual machine provides for tools such as debuggers and profilers. The JVM TI replaces the legacy JVMPI and JVMDI interfaces.

JVMDI   An acronym for *Java virtual machine debug interface*. A legacy programming interface used by debuggers and other programming tools.

JVMPI An acronym for *Java virtual machine profiler interface*. A legacy programming interface intended for tools vendors to develop profilers that work in conjunction with Sun's Java virtual machine implementation.

keyboard shortcut A single keystroke or series of keystrokes to perform an IDE-related action.

keymap A group of profiles, where each profile is made up of several keyboard shortcuts associated with user-initiated actions.

Keymap panel A panel in the Options window that configures for the selection and management of keymap profiles.

keymap profiles A grouping of shortcuts defined with their actions and categories.

keyword A word in the Java programming language that cannot be used as an identifier (in other words, a variable or method name). Java SE 6 maintains 50 keywords, each designed to be used for a specific purpose.

left margin The margin to the left side of the source editor containing line numbers and annotation glyphs.

library Set of compiled classes that add functionality to a Java application.

light bulb A diagnostic indicator in the left margin relative to a warning or error in the source code.

line numbers Consecutive line numbers in the left margin of the source editor representing the numeration of source code lines.

live code template A code template that includes editable fields within the "live" expanded text. The editable fields are highlighted in blue and are traversable by pressing TAB.

Loaded Classes window A debugger window that lists the loaded classes for the current debugging session. Right-clicking a class and choosing Show In Instances View will open the Instances window with related information.

Local History   NetBeans tracks the diffs between file save events. Local History enables developers to roll back to earlier code snapshots and to compare changes. Changes are tracked over a short period—usually days. It can be thought of as a lightweight version control system.

locale   A geographical, political, or cultural region.

localization (i10n)   Process of translating an application into a different language and adapting it to a locale.

Matisse   Matisse was the Sun internal project name of NetBeans GUI Builder.

Maven   A project software management tool designed for the management of builds, reports, and documentation of enterprise Java projects. It provides a standard structure and process for generating project artifacts. It manages a project's dependencies and pulls them from a central repository. A project and its dependencies are described in a `pom.xml` file. NetBeans supports Maven-based projects and can open a Maven-based project without additional project configuration.

Mercurial   A distributed version control system that keeps track of work and changes for a set of files. Unlike with CVS or Subversion, each Mercurial instance contains the entire copy of the repository. That is, each copy contains the complete history of the project. Changes are pushed or pulled between repositories. Thus, to use the parlance of CVS/Subversion, developers are always working on their own branch. Mercurial is used by the NetBeans team and is well supported by the IDE. The primary Mercurial executable is `hg`. NetBeans requires the native Mercurial binaries. Mercurial is similar to Git.

method   A subroutine that contains the code for performing operations in a class.

MIME type   An acronym that stands for *Multipurpose Internet Mail Extensions*. It is a standard used to define the type of data. It was originally created to define extended e-mail formats.

module   A collection of Java classes that provides a specific feature to an application.

mutator method   A method used to set the value of a variable.

MVC   An acronym for *Model-View-Controller architecture*. A design pattern separating business and presentation logic into model, view, and controller functional areas. The model represents the state of components. The view represents the components on the screen. The controller represents the functionality that ties the user-interface components to events.

MySQL   An open-source relational database.

Navigator window   A window that provides a view of a selected node in the Projects window or Source Editor.

nbproject   The directory under the root of a project that contains the settings for the project. This directory is created under the project root. It contains `project.xml`, `build-impl.xml`, and `project.properties` files, among others.

NetBeans APIs   Public classes and interfaces that developers use to create NetBeans modules.

NetBeans GUI Builder   A tool in NetBeans for constructing graphical user interfaces (GUIs). It was formerly the Matisse project. The NetBeans GUI builder generates Java code.

NetBeans JavaScript Debugger   A set of tools that aid in the process of inspecting, monitoring, and debugging JavaScript code.

NetBeans Modules   A group of Java classes that provides NetBeans with a specific feature.

NetBeans Platform   A Swing-based application framework for building desktop applications. It provides common infrastructure for handling menus, documents, settings, and so on.

NetBeans Profiler   A core NetBeans module that profiles local and remote Java applications.

netbeans.conf   A NetBeans configuration file that passes startup parameters to NetBeans. This file has two versions: a global instance and a local instance. The global instance is stored in the installation directory `${nb-install}/etc/netbeans.conf`. The local instance can be found in `${userdir}/etc/netbeans.conf`. Settings in the local file override global settings.

ODBC　An acronym for *Open Database Connectivity*. A database-connectivity API that provides a standard set of routines for which an application can access databases.

package　A statement at the beginning of a class that organizes a class into a namespace.

panel　A GUI component in which other components can be attached including other panels.

path variables　An abstraction in NetBeans for defining a path that may vary across machines. Path variables are defined by choosing Tools | Variables. The variables are substituted into the NetBeans project files in lieu of either absolute or relative paths.

plugin　A module that adds functionality to the NetBeans IDE such as support for version control systems or code quality tools. It is managed using the Plugin Manager.

Plugin Manager　A configuration tool in NetBeans that is accessed by choosing Tools | Plugins. It manages external plugins, which add functionality to the NetBeans IDE.

POSIX　An acronym that stands for *Portable Operating System Interface for Unix*. It is a group of standards defined by IEEE (Institute of Electrical and Electronics Engineers). The standards cover APIs and command-line utilities.

private.properties　A configuration file stored under `nbproject/private`. It contains settings that are specific to a particular machine/user. Since this file is specific to a particular user/machine, it should not be checked into version control. Settings such as certificate parameters for signing JAR files are typically stored in this properties file.

profiler　A tool for performing dynamic analysis on code. This often includes recording and analyzing memory, CPU, and threading usage. The objective is to understand and troubleshoot application performance issues such as memory leaks, deadlocks, and busy loops. NetBeans includes a built-in profiler tool.

project.xml   A configuration file that is used by NetBeans. NetBeans stores basic information about the project in this file including the project name, source directories, and mappings of menus to Ant tasks among many others. It is stored in the `nbproject` directory.

RDBMS   An acronym for *Relational Database Management System*. A type of database management system that organizes its data in the form of interrelated tables.

refactoring   The process of changing the internal structure of code without changing its external behavior.

relative path   A path that is not anchored to the root of a drive. Its resolution depends upon the current path. For example, `../usr/bin` is a relative path. If the current path were `/home/user/Documents`, this path would resolve to `/home/usr/bin`.

resource bundle   A bundle that contains locale-specific objects. It is identified by a locale, and querying with a key retrieves values. It is a key piece of Java's internationalization support. The primary interface is defined in `java.util.ResourceBundle` with two subclasses: `ListResourceBundle` and `PropertyResourceBundle`.

Ruby   A dynamic object-oriented programming language, similar to Java but less strictly typed.

servlet   A pure-Java program that functions in response to an HTTP request.

Sessions window   A debugger window that lists all running debug sessions.

setter   A simple public method that accepts one argument and is used to set the value of an instance variable.

Shale   A framework based on JavaServer Faces providing integration links for other frameworks.

source editor   A collection of editors including Java, JSP, HTML, and XML source editors.

Sources window   A debugger window that lists source code files that may be available to the debugger.

Spring Framework   An open-sorce application framework. It provides a number of services and is considered to be an alternative to Java EE.

SQL   An acronym for *Structured Query Language*. A software language designed for retrieval and management of information in RDBMS systems.

standard project   A type of NetBeans project that uses an IDE-generated build script to compile, run, and debug an application. Projects that are standard projects include Java Application, Java Desktop Application, Java Class Library, Java Project with Existing Sources, Web Application, and Web Application with Existing Sources.

static analysis   Analysis of an application carried out without executing the application.

Struts   A framework for creating enterprise-ready Java web applications that utilize an MVC architecture.

subclass   A term for a class that is derived from another class through inheritance. This may also be called a child class.

Subversion   An open source version control system supported by NetBeans. It possesses client/server architecture and was developed as a replacement for CVS. NetBeans requires Subversion native executables to be installed. For secure shell (SSH) support, plink must also be installed on Windows.

Sun SPOT   An embedded development platform that runs Java. The platform is open source with kits available from Oracle. Sun SPOT can be used to control servos and LEDs, and to interact with other external devices. They communicate wirelessly and support mesh networks.

superclass   A term that describes a class used to derive other classes through inheritance. This may also be called a parent class or base class.

SvnAnt   An Ant task that performs common SVN operations for interfacing the Subversion version control system.

Swing API   A rich GUI API complete with an event model that is used for creating and managing user interfaces.

Threads window   A debugger window that lists all of the threads in the current debugging session.

Tomcat   A web container for Java Servlets and JavaServer Pages.

UML   An acronym for *Unified Modeling Language*. A specification that defines a modeling language for the specification, presentation, construction, and documentation of object-oriented system elements.

variable   A term for a symbolic reference to data in Java code.

Variables window   A debugging-related window that lists the variables in the current call.

version control system (VCS)   A software system for managing file revisions among one or more users. It tracks the history of the files allowing changes to be compared and traced. In addition, it merges changes when one or more users concurrently edit the same file. NetBeans supports three version control systems in its default distributions: CVS, Mercurial, and Subversion.

Visual Web JSF Framework   A NetBeans Module, based on drag and drop functionality that extends the JavaServer Faces standards, providing a visual approach to web application design.

VM Telemetry window   A window that displays information on thread activity, memory heap, and garbage collection of the virtual machine.

WAR file   A Web Archive file with the extension `.war` used for deploying web applications.

Watches window   A debugger window that lists specified variables and expressions to watch while in a debugging session.

web server   Software that hosts websites, supports various protocols, and executes server-side applications such as servlets.

window   A generic term for frames and dialog boxes.

XML   An acronym for *Extensible Markup Language*. A general-purpose specification used for creating markup languages. This specification allows for the creation of custom tags in structured text files. Web-based solutions make common use of XML files as configuration, deployment descriptor, and tag library files.

INDEX

A

Absolute Layout, 198, 206
Absolute Layout library, 199
Absolute Path option, 186
absolute paths, 55, 186
Abstract Controller option, 270
accessor (getter) method, 392,
    418–419
Add JAR/Folder tab, 51, 53, 56,
    183, 186
Add Library tab, 51, 52, 56, 183–185
Add Project tab, 51, 183
AJAX framework, 273
alignment, 344
Allow Offline option, 234
anchors, 209
annotation glyphs, 358, 359, 367
annotations, displaying in CVS,
    112–113
Annotations panel, 352, 353
Ant
    configuring, 9, 10–13
    considerations, 146
    described, 10, 145
    running targets, 148, 149–150
    templates, 146
    versions, 11
    vs. Maven, 145–146
Ant files
    example of, 10–11
    naming patterns, 149
    profiling and, 541
    targets/action mappings,
        81, 89–90
Ant scripts
    build hooks, 150–152
    considerations, 146
    custom properties, 152

    customizing, 150–152
    main, 148
    troubleshooting, 152
    unit tests and, 524, 526
Ant tab, 9, 10–13
Ant targets, 148, 149–150
Apache Ant. *See* Ant
Apache Commons IO library, 56–57
Apache Geronimo server, 281
Apache MyFaces, 273
Apache Tomcat server, 281, 293
APIs (application program
    interfaces)
    deprecated, 289
    Java EE, 173
    Java SE, 180
    Refactoring API, 389
Appearance tab, 9, 13
Applet Descriptor option, 235
Application Descriptor option, 235
Application Frameworks
    Forums, 269
application program interfaces.
    See APIs
application servers, 279, 281,
    282–284. *See also* servers
application shell, 196
applications. *See also* projects
    attaching profilers to, 541–547
    basic, 195
    database, 195–197, 199
    debugging. *See* debugging
    dependencies, 25, 46–55
    desktop. *See* desktop
      applications
    enterprise, 262, 294, 534
    JWS, 234–240
    local. *See* desktop applications

    monitoring, 547–558
    optimizing, 535–537
    profiling, 537
    remote. *See* web applications
    templates. *See* templates
    testing. *See* unit testing
    undeploying, 295–296
    VWJ, 275–279
    web. *See* web applications
Attach Profiler option, 538,
    541–547
Automatic Internationalization
    option, 18
Available Plugins tab, 36
AWG components, 203, 218
AWG GUI Forms, 193, 205
AWT, described, 193
AWT GUIs, 191

B

Beans Binding
    considerations, 16, 17, 198
    JavaBeans and, 225–227
    overview, 222–223
    synthetic properties, 227–228
    using, 223–229
Beans Binding library, 198, 199
Beans category, 203
best practices refactorings, 392,
    393–402
binding. *See* Beans Binding
Binding category, 204
Border Layout, 206
Box Layout, 206
brace placement, 344
branching, 95, 110–112, 130
breakpoint glyphs, 475, 476, 477

breakpoint markers, 475
breakpoints
    applying conditions to, 484
    behavior of, 22
    class, 478–479
    described, 475
    dynamic creation of, 22
    exception, 479–480
    field, 483
    line, 476, 477–478
    listing, 491
    method, 480–481
    nonline, 476
    setting, 475–485
    thread, 482
Breakpoints window, 491
browsers
    configuring, 7–8
    default, 7–8
    displaying at runtime, 293
    Firefox, 8, 83, 498, 499, 500
    Internet Explorer, 8, 498–499
    JavaScript and, 24, 25
    selecting, 7–8
    supported by NetBeans, 24, 25
Bugzilla, 20
build changes, 147
build failures, 531
build files/processes, 93, 145–154
build hooks, 150–152
build settings, 288–293
build systems. *See* Ant; Maven
build-impl.xml file, 148, 151
build.xml file, 147, 148, 151, 286, 288
business logic, 279
byte code, 533, 535, 538, 566

C

C++ editor, 340
C++ plugins, 34
cache files, 44
calibration, 538–540
Call Stack window, 489–490
camel case navigation, 343–344

capitalization settings, 14
Card Layout, 206
cast creation, 366–367
Change Method Parameters
    command, 392, 402–404
Checkstyle plugin, 496
class breakpoints, 478–479
class importing hints, 363–364
class libraries, 50–51, 263
class variables, 18
classes
    copying, 399
    fully qualified names, 20
    loaded, 490–491
    moving between packages,
        398–399
    moving to subclasses, 407
    moving up, 412–413
    multiple copies of, 54
    naming/renaming, 20, 392,
        396–397
    testing with JUnit, 517, 519–523
Classpath tab, 50
classpaths, 180–190
    code completion, 83
    compilation and, 180–184,
        188, 190
    compile, 48, 181, 188
    compile test, 48, 181, 188
    considerations, 181
    debugging and, 48–49, 180,
        183, 190
    desktop applications, 180–190
    differences between, 188–189
    editing, 182–187, 184
    free-form projects, 84–85
    Java EE projects, 188
    Java SE projects, 188–189
    Java Web, 188
    managing, 180–190
    multiple, 181
    populating, 190
    problems with, 189
    project type and, 188–189
    relationships between, 181, 182

removing entries, 51, 184
    run, 188
    run tests, 188
    test, 48, 181, 188, 524
    types, 48–49, 181–182
    variables, 189–190
code. *See also* scripts
    after-all-set, 215
    auto-completion. *See* code
        completion
    custom creation, 215
    customizing, 216–218
    debugging. *See* debugging
    errors in. *See* errors
    expanded, 20
    folded, 20, 343
    generating, 215, 368–375
    history, 30, 31–32
    inefficient, 28
    locked, 213–214
    navigating, 213–218
    post-adding, 215
    post-creation, 215
    post-declaration, 215
    post-init, 215
    post-listeners, 215
    pre-adding, 215
    pre-creation, 215
    pre-declaration, 215
    pre-init, 215
    refactoring. *See* refactoring
    renaming items in, 396–397
    safely deleting elements in,
        399–402
    simplifying, 402–404
    spacing in, 344
    stepping through, 485–487
    templates. *See* templates
    using existing, 172–179,
        260–264
    version control. *See* version
        control systems
Code category, 204
code completion
    classpaths, 83

Code Customizer, 217, 218
described, 368
libraries and, 151
list box stimuli, 369
settings, 344–346
source level and, 82
usage, 368–369
Code Completion panel, 344–346
code completion popups, 344–346, 368–369
Code Customizer, 216–218
code folding, 20, 343
code profilers. See profilers
code properties, 217, 218
Code Templates panel, 346–347, 370–371
code wrapping, 344
Codebase option, 234
Codebase Preview option, 234
color
background/foreground, 351, 352–354
error marks, 360–361
file version status, 99, 101
in GUI editor, 20
highlighting, 351–354
settings, 350, 351–354
color-blindness-profile request, 351
compilation, 180–184, 188, 190
compilation errors, 60, 531
compile classpath, 48, 181, 188
compile test classpath, 48, 181, 188
compilers, 289, 535, 566
compile/runtime classpath, 48
Compiling panel, 289
Component Descriptor option, 235
component tags, 278
Concurrent Versions System. See CVS
configuration, 3–63. See also Options window
Ant, 9, 10–13
appearance, 9, 13
code profiler, 10, 28–29
colors, 7

debugger, 10, 20–24
editor, 7
Editor panel, 341–349
external libraries, 49–51
file comparison, 9, 13–15
file settings, 9, 15
fonts, 7
Fonts & Colors panel, 350–354
general, 7–8
GUI Builder, 9, 16–20
import/export functionality, 7
issue tracking, 10, 20, 21
JavaScript, 10, 20–24
JDK, 57–63
keyboard shortcuts, 354–356
keymap, 7, 354–356
libraries, 49–51, 56–57
Maven, 10, 24–27
miscellaneous, 7, 9–34
Plugin Manager, 34–42
proxy settings, 8–9
shortcut keys, 7
Source Editor, 341–356
tasks, 10, 30
usage statistics, 9
versioning, 10, 30–34
web browsers, 7–8
configuration directories, 43–46
configuration files, 15, 43–46, 270
configuration groups, 6–34
Connection mode, 202
constants, 375, 415
constructors, 22, 213, 369, 416–417, 486
content
adding to library, 56
changes to, 101
merged, 115
new, 101
static, 444
WAR, 290
WEB-INF, 86, 263
content panel, 6
context path, 86, 293
Continue command, 487

continuous integration server, 528–532
control properties, 207
Convert Anonymous To Inner command, 414
cookies, 453, 458–459
Copy command, 399
Copy To Libraries Folder option, 186
CPU performance, 559–568
Create, Read, Update, Delete. See CRUD
CRUD (Create, Read, Update, Delete), 192
CRUD form, 316
CRUD operations, 196
Custom MBeans, 294
Customize Library dialog box, 186, 187
CVS (Concurrent Versions System), 102–116. See also version control systems
annotation display, 112–113
branching, 110–112
checking out projects, 104–107
committing changes, 109–110
considerations, 30
displaying changes, 107–109
displaying revisions, 113
history searches, 113–114
importing projects into, 103–104
overview, 31, 96, 102
project roots, 103, 105, 107
resolving conflicts, 114–116
reverting changes, 114
tagging, 110–112
updating projects, 109
CVS Root, 103, 105, 107

D

data binding, 191. See also Beans Binding
data usage, 349
database applications, 195–197, 199
database connections, 196, 316–319

database connectivity, 310–311
Database Explorer, 312–319
    considerations, 310, 311–312
    context menus, 328
    described, 312
    integration, 327–328
    interfacing with database via,
      320, 324–325
database integration, 316, 327–328
databases
    considerations, 310
    debug mode, 327
    Java, 318–319
    JDBC-supported, 316–318
    SQL Editor, 319–323
    support components, 319–328
    working with, 310–329
Debug menu, 473, 475, 485
debug mode, 327
Debugger Console, 22
debuggers, 471–500
    active, 497
    alternate platforms, 496
    attaching, 495–497
    configuring, 10, 20–24
    Firebug, 498, 499
    Java Debugger, 10, 20–24
    JDPA, 495–496
    local, 472–494
    remote, 494–500
    requirements for, 499
    settings, 10, 20–24, 497
debugging
    breakpoints. *See* breakpoints
    classpaths and, 48–49, 180,
      183, 190
    client-side, 497–500
    considerations, 472, 473
    desktop applications, 472–494
    with external libraries, 46–57
    free-form projects, 93–95
    information about, 289
    JVM and, 495
    listing sessions, 491–492
    local, 472–494

local vs. remote, 494–497
opening project in IDE, 495
remote, 494–500
server-side, 497, 500
session states, 491
starting session, 473–475, 495
vs. profiling, 533
web applications, 497–500
debugging support windows, 487–494
Debugging window, 493
dependencies
    adding projects as, 51, 52,
      183, 184
    applications, 25, 46–55
    folders, 186
    JAR files, 186, 198, 199, 238
    libraries, 46–55, 182, 186,
      187, 198
    moving up/down, 51, 54,
      184, 404
    reordering, 51, 54
deployment descriptors, 279–280
deprecated APIs, 289
Design mode, 201, 202
desktop applications, 171–255.
    See also Java SE projects
    Beans Binding, 222–229
    choosing project, 174
    choosing sources/test
      packages, 176
    classpaths, 180–190
    creating executable JARs,
      231–234
    creating forms, 191–230
    creating from existing sources,
      172–179
    debugging, 472–494
    deploying via Java Web Start,
      234–240
    event listeners, 218–222
    GUI Builder. *See* GUI Builder
    includes/excludes, 176–178
    internationalization support,
      229–230
    monitoring, 547–558

navigating generated code,
    213–218
packaging/distributing projects,
    230–240
project dependencies, 198–199
specifying name/location,
    174–175
templates, 180–181, 192, 195
working with layouts, 205–213
diagnostic glyphs, 358, 359, 367
diagnostic highlighting, 358–360
diagnostic icons, 357–358
diagnostic marks, 360–361
diff engine, 13–15, 100
Diff panel, 352–354
Diff tab, 9, 13–15
diff utility
    overview, 100–102
    settings, 352–354
Dig, Danny, 389
directories
    configuration, 43–46
    deleting empty, 31
    home, 43, 44
    ignoring, 15–16
    NetBeans versions and, 5
    NetBeans-specific, 44
    pruning, 31
    source, 263
    standard projects, 147–148
    test, 263
dist file, 147
Documenting panel, 290–292
documents. *See* files
Downloaded tab, 37
drivers
    JDBC, 188, 313–315
    registrations, 313–315
dynamic resizing, 206–212

E

Edit button, 8, 54, 186
Edit Jar Reference Library dialog box,
    186, 187

Edit tab, 51, 54, 184
editable fields, 368, 371, 372
Editor configuration group, 7
editor hints, 347, 348, 362–367
Editor panel configurations, 341–349
Editor window, 200–201, 204, 212
EJB projects, 188, 195
EJB-QL (Enterprise JavaBeans Query Language), 203
elements
    refactoring commands and, 393
    renaming, 392, 396–397
    safely deleting, 399–402
Encapsulate Fields command, 418–419
enterprise applications, 262, 294, 534
Enterprise JavaBeans Query Language. See EJB-QL
Entity Manager, 203
Ergonomics feature, 535, 536
error marks, 360–361
error stripe diagnostic marks, 360–361
errors. See also troubleshooting
    annotation glyphs, 358, 359, 367
    client, 442
    compilation, 60, 531
    correcting, 357–362
    diagnostic icons, 357–358
    fatal, 533
    in files, 360
    highlighting, 357, 358–360
    linked to source code, 361–362
    mismatching certificates, 238
    out of memory, 29, 46
    server, 442
error/warning icons, 357–358
event listeners, 218–222
events, 204, 207, 218, 219
Events category, 204
exception breakpoints, 479–480
Export button, 7
Export dialog box, 7, 8
export/import functionality, 7, 8
expressions, evaluating, 204, 484, 486

Extensible Markup Language. See XML
extensions, file, 15, 340
Extract Interface command, 407–409
Extract Superclass command, 409–410

F

Facelets, 271, 272
faces-config.xml file, 280
fatal errors, 533
field breakpoints, 483
fields
    editable, 368, 371, 372
    encapsulating, 418–419
    introducing new statements for, 416
    missing, 365–366
    moving to subclasses, 407
    moving to superclasses, 404–406
    renaming, 392, 396–397
file associations, 15
file comparisons, 13–15
file diff utility. See diff utility
file difference engine, 13–15
file extensions, 15, 340
files
    Ant. See Ant files
    build, 93, 145–154
    cache, 44
    comparing. See diff utility
    configuration, 15, 43–46, 270
    deploy on save, 293
    encoded, 83
    errors in, 360
    HTML, 15, 79, 235, 444
    ignoring, 15–16
    JAR. See JAR files
    JNLP, 235–238
    JSF, 271–272, 277, 278
    JSP, 289
    NBM, 35
    recent, 13
    safely deleting, 399–402

searching history of, 113–114
serializing components, 215
settings, 9, 15
source, 147
standard projects, 147–148
templates, 371
test, 147
WAR, 290, 294, 295, 529
XHTML, 15
XML, 270, 279, 526–527
ZIP, 627
Files tab, 9, 15–16
filter sets, 562
Find Usages command, 392, 395–396
FindBugs plugin, 496
Firebug debugger, 498, 499
Firefox browser, 8, 83, 498, 499, 500
firewalls, 8
Flow Layout, 206
Fold Generated Code option, 20
folders
    adding to projects, 51, 53, 56, 183, 186
    dedicated, 174, 263
    dependencies, 186
    JAR, 51, 53
    libraries, 50–56, 174, 183–186, 262, 263
    project, 80, 174, 176, 186, 262
    sources package, 263
    test package, 263
    web, 86, 263
Fonts & Colors configurations, 7, 350–354
Formatting panel, 344
forms
    AWG GUI, 193, 205
    creating with GUI Builder, 191–230
    creating with layouts, 205–213
    dynamic screen resizing, 206–212
    layouts, 205–213
    properties, 220
    resource bundles, 229–230

forms (*continued*)
Swing GUI, 193, 205
templates, 193
types of, 205
Fowler, Martin, 389, 421
Free Design layout
creating, 212–213
guidelines, 208–209
overview, 201, 206, 207–210
free-form projects, 78–95. *See also*
projects
classpaths, 84–85, 188
considerations, 53, 78–79,
178, 188
creating, 79–87, 94–95, 153–154
debugging, 93–95
as dependencies, 53
JUnit integration, 91
names, 80
overview, 78–79
profiling, 91–92
settings, 87–90
vs. Java SE projects, 173
free-form web applications, 85–87

G

garbage collectors
memory analysis and, 577,
578, 580
overview, 535–536
types of, 536
General configuration group, 7–8
General panel, 342–344
generalization/realization refactorings,
392, 404–411
Generate Components As group, 18
Generate Debugging Info
property, 473
genfiles.properties file, 147, 148
getter (accessor) method, 392,
418–419
Git system, 96
GlassFish application servers
considerations, 268
deployment to, 293–294

HSSM setup, 444–445
monitoring HTTP requests,
446–447
Sun GlassFish Server, 281
undeployment, 295
Global Filters, 562–563
global libraries, 50–53, 56–57, 562
Grails framework, 266
graphical user interfaces. *See* GUIs
Grid Layout, 207
Gridbag Layout, 206, 210–211, 213
GridBag layout manager,
210–211, 213
GridBagLayout Customizer, 207,
210–211
Groovy editor, 340
Groovy language, 266
Group Layout, 198
GroupLayout class, 198
GroupLayout code, 18
GUI assistant, 20
GUI Builder
Beans Binding, 222–229
considerations, 192–193, 195
creating forms with, 191–230
GUI Editor, 192–204
navigating, 199–204
navigating generated code,
213–218
overview, 16–20
GUI Builder tab, 9, 16–20
GUI Editor, 20, 192–204
GUI Editor toolbar, 201
guidelines, 208–209
Guiding Line Color option, 20
GUIs (graphical user interfaces). *See
also* user interfaces
internationalization, 191–192
templates, 193, 195

H

heap dumps, 29, 574, 587–588, 593
heaps
analysis, 29
memory leaks and, 548

settings, 535, 536–537
size, 46
HeapWalker, 28, 29, 587–594
HeapWalker instances, 591
HelloWorld project, 371–372
Hibernate classes, 49
Hibernate tool, 25
highlighting errors, 357, 358–360
Highlighting panel, 351–352
highlighting settings, 350, 351–354
hints
editor, 347, 348, 362–367
Java, 366
live code templates, 372–374
Hints panel, 347, 348
history, local, 30, 31–32, 98, 141–145
history searches
CVS, 113–114
SQL commands, 323
Subversion, 125–126
home directory, 43, 44
HSSM (HTTP Server-Side Monitor),
437–460
overview, 438–459
setting up, 443–447
using, 447–460
HSSM records
analyzing, 451–456
managing, 448–451
replaying, 456–460
HTML editor, 340
HTML files, 15, 79, 235, 444
HTTP (HyperText Transfer
Protocol), 438, 439–443
HTTP headers, 440, 441, 455,
459–460
HTTP Monitor. *See* HSSM
HTTP request methods, 440
HTTP request monitoring.
See HSSM
HTTP response status codes, 440–443
HTTP Server-Side Monitor. *See*
HSSM
HTTP stack, 439
HTTP standard, 450
Hudson instances, 529–530

Hudson jobs, 513
Hudson servers, 513, 528–532
HyperText Transfer Protocol.
    See HTTP

I

ICEfaces, 265, 273–275
Icon option, 234
IDE/server integration, 284–285
IE (Internet Explorer), 8
Import button, 7
import statements, 363–364
import/export functionality, 7, 8
importing libraries, 56–57, 184
importing projects
    into CVS, 103–104
    into Mercurial, 134–135
    into Subversion, 119–122
include patterns, 177
indents, 344
inherited methods, 366–367
initComponents method, 213
Inspector window, 204
Install4j program, 232
installation, 43
Installed tab, 38–39
instrumentation schemes, 565
interfaces
    copying, 399
    creating, 407–409
    moving between packages,
        398–399
    renaming, 392, 396–397
    user. *See* user interfaces
internationalization, 18, 191–192,
    229–230
Internet Explorer (IE), 8,
    498–499
Introduce Constant command, 415
Introduce Field command, 416
Introduce Method command,
    416–417
Introduce Variable command, 414
Inversion of Control. *See* IoC
IoC Container, 270

J

IoC (Inversion of Control)
    principle, 270
Issue tracking tab, 10, 20, 21
IzPack program, 232

JAR archives, 35
Jar Bundler, 232
JAR files
    adding to projects, 51, 53, 56,
        183, 186
    dedicated library folder for, 263
    dependencies, 186, 198,
        199, 238
    double-clickable, 231
    executable, 231–234, 240
    paths to, 54
    RXTX, 47
JAR folders, 51, 53
Java 4.5 annotations, 516
Java applications. *See* applications
Java Business Integration (JBI)
    Service Assemblies, 294
Java Community Process, 271
Java databases. *See* databases
Java DB database server, 318–319
Java Debug Interface (JDI), 495
Java Debug Wire Protocol
    (JDWP), 496
Java Debugger, 10, 20–24. *See also*
    debuggers
Java Development Kit. *See* JDK
Java editor, 340
Java EE (Enterprise Edition), 86,
    263, 293
Java EE APIs, 173
Java EE projects, 86, 146–150,
    188, 273
Java EE web applications. *See* web
    applications
Java elements
    refactoring commands and, 393
    renaming, 392, 396–397
    safely deleting, 399–402
Java Enterprise Edition. *See* Java EE

Java Free-Form Project template, 79
Java free-form projects. *See* free-form
    projects
Java heap dumps, 29, 574,
    587–588, 593
Java heap size, 46
Java hints, 366
Java language
    configurable items in, 344
    licensing issues, 58
    templates. *See* templates
    versions, 58
Java layouts, 205–213
Java Management Extension
    (JMX), 547
Java ME projects, 188
Java Persistence API (JPA),
    48–49, 195
Java Persistence category, 203
Java Platform Debugger Architecture
    (JPDA), 495–496
Java Platform Manager, 58–63
Java platforms, 51, 58–63, 183, 198
Java Properties editor, 340
Java Runtime Environments (JREs),
    45, 154, 155
Java SE (Standard Edition),
    172–173, 180
Java SE APIs, 180
Java SE desktop applications.
    See desktop applications
Java SE projects
    Beans Binding, 222–229
    choosing location,
        174–175, 195
    classpath types, 181–182
    classpaths. *See* classpaths
    configuring libraries for, 173,
        191, 198–199
    considerations, 147, 149, 150,
        173, 178, 180
    creating, 174–179
    dependencies, 198–199
    deploying, 234–240
    differences between classpaths,
        188–189

Java SE projects (*continued*)
    editing classpaths, 182–187
    executable JAR files, 231–234
    generating event listeners,
       218–222
    internationalization, 229–230
    Java layouts, 205–213
    naming, 174, 175, 195
    navigating generated code,
       213–218
    packaging/distributing, 230–240
    templates, 180–181
    vs. free-form projects, 173
Java Source Code Editor, 277
Java Specification Request. *See* JSR
Java Standard Edition. *See* Java SE
Java Virtual Machine. *See* JVM
Java web applications. *See* web
  applications
Java Web Start (JWS), 232, 234–240
JavaBeans, 225–227
java.class.path property, 189
Javadoc
    settings, 290–292
    using, 56–59
JavaFX projects, 188, 6:s
JavaRanch, 269
JavaScript
    settings, 10, 20–24
    versions, 24
    web browsers and, 24, 25
JavaScript tab, 10, 20–24
JavaServer Faces. *See* JSF
JavaServer Pages. *See* JSP
JBI (Java Business Integration)
  Service Assemblies, 294
JBoss server, 281
JBuddy Messenger, 547
JButton events, 219
JDBC driver registrations, 313–315
JDBC drivers, 188, 313–315
JDBC-supported databases, 316–318
JDI (Java Debug Interface), 495
JDK (Java Development Kit), 57–63
    adding/removing, 58–62
    alternative implementations, 58

configuring into projects,
    154–157
considerations, 45
developing with, 57–63
versions, 57–58, 154, 156–157
JDWP (Java Debug Wire
  Protocol), 496
Jerry server, 281
jhat tool, 587, 591
JIT (just-in-time) compiler, 535, 566
jmap tool, 587
Jmol application
    considerations, 173
    described, 178
    exercise, 178–179
    running, 240
JMX (Java Management
  Extension), 547
JNLP files, 235–238
JPA (Java Persistence API),
  48–49, 195
JPA Query, 203
JPDA (Java Platform Debugger
  Architecture), 495–496
JREs (Java Runtime Environments),
  45, 154, 155
JRockit, 58
JSF (JavaServer Faces), 265, 271–279
JSF editor, 340
JSF files, 271–272, 277, 278
JSF framework, 265, 268
JSF libraries, 268, 272
JSF specification, 269, 273
JSP (JavaServer Pages), 281, 289
JSP Editor, 277, 340
JSP files, 289
JSP specification, 281
JSR (Java Specification Request), 281
JSR 295. *See* Beans Binding
JSR specification, 281
JUnit, 512–532. *See also* unit testing
    basics, 513–515
    continuous integration support,
      528–532
    creating tests/test suites,
      517–523

    executing tests, 526
    execution options, 525
    Hudson servers, 528–532
    rerunning tests, 526
    resources, 515
    running tests, 524–527, 528
    templates, 517
    test results, 525–527
    testing for existing classes, 517,
      519–523
    unit testing classpath, 518, 524
    unit testing with Hudson, 532
    versions, 515–517, 519
JUnit integration, 91
JUnit reports, 526–527
just-in-time (JIT) compiler, 535, 566
JVM (Java Virtual Machine)
    calibration, 538–540
    debugging and, 495
    garbage collectors, 535–536
    heap size, 535, 536–537
    optimizing, 535
    SunSpots and, 42
JVM TI (JVM Tools Interface), 496
JVM Tools Interface (JVM TI), 496
JWS (Java Web Start), 232, 234–240

K

Kenai project, 311
keyboard shortcuts, 629–638, 354–356
Keymap configuration group, 7
Keymap panel configurations,
  354–356
Keymap profiles, 355
keywords, 350, 351

L

language categories, 350
Layout Generation Style option, 18
layout managers, 205–213
layouts
    Java, 205–213
    overview, 205–206
    working with, 205–213

libraries
    adding, 51, 52–54, 183,
       184–185
    adding content to, 56
    adding to projects, 47, 51, 52,
       56, 183–185
    Apache Commons IO, 56–57
    Beans Binding, 198, 199
    class, 50–51, 263
    configuring, 49–51, 56–57
    considerations, 50
    creating, 50–51, 184
    debugging with, 46–57
    dependencies, 46–55, 182, 186,
       187, 198
    editing, 51, 54
    external, 46–57, 49
    global, 50–53, 56–57, 562
    importing, 56–57, 184
    Java EE, 262, 263–264
    Java SE, 173, 191, 198–199
    JSF, 268, 272
    layout, 185
    listed, 50
    location, 50, 55
    naming, 50
    paths to, 54–57
    project, 51–54, 174, 183
    removing, 51, 54
    reordering dependencies, 51, 54
    selecting, 50–51
    server, 50–51
    shared, 47, 53, 54–57
    splitting, 47
    storage of, 174, 262
    Test Libraries, 517
    web frameworks, 268, 269
libraries folder, 50–56, 174, 183–186,
    262, 263
Library classpath, 50, 51
Library Manager, 49–51
light bulb glyph, 362–364
line breakpoints, 476, 477–478
lines, blank, 344
Linux systems
    installing NetBeans on, 627
    settings. *See* Options window

LiquiBase, 328, 529
Listener Generation Style option, 18
listener logic, 18
listeners, 18, 218–222
live code templates, 368, 372–375
Live Results view, 566, 567, 582–584
Loaded Classes window, 490–491
local applications. *See* desktop
    applications
local debugging, 472–494
Local History feature, 30–32, 98,
    141–145
local variables, 215
localization, 229–230
locked code, 213–214

M

Mac OS X
    installers, 232
    installing NetBeans on,
      624–627
    preferences. *See* Options window
macro settings, 344, 345
Macros panel, 347, 349
Mark Occurrences panel, 347, 348
Matisse. *See* GUI Editor
Maven
    goal definitions, 26, 27
    overview, 24–26, 145–146
    settings, 10, 24–27
    versions, 26
    vs. Ant, 145–146
Maven Pom (Project Object
    Model), 25
Maven tab, 10, 24–27
member variable declaration, 213
member variables, 213
memory
    allocation, 584–587
    monitoring usage, 548
    out of memory errors, 29, 46
    usage overview, 577–587
memory analysis, 577–580
memory dumps, 28
Memory (GC) graph, 550–551, 553
Memory Heap graph, 550, 10;43

memory leaks, 28, 29, 548, 590
memory profiling, 577–587
    described, 577, 587
    initiating session, 577
    searching for String instances,
      593–594
    settings, 577–578
memory snapshots
    comparing, 584–585
    evaluating, 586–587
Mercurial, 32–33. *See also* version
    control systems
    cloning projects, 135–137, 141
    committing changes, 137–138
    displaying changes, 139–140
    initializing/importing projects,
      134–135
    overview, 96, 133–134
    reverting changes, 139
    settings, 134
    updating projects, 138–139
method breakpoints, 480–481
method stepping, 20, 22–23
methods
    changing signature, 402–404
    inherited, 366–367
    introducing, 416–417
    missing, 364–365
    moving to subclasses, 407
    moving to superclasses, 404–406
    naming/renaming, 219, 392,
      396–397
    root, 534, 567, 569–571, 579
    synthetic, 22
MIME (Multipurpose Internet Mail
    Extensions), 15
MIME types, 16
Miscellaneous configuration group,
    7, 9–34
Model-View-Controller (MVC), 265
modules. *See* plugins
monitoring
    desktop applications, 547–558
    memory usage, 548
    performing, 548–549
    settings, 548–550
    thread usage, 548

Move command, 392, 398–399
Move Down tab, 51, 184, 492
Move Inner To Outer command, 412–413
Move Up tab, 51, 184, 404, 492
Multipurpose Internet Mail Extensions. *See* MIME
mutator (setter) method, 392, 418–419
MVC (Model-View-Controller), 265
MySQL Sakila database, 320, 324–326
MySQL server integration, 320

N

nblibraries.properties file, 55
.nbm extension, 35
NBM files, 35
nbproject directory, 147, 148
.netbeans directory, 43, 44
NetBeans IDE
    advantages of, 4
    appearance, 9, 13, 14
    becoming proficient in, 4
    configuring. *See* configuration
    initiating profiling sessions, 537
    installing, 43, 617–627
    issue tracking, 20, 21
    keyboard shortcuts, 629–638, 354–356
    multiple instances of, 44
    new features, 612–616
    OS Independent Zip, 627
    overview, 4
    plugins for. *See* plugins
    resetting defaults, 5
    supported technologies, 611
    uninstalling, 43
    versions, 5, 44, 609–616
NetBeans Keymap, 629–638
NetBeans Modules projects, 146, 147
NetBeans Plugin Portal, 40, 271, 274, 282
NetBeans Profiler, 533–594. *See also* profiling
    attaching profiler, 541–547

    calibration, 538–540
    capuring snapshots, 567–568, 580–582
    CPU performance, 559–568
    HeapWalker, 587–594
    launching, 537–541
    monitoring desktop applications, 547–558
    overview, 512, 533–535
    profiling points, 569–576
    root methods, 570–571
    Telemetry Overview, 550–554
    thread monitoring, 554–556
    viewing live results, 582–584
netbeans.conf file, 43–46
Null Layout, 207

O

object allocations, 578, 580–582
Object Query Language (OQL), 534, 588–594
OpenJDK, 58
OpenSolaris systems, 623–624
operating systems. *See also* specific operating systems
    appearance of, 13
    calibration comparisons, 540
    environment settings, 588
    versions, 589
Options window, 5–34. *See also* configuration
    Editor configuration group, 7
    Editor panel, 341–349
    Fonts & Colors configuration group, 7
    Fonts & Colors panel, 350–354
    General configuration group, 7–8
    Import/Export buttons, 7
    Keymap configuration group, 7
    Keymap panel, 354–356
    Miscellaneous configuration group, 7, 9–34
    overview, 5–7
    panel selectors, 341
    Source Editor, 341–356

OQL (Object Query Language), 534, 588–594
Oracle ADF Faces, 273
Oracle GlassFish Server, 281
Oracle OC4J server, 281
Oracle WebLogic server, 281, 283
organizational refactorings, 392, 412–419
OutOfMemoryError options, 29, 46
Output window
    diagnostic messages, 361–362
    SQL Command Execution window, 326–327
OW2 JonAS server, 281

P

Package Maker, 232
packages
    moving classes between, 398–399
    renaming, 392, 396–397
Packaging panel, 290
PageFlow mode, 280
Palette window, 203
Path From Variable option, 186
path variables, 189–190
paths
    absolute, 55, 186
    context, 86, 293
    relative, 186
    from variables, 186
Pause command, 487
Perforce system, 96
performance
    analysis of, 559–568
    CPU, 559–568
    heap size and, 537
    monitoring, 566–567
    problems with, 533
    settings, 559–565
PHP editor, 340
pid (process identifier), 587
Plain Old Java Objects (POJOs), 270
Plugin Manager, 34–42, 96, 282
plugins
    activated, 39

adding to list, 37
available, 35, 36, 40
C++, 34
checking for, 34
Checkstyle, 496
considerations, 34
deactivated, 38, 39
downloaded, 37
FindBugs, 496
information about, 36, 40
installed, 35, 36, 38–39
listed, 35, 38
location of, 44
managing, 34–42, 96, 282
manually downloaded, 35
NetBeans Plugin Portal, 40, 271, 273, 282
PMD, 496
searching for, 38
server-support, 282
settings, 34–42
status of, 38, 39
SunSpot, 42
uninstalled, 36, 39
updates, 34, 35, 36, 40
Visual Web ICEfaces, 273
PMD plugin, 496
POJOs (Plain Old Java Objects), 270
preferences. *See* Options window
private directory, 148
private.properties file, 148, 152
Procedures node, 327
process identifier (pid), 587
Profile Main Project option, 537–541
Profiler tab, 10, 28–29
profilers. *See also* NetBeans Profiler
    attaching to applications, 541–547
    configuring, 10, 28–29
profiling, 532–594
    calibration, 538–540
    controls, 551–552
    CPU performance, 559–568
    described, 512
    free-form projects, 91–92
    Java applications, 537
    local, 542

memory. *See* memory profiling
monitoring desktop applications, 547–558
options for, 537–538
purpose of, 533
remote, 542
vs. debugging, 533
profiling points, 569–576
profiling sessions, 551–552
programs. *See* applications
project folders, 80, 174, 176, 186, 262
project libraries, 51–54, 174, 183
Project Properties dialog box, 49, 155, 182, 288–293
project.properties file, 147, 152
projects. *See also* applications
    adding as dependency, 51, 52, 183, 184
    adding folders to, 51, 53, 56, 183, 186
    adding JAR files to, 51, 53, 56, 183, 186
    adding libraries to, 47, 51, 52, 56, 183–185
    configuring JDK into, 154–157
    creating, 174, 175
    dependencies, 198–199
    EJB, 188, 195
    free-form. *See* free-form projects
    HelloWorld, 371–372
    includes/excludes, 176–178
    Java EE, 86, 146, 147, 188, 273
    Java ME, 188
    Java SE. *See* Java SE projects
    JavaFX, 188, 340
    location, 174, 175
    names, 80, 174, 175
    NetBeans Modules, 146, 147
    setting as main project, 174, 262
    sharing, 54
    standard, 147–149, 524
    structure, 147–149
    templates. *See* templates
    types of, 147
    version control. *See* version control systems
    web free-form, 78, 79, 146

Projects window, 357–358
properties
    Ant scripts, 152
    Beans Binding, 227–228
    code, 217, 218
    servers, 284
    settings, 200, 204, 217–220
    synthetic, 227–228
Properties category, 204
Properties window, 200, 204, 217–220
proxy settings, 8–9, 105
Pull Up command, 404–406
Push Down command, 407

Q

Quick Filter, 561–562

R

Rational ClearCase system, 96
Redo command, 420
refactoring, 387–421
    architecture, 389–391
    best practices, 392, 393–402
    categories/descriptions, 391–393
    common processes, 421
    considerations, 399, 406, 418
    examples of, 388
    generalization/realization, 392, 404–411
    Java elements, 393
    management, 393, 419–421
    organizational, 392, 412–419
    overview, 388–389
    process flow, 389–390
    purpose of, 388
    refactoring management, 393, 419–421
    resources for, 389
    simplication, 392, 402–404
    undo/redo functions, 420
Refactoring API, 389
refactoring catalog, 421
refactoring commands, 392–420. *See also* specific commands
Relative Path option, 186

relative paths, 186
relative URLs, 293
remote debugging, 494–500
Remove tab, 51, 184
Rename command, 392, 396–397
repositories, 25–26
request URI, 458
resource bundles, 18, 229–230
RichFaces Palette, 265, 273
root methods, 534, 567, 569–571, 579
Ruby editor, 340
run classpath, 48, 181–182, 188
Run panel, 293
run test classpath, 48, 181, 182, 188
Run To Cursor command, 486–487
RXTX JAR files, 47
RXTX library, 47

S

Safely Delete command, 399–402
Sakila database, 320, 324–326
scripts. *See also* code
   Ant. *See* Ant scripts
   build, 241
   database, 529
   SQL, 310
   start, 542
SDKs (software development kits), 58
searches
   in CVS, 113–114
   history. *See* history searches
   plugins, 38
   SQL commands, 323
   for String instances, 593–594
   in Subversion, 125–126
   for ToDo notes, 30
Selection Border Color option, 20
Selection mode, 202
Self-Signed option, 235
server instances, 281–285
server libraries, 50–51
server log file, 284
servers
   Apache Geronimo, 281
   Apache Tomcat, 281, 293

application, 279, 281, 282–284
continuous integration, 528–532
controlling, 284–285
debug mode, 284
external, 446
GlassFish. *See* GlassFish application servers
Hudson, 513, 528–532
profile mode, 284
properties, 284
refreshing, 284
registered, 263, 284
removing instances, 284
settings, 262–263
SJSAS, 444–445
starting/stopping, 284
supported, 281
target, 263, 272, 293
Tomcat Web Server, 443–444
updates to, 284, 285
web, 279, 281–285, 443–448
WebLogic, 281, 283
server-support plugins, 282
Services window, 310, 311
Servlet specification, 281
Sessions window, 491–492
Set Component Names option, 18
setter (mutator) method, 392, 418–419
Settings tab, 39–41
shared libraries, 47
shortcuts. *See* keyboard shortcuts
Show Assistant option, 20
Simple Form Controller option, 270
simplication refactorings, 392, 402–404
SJSAS (Sun Java System Application Server), 444–445
snapshots
   capturing manually, 581
   capturing via profile points, 581, 582
   capuring, 567–568, 580–582
   object allocations, 580–582
   of profile data, 567–568

saving, 568
settings, 28, 568
software development kits (SDKs), 58
source code. *See* code
source directories, 263
Source Editor, 339–376
   annotation glyphs, 358, 359, 367
   build/compile messages, 361–362
   camel case navigation, 343–344
   changing behavior of, 356
   code completion, 344–346, 368–369
   code folding, 343
   diagnostic highlighting, 358–360
   diagnostic icons, 357–358
   editor hints, 347, 348, 362–367
   error correction, 357–362
   error stripe diagnostic marks, 360–361
   generating code, 368–375
   language editors in, 340
   macros, 347, 349
   modifying behavior of, 341–356
   overview, 340
   settings, 341–356
source files, 147
Source mode, 201
Source view, 201, 220
sources, 181
sources package folders, 263
Sources window, 492–493
Spring Framework, 265, 268, 270
Spring Source, 270
Spring Web MVC, 265
Spring XML configuration file, 270
SQL Editor, 319–323
SQL scripts, 310
SQL Table Viewer, 325–326
src file, 147
static initializers, 22
step filters, 20, 22–23
Step Into command, 486
Step Into Next Method command, 486
Step Out command, 486
Step Over command, 486

Step Over Expression command, 486
String instances, 593–594
Struts Framework, 265, 268–270
Subversion. *See* SVN
Sun GlassFish Server, 281
Sun Java System Application Server
    (SJSAS), 444–445
Sun Java System Web Server, 281
SunSpot plugin, 42
superclasses
    creating, 409–410
    moving fields/methods to,
        404–406
supertypes, converting types to,
    410–411
SVN (Subversion), 116–132. *See also*
    version control systems
    checking out projects,
        122–123, 132
    commiting changes, 127
    copying items, 130–132
    displaying changes, 124–125
    file locking and, 194
    history searches, 125–126
    importing projects into,
        119–122
    overview, 96, 116–117
    project relocation, 123–124
    resolving conflicts, 128–130
    reverting changes, 125
    settings, 33–34, 117–118,
        130, 131
    updating projects, 126–127
    versions, 117
Swing Application Framework,
    193, 199
Swing Application Framework
    library, 199
Swing components, 191, 203, 218,
    222, 229
Swing controls, 193, 203, 224, 227
Swing GUI Forms, 193, 205
Swing GUIs, 191
Swing Layout Extensions library,
    198, 199
Swing widgets, 203

Syntax panel, 350–351
synthetic methods, 22
System.currentTimeMillis(), 539

T

TAB key behaviors, 344, 345
tables, working with, 325–326, 327
Tables node, 327
tagging, 95, 110–112, 130
Tapestry framework, 271
target server, 263, 272, 293
targets
    Ant, 148, 149–150
    listed, 149, 150
    XML, 286, 287–288
task settings, 10, 30
tasks, described, 30
Tasks tab, 10, 30
TCP ports, 28
telemetry information, 550–554
Telemetry Overview, 550–554
templates
    Ant, 146
    applications, desktop, 180–181,
        192, 195
    applications, free-form,
        78–79, 146
    applications, web, 270–272,
        276, 278
    code, 639–648, 346–347,
        370–371, 375
    facelets, 271
    files, 371
    forms, 193
    free-form projects, 78–79, 146
    GUI, 193, 195
    JUnit, 517
    JWS, 235
    live code, 368, 372–375
    projects, 146, 147, 328
test classpaths, 48, 181, 188, 524
test dependencies, 48
test directories, 263
test file, 147
test files, 147

Test Libraries, 517
test package folders, 263
test sources, 181
testing. *See* JUnit; unit testing
text field binding, 224–225, 229
thread breakpoints, 482
thread leaks, 548
threads
    in current debugging session,
        492, 493
    deadlocking, 557–558
    debugger, 22
    monitoring usage, 548
    states, 492, 555
    timeline, 555
    viewing, 554–556
Threads window, 492
Threads/Loaded Classes graph,
    550–551, 554
ToDo notes, 30
Tomcat Web Server, 443–444
tooltips, 360–361, 363
TopLink Essentials, 199
TopLink Essentials library, 199
troubleshooting. *See also* errors
    Ant scripts, 152
    classpath problems, 189
    debugger and, 20
    locked code, 213–214
    performance problems, 533
type parameters, 215
types, converting to supertypes,
    410–411

U

UIs. *See* user interfaces
undeployment, 295–296
Undo command, 420
uninstalling NetBeans, 43
unit testing, 512–532. *See also* JUnit
    creating tests/test suites,
        517–523
    described, 512
    failed tests, 531
    test suites, 514–515

universal resource locators (URLs), 13, 293
updates
    plugins, 34, 35, 36, 40
    servers, 284, 285
Updates tab, 34, 35
URLs (universal resource locators), 13, 293
usage statistics, 9
Use Supertype Where Possible command, 410–411
user interfaces (UIs). *See also* GUI entries
    basic, 196
    binding to beans, 225–227
    creating, 193, 206, 213
    dynamic screen resizing, 206–212
    editing, 193
    JSF and, 271–273
    layouts, 205–213
    library configuration, 49
    settings, 13

V

varargs (variable arguments), 404
variable arguments (varargs), 404
variable formatters, 20, 23–24
variables
    classes, 18
    classpaths, 189–190
    formatting, 20, 23–24
    introducing new statements for, 414
    local, 215
    members, 213
    missing, 365–366
    modifiers, 215
    names, 215
    paths, 189–190
    paths from, 186
    unknown, 189
Variables Modifier option, 18
Variables window, 488–489

VCSs. *See* version control systems
-verbose flag, 189
version control systems (VCSs), 92–145
    best practices, 96
    Concurrent Versions System. *See* CVS
    diff utility. *See* diff utility
    listed, 96
    Local History feature, 30, 31–32, 98, 141–145
    Mercurial. *See* Mercurial
    overview, 10, 95–98
    Subversion. *See* SVN
    version control submenus, 97–98
    visual feedback, 99
versioning settings, 10, 30–34
Versioning tab, 10, 30–34
Views node, 327
virtual machine. *See* VM
Visual Designer, 277
visual editors, 279–280
visual web frameworks, 272–281
Visual Web ICEfaces Framework, 265, 273–275
Visual Web JSF. *See* VWJ
VM (virtual machine) options, 293
VM Telemetry Overview, 550–554
VWJ applications, 275–279
VWJ (Visual Web JSF) framework, 265, 272–281
VWJ toolset, 276

W

WAR content, 290
WAR file, 290, 294, 295, 529
warning/error icons, 357–358
Watches window, 489
web applications, 259–297. *See also* applications
    adding web frameworks, 266–268
    build settings, 288–293
    choosing location, 262

    choosing project, 261
    choosing sources/libraries, 263–264
    common development tasks, 286–288
    creating from existing sources, 260–264
    debugging, 497–500
    deploying, 293–294
    free-form, 85–87
    IDE/server integration, 284–285
    JSF applications, 275–279
    naming, 262
    NetBeans frameworks, 265–272
    server instances, 281–285
    server-related settings, 262–263
    templates, free-form, 78, 79, 146
    templates, Java EE, 270, 271–272, 276, 278
    undeploying, 295–296
    using web frameworks, 268–272
    visual editors, 279–280
    visual web frameworks, 272–281
web browsers
    configuring, 7–8
    default, 7–8
    displaying at runtime, 293
    Firefox, 8, 83, 498, 499, 500
    Internet Explorer, 8, 498–499
    JavaScript and, 24, 25
    selecting, 7–8
    supported by NetBeans, 24, 25
web folders, 263
web frameworks, 265–272. *See also* specific frameworks
    adding, 266–268
    concepts, 268–272
    described, 265
    legacy, 271
    libraries, 268, 269
    listed, 265
Web Free-Form Application template, 78, 79, 146
web free-form projects, 85–87, 146